DIMENSIONS OF THE WRITING

CHOOSING
PURPOSE AND AUDIENCE

COLLECTING

OBSERVING

Sensory details
Comparisons and images
Changes
What is not there

REMEMBERING

Specific scenes
Changes and conflict
Connections between
   past and present

READING

Active reading
Annotating
Summarizing
Responding

INVESTIGATING

Asking questions
Interviews
Questionnaires
Library research

SHAPING

Chronological order
Spatial order
Comparison/contrast
Definition
Example

Focusing and narrowing subject
Introductions
Body paragraphs
Conclusions

Causal analysis
Process analysis
Dialogue
Image
Voice and persona

DRAFTING

Planning
Re-reading
Talking

Reconsidering purpose and audience
Starting at the beginning
Starting at the middle

Writing nonstop
Stopping when you
   know what comes next

REVISING AND EDITING

MAJOR CHANGES

Changing purpose or audience
Collecting new information, ideas,
   evidence, examples
Reshaping paragraphs or reorganizing an essay
Choosing a new point of view

MINOR CHANGES

Revising sentences, transitions,
   word choice
Editing for grammar, punctuation,
   usage
Proofreading for spelling and mechanics

THE PRENTICE HALL GUIDE
FOR COLLEGE WRITERS

FOURTH EDITION

THE PRENTICE HALL GUIDE FOR COLLEGE WRITERS

STEPHEN REID

COLORADO STATE UNIVERSITY

PRENTICE HALL, UPPER SADDLE RIVER, NJ 07458

Library of Congress Cataloging-in-Publication Data
Reid, Stephen, 1940—
        The Prentice Hall guide for college writers/Stephen Reid. —4th ed.
        p.   cm.
    Includes index.
    ISBN 0–13–621855-5
    1. English language—Rhetoric.   2. Report Writing.   I. Title.
    PE1408.R424   1998
    808'.042—DC21   97-13715
                                                                        CIP

Editor-in-Chief: Charlyce Jones Owen
Executive Editor: Leah Jewell
Assistant Development Editor: Kara Hado
Director of Production and Manufacturing: Barbara Kittle
Senior Managing Editor: Bonnie Biller
Production Editor: Randy Pettit
Manufacturing Manager: Nick Sklitsis
Prepress and Manufacturing Buyer: Mary Ann Gloriande
Marketing Director: Gina Sluss
Marketing Manager: Rob Mejia
Creative Design Director: Leslie Osher
Cover and Interior Design: Carmella Periera
Photo Researcher: Barbara Salz
Cover Art: Thomas McKnight "Riviera Villa" © 1998 Thomas McKnight, Inc.

This book was set in 10/12.5 Adobe Caslon by Clarinda Corp.
and printed and bound by World Color.
The cover was printed by Phoenix Color Corp.

© 1998, 1995, 1992, 1989 by Prentice-Hall Inc.
Simon & Schuster/A Viacom Company
Upper Saddle River, New Jersey 07458

For permission to use copyrighted material, grateful
acknowledgment is made to the copyright holders listed
on page xxix–xxxi, which is considered an extension of this
copyright page.

Printed in the United States of America

10 9 8 7 6 5 4 3 2

ISBN   0-13-621855-5
       0-13-621848-2 (Brief Edition)
       0-13-621863-6 (Annotated Instructor's Edition)

Prentice-Hall International (UK) Limited, *London*
Prentice-Hall of Australia Pty. Limited, *Sydney*
Prentice-Hall Canada Inc., *Toronto*
Prentice-Hall Hispanoamerica, S.A., *Mexico*
Prentice-Hall of India Private Limited, *New Delhi*
Prentice-Hall of Japan, Inc., *Tokyo*
Simon & Schuster Asia Pte. Ltd., *Singapore*
Editora Prentice-Hall do Brasil, Ltda., *Rio de Janeiro*

BRIEF CONTENTS

CONTENTS

～

~

~

THEMATIC CONTENTS

The Prentice Hall Guide for College Writers, fourth edition, contains excerpts and selections from over 50 writers. Thematic clusters are indicated below. Asterisk (*) indicates complete essay.

~

ADVERTISING AND THE MEDIA

~

DEPENDENCY AND DYSFUNCTION

PREFACE

As we move to the new millennium, we are witnessing a dramatic change in the contexts for the teaching of writing. The recent explosion of World Wide Web sites, the increasing ease of access to the Internet, and the expanding number of computer classrooms and terminals available to student writers have revolutionized the teaching and practice of writing. On the Internet, writers can quickly access an incredible range of information, both about specific subjects and about the process of writing and revising. On local networks, students can continue conversations started in print media or in the classroom, get and receive peer advice about drafting and revision, and access teacher response. Distance learning becomes a practical reality, as students sitting at computers in different cities or countries can communicate as easily as students sitting at adjoining computers.

The more things change, however, the more they remain the same. Writers still need to learn critical reading skills. They still need to assess rhetorical contexts, establish rhetorical purpose, consider their audiences and readers, develop and organize their ideas, and learn how to revise and edit their writing to meet the rhetorical situation. They still need to learn to work cooperatively and collaboratively to create a writing community. Computers and networks are merely electronic means for communicating—for putting people in contact with people, writers in contact with readers. Computers and networks can continue teachers' efforts to communicate with their students and to center their curriculum on the students' reading, writing, and revising.

In its fourth edition, *The Prentice Hall Guide for College Writers* retains an emphasis on aims and purposes for reading and writing, on a clear sequence of chapters that move from expressive to argumentative writing, and on extensive, integrated writing process advice that helps students learn to read, write, and revise. Providing ongoing support for both students and teachers during the reading, writing, and revising processes remains the overriding goal of this text.

Continued in the fourth edition is an emphasis on critical reading and responding to texts. Chapter Five, "Reading," uses the summary/response essay as a means to teach active and critical reading, accurate summarizing, and focused responding to texts. Drawing on reader-response theories and psycho-linguistic research, Chapter Five provides a variety of activities to promote active reading and critical responding.

New to the fourth edition is a focus on using and evaluating sources from the Internet and the World Wide Web. First, five new essays, scattered throughout the text, give students information about the Internet—what it is, how to use it, and how it affects writing and learning. Second, an expanded section on locating, evaluating, and documenting Internet and Web sources help students use electronic resources in their writing. Finally, the fourth edition contains over fifteen new professional essays by writers such as John Muir, Horace Miner, Mike Rose, Elayne Rapping, Neil Postman, Edward Koch, and Mike Royko. The additional essays help create thematic clusters of topics that reappear throughout the text: Race and Cultural Diversity, Gender Roles, Technology and the Internet, Environmental Issues, Education, Literacy and Language, Advertising and the Media, and Dependency and Dysfunction. See the Thematic Contents (following the table of contents) for a complete listing.

Finally, *The Prentice Hall Guide for College Writers* continues to showcase student writing, featuring the work of more than forty student writers from several colleges and universities. The fourth edition contains twenty-three full-length student essays and ten essays with sample prewriting materials and drafts.

KEY FEATURES

Continuing in the fourth edition of *The Prentice Hall Guide for College Writers* is a wide range of noteworthy features:

LOGICAL SEQUENCE OF PURPOSE-BASED CHAPTERS

Aims and purposes, not rhetorical strategies, guide each writing assignment. Early chapters focus on invention strategies (observing, remembering, reading, and investigation), while later chapters emphasize exposition and argumentation (explaining, evaluating, problem solving, and arguing).

FOCUS ON WRITING PROCESSES   Every major chapter contains techniques, professional and student samples, journal exercises, reading and writing activities, collaborative activities, peer-response guidelines, and revision suggestions designed to assist students with their work-in-progress.

JOURNAL WRITING   Throughout the text, write-to-learn activities help writers improve their critical reading skills, "warm up" for each assignment, and practice a variety of invention and shaping strategies.

MARGINAL QUOTATIONS   Nearly a hundred short quotations by composition teachers, researchers, essayists, novelists, and poets personalize for the inexperienced writer a larger community of writers still struggling with the same problems that each student faces.

ANNOTATED INSTRUCTOR'S EDITION (AIE)   In the margins of the Annotated Instructor's Edition are hundreds of teaching tips and suggestions for assignments and group activities. (0-13-621863-6)

Designed to accompany the Annotated Instructor's Edition, *Teaching Composition with the Prentice Hall Guide* contains sections on composition theory, policy statements, lesson plans, collaborative writing, writing in a computer classroom, small-group learning, write-to-learn exercises, reading/writing exercises, prereading journal assignments, writing assignments, suggestions for student conferences, and responding to and evaluating writing, as well as an annotated bibliography of articles about teaching writing. Also included are chapter commentaries and answers to discussion questions. (0-13-645458-5)

Available for a nominal fee, the *Critical Thinking Skills Journal* provides students with additional exercises and freewriting activities, as well as opportunities to consider and respond to opposing viewpoints. (0-13-645532-8)

AN INTRODUCTION TO MYTHS AND RITUALS FOR WRITING   Chapter One, "Writing Myths and Rituals," discounts some common myths about college writing courses, introduces the notion of writing rituals, and outlines the variety of journal writing used throughout the text. Rituals are crucial for all writers but especially so for novice writers. Effective rituals are simply those behavioral strategies that complement the cognitive and social strategies of the writing process. Illustrating a variety of possible writing rituals are quotations from a dozen professional writers on the nature of writing. These short quotations continue throughout the book, reminding students that writing is not some magical process, but rather a madness that has a method to it, a love that is built from labor, and a learning that is born of reading, thinking, observing, remembering, discussing, and writing.

AN ORIENTATION TO RHETORICAL SITUATION AND TO WRITING PROCESSES   Chapter Two, "Purposes and Processes for Writing," bases the writing process in the rhetorical situation (writer, subject, purpose, text, and audience). It restores the writer's intent or purpose (rather than a thesis sentence or a rhetorical strategy) as the driving force during the writing process. It demonstrates how meaning evolves from a variety of recursive, multidimensional, and hierarchical activities that we call the writing process. Finally, it reassures students that, because individual writing and learning styles differ, they will be encouraged to discover and articulate their own processes from a range of appropriate possibilities.

AIMS AND PURPOSES FOR WRITING   The text then turns to specific purposes and assignments for writing. Chapters Three through Six ("Observing," "Remembering," "Reading," and "Investigating") focus on invention strategies. These chapters illustrate how writing to learn is a natural part of learning to write. To promote reading, writing, discussing, revising, and learning, these chapters introduce four sources of invention—*observing* people, places, events, and objects; *remembering* people, places, and events; *reading and responding* to texts; and *investigating* information through interviews, surveys, and written sources. Although students write essays intended for a variety of audiences in each of these chapters, the emphasis is on invention strategies and on writer-based purposes for writing. Although this text includes expressive and transactional elements in every assignment, the direction of the overall sequence of assignments is from the more personal forms of discourse to the more public forms.

Chapters Seven through Ten ("Explaining," "Evaluating," "Problem Solving," and "Arguing") emphasize subject- and audience-based purposes. The sequence in these chapters moves the student smoothly from exposition to argumentation (acknowledging the obvious overlapping), building on the skills and sociocognitive strategies of the previous chapters. The teacher may, in fact, use Chapters Seven through Ten as a minicourse in argument, teaching students how to develop and argue claims of fact, claims of cause and effect, claims about values, and claims about solutions or policies.

RESPONDING TO LITERATURE   Chapter Eleven guides students through the process of writing interpretive essays about short fiction, using many of the critical reading strategies, invention techniques, and shaping strategies practiced in the earlier chapters. This chapter contains three short fiction works and two student essays.

RESEARCH PAPER   Chapter Twelve ("Writing a Research Paper") draws on all the cognitive and social strategies presented in the first eleven chapters. Research papers are written for specific purposes and audiences, too, but the invention, composing, and revising processes are more extended. This chapter helps students select and plan their projects, use the library, find Internet sources, evaluate and document electronic and print sources, record their progress, and test ideas in research logs—learning all the while to integrate the information they gather with their own experiences and ideas.

HANDBOOK   A brief handbook includes a review of basic sentence elements, sentence structure and grammar, diction and style, and punctuation and mechanics.

ACKNOWLEDGMENTS

This textbook builds on the work of hundreds of teachers and researchers. Its most obvious and immediate debts are to James Kinneavy, Frank D'Angelo, Donald Murray, Rise Axelrod and Charles Cooper, Jeanne Fahnestock and Marie Secor, Linda Flower and John Hayes, Patricia Bizzell, Maxine Hairston, Frank Smith, Louise Rosenblatt, and Lynn Troyka. Beyond these are many other writers whose theories and practices contribute to this textbook: David Bartholomae, Ann Berthoff, James Britton, Kenneth Bruffee, Richard Coe, Robert Connors, Edward Corbett, Peter Elbow, Caroline Eckhardt and David Stewart, Janet Emig, Richard Fulkerson, Toby Fulwiler, George Hillocks, Richard Larson, Erika Lindemann, Stephen North, Mike Rose, Mina Shaughnessy, and Stephen Toulmin.

Since teaching writing is always a situated enterprise, I would like to thank the members of the composition faculty and staff at Colorado State University whose teaching expertise and enthusiasm have improved every page of the text and the teacher's manual: Kate Kiefer, Mike Palmquist, Donna LeCourt, Jon Leydens, Kathy Northcut, Mark Bruce, Bob White, and Laura Thomas.

In addition, the following teachers offered excellent advice about changes and additions for the fourth edition: William S. Buck, Central Oregon Community College; Marie B. Czarnecki, Mohawk Valley Community College; Gabriel Decio, McHenry County College; Cynthia Haynes, University of Texas at Dallas; Paul Heikler, Virginia

Tech; William T. Hope, Jefferson Community College; Elizabeth Metzger, University of South Florida; Tramble T. Turner, Pennsylvania State University, Abington Campus; Kathleen Walsh, Central Oregon Community College. Previous editions have benefited from suggestions by Sue V. Lape—Columbus State Community College; Jim Moody— South Suburban College; Clayton G. Holloway—Hampton University; Winifred Morgan—Edgewood College; Michael Hogan—A.E. Missouri State University; James C. McDonald—University of S. Louisiana; Sarah Liggett—Louisiana State University; Paula Gillespie—Marquette University.

For the expert crew at Prentice Hall, I am especially grateful. Phil Miller, a fine editor and friend, has enthusiastically supported this text from the first edition. Kara Hado provided ongoing editorial and organizational assistance, while Barbara Christenberry clarified the manuscript at every turn. To Gina Sluss, Tracy Augustine, Jane Pohlenz, and Rob Mejia, I can only say thanks for being such professionals—and for being such good friends.

Finally, I wish to thank my family—Joy, Shelley, Michael, Gus, and Loren—for their continued patience and active support.

—Stephen Reid

The New York Times and Prentice Hall are sponsoring Themes of the Times, a program designed to enhance student access to current information of relevance in the classroom.

Through this program, the core subject matter provided in the text is supplemented by a collection of time-sensative articles from one of the world's most distinguished newspapers, *The New York Times*. These articles demonstrate the vital, ongoing connection between what is learned in the classroom and what is happening in the world around us.

To enjoy the wealth of information of *The New York Times* daily, a reduced subscription rate is available in deliverable areas. For information, call toll-free: 1-800-631-1222. Prentice Hall and *The New York Times* are proud to cosponsor Themes of the Times. We hope it will make the reading of both textbooks and newspapers a more dynamic, involving process.

ABCNEWS

ABC News/Prentice Hall Video Library for Composition, Volume II (0-13-149030-3)

This text is accompanied by a videocassette from ABC News and Prentice Hall, which contains nine video segments, one for each of the nine chapters on purposes for writing. These videos were selected from such award-winning news programs as *20/20, World News Tonight/American Agenda, Nightline,* and *PrimeTime Live.*

ABC NEWS annotations in the Annotated Instructor's Edition indicate tie-ins between the video library and the text and show professors how to use the videos as springboards for writing and/or as "texts" for analyzing rhetorical strategies.

A video guide, the *ABC News/Prentice Hall Video Guide for Composition,* by William Costanzo of Westchester Community College, provides a synopsis for and transcripts of each video; an overview of how to use the video library in class, and teaching notes organized three ways: by textbook chapter, by video selection, and by rhetorical strategies.

CREDITS

Edward Abbey, excerpt from "The Damnation of a Canyon," from *Beyond the Wall* by Edward Abbey. Copyright © 1984 by Edward Abbey. Reprinted by permission of Henry Holt and Company, Inc. **Vicki Alexander and Grace Lyu-Volckhausen,** excerpt from "Black–Asian Conflict: Where Do We Begin?" Originally appeared in *Ms.* magazine, November/December 1991 issue. Reprinted by permission of Ms. Magazine. © 1991. **Russell Baker,** "Writing for Myself" (editor's title), excerpt from *Growing Up,* © 1982 by Russell Baker. Reprinted by permission of Congdon & Weed, Inc. **Toni Cade Bambara,** "The Lesson," from *Gorilla, My Love* by Toni Cade Bambara. Copyright © 1972 by Toni Cade Bambara. Reprinted by permission of Random House, Inc. **Wendell Berry,** excerpt from "Solving for Pattern," from *The Gift of Good Land* by Wendell Berry. Copyright © 1981 by Wendell Berry. Reprinted by permission of North Point Press, a division of Farrar, Straus & Giroux, Inc. *Consumers Reports* excerpt from "How Much Car for $3990?" Copyright 1986 by Consumers Union of United States, Inc., Mount Vernon, NY 10553. Excerpt by permission of *Consumers Reports,* February 1986. **Annie Dillard,** "The Snake," selected excerpt from *Pilgrim at Tinker Creek.* Copyright © 1974 by Annie Dillard. Reprinted by permission of HarperCollins Publishers, Inc. **Barbara Ehrenreich,** "Teach Diversity—with a Smile," from *Time* magazine, April 08, 1991. Copyright 1991 Time Inc. Reprinted by permission. **James Gorman,** "Man, Bytes, Dog." Reprinted by permission; © 1984 James Gorman. Originally in *The New Yorker.* **Stephen Jay Gould,** "Darwin's Middle Road." Reprinted from *The Panda's Thumb: More Reflections in Natural History* by Stephen Jay Gould, with the permission of W. W. Norton & Company, Inc. Copyright © 1980 by Stephen Jay Gould. **Lewis Grossberger,** "The Triumph of the Wheel," from *Rolling Stone,* December 04, 1986 by Straight Arrow Publishers Company, L.P. 1986. All rights reserved. Reprinted by permission. **Gilbert Highet,** "The Gettysburg Address." excerpt from *A Clerk of Oxenford.* Reprinted by permission of Curtis Brown, Ltd. Copyright © 1954 by Gilbert Highet. **Roy Hoffman,** "On Keeping a Journal," *Newsweek On Campus,* October 1983, Newsweek, Inc. All rights reserved. **Marjorie Hope and James Young,** excerpt from "Making the Case for Full Employment," *The Christian Century,* August 26, 1987. Reprinted by permission of *The Christian Century* magazine. **Gary Larson,** "The Far Side" cartoon is reprinted by permission of Chronicle Features, San Francisco. **Robert Kiely,** "Armageddon, Complete and Uncut," from *The New York Times,* June 05, 1990, Copyright © 1990 by The New York Times Company. Reprinted by permission. **Martin Luther King, Jr.,** excerpt from "Letter from Birmingham Jail–April 16, 1963," from *Why We Can't Wait.* Reprinted by arrangement with the heirs to the estate of Martin Luther King, Jr., c/o Joan Daves Agency as agent for the proprietor. Copyright 1963 by Martin Luther King, Jr., copyright renewed 1991 by Coretta Scott King. **Jonathan Kozol,** excerpt from *Illiterate America.* Reprinted by permission of Anchor Press, a division of Bantam, Doubleday, Dell Publishing Group, Inc. **Jeff Meer,** "Date Rape: Familiar Strangers." Reprinted with permission from *Psychology Today*

THE PRENTICE HALL GUIDE
FOR COLLEGE WRITERS

1 WRITING MYTHS AND RITUALS

Grandma Moses: *Catching the Thanksgiving Turkey.* Copyright © 1987,
Grandma Moses Properties Co., New York.
Anna Mary Robertson Moses (1860–1961), better known as "Grandma Moses," became
famous in old age for her paintings of rural America.

ONE MYTH ABOUT WRITING I HAVE BELIEVED MY WHOLE LIFE IS THAT "GOOD WRITERS ARE BORN, NOT MADE." MY ATTITUDE WHEN BEGINNING THIS WRITING COURSE WAS one of apprehension and dread. I wondered if I *could* improve my writing, or if I was destined to receive B's and C's on every essay for the rest of my life. This writing class has given me concrete examples and suggestions for improvement—not just grammar or essay maps. The freewriting is such a great help that whenever I'm stuck I immediately turn to my ten-minute freewriting to open up blocked passages. Once I get past my writer's block, I see that I can be a good writer.

❦

FOR ME, THE MOST EFFECTIVE WRITING RITUAL IS TO GATHER UP ALL OF MY STUFF—LEGAL PAD AND PENCIL, NOTES, DICTIONARY, AND THESAURUS—AND GET ON MY bike, ride to campus, and set myself up in the art lounge in the student center. During the week, I'll do this in the evening after dinner. On a weekend, I go any time from 10 a.m. to midnight. I don't write effectively at home because there are always distractions. Some people will be moving around and I'll go see who they are and what they're doing, or I'll go get a cup of coffee or a piece of toast, or I'll snap on the TV, ignoring that tiny voice inside saying, "Get busy—you have to get this done!" So what makes the art lounge better? Simple—no distractions. I can lay out all of my stuff, get a cup of coffee, and go to work. All around me people are doing the same thing, and somehow all of those hardworking people are an encouragement. The art lounge is always quiet, too—quieter than the library—and it doesn't smell like the library.

A writer is someone who writes, that's all.
—GORE VIDAL, NOVELIST AND SOCIAL COMMENTATOR

❦

I've always disliked words like inspiration. Writing is probably like a scientist thinking about some scientific problem or an engineer about an engineering problem.
—DORIS LESSING, AUTHOR OF ESSAYS AND FICTION, INCLUDING THE GOLDEN NOTEBOOK

❦

I always worked until I had something done and I always stopped when I knew what was going to happen next. That way I could be sure of going on the next day.
—ERNEST HEMINGWAY, JOURNALIST AND NOVELIST, AUTHOR OF THE OLD MAN AND THE SEA

I work at my writing as an athlete does at . . . training, taking it very seriously. What is important is the truth in it and the way that truth is expressed.

—EDNA
O'BRIEN,

NOVELIST AND
PLAYWRIGHT

AS YOU BEGIN A COLLEGE WRITING COURSE, YOU NEED TO GET RID OF SOME MYTHS ABOUT WRITING THAT YOU MAY HAVE BEEN PACKING AROUND FOR SOME TIME. DON'T allow misconceptions to ruin a good experience. Here are a few common myths about writing, followed by some facts compiled from the experiences of working writers.

MYTH: "Good writers are born, not made. A writing course really won't help my writing."

FACT: *Writers acquire their skills the same way athletes do—through practice and hard work.* There are very few "born" writers. Most writers—even professional writers and journalists—are not continually inspired to write. In fact, they often experience "writer's block"—the stressful experience of staring helplessly at a piece of paper, unable to think or to put words down on paper. A writing course will teach you how to cope with your procrastination, anxiety, lack of "inspiration," and false starts by focusing directly on solving the problems that occur during the writing process.

MYTH: "Writing courses are just a review of boring grammar and punctuation. When teachers read your writing, the only thing they mark is that stuff, anyway."

FACT: *Learning and communicating—not grammar and punctuation—come first in college writing courses.* Knowledge of grammar, spelling, punctuation, and usage is essential to editing, but it is secondary to discovering ideas, thinking, learning, and communicating. In a writing course, students learn to revise and improve the content and organization of each other's writing. *Then* they help each other edit for grammar, punctuation, or spelling errors.

MYTH: "College writing courses are really 'creative writing,' which is not what my major requires. If I wanted to be another Shakespeare and write poetry, I'd change my major."

FACT: *Writing courses emphasize rhetoric, not poetry.* Rhetoric involves practicing the most effective means or strategies for informing or persuading an audience. All writing—even technical or business writing—is "creative." Deciding what to write, how to write it, how best to get your reader's attention, and how to inform or persuade your reader requires creativity and imagination. Every major requires the skills that writing courses teach: exploring new ideas, learning concepts and processes, communicating with others, and finding fresh or creative solutions to problems.

MYTH: "Writing courses are not important in college or the real world. I'll never have to write, anyway."

FACT: *Writing courses do have a significant effect on your success in college, on the job, and in life.* Even if you don't have frequent, formal writing assignments in other courses, writing improves your note-taking, reading comprehension, and thinking skills. When you do have other written tasks or assignments, a writing course teaches you to *adapt* your writing to a variety of different purposes and audiences—whether you are writing a lab report in biology, a letter to an editor, a complaint to the Better Business Bureau, or a memorandum to your boss. Taking a writing course helps you express yourself more clearly, confidently, and persuasively—a skill that comes in handy whether you're writing a philosophy essay, a job application, or a love letter.

The most important fact about writing is that *you are already a writer.* You have been writing for years. A writer is someone who writes, not someone who writes a nationally syndicated newspaper column, publishes a bestseller, or wins a Pulitzer Prize. To be an effective writer, you don't have to earn a million dollars; you just have to practice writing often enough to get acquainted with its personal benefits for you and its value for others.

■ WARM-UP EXERCISE: FREEWRITING Put this book aside—right now—and take out pencil or pen and a piece of paper. Use this free exercise (private, unjudged, ungraded) to remind yourself that you are already a writer. Time yourself for five minutes. Write on the first thing that comes to mind—*anything whatsoever.* Write nonstop. Keep writing even if you have to write, "I can't think of anything to say. This feels stupid!" When you get an idea, pursue it.

When five minutes are up, stop writing and reread what you have written. Whether you write about a genuinely interesting topic or about the weather, freewriting is an excellent way to warm up, to get into the habit of writing, and to establish a writing ritual.

WRITING FITNESS:
RITUALS AND PRACTICE

Writing is no more magic or inspiration than any other human activity that you admire: figure skating at the Olympics, rebuilding a car engine, cooking a gourmet meal, or acting in a play. Behind every human achievement are many unglamorous hours of practice—working and sweating, falling flat on your face, and picking yourself up again. You can't learn to write just by reading some chapters in a textbook or by memorizing other people's advice. You need help and advice, but you also need practice. Consider the following parable about a Chinese painter:

A rich patron once gave money to the painter Chu Ta, asking him to paint a picture of a fish. Three years later, when he still had not received the painting, the patron went to Chu Ta's house to ask why the picture was not done. Chu Ta did not answer but dipped a brush in ink and with a few strokes drew a splendid fish. "If it is so easy," asked the patron, "why didn't you give me the picture three years ago?" Again, Chu Ta did not answer. Instead, he opened the door of a large cabinet. Thousands of pictures of fish tumbled out.

Most writers develop little rituals that help them practice their writing. A ritual is a *repeated pattern of behavior* that provides structure, security, and a sense of progress to the one who practices it. Creating your own writing rituals and making them part of your regular routine will help reduce that dreaded initial panic and enable you to call upon your writing process with confidence when you need it.

PLACE, TIME, AND TOOLS

Some writers work best in pen and ink, sprawled on their beds in the afternoon while pets snooze on nearby blankets. Others start at 8 A.M. and rely on hard chairs, clean tables, and a handful of number 2 pencils sharpened to needle points. Still others are most comfortable with their keyboards and word processors at their desks or in the computer lab. Legal-sized pads help some writers produce, while others feel motivated by spiral notebooks with pictures of mountain streams on the covers. Only you can determine which place, time, and tools give you the best support as a writer.

The place where you write is also extremely important. If you are writing in a computer lab, you have to adapt to that place, but if you write a draft in longhand or on your own word processor, you can choose the place yourself. In selecting a place, keep the following tips in mind:

- **Keep distractions minimal.** Some people simply can't write in the kitchen, where the refrigerator is distractingly close, or in a room that has a TV in it. On the other hand, a public place—a library, an empty classroom, a cafeteria—can be fine as long as the surrounding activity does not disturb you.
- **Control interruptions.** If you can close the door to your room and work without interruptions, fine. But even then, other people often assume that you want to take a break when they do. Choose a place where you can decide when it's time to take a break.
- **Have access to notes, journal, textbooks, sources, and other materials.** If the place is totally quiet but you don't have room to work or access to important notes or sources, you still may not make much progress. Whatever you need—a desk to spread your work out on,

access to notes and sources, extra pens, or computer disks—make sure your place has it.

The time of day you write and the tools you write with can also affect your attitude and efficiency. Some people like to write early in the morning, before their busy days start; others like to write in the evening, after classes or work. Whatever time you choose, try to write regularly—at least three days a week—at about the same time. If you're trying to get in shape by jogging, swimming, or doing aerobics, you wouldn't exercise for five straight hours on Monday and then take four days off. Like exercise, writing requires regular practice and conditioning.

Your writing tools—pen, pencil, paper, legal pads, four-by-six-inch note-cards, notebooks, computer—should also be comfortable for you. Some writers like to make notes with pencil and paper and write drafts on computers, some like to do all composing on computers. As you try different combinations of tools, be aware of how you feel and whether your tools make you more effective. If you feel comfortable, it will be easier to establish rituals that lead to regular practice.

Rituals are important because they help you with the most difficult part of writing—getting started. So use your familiar place, time, and tools to trick yourself into getting some words down on paper. Your mind will devise clever schemes to avoid writing those first ten words—watching TV, balancing your checkbook, drinking some more coffee, or calling a friend and whining together about all the writing you have to do. But if your body has been through the ritual before, it will walk calmly to your favorite place, where all your tools are ready (perhaps bringing the mind kicking and screaming all the way). Then, after you get the first ten words down, the mind will say, "Hey, this isn't so bad—I've got something to say about that!" And off you'll go.

Each time you perform your writing ritual, the *next* time you write will be that much easier. Soon, your ritual will let you know: *"This is where you write. This is when you write. This is what you write with."* No fooling around. Just writing.

Writers are notorious for using any reason to keep from working: overresearching, retyping, going to meetings, waxing the floors—anything.
—GLORIA STEINEM,
FORMER EDITOR OF
MS. MAGAZINE

FRANK AND ERNEST ©by Bob Thaves

I am by nature lazy, sluggish and of low energy. It constantly amazes me that I do anything at all.

—MARGARET ATWOOD,

WHO HAS MANAGED TO PRODUCE NUMEROUS BOOKS OF FICTION AND POETRY

Since I began writing I have always played games. . . . I have a playful nature; I have never been able to do things because it is my duty to do them. If I can find a way to do my duty by playing a game, then I can manage.

—MARIA IRENE FORNES,

OBIE AWARD–WINNING PLAYWRIGHT

ENERGY AND ATTITUDE

Once you've tricked yourself into the first ten words, you need to keep your attitude positive and your energy high. When you see an intimidating wall starting to form in front of you, don't ram your head into it; figure out a way to sneak around it. Try these few tricks and techniques:

- *Start anywhere, quickly.* No law says that when you sit down to write a draft, you have to "begin at the beginning." If the first sentence is hard to write, begin with the first thoughts that come to mind. Or begin with a good example from your experience. Use that to get you going; then come back and rewrite your beginning after you've figured out what you want to say.
- *Write the easiest parts first.* Forcing yourself to start a piece of writing by working on the hardest part first is a sure way to make yourself hate writing. Take the path of least resistance. If you can't get your thesis to come out right, jot down more examples. If you can't think of examples, go back to brainstorming.
- *Keep moving.* Once you've plunged in, write as fast as you can— whether you are scribbling ideas out with a pencil or hitting the keys of a typewriter or a computer. Maintain your momentum. Reread if you need to, but then plunge ahead.
- *Quit when you know what comes next.* When you do have to quit for the day, stop at a place where you know what comes next. Don't drain the well dry; stop in the middle of something you know how to finish. Make a few notes about what you need to do next and circle them. Leave yourself an easy place to get started next time.

One of the most important strategies for every writer is to *give yourself a break from the past and begin with a fresh image.* In many fields—mathematics, athletics, art, engineering—some people are late bloomers. Don't let that C or D you got in English back in the tenth grade hold you back now like a ball and chain. Imagine yourself cutting the chain and watching the ball roll away for good. Now you are free to start fresh with a clean slate. Your writing rituals should include only positive images about the writer you are right now and realistic expectations about what you can accomplish.

- *Visualize yourself writing.* Successful athletes know how to visualize a successful tennis swing, a basketball free throw, or a baseball swing. When you are planning your activities for the day, visualize yourself writing at your favorite place. Seeing yourself doing your writing will enable you to start writing more quickly and maintain a positive attitude.
- *Discover and emphasize the aspects of writing that are fun for you.* Emphasize whatever is enjoyable for you—discovering an idea, getting the organization of a paragraph to come out right, clearing the

unnecessary words and junk out of your writing. Concentrating on the parts you enjoy will help you make it through the tougher parts.

- *Set modest goals for yourself.* Don't aim for the stars; just work on a sentence. Don't measure yourself against some great writer; be your own yardstick. Compare what you write to what *you* have written before.
- *Congratulate yourself for the writing you do.* Writing is hard work; you're using words to create ideas and meanings literally out of nothing. So pat yourself on the back occasionally. Keep in mind the immortal words of comedian and playwright Steve Martin: "I think I did pretty well, considering I started out with nothing but a bunch of blank paper."

KEEPING A JOURNAL

Many writers keep some kind of notebook in which they write down their thoughts for later use. Some writers call it a "journal," a place for their day-to-day thoughts. Other writers call it a "daybook," a place to record ideas, collected information, possible outlines, titles, questions—anything related to the process of writing, thinking, and learning. Scientists and social scientists keep daily logs in which they record data or describe behavior. The word "journal" is the general term referring to "a place for daily writing." Whatever you call it, it should become part of your writing ritual. In it should go all kinds of writing. Bits and pieces of experience or memory that might come in handy later. Summary/responses of essays you read. In-class write-to-learn entries. Plans for writing your essays. A log of your writing plans and the writing problems you face. Postscripts on your writing process. Your journal is a place to practice, a closet where all your "fish paintings" go.

As the following list indicates, there are many kinds of journal entries, but they fall into three categories: *Reading Entries, Write-to-Learn Entries,* and *Writing Entries.* Reading entries help you understand and actively respond to student or professional writing. Write-to-learn entries help you summarize, react to, or question ideas or essays discussed in class. Writing entries help you warm up, test ideas, make writing plans, practice rhetorical strategies, or solve specific writing problems. All three kinds of journal writing, however, take advantage of the unique relationship between thinking, writing, and learning. Simply put, writing helps you learn what you know (and don't know) by shaping your thoughts into language.

Reading Entries

- *Prereading journal entries.* Before you read an essay, read the headnote and write for five minutes on the topic of the essay—what you know about the subject, what related experiences you have had, and what

I carry a journal with me almost all the time . . .

—NTOZAKE SHANGE,

AUTHOR OF THE PLAY FOR COLORED GIRLS WHO HAVE CONSIDERED SUICIDE WHEN THE RAINBOW IS ENUF

The most valuable writing tool I have is my daybook. . . . I write in my lap, in the living room or on the porch, in the car or an airplane, in meetings at the university, in bed, or sitting down on a rock wall during a walk. . . . It is always a form of talking to myself, a way of thinking on paper.

—DONALD MURRAY,

JOURNALIST, AUTHOR OF BOOKS AND ESSAYS ABOUT WRITING

opinions you hold. After you write your entry, the class can discuss the topic before you read the essay. The result? Your reading will be more active, engaged, and responsive.

- *Double-entry logs.* Draw a line vertically down a sheet of paper. On the left-hand side, summarize key ideas as you reread an essay. On the right-hand side, write down your reactions, responses, and questions. Writing while you read helps you understand and respond more thoroughly.
- *Essay annotations.* Writing your comments in the margin as you read is sometimes more efficient than writing separate journal entries. Also, in a small group in class, you can share your annotations and collaboratively annotate a copy of the essay.
- *Vocabulary entries.* Looking up unfamiliar words in a dictionary and writing out definitions in your journal will make you a much more accurate reader. Often an essay's thesis, meaning, or tone will hinge on the meanings of a few key words.
- *Summary/response entries.* Double-entry logs help you understand while you reread, but a short one-paragraph summary and one-paragraph response after you finish your rereading helps you focus on both the main ideas of a passage and your own key responses.

Write-to-Learn Entries

- *Lecture/discussion entries.* At key points in a class lecture or discussion, your teacher may ask you to write for five minutes by responding to a few questions: What is the main idea of the discussion? What one question would you like to ask? How does the topic of discussion relate to the essay that you are currently writing?
- *Responses to essays.* Before discussing an essay, write for a few minutes to respond to the following questions: What is the main idea of this essay? What do you like best about the essay? What is confusing, misleading, or wrong in this essay? What strategies illustrated in this essay will help you with your own writing?
- *Time-out responses.* During a controversial discussion or argument about an essay, your teacher may stop the class, take time out, and ask you to write for five minutes to respond to several questions: What key issue is the class debating? What are the main points of disagreement? What is your opinion? What evidence, either in the essay or in your experience, supports your opinion?

Writing Entries

- *Warming up.* Writing, like any other kind of activity, improves when you loosen up, stretch, get the kinks out, practice a few lines. Any daybook or journal entry gives you a chance to warm up.

- *Collecting and shaping exercises.* Some journal entries will help you collect information by observing, remembering, or investigating people, places, events, or objects. You can also record quotations or startling statistics for future writing topics. Other journal entries suggested in each chapter of this book will help you practice organizing your information. Strategies of development, such as comparison/contrast, definition, classification, or process analysis will help you discover and shape ideas.
- *Writing for a specific audience.* In some journal entries, you need to play a role. Imagine that you are in a specific situation, writing for a defined audience. For example, you might write a letter of application for a job or letter to a friend explaining why you've chosen a certain major.
- *Revision plans and postscripts.* Your journal is also the place to keep a log—a running account of your writing plans, revision plans, problems, and solutions. Include your research notes, peer responses, and postscripts on your writing process in this log.
- *Imitating styles of writers.* Use your journal to copy passages from writers you like. Practice imitating their styles on different topics. Also, try simply transcribing a few paragraphs. Even copying effective writers' words will reveal some of their secrets for successful writing.
- *Writing free journal entries.* Use your journal to record ideas, reactions to people on campus, events in the news, reactions to controversial articles in the campus newspaper, conversations after class or work, or just your private thoughts.

For each of these writing entries, let your ideas flow easily. Don't stop to fix spelling or punctuation. Focus on key images from your train of thought.

Below is a sample of a freewriting entry. The author, Terri Ciccarello, had originally decided to write about a bumper sticker that she had seen, but the more she wrote, the more it suggested related ideas to her. Although she

I just bought a bumper sticker, white writing on black that reads, "Are we having fun yet?" It struck me as funny. The purpose of that bumper sticker for those who display it is to make a statement about a way of life. Are we having fun yet? It conveys a sense of dissatisfaction at the way life is supposed to be. It's an attitude. Why does it have to be structured the way it is? Does everyone have to fit in? Is this it? Is this all? Are we having fun yet? Are we supposed to be? When do I get to do what I want to do? Why don't things go my way? Can't I play by my own rules?

That seems like a lot of "message" in one little saying, but when I read it for the first time, that's what it brought to my mind. So, I was part of the audience. I think a lot of people, especially young people are the intended audience for this sticker. Young people who are still idealistic; who think that maybe there is still time to change the world. Young people who are brought into a society they didn't organize and if they had, it would have been done differently. Young people who want to be individuals when they "grow up," not just another nameless faceless joe blow on the street. Are we having fun yet? When is it our turn to run the show?

Terri Ciccarello

never wrote an essay about that bumper sticker, the theme of being an individual and wanting to make the world a better place was an undercurrent in several of her essays. Articulating these questions helped her discover what she wanted to write about.

■   **WARMING UP: JOURNAL EXERCISES**   Choose three of the exercises below and write for ten minutes on each. Date and number each entry.

1. Make an "authority" list of activities, subjects, ideas, places, people, or events that you already know something about. List as many topics as you can. If your reaction is, "I'm not really an *authority* on anything," then imagine you've met someone from another school, state, country, or historical period. Regarding that person as your audience, what are you an "authority" on?

2. Choose one activity, sport, or hobby that you do well and that others might admire you for. In the form of a letter to a friend, describe the steps or stages of the process through which you acquired that skill or ability.

3. In two or three sentences, complete the following thought: "I have trouble writing because . . ."

4. In a few sentences, complete the following thought: "In my previous classes and from my own writing experience, I've learned that the three most important rules about writing are . . ."

5. Describe your own writing rituals. *When, where,* and *how* do you write best?

6. Write an open journal entry. Describe events from your day, images, impressions, bits of conversation—anything that catches your interest. For possible ideas for open journal entries, read the following essay by Roy Hoffman.

ON KEEPING A JOURNAL

Roy Hoffman

In a Newsweek On Campus *essay, Roy Hoffman describes his own experience, recording events and trying out ideas just as an artist doodles on a sketch pad. Your own journal entries about events, images, descriptions of people, and bits of conversation will not only improve your writing but will also become your own personal time capsule, to dig up and reread in the year 2020.*

Wherever I go I carry a small notebook in my coat or back pocket for thoughts, observations and impressions. As a writer I use this notebook as an artist would a sketch pad, for stories and essays, and as a sporadic journal of my comings and goings. When I first started keeping notebooks, though, I was not yet a professional writer. I was still in college.

I made my first notebook entries . . . just after my freshman year, in what was actually a travel log. A buddy and I were setting out to trek from our Alabama hometown to the distant tundra of Alaska. With unbounded enthusiasm I began: "Wild, crazy ecstasy wants to wrench my head from my body." The log, written in a university composition book, goes on to chronicle our adventures in the land where the sun never sets, the bars never close and the prepipeline employment prospects were so bleak we ended up taking jobs as night janitors.

When I returned to college that fall I had a small revelation: the world around me of libraries, quadrangles, Frisbees and professors was as rich with material for my journals and notebooks as galumphing moose and garrulous fishermen.

These college notebooks, which built to a pitch my senior year, are gold mines to me now. Classrooms, girlfriends, cups of coffee and lines of poetry—from mine to John Keats's—float by like clouds. As I lie beneath these clouds again, they take on familiar and distinctive shapes.

Though I can remember the campus's main quadrangle, I see it more vividly when I read my description of school on a visit during summer break: "the muggy, lassitudinal air . . . the bird noises that can not be pointed to, the summer emptiness that grows emptier with a few students squeaking by the library on poorly oiled bicycles." An economics professor I fondly remember returns with less fondness in my notebooks, "staring down at the class with his equine face." And a girl I had a crush on senior year, whom I now recall mistily, reappears with far more vitality as "the ample, slightly-gawky, whole-wheat, fractured object of my want gangling down the hall in spring heat today."

When, in reading over my notebooks, I am not peering out at quadrangles, midterm exams, professors or girlfriends, I see a portrait of my parents and hometown during holidays and occasional weekend breaks. Like a wheel, home revolves, each turn regarded differently depending on the novel or political essay I'd been most influenced by the previous semester.

Mostly, though, in wandering back through my notebooks, I meet someone who could be my younger brother: the younger version of myself. The younger me seems moodier, more inquisitive, more fun-loving and surprisingly eager to stay up all night partying or figuring out electron orbitals for a 9 a.m. exam. The younger me wanders through a hall of mirrors of the self, writes of "seeing two or three of myself on every corner," and pens long meditations on God and society before scribbling in the margin, "what a child I am." The younger me also finds humor in trying to keep track of this hall of mirrors, commenting in ragged verse.

> *I hope that one day*
> *Some grandson or cousin*
> *Will read these books,*
> *And know that I was*
> *Once a youth*
> *Sitting in drugstores with*
> *Anguished looks.*
> *And poring over coffee,*
> *And should have poured*
> *The coffee*
> *Over these lines.*

I believe that every college student should attempt to keep some form of notebook, journal or diary. A notebook is a secret garden in which to dance, sing, muse, wander, perform handstands, even cry. In the privacy of this little book, you can make faces, curse, turn somersaults and ask yourself if you're *really* in love. A notebook or journal is one of the few places you can call just your own.

. . . Journal writing suffers when you let someone, in your mind, look over your shoulder. Honesty wilts when a parent, teacher or friend looms up in your imagination to discourage you from putting your *true* thoughts on the page. Journal writing also runs a related hazard: the dizzying suspicion that one day your private thoughts, like those of Samuel Pepys or Virginia Woolf, will be published in several volumes and land up required reading for English 401. How can you write comfortably when the eyes of all future readers are upon you? Keep your notebooks with the abandon of one who knows his words will go up in smoke. Then you might really strike fire a hundred years or so from now if anyone cares to pry.

By keeping notebooks, you improve your writing ability, increasing your capacity to communicate both with yourself and others. By keeping notebooks, you discover patterns in yourself, whether lazy ones that need to be broken or healthy ones that can use some nurturing. By keeping notebooks, you heighten some moments and give substance to others: even a journey to the washateria offers potential for some offbeat journal observations. And by keeping notebooks while still in college, you chart a terrain that, for many, is more dynamically charged with ideas and discussions than the practical, workaday world just beyond. Notebooks, I believe, not only help us remember this dynamic charge, but also help us sustain it.

Not long ago, while traveling with a friend in Yorktown, Va., I passed by a time capsule buried in the ground in 1976, intended to be dug up in 2076. Keeping notebooks and journals is rather like burying time capsules into one's own life. There's no telling what old rock song, love note, philosophical complaint or rosy Saturday morning you'll unearth when you dig up these personal time capsules. You'll be able to piece together a remarkable picture of where you've come from, and may well get some important glimmers about where you're going.

2 PURPOSES AND PROCESSES FOR WRITING

Paul Klee *Nekropolis*, 1879–1940 Swiss Christie's, London

S A CHINESE-AMERICAN WOMAN GROWING UP IN AMER-ICA, YOU DECIDE TO WRITE ABOUT THE DIFFICULTY OF LIVING IN TWO CULTURES. YOU RECALL HOW, DURING your childhood, you rebelled against your mother when she insisted that you learn about your Chinese heritage. You remember how much you hated your Chinese school and how embarrassed you were that your mother could not speak English properly. As you grew older, however, you realized the price you paid for your assimilation into American culture. After discussing this conflict with your friends, you decide to describe your experiences to others who share them or who may want to know what you learned. At that point, you write an autobiographical account of your experiences and send it to a metropolitan newspaper.

❧

VETERAN SMOKER, YOU HAVE BECOME INCREASINGLY IRRITATED AT THE NONSMOKING REGULATIONS THAT HAVE APPEARED IN RESTAURANTS, BUSINESSES, AND other public places. And it's not just the laws that are irritating, but the holier-than-thou attitude of people who presume that what's good for them should be good for you. Nonsmoking laws seem to give people license to censure your behavior while totally ignoring their own offensive behavior: polluting the atmosphere with hydrocarbons, fouling the aquifers with fertilizers, and generally corrupting the social air with odors of false superiority. So after one particularly memorable experience, you write a letter to the editor of the local paper, intending not only to express your own frustration but also to satirize all those smug do-gooders.

THE WRITING FOR THIS COURSE (AND THE STRUCTURE OF THIS TEXTBOOK) STARTS WITH THE PREMISE THAT EFFECTIVE COMMUNICATION BEGINS WITH LEARNING. IT ALSO assumes that learning results—at least in part—from your written efforts to make connections and see relationships between your own observations and experience and the written or collected knowledge of others. There are four important sources for learning, writing, and communication:

- observing and describing the world around you
- remembering and drawing on your experiences
- reading and responding to textual material
- investigating knowledge through interviews, surveys, and library sources.

Writing, as a means of learning and communicating, begins with what you see and have experienced. It then makes use of what you're reading in texts, hearing in lectures, finding out at work, or learning from friends and family.

■ FREEWRITING: INVENTORY OF YOUR WRITING

Before you read further in this chapter, take out a pen or pencil and a piece of paper and inventory what you have written in the last year or two. Brainstorm a list of everything you can think of: grocery lists, letters, wedding invitations, reports, school essays, notes to friends, applications for jobs, memos to your boss. Then for one of your longer writing projects, jot down several sentences describing the situation that called for that piece of writing—*when* you did it, *whom* you wrote it for, *what* its purpose was, *where* you wrote it, and *how* you went about writing it.

Most good writing has a personal dimension. It may be about the writer personally or it may address a subject or an idea the writer cares about. It begins with honesty, curiosity, inquiry, and even vulnerability. Good writers assert themselves, knowing that they are vulnerable to other people's criticism. They take risks—sometimes writing on subjects they don't completely understand—knowing that taking their thoughts to a public forum is one way to actively engage the information that threatens to overwhelm them. By continually probing and learning, being honest with themselves, and accepting risks, writers can use their writing to teach themselves as well as their readers.

WRITING FOR MYSELF

Russell Baker

For many years, Russell Baker wrote humorous essays for The New York Times. *Before that, however, he was just a writer—someone who wrote about his experiences, what he was learning or was curious about, or what he found amusing or absurd. In this selection from his autobiography,* Growing Up, *Baker describes how bored he was as a student required to write "compositions," until he found a topic that had a personal dimension for him. The essay he wrote for his composition class, on the art of eating spaghetti, taught Baker an important truth: Writers should write honestly about topics that are important—even fun—for them.*

The notion of becoming a writer had flickered off and on in my head since the Belleville days, but it wasn't until my third year in high school that the possibility took hold. Until then I'd been bored by everything associated with English courses. I found English grammar dull and baffling. I hated the assignments to turn out leaden, lackluster paragraphs that were agonies for teachers to read and for me to write. The classics thrust on me to read seemed as deadening as chloroform.

When our class was assigned to Mr. Fleagle for third-year English I anticipated another grim year in that dreariest of subjects. Mr. Fleagle was notorious among City students for dullness and inability to inspire. He was said to be stuffy, dull, and hopelessly out of date. To me he looked to be sixty or seventy and prim to a fault. He wore primly severe eyeglasses, his wavy hair was primly cut and primly combed. He wore prim vested suits with neckties blocked primly against the collar buttons of his primly starched white shirts. He had a primly pointed jaw, a primly straight nose, and a prim manner of speaking that was so correct, so gentlemanly, that he seemed a comic antique.

I anticipated a listless, unfruitful year with Mr. Fleagle and for a long time was not disappointed. Late in the year we tackled the informal essay. Mr. Fleagle distributed a homework sheet offering us a choice of topics. None was quite so simpleminded as "What I Did on My Summer Vacation," but most seemed to be almost as dull. I took the list home and dawdled until the night before the essay was due. Sprawled on the sofa, I finally faced up to the grim task, took the list out of my notebook, and scanned it. The topic on which my eye stopped was "The Art of Eating Spaghetti."

This title produced an extraordinary sequence of mental images. Surging up out of the depths of memory came a vivid recollection of a night in Belleville when all of us were seated around the supper table—Uncle Allen, my mother, Uncle Charlie, Doris, Uncle Hal—and Aunt Pat served spaghetti for supper. Spaghetti was an exotic treat in those days. Neither Doris nor I had ever eaten spaghetti, and none of the adults had enough experience to be good at it. All the good humor of Uncle Allen's house reawoke in my mind as I recalled the laughing arguments we had that night about the socially respectable method for moving spaghetti from plate to mouth.

Suddenly I wanted to write about that, about the warmth and good feeling of it, but I wanted to put it down simply for my own joy, not for Mr. Fleagle. It was a moment I wanted to recapture and hold for myself. I wanted to relive the pleasure of an evening at New Street. To write it as I wanted, however, would violate all the rules of formal composition I'd learned in school, and Mr. Fleagle would surely give it a failing grade. Never mind. I would write something else for Mr. Fleagle after I had written this thing for myself.

When I finished it the night was half gone and there was no time left to compose a proper, respectable essay for Mr. Fleagle. There was no choice next morning but to turn in my private reminiscence of Belleville. Two days passed before Mr. Fleagle returned the graded papers, and he returned everyone's but mine. I was bracing myself for a command to report to Mr. Fleagle immediately after school for discipline when I saw him lift my paper from his desk and rap for the class's attention.

"Now, boys," he said. "I want to read you an essay. This is titled, 'The Art of Eating Spaghetti.'"

And he started to read. My words! He was reading my words out loud to the entire class. What's more, the entire class was listening. Listening attentively. Then somebody laughed, then the entire class was laughing, and not in contempt and ridicule, but with openhearted enjoyment. Even Mr. Fleagle stopped two or three times to repress a small prim smile.

I did my best to avoid showing pleasure, but what I was feeling was pure ecstasy at this startling demonstration that my words had the power to make people laugh. In the eleventh grade, at the eleventh hour as it were, I had discovered a calling. It was the happiest moment of my entire school career. When Mr. Fleagle finished he put the final seal on my happiness by saying, "Now that, boys, is an essay, don't you see. It's—don't you see—it's of the very essence of the essay, don't you see. Congratulations, Mr. Baker."

> *The writer may write to inform, to explain, to entertain, to persuade, but whatever the purpose there should be first of all, the satisfaction of the writer's own learning. . . .*
>
> **—DONALD MURRAY,**
> TEACHER AND PULITZER PRIZE–WINNING JOURNALIST

PURPOSES FOR WRITING

Getting a good grade, making a million dollars, or contributing to society may be among your motives for writing. However, as a writer, you also have more specific purposes for writing. These purposes help you make key decisions about content, structure, and style. When your main purpose is to *express* your feelings, you may write a private entry in your journal. When your main purpose is to *explain* how your sales promotion increased the number of your company's customers, you may write a factual report to your boss. When your main purpose is to *persuade* others to see a movie that you like, you may write a review for the local newspaper. In each case, the intended purpose— your desired effect on your audience—helps determine what you write and how you write it.

WRITER-BASED PURPOSES

Because writing is, or should be, for yourself first of all, everything you write involves at least some purpose that benefits you. Of course, expressing yourself is a fundamental purpose of all writing. Without the satisfaction of expressing your thoughts, feelings, reactions, knowledge, or questions, you might not make the effort to write in the first place.

A closely related purpose is learning: Writing helps you discover what you think or feel, simply by using language to identify and compose your thoughts. Writing not only helps you form ideas, but actually promotes observing and remembering. If you write down what you observe about people, places, or things, you can actually "see" them more clearly. Similarly, if you write down facts, ideas, experiences, or reactions to your readings, you will remember them longer. Writing and rewriting facts, dates, definitions, impressions, or personal experiences will improve your powers of recall on such important occasions as examinations and job interviews.

SUBJECT- AND AUDIENCE-BASED PURPOSES

Although some writing is intended only for yourself—such as entries in a diary, lists, class notes, reminders—much of your writing will be read by others, by those readers who constitute your "audience."

- You may write to *inform* others about a particular subject—to tell them about the key facts, data, feelings, people, places, or events.
- You may write to *explain* to your readers what something means, how it works, or why it happens.
- You may write to *persuade* others to believe or do something—to convince others to agree with your judgment about a book, record, or restaurant, or to persuade them to take a certain class, vote for a certain candidate, or buy some product you are advertising.

I think writing is really a process of communication. . . . It's the sense of being in contact with people who are part of a particular audience that really makes a difference to me in writing.

—SHERLEY ANN WILLIAMS,

POET, CRITIC, AND NOVELIST

- You may write to *explore* ideas and "truths," to examine how your ideas have changed, to ask questions that have no easy answers, and then to share your thoughts and reflections with others.
- You may write to *entertain*—as a primary purpose in itself or as a purpose combined with informing, explaining, persuading, or exploring. Whatever your purposes may be, good writing both teaches and pleases. Remember, too, that your readers will learn more, remember more, or be more convinced when your writing contains humor, wit, or imaginative language.

COMBINATIONS OF PURPOSES

In many cases, you write with more than one purpose in mind. Purposes may appear in combinations, connected in a sequence, or actually overlapping. Initially, you may take notes about a subject to learn and remember, but later you may want to inform others about what you have discovered. Similarly, you may begin by writing to express your feelings about a movie that you loved or that upset you; later, you may wish to persuade others to see it—or not to see it.

Purposes can also contain each other, like Chinese boxes, or overlap, blurring the distinctions. An explanation of how an automobile works will contain information about that vehicle. An attempt to persuade someone to buy an automobile may contain an explanation of how it handles and information about its body style or engine. Usually, writing to persuade others will contain explanations and basic information, but the reverse is not necessarily true; you can write simply to give information, without trying to persuade anyone to do anything.

Writing, as a rhetorical act, is carried out within a web of purpose.
—LINDA FLOWER,
TEACHER AND RESEARCHER IN COMPOSITION

SUBJECT, PURPOSE, AND THESIS

The *thesis, claim,* or *main idea* in a piece of writing is related to your purpose. As a writer, you usually have a purpose in mind that serves as a guide while you gather information about your subject and think about your audience. However, as you collect and record information, impressions, and ideas you gradually narrow your subject to a specific topic and thus clarify your purpose. You bring your purpose into sharper and sharper focus—as if progressing on a target from the outer circles to the bull's-eye—until you have narrowed your purpose down to a central thesis. The thesis is the dominant idea, explanation, evaluation, or recommendation that you want to impress upon your readers.

The following examples illustrate how a writer moves from a general subject, guided by purpose, to a specific thesis or claim.

SUBJECT	PURPOSE	THESIS, CLAIM, OR MAIN IDEA
childhood experiences	To *express* your feelings and explain how one childhood experience was important.	The relentless competition between me and my sisters distorted my easygoing personality.
heart disease	To *inform* readers about relationships between Type A personalities and heart attacks.	Type A personalities do not necessarily have an abnormally high risk of suffering heart attacks.
the death penalty	To *persuade* readers that the death penalty should be used.	Despite our belief that killing is wrong, a state-administered death penalty is fair, just, and humane.

PURPOSE AND AUDIENCE

Writing for yourself is relatively easy; after all, you already know your audience and can make spontaneous judgments about what is essential and what is not. However, when your purpose is to communicate to other readers, you need to analyze your audience. Your writing will be more effective if you can anticipate what your readers know and need to know, what they are interested in, and what their beliefs or attitudes are. As you write for different readers, you will select different kinds of information, organize it in different ways, or write in a more formal or less formal style.

■ FREEWRITING: WRITING FOR DIFFERENT AUDIENCES

Before you read further, get a pen or pencil and several sheets of paper and do the following exercise:

1. For your eyes only, write about what you did at a recent party. Write for four minutes.
2. On a second sheet of paper, describe for the members of your writing class what you did at this party; you will read it aloud to the class. Stop after four minutes.
3. On a third sheet of paper, write a letter to one of your parents describing what you did at the party. Stop after four minutes.

AUDIENCE ANALYSIS

If you are writing to communicate to other readers, analyzing your probable audience will help you answer some basic questions:

- How much information or evidence is enough? What should I assume my audience already knows? What should I not tell them? What do they believe? Will they readily agree with me or will they be antagonistic?
- How should I organize my writing? How can I get my readers' attention? Can I just describe my subject and tell a story or should I analyze everything in a logical order? Should I put my best examples or arguments first or last?
- Should I write informally, with simple sentences and easy vocabulary, or should I write in a more elaborate or specialized style, with technical vocabulary?

Analyze your audience by considering the following questions. As you learn more about your audience, the possibilities for your own role as a writer will become clearer.

1. **Audience profile.** How narrow or broad is your audience? Is it a narrow and defined audience—a single person, such as your Aunt Mary, or a group with clear common interests, such as the zoning board in your city or the readers of *Organic Gardening*? Is it a broad and diverse audience: educated readers who wish to be informed on current events, American voters as a whole, or residents of your state? Do your readers have identifiable roles? Can you determine their age, sex, economic status, ethnic background, or occupational category?

2. **Audience–subject relationship.** Consider what your readers know about your subject. If they know very little about it, you'll need to explain the basics; if they already know quite a bit, you can go straight to more difficult or complex issues. Also estimate their probable attitude toward this subject. Are they likely to be sympathetic or hostile?

3. **Audience–writer relationship.** What is your relationship with your readers? Do you know each other personally? Do you have anything in common? Will your audience be likely to trust what you say or will they be skeptical about your judgments? Are you the expert on this particular subject and the readers the novices? Or are you the novice and your readers the experts?

4. **Writer's role.** To communicate effectively with your audience, you should also consider your own role or perspective. Of the many roles that you could play (friend, big sister or brother, student of psychology, music fan, employee of a fast-food restaurant, and so on), choose one that will be effective for your purpose and audience. If, for example, you are writing to sixth-graders about nutrition, you could choose the perspective of a concerned older brother or sister. Your writing might be more effective, however, if you assume the role of a person who has worked in fast-food restaurants for three years and knows what goes into hamburgers, french fries, and milkshakes.

Writers may write to real audiences, or they may create audiences. Sometimes the relationship between writer and reader is real (sister writing to brother), so the writer starts with a known audience and writes accordingly. Sometimes, however, writers begin and gradually discover or create an audience in the process of writing. Knowing the audience guides the writing, but the writing may construct an audience as well.

THE WRITING SITUATION

Taken together, the writer's purpose or aim, the subject, and the probable audience (whether yourself or others) define the writing situation. Sometimes an instructor or employer assigns you a specific writing situation. At other times, you yourself construct a situation from scratch.

The components of the writing situation—writer, subject, purpose, thesis, and audience—are so interrelated that a change in one may affect the other three. As you write, therefore, you do not always follow a step-by-step order. You may begin, for example, with a specific audience on which you wish to make an impression; as you analyze the audience, you decide what subject and purpose would be most appropriate. Conversely, you may start with an interesting subject but no clear sense of purpose or audience. Or you may be asked to write for a certain audience and then you discover that its needs and expectations have led you to discover or modify your purpose or subject. In short, subject, purpose, thesis, and audience are all modified, reconsidered, and revised as you write.

The following examples illustrate how subject, purpose, and audience combine to define a writing situation.

In response to a request by an editor of a college recruiting pamphlet, a student decides to write an essay explaining the advantages of the social and academic life at his university. According to the editor, the account needs to be realistic but should also promote the university. It shouldn't be too academic and stuffy—the college catalogue itself contains all the basic information—but it should give high school seniors a flavor of college life. The student decides to write a narrative account of his most interesting experiences during his first week at college.

A student majoring in journalism reads about correspondents' accounts of restrictions during the Persian Gulf conflict. The military limited reporters to carefully controlled "pools," and during the ground offensive, television journalists' tapes were mysteriously delayed or lost until after the ground war was over. Following a class debate on the public's right to know versus the military's need to maintain secrecy in times of war, the student investigates specific incidents to see if the military exercised unnecessary or excessive censorship. The student researches these incidents and reports her findings in a letter to her congressional representative, asking for a further investigation of certain cases of alleged censorship.

PURPOSE AND AUDIENCE

IN TWO ESSAYS

The two short essays that follow appeared as columns in newspapers. Both relate the writers' own experiences. They are similar in form but have different purposes and appeal to different kinds of readers. As you read each essay, decide which one you find more interesting—and why.

THE STRUGGLE TO BE AN ALL-AMERICAN GIRL

Elizabeth Wong

It's still there, the Chinese school on Yale Street where my brother and I used to go. Despite the new coat of paint and the high wire fence, the school I knew 10 years ago remains remarkably, stoically the same.

Every day at 5 p.m., instead of playing with our fourth- and fifth-grade friends or sneaking out to the empty lot to hunt ghosts and animal bones, my brother and I had to go to Chinese school. No amount of kicking, screaming, or pleading could dissuade my mother, who was solidly determined to have us learn the language of our heritage.

Forcibly, she walked us the seven long, hilly blocks from our home to school, depositing our defiant tearful faces before the stern principal. My only memory of him is that he swayed on his heels like a palm tree, and he always clasped his impatient twitching hands behind his back. I recognized him as a repressed maniacal child killer, and knew that if we ever saw his hands we'd be in big trouble.

We all sat in little chairs in an empty auditorium. The room smelled like Chinese medicine, and imported faraway mustiness. Like ancient mothballs or dirty closets. I hated that smell. I favored crisp new scents. Like the soft French perfume that my American teacher wore in public school.

Although the emphasis at the school was mainly language—speaking, reading, writing—the lessons always began with an exercise in politeness. With the entrance of the teacher, the best student would tap a bell and everyone would get up, kowtow, and chant, "sing san ho," the phonetic for "How are you, teacher?"

Being ten years old, I had better things to learn than ideographs copied painstakingly in lines that ran right to left from the tip of a *moc but*, a real ink pen that had to be held in an awkward way if blotches were to be avoided. After all, I could do the multiplication tables, name the satellites of Mars, and write reports on "Little Women" and "Black Beauty." Nancy Drew, my favorite book heroine, never spoke Chinese.

The language was a source of embarrassment. More times than not, I had tried to disassociate myself from the nagging loud voice that followed me wherever I wandered in the nearby American supermarket outside Chinatown. The voice belonged to my grandmother, a fragile woman in her seventies who could outshout the best of the street vendors. Her humor was raunchy, her Chinese rhythmless, patternless. It was quick, it was loud, it was unbeautiful. It was not like the quiet, lilting romance of French or the gentle refinement of the American South. Chinese sounded pedestrian. Public.

In Chinatown, the comings and goings of hundreds of Chinese on their daily tasks sounded chaotic and frenzied. I did not want to be thought of as mad, as talking gibberish. When I spoke English, people nodded at me, smiled sweetly, said encouraging words. Even the people in my culture would cluck and say that I'd do well in life. "My, doesn't she move her lips fast," they would say, meaning that I'd be able to keep up with the world outside Chinatown.

My brother was even more fanatical than I about speaking English. He was especially hard on my mother, criticizing her, often cruelly, for her pidgin speech—smatterings of Chinese scattered like chop suey in her conversation. "It's not 'What it is,' Mom," he'd say in exasperation. "It's 'What is it, what is it, what is it!'" Sometimes Mom might leave out an occasional "the" or "a," or perhaps a verb of being. He would stop her in mid-sentence: "Say it again, Mom. Say it right." When he tripped over his own tongue, he'd blame it on her: "See, Mom, it's all your fault. You set a bad example."

After two years of writing with a *moc but* and reciting words with multiples of meanings, I finally was granted a cultural divorce. I was permitted to stop Chinese school.

I thought of myself as multicultural. I preferred tacos to egg rolls; I enjoyed Cinco de Mayo more than Chinese New Year.

At last, I was one of you; I wasn't one of them.

Sadly, I still am.

I'M O.K., BUT YOU'RE NOT

Robert Zoellner

The American novelist John Barth, in his early novel, *The Floating Opera*, remarks that ordinary, day-to-day life often presents us with embarrassingly obvious, totally unsubtle patterns of symbolism and meaning—life in the midst of death, innocence vindicated, youth versus age, etc.

The truth of Barth's insight was brought home to me recently while having breakfast in a lawn-bordered restaurant on College Avenue near the Colorado State University campus. I had asked to be seated in the smoking section of the restaurant—I have happily gone through three or four packs a day for the past 40 years.

As it happened, the hostess seated me—I was by myself—at a little two-person table on the dividing line between the smoking and non-smoking sections. Presently, a well-dressed couple of advanced years, his hair a magisterial white and hers an electric blue, were seated in the non-smoking section five feet away from me.

It was apparent within a minute that my cigarette smoke was bugging them badly, and soon the husband leaned over and asked me if I would please stop smoking. As a chronic smokestack, I normally comply, out of simple courtesy, with such requests. Even an addict such as myself can quit for as long as 20 minutes.

But his manner was so self-righteous and peremptory—he reminded me of Lee Iacocca boasting about Chrysler—that the promptings of original sin, always a problem with me, took over. I quietly pointed out that I was in the smoking section—if only by five feet—and that that fact meant that I had met my social obligation to non-smokers. Besides, the idea of morning coffee without a cigarette was simply inconceivable to me—might as well ask me to vote Republican.

The two of them ate their eggs-over-easy in hurried and sullen silence, while I chain-smoked over my coffee. As well as be hung for a sheep as a lamb, I reasoned. Presently they got up, paid their bill, and stalked out in an ambiance of affronted righteousness and affluent propriety.

And this is where John Barth comes in. They had parked their car—a diesel Mercedes—where it could be seen from my table. And in the car, waiting impatiently, was a splendidly matched pair of pedigreed poodles, male and female.

Both dogs were clearly in extremis, and when the back door of the car was opened, they made for the restaurant lawn in considerable haste. Without ado (no pun intended), the male did a doo-doo that would have done credit to an animal twice his size, and finished off with a leisurely, ruminative wee-wee. The bitch of the pair, as might be expected of any well-brought-up female of Republican proclivities, confined herself to a modest wee-wee, fastidious, diffident, and quickly executed.

Having thus polluted the restaurant lawn, the four of them marshalled their collective dignity and drove off in a dense cloud of blue smoke—that lovely white Mercedes was urgently in need of a valve-and-ring job, its emission sticker an obvious exercise in creative writing.

As I regretfully watched them go—after all, the four of them had made my day—it seemed to me that they were in something of a hurry, and I uncharitably wondered if the husband was not anxious to get home in order to light the first Fall fire in his moss-rock fireplace, or apply the Fall ration of chemical fertilizer to his doubtlessly impeccable lawn, thus adding another half-pound of particulates to the local atmosphere and another 10 pounds of nitrates and other poisons to the regional aquifers. But that, of course, is pure and unkindly speculation.

In any case, the point of this real-life vignette, as John Barth would insist, is obvious. The current controversy over public smoking in Fort Collins is a clear instance of selective virtue at work, coming under the rubric of, what I do is perfectly OK, but what you do is perfectly awful.

QUESTIONS FOR WRITING AND DISCUSSION

1. Choosing only one adjective to describe your main reaction to each essay, answer the following question: "When I finished the _____ [Wong, Zoellner] essay, I was _____ [intrigued, bored, amused, irritated, curious, confused, or _____] because _____. Explain your choice of adjectives in one or two sentences.

2. Referring to specific passages, explain the purpose and state the thesis or main point of each essay.

3. What personality or role does each writer project? Drawing from evidence in the essay, describe what you think both writers would be like if you met them.

4. Both of these essays appeared in newspapers. What kind of reader would find each essay interesting? What kind of reader would not enjoy each essay? For each essay, find examples of specific sentences, word choices, vocabulary, experiences, or references to culture or politics that would appeal to one reader but perhaps irritate another.

5. These two essays are similar in form—they are both informal essays narrating personal experiences and explaining what each

I don't see writing as communication of something already discovered, as "truths" already known. Rather, I see writing as a job of experiment. It's like any discovery job; you don't know what's going to happen until you try it.

—WILLIAM STAFFORD,

TEACHER, POET, AND ESSAYIST

writer discovered or learned. There are differences, however, in structure and style. What differences do you notice in the way each essay begins and concludes, in the order of the paragraphs, and in vocabulary or style of the sentences?

DIMENSIONS OF THE PROCESS

Processes for writing vary from one writer to the next and from one writing situation to the next. Most writers, however, can identify four basic stages, or dimensions, of their writing process: collecting, shaping, drafting, and revising. The writing situation may precede these stages—particularly if you are assigned a subject, purpose, audience, and form. Usually, however, you continue to narrow your subject, clarify your purpose, meet the needs of your audience, and modify your form as you work through the dimensions of your writing process.

COLLECTING

Mark Twain, author of *Huckleberry Finn,* once observed that if you attempt to carry a cat around the block by its tail, you'll gain a whole lot of information about cats that you'll never forget. You may collect such firsthand information, or you may rely on the data, experience, or expertise of others. In any case, writers constantly collect facts, impressions, opinions, and ideas that are relevant to their subjects, purposes, and audiences. Collecting involves observing, remembering, imagining, thinking, reading, listening, writing, investigating, talking, taking notes, and experimenting. Collecting also involves thinking about the relationships among the bits of information that you have collected.

SHAPING

Writers focus and organize the facts, examples, and ideas that they have collected into the recorded, linear form that is written language. When a hurricane hits the Gulf Coast, for example, residents of Texas, Louisiana, Mississippi, Alabama, and Florida are likely to collect an enormous amount of data in just a few hours. Rain, floods, tree limbs snapping in the wind, unboarded windows shattering, sirens blaring—all of these events occur nearly simultaneously. If you try to write about such devastation, you need to narrow your focus (you can't describe everything that happened) and organize your information (you can't describe all of your experiences at the same time).

A chronological order is just one of the shapes that a writer may choose to develop and organize experience. Such shaping strategies also help writers collect additional information and ideas. Reconstructing a chronological order, for example, may suggest some additional details—perhaps a wet, miserable-looking dog running through the heavy downpour—that you might not otherwise have remembered.

DRAFTING

At some point, writers actually write down a rough version of what will evolve into the finished piece of writing. Drafting processes vary widely from one writer to the next. Some writers prefer to reread their collecting and shaping notes, find a starting point, and launch themselves—figuring out what they want to say as they write it. Other writers start with a plan—a mental strategy, a short list, or an outline—of how they wish to proceed. Whatever approach you use in your draft, write down as much as possible: You want to see whether the information is clear, whether your overall shape expresses and clarifies your purpose, and whether your content and organization meet the needs and expectations of your audience.

REVISING

When writers revise rough drafts, they literally "resee" their subjects—and then modify drafts to fit new visions. Revision is more than just tinkering with a word here and there; revision leads to larger changes—new examples or details, a different organization, or a new perspective. You accomplish these changes by adding, deleting, substituting, or reordering words, sentences, and paragraphs. Although revision begins the moment you get your first idea, most revisions are based on the reactions—or anticipated reactions—of the audience to your draft. You often play the role of audience yourself by putting the draft aside and rereading it later when you have some distance from your writing. Wherever you feel readers might not get your point, you revise to make it clearer. You may also get feedback from readers in a class workshop, suggesting that you collect more or different information, alter the shape of your draft to improve the flow of ideas, or clarify your terminology. As a result of your rereading and your readers' suggestions, you may change your thesis or write for an entirely different audience.

Editing—in contrast to revising—focuses on the minor changes that you make to improve the accuracy and readability of your language. You usually edit your essay to improve word choice, grammar, usage, or punctuation. You also use a computer spell-check program and proofread to catch typos and other surface errors.

The writing process is not linear, moving smoothly in one direction from start to finish. It is messy, recursive, convoluted, and uneven. Writers write, plan, revise, anticipate, and review throughout the writing process. . . .

—MAXINE HAIRSTON,

TEACHER AND AUTHOR OF ARTICLES AND TEXTBOOKS ON WRITING

We must and do write each our own way.

—EUDORA WELTY,

NOVELIST AND ESSAYIST

THE WHOLE PROCESS

In practice, a writer's process rarely follows the simple, consecutive order that these four stages or dimensions suggest. The writing process is actually recursive: It begins at one point, goes on to another, comes back to the first, jumps to the third, and so forth. A stage may last hours or only a second or two. While writing a letter to a friend, you may collect, shape, revise, and edit in one quick draft; a research paper may require repeated shaping over a two-week period. As writers draft, they may correct a few mistakes or typos, but they may not proofread until many days later. In the middle of reorganizing an essay, writers often reread drafts, go back and ask more questions, and collect more data. Even while editing, writers may throw out several paragraphs, collect some additional information, and draft new sections.

In addition to the recursive nature of the writing process, keep in mind that writing often occurs during every stage, not just during drafting and revising. During collecting, you will be recording information and jotting down ideas. During shaping, you will be writing out trial versions that you may use later when you draft or revise. Throughout the writing process, you use your writing to modify your subject, purpose, audience, and form.

The most important point to keep in mind is that the writing process is unique to each writer and to each writing situation. What works for one writer may be absolutely wrong for you. Some writers compose nearly everything in their heads. Others write only after discussing the subject with friends or drawing diagrams and pictures.

During the writing process, you need to experiment with several collecting, shaping, and drafting strategies to see what works best for you and for a particular piece of writing. As long as your process works, however, it's legitimate—no matter how many times you backtrack and repeat stages. When you are struggling with a piece of writing, remember that numerous revisions are a normal part of the writing process—even for most professionals.

Circling back over what you have already written—to sharpen your thesis, improve the organization, tighten up a paragraph, or add specific details to your examples—is likely to be the most time consuming, yet worthwhile, part of your writing process. Most professional writers testify to the necessity and value of writing numerous drafts. When you are reworking a piece of writing, scrawling revisions over what you had hoped would be your finished product, remember what Nobel laureate Isaac Bashevis Singer once pointed out: "The wastepaper basket is the writer's best friend."

WRITING WITH A COMPUTER

Some students who are taking college writing courses have never used computers for writing essays or papers. If you are one of those students, don't panic. Most schools have computer laboratories with well-trained, knowledgeable staff who will help you learn how to write with a computer. Over the period of the semester, you'll become more comfortable at a keyboard and less worried when you press the wrong key or accidentally delete a sentence or paragraph. Gradually, you'll learn when you still want to use a pencil and paper and when you want to compose and revise on the computer. In the long run, the computer's revision capabilities and high-quality printing—not to mention its access to the Internet—will make your writing faster, easier, and more professional looking.

Many students, however, already have experience with computers. They have written papers on personal computers with one of the popular word-processing programs, such as Microsoft Word, Windows, or WordPerfect. They have struggled through the frustration of learning to type, learning a word-processing program, and revising on a computer screen because they know the potential benefits are great. Now, they can create files for each of their courses or papers, and they know how to find information, draft, reorganize, revise, and edit their essays. If you are one of those students, you may learn how to make your writing even more efficient and productive by using your computer lab's updated equipment.

Usually, college computer writing laboratories or classrooms provide additional software programs to assist with the writing and revising processes. First, the lab computers may have some composing software—such as Blue Pencil, Writer's Helper, or Daedelus—that prompts writers to freewrite, brainstorm, dialogue, question, outline, organize, and revise. In addition, the lab computers have spelling checkers, thesauruses, and even style checkers to help with editing. Today, however, many college computer labs or classrooms have added two new capabilities that transform the computer from a writing machine into a high-tech communicating and information gathering tool. These two technologies are *networks* and *hypertexts*.

Networks are created when several computers are linked so that they can communicate with each other. Compared to a stand-alone computer, networked computers offer special advantages both within the writing classroom and outside of the classroom. In the writing classroom or laboratory, writers can communicate with each other and with their teachers in a variety of ways. First, they can use electronic mail (e-mail) to send messages or even entire files to their peers or to teachers. Teachers and students can read drafts and offer suggestions while a student is revising. In

For better or worse, less of me will remain unsaid because of the speed and ease and even intimacy of computer-assisted writing.

—PETER R. STILLMAN,

TEACHER AND ESSAYIST

WRITING WITH COMPUTERS

The computer can assist you both as a writing tool and as a networking tool. Listed in the left-hand column are writing activities that a stand-alone computer provides. Listed in the right-hand column are the additional capabilities of computers tied into a network.

The Computer as a Writing Tool
- Freewriting
- Brainstorming
- Double-entry reading log
- Answers to "Wh" questions
- Insert/delete sentences
- Move paragraphs
- Style/usage checkers
- Thesaurus
- Spelling checker
- Print preview

The Computer as a Networking Tool
- Access to bulletin boards
- E-mail messages
- E-mail essays or files
- "Chat" dialogues
- Access to on-line library catalogs
- Access to the Internet and the World Wide Web

---

addition, some networked classrooms allow writers to send messages or "chat" with each other on their computers, just as they might sit and talk across a table. Finally, some classrooms or labs have electronic bulletin boards available for public comment and reaction. A writer can electronically send his or her essay draft to a bulletin board and have students in the class comment on his or her work-in-progress. If the class agrees, a writer's essay or his or her bulletin board comments can be anonymous or identified by a fictional name.

In addition to facilitating communication within a classroom, many computers can access the Internet and the World Wide Web in order to tap an incredible array of information sources across the campus and around the world. With immediate access to library on-line catalogs, writers don't have to make repeated trips across campus to the library to find information for their essays. In a few minutes, they can check the holdings of their library and—if they wish—the holdings of dozens of other libraries. In some cases, they can print out bibliographic information, abstracts of articles, or even entire articles without leaving their computer. Networked computers also help writers reach beyond the campus. Networked computers offer access to the information superhighway through the Internet and the World Wide Web. Overall, networked computers offer several key advantages for writers: They save time, paper, and printing costs; they give writers quick access to information; and they electronically reinforce the idea that a writing class is a supportive, interactive learning community.

While most people are familiar with some relatively simple hypertext sites on the World Wide Web, not everyone has visited one of the sophisticated academic hypertext environments that already exist at some websites and in some compact disk (CD-ROM) formats. A hypertext is simply a computer-based system that allows readers and writers to take multiple paths through a network of available passages or texts. For example, if you were learning about computer technology in a hypertext format, you might be able to select the word "hypertext" from a menu on your screen and get any of the following: a short history of hypertexts; a comment on the difference between hypertext and hypermedia (hypermedia usually adds graphics, sound, and/or animation); a definition of "virtual reality"; or a bibliography of articles about the uses of hypertext in computer classrooms. Instead of having to read through a whole chapter in conventional print format, hypertexts allow you to select what you want to learn next. By combining the technologies of television, audio, compact disks (CDs), networks, and computers, hypertexts are already changing how we access information, how we learn, and even how we communicate with other people.

■ WARMING UP: JOURNAL EXERCISES The following exercises will help you review and practice the topics the lab covered in this chapter. In addition, you may discover a subject for your own writing. Choose three of the following entries, and write for ten minutes on each.

1. Reread your "authority" list from Chapter 1. Choose one of those subjects and then explain your purpose and a possible audience for that subject.

2. Find a sample of writing from a magazine or newspaper article, an advertisement, a letter, or even from graffiti on walls. What is the purpose of that writing? Who is the intended audience? Why is the writing effective or ineffective?

3. Read Neil Petrie's essay and postscript at the end of this chapter. Then find the best paper you've written during the past year or two and write a "postscript" for it. Describe (a) the writing situation, (b) your purpose, and (c) the process you used to write it.

4. If you have already been given a writing assignment in another course, explain the purpose and the intended audience for that assignment. What might be your process for writing that essay?

5. During the first week of the term, one of your friends, Mark Lindstrom, is in an accident and is hospitalized. While still under the effects of anesthesia, he scribbles the following note for you to mail to his parents.

> Dear Mom and Dad,
>
> I arrived here last week. The trip was terrible. Dr. Stevens says that my leg will be better soon. My roommate is very strange. The police say my money is gone forever.
>
> Please send $1,500 to my new address right away.
>
> Thanks!
>
> Your loving son
>
> Mark

Because you were at the accident and can fill in the details, Mark asks you to explain everything to his parents. Write a short letter to them. Next, write a paragraph to your best friend that describes what happened to Mark.

6. Write an open-journal entry. Writing for yourself, describe one event from your week that upset or angered you. What did you learn from this event?

7. Explore the availability of computers on your campus. Where is the English Department computer lab? What services does it offer? What other computer facilities are available?

A WRITING PROCESS AT WORK:
COLLECTING AND SHAPING

ATHLETES AND EDUCATION

Neil H. Petrie

In the following essay that appeared in The Chronicle of Higher Education, *Neil H. Petrie argues that colleges have a hypocritical attitude toward student athletes. Although most universities claim that their ath-*

letes—both male and female—are in college to get a good education, in reality, the pressures on athletes compromise their academic careers. The problem, Petrie argues, is not the old cliché that jocks are dumb, but that the endless hours devoted to practice or spent on road trips drain even the good student-athlete's physical and mental energies. Colleges point with pride to a tiny number of athletes who become professionals, but much more frequently the collegiate system encourages athletes to settle for lower grades and incomplete programs. In far too many cases, athletes never graduate. These are the students that, as Petrie says, "the system uses and then discards after the final buzzer."

I have spent all my adult life in academe, first as a student and then as a professor. During that time I have seen many variations in the role of inter-collegiate athletics in the university, and I've developed sharply split opinions on the subject. On one hand, I despise the system, clinging as it does to the academic body like a parasite. On the other hand, I feel sympathy and admiration for most of the young athletes struggling to balance the task of getting an education with the need to devote most of their energies to the excessive demands of the gym and the field. **(1)**

My earliest experiences with the intrusion of athletics into the classroom came while I was still a freshman at the University of Colorado. While I was in my English professor's office one day, a colleague of hers came by for a chat. Their talk turned to the football coach's efforts to court the favor of the teachers responsible for his gladiators by treating them to dinner and a solic-itous discussion of the academic progress of the players. I vividly recall my professor saying, "He can take me out to dinner if he wants, but if he thinks I'll pass his knuckleheads just because of that, he'd better think again." **(2)**

Later, as a graduate teaching fellow, a lecturer, and then an assistant pro-fessor of English, I had ample opportunity to observe a Division I university's athletics program. I soon discovered that the prevailing stereotypes did not always apply. Athletes turned out to be as diverse as any other group of stu-dents in their habits, tastes, and abilities, and they showed a wide range of strategies for coping with the stress of their dual roles. **(3)**

Some of them were poor students. An extreme example was the All-American football player (later a successful pro) who saw college only as a step to a six-figure contract and openly showed his disdain for the educational process. Others did such marginal work in my courses that I got the feeling they were daring me to give them D's or F's. One woman cross-country star, who almost never attended my composition class, used to push nearly illiter-ate essays under my office door at odd hours. **(4)**

Yet many athletes were among the brightest students I had. Not so sur-prising, when you consider that, in addition to physical prowess, success in athletics requires intelligence, competitive drive, and dedication—all qualities that can translate into success in the classroom as well as on the field. The trouble is that the grinding hours of practice and road trips rob student athletes of precious study time and deplete their reserves of mental and physical energy. A few top athletes have earned A's; most are content to settle for B's or C's, even if they are capable of better. **(5)**

The athletes' educational experience can't help being marred by their numerous absences and divided loyalties. In this respect, they are little different from the students who attempt to go to college while caring for a family or working long hours at an outside job. The athletes, however, get extra help in juggling their responsibilities. Although I have never been bribed or threatened and have never received a dinner invitation from a coach, I am expected to provide extra time and consideration for athletes, far beyond what I give other students. **(6)**

Take the midterm grade reports, for example. At my university, the athletic department's academic counselor sends progress questionnaires to every teacher of varsity athletes. While the procedure shows admirable concern for the academic performance of athletes, it also amounts to preferential treatment. It requires teachers to take time from other teaching duties to fill out and return the forms for the athletes. (No other students get such progress reports.) If I were a cynic it would occur to me that the athletic department might actually be more concerned with athletes' eligibility than with their academic work. **(7)**

Special attendance policies for athletes are another example of preferential treatment. Athletes miss a lot of classes. In fact, I think the road trip is one of the main reasons that athletes receive a deficient education. You simply can't learn as much away from the classroom and the library as on the campus. Nevertheless, professors continue to provide make-up tests, alternative assignments, and special tutoring sessions to accommodate athletes. Any other student would have to have been very sick or the victim of a serious accident to get such dispensations. **(8)**

It is sad to see bright young athletes knowingly compromise their potential and settle for much less education than they deserve. It is infuriating, though, to see the ones less gifted academically exploited by a system that they do not comprehend and robbed of any possible chance to grow intellectually and to explore other opportunities. **(9)**

One specific incident illustrates for me the worst aspects of college athletics. It wasn't unusual or extraordinary—just the all-too-ordinary case of an athlete not quite good enough to make a living from athletics and blind to the opportunity afforded by the classroom. **(10)**

I was sitting in my office near the beginning of a term, talking to a parade of new advisees. I glanced up to see my entire doorway filled with the bulk of a large young man, whom I recognized as one of our basketball stars from several seasons ago who had left for the pros and now apparently come back. **(11)**

Over the next hour I got an intensive course on what it's like to be a college athlete. In high school, John had never been interested in much outside of basketball, and, like many other indifferent students, he went on to junior college on an athletic scholarship. After graduating, he came to the university, where he played for two more years, finishing out his eligibility. He was picked in a late round of the N.B.A. draft and left college, but in the end he turned out to be a step too slow for the pros. By that time he had a family to support, and when he realized he could never make a career of basketball, he decided to return to college. **(12)**

We both knew that his previous academic career hadn't been particularly focused, and that because of transferring and taking minimum course loads during the basketball season, he wouldn't be close to a degree. But I don't think either one of us was prepared for what actually emerged from our examination of his transcripts. It was almost as if he had never gone beyond high school. His junior-college transcript was filled with remedial and nonacademic courses. **(13)**

Credit for those had not transferred to the university. Over the next two years he had taken a hodgepodge of courses, mostly in physical education. He had never received any advice about putting together a coherent program leading to a degree. In short, the academic side of his college experience had been completely neglected by coaches, advisers, and, of course, John himself. **(14)**

By the time we had evaluated his transcripts and worked out a tentative course of study, John was in shock and I was angry. It was going to take him at least three years of full-time study to complete a degree. He thanked me politely for my time, picked up the planning sheets, and left. I was ashamed to be a part of the university that day. Why hadn't anyone in the athletic department ever told him what it would take to earn a degree? Or at least been honest enough to say, "Listen, we can keep you eligible and give you a chance to play ball, but don't kid yourself into thinking you'll be getting an education, too." **(15)**

I saw John several more times during the year. He tried for a while. He took classes, worked, supported his family, and then he left again. I lost track of him after that. I can only hope that he found a satisfying job or completed his education at some other institution. I know people say the situation has improved in the last few years, but when I read about the shockingly low percentages of athletes who graduate, I think of John. **(16)**

Colleges give student athletes preferential treatment. We let them cut classes. We let them slide through. We protect them from harsh realities. We applaud them for entertaining us and wink when they compromise themselves intellectually. We give them special dorms, special meals, special tutors, and a specially reprehensible form of hypocrisy. **(17)**

I can live with the thought of the athletes who knowingly use the college-athletics system to get their pro contracts or their devalued degrees. But I have trouble living with the thought of the ones whom the system uses and then discards after the final buzzer. **(18)**

ON WRITING "ATHLETES AND EDUCATION"

In the following postscript on his writing process, Neil Petrie describes why he wanted to write the paper, how he collected material to support his argument, and how he shaped and focused his ideas as he wrote. His comments illustrate how his purpose—to expose the hypocrisies of collegiate athletics— guided his writing of the essay. In addition, Petrie explains that other key questions affected the shape of his essay: how he should begin, where he should use his best example, and what words he should choose.

This essay has its origin, as all persuasive writing should, in a strongly held opinion. I'm always more comfortable if I care deeply about my subject matter. As a teacher, I hold some powerful convictions about the uneasy marriage of big-time athletics and higher education, and so I wanted to write an essay that would expose what I think are the dangers and hypocrisies of that system.

At the beginning of my essay, I wanted to establish some authority to lend credibility to my argument. Rather than gather statistics on drop-out rates of student athletes or collect the opinions of experts, I planned to rely on my own experiences as both a student and teacher. I hoped to convince my readers that my opinions were based on the authority of firsthand knowledge. In this introduction I was also aware of the need to avoid turning off readers who might dismiss me as a "jock hater." I had to project my negative feelings about the athletic system while maintaining my sympathy with the individual student athletes involved in that system. The thesis, then, would emerge gradually as I accumulated the evidence; it would be more implied than explicitly stated.

Gathering the material was easy. I selected a series of examples from my personal experiences as a college student and instructor, as well as anecdotes I'd heard from other instructors. Most of these stories were ones that I had shared before, either in private discussions with friends or in classrooms with students. Shaping the material was a little tougher. As I began thinking about my examples and how to order them, I saw that I really wanted to make two main points. The first was that most colleges give preferential treatment to athletes. The second point was that, despite the extra attention, the success of the athlete's academic career is often ignored by all parties involved. Many of my examples, I realized, illustrated the varieties of pressures put upon both athletes and instructors to make sure that the students at least get by in class and remain eligible. These examples seemed to cluster together because they showed the frustrations of teachers and the reactions of athletes trying to juggle sports and academics. This group would make a good introduction to my general exposé of the system. But I had one more example I wanted to use that seemed to go beyond the cynicism of some athletes or the hypocrisy of the educators. This was the case of John, an athlete who illustrated what I thought were the most exploitative aspects of varsity athletics. I originally planned on devoting the bulk of my essay to this story and decided to place it near the end where it would make my second point with maximum emotional effect.

A two-part structure for the essay now emerged. In the first segment following my introductory paragraph, I gave a series of shorter examples, choosing to order them in roughly chronological order (paragraphs 2–4). I then moved from these specific details to a more general discussion of the demands placed upon both students and teachers, such as lengthy practice time, grade reports, road trips, and special attendance policies. This concluded my description of the way the system operates (paragraphs 5–8).

Then it was time to shift gears, to provide a transition to the next part of my essay, to what I thought was my strongest example. I wanted the story of John to show how the system destroyed human potential. To do this, I needed to increase the seriousness of the tone in order to persuade the reader that I was dealing in more than a little bureaucratic boondoggling. I tried to set the tone by my word choice: I moved from words such as "sad," "compromise," and "settle" to words with much stronger emotional connotations such as "infuriating," "exploited," and "robbed," all in a single short transitional paragraph (paragraph 9).

I then introduced my final extended example in equally strong language, identifying it as a worst-case illustration (paragraph 10). I elaborated on John's story, letting the details and my reactions to his situation carry the more intense outrage that I was trying to convey in this second part of the essay (paragraphs 10–16). The first version that I tried was a rambling narrative that had an overly long recounting of John's high school and college careers. So I tightened this section by eliminating such items as his progress through the ranks of professional basketball and his dreams of million-dollar contracts. I also cut down on a discussion of the various courses of study he was considering as options. The result was a sharper focus on the central issue of John's dilemma: the lack of adequate degree counseling for athletes.

After my extended example, all that was left was the conclusion. As I wrote, I was very conscious of using certain devices, such as the repetition of key words and sentence patterns in paragraph seventeen ("We let them

. . . We let them . . . We protect them . . . We applaud them . . . We give them . . . ") to maintain the heightened emotional tone. I was also conscious of repeating the two-part structure of the essay in the last two paragraphs. I moved from general preferential treatment (paragraph 17) to the concluding and more disturbing idea of devastating exploitation (paragraph 18).

On the whole, I believe that this essay effectively conveys its point through the force of accumulated detail. My personal experience was the primary source of evidence, and that experience led naturally to the order of the paragraphs and to the argument I wished to make: that while some athletes knowingly use the system, others are used and exploited by it.

QUESTIONS FOR WRITING AND DISCUSSION

1. In your journal, describe how your extracurricular activities (athletics, jobs, clubs, or family obligations) have or have not interfered with your education. Recall one specific incident that illustrates how these activities affected your classwork—either positively or negatively.

2. Describe Petrie's audience and purpose for this essay. What sentences reveal his intended audience? What sentences reveal his purpose? What sentences contain his thesis, claim, or main idea? Do you agree with that thesis? Why or why not?

3. Reread Petrie's postscript. Based on his comments and on your reading of the essay, how does Petrie describe or label each of the following sections of his essay:

   paragraphs 1–4
   paragraphs 5–8
   paragraphs 9
   paragraphs 10–16
   paragraphs 17–18.

4. Who do you think is most to blame for the situation that Petrie describes: The athletes themselves? The colleges for paying their scholarships and then ignoring them when they drop out? The students and alumni who pay to see their teams win?

5. Petrie does not explicitly suggest a solution to the problem that he describes. Assume, however, that he has been asked by the president of his university to propose a solution. Write the letter that you think Petrie would send to the president.

A WRITING PROCESS AT WORK:

DRAFTING AND REVISING

While drafting and revising, writers frequently make crucial changes in their ideas and language. The first scribbled sentences, written primarily for ourselves, are often totally different from what we later present to other people in final, polished versions. Take, for example, the final version of Abraham Lincoln's Gettysburg Address. It begins with the famous lines "Four score and seven years ago our fathers brought forth on this continent a new nation . . ." But his first draft might well have begun, "Eighty-seven years ago, several politicians and other powerful men in the American Colonies got together and decided to start a new country . . ." It is difficult to imagine that language ingrained in our consciousness was once drafted, revised, drafted again, and edited, as the author or authors added, deleted, reordered, and otherwise altered words, sentences, and ideas. In fact, it usually was.

Carl Becker's study of the American Declaration of Independence assembles the early drafts of that famous document and compares them with the final version. Shown below is Thomas Jefferson's first draft, with revisions made by Benjamin Franklin, John Adams, and other members of the Committee of Five that was charged with developing the new document.

Thomas Jefferson's Rough Draft of the Opening Sentences of the Declaration of Independence

When in the course of human events it becomes necessary for a people to [*one* inserted above] [a struck]

~~dissolve the political bonds which have connected them with another, and to~~ advance from that subordination in which they have hitherto remained, & to

assume among the powers of the earth the ~~equal & independent~~ station to [*separate and equal* inserted above]

which the laws of nature & of nature's god entitle them, a decent respect to

the opinions of mankind requires that they should declare the causes which

impel them to ~~the change.~~ [*the separation.* inserted above] *self-evident*

We hold these truths ~~to be sacred & undeniable~~; that all men are created eq

they are endowed by their creator with

~~& independent~~; that ~~from that equal creation they derive in rights~~ inherent

rights; that   these

& inalienable among ~~which~~ are ~~the preservation of~~ life, ~~&~~ liberty, & the

pursuit of happiness. . . .

The Final Draft of the Opening Sentences of the Declaration of Independence, as Approved on July 4, 1776.

When in the Course of human events, it becomes necessary for one people to dissolve the political bands, which have connected them with another, and to assume among the powers of the earth, the separate and equal station to which the Laws of Nature and of Nature's God entitle them, a decent respect to the opinions of mankind requires that they should declare the causes which impel them to the separation.

We hold these truths to be self-evident, that all men are created equal, that they are endowed by their Creator with certain unalienable Rights, that among these are Life, Liberty and the pursuit of Happiness.

QUESTIONS FOR WRITING AND DISCUSSION

1. Describe your reaction to the "rough draft" of the Declaration of Independence. Where did it seem strange or make you feel uncomfortable?

2. Select one change in a sentence that most improved the final version. Explain how the revised wording is more effective.

3. Find one change in a word or phrase that constitutes an alteration in meaning rather than just a choice of "smoother" or more appropriate language. How does this change affect the meaning?

4. Upon rereading this passage from the Declaration of Independence, one reader wrote, "I was really irritated by that 'all men are created equal' remark. The writers were white, free, well-to-do, Anglo-Saxon, mostly Protestant males discussing their own 'unalienable rights.' They sure weren't discussing the 'unalienable rights' of female Americans or of a million slaves or of nonwhite free Americans!" Revise the passage from the Declaration of Independence using this person as your audience.

3 OBSERVING

Leonardo da Vinci. *Mona Lisa.* Louvre, Paris, France.

IN THE FAR CORNER OF A FRIEND'S LIVING ROOM IS A LIGHTED AQUARIUM. INSTEAD OF WATER, THE AQUARIUM HAS A FEW INCHES OF WHITE SAND, A DISH OF WATER, and a small piece of pottery. When you ask about the aquarium, your friend excitedly says, "You mean you haven't met Nino?" In a matter of seconds, you have a small, tannish-brown snake practically in your lap, and your friend is saying, "This is Nino. She—or he—is an African sand boa." You imagined that all boa constrictors were those huge snakes that suffocated and then swallowed babies. "Actually," replies your friend, "Nino is very shy. She prefers to burrow in the sand." The snake is fascinating. It is only fifteen inches long, with a strong, compact body and a stub tail. Before it burrows into your coat pocket, you observe it closely so you can describe it to your younger brother, who loves all kinds of snakes.

❧

IN THE PHYSICS LABORATORY, YOU'RE DOING AN EXPERIMENT ON LIGHT REFRACTION. YOU NEED TO OBSERVE HOW LIGHT RAYS BEND AS THEY GO THROUGH WATER, SO you take notes describing the procedure and the results. During each phase of the experiment, you observe and record the angles of refraction. The data and your notes will help you write up the lab report that is due next Monday.

My task . . . is, by the power of the written word, to make you hear, to make you feel— it is, before all, to make you see.
—JOSEPH CONRAD, AUTHOR OF <u>HEART OF DARKNESS</u> AND OTHER NOVELS

❧

Seeing is of course very much a matter of verbalization. Unless I call my attention to what passes before my eyes, I simply won't see it.
—ANNIE DILLARD, NATURALIST AND AUTHOR OF <u>PILGRIM AT TINKER CREEK</u>

O BSERVING IS ESSENTIAL TO GOOD WRITING. WHETHER YOU ARE WRITING IN A JOURNAL, DOING A LABORATORY REPORT FOR A SCIENCE CLASS, DASHING OFF A MEMO AT WORK, OR writing a letter to the editor of a newspaper, keen observation is essential. Writing or verbalizing what you see helps you discover and learn more about your environment. Sometimes your purpose is limited to yourself: You observe and record to help you understand your world or yourself better. At other times, your purpose extends to a wider audience: You want to share what you have learned with others to help them learn as well. No matter who your audience is or what your subject may be, however, your task is to see and to help your readers see.

Of course, observing involves more than just "seeing." Good writers draw on all their senses: sight, smell, touch, taste, hearing. In addition, however, experienced writers also notice what is *not* there. The smell of food that should be coming from the kitchen but isn't. A friend who usually is present but now is absent. The absolute quiet in the air that precedes an impending storm. Writers should also look for *changes* in their subjects—from light to dark, from rough to smooth, from bitter to sweet, from noise to sudden silence. Good writers learn to use their previous *experiences* and their *imaginations* to draw comparisons and create images. Does a sea urchin look and feel like a pincushion with the pins stuck in the wrong way? Does the room feel as cramped and airless as the inside of a microwave oven? Finally, good writers write from a specific point of view or role: a student describing basic laws of physics or an experienced worker in a mental health clinic describing the clientele.

Depending on your purpose and audience, writing from observation can be relatively *objective,* as when you record what is actually, demonstrably there; or it can be more *subjective,* as when you suggest how you feel, think, or react to a subject. For example, you might describe a bicycle objectively as a "secondhand blue Bridgestone MB-3 mountain bike with a 25-inch Ritchey Logic frame, Shimano Deore DX derailleurs, a Shimano crank, Dia Compe brakes, and an Avocet saddle." You might need to communicate that kind of objective information to a prospective buyer or to an employee in a cycle repair shop. On the other hand, you may wish to communicate the bicycle's subjective feel—how easily it pedals, how it cranks up steep, rocky trails, or how solid it feels on rough terrain. In most situations, however, good writers describe their subjects both objectively and subjectively. They use some objectivity for accuracy and specific detail and some subjectivity to suggest the value or relevance of subjects in a human environment.

The key to effective observing is to *show* your reader the person, place, event, or object through *specific detail.* Good description allows the reader to draw general conclusions based on specific detail. Rather than just telling a reader, "This bicycle has good technical components," the writer should show or describe how it feels as she rides it. If your reader is going to learn from your observations, you need to give the *exact details that you learned from,* not just your conclusions or generalizations. Even in writing, experience is the best teacher, so use specific details to communicate the feel, the data, the sights and sounds and smells. Whether you are a tourist describing the cliff dwellings at Mesa Verde, a salesperson analyzing consumer preferences for your boss, a physicist presenting data on a new superconducting material to other physicists, or a social worker putting together the details of a child-abuse case, your first task is to describe your subject—to show your readers, to make them *see.*

TECHNIQUES FOR WRITING
ABOUT OBSERVATIONS

. . . Not that it's raining, but the feel of being rained upon.

—E. L. DOCTOROW,

AUTHOR OF <u>RAGTIME</u> AND OTHER NOVELS

The short passages that follow all use specific techniques for observing people, places, objects, or events. Some emphasize objective detail; some recreate subjective reactions or feelings. In all the passages, however, the writer *narrows* or *limits* the scope of the observation and selects specific details. The result is some *dominant idea.* The dominant idea reflects the writer's purpose for that particular audience. As you read these excerpts, notice how the authors use the following six techniques for recording vivid observations:

- **Giving sensory details (sight, sound, smell, touch, taste).** Also include *actual dialogue* and *names of things* where appropriate. Good writers often "zoom in" on crucial details.
- **Using comparisons and images.** To help readers visualize the unfamiliar (or see the commonplace in a new light), writers often draw comparisons and use evocative images.
- **Describing what is *not* there.** Sometimes keen observation requires stepping back and noticing what is absent, what is not happening, or who is not present.
- **Noting changes in the subject's form or condition.** Even when the subject appears static—a landscape, a flower, a building—good writers look for evidence of changes, past or future: a tree being enveloped by tent worms, a six-inch purple-and-white iris that eight hours earlier was just a green bud, a sandstone exterior of a church being eroded by acid rain.

- **Writing from a distinct point of view.** Good writers assume distinct roles; in turn, perspective helps clarify what they observe. A lover and a botanist, for example, see entirely different things in the same red rose. *What* is seen depends on *who* is doing the seeing.
- **Focusing on a dominant idea.** Good writers focus on those details and images that clarify the main ideas or discoveries. Discovery often depends on the *contrast* between the reality and the writer's expectations.

These six techniques are illustrated in the following two paragraphs by Karen Blixen, who wrote *Out of Africa* under the pen name Isak Dinesen. A Danish woman who moved to Kenya to start a coffee plantation, Blixen knew little about the animals in Kenya Reserve. In this excerpt from her journals, she describes a startling change that occurred when she shot a large iguana. (The annotations in the margin identify all six observing techniques.)

Role: A newcomer to the Reserve

Comparisons and images

Sensory details
Comparisons and images

In the Reserve I have sometimes come upon the Iguana, the big lizards, as they were sunning themselves upon a flat stone in a riverbed. They are not pretty in shape, but nothing can be imagined more beautiful than their coloring. They shine like a heap of precious stones or like a pane cut out of an old church window. When, as you approach, they swish away, there is a flash of azure, green and purple over the stones, the color seems to be standing behind them in the air, like a comet's luminous tail.

Changes in condition
Sensory detail

What is not there
Dominant idea: now colorless and dead

Once I shot an Iguana. I thought that I should be able to make some pretty things from his skin. A strange thing happened then, that I have never afterwards forgotten. As I went up to him, where he was lying dead upon his stone, and actually while I was walking the few steps, he faded and grew pale, all color died out of him as in one long sigh, and by the time that I touched him he was grey and dull like a lump of concrete. It was the live impetuous blood pulsating within the animal, which had radiated out all that glow and splendor. Now that the flame was put out, and the soul had flown, the Iguana was as dead as a sandbag.

OBSERVING PEOPLE

Observing people—their dress, facial features, body language, attitudes, behavior, skills, quirks, habits, and conversation—is a pastime that we all share. When writers describe people, however, they zero in on specific details that fit overall patterns or impressions. In an *Esquire* magazine article, for example, Joseph Nocera profiles Steven Jobs, the cocreator of the Apple and Macintosh computers and the ex-chairman of the board of Apple Computer. All of Nocera's details reinforce his dominant idea that Steven Jobs is a temperamental boy genius.

> With personal computers so ubiquitous today, you tend to forget that . . . the Apple II, the machine that began it all, was unleashed upon an unsuspecting world in 1977. You forget, that is, until you sit in a room full of people who have built them and realize how young they are. Jobs himself is only thirty-one. If anything, he looks younger. He is lithe and wiry. He is wearing faded jeans (no belt), a white cotton shirt (perfectly pressed), and a pair of brown suede wing-tipped shoes. There is a bounce to his step that betrays a certain youthful cockiness; the quarterback of your high school football team used to walk that way. His thin, handsome face does not even appear to need a daily shave. And that impression of eternal youth is reinforced by some guileless, almost childlike traits: by the way, for instance, he can't resist showing off his brutal, withering intelligence whenever he's around someone he doesn't think measures up. Or by his almost willful lack of tact. Or by his inability to hide his boredom when he is forced to endure something that doesn't interest him, like a sixth grader who can't wait for class to end.

Role: writer as an outsider looks objectively at jobs, is probably older

Dominant idea: youth
Sensory detail: visual description

Comparison and image

What is not there: facial hair

What is not there: tact

Comparison

OBSERVING PLACES

In the following excerpt from *Brown Girl, Brownstones,* Paule Marshall creates a catalog of the sights, sounds, and smells of a Brooklyn street during the Great Depression of the 1930s. In this paragraph, she records a typical Saturday night on Fulton Street: the bright lights, the clamorous street activity, the mixed odors of foods, and the faces of the street people. The specific details contribute to the overall idea of vibrant, chaotic energy.

> Unlike Chauncey Street, Fulton Street this summer Saturday night was a whirling spectrum of neon signs, movie marquees, bright-lit store windows and sweeping yellow streamers of light from the cars. It was canorous voices, hooted laughter and curses ripping the night's warm cloak; a welter of dark faces and gold-etched teeth; children crying high among the fire escapes of the tenements; the subway rumbling below; the unrelenting wail of a blues spilling from a bar; greasy counters and fish sandwiches and barbecue and hot sauce; trays of chitterlings and hog maws and fat back in the meat stores; the trolley's insistent clangor; a man and woman in a hallway

bedroom, sleeping like children now that the wildness had passed; a drunken woman pitching along the street; the sustained shriek of a police car and its red light stabbing nervously at faces and windows. Fulton Street on Saturday night was all beauty and desperation and sadness.

Compare Marshall's portrait of the clamorous activity on Fulton Street with John Muir's evocative description of California and the Yosemite Valley, written 130 years ago. John Muir, of course, was the founder of the Sierra Club, whose first mission was to preserve the vision of Yosemite that Muir paints in the following paragraphs. Notice how Muir uses all of the key techniques for observing as he vividly describes the California Sierra.

Arriving by the Panama steamer, I stopped one day in San Francisco and then inquired for the nearest way out of town. "But where do you want to go?" asked the man to whom I had applied for this important information. "To any place that is wild," I said. This reply startled him. He seemed to fear I might be crazy and therefore the sooner I was out of town the better, so he directed me to the Oakland ferry.

So on the first of April, 1868, I set out afoot for Yosemite. It was the bloom-time of the year over the lowlands and coast ranges; the landscapes of the Santa Clara Valley were fairly drenched with sunshine, all the air was quivering with the songs of the meadow-larks, and the hills were so covered with flowers that they seemed to be painted. Slow indeed was my progress through these glorious gardens, the first of the California flora I had seen. Cattle and cultivation were making few scars as yet, and I wandered enchanted in long wavering curves, knowing by my pocket map that Yosemite Valley lay to the east and that I should surely find it.

Looking eastward from the summit of the Pacheco Pass one shining morning, a landscape was displayed that after all my wanderings still appears as the most beautiful I have ever beheld. At my feet lay the Great Central Valley of California, level and flowery, like a lake of pure sunshine, forty or fifty miles wide, five hundred miles long, one rich furred garden of yellow *Compositae*. And from the eastern boundary of this vast golden flower-bed rose the mighty Sierra, miles in height, and so gloriously colored and so radiant, it seemed not clothed with light, but wholly composed of it, like the wall of some celestial city. Along the top and extending a good way down, was a rich pearl-gray belt of snow; below it a belt of blue and dark purple, marking the extension of the forests; and stretching along the base of the range a broad belt of rose-purple; all these colors, from the blue sky to the yellow valley smoothly blending as they do in a rainbow, making a wall of light ineffably fine. Then it seemed to me that the Sierra should be called, not the Nevada or Snowy Range, but the Range of Light.

In general views no mark of man is visible upon it, nor anything to suggest the wonderful depth and grandeur of its sculpture. None of its magnificent forest-crowned ridges seems to rise much above the general level to publish its wealth. No great valley or river is seen, or group of well-marked features of any kind standing out as distinct pictures. Even the summit peaks, marshaled in glorious array so high in the sky, seem comparatively regular in form. Nevertheless the whole range five hundred miles long is furrowed with canyons 2,000 to 5,000 feet deep, in which once flowed majestic glaciers, and in which now flow and sing the bright rejoicing rivers.

OBSERVING OBJECTS

In observing an inanimate object such as a cookie, Paul Goldberger brings his special point of view—architecture critic for *The New York Times*—to his description. He totally ignores the cookie's taste, ingredients, and calories, focusing instead on the architectural relationships of function and form. Goldberger's architectural perspective helps focus his observations, creating a dominant idea for each passage.

Sugar Wafer (Nabisco)   There is no attempt to imitate the ancient forms of traditional, individually baked cookies here—this is a modern cookie through and through. Its simple rectangular form, clean and pure, just reeks of mass production and modern technological methods. The two wafers, held together by the sugar-cream filling, appear to float . . . this is a machine-age object.

Fig Newton (Nabisco)   This, too, is a sandwich but different in every way from the Sugar Wafer. Here the imagery is more traditional, more sensual even; a rounded form of cookie dough arcs over the fig concoction inside, and the whole is soft and pliable. Like all good pieces of design, it has an appropriate form for its use, since the insides of Fig Newtons can ooze and would not be held in place by a more rigid form. The thing could have had a somewhat different shape, but the rounded tip is a comfortable, familiar image, and it's easy to hold. Not a revolutionary object but an intelligent one.

OBSERVING EVENTS

Observing events requires weaving specific details about people, places, and objects into some chronological order, as in the following account of a rhythm-and-blues performance by Bobby "Blue" Bland. The paragraph, taken from Peter Guralnick's *Lost Highway: Journeys & Arrivals of American Musicians,* demonstrates how vivid, specific details (names of singers, a description of barefoot dancing, titles of songs, the recording of actual dialogue and lyrics) create a dominant idea: a single night's performance blurs into an endless series of one-night stands.

Every night it is exactly the same. The band, a brass-heavy ten pieces with dilapidated reading stands that say "Mel Jackson/MFs Bobby Bland's Revue," does a desultory thirty-minute set. Then Burnett Williams, singer, valet, bus driver, and all-around good fellow, swings affably into a succession of Al Green numbers and current soul hits. The band plays dispiritedly behind him; even the bandleader, Mel Jackson, has disappeared from the stand; but Burnett always works up a sweat, finishing out his segment with shoes kicked off, doing the barefoot to the strains of "Love and Happiness." This invariably cracks up Mel Jackson, who reappears precisely at this point, dapper, diminutive, very much in charge. His eyes gleam and dart skittishly about the room as he laughs out loud, proclaims, "That boy doing some barefooting!" and gives Burnett a soul slap and quick little hug as the warm-up singer departs from the stage, his shoes held delicately aloft. Then it's Show Time, Ladies and Gentlemen, a Young Man Who Needs No Introduction, he'll Take Care of You, Further on Up the Road, won't let you Cry No More, cause when you Cry Cry Cry he just wants to Turn On Your Lovelights, well he's a Good-Time Charlie, and You're the One (That He Adores), but now The Feeling is Gone and he's Two steps From the Blues. The string of hits becomes a litany, a numbing incantation. Audience talk becomes louder and more distracted, and then Bobby "Blue" Bland appears, big shambling, sleepy-eyed, a cigarette between his fingers, tongue licking at the edge of his lips. He plays aimlessly for a moment with the microphone, his eyes cast upwards as if for inspiration, the band kicks off, and that smooth, mellow, almost hornlike voice slides in among the three trumpets, trombone, and saxophone (guitar, bass, two drummers, and occasionally a piano round out the band). "I pity the fool/I pity the fool that falls in love with you. . . ." It is ten-thirty, and Bobby "Blue" Bland is just going to work.

■ **WARMING UP: JOURNAL EXERCISES** The following topics will help you practice close, detailed observation and may possibly suggest a subject for your assignment on observing. Read the following exercises and then write on the two or three that interest you the most.

1. Go to a public place (library, bar, restaurant, hospital emergency room, gas station, laundromat, park, shopping mall, hotel lobby, police station, beach, skating rink, beauty salon, city dump, tennis court, church, etc.). Sit and observe everything around you. Use your pencil to help you see, both by drawing sketches and by recording sensory details in words. What do you see that you haven't noticed before? Then *narrow* your attention to a single

For Godsake, keep your eyes open. Notice what's going on around you.
—WILLIAM BURROUGHS,
NOVELIST

person, *focus* on a restricted place, or *zoom in* on a single object. What do you see that you haven't noticed before?

2. Buy a piece of fruit or a vegetable. An apple, orange, pear, carrot, or onion will do, but if possible find a persimmon, pawpaw, mango, pineapple, guava, pomegranate, coconut, passion fruit, artichoke, cauliflower, broccoli, jicama, bok choy, or rutabaga. Sit down somewhere and look at it. Record your impressions. Hold it close to your ear and shake it. Record your impressions. Scrape your fingernail over the surface. Rub it against your cheek. Record your impressions. Close your eyes and sample it with your tongue. Record your impressions. Scratch the surface with a utensil. Now close your eyes and smell it. Record your impressions. Peel it or take it apart. Describe what it looks like now. Take a bite out of it. Record your impressions.

3. Find a place where people (either friends or strangers) are talking (over lunch, at a bar, at a party). For ten or fifteen minutes, record the conversation word for word. To keep friends from being self-conscious, tell them that you're doing homework. If you're eaves-dropping on strangers, be as inconspicuous as possible. Your purpose is to record as much of the dialogue as possible, with the pauses, interruptions, *"uh's* and *er's,"* unfinished sentences, slang—everything *exactly* as you hear it.

4. In one of your classes, use your repeated observations of the total learning environment (the room, the seating arrangements, the blackboards, the audiovisual or computer equipment, the teacher, the daily teaching or learning rituals, and the students) to specu-late on who has authority, how knowledge is created or communi-cated, and what the learning goals are for this course.

5. *Obnoxious,* the dictionary says, means "highly disagreeable, offen-sive, irritating, odious." Describe the most obnoxious person you know by giving at least two detailed examples of his or her behav-ior. Or do just the reverse: Tell how the most obnoxious person you know would describe you.

6. Go to a gallery, studio, or museum where you can observe sculp-ture, paintings, or other works of art. Choose one work of art and draw it. Then describe it as fully as possible. Return to the gallery the next day, reread your first description, observe the work again, and add details that you didn't notice the first time.

7. Visit a local park. Pretend that you are a landscape architect, a photographer, a bird-watcher, an entomologist, an engineer build-ing a road, a jogger, or a mother with two small children. Describe

what you see. Now choose another role—you're a social worker, a woman alone in a park at night, a person without a home, a Secret Service agent assigned to protect the President of the United States, a Saint Bernard, or a sixth-grader just out of school for the day. Describe what you see. Then reread both descriptions. Compare them. Briefly, explain how and why they are similar or dissimilar.

8. After every episode of *Beverly Hills 90210,* Danny Drennen, a writer who lives in New York City, spends nearly six hours writing a detailed account of the events of the show. After reading the following paragraphs from one of Drennen's recent accounts, watch a TV show of your own choosing and write an account, imitating Drennen's descriptive, humorous style. (To check other accounts by Danny Drennen, visit his "90210 Weekly Wrapup" at his website, Inquisitor Mediarama.)

So this show starts off in the Clare/Donna/Kelly Compound, and Clare is like, "I'm sorry, Kelly, I just don't think it's a good idea," and Donna "Transformer Barbie" Martin, sitting uncomfortably on the chintz armchair and wearing a white bathrobe embroidered with blue cloud-looking things, is like, "Are you sure Tara doesn't have anyplace else to stay?" Kelly "My Eyebrows Are Back" Taylor is wearing a blue pajama top and is sitting in the brown-and-white cowhide chair, which goes so well with any decor, and her hair is about twelve shades lighter than last time, and she is like, "Yeah, she has someplace else to go—the streets. That was her former address." Then we switch to a colorized version of *The Munsters* because there's Lily Munster—NO WAIT!—It's Clare, wearing a lilac print blouse over a gray T-shirt thing and black pants, and someone should define the word "subtle highlights" to the person who does Clare's hair, because I think they left the coloring on too long. Clare is like, "My point exactly," and Donna is like, "Look, Tara is sweet— I just wish we knew her better," and Clare is like, "How long would this arrangement be for? I mean, when would she move out?" and Kelly is like, "It would only be for a couple of weeks."

So then . . . Tara and Kelly are in the kitchen making breakfast, and Tara is making coffee and asking whether she can have some of Clare's juice, and Kelly is all, "Pour me some too" and that finishes off the juice. Tara is all freaking out, and Kelly is all reassuring her that "We all share around here," and then the door opens, and all of a sudden we are watching a 1950s horror movie because Vampira is walking in the door—NO WAIT! It's Clare, wearing an atrociously horrendous chartreuse blouse over a bright orange T-shirt with pegged black pants and Romanesque wrap-up sandals and carrying a vermilion leather bag, and with her is Donna, equally horrifying in a too short long-sleeved almost-shiny gray and white-striped sweater-ish thing over a cut-off T-shirt and gray camel-toe hiphugger pants and vinyl white sandals and a sad, sad macramé bag and big old metal barrettes in her hair. . . .

Over at Casa Walsh, Brandon "VO5" Walsh is hunting and pecking away at his PowerBook, and can someone please explain to Brandon that the WHOLE POINT of the Apple PowerBook keyboard is that you can rest your wrists ON THE KEYBOARD part of the computer to make typing easier, and therefore there is no reason why he should be arching his hands in from the side like that. Val walks in and goes, "Hey," and Brandon in his car-salesman voice goes, "Hey Val, how's it going," without even looking up, and Val goes, "Colin's looking at jail time no matter how you cut it," and Brandon goes, "Ooh—I guess you've got to commit murder to get away with anything in this town," and HOW OBNOXIOUS is that? I mean, here you are living in the most exclusive neighborhood in L.A. where rich white men get away with major crimes EACH AND EVERY DAY, and beyond which nine out of ten movies that come out of Hollywood are MAJOR CRIMES AGAINST HUMAN-ITY, not to mention particular television shows that shall remain nameless, and if rampant bad taste via television programming were a crime, L.A. would be turned into a huge prison and Jason Priestly would be serving fifty years to life. So Val goes, "Fine," and Brandon goes, "Fine," and Val goes, "Fine," and Brandon goes, "Fine," and Val screws up her face at Brandon and gets up to leave, and as she exits Brandon goes, "Fine," and Val goes, "Fine," and Brandon goes back to making clickety-clack typewriter noises with his PowerBook.

OBSERVING:

PROFESSIONAL WRITING

THE SNAKE

Annie Dillard

Annie Dillard was born in Pittsburgh in 1945 and received her B.A. and M.A. degrees from Hollins College. She has published a book of poetry, Tickets for a Prayer Wheel *(1974), columns and essays for* Living Wilderness, Harper's, *and the* Atlantic, *and several books, including* An

American Childhood (1987), A Writing Life *(1989), and* Modern American Memoirs *(1995). In the following selection from* Pilgrim at Tinker Creek (1974), *Dillard carefully observes a snake, a poisonous copperhead, as it lies on a sandstone quarry ledge at twilight. To her surprise, a mosquito alights on the snake and goes about its business of drilling through the scaly skin and sucking the snake's blood. Observing this bizarre episode, Dillard wonders about the laws of biological survival: "A little blood here, a chomp there, and still we live, trampling the grass? Must everything whole be nibbled?"*

There was a snake at the quarry with me tonight. It lay shaded by cliffs on a flat sandstone ledge above the quarry's dark waters. I was thirty feet away, sitting on the forest path overlook, when my eye caught the dark scrawl on the rocks, the lazy sinuosity that can only mean snake. I approached for a better look, edging my way down the steep rock cutting, and saw that the snake was only twelve or thirteen inches long. Its body was thick for its length. I came closer still, and saw the unmistakable undulating bands of brown, the hourglasses: copperhead. **(1)**

I never step a foot out of the house, even in winter, without a snakebite kit in my pocket. Mine is a small kit in rubber casing about the size of a shotgun shell; I slapped my pants instinctively to fix in my mind its location. Then I stomped hard on the ground a few times and sat down beside the snake. **(2)**

The young copperhead was motionless on its rock. Although it lay in a loose sprawl, all I saw at first was a camouflage pattern of particolored splotches confused by the rushing speckles of light in the weeds between us, and by the deep twilight dark of the quarry pond beyond the rock. Then suddenly the form of its head emerged from the confusion: burnished brown, triangular, blunt as a stone ax. Its head and the first four inches of its body rested on airy nothing an inch above the rock. I admired the snake. Its scales shone with newness, bright and buffed. Its body was perfect, whole and unblemished. I found it hard to believe it had not just been created on the spot, or hatched fresh from its mother, so unscathed and clean was its body, so unmarked by any passage. **(3)**

Did it see me? I was only four feet away, seated on the weedy cliff behind the sandstone ledge; the snake was between me and the quarry pond. I waved an arm in its direction: nothing moved. Its low-forehead glare and lipless reptile smirk revealed nothing. How could I tell where it was looking, what it was seeing? I squinted at its head, staring at those eyes like the glass eyes of a stuffed warbler, at those scales like shields canted and lapped just so, to frame an improbable, unfathomable face. **(4)**

Yes, it knew I was there. There was something about its eyes, some alien alertness . . . what on earth must it be like to have scales on your face? All right then, copperhead. I know you're here, you know I'm here. This is a big night. I dug my elbows into rough rock and dry soil and settled back on the hillside to begin the long business of waiting out a snake. **(5)**

The only other poisonous snake around here is the timber rattler, *Crotalus horridus horridus*. These grow up to six feet long in the mountains, and as big as your thigh. I've never seen one in the wild; I don't know how many have seen me. I see copperheads, though, sunning in the dust, disappearing into rock cliff chinks, crossing dirt roads at twilight. Copperheads have no rattle, of course, and, at least in my experience, they do not give way. You walk around a copperhead—if you see it. Copperheads are not big enough or venomous enough to kill adult humans readily, but they do account for far and away the greatest number of poisonous snakebites in North America: there are so many of them, and people, in the Eastern woodlands. It always interests me when I read about new studies being done on pit vipers; the team of herpetologists always seems to pick my neck of the woods for its fieldwork. I infer that we have got poisonous snakes as East Africa has zebras or the tropics have orchids—they are our specialty, our stock-in-trade. So I try to keep my eyes open. But I don't worry: you have to live pretty far out to be more than a day from a hospital. And worrying about getting it in the face from a timber rattler is like worrying about being struck by a meteorite: life's too short. Anyway, perhaps the actual bite is painless. . . . **(6)**

The copperhead in front of me was motionless; its head still hung in the air above the sandstone rock. I thought of poking at it with a weed, but rejected the notion. Still, I wished it would do something. Marston Bates tells about an English ecologist, Charles Elton, who said, with his Britishness fully unfurled, "All cold-blooded animals . . . spend an unexpectedly large proportion of their time doing nothing at all, or at any rate nothing in particular." That is precisely what this one was doing. **(7)**

I noticed its tail. It tapered to nothingness. I started back at the head and slid my eye down its body slowly: taper, taper, taper, scales, tiny scales, air. Suddenly the copperhead's tail seemed to be the most remarkable thing I had ever seen. I wished I tapered like that somewhere. What if I were a shaped balloon blown up through the tip of a finger? **(8)**

Here was this blood-filled, alert creature, this nerved rope of matter, really here instead of not here, splayed soft and solid on a rock by the slimmest of chances. It was a thickening of the air spread from a tip, a rush into being, eyeball and blood, through a pin-hole rent. Every other time I had ever seen this rock it had been a flat sandstone rock over the quarry pond; now it hosted and bore this chunk of fullness that parted the air around it like a driven wedge. I looked at it from the other direction. From tail to head it spread like the lines of a crescendo, widening from stillness to a turgid blast; then at the bulging jaws it began contracting again, diminuendo, till at the tip of its snout the lines met back at the infinite point that corners every angle, and that space once more ceased being a snake. **(9)**

While this wonder engaged me, something happened that was so unusual and unexpected that I can scarcely believe I saw it. It was ridiculous. **(10)**

Night had been rising like a ground vapor from the blackened quarry pool. I heard a mosquito sing in my ear; I waved it away. I was looking at the copperhead. The mosquito landed on my ankle; again, I idly brushed it off. To my utter disbelief, it lighted on the copperhead. It squatted on the copperhead's back near its "neck," and bent its head to its task. I was riveted. I couldn't see the mosquito in great detail, but I could make out its lowered head that seemed to bore like a well drill through surface rock to fluid. Quickly I looked around to see if I could find anyone—any hunter going to practice shooting beer cans, any boy on a motorbike—to whom I could show this remarkable sight while it lasted. **(11)**

To the best of my knowledge, it lasted two or three full minutes; it seemed like an hour. I could imagine the snake, like the frog sucked dry by the giant water bug, collapsing to an empty bag of skin. But the snake never moved, never indicated any awareness. At last the mosquito straightened itself, fumbled with its forelegs about its head like a fly, and sluggishly took to the air, where I lost it at once. I looked at the snake; I looked beyond the snake to the ragged chomp in the hillside where years before men had quarried stone; I rose, brushed myself off, and walked home. **(12)**

Is this what it's like, I thought then, and think now: a little blood here, a chomp there, and still we live, trampling the grass? Must everything whole be nibbled? Here was a new light on the intricate texture of things in the world, the actual plot of the present moment in time after the fall: the way we the living are nibbled and nibbling—not held aloft on a cloud in the air but bumbling pitted and scarred and broken through a frayed and beautiful land. **(13)**

VOCABULARY

In your journal, write down the meanings of the following words:

- the lazy *sinuosity* **(1)**
- *undulating* bands **(1)**
- team of *herpetologists* **(6)**
- *splayed* soft and solid **(9)**
- lines of a *crescendo* **(9)**
- *diminuendo* **(9)**
- in time after the *fall* **(13)**

QUESTIONS FOR WRITING AND DISCUSSION

1. If you have ever seen a snake or reptile up close, describe the snake (and the experience) in a paragraph.

2. Using only the details and description provided by Dillard, write a paragraph describing and characterizing the copperhead. Now, compare the paragraph you wrote in Question 1 with the details that Dillard gives. What does she describe that you did not? What did you notice that she doesn't?

3. Reread Dillard's essay, annotating for sensory details, images, descriptions of what is not there, and changes in her subject. Cite two specific examples (phrases or sentences) for each of these four observing techniques. Which of these techniques does she use most frequently? Which does she use most effectively?

4. In addition to observing her subject, Dillard describes herself and her relationship to the snake. Find three specific instances of this strategy. If she omitted these descriptions of herself, would her essay be more effective? Explain.

5. Observing essays focus on a discovery, a dominant idea, or a perceived general law. Professor Louis Agassiz, a famous naturalist, once said: "Facts are stupid things until brought into connection with some general law." What "facts" does Dillard observe? What general law does she perceive? In which sentences does Dillard connect observed facts with her general law or dominant idea?

O B S E R V I N G   W O L V E S

Farley Mowat

Farley Mowat was born in Ontario in 1921 and received a B.A. from the University of Toronto. He has published over fifty books of fiction and non-fiction, including People of the Deer *(1952),* Never Cry Wolf *(1963), and* Woman in the Mists: The Story of Dian Fossey and the Mountain Gorillas of Africa *(1987).* Never Cry Wolf, *from which "Observing Wolves" was taken, describes how the Canadian government sent Mowat to the Keewatin Barren Lands in the Northwest Territories to prove that the wolves were decimating the caribou herds—and thus should be exterminated. After observing wolves for a few short days, however, Mowat realized that "the centuries-old and universally accepted human concept of wolf character was a palpable lie. . . . I made my decision that, from this hour onward, I would go open-minded into the lupine world and learn to see and know the wolves, not for what they were supposed to be, but for what they actually were." In the first scene, Mowat learns how wolves establish territories; in the second, he discovers something about their diet. Mowat also gives names to each wolf that he observes: Angeline is a female wolf, George is her mate, and Uncle Albert is a male attached to the group.*

I

During the next several weeks I put my decision into effect with the thoroughness for which I have always been noted. I went completely to the wolves. To begin with I set up a den of my own as near to the wolves as I could conveniently get without disturbing the even tenor of their lives too much. After all, I *was* a stranger, and an unwolflike one, so I did not feel I should go too far too fast. **(1)**

Abandoning Mike's cabin (with considerable relief, since as the days warmed up so did the smell) I took a tiny tent and set it up on the shore of the bay immediately opposite to the den esker. I kept my camping gear to the barest minimum—a small primus stove, a stew pot, a teakettle, and a sleeping bag were the essentials. I took no weapons of any kind, although there were times when I regretted this omission, even if only fleetingly. The big telescope was set up in the mouth of the tent in such a way that I could observe the den by day or night without even getting out of my sleeping bag. **(2)**

During the first few days of my sojourn with the wolves I stayed inside the tent except for brief and necessary visits to the out-of-doors which I always undertook when the wolves were not in sight. The point of this personal concealment was to allow the animals to get used to the tent and to accept it as only another bump on a very bumpy piece of terrain. Later, when the mosquito population reached full flowering, I stayed in the tent practically all of the time unless there was a strong wind blowing, for the most bloodthirsty beasts in the Arctic are not wolves, but the insatiable mosquitoes. **(3)**

My precautions against disturbing the wolves were superfluous. It had required a week for me to get their measure, but they must have taken mine at our first meeting; and, while there was nothing overtly disdainful in their evident assessment of me, they managed to ignore my presence, and indeed my very existence, with a thoroughness which was somehow disconcerting. **(4)**

Quite by accident I had pitched my tent within ten yards of one of the major paths used by the wolves when they were going to, or coming from, their hunting grounds to the westward; and only a few hours after I had taken up residence one of the wolves came back from a trip and discovered me and my tent. He was at the end of a hard night's work and was clearly tired and anxious to go home to bed. He came over a small rise fifty yards from me with his head down, his eyes half-closed, and a preoccupied air about him. Far from being the preternaturally alert and suspicious beast of fiction, this wolf was so self-engrossed that he came straight on to within fifteen yards of me, and might have gone right past the tent without seeing it at all, had I not banged my elbow against the teakettle, making a resounding clank. The wolf's head came up and his eyes opened wide, but he did not stop or falter in his pace. One brief, sidelong glance was all he vouchsafed to me as he continued on his way. **(5)**

It was true that I wanted to be inconspicuous, but I felt uncomfortable at being so totally ignored. Nevertheless, during the two weeks which followed, one or more wolves used the track past my tent almost every night—and never, except on one memorable occasion, did they evince the slightest interest in me. **(6)**

By the time this happened I had learned a good deal about my wolfish neighbors, and one of the facts which had emerged was that they were not nomadic roamers, as is almost universally believed, but were settled beasts and the possessors of a large permanent estate with very definite boundaries. **(7)**

The territory owned by my wolf family comprised more than a hundred square miles, bounded on one side by a river but otherwise not delimited by geographical features. Nevertheless there *were* boundaries, clearly indicated in wolfish fashion. **(8)**

Anyone who has observed a dog doing his neighborhood rounds and leaving his personal mark on each convenient post will have already guessed how the wolves marked out *their* property. Once a week, more or less, the clan made the rounds of the family lands and freshened up the boundary markers—a sort of lupine beating of the bounds. This careful attention to property rights was perhaps made necessary by the presence of two other wolf families whose lands abutted on ours, although I never discovered any evidence of bickering or disagreements between the owners of the various adjoining estates. I suspect, therefore, that it was more of a ritual activity. **(9)**

In any event, once I had become aware of the strong feeling of property rights which existed amongst the wolves, I decided to use this knowledge to make them at least recognize my existence. One evening, after they had gone off for their regular nightly hunt, I staked out a property claim of my own, embracing perhaps three acres, with the tent at the middle, and *including a hundred-yard long section of the wolves' path.* **(10)**

Staking the land turned out to be rather more difficult than I had anticipated. In order to ensure that my claim would not be overlooked, I felt obliged to make a property mark on stones, clumps of moss, and patches of vegetation at intervals of not more than fifteen feet around the circumference of my claim. This took most of the night and required frequent returns to the tent to consume copious quantities of tea; but before dawn brought the hunters home the task was done, and I retired, somewhat exhausted, to observe results. **(11)**

I had not long to wait. At 0814 hours, according to my wolf log, the leading male of the clan appeared over the ridge behind me, padding homeward with his usual air of preoccupation. As usual he did not deign to glance at the tent; but when he reached the point where my property line intersected the trail, he stopped as abruptly as if he had run into an invisible wall. He was only fifty yards from me and with my binoculars I could see his expression very clearly. **(12)**

His attitude of fatigue vanished and was replaced by a look of bewilderment. Cautiously he extended his nose and sniffed at one of my marked bushes. He did not seem to know what to make of it or what to do about it. After a minute of complete indecision he backed away a few yards and sat down. And then, finally, he looked directly at the tent and at me. It was a long, thoughtful, considering sort of look. **(13)**

Having achieved my object—that of forcing at least one of the wolves to take cognizance of my existence—I now began to wonder if, in my ignorance, I had transgressed some unknown wolf law of major importance and would have to pay for my temerity. I found myself regretting the absence of a weapon as the look I was getting became longer, yet more thoughtful, and still more intent. **(14)**

I began to grow decidedly fidgety, for I dislike staring matches, and in this particular case I was up against a master, whose yellow glare seemed to become more baleful as I attempted to stare him down. **(15)**

The situation was becoming intolerable. In an effort to break the impasse I loudly cleared my throat and turned my back on the wolf (for a tenth of a second) to indicate as clearly as possible that I found his continued scrutiny impolite, if not actually offensive. **(16)**

He appeared to take the hint. Getting to his feet he had another sniff at my marker, and then he seemed to make up his mind. Briskly, and with an air of decision, he turned his attention away from me and began a systematic tour of the area I had staked out as my own. As he came to each boundary marker he sniffed it once or twice, then carefully placed his mark on the outside of each clump of grass or stone. As I watched I saw where I, in my ignorance, had erred. He made *his* mark with such economy that he was able to complete the entire circuit without having to reload once, or, to change the simile slightly, he did it all on one tank of fuel. **(17)**

The task completed—and it had taken him no longer than fifteen minutes—he rejoined the path at the point where it left my property and trotted off towards his home—leaving me with a good deal to occupy my thoughts. **(18)**

II

After some weeks of study I still seemed to be as far as ever from solving the salient problem of how the wolves made a living. This was a vital problem, since solving it in a way satisfactory to my employers was the reason for my expedition. **(19)**

Caribou are the only large herbivores to be found in any numbers in the arctic Barren Lands. Although once as numerous as the plains buffalo, they had shown a catastrophic decrease during the three or four decades preceding my trip to the Barrens. Evidence obtained by various Government agencies from hunters, trappers and traders seemed to prove that the plunge of the caribou toward extinction was primarily due to the depredations of the wolf.

It therefore must have seemed a safe bet, to the politicians-cum-scientists who had employed me, that a research study of wolf–caribou relationships in the Barrens would uncover incontrovertible proof with which to damn the wolf wherever he might be found, and provide a more than sufficient excuse for the adoption of a general campaign for his extirpation. **(20)**

I did my duty, but although I had searched diligently for evidence which would please my superiors, I had so far found none. Nor did it appear I was likely to. **(21)**

Toward the end of June, the last of the migrating caribou herds had passed Wolf House Bay heading for the high Barrens some two or three hundred miles to the north, where they would spend the summer.

Whatever my wolves were going to eat during those long months, and whatever they were going to feed their hungry pups, it would not be caribou, for the caribou were gone. But if not caribou, what *was* it to be? **(22)**

I canvassed all the other possibilities I could think of, but there seemed to be no source of food available which would be adequate to satisfy the appetites of three adult and four young wolves. Apart from myself (and the thought recurred several times) there was hardly an animal left in the country which could be considered suitable prey for a wolf. Arctic hares were present; but they were very scarce and so fleet of foot that a wolf could not hope to catch one unless he was extremely lucky. Ptarmigan and other birds were numerous; but they could fly, and the wolves could not. Lake trout, arctic grayling and whitefish filled the lakes and rivers; but wolves are not otters. **(23)**

About this time I began having trouble with mice. The vast expanses of spongy sphagnum bog provided an ideal milieu for several species of small rodents who could burrow and nest-build to their hearts' content in the ready-made mattress of moss. **(24)**

They did other things too, and they must have done them with great frequency, for as June waned into July the country seemed to become alive with little rodents. The most numerous species were the lemmings, which are famed in literature for their reputedly suicidal instincts, but which, instead, *ought* to be hymned for their unbelievable reproductive capabilities. Red-backed mice and meadow mice began invading Mike's cabin in such numbers that it looked as if *I* would soon be starving unless I could thwart their appetites for my supplies. *They* did not scorn my bread. They did not scorn my bed, either; and when I awoke one morning to find that a meadow mouse had given birth to eleven naked offspring inside the pillow of my sleeping bag, I began to know how Pharaoh must have felt when he antagonized the God of the Israelites. **(25)**

I suppose it was only because my own wolf indoctrination had been so complete, and of such a staggeringly inaccurate nature, that it took me so long to account for the healthy state of the wolves in the apparent absence of any game worthy of their reputation and physical abilities. The idea of wolves not only eating, but actually thriving and raising their families on a diet of mice was so at odds with the character of the mythical wolf that it was really too ludicrous to consider. And yet, it was the answer to the problem of how my wolves were keeping the larder full. **(26)**

Angeline tipped me off. **(27)**

Late one afternoon, while the male wolves were still resting in preparation for the night's labors, she emerged from the den and nuzzled Uncle Albert until he yawned, stretched and got laboriously to his feet. Then she left the den site at a trot, heading directly for me across a broad expanse of grassy muskeg, and leaving Albert to entertain the pups as best he could. **(28)**

There was nothing particularly new in this. I had several times seen her conscript Albert (and on rare occasions even George) to do duty as a babysitter while she went down to the bay for a drink or, as I mistakenly thought, simply went for a walk to stretch her legs. Usually her peregrinations took her to the point of the bay farthest from my tent where she was hidden from sight by a low gravel ridge; but this time she came my way in full view and so I swung my telescope to keep an eye on her. **(29)**

She went directly to the rocky foreshore, waded out until the icy water was up to her shoulders, and had a long drink. As she was doing so, a small flock of Old Squaw ducks flew around the point of the Bay and pitched only a hundred yards or so away from her. She raised her head and eyed them speculatively for a moment, then waded back to shore, where she proceeded to act as if she had suddenly become demented. **(30)**

Yipping like a puppy, she began to chase her tail; to roll over and over among the rocks; to lie on her back; to wave all four feet furiously in the air; and in general to behave as if she were clean out of her mind. **(31)**

I swung the glasses back to where Albert was sitting amidst a gaggle of pups to see if he, too, had observed this mad display, and, if so, what his reaction to it was. He had seen it all right, in fact he was watching Angeline with keen interest but without the slightest indication of alarm. **(32)**

By this time Angeline appeared to be in the throes of a manic paroxysm, leaping wildly into the air and snapping at nothing, the while uttering shrill squeals. It was an awe-inspiring sight, and I realized that Albert and I were not the only ones who were watching it with fascination. The ducks seemed hypnotized by curiosity. So interested were they that they swam in for a closer view of this apparition on the shore. Closer and closer they came, necks outstretched, and gabbling incredulously among themselves. And the closer they came, the crazier grew Angeline's behavior. **(33)**

When the leading duck was not more than fifteen feet from shore, Angeline gave one gigantic leap towards it. There was a vast splash, a panic-stricken whacking of wings, and then all the ducks were up and away. Angeline had missed a dinner by no more than inches. **(34)**

This incident was an eye-opener since it suggested a versatility at food-getting which I would hardly have credited to a human being, let alone to a mere wolf. However, Angeline soon demonstrated that the charming of ducks was a mere side line. **(35)**

Having dried herself with a series of energetic shakes which momentarily hid her in a blue mist of water droplets, she padded back across the grassy swale. But now her movements were quite different from what they had been when she passed through the swale on the way to the bay. **(36)**

Angeline was of a rangy build, anyway, but by stretching herself so that she literally seemed to be walking on tiptoe, and by elevating her neck like a camel, she seemed to gain several inches in height. She began to move infinitely slowly upwind across the swale, and I had the impression that both ears were cocked for the faintest sound, while I could see her nose wrinkling as she sifted the breeze for the most ephemeral scents. **(37)**

Suddenly she pounced. Flinging herself up on her hind legs like a horse trying to throw its rider, she came down again with driving force, both forelegs held stiffly out in front of her. Instantly her head dropped; she snapped once, swallowed, and returned to her peculiar mincing ballet across the swale. Six times in ten minutes she repeated the straight-armed pounce, and six times she swallowed—without my having caught a glimpse of what it was that she had eaten. The seventh time she missed her aim, spun around, and began snapping frenziedly in a tangle of cotton grasses. This time when she raised her head I saw, quite unmistakably, the tail and hind quarters of a mouse quivering in her jaws. One gulp, and it too was gone. **(38)**

Although I was much entertained by the spectacle of one of this continent's most powerful carnivores hunting mice, I did not really take it seriously. I thought Angeline was only having fun; snacking, as it were. But when she had eaten some twenty-three mice I began to wonder. Mice are small, but twenty-three of them adds up to a fair-sized meal, even for a wolf. **(39)**

It was only later, by putting two and two together, that I was able to bring myself to an acceptance of the obvious. The wolves of Wolf House Bay, and, by inference at least, all the Barren Land wolves who were raising families outside the summer caribou range, were living largely, if not almost entirely, on mice. **(40)**

VOCABULARY

In your journal, write down the meanings of the following words:

- the den *esker* **(2)**
- *superfluous* **(4)**
- somehow *disconcerting* **(4)**
- *preternaturally* **(5)**
- *evince* the slightest interest **(6)**

- *lupine* **(9)**
- *extirpation* **(20)**
- her *peregrinations* **(29)**

QUESTIONS FOR WRITING AND DISCUSSION

1. Describe what you knew about wolves before you read Mowat's description. Which parts of Mowat's description agreed with your preconceptions? Which parts gave you new information or a different opinion?

2. What equipment and habits of observation does the narrator employ in his study of wolves?

3. *What* is observed depends on who is doing the observing. Describe the narrator's behavior and personality. How do his preconceptions affect what he observes? Should a scientific observer interfere with the lives of the wolves, as the narrator does? What does the narrator learn?

4. Four keys to effective description are repeated observation, attention to sensory details, noticing changes in the subject or the subject's behavior, and noticing what is not present. Find examples of each of these four strategies in this essay.

5. Reread Dillard's "The Snake." What are the similarities and differences between Mowat's and Dillard's methods of observation, their voices as observers, and their discoveries?

6. Naturalists have recently reintroduced wolves into Yellowstone National Park. Nearby ranchers, however, are fearful that the wolves will leave the park and kill livestock. How would Mowatt respond to this debate? Write a letter that Mowat might send to a rancher whose lands adjoin the park and who is worried about losing livestock—or who in fact has already lost livestock—to marauding wolves. You may wish to read additional chapters from *Never Cry Wolf.*

BODY RITUAL AMONG THE NACIREMA

Horace Miner

Anthropologist Horace Miner (1912–) was born in St. Paul, received his A.B. degree from the University of Kentucky, and earned his Ph.D. from the University of Chicago. In addition to teaching sociology and anthropology at the University of Michigan, Horace Miner has done research in Morocco, Uganda, Nigeria, and Algeria. His publications include Culture and Agriculture *(1949),* Principles of Sociology *(1956),* The Primitive City of Timbuctoo *(1965), and* The City in Modern Africa *(1967). "Body Ritual Among the Nacirema," (pronounced Na si ree' ma) was first published in* American Anthropologist, *in 1956. In this essay, Miner reveals his lifelong interest in the ritual behavior of exotic tribes of peoples. Throughout the essay, Miner observes and describes the daily rites and magical practices associated with the body rituals of this remarkable tribe.*

The anthropologist has become so familiar with the diversity of ways in which different peoples behave in similar situations that he is not apt to be surprised by even the most exotic customs. In fact, if all of the logically possible combinations of behavior have not been found somewhere in the world, he is apt to suspect that they must be present in some yet undescribed tribe. This point has, in fact, been expressed with respect to clan organization by Murdock (1947:71). In this light, the magical beliefs and practices of the Nacirema present such unusual aspects that it seems desirable to describe them as an example of the extremes to which human behavior can go. **(1)**

Professor Linton first brought the ritual of the Nacirema to the attention of anthropologists twenty years ago (1936:326), but the culture of this people is still very poorly understood. They are a North American group living in the territory between the Canadian Cree, the Yaqui and Tarahumare of Mexico, and the Carib and Arawak of the Antilles. Little is known of their origin, although tradition states that they came from the east. According to Nacirema mythology, their nation was originated by a culture hero, Notgnihsaw, who is otherwise known for two great feats of strength—the throwing of a piece of wampum across the river Pa-To-Mac and the chopping down of a cherry tree in which the Spirit of Truth resided. **(2)**

Nacirema culture is characterized by a highly developed market economy which has evolved in a rich natural habitat. While much of the people's time is devoted to economic pursuits, a large part of the fruits of these labors and a considerable portion of the day are spent in ritual activity. The focus of this activity is the human body, the appearance and health of which loom as a dominant concern in the ethos of the people. While such a concern is certainly not unusual, its ceremonial aspects and associated philosophy are unique. **(3)**

The fundamental belief underlying the whole system appears to be that the human body is ugly and that its natural tendency is to debility and disease. Incarcerated in such a body, man's only hope is to avert these characteristics through the use of the powerful influences of ritual and ceremony. Every household has one or more shrines devoted to this purpose. The more powerful individuals in the society have several shrines in their houses and, in fact, the opulence of a house is often referred to in terms of the number of such ritual centers it possesses. Most houses are of wattle and daub construction, but the shrine rooms of the more wealthy are walled with stone. Poorer families imitate the rich by applying pottery plaques to their shrine walls. **(4)**

While each family has at least one such shrine, the rituals associated with it are not family ceremonies but are private and secret. The rites are normally only discussed with children, and then only during the period when they are being initiated into these mysteries. I was able, however, to establish sufficient rapport with the natives to examine these shrines and to have the rituals described to me. **(5)**

The focal point of the shrine is a box or chest which is built into the wall. In this chest are kept the many charms and magical potions without which no native believes he could live. These preparations are secured from a variety of specialized practitioners. The most powerful of these are the medicine men, whose assistance must be rewarded with substantial gifts. However, the medicine men do not provide the curative potions for their clients, but decide what the ingredients should be and then write them down in an ancient and secret language. This writing is understood only by the medicine men and by the herbalists who, for another gift, provide the required charm. **(6)**

The charm is not disposed of after it has served its purpose, but is placed in the charm-box of the household shrine. As these magical materials are specific for certain ills, and the real or imagined maladies of the people are many, the charm-box is usually full to overflowing. The magical packets are so numerous that people forget what their purposes were and fear to use them again. While the natives are very vague on this point, we can only assume that the idea in retaining all the old magical materials is that their presence in the charm-box, before which the body rituals are conducted, will in some way protect the worshipper. **(7)**

Beneath the charm-box is a small font. Each day every member of the family, in succession, enters the shrine room, bows his head before the charm-box, mingles different sorts of holy water in the font, and proceeds with a brief rite of ablution. The holy waters are secured from the Water Temple of the community, where the priests conduct elaborate ceremonies to make the liquid ritually pure. **(8)**

In the hierarchy of magical practitioners, and below the medicine men in prestige, are specialists whose designation is best translated "holy-mouth-men." The Nacirema have an almost pathological horror of and fascination with the mouth, the condition of which is believed to have a supernatural influence on all social relationships. Were it not for the rituals of the mouth, they believe that their teeth would fall out, their gums bleed, their jaws shrink, their friends desert them, and their lovers reject them. They also believe that a strong relationship exists between oral and moral characteristics.

For example, there is a ritual ablution of the mouth for children which is supposed to improve their moral fiber. **(9)**

The daily body ritual performed by everyone includes a mouth-rite. Despite the fact that these people are so punctilious about care of the mouth, this rite involves a practice which strikes the uninitiated stranger as revolting. It was reported to me that the ritual consists of inserting a small bundle of hog hairs into the mouth, along with certain magical powders, and then moving the bundle in a highly formalized series of gestures. **(10)**

In addition to the private mouth-rite, the people seek out a holy-mouth-man once or twice a year. These practitioners have an impressive set of paraphernalia, consisting of a variety of augers, awls, probes, and prods. The use of these objects in the exorcism of the evils of the mouth involves almost unbelievable ritual torture of the client. The holy-mouth-man opens the client's mouth and, using the above mentioned tools, enlarges any holes which decay may have created in the teeth. Magical materials are put into these holes. If there are no naturally occurring holes in the teeth, large sections of one or more teeth are gouged out so that the supernatural substance can be applied. In the client's view, the purpose of these ministrations is to arrest decay and to draw friends. The extremely sacred and traditional character of the rite is evident in the fact that the natives return to the holy-mouth-men year after year, despite the fact that their teeth continue to decay. **(11)**

It is to be hoped that, when a thorough study of the Nacirema is made, there will be careful inquiry into the personality structure of these people. One has but to watch the gleam in the eye of a holy-mouth-man, as he jabs an awl into an exposed nerve, to suspect that a certain amount of sadism is involved. If this can be established, a very interesting pattern emerges, for most of the populations shows definite masochistic tendencies. It was to these that Professor Linton referred in discussing a distinctive part of the daily body ritual which is performed only by men. This part of the rite involves scraping and lacerating the surface of the face with a sharp instrument. Special women's rites are performed only four times during each lunar month, but what they lack in frequency is made up in barbarity. As part of this ceremony, women bake their heads in small ovens for about an hour. The theoretically interesting point is that what seems to be a preponderantly masochistic people have developed sadistic specialists. **(12)**

The medicine men have an imposing temple, or *latipso*, in every community of any size. The more elaborate ceremonies required to treat very sick patients can only be performed at this temple. These ceremonies involve not only the thaumaturge but a permanent group of vestal maidens who move sedately about the temple chambers in distinctive costume and headdress. **(13)**

The *latipso* ceremonies are so harsh that it is phenomenal that a fair proportion of the really sick natives who enter the temple ever recover. Small children whose indoctrination is still incomplete have been known to resist attempts to take them to the temple because "that is where you go to die." Despite this fact, sick adults are not only willing but eager to undergo the protracted ritual purification, if they can afford to do so. No matter how ill the supplicant or how grave the emergency, the guardians of many temples will not admit a client if he cannot give a rich gift to the custodian. Even after one has gained admission and survived the ceremonies, the guardians will not permit the neophyte to leave until he makes still another gift. **(14)**

The supplicant entering the temple is first stripped of all his or her clothes. In every-day life the Nacirema avoids exposure of his body and its natural functions. Bathing and excretory acts are performed only in the secrecy of the household shrine, where they are ritualized as part of the body-rites. Psychological shock results from the fact that body secrecy is suddenly lost upon entry into the *latipso*. A man, whose own wife has never seen him in an excretory act, suddenly finds himself naked and assisted by a vestal maiden while he performs his natural functions into a sacred vessel. This sort of ceremonial treatment is necessitated by the fact that the excreta are used by a diviner to ascertain the course and nature of the client's sickness. Female clients, on the other hand, find their naked bodies are subjected to the scrutiny, manipulation, and prodding of the medicine men. **(15)**

Few supplicants in the temple are well enough to do anything but lie on their hard beds. The daily ceremonies, like the rites of the holy-mouth-men, involve discomfort and torture. With ritual precision, the vestals awaken their miserable charges each dawn and roll them about on their beds of pain while performing ablutions, in the formal movements of which the maidens are highly trained. At other times they insert magic wands in the supplicant's mouth or force him to eat substances which are supposed to be healing. From time to time the medicine men come to their clients and jab magically treated needles into their flesh. The fact that these temple ceremonies may not cure, and may even kill the neophyte, in no way decreases the people's faith in the medicine men. . . . **(16)**

In conclusion, mention must be made of certain practices which have their base in native esthetics but which depend upon the pervasive aversion to the natural body and its functions. There are ritual fasts to make fat people thin and ceremonial feasts to make thin people fat. Still other rites are used to make women's breasts larger if they are small, and smaller if they are large. General dissatisfaction with breast shape is symbolized in the fact that the ideal form is virtually outside the range of human variation. A few women afflicted with almost inhuman hypermammary development are so idolized that they make a handsome living by simply going from village to village and permitting the natives to stare at them for a fee. **(17)**

Reference has already been made to the fact the excretory functions are ritualized, routinized, and relegated to secrecy. Natural reproductive functions are similarly distorted. Intercourse is a taboo as a topic and scheduled as an act. Efforts are made to avoid pregnancy by the use of magical materials or by limiting intercourse to certain phases of the moon. Conception is actually very infrequent. When pregnant, women dress so as to hide their condition. Parturition takes place in secret, without friends or relatives to assist, and the majority of women do not nurse their infants. **(18)**

Our review of the ritual life of the Nacirema has certainly shown them to be a magic-ridden people. It is hard to understand how they have managed to exist so long under the burdens which they have imposed on themselves. But even such exotic customs as these take on real meaning when they are viewed with the insight provided by Malinowski when he wrote (1948:70):

> Looking from far and above, from our high places of safety in the developed civilization, it is easy to see all the crudity and irrelevance of magic. But without its power and guidance early man could not have mastered his practical difficulties as he has done, nor could man have advanced to the higher stages of civilization. **(19)**

References

Linton, Ralph. 1936. *The Study of Man.* New York: D. Appleton-Century Co.

Malinowski, Bronislaw. 1948. *Magic, Science, and Religion.* Glencoe: The Free Press.

Murdock, George P. 1949. *Social Structure.* New York: The Macmillan Co.

VOCABULARY

In your journal, write down the meanings of the following words:

- *wattle* and *daub* construction **(4)**
- *herbalists* **(6)**
- brief *rite* of *ablution* **(8)**
- so *punctilious* **(10)**
- set of *paraphernalia* **(11)**
- *preponderantly masochistic* people **(12)**
- *thaumaturge* **(13)**
- *neophyte* **(14)**
- *supplicant* **(15)**
- *parturition* **(18)**

QUESTIONS FOR WRITING AND DISCUSSION

1. A writer's *persona* is the voice, role, or personality he or she assumes while writing. Find at least three passages which reveal the *persona* that Horace Miner uses to describe the Nacirema.

2. At what point in the essay did you become aware of the true identity of the Nacirema? Reread the first three paragraphs. What clues does Miner provide?

3. Readers gradually realize that the "shrines" Miner discusses are actually bathrooms. Identify other key terms that Miner uses, such as "pottery plaques," "charms," "medicine men," "small font," "Water Temple," and "holy-mouth-men." Find and then explain the other anthropological terms that Miner uses.

4. Throughout the essay, Miner uses academic, anthropological language and sentence patterns. Locate a recent copy of *American Anthropologist*. Compare Miner's essay with one of the essays you locate. Explain how these two essays are similar or different in terms of content, vocabulary, and sentence structure.

5. Reread Miner's essay, annotating for sensory details, images, descriptions of what is not there, and changes in the subject. Is Miner's essay as descriptively vivid as Dillard's or Mowat's? Should he give a more vivid and detailed description of these body rituals? Choose one of Miner's descriptive paragraphs and explain why it should or should not have more sensory details.

6. Irony involves saying one thing but meaning something else—usually the direct opposite. Find three passages where Miner is being ironic or satiric. What words or phrases lead you to believe that Miner's tone at that point is ironic or satiric?

7. For an essay of your own, locate and describe, in anthropological terms, the culture, behavior, and rituals of a specific group of people. The group might be high school students, dorm residents, fitness enthusiasts, cooks, artists, adults, or another identifiable group. Or imagine how an anthropologist from another planet might describe you and your friends. Of course, avoid gender or racist stereotypes.

OBSERVING:

THE WRITING PROCESS

■ **ASSIGNMENT FOR OBSERVING**   Do a piece of writing in which you observe a specific person, place, object, or event. Your goal is to show how specific, observed details create dominant ideas about the person, place, object, or event. Your initial purpose is to use your writing to help you observe, discover, and learn about your subject; your final purpose will be to show your reader what you have seen and learned.

Important: Repeated observation is essential. Choose some *limited* subject—a person or small group of people, a specific place, a single object or animal, or a recurring event—that *you can reobserve over a period of several days during the writing process.*

CHOOSING A SUBJECT

If one of your journal entries suggested an interesting subject, try the collecting and shaping strategies. If none of those exercises caught your interest, consider the following ideas:

- Think about your current classes. Do you have a class with a laboratory—chemistry, physics, biology, engineering, animal science, horticulture, industrial sciences, physical education, social work, drawing, pottery—in which you have to make detailed observations? Use this assignment to help you in one of those classes: Write about what you observe and learn during one of your lab sessions.
- Seek out a new place on campus that is off your usual track. Check the college catalog for ideas about places you haven't yet seen: a theater where actors are rehearsing, a greenhouse, a physical education class in the martial arts, a studio where artists are working, a computer laboratory, or an animal research center. Or visit a class you wouldn't take for credit. Observe, write, and learn about what's there and what's happening.
- Get a copy of the Yellow Pages for your town or city. Open to a page at random and place your finger on the page. If it lands on an advertisement for a nearby store, take your notebook there for a visit. Describe the chocolate mousse at a restaurant, an expensive wine at a liquor store, a new car at a dealership, a headstone at a burial-monument company, a twelve-string guitar at a music shop—whatever you would like to learn about through careful observation.

We don't take in the world like a camera or a set of recording devices. The mind is an agent, not a passive receiver. . . . The active mind is a composer and everything we respond to, we compose.

—ANN BERTHOFF,

AUTHOR AND TEACHER

As you write on your subject, consider a tentative audience and purpose. Who might want to know what you learn from your observations? What do you need to explain? What will readers already know? Jot down tentative ideas about your subject, audience, and purpose. Remember, however, that these are not cast in concrete: You may discover some new idea, focus, or angle as you write.

"Write about dogs!"

COLLECTING

Once you have chosen a subject from your journal or elsewhere, begin collecting information. Depending on your purpose, your topic, or even your personal learning preferences, some activities will work better than others. However, you should *practice* all of these activities to determine which is most successful for you and most appropriate to your topic. During these collecting activities, go back and *reobserve your subject.* The second or third time you go back, you may see additional details or more actively understand what you're seeing.

Sketching Begin by *drawing* what you see. The essayist Samuel Scudder says that pen or pencil can be "the best of eyes." Your drawing doesn't have to be great art to suggest other details, questions, or relationships that may be important. Instead of trying to cover a wide range of objects, try to narrow and focus on one limited subject and draw it in detail.

Here's an example. Writing student Brad Parks decided to visit an Eskimo art display at a local gallery. As part of his observing notes, he drew the above sketches of Eskimo paintings. As he drew, he made notes in the margins of his sketches and zoomed in for more detail on one pair of walruses.

Taking Double-Entry Notes   Taking notes in a double-entry format is a simple but effective system for recording observed details. Draw a vertical line down the middle of a page in your journal. On the left-hand side, record bits of description and sensory details. On the right-hand side, jot down your reactions, thoughts, or ideas. On the left-hand side, make your observed details as *objective* as possible. Comments on the right-hand side will be more *subjective*, noting your impressions, reactions, comparisons, and images, as well as additional questions and ideas.

SENSORY DETAILS, FACTS, DATA	IMPRESSIONS, REACTIONS, IDEAS, QUESTIONS
size, color, shape, sounds, smell, touch, taste, actions, behavior	impressions, associations, feelings, reactions, ideas, images, comparisons, related thoughts, questions

Answering Questions To help you describe the person, place, object, or event, write a short response in your journal to each of the following questions:

- What exactly is it? Can you *define* this person, place, object, or event? If it's an object, are its parts related? Who needs it, uses it, or produces it?
- How much could it change and still be recognizable?
- Compare and contrast it. How is it similar to or different from other comparable people, places, things, or events?
- From what points of view is it usually seen? From what point of view is it rarely seen?

Freewriting Freewriting means exactly what it says. Write about your subject, nonstop, for five to ten minutes. Sometimes you may have to write, "I can't think of anything" or "This is really stupid," but keep on writing. Let your words and ideas suggest other thoughts and ideas. For observing, the purpose of freewriting is to let your *imagination* work on the subject, usually *after* you have observed and recorded specific details. Freewriting on your subject will also develop more *associations* or *comparisons* for the right-hand side of your double-entry log. It should also help you to identify a dominant idea for your details.

SHAPING

To focus once again on the shaping process, consider your subject, purpose, and audience. Has your purpose changed? Can you narrow your subject to a specific topic? You may know the answers to some questions immediately; others you may not know until after you complete your first draft. Jot down your current responses to the following questions:

- *Subject:* What is your general subject?
- *Specific topic:* What aspect of your subject are you interested in? Try to *narrow* your field or limit your focus.
- *Purpose:* Why is this topic interesting or important to you or to others? From what point of view will you be writing? What is the *dominant idea* you are trying to convey?
- *Audience:* Who are your readers? What are these readers like and why might they be interested in this topic? How can you direct your description of your subject to your particular audience?

With answers to these questions in mind, you should experiment with several of the following shaping strategies. These strategies will not only organize your specific examples but may also suggest related ideas to improve your description.

> *Your audience is one single reader. I have found that sometimes it helps to pick out one person—a real person you know, or an imagined person and write to that one.*
>
> **—JOHN STEINBECK,** NOVELIST

As you practice these strategies, try to *focus* on your subject. In a profile of a person, for example, focus on key facial features or revealing habits or mannerisms. If you're writing about a place or an event, narrow the subject. Describe, for instance, the street at night, a spider spinning a web in a windowsill, a man in a laundromat banging on a change machine, a bird hovering in mid-air, a photograph, a fish. Write in depth and detail about a *limited* subject.

With a limited subject, a shaping strategy such as spatial order, classification, or comparison/contrast will organize all the specific details for your audience. Shaping strategies give you ways of seeing relationships among the many bits of your description and of presenting them in an organized manner for your reader. Seeing these relationships will also help you discover and communicate the *dominant idea* to your reader.

Spatial Order   Spatial order is a simple way to organize your descriptive details. Choose some sequence—left to right, right to left, bottom to top—and describe your observed details in that sequence. In the following description of his "trashed" dorm room, Dale Furnish, a student who was the victim of a prank, uses spatial order. The italicized words illustrate the spatial order.

> As I walked in the door, I could hardly believe that this scene of destruction used to be my room. *Along the left hand wall,* nearly hiding my desk and mirror, was a pile of beer cans and bottles, paper cups and old crumpled newspapers. The small window *on the far wall* was now covered with the mattress of the bed, and the frame of the bunk bed stood on end. The clothes closet, *to the right of the window,* looked as though it were a giant washing machine which had just gone through spin cycle—clothes were plastered all over, and only four hangers remained, dangling uselessly on the pole. *On the right wall,* where the bed had been, was the real surprise. Tied to the heating pipe was a mangy looking sheep. I swear. It was a real sheep. As I looked at it, it turned to face me and loudly and plaintively said, "Baaaa." *Behind me,* in the hall, everyone began laughing. I didn't know whether to laugh or cry.

Chronological Order   Chronological order is simply the time sequence of your observation. In the following passage, Gregory Allen, writing from his point of view as a five-foot-six-inch guard on a basketball team, describes sights, sounds, and his feelings during a pickup game. The italicized words emphasize the chronological order.

> The game *begins.* The guy checking me is about 6'1", red hair, freckles, and has no business on the court. He looks slow, so I decide to run him to tire him. I dribble twice, pump fake, and the guy goes for it, thinking that he's going to block this much smaller guy's shot. *Then* I leap, flick my wrist, and the ball glides through the air and

flows through the net with a swish as the net turns upside down. I come down and realize that I have been scratched. *Suddenly,* I feel a sharp pain as sweat runs into the small red cut. I wipe the blood on my shorts and *continue playing* the game. *After* that first play, I begin to hear the common song of the game. There's the squeak of the high-top Nike sneakers, the bouncing ball, the shuffle of feet. *Occasionally,* I hear "I'm open!" "Pass the ball!" "Augghh!" And *then,* "Nice play, man!"

Comparison/Contrast   If what you've observed and written about your subject so far involves seeing similarities or differences, you may be able to use comparison/contrast as a shaping strategy—either for a single paragraph or for a series of paragraphs. The following two paragraphs, for example, are taken from Albert Goldman's biography of Elvis Presley, entitled *Elvis.* In these paragraphs, Goldman's dominant idea depends on the striking contrast between what he finds on the front lawn of Graceland, the rock star's mansion in Memphis, and what he notices when he steps through the front door.

> Prominently displayed on the front lawn is an elaborate creche. The stable is a full-scale adobe house strewn with straw. Life-sized are the figures of Joseph and Mary, the kneeling shepherds and Magi, the lambs and ewes, as well as the winged annunciatory angel hovering over the roof beam. Real, too, is the cradle in which the infant Jesus sleeps.

> When you step through the ten-foot oak door and enter the house, you stop and stare in amazement. Having just come from the contemplation of the tenderest scene in the Holy Bible, imagine the shock of finding yourself in a *whorehouse!* Yet there is no other way to describe the drawing room of Graceland except to say that it appears to have been lifted from some turn-of-the-century bordello down in the French Quarter of New Orleans. . . . The room is a gaudy melange of red velour and gilded tassels, Louis XV furniture and porcelain bric-a-brac, all informed by the kind of taste that delights in a ceramic temple d'amour housing a miniature Venus de Milo with an electrically simulated waterfall cascading over her naked shoulders.

Examine once again your collecting notes about your subject. If there are striking similarities or differences between the two parts or between various aspects of your subject, perhaps a comparison or contrast structure will organize your details.

Classification   Classifying people, events, or things by *types* may provide a shape that you can use for either a paragraph or a whole essay. In the following paragraph from "Speedway," an essay on racing at the Indianapolis 500, cultural critic Paul Fussell categorizes spectators into three social classes: the middle classes, or "middles"; the high proletarians, or "high proles"; and the "uglies."

> I'd say the people can be divided into three social classes: the middles, who on race day tend, in homage to the checkered flag, to dress all in black and white and who sit in reserved seats; the high proles, who watch standing or lolling in the infield, especially at the turns, "where the action is"; and the uglies, the overadvertised, black-leathered, beer-sodden, pot-headed occupiers of that muddy stretch of ground in the infield at the first turn, known as the Snake Pit. These are the ones who, when girls pass, spiritlessly hold up signs reading "Show Us Your T__s." The uglies are sometimes taken to be the essence of Indy, and they are the people who, I think, Frank Deford has in mind when he speaks of "barbarians." But they are not the significant Indy audience. The middle class is all those people arriving at the Speedway in cars bearing Purdue and Indiana State stickers.

Classification is often a useful method of shaping description. To see if it is appropriate for your subject, ask "What types do you observe?" The answer may lead to categories or types that you had failed to observe, and the categories may provide a shape you can adopt.

Definition   Definition is the essence of observation. Defining a person, place, or object requires stating its exact meaning and describing its basic qualities. Literally, a definition sets the boundaries, indicating, for example, how an apple is distinct from an orange or how a canary is different from a sparrow. Definition, however, is a catchall term for a variety of strategies. It uses classification and comparison as well as description. It often describes a thing by negation—by saying what it is not. For example, Sidney Harris, a columnist for many years for the *Chicago Daily News,* once defined a "jerk" by referring to several types of people ("boob," "fool," "dope," "bore," "egotist" "nice person," "clever person") and then compared or contrasted these terms to show where "jerk" leaves off and "egotist" begins. In the following excerpt, Harris also defines by negation, saying that a jerk has no grace and is tactless. The result, when combined with a description of qualities he has observed in jerks, is definition.

> Thinking it over, I decided that a jerk is basically a person without insight. He is not necessarily a fool or a dope, because some extremely clever persons can be jerks. In fact, it has little to do with intelligence as we commonly think of it; it is, rather, a kind of subtle but persuasive aroma emanating from the inner part of the personality.

> I know a college president who can be described only as a jerk. He is not an unintelligent man, or unlearned, nor even unschooled in the social amenities. Yet he is a jerk *cum laude,* because of a fatal flaw

in his nature—he is totally incapable of looking into the mirror of his soul and shuddering at what he sees there.

A jerk, then, is a man (or woman) who is utterly unable to see himself as he appears to others. He has no grace, he is tactless without meaning to be, he is a bore even to his best friends, he is an egotist without charm. All of us are egotists to some extent, but most of us—unlike the jerk—are perfectly and horribly aware of it when we make asses of ourselves. The jerk never knows.

At this stage in the writing process, you have already been defining your subject simply by describing it. But you may want to use a deliberately structured definition, as Harris does, to shape your observations.

Simile, Metaphor, and Analogy   Simile, metaphor, and analogy create vivid word pictures or *images* by making *comparisons*. These images may take up only a sentence or two, or they may shape several paragraphs.

- A *simile* is a comparison using "like" or "as": A is like B. "George eats his food like a vacuum cleaner."
- A *metaphor* is a direct or implied comparison suggesting that A is B: "At the dinner table, George is a vacuum cleaner."
- An *analogy* is an extended simile or metaphor that builds a point-by-point comparison into several sentences, a whole paragraph, or even a series of paragraphs. Writers use analogy to explain a difficult concept, idea, or process by comparing it with something more familiar or easier to understand.

If the audience, for example, knows about engines but has never seen a human heart, a writer might use an analogy to explain that a heart is like a simple engine, complete with chambers or cylinders, intake and exhaust valves, and hoses to carry fuel and exhaust.

As an illustration of simile and metaphor, notice how Joseph Conrad, in the following brief passage from *Heart of Darkness,* begins with a simile and then continues to build on his images throughout the paragraph. Rather than creating a rigid structural shape for his details (as classification or comparison/contrast would do), the images combine and flow like the river he is describing.

Going up that river was like travelling back to the earliest beginnings of the world, when vegetation rioted on the earth and the big trees were kings. An empty stream, a great silence, an impenetrable forest. The air was warm, thick, heavy, sluggish. There was no joy in the brilliance of sunshine. The long stretches of the waterway ran on, deserted, into the gloom of overshadowed distances. On silvery sandbanks hippos and alligators sunned themselves side by side. The broadening waters flowed through a mob of wooded islands; you lost your way on that river as you would in a desert, and butted all day long against shoals, trying to find the channel, till you thought yourself bewitched and cut off for ever from everything you had known once—somewhere—far away—in another existence perhaps.

An analogy helps shape the following paragraph by Carl Sagan, author of *The Dragons of Eden* and *Cosmos*. To help us understand a difficult concept, the immense age of the Earth—(and, by comparison, the relatively tiny span of human history)—Sagan compares the lifetime of the universe to something simple and familiar: the calendar of a single year.

The most instructive way I know to express this cosmic chronology is to imagine the fifteen-billion year lifetime of the universe . . . compressed into the span of a single year. . . . It is disconcerting to find that in such a cosmic year the Earth does not condense out of interstellar matter until early September; dinosaurs emerge on Christmas Eve; flowers arise on December 28th; and men and women originate at 10:30 P.M. on New Year's Eve. All of recorded history occupies the last ten seconds of December 31; and the time from the waning of the Middle Ages to the present occupies little more than one second.

Consider whether a good analogy would help you shape one or more paragraphs in your essay. Ask yourself: "What is the most difficult concept or idea I'm trying to describe?" Is there an extended point-by-point comparison—an analogy—that would clarify it?

Title, Introduction, and Conclusion   Depending on your purpose and audience, you may want a *title* for what you're writing. At the minimum, titles—like labels—should accurately indicate the contents in the package. In addition, however, good titles capture the reader's interest with some catchy phrasing or imaginative language—something to make the reader want to "buy" the package. Annie Dillard uses the simple label, "The Snake," for her essay. Horace Miner uses a more descriptive and intriguing title for his essay, "Body Ritual Among the Nacirema." Readers are undoubtedly curious about this strange tribe called the "Nacirema" and want to learn about their rituals. If a title is appropriate for your observation, write out several possibilities in your journal.

The introduction should set up the context for the reader—*who, what, when, where,* and *why*—so that readers can orient themselves. Depending on your audience and purpose, introductions can be very brief, pushing the reader quickly into the scene, or they can take more time, easing readers into the setting. Annie Dillard begins with a dramatic sentence: "There was a snake at the quarry with me tonight." Stephen White, in his essay about Mesa Verde at the end of this chapter, begins more mysteriously: "It is difficult for me to say exactly what it was that drew me to this solitary place." White doesn't tell his reader that he's talking about Mesa Verde until the second paragraph.

Conclusions should wrap up the observation, providing a sense of completeness. Conclusions vary, depending upon a writer's purpose and audience, but they tend to be of two types or have two components: a *summary* and a *reference* to the introduction. Dillard's final paragraph is of the first type. She states the whole point of her discovery: "Is this what it's like, I thought then, and think now. . . . Must everything whole be nibbled?" Mowat uses both components when he concludes his essay. Part II of his essay ends by referring to and then answering the central question of his expedition, that is, how do wolves survive? "The wolves of Wolf House Bay" Mowat tells us, "were living largely, if not almost entirely, on mice."

As you work on shaping strategies and drafting, make notes about possible titles, appropriate introductions, or effective conclusions for your written observations.

DRAFTING

Reread Journal Entries and Notes from Collecting and Shaping   Before you start drafting, review your material so you aren't writing cold. Stop and reread everything you've written on your subject. You're not trying to memorize particular sentences or phrases; you're just getting it all fresh in your mind, seeing what you still like and discarding details that are no longer relevant.

Reobserve Your Subject   If necessary, go back and observe your subject again. One more session may suggest an important detail or idea that will help you get started writing.

Reexamine Purpose, Audience, Dominant Idea, and Shape   After all your writing and rereading, you may have some new ideas about your purpose, audience, or dominant idea. Take a minute to jot these down in your journal. Remember that your specific details should show the main point or dominant idea, whether you state it explicitly or not.

The idea is to get the pencil moving quickly.

—BERNARD MALAMUD, NOVELIST

Next, if the shaping strategies suggested an order for your essay, use it to guide your draft. You may, however, have only your specific details or a general notion of the dominant idea you're trying to communicate to your reader. In that case, you may want to begin writing and work out a shape or outline as you write.

Create a Draft   With the above notes as a guide, you are ready to start drafting. Work on establishing your ritual: Choose a comfortable, familiar place with the writing tools you like. Make sure you'll have no interruptions.

Try to write nonstop. If you can't think of a word, substitute a dash. If you can't remember how to spell a word, don't stop to look it up now—keep writing. Write until you reach what feels like the end. If you do get stuck, *reread* your last few lines or some of your writing process materials. Then go back and pick up the thread. Don't stop to count words or pages. You should shoot for more material than you need because it's usually easier to cut material later, when you're revising, than to add more if you're short.

REVISING

Gaining Distance and Objectivity Revising, of course, has been going on since you put your first sentence down on paper. You've changed ideas, thought through your subject again, and observed your person, place, object, or event. After your rough draft is finished, your next step is to revise again to resee the whole thing. But before you do, you need to let it sit at least twenty-four hours, to get away from it for a while, to gain some distance and perspective. Relax. Congratulate yourself.

About the time you try to relax, however, you may get a sudden temptation—even an overwhelming urge—to have someone else read it—immediately! Usually, it's better to resist that urge. Chances are, you will want to have someone else read it either because you're bubbling with enthusiasm and you want to share it or because you're certain that it's all garbage and you want to hear the bad news right away. Most readers will not find it either as great as you hope *or* as awful as you fear. As a result, their offhand remarks may seem terribly insensitive or condescending. In a day or so, however, you'll be able to see your writing more objectively: Perhaps it's not great yet, but it's not hopeless, either. At that point, you're ready to get some feedback and start your revisions.

Rereading and Responding to Your Readers When you've been away from the draft for a while, you are better able to see the whole piece of writing. Start by rereading your own draft and making marginal notes. Don't be distracted by spelling errors or typos; concentrate on the quality of the details and the flow of the sentences. Focus on the overall effect you're creating, see if your organization still makes sense, and check to make sure that all the details support the dominant idea. Now you're ready to get some peer feedback. Depending on the reactions of your readers, you may need to change the point of view, add a few specific examples or some comparisons or images, fix the organization of a paragraph, reorder some details, delete some sentences, or do several of the above. Be prepared, however, to rewrite several paragraphs to help your readers really see what you are describing.

PEER RESPONSE

The instructions below will help you give and receive constructive advice about the rough draft of your observing essay. You may use these guidelines for an in-class workshop, a take-home review, or a computer e-mail response.

Writer: Before you exchange drafts with another reader, write out the following information about your rough draft:

1. What is the dominant impression that you want your description to make? What overall idea or impression do you want your reader to have?

2. What paragraph(s) contains your best and most vivid description? What paragraph(s) still need some revision?

3. Explain one or two things you would like your reader to comment on as he or she responds to your draft.

Reader: First, without making any marks, read the entire draft from start to finish. As you *reread* the draft, answer the following questions.

1. What *dominant impression* does the draft create? Does the dominant impression your received agree with the writer's own idea? If not, how might the writer better achieve that overall impression?

2. Look at the writer's responses to Question 2. Does the writer, in fact, use vivid description in his or her best paragraph(s)? How might the paragraphs that the writer says need revision be improved? Review the six techniques for descriptive writing at the beginning of this chapter. Where or how might the writer improve the *sensory details, images,* descriptions of what is *not there, changes* in the subject, or *point of view?* Offer specific suggestions.

3. Reread the assignment for this essay. Explain how this essay should be revised to more clearly *meet the assignment.*

4. List the *two most important things* this writer should work on as he or she revises this draft. Explain why these are important.

Guidelines for Revision

As you revise your essay, keep the following tips and checklist questions in mind:

- **Reexamine your purpose and audience.** Are you doing what you intended? If your purpose or audience has changed, what other changes do you need to make as you revise?
- **Pay attention to the advice your readers give you, but don't necessarily make all the changes they suggest.** Ask them *why* something should be changed. Ask them specifically *where* something should be changed.
- **Consider your point of view.** Would changing to another point of view clarify what you are describing?
- **Consider your vantage point.** Do you have a bird's-eye view, or are you observing from a low angle? Do you zoom in for a close-up of a person or object? Would a different vantage point fit your purpose and audience?
- **Make sure you are using sensory details where appropriate.** Remember, you must *show* your reader the details you observe. If necessary, *reobserve* your subject.
- **Do all your details and examples support your dominant idea?** Reread your draft and omit any irrelevant details.
- **What is *not* present in your subject that might be important to mention?**
- **What changes occur in the form or function of your subject?** Where can you describe those changes more vividly?
- **Make comparisons if they will help you or your reader understand your subject better.** Similes, metaphors, or analogies may describe your subject more vividly.
- **Does what you are observing belong to a class of similar objects?** Would classification organize your writing?
- **Be sure to cue or signal your reader with appropriate transition words.** Transitions will improve the coherence or flow of your writing.
  - *Spatial Order:* on the left, on the right, next, above, below, higher, lower, farther, next, beyond
  - *Chronological Order:* before, earlier, after, afterward, thereafter, then, from then on, the next day, shortly, by that time, immediately, slowly, while, meanwhile, until, now, soon, within an hour, first, later, finally, at last
  - *Comparison/Contrast:* on one hand, on the other hand, also, similarly, in addition, likewise, however, but, yet, still, although, even so, nonetheless, in contrast.
- **Revise sentences for clarity, conciseness, emphasis, and variety.**
- **When you have revised your essay, edit your writing for correct spelling and appropriate word choice, punctuation, usage, and grammar.**

I went for years not finishing anything. Because, of course, when you finish something you can be judged. . . .

—ERICA JONG,

AUTHOR OF FEAR OF FLYING

■ POSTSCRIPT ON THE WRITING PROCESS When you've finished writing this assignment, do one final journal entry. Briefly, answer the following questions:

1. What was the hardest part of this writing assignment for you?

2. Put brackets ([ ]) around the paragraph containing your most vivid sensory details. Explain what makes this paragraph so vivid.

3. What exercise, practice, strategy, or workshop was the "breakthrough" for you? What led you to your discovery or dominant idea?

4. State in one sentence your discovery or the dominant idea of your essay.

5. What did you learn about your writing ritual and process? What did you learn about observing?

OBSERVING:

STUDENT WRITING

PERMANENT TRACINGS

Jennifer Macke

Jennifer Macke, a student in Professor Rachel Henne-Wu's class at Owens Community College in Findlay, Ohio, decided to write her observing essay about a tattoo parlor. She visited the Living Color Tattoo Parlor and took notes on the office, the clientele, the conversations, the artwork of the tattoos, and the owner of the establishment. Ms. Macke wrote that her preconceptions about tattoo parlors were that they were "smoke-filled, dimly lit places" where "undesirables gathered." Gradually, her impressions changed as she saw firsthand the high quality of the tattoos and the remarkable artistry of the tattoos. Reprinted below are some of her original notes, questions and answers, an outline, and the final version of her essay.

NOTES ON A VISIT

—A couple with a young school-aged daughter looks at the artwork on the walls for about 15 minutes before saying anything to the owner. They are looking for a design for the wife for her birthday. They appear to be a typical young couple with a limited amount of money. They ask how much a particular design will be and say they will have to save for it. "How much for this ankle bracelet?" he says. "It'll run you between $45 and $60, depending on how thick you want the rose vine," Gasket says.

—Two Latino men enter the waiting room. One peeks his head into the office and says, "I'm here early for my appointment because I'm not sure exactly what I want. Do you have any books or more pictures I can look through?" Gasket gives him six photo albums full of ideas (designs).

—Five young adult black men enter. They begin browsing through the photos on the wall. There are designs with prices below them so you know what it costs without asking. They too look through the photo albums the Latinos left on the floor. One of the black guys announces, "I'll go first 'cause I want to get it over with." One says, "I'm not going to do this. I can't stand the sound of that needle!" Gasket looks at me and says, "It's amazing how many people just think all you have to do is walk through the door like a walk-in barber shop. They don't know I'm booked for at least a week. During the summer, it's three weeks."

—The phone rings and since his daughter, who normally works there, is gone to visit her mother, he tells me to pick it up. The guy on the other end says, "My uncle wants to know if Jeff's cousin works here?" I relay the message to the owner and he replies, "Yes, that's me." Back on the phone, "He says he's the best in the business. Does he have any time today?" Gasket says, "Here we go again." I tell the guy it will be a week. He says, "OK, I'll call back then." I tell Gasket what he said and he comments, "He'll call back next week, and I'll have to tell him it'll be another week. You would not believe the intelligence level of some people."

—The next girl is going to have lips tattooed on her right hip. She is a petite nurse whom you would never guess would even consider such a thing. Her husband put lipstick on and kissed a napkin which she brought to use for the pattern. Gasket took a photocopy of this and made a transfer from it to use as the template. She dropped her shorts to expose where the art would be placed. She lay down on the table which Gasket explained he had gotten in trade for a tattoo. He also said the stirrups were still in the drawer. The girl smiled and talked the whole time he worked. At one point, he asked her, "Does it hurt?" She said, "No." He said, "I can go deeper!" She said, "Are you supposed to?" He said, laughing, "It's just a joke. If I see someone who's comfortable, I'll ask them this." It only took about 30 minutes to complete this one. You would swear someone just kissed her with bright red lipstick. It's amazing how realistic his work looks.

QUESTIONS AND ANSWERS

1. "Why do people get tattoos?"
   "A tattoo is a very personal thing. It's an expression of one's self."

2. "Does it hurt to get a tattoo?"
   "It all depends on the placement and the person. Guys tend to be bigger wimps. I'd rather do women any day. The most painful areas are the ankle and higher up on the belly. I've had the pain described as something annoying but not necessarily painful to such a point that they cannot stand it. I've never had anyone pass out, though."

3. "What kind of person gets a tattoo?"
   "There's not one particular type of person who gets a tattoo. I once had a call from some lawyers from Findlay. They wanted to know if they had five or so people who wanted a tattoo, would I come over? I said, yes, and I tattooed six lawyers at a party."

4. "What is the process of getting a tattoo?"
   "Depending if it will be freehand or something the people bring in, it starts with drawing the art. It is drawn either on the person or on carbon paper backwards. The carbon design is transferred to the skin with Speed Stick deodorant. The outline is applied first. As the single needle picks up and sews into the skin, excess ink covers the work area."

   As Gasket works, it's hard to see the actual area he's working on because of the excess ink. When asked how he can work with the excess ink obstructing the guidelines, he says he just knows where the line goes. (I wouldn't.) Once the outline is complete he changes to use a 3 or 4 needle set, depending on the coverage necessary. He colorizes the art which brings it to life. After it's complete, he puts a thick coat of bacitracin on and covers it with a gauze bandage. The gauze must remain on for one and a half to two hours.

5. "What is the most common place for a tattoo?"
   "Placement runs in cycles, sometimes the upper arm, sometimes the ankle." While we were talking, a man came in with one on the back of his neck.

6. "How expensive are tattoos?"
   The minimum is $30. Depending on how detailed and how big. Gasket has bartered for the tattoos, too.

7. "Do most people get more than one tattoo?"
   "I've seen people go through life with only one or maybe two, but it's said when you get your third, you're hooked. You'll be back for more."

8. "Are there Health Department requirements?"

   "At the beginning, the requirements (laws) weren't very strict. I knew I wanted to be super sterile, so I put my needles and equipment through a much stricter procedure. Since then, the Health Department has taken on my policy and requires everyone to process their stuff like me. They drop in to make sure the laws are being followed."

9. "How many times do you use your needles?"

   "They are single application needles, but they still need to be sterilized. People ask me if they can watch their needles being sterilized so they can make sure. I say fine, but it will be 2 and 1/2 hours until I can work on you."

OUTLINE

Working Thesis: "Gasket's creative artistic ability and perfectionist work ethic make his designs worth sewing into your body for a lifetime."

    I. Describe the Tattoo Parlor
        A. Outer area (waiting room)
        B. Inner office

    II. Describe the owner
        A. The way he looks
        B. The way he feels about his work

    III. Describe the people
        A. People getting a tattoo
        B. People not getting a tattoo

FINAL VERSION

PERMANENT TRACINGS

At first glance, the Living Color Tattoo Parlor appears to be just another typical tattoo establishment. You enter through a glass door only to find a waiting room with the decor reminiscent of the 1970's. The dark paneled walls display numerous types of artwork that range from pencil sketching to color Polaroid snapshots of newly completed tattoos. The gold and green davenport looks like it came from a Saturday morning garage sale. The inner office is celery green with a dental chair and an obstetrics' table that the owner bartered for a tattoo (the stirrups are still in the drawer). A filing cabinet, desk, and copy machine make you feel like you're in a professional office. The sterilizer is in plain sight and is in operation. Bottle after bottle of brightly colored inks are neatly arranged on a tiered wooden stand. The sound of the oscillating fan that cools the client interrupts the buzz of the needle sewing the paint into the client's skin. A freeze-dried turtle is displayed on a table in the office. **(1)**

I still wondered, though. Could tattoos actually be a form of art? **(2)**

As soon as I could, I asked the owner, a man called "Gasket," about his occupation. "I was a suit for 15 years and now I can work as much as I want. There's always somebody wanting a tattoo or something pierced," Gasket said. He's often asked if he'll scratch out the name of a previous girlfriend, and he always replies that he would never even consider it. "That would be defacement," he said. "When I'm done, the design should look better than when I started." Gasket is not his given name but one he acquired because of his expert repair work on Harley Davidson motorcycles. Gasket is the owner of this establishment, and to look at him, you would never guess he is a college-educated engineer. His long curly, graying hair flows from under his Harley hat, and examples of his handiwork are visible under the rolled up sleeves of his black Harley T-shirt. The harshness of his heavily bearded face is softened by his slate-blue eyes that mirror his gentle demeanor. If you look past his casual exterior, you will find a code of steel. "At the beginning, the laws weren't very strict. I knew I wanted to be super sterile, so I put my single use needles and equipment through a much stricter procedure. Since then, the Health Department has taken on my policy and requires everyone to process their stuff like me," he said. **(3)**

The appearance of the Living Color Tattoo Parlor may be typical, but two things are distinctly different: the quality and the creativity of the tattoo designs. A young college couple from Toledo was asked why they would drive to Fremont for an appointment. They answered, "Gasket's the best! We wouldn't trust something that's going to be on our body for the rest of our lives to someone other than him." **(4)**

"I already have two tattoos from you, and I love your work," a middle-aged woman said. Displaying two greeting cards, she asks, "Is it possible to get a combination of these two designs?" **(5)**

"I can create anything you want," Gasket said. **(6)**

"I'll have to wait a couple of weeks because I'm not working much and my other bills come first," she said. **(7)**

"Yes, you have to get your priorities straight. When you're ready, I'm here," he said. **(8)**

Gasket is performing his tattoo magic on a young college female. He's creating a rose with a heart stem wrapping around her belly button, which is pierced. The girl is nervously seated in the green dental chair which is tilted back to flatten the skin surface. First, Gasket draws the sketch on her belly. He covers his hands with a thin layer of latex once the exact position and specific details are decided upon. A small device resembling a fountain pen with a brightly colored motor and a single needle moving at 1000 rpm is used to apply the black outline first. As the needle moves up and down, it picks up small amounts of ink and deposits it just under the surface of the skin. When asked how he can work with the excess ink obstructing the guidelines, he simply said he just knows where the line goes. This is a difficult task because unlike a paint-by-number design, the image not only has to be in his mind but he also has to have the artistic ability to convert the image to the skin. The girl asks a pain-filled question, "How much longer?" **(9)**

"I can stop and let you take a break at any time," Gasket says. His soft tone and slow-paced voice help soothe the girl. "The higher up on the belly, the more painful," he says. The process of colorizing the tattoo begins once the outline is complete. This is accomplished with a three or four needle set, depending on the amount of coverage desired. It takes about 45 minutes to complete the multi-colored masterpiece which is literally sewn into her skin. Some of Gasket's designs can be compared to Picasso's' brilliantly colored dreamlike images. Upon completion, the girl is directed to a full-length mirror to inspect her permanently altered abs. **(10)**

"It looks fantastic!" she exclaims. "I was a little vague on how I pictured it would look, but it looks even better than I had imagined. I'm thrilled." **(11)**

Once thought of as green-toned disfigurements that only drunken sailors and lowlife people would don, tattoos are now high fashion. Now it is possible to see skin art on TV stars, sports superstars, and a multitude of individuals you might not suspect. The future of this trendy fashion has its roots firmly planted in today's society. Young people seem to be one of its biggest supporters. **(12)**

"I'll go first 'cause I want to get it over with," one young black man states to his four companions. **(13)**

"I'm not going to do this. I can't stand the sound of that needle!" another man proclaims. **(14)**

"It's amazing how many people just think all you have to do is walk through the door like a walk-in barber shop. They don't know I'm booked for at least a week. During the summer, it's three weeks," Gasket claims. He explains this to the young men who make appointments. They leave, disappointed. **(15)**

Gasket's tattoo designs can be compared to the famous fashion designs by Bob Mackie. Like Mackie's one-of-a-kind designs, they are not mass produced, but are hand-sewn for a specific individual. As I left, my first impression of the Living Color Tattoo Parlor was changed by the incredibly beautiful skin art and the comments of the satisfied clients. For many, Gasket's artistic ability and perfectionism make his designs worth sewing into your body for a lifetime. **(16)**

QUESTIONS FOR WRITING AND DISCUSSION

1. Review the techniques for writing observing papers at the beginning of the chapter. Which paragraph(s) in Macke's essay have the best sensory detail, images, comparisons, and other effective bits of description? Which paragraphs might use more descriptive detail?

2. Macke describes the office, the owner, the customers, the process of tattooing, and the prices of a tattoo. Should she also describe several of the tattoos? Should she describe the colors in a typical tattoo? If she did these descriptions, where might she put them in her essay?

3. Reread Macke's notes of her visit, including her questions and answers. What interesting ideas and descriptions in her notes might be included in her final draft? Why might Macke have left these details out? Assume that you are a peer reader for Macke's essay. Fill out the peer response questions printed earlier in this chapter so you can help her with a revision of her essay.

4. List the three things that you like best about Macke's essay. Which of her strategies might work for a revision of your own essay? Make a revision plan for your own essay, based on what you learned from reading "Permanent Tracings."

EMPTY WINDOWS

Stephen White

In this essay written for Professor John Boni at Colorado State University, Stephen White describes both what his senses tell him and what he can only imagine about the Anasazi, the ancient Native Americans who more than a thousand years ago built the cliff dwellings at Mesa Verde in southwestern Colorado. Writing about those empty dwellings with their darkened windows, White says, "Perhaps there lurks, behind every blackened window, a certain unexplainable something we can never understand."

It is difficult for me to say exactly what it was that drew me to this solitary place and held me here, virtually entranced, the entire day. It's the silence, maybe, or the empty houses perched precariously on the canyon wall below me. Or, could it be the knowledge that something seemingly nonexistent does indeed exist? **(1)**

I awoke this morning with a sense of unexplainable anticipation gnawing away at the back of my mind, that this chilly, leaden day at the Mesa Verde would bring something new and totally foreign to any of my past experiences. It was a sensation that began to permeate my entire being as I sat crouched before my inadequate campfire, chills running up my spine. Chills which, I am certain, were due not entirely to the dreary gray of a winter "sunrise." **(2)**

It had been my plan to travel the so-called Ruins Road early today, and then complete my visit here, but as I stopped along the road and stood scanning the opposite wall of the canyon for ruins, I felt as if some force had seized control of my will. I was compelled to make my way along the rim. **(3)**

Starting out upon the rock, I weaved in and out repeatedly as the gaping emptiness of the canyon and the weathered standstone of the rim battled one another for territory. At last arriving here, where a narrow peninsula of canyon juts far into the stone, I was able to peer back into the darkness of a cave carved midway in the vertical wall opposite, within whose smoke blackened walls huddle, nearly unnoticeable, the rooms of a small crumbled ruin. **(4)**

They are a haunting sight, these broken houses, clustered together down in the gloom of the canyon. It presents a complete contrast to the tidy, excavated ruins I explored yesterday, lost within a cluster of tourists and guided by a park ranger who expounded constantly upon his wealth of knowledge of excavation techniques and archaeological dating methods. The excavated ruins seemed, in comparison, a noisy, almost modern city, punctuated with the clicking of camera shutters and the bickering of children. Here it is quiet. The silence is broken only by the rush of the wind in the trees and the trickling of a tiny stream of melting snow springing from ledge to ledge as it makes its way down over the rock to the bottom of the canyon. And this small, abandoned village of tiny houses seems almost as the Indians left it, reduced by the passage of nearly a thousand years to piles of rubble through which protrude broken red adobe walls surrounding ghostly jet black openings, undisturbed by modern man. **(5)**

Those windows seem to stare back at me as my eyes are drawn to them. They're so horribly empty, yet my gaze is fixed, searching for some sign of the vitality they must surely have known. I yearn for sounds amidst the silence, for images of life as it once was in the bustling and prosperous community of cliff dwellers who lived here so long ago. It must have been a sunny home when the peaceful, agrarian Anasazi, or ancient ones, as the Navajo call them, lived and dreamed their lives here, wanting little more than to continue in their ways and be left alone, only to be driven away in the end by warring people with whom they could not contend. **(6)**

I long to hear, to see, and to understand, and though I strain all my senses to their limits, my wishes are in vain. I remain alone, confronted only by the void below and the cold stare of those utterly desolate windows. I know only an uneasy sensation that I am not entirely alone, and a quick, chill gust gives birth once again to that restless shiver tracing its path along the length of my spine. **(7)**

As a gray afternoon fades into a gray evening, I can find neither a true feeling of fear nor one of the quiet serenity one would expect to experience here. It is comforting for me to believe that it was the explorer in me which brought me here, to feel that I was lured to stand above this lonely house by that same drive to find and explore the unknown which motivated the countless others who have come here since seeking knowledge and understanding of the ancient people of the "Green Table." Yet as I begin the journey back to my car and the security of an evening fire, I remain uncomfortably unconvinced. **(8)**

Perhaps the dreariness of a cloudy day united with my solitude to pave a mental pathway for illusion and mystery. Or perhaps all homes are never truly empty, having known the multitude of experience which is human life. Perhaps there lurks, behind every blackened window, a certain unexplainable something we can never understand. I know only that the Indian has long respected these places and given them wide berth, leaving their sanctity inviolate. **(9)**

QUESTIONS FOR WRITING AND DISCUSSION

1. Describe a similar experience you have had with an empty room or vacant house. White says that "perhaps all homes are never truly empty, having known the multitude of experience which is human life." Based on your experience, do you agree with him?

2. Through his description, what did White help you "see" about the Anasazi and their cliff dwellings? What did you learn?

3. Consider once again the basic techniques for observing—using sensory detail, comparisons, and images; describing what is not there; noting changes; and writing from a clear point of view. Which ones does White use most effectively? Cite an example of each technique from his essay.

4. In which paragraphs does White use each of the following shaping strategies: spatial order, chronological order, comparisons or contrasts, and simile, metaphor, or analogy? Which strategies did you find most effective in organizing the experience for you as a reader?

4 REMEMBERING

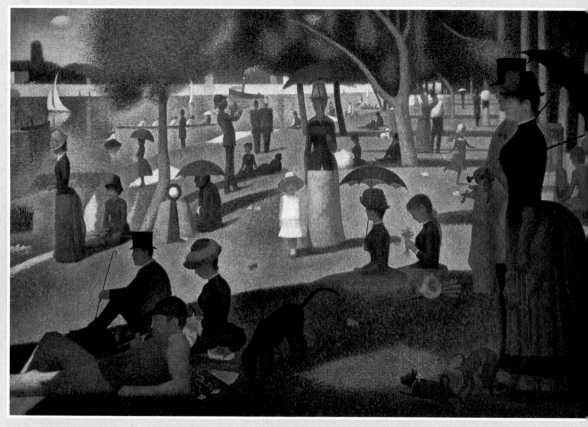

George Seurat, French, 1859–1891. *A Sunday on La Grande Jatte, 1884.* Oil on canvas, 1884–86, 207.5 x 308 cm, Helen Birch Bartlett Memorial Collection, 1926.224

T HIS MORNING YOU ACCIDENTALLY RAN INTO A CERTAIN PERSON WHOM YOU KNEW SEVERAL YEARS AGO, AND FOR SEVERAL HOURS YOU'VE BEEN IN A BAD MOOD. YOU CALLED your best friend, but no one answered the phone. You went to class and then for your usual jog, but you pooped out after only half a mile. You even watched a game show on television in the middle of the afternoon and ate half a bag of potato chips, but you still felt lousy. You yell at the television: "Why do I always react this way when I see that person?" But the television has no reply. So you grab some paper and begin scrawling out every memory you have of your experiences with the person you ran into this morning, hoping to understand your feelings.

❧

Y OU AND SEVERAL COWORKERS HAVE FORMED A COMMITTEE TO DRAFT A REPORT FOR YOUR COMPANY'S VICE PRESIDENT IN CHARGE OF PERSONNEL. YOU HAVE GRIEVANCES ABOUT workload, pay scale, daily procedures, and the attitudes of supervisors. Your report needs to recommend changes in current policies. The committee decides that each person will contribute part of the report by describing actual incidents that have had negative effects on efficiency and human relations. You decide to describe a day last June when your immediate supervisor expected you to learn a new word-processing system and at the same time meet a 3:00 P.M. deadline for a thirty-seven-page budget analysis.

For me the initial delight is in the surprise of remembering something I didn't know I knew.
—ROBERT FROST,
POET

❧

The fact is that there's no understanding the future without the present, and no understanding where we are now without a glance, at least, to where we have been.
—JOYCE MAYNARD,
COLUMNIST AND AUTHOR OF LOOKING BACKWARD: A CHRONICLE OF GROWING UP OLD IN THE SIXTIES

T HE HUMAN BRAIN IS A PACK RAT: NOTHING IS TOO SMALL, OBSCURE, OR MUNDANE FOR THE BRAIN'S COLLECTION. OFTEN THE BRAIN COLLECTS AND DISCARDS INFORMATION WITHOUT regard to our wishes. Out of the collection may arise, with no warning, the image of windblown whitecaps on a lake you visited more than five years ago, the recipe for Uncle Joe's incomparable chili, or even the right answer to an exam question that you've been starting at for the past fifteen minutes.

Remembering is sometimes easy, sometimes difficult. Often careful concentration yields nothing, while the most trivial occurrence—an old song on a car radio, the acrid smell of diesel exhaust, the face of a stranger—will trigger a flood of recollections. Someone tells a story and you immediately recall incidents, funny or traumatic, from your own life. Some memories, however, are nagging and troublesome, keeping you awake at night, daring you to deal with them. You pick at these memories. Why are they so important? You write about them, usually to probe that mystery of yesterday and today. Sights, sounds, or feelings from the present may draw you to the past, but the past leads, just as surely, back to the present.

Time passes and the past becomes the present. . . . These presences of the past are there in the center of your life today. You thought . . . they had died, but they have just been waiting their chance.

—CARLOS FUENTES,

Direct observations are important to learning and writing, but so are your memories, experiences, and stories. You may write an autobiographical account of part of your life, or you may recall a brief event, a person, or a place just as an example to illustrate a point. Whatever form your writing from memory takes, however, your initial purpose is to remember experiences so that you can understand yourself and your world. The point is not to write fiction, but to practice drawing on your memories and to write vividly enough about them so that you and others can discover and learn.

The value of remembering lies exactly here: Written memories have the power to teach you and, through *empathy* with your readers, to inform or convince them as well. At first, you may be self-conscious about sharing your personal memories. But as you reveal these experiences, you realize that your story is worth telling—not because you're such an egotist, but because sharing experiences helps everyone learn.

TECHNIQUES FOR WRITING
ABOUT MEMORIES

Writing vividly about memories includes all the skills of careful observing, but it adds several additional narrative strategies. Listed below are five techniques that writers use to compose effective remembering essays. As you read the essays that follow in this chapter, notice how each writer uses these techniques. Then, when you write your own remembering essay, use these techniques in your own essay. Remember: Not all writing about memories uses all five techniques, but one or two of them may transform a lifeless or boring account into an effective narrative.

- Using *detailed observation* **of people, places, and events.** Writing vividly about memories requires many of the skills of careful observation. Give actual dialogue where appropriate.
- **Creating specific scenes set in time and space.** Show your reader the actual events; don't just tell about events. Narrate specific incidents as they actually happened. Avoid monotonously summarizing events or presenting just the conclusions (for instance, "those experiences really changed my life").
- **Noting** *changes, contrasts,* **or** *conflicts.* Changes in people or places, contrasts between two different memories or between memories of expectations and realities, and conflicts between people or ideas—any of these may lead to the meaning or importance of a remembered person, place, or event.
- **Making** *connections* **between past events, people, or places and the present.** The main idea of a narrative often grows out of changes and conflicts or arises from the connections you make between past and present.
- **Discovering and focusing on a main idea.** A remembering essay is not a random narrative of the writer's favorite memories. A narrative should have a clear main point, focus on a main idea, or make a discovery. The essay should clearly show why the memories are important.

All of these techniques are important, but you should also keep several other points in mind. Normally, you should write in the *first person,* using "I" or "we" throughout the narrative. Although you will usually write in *past tense,* sometimes you may wish to lend immediacy to the events by retelling them in the *present tense,* as if they are happening now. Finally, you may choose straightforward *chronological order,* or you may begin near the end and use a *flashback* to tell the beginning of the story.

The key to effective remembering, however, is to get beyond *generalities and conclusions* about your experiences ("I had a lot of fun—those days really changed my life"). Your goal is to recall *specific incidents set in time and place* that *show* how and why those days changed your life. The specific incidents should show your *main point* or *dominant idea.*

The following passage by Andrea Lee began as a journal entry during a year she spent in Moscow and Leningrad following her graduation from college. She then combined these firsthand observations with her memories and published them in a collection called *Russian Journal.* She uses first person and, frequently, present tense as she describes her reactions to the sights of Moscow. In these paragraphs, she weaves observations and memories together to show her main idea: The contrast between American and Russian advertising helped her understand both the virtues and the faults of American commercialism. (The annotations in the margin illustrate how Lee uses all five remembering techniques.)

Specific scene

In Mayakovsky Square, not far from the Tchaikovsky Concert Hall, a big computerized electric sign sends various messages flashing out into the night. An outline of a taxi in green dots is accompanied by the words: "Take Taxis—All Streets Are Near." This is replaced by multicolored human figures and a sentence urging Soviet citizens to save in State banks. The bright patterns and messages come and go, making this one of the most sophisticated examples of advertising in Moscow. Even on chilly nights when I pass through the square, there is often a little group of Russians standing in front of the sign, watching in fascination for five and ten minutes as the colored dots go through their magical changes. The first few times I saw this, I chuckled and recalled an old joke about an American town so boring that people went out on weekends to watch the Esso sign.

Detailed observation

Connections past and present

Advertising, of course, is the glamorous offspring of capitalism and art: why advertise in a country where there is only one brand, the State brand, of anything, and often not enough even of that? There is nothing here comparable to the glittering overlay of commercialism that Americans, at least, take for granted as part of our cities; nothing like the myriad small seductions of the marketplace, which have led us to expect to be enticed. The Soviet political propaganda posters that fill up a small part of the Moscow landscape with their uniformly cold red color schemes and monumental robot-faced figures are so unappealing that they are dismissable.

Contrast

Main idea

Detailed observation

I realize now, looking back, that for at least my first month in Moscow, I was filled with an unconscious and devastating disappointment. Hardly realizing it, as I walked around the city, I was looking for the constant sensory distractions I was accustomed to in America. Like many others my age, I grew up reading billboards and singing advertising jingles; my idea of beauty was shaped—perniciously, I think—by the models with the painted eyes and pounds of shining hair whose beauty was accessible on every television set and street corner.

Connections past and present

Contrast and change

Main idea

REMEMBERING PEOPLE

In the following passage from the introduction to *The Way to Rainy Mountain,* N. Scott Momaday remembers his grandmother. While details of place and event are also recreated, the primary focus is on the character of his grandmother as revealed in several *specific,* recurring actions. Momaday does not give us generalities about his feelings (for instance, "I miss my grandmother a lot, especially now that she's gone"); instead, he begins with specific memories of scenes that *show* how he felt.

A writer is a reader moved to emulation.

—SAUL BELLOW,

AUTHOR OF HENDERSON THE RAIN KING

> Now that I can have her only in memory, I see my grandmother in the several postures that were peculiar to her: standing at the wood stove on a winter morning and turning meat in a great iron skillet; sitting at the south window, bent above her beadwork, and afterwards, when her vision failed, looking down for a long time into the fold of her hands; going out upon a cane, very slowly as she did when the weight of age came upon her; praying. I remember her most often at prayer. She made long, rambling prayers out of suffering and hope, having seen many things. I was never sure that I had the right to hear, so exclusive were they of all mere custom and company. The last time I saw her she prayed standing by the side of her bed at night, naked to the waist, the light of a kerosene lamp moving upon her dark skin. Her long, black hair, always drawn and braided in the day, lay upon her shoulders and against her breasts like a shawl. I do not speak Kiowa, and I never understood her prayers, but there was something inherently sad in the sound, some merest hesitation upon the syllables of sorrow. She began in a high and descending pitch, exhausting her breath to silence; then again and again—and always the same intensity of effort, of something that is, and is not, like urgency in the human voice. Transported so in the dancing light among the shadows of her room, she seemed beyond the reach of time. But that was illusion; I think I knew then that I should not see her again.

REMEMBERING PLACES

In the following passage from *Farewell to Manzanar,* Jeanne Wakatsuke Houston remembers the place in California where, as Japanese-Americans, her family was imprisoned during World War II. As you read, look for specific details and bits of description that convey her main idea.

In Spanish, Manzanar means "apple orchard." Great stretches of Owens Valley were once green with orchards and alfalfa fields. It has been a desert ever since its water started flowing south into Los Angeles, sometime during the twenties. But a few rows of untended pear and apple trees were still growing there when the camp opened, where a shallow water table and kept them alive. In the spring of 1943 we moved to block 28, right up next to one of the old pear orchards. That's where we stayed until the end of the war, and those trees stand in my memory for the turning of our life in camp, from the outrageous to the tolerable.

Papa pruned and cared for the nearest trees. Late that summer we picked the fruit green and stored it in a root cellar he had dug under our new barracks. At night the wind through the leaves would sound like the surf had sounded in Ocean Park, and while drifting off to sleep, I could almost imagine we were still living by the beach.

REMEMBERING EVENTS

In the following essay, called "The Boy's Desire," Richard Rodriguez recalls a particular event from his childhood that comes to mind when he remembers Christmas. In his memory, he sorts through the rooms in his house on 39th Street in Sacramento, recalling old toys: a secondhand bike, games with dice and spinning dials, a jigsaw puzzle, and a bride doll. In this passage, Rodriguez describes both the effort to remember and the memory itself—the one memory that still "holds color and size and shape." Was it all right, he wonders, that a boy should have wanted a doll for Christmas?

The fog comes to mind. It never rained on Christmas. It was never sharp blue and windy. When I remember Christmas in Sacramento, it is in gray: The valley fog would lift by late morning, the sun boiled haze for a few hours, then the tule fog would rise again when it was time to go into the house.

The haze through which memory must wander is thickened by that fog. The rooms of the house on 39th Street are still and dark in late afternoon, and I open the closet to search for old toys. One year there was a secondhand bike. I do not remember a color. Perhaps it had no color even then. Another year there were boxes of games that rattled their parts—dice and pegs and spinning dials. Or perhaps the rattle is of a jigsaw puzzle that compressed into an image . . . of what? of Paris? a litter of kittens? I cannot remember. Only one memory holds color and size and shape: brown hair, blue eyes, the sweet smell of styrene.

That Christmas I announced I wanted a bride doll. I must have been seven or eight—wise enough to know not to tell anyone at school, but young enough to whine out my petition from early November.

My father's reaction was unhampered by psychology. A shrug—"Una muñeca?"—a doll, why not? Because I knew it was my mother who would choose all the presents, it was she I badgered. I wanted a bride doll! "Is there something else you want?" she wondered. No! I'd make clear with my voice that nothing else would appease me, "We'll see," she'd say, and she never wrote it down on her list.

By early December, wrapped boxes started piling up in my parents' bedroom closet, above my father's important papers and the family album. When no one else was home, I'd drag a chair over and climb up to see . . . Looking for the one. About a week before Christmas, it was there. I was so certain it was mine that I punched my thumb through the wrapping paper and the cellophane window on the box and felt inside—lace, two tiny, thin legs. I got other presents that year, but it was the doll I kept by me. I remember my mother saying I'd have "to share her" with my younger sister—but Helen was four years old, oblivious. The doll was mine. My arms would hold her. She would sleep on my pillow.

And the sky did not fall. The order of the universe did not tremble. In fact, it was right for a change. My family accommodated itself to my request. My brother and sisters played round me with their own toys. I paraded my doll by the hands across the floor.

The other day, when I asked my brother and sisters about the doll, no one remembered. My mother remembers. "Yes," she smiled. "One year there was a doll."

The closet door closes. (The house on 39th Street has been razed for a hospital parking lot.) The fog rises. Distance tempts me to mock the boy and his desire. The fact remains: One Christmas in Sacramento I wanted a bride doll, and I got one.

■ WARMING UP: JOURNAL EXERCISES The following topics will help you practice writing about your memories. Read all of the following exercises, and then write on three that interest you the most. If another idea occurs to you, write a free entry about it.

Some very small incident that takes place today may be the most important event that happens to you this year, but you don't know that when it happens. You don't know it until much later.

—TONI MORRISON,

NOBEL PRIZE–WINNING AUTHOR OF BELOVED AND SONG OF SOLOMON

1. Select one moment in your past that either changed your life or showed you how your life had already changed. What was the event? What were you like before—and afterward?

2. Go through old family photographs and find one of yourself, taken at least five years ago. Describe the person in the photograph— what he or she did, thought, said, or hoped. How is that person like or unlike the person you are now?

3. Remember the first job you had. How did you get it, and what did you do? What mistakes did you make? What did you learn? Were there any humorous or serious misunderstandings between you and others?

4. Pick a favorite record from your collection—one that you've owned for a few years—and play one track. As you listen, write down the associations or memories that come to mind. What were you doing when you first heard the song? What other people, places, or events does it remind you of?

5. What were your earliest memories? Choose one particular event. How old were you? What was the place? Who were the people around you? What happened? After you write down your earliest memories, call members of your family, if possible, and interview them for their memories of this incident. How does what you actually remember differ from what your family tells you? Revise your first memory to incorporate additional details provided by your family.

6. At some point in the past, you may have faced a conflict between what was expected of you—by parents, friends, family, coach, or employer—and your own personality or abilities. Describe one occasion when these expectations seemed unrealistic or unfair. Was the experience entirely negative or was it, in the long run, positive?

7. At at least one point in our lives, we have felt like an outsider. In a selection earlier in this chapter, for instance, Richard Rodriguez recalls feelings of being different, rejected, or outcast. Write about an incident when you felt alienated from your family, peers, or social group. Focus on a key scene or scenes that show what happened, why it was important, and how it affects you now.

8. Read Helen Keller's or Mike Rose's essay later in this chapter and write your own literacy narrative. What are your early memories about learning to read and write? At what points did you struggle or fail? When did you most enjoy reading or writing?

REMEMBERING:

PROFESSIONAL WRITING

THE DAY LANGUAGE CAME INTO MY LIFE

Helen Keller

At the age of eighteen months, Helen Keller (1880–1968) lost her sight and hearing as a result of illness. During the next five years of her childhood, Keller became increasingly wild and unruly as she struggled against her dark and silent world. In "The Day Language Came into My Life," Keller remembers how, at age seven, her teacher, Anne Sullivan, arrived and taught her the miracle of language. After learning sign language and braille, Keller began her formal schooling and—with continued help from Sullivan—eventually graduated with honors from Radcliffe College. In her adult years, Keller became America's best-loved ambassador for the blind and disabled. She met nearly every American president, traveled to dozens of countries to speak on behalf of blind and deaf people, and wrote several books, including The Story of My Life *(1903),* The World I Live In *(1908), and* Midstream: My Later Life *(1930). The story of Anne Sullivan's teaching is told in William Gibson's Pulitzer Prize–winning play,* The Miracle Worker.

The most important day I remember in all my life is the one on which my teacher, Anne Mansfield Sullivan, came to me. I am filled with wonder when I consider the immeasurable contrast between the two lives which it connects. It was the third of March 1887, three months before I was seven years old. **(1)**

On the afternoon of that eventful day, I stood on the porch, dumb, expectant. I guessed vaguely from my mother's signs and from the hurrying to and fro in the house that something unusual was about to happen, so I went to the door and waited on the steps. The afternoon sun penetrated the mass of honeysuckle that covered the porch and fell on my upturned face. My fingers lingered almost unconsciously on the familiar leaves and blossoms which had just come forth to greet the sweet southern spring. I did not know what the future held of marvel or surprise for me. Anger and bitterness had preyed upon me continually for weeks and a deep languor had succeeded this passionate struggle. **(2)**

Have you ever been at sea in a dense fog, when it seemed as if a tangible white darkness shut you in, and the great ship, tense and anxious, groped her way toward the shore with plummet and sounding-line, and you waited with beating heart for something to happen? I was like that ship before my education began, only I was without compass or sounding-line and had no way of knowing how near the harbor was. "Light! give me light!" was the wordless cry of my soul, and the light of love shone on me in that very hour. **(3)**

I felt approaching footsteps. I stretched out my hand as I supposed to my mother. Someone took it, and I was caught up and held close in the arms of her who had come to reveal all things to me, and, more than all things else, to love me. **(4)**

The morning after my teacher came she led me into her room and gave me a doll. The little blind children at the Perkins Institution had sent it and Laura Bridgman had dressed it; but I did not know this until afterward. When I had played with it a little while, Miss Sullivan slowly spelled into my hand the word "d-o-l-l." I was at once interested in this finger play and tried to imitate it. When I finally succeeded in making the letters correctly I was flushed with childish pleasure and pride. Running downstairs to my mother I held up my hand and made the letters for doll. I did not know that I was spelling a word or even that words existed; I was simply making my fingers go in monkeylike imitation. In the days that followed I learned to spell in this uncomprehending way a great many words, among them *pin, hat, cup* and a few verbs like *sit, stand* and *walk*. But my teacher had been with me several weeks before I understood that everything has a name. **(5)**

One day, while I was playing with my new doll, Miss Sullivan put my big rag doll into my lap also, spelled "d-o-l-l" and tried to make me understand that "d-o-l-l" applied to both. Earlier in the day we had had a tussle over the words "m-u-g" and "w-a-t-e-r." Miss Sullivan had tried to impress it upon me that "m-u-g" is *mug* and that "w-a-t-e-r" is *water*, but I persisted in confounding the two. In despair she had dropped the subject for the time, only to renew it at the first opportunity. I became impatient at her repeated attempts and, seizing the new doll, I dashed it upon the floor. I was keenly delighted when I felt the fragments of the broken doll at my feet. Neither sorrow nor regret followed my passionate outburst. I had not loved the doll. In the still, dark world in which I lived there was no strong sentiment or tenderness. I felt my teacher sweep the fragments to one side of the hearth, and I had a sense of satisfaction that the cause of my discomfort was removed. She brought me my hat, and I knew I was going out into the warm sunshine. This thought, if a wordless sensation may be called a thought, made me hop and skip with pleasure. **(6)**

We walked down the path to the well-house, attracted by the fragrance of the honeysuckle with which it was covered. Someone was drawing water and my teacher placed my hand under the spout. As the cool stream gushed over one hand she spelled into the other the word *water*, first slowly, then rapidly. I stood still, my whole attention fixed upon the motions of her fingers. Suddenly I felt a misty consciousness as of something forgotten—a thrill of returning thought; and somehow the mystery of language was revealed to me. I knew then that "w-a-t-e-r" meant the wonderful cool something that was flowing over my hand. The living word awakened my soul, gave it light, hope, joy, set it free! There were barriers still, it is true, but barriers that could in time be swept away. **(7)**

I left the well-house eager to learn. Everything had a name, and each name gave birth to a new thought. As we returned to the house every object which I touched seemed to quiver with life. That was because I saw every-thing with the strange, new sight that had come to me. On entering the door I remembered the doll I had broken. I felt my way to the hearth and picked up the pieces. I tried vainly to put them together. Then my eyes filled with tears; for I realized what I had done, and for the first time I felt repentance and sorrow. **(8)**

I learned a great many new words that day. I do not remember what they all were; but I do know that *mother, father, sister, teacher* were among them—words that were to make the world blossom for me, "like Aaron's rod, with flowers." It would have been difficult to find a happier child than I was as I lay in my crib at the close of that eventful day and lived over the joys it had brought me, and for the first time longed for a new day to come. **(9)**

VOCABULARY

In your journal, write the meaning of the following words:

- I stood on the porch, *dumb* **(2)**
- a deep *languor* **(2)**
- with *plummet* and *sounding-line* **(3)**
- no strong *sentiment* **(6)**
- like *Aaron's rod* **(9)**

QUESTIONS FOR WRITING AND DISCUSSION

1. Write for five minutes, recalling your earliest memories with read-ing, speaking, or writing. Focus on one specific incident. How old were you? Where were you? What were you reading or writing?

2. Helen Keller's books have been translated into more than fifty lan-guages. Explain why you believe her story, as illustrated in this essay, has such universal appeal.

3. In paragraph 3, Keller uses an analogy to explain her feelings and her state of mind before language opened her life. Identify the extended comparison. What "difficult concept" does Keller explain through her analogy?

4. In paragraph 8, Keller says, "Everything had a name, and each name gave birth to a new thought." Explain what Keller means by using examples of the names of things from your own life.

5. Contrast Keller's actions and feelings before she discovers language to her actions and feeling afterward. In addition to learning words, how do her feelings and personality change?

6. A century ago, when Helen Keller was learning to read and speak, people who were blind and deaf were classified by the law as "idiots." Describe one experience you have had with a disabled person. Based on that experience, explain how Americans' attitudes toward people with some disability have (or have not) improved.

LIVES ON THE BOUNDARY

Mike Rose

Mike Rose was born to Italian immigrant parents in 1944, and his family moved to Los Angeles where he attended Our Lady of Mercy, a private Catholic school. He continued his education at Loyola University, graduating in 1966, and went on to earn his Ph.D from UCLA in 1981. Rose currently teaches at UCLA, and is the author of numerous articles and books, including When a Writer Can't Write: Studies in Writer's Block and Other Composing Problems *(1985),* Lives on the Boundary *(1989), and* Possible Lives: The Promise of Public Education in America *(1995). In the following selection, taken from the second chapter of* Lives on the Boundary, *Rose recalls how he was originally misplaced in a high school vocational track and then was shifted to college prep courses. Rose focuses his memories on his fellow students in the Voc. Ed. track and on one English teacher, Jack MacFarland, who opened his mind to the world of books and ideas and who helped him get to college and live "beyond the limiting boundaries" of his South Los Angeles neighborhood.*

My parents used to say that their son would have the best education they could afford. Maybe I would be a doctor. There was a public school in our neighborhood and several Catholic schools to the west. They had heard that quality schooling meant private, Catholic schooling, so they somehow got the money together to send me to Our Lady of Mercy, fifteen or so miles southwest of Ninety-first and Vermont. **(1)**

It took two buses to get to Our Lady of Mercy. The first started deep in South Los Angeles and caught me at midpoint. The second drifted through neighborhoods with trees, parks, big lawns, and lots of flowers. The rides were long but were livened up by a group of South L.A. veterans whose parents also thought that Hope had set up shop in the west end of the county. There was Christy Biggars, who, at sixteen, was dealing and was, according to rumor, a pimp as well. There were Bill Cobb and Johnny Gonzales, grease-pencil artists extraordinaire, who left Nembutal-enhanced swirls of "Cobb" and "Johnny" on the corrugated walls of the bus. And then there was Tyrrell Wilson. Tyrrell was the coolest kid I knew. He ran the dozens like a metric halfback, laid down a rap that outrhymed and outpointed Cobb, whose rap was good but not great— the curse of a moderately soulful kid trapped in white skin. But it was Cobb who would sneak a radio onto the bus, and thus underwrote his patter with Little Richard, Fats Domino, Chuck Berry, the Coasters, and Ernie K. Doe's mother-in-law, an awful woman who was "sent from down below." And so it was that Christy and Cobb and Johnny G. and Tyrrell and I and assorted others picked up along the way passed our days in the back of the bus, a funny mix brought together by geography and parental desire. **(2)**

Entrance to school brings with it forms and releases and assessments. Mercy relied on a series of tests, mostly the Stanford-Binet, for placement, and somehow the results of my tests got confused with those of another student named Rose. The other Rose apparently didn't do very well, for I was placed in the vocational track, a euphemism for the bottom level. Neither I nor my parents realized what this meant. We had no sense that Business Math, Typing, and English-Level D were dead ends. The current spate of reports on the schools criticizes parents for not involving themselves in the education of their children. But how would someone like Tommy Rose, with his two years of Italian schooling, know what to ask? And what sort of pressure could an exhausted waitress apply? The error went undetected, and I remained in the vocational track for two years. What a place. **(3)**

Students will float to the mark you set. I and the others in the vocational classes were bobbing in pretty shallow water. Vocational education has aimed at increasing the economic opportunities of students who do not do well in our schools. Some serious programs succeed in doing that, and through exceptional teachers—like Mr. Gross in *Horace's Compromise*—students learn to develop hypotheses and troubleshoot, reason through a problem, and communicate effectively—the true job skills. The vocational track, however, is most often a place for those who are just not making it, a dumping ground for the disaffected. There were a few teachers who worked hard at education; young Brother Slattery, for example, combined a stern voice with weekly quizzes to try to pass along to us a skeletal outline of world history. But mostly the teachers had no idea of how to engage the imaginations of us kids who were scuttling along at the bottom of the pond. **(4)**

But I did learn things about people and eventually came into my own socially. I liked the guys in Voc. Ed. Growing up where I did, I understood and admired physical prowess, and there was an abundance of muscle here. There was Dave Snyder, a sprinter and a halfback of true quality. Dave's ability and his quick wit gave him a natural appeal, and he was welcome in any clique, through he always kept a little independent. It was a testament to his independence that he included me among his friends—I eventually went out for track, but I was no jock. Owing to the Latin alphabet and a dearth of Rs and Ss, Snyder sat behind Rose, and we started exchanging one-liners and became friends. **(5)**

There was Ted Richard, a much-touted Little League pitcher. He was chunky and had a baby face and came to Our Lady of Mercy as a seasoned street fighter. Ted was quick to laugh and he had a loud, jolly laugh, but when he got angry he'd smile a little smile, the kind that simply raises the corner of the mouth a quarter of an inch. For those who knew, it was an eerie signal. Those who didn't found themselves in big trouble, for Ted was very quick. He loved to carry on what we would come to call philosophical discussions: What is courage? Does God exist? He also loved words, enjoyed picking up big ones like *salubrious* and *equivocal* and using them in our conversations—laughing at himself as the word hit a chuckhole rolling off his tongue. Ted didn't do all that well in school—baseball and parties and testing the courage he'd speculated about took up his time. His textbooks were *Argosy* and *Field and Stream*, whatever newspapers he'd find on the bus stop—from the *Daily Worker* to pornography—conversations with uncles or hobos or businessmen he'd meet in a coffee shop, *The Old Man and the Sea*. With hindsight, I can see that Ted was developing into one of those rough-hewn intellectuals whose sources are a mix of the learned and the apocryphal, whose discussions are both assured and sad. **(6)**

And then there was Ken Harvey. Ken was good-looking in a puffy way and had a full and oily ducktail and was a car enthusiast . . . a hodad. One day in religion class, he said the sentence that turned out to be one of the most memorable of the hundreds of thousands I heard in those Voc. Ed. years. We were talking about the parable of the talents, about achievement, working hard, doing the best you can do, blah-blah-blah, when the teacher called on the restive Ken Harvey for an opinion. Ken thought about it, but just for a second, and said (with studied, minimal affect), "I just wanna be average." That woke me up. Average?! Who wants to be average? Then the athletes chimed in with the clichés that make you want to laryngectomize them, and the exchange became a platitudinous melee. At the time, I thought Ken's assertion was stupid, and I wrote him off. But his sentence has stayed with me all these years, and I think I am finally coming to understand it. . . . **(7)**

My own deliverance from the Voc. Ed. world began with sophomore biology. Every student, college prep to vocational, had to take biology, and unlike the other courses, the same person taught all sections. When teaching the vocational group, Brother Clint probably slowed down a bit or omitted a little of the fundamental biochemistry, but he used the same book and more or less the same syllabus across the board. If one class got tough, he could get tougher. He was young and powerful and very handsome, and looks and physical strength were high currency. No one gave him any trouble. **(8)**

I was pretty bad at the dissecting table, but the lectures and the textbook were interesting: plastic overlays that, with each turned page, peeled away skin, then veins and muscle, then organs, down to the very bones that Brother Clint, pointer in hand, would tap out on our hanging skeleton. Dave Snyder was in big trouble, for the study of life—versus the living of it—was sticking in his craw. We worked out a code for our multiple-choice exams. He'd poke me in the back: once for the answer under A, twice for B, and so on; and when he'd hit the right one, I'd look up to ceiling as though I were lost in thought. Poke: cytoplasm. Poke, poke: methane. Poke, poke, poke: William Harvey. Poke, poke, poke, poke: islets of Langerhans. This didn't work out perfectly, but Dave passed the course, and I mastered the dreamy look of a guy on a record jacket. And something else happened. Brother Clint puzzled over this Voc. Ed. kid who was racking up 98s and 99s on his tests. He checked the school's records and discovered the error. He recommended that I begin my junior year in the College Prep program. According to all I've read since, such a shift, as one report puts it, is virtually impossible. Kids at that level rarely cross tracks. The telling thing is how chancy both my placement into and exit from Voc. Ed. was; neither I nor my parents had anything to do with it. I lived in one world during spring semester, and when I came back to school in the fall, I was living in another. **(9)**

Switching to College Prep was a mixed blessing. I was an erratic student. I was undisciplined. And I hadn't caught onto the rules of the game: Why work hard in a class that didn't grab my fancy? I was also hopelessly behind in math. Chemistry was hard; toying with my chemistry set years before hadn't prepared me for the chemist's equations. Fortunately, the priest who taught both chemistry and second year algebra was also the school's athletic director. Membership on the track team covered me; I knew I wouldn't get lower than a C. U.S. history was taught pretty well, and I did okay. But civics was taken over by a football coach who had trouble reading the textbook aloud—and reading aloud was the centerpiece of his pedagogy. College Prep at Mercy was certainly an improvement over the vocational program—at least it carried some status—but the social science curriculum was weak, and the mathematics and physical sciences were simply beyond me. . . . **(10)**

Jack MacFarland couldn't have come into my life at a better time. Mr. MacFarland had a master's degree from Columbia and decided, at twenty-six, to find a little school and teach his heart out. He never took any credentialing courses, couldn't bear to, he said, so he had to find employment in a private system. He ended up at Our Lady of Mercy teaching five sections of senior English. He was a beatnik who was born too late. His teeth were stained, he tucked his sorry tie in between the third and fourth buttons of his shirt, and his pants were chronically wrinkled. At first, we couldn't believe this guy, thought he slept in his car. But within no time, he had us so startled with work that we didn't much worry about where he slept or if he slept at all. We wrote three or four essays a month. We read a book every two to three weeks, starting with the *Iliad* and ending up with Hemingway. He gave us a quiz on the reading every other day. He brought a prep school curriculum to Mercy High. **(11)**

MacFarland's lectures were crafted, and as he delivered them he would pace the room jiggling a piece of chalk in his cupped hand, using it to scribble on the board the names of all the writers and philosophers and plays and novels he was weaving into his discussion. He asked questions often, raised everything from Zeno's paradox to the repeated last line of Frost's "Stopping by Woods on a Snowy Evening." He slowly and carefully built up our knowledge of Western intellectual history—with facts, with connections, with speculations. We learned about Greek philosophy, about Dante, the Elizabethan world view, the Age of Reason, existentialism. He analyzed poems with us, had us reading sections from John Ciardi's *How Does a Poem Mean?*, making a potentially difficult book accessible with his own explanations. We gave oral reports on poems Ciardi didn't cover. We imitated the styles of Conrad, Hemingway, and *Time* magazine. We wrote and talked, wrote and talked. The man immersed us in language. **(12)**

Even MacFarland's barbs were literary. If Jim Fitzsimmons, hung over and irritable, tried to smart-ass him, he'd rejoin with a flourish that would spark the indomitable Skip Madison—who'd lost his front teeth in a hapless tackle—to flick his tongue through the gap and opine, "good chop," drawing out the single "o" in stinging indictment. Jack MacFarland, this tobacco-stained intellectual, brandished linguistic weapons of a kind I hadn't encountered before. Here was this *egghead,* for God's sake, keeping some pretty difficult people in line. And from what I heard, Mike Dweetz and Steve Fusco and all the notorious Voc. Ed. crowd settled down as well when MacFarland took the podium. Though a lot of guys groused in the schoolyard, it just seemed that giving trouble to this particular teacher was a silly thing to do. Tomfoolery, not to mention assault, had no place in the world he was trying to create for us, and instinctively everyone knew that. If nothing else, we all recognized MacFarland's considerable intelligence and respected the hours he put into his work. It came to this: The troublemaker would look foolish rather than daring. Even Jim Fitzsimmons was reading *On the Road* and turning his incipient alcoholism to literary ends. **(13)**

There were some lives that were already beyond Jack MacFarland's ministrations, but mine was not. I started reading again as I hadn't since elementary school. I would go into our gloomy little bedroom or sit at the dinner table while, on the television, Danny McShane was paralyzing Mr. Moto with the atomic drop, and work slowly back through *Heart of Darkness,* trying to catch the words in Conrad's sentences. I certainly was not MacFarland's best student; most of the other guys in College Prep, even my fellow slackers, had better backgrounds than I did. But I worked very hard, for MacFarland had hooked me. He tapped my old interest in reading and creating stories. He gave me a way to feel special by using my mind. And he provided a role model that wasn't shaped on physical prowess alone, and something inside me that I wasn't quite aware of responded to that. Jack MacFarland established a literacy club, to borrow a phrase of Frank Smith's, and invited me—invited all of us—to join. **(14)**

In my last semester of high school, I elected a special English course fashioned by Mr. MacFarland, and it was through this elective that there arouse at Mercy a fledgling literati. Art Mitz, the editor of the school news-paper and a very smart guy, was the kingpin. He was joined by me and Mark Dever, a quiet boy who wrote beautifully and who would die before he was forty. MacFarland occasionally invited us to his apartment, and those visits became the high point of our apprenticeship: We'd clamp on our training wheels and drive to his salon. **(15)**

He lived in a cramped and cluttered place near the airport, tucked away in the kind of building that architectural critic Reyner Banham calls a *ding-bat.* Books were all over: stacked, piled, tossed, and crated, underlined and dog eared, well worn and new. Cigarette ashes crusted with coffee in saucers or spilled over the sides of motel ashtrays. The little bedroom had, along two of its walls, bricks and boards loaded with notes, magazines, and oversized books. The kitchen joined the living room, and there was a stack of German newspapers under the sink. I had never seen anything like it: a great flophouse of language furnished by City Lights and Café le Metro. I read every title. I flipped through paperbacks and scanned jackets and memorized names: Gogol, *Finnegan's Wake,* Djuna Barnes, Jackson Pollock, *A Coney Island of the Mind,* F. O. Matthiessen's *American Renaissance,* all sorts of Freud, *Troubled Sleep,* Man Ray, the *Education of Henry Adams,* Richard Wright, *Film as Art,* William Butler Yeats, Marguerite Duras, *Redburn,* a *Season in Hell, Kapital.* On the cover of Alain-Fournier's *The Wanderer* was an Edward Gorey draw-ing of a young man on a road winding into dark trees. By the hotplate sat a strange Kafka novel called *Amerika,* in which an adolescent hero crosses the Atlantic to find the Nature Theater of Oklahoma. Art and Mark would be talking about a movie or the school newspaper, and I would be consuming my English teacher's library. It was heady stuff. I felt like a Pop Warner athlete on steroids. **(16)**

Let me be the first to admit that there was a good deal of adolescent pas-sion in this embrace of the avant-garde: self-absorption, sexually charged pedantry, an elevation of the odd and abandoned. Still it was a time during which I absorbed an awful lot of information: long lists of titles, images from expressionist paintings, new wave shibboleths, snippets of philosophy, and names that read like Steve Fusco's misspellings—Goethe, Nietzche, Kierkegaard. Now this is hardly the stuff of deep understanding. But it was an introduction, a phrase book, a Baedeker to a vocabulary of ideas, and it felt good at the time to know all these words. With hindsight I realize how layered and important that knowledge was. **(17)**

It enabled me to do things in the world. I could browse bohemian bookstores in far-off, mysterious Hollywood; I could go to the Cinema and see events through the lenses of European directors; and, most of all, I could share an evening, talk that talk, with Jack MacFarland, the man I most admired at the time. Knowledge was becoming a bonding agent. Within a year or two, the persona of the disaffected hipster would prove too cynical, too alienated to last. But for a time it was new and exciting: It provided a critical perspective on society, and it allowed me to act as though I were living beyond the limiting boundaries of South Vermont. **(18)**

VOCABULARY

In your journal, write the meanings of the following words:

- a *euphemism* for the bottom level **(3)**
- picking up big ones like *salubrious* and *equivocal* **(6)**
- a mix of the learned and the *apocryphal* **(6)**
- centerpiece of his *pedagogy* **(10)**
- turning his *incipient* alcoholism to literary ends **(13)**
- beyond Jack MacFarland's *ministrations* **(14)**
- this embrace of the *avant-garde* **(17)**
- new wave *shibboleths* **(17)**
- a *Baedeker* to a vocabulary of ideas **(17)**

QUESTIONS FOR WRITING AND DISCUSSION

1. The title of Mike Rose's book is *Lives on the Boundary*. In this selection, what "boundaries" do the Voc. Ed. students face? What boundaries does Rose face? Which of these boundaries is Rose able to cross? (How are these boundaries similar to or different from the boundaries you faced growing up?)

2. Effective remembering essays build on detailed descriptions. Review the *observing* techniques from Chapter 3. Of the techniques discussed there (using sensory details and images, describing what is not present, noting changes, writing from a point of view, and focusing on a dominant idea), which does Rose use most

effectively? To support your choice(s), find examples from Rose's essay.

3. Review the remembering techniques listed early in this chapter. Which does Rose use most effectively in his essay? Cite examples to support your choice(s). Which techniques might he add to his essay? Where, for example, might Rose use dialogue to recreate a school scene more vividly?

4. In his essay, Rose creates two voices which represent him as a high school student and as a forty year-old man looking back on his early education. Find examples that illustrate each of these voices. (Should Rose interrupt the narration about his high school years with his older reflections? Why or why not?)

5. Write your own remembering essay describing a particular teacher from high school or college who impressed you or influenced the direction of your life. Recall scenes from this time in your life that illustrate how this teacher changed your life.

BEAUTY: WHEN THE OTHER DANCER IS THE SELF

Alice Walker

The author of the Pulitzer Prize–winning novel The Color Purple *(1983), Alice Walker has written works of fiction and poetry, including* Love and Trouble: Stories of Black Women *(1973),* Meridian *(1976), and* Revolutionary Petunias and Other Poems *(1973). "Beauty: When the Other Dancer Is the Self" originally appeared in* Ms. *magazine and was revised and published in her collection of essays,* In Search of Our Mother's Gardens *(1983). Walker, a former editor of* Ms., *refers in this essay to Gloria Steinem and an interview published in* Ms. *entitled, "Do You Know This Woman? She Knows You—A Profile of Alice Walker." As you read the essay reprinted here, consider Walker's purpose: Why is she telling us—total strangers—about a highly personal and traumatic event that shaped her life?*

It is a bright summer day in 1947. My father, a fat, funny man with beautiful eyes and a subversive wit, is trying to decide which of his eight children he will take with him to the county fair. My mother, of course, will not go. She is knocked out from getting us ready: I hold my neck stiff against the pressure of her knuckles as she hastily completes the braiding and then beribboning of my hair. **(1)**

My father is the driver for the rich old white lady up the road. Her name is Miss Mey. She owns all the land for miles around, as well as the house in which we live. All I remember about her is that she once offered to pay my mother thirty-five cents for cleaning her house, raking up piles of her magnolia leaves, and washing her family's clothes, and that my mother—she of no money, eight children, and a chronic earache—refused it. But I do not think of this in 1947. I am two-and-a-half years old. I want to go everywhere my daddy goes. I am excited at the prospect of riding in a car. Someone has told me fairs are fun. That there is room in the car for only three of us doesn't faze me at all. Whirling happily in my starchy frock, showing off my biscuit polished patent leather shoes and lavender socks, tossing my head in a way that makes my ribbons bounce, I stand, hands on hips, before my father. "Take me, Daddy," I say with assurance, "I'm the prettiest!" **(2)**

Later, it does not surprise me to find myself in Miss Mey's shiny black car, sharing the backseat with the other lucky ones. Does not surprise me that I thoroughly enjoy the fair. At home that night I tell all the unlucky ones about the merry-go-round, the man who eats live chickens, and the abundance of Teddy bears, until they say: that's enough, baby Alice. Shut up now, and go to sleep. **(3)**

It is Easter Sunday, 1950. I am dressed in a green, flocked scalloped-hem dress (handmade by my adoring sister Ruth) that has its own smooth satin petticoat and tiny hot-pink roses tucked into each scallop. My shoes, new T-strap patent leather, again highly biscuit polished. I am six years old and have learned one of the longest Easter speeches to be heard in church that day, totally unlike the speech I said when I was two: "Easter lilies / pure and white / blossom in / the morning light." When I rise to give my speech I do so on a great wave of love and pride and expectation. People in the church stop rustling their new crinolines. They seem to hold their breath. I can tell they admire my dress, but it is my spirit, bordering on sassiness (womanishness), they secretly applaud. **(4)**

"That girl's a little *mess*," they whisper to each other, pleased. **(5)**

Naturally I say my speech without stammer or pause, unlike those who stutter, stammer, or, worst of all, forget. This is before the word "beautiful" exists in people's vocabulary, but "Oh, isn't she the *cutest* thing!" frequently floats my way. "And got so much sense!" they gratefully add . . . for which thoughtful addition I thank them to this day. **(6)**

It was great fun being cute. But then, one day, it ended. **(7)**

I am eight years old and a tomboy. I have a cowboy hat, cowboy boots, checkered shirt and pants, all red. My playmates are my brothers, two and four years older than I. Their colors are black and green, the only difference in the way we are dressed. On Saturday nights we all go to the picture show, even my mother; Westerns are her favorite kind of movie. Back home, "on the ranch," we pretend we are Tom Mix, Hopalong Cassidy, Lash LaRue (we've even named one of our dogs Lash LaRue); we chase each other for hours rustling cattle, being outlaws, delivering damsels from distress. Then my parents decide to buy my brothers guns. These are not "real" guns. They shoot "BBs," copper pellets my brothers say will kill birds. Because I am a girl, I do not get a gun. Instantly I am relegated to the position of Indian. Now there appears a great distance between us. They shoot and shoot at everything with their new guns. I try to keep up with my bow and arrows. **(8)**

One day while I am standing on top of our makeshift "garage"—pieces of tin nailed across some poles—holding my bow and arrow and looking out toward the fields, I feel an incredible blow in my right eye. I look down just in time to see my brother lower his gun. **(9)**

Both brothers rush to my side. My eye stings, and I cover it with my hand. "If you tell," they say, "we will get a whipping. You don't want that to happen, do you?" I do not. "Here is a piece of wire," says the older brother, picking it up from the roof; "say you stepped on one end of it and the other flew up and hit you." The pain is beginning to start. "Yes," I say. "Yes, I will say that is what happened." If I do not say this is what happened, I know my brothers will find ways to make me wish I had. But now I will say anything that gets me to my mother. **(10)**

Confronted by our parents we stick to the lie agreed upon. They place me on a bench on the porch and I close my left eye while they examine the right. There is a tree growing from underneath the porch, that climbs past the railing to the roof. It is the last thing my right eye sees. I watch as its trunk, its branches, and then its leaves are blotted out by the rising blood. **(11)**

I am in shock. First there is intense fever, which my father tries to break using lily leaves bound around my head. Then there are chills: my mother tries to get me to eat soup. Eventually, I do not know how, my parents learn what has happened. A week after the "accident" they take me to see a doctor. "Why did you wait so long to come?" he asks, looking into my eye and shaking his head. "Eyes are sympathetic," he says. "If one is blind, the other will likely become blind too." **(12)**

This comment of the doctor's terrifies me. But it is really how I look that bothers me most. Where the BB pellet struck there is a glob of whitish scar tissue, a hideous cataract, on my eye. Now when I stare at people—a favorite pastime, up to now—they will stare back. Not at the "cute" little girl, but at her scar. For six years I do not stare at anyone because I do not raise my head. **(13)**

Years later, in the throes of a mid-life crisis, I ask my mother and sister whether I changed after the "accident." "No," they say, puzzled. "What do you mean?" **(14)**

What do I mean? **(15)**

I am eight, and for the first time, doing poorly in school, where I have been something of a whiz since I was four. We have just moved to the place where the "accident" occurred. We do not know any of the people around us because this is a different county. The only time I see the friends I knew is when we go back to our old church. The new school is the former state penitentiary. It is a large stone building, cold and drafty, crammed to overflowing with boisterous, ill-disciplined children. On the third floor there is a huge circular imprint of some partition that has been torn out. **(16)**

"What used to be here?" I ask a sullen girl next to me on our way past it to lunch. **(17)**

"The electric chair," says she. **(18)**

At night I have nightmares about the electric chair, and about all the people reputedly "fried" in it. I am afraid of the school, where all the students seem to be budding criminals. **(19)**

"What's the matter with your eye?" they ask, critically. **(20)**

When I don't answer (I cannot decide whether it was an "accident" or not), they shove me, insist on a fight. **(21)**

My brother, the one who created the story about the wire, comes to my rescue. But then brags so much about "protecting" me, I become sick. **(22)**

After months of torture at the school, my parents decide to send me back to our old community to my old school. I live with my grandparents and the teacher they board. But there is no room for Phoebe, my cat. By the time my grandparents decide there is room, and I ask for my cat, she cannot be found. Miss Yarborough, the boarding teacher, takes me under her wing, and begins to teach me to play the piano. But soon she marries an African—a "prince," she says—and is whisked away to his continent. **(23)**

At my old school there is at least one teacher who loves me. She is the teacher who "knew me before I was born" and bought my first baby clothes. It is she who makes my life bearable. It is her presence that finally helps me turn on the one child at the school who continually calls me "one-eyed bitch." One day I simply grab him by his coat and beat him until I am satisfied. It is my teacher who tells me my mother is ill. **(24)**

My mother is lying in bed in the middle of the day, something I have never seen. She is in too much pain to speak. She has an abscess in her ear. I stand looking down on her, knowing that if she dies, I cannot live. She is being treated with warm oils and hot bricks held against her cheek. Finally a doctor comes. But I must go back to my grandparents' house. The weeks pass, but I am hardly aware of it. All I know is that my mother might die, my father is not so jolly, my brothers still have their guns, and I am the one sent away from home. **(25)**

"You did not change," they say. **(26)**

Did I imagine the anguish of never looking up? **(27)**

I am twelve. When relatives come to visit I hide in my room. My cousin Brenda, just my age, whose father works in the post office and whose mother is a nurse, comes to find me. "Hello," she says. And then she asks, looking at my recent school picture which I did not want taken, and on which the "glob" as I think of it is clearly visible, "You still can't see out of that eye?" **(28)**

"No," I say, and flop back on the bed over my book. **(29)**

That night, as I do almost every night, I abuse my eye. I rant and rave at it, in front of the mirror. I plead with it to clear up before morning. I tell it I hate and despise it. I do not pray for sight. I pray for beauty. **(30)**

"You did not change," they say. **(31)**

I am fourteen and baby-sitting for my brother Bill who lives in Boston. He is my favorite brother and there is a strong bond between us. Understanding my feelings of shame and ugliness, he and his wife take me to a local hospital where the "glob" is removed by a doctor named O. Henry. There is still a small bluish crater where the scar tissue was, but the ugly white stuff is gone. Almost immediately I become a different person from the girl who does not raise her head. Or so I think. Now that I've raised my head, I win the boyfriend of my dreams. Now that I've raised my head, I have plenty of friends. Now that I've raised my head, classwork comes from my lips as faultlessly as Easter speeches did, and I leave high school as valedictorian, most popular student and *queen,* hardly believing my luck. Ironically, the girl who was voted most beautiful in our class (and was) was later shot twice through the chest by a male companion, using a "real" gun, while she was pregnant. But that's another story in itself. Or, is it? **(32)**

"You did not change," they say. **(33)**

It is now thirty years since the "accident." A beautiful journalist comes to visit and to interview me. She is going to write a cover story for her magazine that focuses on my last book. "Decide how you want to look on the cover," she says. "Glamorous, or whatever." **(34)**

Never mind "glamorous," it is the "whatever" that I hear. Suddenly all I can think of is whether I will get enough sleep the night before the photography session: if I don't, my eye will be tired and wander, as blind eyes will. **(35)**

At night in bed with my lover I think up reasons why I should not appear on the cover of a magazine. "My meanest critics will say I've sold out," I say. "My family will now realize I write scandalous books." **(36)**

"But what's the real reason you don't want to do this?" he asks. **(37)**

"Because in all probability," I say in a rush, "my eye won't be straight." **(38)**

"It will be straight enough," he says. Then, "Besides, I thought you'd made your peace with that." **(39)**

And I suddenly remember that I have. **(40)**

I remember:

I am talking to my brother Jimmy, asking if he remembers anything unusual about the day I was shot. He does not know I consider that day the last time my father, with his sweet home remedy of cool lily leaves, "chose" me, and that I suffered and raged inside because of this. "Well," he says, "all I remember is standing by the side of the highway with Daddy, trying to flag down a car. A white man stopped, but when Daddy said he needed somebody to take his little girl to the doctor, he drove off." **(41)**

I remember:

I am in the desert for the first time. I fall totally in love with it. I am so overwhelmed by its beauty, I confront for the first time, consciously, the meaning of the doctor's words years ago: "Eyes are sympathetic. If one is blind, the other will likely become blind too." I realize I have dashed about the world madly, looking at this, looking at that, storing up images against the fading of the light. But I might have missed seeing the desert! The shock of that possibility—and gratitude for over twenty-five years of sight—sends me literally to my knees. Poem after poem comes—which is perhaps how poets pray.

On Sight

I am so thankful I have seen
The Desert
And the creatures in the desert
And the desert Itself.
The desert has its own moon
Which I have seen
With my own eye
There is no flag on it.
Trees of the desert have arms
All of which are always up
That is because the moon is up
The sun is up
Also the sky
The stars
Clouds
None with flags.
If there were flags, I doubt
the trees would point.
Would you? **(42)**

But mostly, I remember this:

I am twenty-seven, and my baby daughter is almost three. Since her birth I have worried over her discovery that her mother's eyes are different from other people's. Will she be embarrassed? I wonder. What will she say? Every day she watches a television program called "Big Blue Marble." It begins with a picture of the earth as it appears from the moon. It is bluish, a little battered-looking, but full of light, with whitish clouds swirling around it. Every time I see it I weep with love, as if it is a picture of Grandma's house. One day when I am putting Rebecca down for her nap, she suddenly focuses on my eye. Something inside me cringes, gets ready to try to protect myself. All children are cruel about physical differences, I know from experience, and that they don't always mean to be is another matter. I assume Rebecca will be the same. **(43)**

But no-o-o-o. She studies my face intently as we stand, her inside and me outside her crib. She even holds my face maternally between her dimpled little hands. Then, looking every bit as serious and lawyerlike as her father, she says, as if it may just possibly have slipped my attention: "Mommy, there's a *world* in your eye." (As in, "Don't be alarmed, or do anything crazy.") And then, gently, but with great interest: "Mommy, where did you *get* that world in your eye?" **(44)**

For the most part, the pain left then. (So what if my brothers grew up to buy even more powerful pellet guns for their sons and to carry real guns themselves. So what if a young "Morehouse man" once nearly fell off the steps of Trevor Arnett Library because he thought my eyes were blue.) Crying and laughing I ran to the bathroom, while Rebecca mumbled and sang herself off to sleep. Yes indeed, I realized, looking into the mirror. There *was* a world in my eye. And I saw that it was possible to love it; that in fact, for all it had taught me, of shame and anger and inner vision, I *did* love it. Even to see it drifting out of orbit in boredom, or rolling up out of fatigue, not to mention floating back at attention in excitement (bearing witness, a friend has called it), deeply suitable to my personality, and even characteristic of me. **(45)**

That night I dream I am dancing to Stevie Wonder's song "Always" (the name of the song is really "As," but I hear it as "Always"). As I dance, whirling and joyous, happier than I've ever been in my life, another bright-faced dancer joins me. We dance and kiss each other and hold each other through the night. The other dancer has obviously come through all right, as I have done. She is beautiful, whole and free. And she is also me. **(46)**

VOCABULARY

In your journal, write the meaning of the following words:

- a *subversive* wit **(1)**
- rustling their new *crinolines* **(4)**
- Eyes are *sympathetic* **(12)**
- a hideous *cataract* **(13)**
- *boisterous*, ill-disciplined children **(16)**
- bearing *witness* **(45)**

QUESTIONS FOR WRITING AND DISCUSSION

1. Why does Alice Walker share this story with us? What memories from your own life did her story trigger? Write them down.

2. What does Walker discover or learn about herself? As a reader, what did you learn about your own experiences by reading this essay?

3. Reread the essay, looking for examples of the following techniques for writing about memories: (1) using detailed observations; (2) creating specific scenes; (3) noting changes, contrasts, or conflicts;

and (4) seeing relationships between past and present. In your opinion, which of these techniques does she use most effectively?

4. What is Walker's main idea in this autobiographical account? State it in your own words. Where in the essay does she state it most explicitly?

5. How many scenes or episodes does Walker recount? List them according to her age at the time. Explain how each episode relates to her main idea.

6. Walker also uses images of sight and blindness to organize her essay. The story begins with a description of a father who has "beautiful eyes" and ends with her dancing in her dream to a song by Stevie Wonder. Catalog the images of sight and blindness from each scene or episode. Explain how, taken together, these images reinforce Walker's main idea.

7. Walker writes her essay in the present tense, and she uses italics not only to emphasize ideas but to indicate the difference between past thoughts and events and the present. List the places where she uses italics. Explain how the italicized passages reinforce her main point.

REMEMBERING:

THE WRITING PROCESS

■ ASSIGNMENT FOR REMEMBERING Write an essay about an important person, place, and/or event in your life. Your purpose is to recall and then use specific examples that *recreate* this memory and *show why* it is so important to you.

As you begin writing, assume that you are writing for yourself or for a small audience of good friends who are interested in your life. Let your writing recreate the experience vividly enough so that your readers can see the main idea that you wish to convey.

Memory is more indelible than ink.

—ANITA LOOS,
AUTHOR OF <u>KISS</u>
<u>HOLLYWOOD GOODBYE</u>

CHOOSING A SUBJECT

If one of the journal-entry exercises suggested a possible subject, try the collecting and shaping strategies below. If none of those exercises led to an interesting subject, consider the following ideas:

- Interview (in person or over the phone) your parents, a brother or sister, or a close friend. What events or experiences do they remember that were important to you?
- Get out a map of your town, city, state, or country and spend a few minutes doing an inventory of places you have been. Make a list of trips you have taken, with dates and years. Which of those places is the most memorable for you?
- Dig out a school yearbook and look through the pictures and the inscriptions that your classmates wrote. Whom do you remember most clearly? What events do you recall most vividly?
- Go to the library and look through news magazines or newspapers from five to ten years ago. What were the most important events of those years? What do you remember about them? Where were you and what were you doing when these events occurred? Which events had the largest impact on your life?
- Choose an important moment in your life, but write from the *point of view* of another person—a friend, family member, or stranger who was present. Let this person narrate the events that happened to you.

Note: Avoid choosing overly emotional topics such as the recent death of a close friend or family member. If you are too close to your subject, responding to your reader's revision suggestions may be difficult. Ask yourself if you can emotionally distance yourself from that subject. If you received a C for that essay, would you feel devastated?

COLLECTING

Once you have chosen a subject for your essay, try the following collecting strategies:

Brainstorming   Brainstorming is merely jotting down anything and everything that comes to mind that is remotely connected to your subject: words, phrases, images, or complete thoughts. You can brainstorm by yourself or in groups, with everyone contributing ideas and one person recording them.

Looping   Looping is a method of controlled freewriting that generates ideas and provides focus and direction. Begin by freewriting about your subject for eight to ten minutes. Then pause, reread what you have written, and *underline* the most interesting or important idea in what you've written so far. Then, using that sentence or idea as your starting point, write for eight to ten minutes more. Repeat this cycle, or "loop," one more time. Each loop should add ideas and details from some new angle or viewpoint, but overall you will be focusing on the most important ideas that you discover.

Clustering Clustering is merely a visual scheme for brainstorming and free-associating about your topic. It can be especially effective for remembering because it helps you sketch relationships among your topics and subtopics. As you can see from the sample sketch that follows, the sketch that you make of your ideas should help you see relationships between ideas or get a rough idea about an order or shape you may wish to use.

SHAPING

First, reconsider your purpose; perhaps it has become clearer or more definite since you recorded it in your journal entry. In your journal, jot down tentative answers for the following questions. If you don't have an answer, go on to the next question.

- *Subject:* What is your general subject?
- *Specific Topic:* What aspect of your subject are you interested in?
- *Purpose:* Why is this topic interesting or important to you or your readers?
- *Main Idea:* What might your main idea be?
- *Audience:* For whom are you writing this? What is your reader like, and why might he or she be interested in this topic?

Narrow and focus your subject. If you're going to write a three-page essay, don't try to cover everything in your life. Focus on one person, one episode, one turning point, one day, even one *part* of one day, and do that in depth and detail.

As you start your shaping activities, use the observing strategies discussed in Chapter 3. *Spatial order* may help you shape your description of a place you are remembering; *classification* or *definition* can shape your memories of people, places, or events. *Similes, metaphors,* and *analogies* will make your writing more vivid and may also suggest a shape or help you develop your subject.

In addition, use the following strategies for shaping written memories. Try each strategy to see if it works for your subject. Although some strategies may not be appropriate, others will work naturally, suggesting ways to shape and develop your writing.

Chronological Order   If you are writing about remembered events, you will probably use some form of chronological order. Try making a *chronological list of the major scenes or events.* Then go through the list, deciding what you will emphasize by telling about each item in detail and what you will pass over quickly. Normally, you will be using a straightforward chronological order, but you may wish to use a flashback, starting in the middle or near the end and then returning to tell the beginning. In his paragraph about a personal relationship, for example, student writer Gregory Hoffman begins the story at the most dramatic point, returns to tell how the relationship began, and then concludes the story.

> Her words hung in the air like iron ghosts. "I'm pregnant," she said as they walked through the park, the snow crackling beneath their feet. Carol was looking down at the ground when she told him, somewhat ashamed, embarrassed and defiant all at once. Their relationship had only started in September, but both had felt the uneasiness surrounding them for the past months. She could remember the beginning so well and in such favor, now that the future seemed so uncertain. The all-night conversations by the bay window, the rehearsals at the university theatre—where he would make her laugh

during her only soliloquy, and most of all the Christmas they had spent together in Vermont. No one else had existed for her during those months. Yet now, she felt duped by her affections—as if she had become an absurd representation of a tragic television character. As they approached the lake he put his arm around her, "Just do what you think is best, babe. I mean, I think you know how I feel." At that moment, she knew it was over. It was no longer "their" decision. His hand touched her cheek in a benedictorial fashion. The rest would only be form now. Exchanging records and clothes with an aside of brief conversation. She would see him again, in the market or at a movie, and they would remember. But like his affection in September, her memory of him would fade until he was too distant to see.

Comparison/Contrast   Although you may be comparing or contrasting people, places, or events from the past, you will probably also be comparing or contrasting the past to the present. You may do that at the beginning, noting how something in the present reminds you of a past person, place, or event. You may do it at the end, as Andrea Lee does in *Russian Journal*. You may do it both at the beginning and at the end, as Richard Rodriguez does in "The Boy's Desire." You may even contrast past and present throughout, as Alice Walker does in "Beauty: When the Other Dancer Is the Self." Comparing or contrasting the past with the present will often clarify your dominant idea.

Image   Sometimes a single mental picture or recurring image will shape a paragraph or two in an essay. Consider how novelist George Orwell, in his essay "Shooting an Elephant," uses the image of a puppet or dummy to describe his feeling at a moment when he realized that, against his better judgment, he was going to have to shoot a marauding elephant in order to satisfy a crowd of two thousand Burmese who had gathered to watch him. The italicized words emphasize the recurring image.

> Suddenly I realized that I should have to shoot the elephant after all. The people expected it of me and I had got to do it; I could feel their *two thousand wills pressing me forward*, irresistibly. And it was at this moment, as I stood there with the rifle in my hands, that I first grasped the hollowness, the futility of the white man's dominion in the East. Here was I, the white man with his gun, standing in front of the unarmed native crowd—*seemingly the leading actor* of the piece; but in reality I was only an absurd *puppet pushed to and fro* by the will of those yellow faces behind. I perceived in this moment that when the white man turns tyrant it is his own freedom that he destroys. He becomes a sort of *hollow, posing dummy*, the *convention-*

alized figure of a sahib. For it is the condition of his rule that he shall spend his life in trying to impress the "natives" and so in every crisis he has got to do what the "natives" expect of him. He *wears a mask,* and his face grows to fit it. I had got to shoot the elephant. I had committed myself to doing it when I sent for the rifle. *A sahib has got to act like a sahib;* he has got to appear resolute, to know his own mind and do definite things.

Voice and Tone   When you have a personal conversation with someone, the way you look and sound—your body type, your voice, your facial expressions and gestures—communicates a sense of personality and attitude, which in turn affects how the other person reacts to what you say. In written language, although you don't have those gestures, expressions, or the actual sound of your voice, you can still create the sense that you are talking directly to your listener.

The term *voice* refers to a writer's personality as revealed through language. Writers may use emotional, colloquial, or conversational language to communicate a sense of personality. Or they may use abstract, impersonal language either to conceal their personalities or to create an air of scientific objectivity.

Tone is a writer's attitude toward the subject. The attitude may be positive or negative. It may be serious, humorous, honest, or ironic; it may be skeptical or accepting; it may be happy, frustrated, or angry. Often voice and tone overlap, and together they help us hear a writer talking to us. In the following passage, we hear student writer Kurt Weekly talking to us directly; we hear a clear, honest voice telling the story. His tone is not defensive or guilty: He openly admits he has a "problem."

> Oh no, not another trash day. Every time I see all those trash containers, plastic garbage bags and junk lined up on the sidewalks, it drives me crazy. It all started when I was sixteen. I had just received my driver's license and the most beautiful Ford pickup. It was Wednesday as I remember and trash day. I don't know what happened. All of a sudden I was racing down the street swerving to the right, smashing into a large green Hefty trash bag filled with grass clippings. The bag exploded, and grass clippings and trash flew everywhere. It was beautiful and I was hooked. There was no stopping me.
>
> At first I would smash one or two cans on the way to school. Then I just couldn't get enough. I would start going out the night before trash day. I would go down the full length of the street and wipe out every garbage container in sight. I was the terror of the neighborhood. This was not a bad habit to be taken lightly. It was an obsession. I was in trouble. There was no way I could kick this on my own. I needed help.

I received that help. One night after an evening of nonstop can smashing, the Arapahoe County Sheriff Department caught up with me. Not just one or a few but the whole department. They were willing to set me on the right path, and if that didn't work, they were going to send me to jail. It was a long, tough road to rehabilitation, but I did it. Not alone. I had the support of my family and the community.

Persona   Related to voice and tone is the *persona*—the "mask" that a writer can put on. Sometimes in telling a story about yourself, you may want to speak in your own "natural" voice. At other times, however, you may change or exaggerate certain characteristics in order to project a character different from your "real" self. Writers, for example, may project themselves as braver and more intelligent than they really are. Or to create a humorous effect, they may create personas who are more foolish or clumsy than they really are. This persona can shape a whole passage. In the following excerpt, James Thurber, a master of autobiographical humor, uses a persona—along with chronological narrative—to shape his account of a frustrating botany class.

I passed all the other courses that I took at my university, but I could never pass botany. This was because all botany students had to spend several hours a week in a laboratory looking through a microscope at plant cells, and I could never see through a microscope. I never once saw a cell through a microscope. This used to enrage my instructor. He would wander around the laboratory pleased with the progress all the students were making in drawing the involved and, so I am told, interesting structure of flower cells, until he came to me. I would just be standing there. "I can't see anything," I would say. He would begin patiently enough, explaining how anybody can see through a microscope, but he would always end up in a fury claiming that I could too see through a microscope but just pretended that I couldn't. "It takes away from the beauty of flowers anyway," I used to tell him. "We are not concerned with beauty in this course," he would say. "We are concerned solely with the mechanics of flowers." "Well," I'd say, "I can't see anything." "Try it just once again," he'd say, and I would put my eye to the microscope and see nothing at all, except now and again a nebulous milky substance—a phenomenon of maladjustment. You were supposed to see a vivid, restless clockwork of sharply defined plant cells. "I see what looks like a lot of milk," I would tell him. This, he claimed, was the result of my not having adjusted the microscope properly, so he would readjust it for me, or rather, for himself. And I would look again and see milk. I finally took a deferred pass, as they called it, and waited a year and tried again. (You had to pass one of the biological sciences or you couldn't graduate.) The professor had come back from vacation brown as a berry, bright-eyed, and eager to explain cell-structure again to his classes. "Well," he said to me, cheerily, when we met in the first laboratory hour of the semester, "we're going to see cells this time, aren't we?" "Yes, sir," I said. Students to the right of me and to the left of me and in front of me were seeing cells; what's more, they were quietly drawing pictures of them in their notebooks. Of course, I didn't see anything.

"We'll try it," the professor said to me, grimly, "with every adjustment of the microscope known to man. As God is my witness, I'll arrange this glass so that you see cells through it or I'll give up teaching. In twenty-two years of botany, I—" He cut off abruptly for he was beginning to quiver all over, like Lionel Barrymore, and he genuinely wished to hold onto his temper; his scenes with me had taken a great deal out of him.

So we tried it with every adjustment of the microscope known to man. With only one of them did I see anything but blackness or the familiar lacteal opacity, and that time I saw, to my pleasure and amazement, a variegated constellation of flecks, specks, and dots. These I hastily drew. The instructor, noting my activity, came back from an adjoining desk, a smile on his lips and his eyebrows high in hope. He looked at my cell drawing. "What's that?" he demanded, with a hint of a squeal in his voice. "That's what I saw," I said. "You didn't, you didn't, you didn't!" he screamed, losing control of his temper instantly, and he bent over and squinted into the microscope. His head snapped up. "That's your eye!" he shouted. "You've fixed the lens so that it reflects! You've drawn your eye!"

Dialogue   Dialogue, which helps to _recreate_ people and events rather than just tell about them, can become a dominant form and thereby shape your writing. Recreating an actual conversation, you could possibly write a whole scene using nothing but dialogue. More often, however, writers use dialogue occasionally for dramatic effect. In the account of his battle with the microscope, for instance, Thurber uses dialogue in the last two paragraphs to dramatize his conclusion:

"We'll try it," the professor said to me, grimly, "with every adjustment known to man. As God is my witness, I'll arrange this glass so that you see cells through it or I'll give up teaching. In twenty-two years of teaching botany, I—". . . ."What's that?" he demanded. . . . "That's what I saw," I said. "You didn't, you didn't, you didn't!" he screamed. . . . "You've fixed the lens so that it reflects! You've drawn your eye!"

I start at the beginning, go on to the end, then stop.

—GABRIEL
GARCÍA
MÁRQUEZ

AUTHOR OF ONE HUNDRED
YEARS OF SOLITUDE

Title, Introduction, and Conclusion In your journal, sketch out several possible titles you might use. You may want a title that is merely an accurate label, such as *Russian Journal* or "The Boy's Desire," but you may prefer something less direct that gets your reader's attention. For example, for his essay about his hat that appears at the end of this chapter, student writer Todd Petry uses the title "The Wind Catcher." As a reader, what do you think about Alice Walker's title, "Beauty: When the Other Dancer Is the Self?"

Introductions or beginning paragraphs take several shapes. Some plunge the reader immediately into the action—as Gregory Hoffman does—and then later fill in the scene and context. Others are more like Kurt Weekly's, announcing the subject—trash cans—and then taking the reader from the present to the past and the beginning of the story: "It all started when I was sixteen. . . ." At some point, however, readers do need to know the context—the *who, what, when,* and *where* of your account.

Conclusions are also of several types. In some, writers will return to the present and discuss what they have learned, as Andrea Lee does in *Russian Journal.* Some, like Alice Walker, end with an image or even a dream. Some writers conclude with dramatic moments, as James Thurber does, or with an emotional scene, as student writer Brooke Selby does in the essay on Kit Carson that appears at the end of this chapter. But many writers will try to tie the conclusion back to the beginning, as Richard Rodriguez does at the end of "The Boy's Desire": "The closet door closes . . . the fog rises." In your journal, experiment with several possibilities until you find one that works for your subject.

I always know the ending; that's where I start.

—TONI
MORRISON,

NOBEL PRIZE–WINNING
NOVELIST

DRAFTING

When you have experimented with the above shaping strategies, reconsider your purpose, audience, and main idea. Have they changed? In your journal, reexamine the notes you made before trying the shaping activities. If necessary, revise your statements about purpose, audience, or main idea based on what you have actually written.

Working from your journal material and from your collecting and shaping activities, draft your essay. It is important *not* to splice different parts together or just recopy and connect segments, for they may not fit or flow together. Instead, reread what you have written, and then start with a clean sheet of paper. If you're working on a computer file, you can start with your list of events or one of your best shaping strategies and expand that file as you draft. Concentrate on what you want to say and write as quickly as possible.

To avoid interruptions, choose a quiet place to work. Follow your own writing rituals. Try to write nonstop. If you cannot think of the right word, put a line or a dash, but keep on writing. When necessary, go back and reread what you have previously written.

REVISING

Revising begins, of course, when you get your first idea and start collecting and shaping. It continues as you redraft certain sections of your essay and rework your organization. In many classes, you will give and receive advice from the other writers in your class. Use the guidelines below to give constructive advice about a remembering essay draft.

The difference between the right word and the nearly right word is the same as that between lightning and the lightning bug.

—MARK TWAIN,
AUTHOR OF THE
ADVENTURES OF
HUCKLEBERRY FINN

PEER RESPONSE

The instructions below will help you give and receive constructive advice about the rough draft of your remembering essay. You may use these guidelines for an in-class workshop, a take-home review, or a computer e-mail response.

Writer: Before you exchange drafts with another reader, write out the following information about your own rough draft.

1. State main idea that you hope your essay will convey.

2. Describe the best *one* or *two* key scenes that your narrative creates.

3. Explain one or two problems that you are having with this draft that you want your reader to focus on.

Reader: Without making any comments, read the *entire* draft from start to finish. As you *reread* the draft, answer the following questions.

1. Locate one or two of the *key scenes* in the narrative. Are they clearly set at an identified time and place? Does the writer use vivid description of the place or the people? Does the writer use dialogue? Does the writer include his or her reflections? Which of these areas need the most attention during the writer's revision? Explain.

2. Write out a *time line* for the key events in the narrative. What happened first, second, third, and so forth? Are there places in the narrative where the time line could be clearer? Explain.

(continued)

3. When you finished reading the draft, *what characters or incidents were you still curious about?* Where did you want more information? What characters or incidents did you want to know more about?

4. What *overall idea* does the narrative convey to you? How does your notion of the main idea compare to the writer's answer to Question 1? Explain how the writer might revise the essay to make the main idea clearer.

5. Answer the *writer's questions* in Question 3.

After you have some feedback from other readers, you need to distance yourself and objectively reread what you have written. Review the advice you received from your peer readers. Remember, you will get both good and bad advice, so *you* must decide what you think is important or not important. If you are uncertain about advice you received from one of your peers, ask for a third or fourth opinion. In addition, most writing centers will have tutors available who can help you sort through the advice you have received on your draft and figure out a revision plan. Especially for this remembering essay, make sure your memories are recreated on paper. Don't be satisfied with suggesting incidents that merely trigger your own memories: You must *show* people and events vividly for your reader.

Guidelines for Revision

- **Reexamine your purpose and audience.** Are you doing what you intended?

- **Revise to make the main idea of your account clearer.** You don't need a "moral" to the story or a bald statement saying "This is why this person was important." Your reader, however, should know clearly why you wanted to write about the memory that you chose.

- **Revise to clarify the important *relationships* in your story.** Consider relationships between past and present, between you and the people in your story, between one place and another place, between one event and another event.

- **Close and detailed observation is crucial.** *Show*, don't just tell. Can you use any of the collecting and shaping strategies for observing discussed in Chapter 3?

- **Revise to show crucial changes, contrasts, or conflicts more clearly.** Keller's and Walker's essays, for instance, illustrate how *conflict* and *change* are central to an effective remembering essay. See if their strategies will work in your essay.

- **Have you used a straight chronological order?** If it works, keep it. If not, would another order be better? Should you begin in the middle and do a flashback? Do you want to move back and forth from present to past or stay in the past until the end?

     If you are using a chronological order, cue your reader by occasionally using transitional words to signal changes:
     then, when, first, next, last, before, after, while, as, sooner, later, initially, finally, yesterday, today

- **Be clear about point of view.** Are you looking back on the past from a viewpoint in the present? Are you using the point of view of yourself as a child or at some earlier point in your life? Are you using the point of view of another person or object in your story?

- **What are the key images in your account?** Should you add or delete an image to show the experience more vividly?

- **What voice are you using?** Does it support your purpose? If you are using a persona, is it appropriate for your audience and purpose?

- **Revise sentences to improve clarity, conciseness, emphasis, and variety.**

- **Check your dialogue for proper punctuation and indentation.** See the essay by Alice Walker in this chapter for a model.

- **When you are relatively satisfied with your draft, edit for correct spelling, appropriate word choice, punctuation, and grammar.**

POSTSCRIPT ON THE WRITING PROCESS

After you finish writing, revising, and editing your essay, you will want to breathe a sigh of relief and turn it in. But before you do, think about the problems that you solved as you wrote this essay. *Remember:* Your major goal for this course is to learn to write and revise more effectively. To do that, you need to discover and adapt your writing processes so you can anticipate and solve the problems you face as a writer. Take a few minutes to answer the following questions. Be sure to hand in this postscript with your essay.

1. Review your writing process. Which collecting, shaping, and revising strategies helped you remember and describe incidents

most quickly and clearly? What problems were you unable to solve?

2. Reread your essay. With a small asterisk [*], identify in the margin of your essay sentences where you used sensory details, dialogue, or images to *show* or recreate the experience for your reader.

3. If you received feedback from your peers, identify one piece of advice that you followed and one bit of advice that you ignored. Explain your decisions.

4. Rereading your essay, what do you like best about it? What parts of your essay need work? What would you change if you had another day to work on this assignment?

REMEMBERING:

STUDENT WRITING

THE WIND CATCHER

Todd Petry

Todd Petry decided to write about his cowboy hat, observing it in the present and thinking about some of the memories that it brought back. His notes, his first short draft paragraphs, and his revised version demonstrate how observing and remembering work together naturally: The details stimulate memories, and memories lead to more specific details.

NOTES AND DETAILS

DETAILS	MORE SPECIFIC DETAILS
Gray	Dirty, dust coated, rain stained cowdung color
Resistol	The name is stained and blurred
Size 7 3/8	
Diamond shape	Used to be diamond shape, now battered, looks abandoned

4" brim	Front tipped down, curled up in back
1" sweat band	blackish
5 yrs. old	still remember the day I bought it
4x beaver	
What it is not:	it is unlike a hat fresh out of the box
What it compares to:	point of crown like the north star like a pancake with wilted edges battered like General Custer's hat
What I remember:	the day I bought the hat a day at Pray Mesa

FIRST DRAFT

THE WIND CATCHER

The other day while I was relaxing in my favorite chair and listening to Ian Tyson, I happened to notice my work cowboy hat hanging on the wall. Now I look at that old hat no less than a dozen times a day without too much thought, but on that particular day, my eyes remained fixed on it and my mind went to remembering.

I still remember I had $100 cash in my pocket the day I went hat shopping. The local tack, feed, and western wear CO-OP was my first and only stop. Finding a hat to meet my general specifications was no big deal. I wanted a gray Resistol, size 7 3/8, with a 4-inch brim and diamond shaped crown. From there on, though, my wants became very particular. I took 30 minutes to find the one that had the right fit, and five times that long to come to terms with the hat shaper. Boy, but I was one proud young fellow the next day when I went to school sporting my new piece of head gear. I've had that wind catcher five years through rough times, but in a way, it really looks better now, without any shape, dirty, and covered with dust and cow-dung.

REVISED VERSION

THE WIND CATCHER

The other day while I was relaxing in my favorite chair and listening to Ian Tyson, I happened to notice my work cowboy hat hanging on the wall. Now I look at that old hat no less than a dozen times a day without too much thought, but on that particular day, my eyes remained fixed on it and my mind went to remembering. **(1)**

I was 15 years old and had $100 cash in my pocket the day I went hat shopping 5 years ago. The local tack, feed, and western wear CO-OP was my first and only stop. Finding a hat to meet my general specifications was no big deal. I wanted a gray 4X Resistol, size 7 3/8, with a 4-inch brim and diamond shaped crown. I wanted no flashy feathers or gaudy hatbands, which in my mind were only for pilgrims. From there on, though, my wants became very particular. I took 30 minutes to find the one that had the right fit, and five times that long to come to terms with the hat shaper. Boy, but I was one proud young fellow the next day when I went to school sporting my new piece of head gear. **(2)**

About that time, Ian Tyson startled me out of my state of reminiscence by singing "Rose in the Rockies," with that voice of his sounding like ten cow elk cooing to their young in the springtime. As I sat there listening to the music and looking at that old hat, I had to chuckle to myself because that wind catcher had sure seen better days. I mean it looked rode hard and put up wet. The gray, which was once as sharp and crisp as a mountain lake, was now faded and dull where the sun had beat down. Where the crown and brim met, the paleness was suddenly transformed into a gritty black which ran the entire circumference of the hat. This black was unlike any paint or color commercially available, being made up of head sweat, dirt, alfalfa dust, and powdered cow manure. Water blemishes from too much rain and snow mottled the brim, adding to the colors' turbidity. Inside the crown and wherever the slope was less than ninety degrees, dust had collected to hide the natural color even more. **(3)**

After awhile, my attention lost interest in the various colors and began to work its way over the hat's shape, which I was once so critical of. General Custer's hat itself could not have looked worse. All signs of uniformity and definite shape had disappeared. The diamond shaped crown, which was once round and smooth, now bowed out on the sides and had edges as blunt as an orange crate. The point, which once looked like the North Star indicating the direction, now was twisted off balance from excessive right hand use. Remembering last spring, how I threw that hat in the face of an irate mother cow during calving, I had to chuckle again. Throwing that hat kept my horse and me out of trouble but made the "off balance look" rather permanent. As I looked at the brim, I was reminded of a three-day-old pancake with all its edges wilted. The back of that brim curled upward like a snake ready to strike, and the front had become so narrow and dipped, it looked like something a dentist would use on your teeth. **(4)**

For probably half an hour I sat looking at the wear and tear on that ancient hat. Awhile back, I remember, I decided to try to make my old hat socially presentable by having it cleaned and blocked, removing those curls and dips and other signs of use. However, when a hat shop refused to even attempt the task, I figured I'd just leave well enough alone. As I scanned my eyes over the hat, I noticed several other alterations from its original form, such as the absent hat band which was born off in the brush on Pray Mesa and the black thread that drew together the edges of a hole in the crown. However, try as I might, I could not for the life of me see where any character had been lost in the brush, or any flair had been covered with cowdung. **(5)**

QUESTIONS FOR WRITING AND DISCUSSION

1. Close observation often leads to specific memories. In the opening paragraph of his revised version, Todd Petry says that "on that particular day, my eyes remained fixed on it and my mind went to remembering." He then recalls the time when he was fifteen years old and bought his hat. Identify two other places where observation leads Petry to remember specific scenes from the past.

2. Petry chose "The Wind Catcher" as the title for his essay. Reread the essay and then brainstorm a list of five other titles that might be appropriate for this short essay. Which title do you like best?

3. Where does Petry most clearly express the main idea of his essay? Write out the main idea in your own words.

KIT CARSON

Brooke Selby

In the following essay, Brooke Selby remembers an Easter reunion that turned out to be a celebration of life in a small western town. As she wrote, Selby says, she tried to "paint a prose portrait of a place which always held an almost spiritual 'specialness' for my family. I closed my eyes and tried to recall actual snapshots from the day; I used those mental images as I searched for the words to describe it."

The town of Kit Carson is often omitted from Colorado maps. One sees just a glimpse from the highway, a square cluster of peeling white frame houses and dingy brown buildings, long bathed in the eastern Colorado dust. To the two hundred and eighty persons who call Kit Carson their home, it is the very center of existence, but to outsiders it is a curious, tattered remnant from farming days: a slow-moving, wind-blown apparition from the past. **(1)**

The highway bisects Kit Carson, seeming almost an incongruity amidst the time-worn face of the town. The only motel lies on the northernmost edge, gaudy and commercial amidst the waving plains grasses. From the road one catches a glimpse of a one room museum, an old red brick drug store, some tired stone churches, rusted screen doors which lead into the musty quiet of the few surviving shops, some deserted buildings with splintered boards nailed across the windows . . . all this in a rapid blur like an old news-reel, flashed by too quickly to grasp any more than a vague impression of deteriorating quiet. Yet from the road, one sees also black windmills, the sentinels of surrounding farms, and huge fields, opulent with crops, so that one knows that there are those who still prosper in this town. **(2)**

My mother was fifteen years old when she left Kit Carson. Times were hard and the farm's livelihood was not dependable enough to support a family of five, so they moved to Denver, with high hopes that an invention of my grandfather's would open the door to new prosperity and financial security. Yet in leaving Kit Carson, they left behind something which became to them a symbol of childhood, a place where innocence was not outdated, where the pace of life still permitted one time to be alone and to dream, and where one could go to escape when the pressures of job and existence became too overbearing. Even now, the mention of Kit Carson evokes nostalgic memories and a burning, longing homesickness among my mother and her brother and sister. The three have all instilled in their children the same sacred image of the town, the same craving to go home, to return to times less strenuous and demanding. It is a different sort of world—although not untouched by the insensitive and often callous times we live in, it remains still a sanctuary, where one can walk out onto the prairie, breathe as deeply as possible, and feel a rare sense of complete inner peace, as if even miracles are possible and God not far away. **(3)**

There are those who cling yet to the town, like children clutching at their mother's skirts, certain that life elsewhere would be only a tarnished replica of life in Kit Carson. My great-grandparents are among these, their beings intricately woven within the fibers of the town's foundation. My great-grandfather will brook no criticism, disapproval, or even hinted dissatisfaction with his town, for it is "God's country" and "those big cities simply aren't fit for even animals to make their home." Outwardly, we scoff at Kit Carson's backwardness; inwardly we all feel its pull, yet we long for an actual confirmation of its magic, to prove to ourselves that it is not simply a land of dreams never realized. Easter brought us closer to this wish. **(4)**

We left early that Sunday morning, being unable to afford the time to go for the entire weekend. There was just the slightest hint of winter's last lingering sighs, as we sleepily crawled into our car. The sun seemed indecisive, resolving first to stretch its healing arms out toward the dormant earth, but then withdrawing its offer, as if uncertain that the spring had truly yet arrived. **(5)**

We spoke little on the trip, all caught up, I think, in our own thoughts and early morning sleepiness. We were restless, anticipating the celebration which lay ahead of us, as over fifty relatives gathered to mark my great-grandparents' sixtieth wedding anniversary. I stared lazily out the window, fixing my gaze on the telephone poles careening down the road, and struggling desperately against the fuzzy blanket of sleep which kept falling over my head. **(6)**

We were met in Kit Carson with a warm and loving welcome, immediately swallowed up in the overflowing concern oozing from each corner of the crowded house. The house was afire with conversation, exclamations, greetings issued to new arrivals, fantastic smells drifting out from the kitchen, and love tumbling from and between every person. Naturally, the occasion centered on my great-grandparents, who beamed proudly at the house filled with their family and loved ones. Both were beautifully dressed for the day. My great-grandmother resembled a velvet, pale pink rose, fragile and perhaps a little faded, yet with pride's stiff spine keeping her ever strong. Great-grandpa was filled with nervous energy, rushing from one group to another and beaming so joyously that an ache rose inside of me at the thought that perhaps soon a photograph would be our only tangible recollection of that grin. **(7)**

The day passed quickly in a blur of flashcubes, singing around the piano, and endless hugs, some from people I couldn't place. The afternoon was winding down, and many were beginning to talk of starting the drives back to their respective homes, when a young cousin ran into the house, shouting to my great-uncle that he should come outside immediately. He disappeared into the back, but shortly, two more young cousins came racing in, both eager to be the first to shout the news. My great-uncle, another romanticist, had several years earlier purchased ten buffalo and set them to graze upon his land, in an attempt to return that which rightfully belonged to the earth. Now one of the buffalo was having a baby and the young cousins were impatient that everyone should come to see. **(8)**

Although a couple of the adults were skeptical at first, the house grew quiet as everyone streamed into the back. My uncle confirmed that one of the buffalo was indeed calving and that the wait would not be long. At first, we all stood, gazing out over the fence into the pasture, laughing and joking about the coincidence of the birth on Easter. Soon, however, we were all caught up in the drama unfolding in front of us. It was a loud silence, so full was it of anticipation and unspoken thought. **(9)**

When a buffalo is in labor, it is on its own. As in the days of the early West, no veterinarian can make its task easier. To come near the animal would be to invite death for oneself or the newborn. It was soon apparent, however, that the mother buffalo was in serious trouble, and we stood in somber silence, voicing whispered prayers for the animals. It was as though a physical bond had those of us on the hillside tightly glued together, for we were straining as one, with frustration at our inability to aid the animals. My uncle paced nervously, almost certain that the birth was to be breech, for it appeared that the small calf's legs were emerging first. We waited what seemed an eon, squinting against the descending sun, and shivering from the slight breeze. **(10)**

It was hard to distinguish calf from mother when it began to appear, for from the distance it looked almost as one. Suddenly, though, my uncle gave a shout, and we could see the tiny calf was born and was standing, leaning its weight against its mother. As one, we all began to cheer and shout and talk in hushed voices about the miracle we had just witnessed. We began to vie with one another for the selection of an appropriate name, and dozens of suggestions were tossed out. Finally, one aunt cried that we should christen it "Resurrection," in light of the occasion and its close brush with death. **(11)**

Again quieted, we straggled back into the house and the prairie once more grew silent. I was the last to return inside and turned for one last glimpse of the newborn creature. In the twilight, the little calf was outlined against the prairie sky, still standing wobbly-kneed and shaky against the big mother buffalo. As I turned back around to return to the house, I saw spring's first flower, poking its head through the earth at the side of the building, and I was overwhelmed with the magnitude of what had just occurred. Kit Carson had confirmed its holiness, its magical potential as a place where miracles do not cease with growing up. I swallowed the lump in my throat and went inside. **(12)**

QUESTIONS FOR WRITING AND DISCUSSION

1. Selby's essay is very much about human feelings and emotions. Stop and think for a moment. What specific feelings did you have as you read the essay?

2. Reread paragraphs 1 and 2. In terms of the rest of the essay, why does Selby spend so much time describing the *town* of Kit Carson? Is it necessary, or could it be deleted? Explain.

3. In writing about remembered people, places, or events, writers should make main ideas obvious without overstating them. What sentences contain the main point that Selby wants to make? (How does paragraph 5, for example, contribute to that thesis?) In your opinion, is Selby's thesis stated too obviously, not stated clearly enough, or given just the proper emphasis?

4. Good writers do not rush a story. They carefully set up the scene, let events develop, and take the time to recount the most important events. Reread this essay. Where do you notice Selby keeping a steady pace by refusing to rush her story?

5. Choose the best paragraph in this essay and copy it into your journal. When you have finished copying the paragraph, reread it. What is it about the sentences that makes them effective?

5 READING

William H. Huggin *Falling Leaves*, 1966; American Private Collection

AS AN ASSIGNMENT IN CLASS, YOU ARE READING AND CRITIQUING AN ARTICLE BY DEBORAH TANNEN ON HOW MEN AND WOMEN RESPOND DIFFERENTLY DURING CLASS CONVERSATIONS. AS YOU read the article, you like the thought-provoking examples, but soon you find yourself becoming frustrated. First, you have trouble locating the main focus of the article, and then you are disturbed by some unsupported assertions that she makes about typical behavior of men and women. Do men really like to argue and dominate class discussions? Do women always benefit from smaller, more intimate group discussions? You reread the article and make notes in the margin. After discussing your reactions with other readers, you write the draft of your summary and response. You argue that readers should expect clearer organization and fewer unsupported assertions about the gender-based differences between men and women.

❧

AFTER DISCUSSING STEREOTYPED AND SEXIST IMAGES IN ADVERTISING, YOU LEAF THROUGH A COPY OF A POPULAR MAGAZINE. A TWO-PAGE ADVERTISEMENT FOR FILA JEANS CATCHES YOUR attention. The first page shows a man in jeans and a jeans jacket in the foreground with football players pictured in the background. The caption at the bottom of the page says, "SOME LIKE THEIR BLUES HARD." On the facing page is a woman curled up in a chair and wearing her blue jeans. Her background photograph shows a woman clad in a bikini. The caption says, "SOME LIKE THEIR BLUES SOFT." For your essay, you describe the features of the ad carefully and then offer your own analysis of the sexist features of the images and the language. The language and the imagery of the Fila jeans ad, you argue, stereotype and alienate the sexes by conveying the idea that men and women are not parallel in nature but are fundamentally separate and different.

If we think of it, all that a University, or final highest School can do for us, is still but what the first School began doing—teach us to read.

—THOMAS CARLYLE,

ON HEROES AND HERO WORSHIP

❧

Reading involves a fair measure of push and shove. You make your mark on a book and it makes its mark on you. Reading is not simply a matter of hanging back and waiting for a piece, or its author, to tell you what the writing has to say.

—DAVID BARTHOLOMAE AND ANTHONY PETROSKY,

AUTHORS OF WAYS OF READING

AT FIRST GLANCE, A CHAPTER ON READING IN A TEXTBOOK ON WRITING MAY CATCH YOU BY SURPRISE. THIS CHAPTER, HOWEVER, IS NOT ABOUT LEARNING YOUR ABC'S OR ABOUT READING *THE CAT in the Hat*. It is about learning to read texts actively and critically. It is about learning how to summarize and respond to what you read. It is about using reading—along with observing and remembering—as a source for your writing.

At the beginning of this chapter, we need define two key terms: "texts" and "reading." Normally, when you think about a "text," you may think of a textbook. A "text," however, can be any graphic matter—a textbook, an essay, a poem, a story, a newspaper editorial, a graph, a design, or an advertisement. Some people expand the definition of "texts" to include any thing or phenomenon in the world. In this widest sense, the layout of a restaurant, the behavior of children on a playground, or clouds in the sky could be "texts" that can be read.

Similarly, the term "reading" has both narrow and broad senses. In a narrow sense, reading is just understanding words on a page. But reading has a variety of wider meanings as well. Reading can mean analyzing, as when an architect "reads" blueprints and knows how to construct a roof. Reading can mean interpreting, as when a sailor "reads" the sky and knows that the day will bring winds and rough weather. Reading can mean making guesses about purpose or intention, as when a woman "reads" her boss's mind or a man "reads" between the lines of a friend's letter. All of these "readings" require close, repeated observation of the text and an ability to engage, analyze, respond to, and interpret the text.

In this chapter, you will practice a fairly specific kind of textual reading. Most of the texts will be essays on academic topics and your reading will be active, critical, and responsive. Implied in active, critical reading is writing. Reading and writing work together to make reading more active and writing more effective. Reading and writing are so inseparable that we sometimes use the phrase "reading/writing" to discuss any reading activity. In addition, there is an essential third dimension to critical reading: discussion. This third dimension can take a variety of forms—sharing ideas in small groups, engaging in a class conversation, posting e-mail responses, or taking sides in a debate. Reading, writing, and discussing are all "reading" activities. We may be able to read the words on a page and write out our reactions, but we must also engage other readers' reactions and points of view in order to fully grasp the possible meanings of a text.

This chapter will show you how to use reading/writing/discussing strategies for three important tasks. First, you will learn how to write short critiques or summary/response essays that are frequent college writing assignments. Second, you will practice reading your peers' drafts and essays actively and critically. Third, you will use critical reading to find information and generate ideas for expository or argumentative essays. Just as observing gives you descriptive strategies and remembering helps you to practice drawing on your personal experience, reading will help you critically analyze ideas, facts, statistics, and arguments—a skill that you will need for many college writing assignments.

TECHNIQUES FOR WRITING ABOUT READING

As you approach your assignments in this chapter, remember that reading, writing, and discussing are all interrelated and interactive strategies. Writing assists reading, discussing, and rereading. Reading and rereading help you discuss and write. Conversations (written and oral) among readers and writers are integral to reading/writing. Focus on the techniques that follow as you write your summary/response or critique.

- **Using active and responsive reading/writing/discussing strategies.** Preview the author's background and the writing context. Prewrite about your own experiences with the subject. Read initially for information and enjoyment. As you reread, make annotations, write questions, or do a double-entry log. Discuss the text with other readers.
- **Summarizing the main ideas or features of the text.** A summary should *accurately* and *objectively* represent the key ideas. Summaries cite the author and title, accurately represent the main ideas, quote directly key phrases or sentences, and describe main features of the text.
- **Responding to or critiquing the ideas in the text.** A response should focus on your ideas and reactions—as distinguished from ideas set forth by the author/text. Types of responses include *analysis* of the argument, organization, or evidence in the text; *agreement or disagreement* with the author/text; or *interpretation* of the text.
- **Supporting the response with evidence.** As supporting evidence for the response, writers should analyze key features of the text, cite evidence from other relevant texts, and/or use examples from personal experience.
- **Combining summary and response into a coherent essay.** Usually, the summary appears first, followed by the reader's response, but

Reading is not a passive process by which we soak up words and information from the page, but an active process by which we predict, sample, and confirm or correct our hypotheses about the written text.

—CONSTANCE WEAVER, AUTHOR OF READING PROCESS AND PRACTICE

Reading . . . is a vital component of rhetorical invention, for it is an important way of participating in the conversation that gives us all of our meanings.

—DOUG BRENT, AUTHOR OF READING AS RHETORICAL INVENTION

be sure to *integrate* the two parts. Focus early on a main idea for your response. Use transitions between the summary and the response.

As you work on these techniques, don't simply read the text, discuss it in class, and then write out your critique. Instead, write notes as you read. Reread the text after class discussion. Reread and discuss the text after you have written your draft. Use the interactive powers of reading/writing/discussing to help you throughout your writing process.

How Readers Read

One of the purposes of this chapter is to show you how readers read. If you know how readers read and how they construct meaning from a text, you will become a more active reader and a more effective writer.

Reading, some theorists believe, involves a three-part process. First, readers bring their *prior experience* (about the subject, about language, and about culture) to their reading. Second, based on their prior experience, readers make *guesses* about how each passage relates to their prior experience and *predictions* about where the text is headed. Finally, as readers continue to read or reread, they *make meaning* or *comprehend* the text by testing (confirming or rejecting) the guesses and predictions that they have made. If readers have limited experiences with the subject or the language, making accurate predictions can be difficult. If readers have a good deal of prior experience, they are more likely to make accurate predictions.

If this theory of reading and comprehension is true, it has three important lessons for any reader/writer:

- **First, prior knowledge about a text and its subject is extremely important.** As a reader, you should activate your prior knowledge *before* reading the text. Doing a prereading journal exercise and discussing the subject with others are excellent strategies to access what you already know.
- **Second, making guesses and predictions enables readers to make meaning.** Making wrong guesses is just as important as making right guesses. Don't worry about making wrong guesses—they are a crucial part of the active reading process.
- **Third, learning to read actively will make you a better writer.** Good writers know the problems that readers have making meaning. Good writers activate their readers' prior knowledge by using examples from their own experience. Good writers preview their main ideas so that their readers can make better guesses. Good writers use transitions or signals to help readers make meaning.

SUMMARIZING AND RESPONDING

TO AN ESSAY

*new structuring
principles.*

**—LOUISE
ROSENBLATT,**

AUTHOR OF THE READER,
THE TEXT, THE POEM

Following is an essay by Barbara Ehrenreich, "Teach Diversity—with a Smile." First, write for five minutes on the suggested Prereading Journal Entry that precedes the essay. The purpose of the journal entry is to allow you to collect your thoughts about the subject *before* you read Ehrenreich's essay. You will be a much more responsive reader if you reflect on your experiences and articulate your opinions *before* you are influenced by the author and her text. If possible, discuss your experiences and opinions with your classmates after you write your entry but before you read the essay. Next, read the introductory note about Barbara Ehrenreich to understand her background and the context for the essay. Finally, practice active reading techniques as you read. Read first for information and enjoyment. Then, reread with a pen in your hand. Either write your comments and questions directly in the text or do a double-entry log, summarizing the main ideas on one side of a piece of paper and writing your questions and reactions on the other.

■ PREREADING JOURNAL ENTRY   Describe the ethnic groups of people who live in your neighborhood or who attended your previous school. List all the groups you can recall. Then choose one of the following terms and briefly explain what it means: *Diversity, multiculturalism,* or *political correctness.* Finally, describe one personal experience that taught you something about diversity or political correctness. What was the experience and how did you react?

TEACH DIVERSITY—WITH A SMILE

Barbara Ehrenreich

Barbara Ehrenreich was born in Butte, Montana, in 1941 and received a B.A. degree from Reed College and a Ph.D. from Rockefeller University. She has been a health policy advisor and a professor of health sciences, but since 1974 she has spent most of her time writing books and articles about socialist and feminist issues. She has received a Ford Foundation award and a Guggenheim fellowship for her writings, which include Fear of Falling: The Inner Life of the Middle Class *(1989),* The Worst Years of Our Lives: Irreverent Notes from a Decade of Greed *(1990), and* The Snarling Citizen: Essays *(1995). Her articles and essays have appeared in* Esquire, Mother Jones, Ms., New Republic, The New York Times Magazine, *and* Time. *The following essay on cultural diversity appeared in* Time *magazine.*

Something had to replace the threat of communism, and at last a workable substitute is at hand. "Multiculturalism," as the new menace is known, has been denounced in the media recently as the new McCarthyism, the new fundamentalism, even the new totalitarianism—take your choice. According to its critics, who include a flock of tenured conservative scholars, multiculturalism aims to toss out what it sees as the Eurocentric bias in education and replace Plato with Ntozake Shange and traditional math with the Yoruba number system. And that's just the beginning. The Jacobins of the multiculturalist movement, who are described derisively as P.C., or politically correct, are said to have launched a campus reign of terror against those who slip and innocently say "freshman" instead of "freshperson," "Indian" instead of "Native American" or, may the Goddess forgive them, "disabled" instead of "differently abled." **(1)**

So you can see what is at stake here: freedom of speech, freedom of thought, Western civilization and a great many professorial egos. But before we get carried away by the mounting backlash against multiculturalism, we ought to reflect for a moment on the system that the P.C. people aim to replace. I know all about it; in fact it's just about all I *do* know, since I—along with so many educated white people of my generation—was a victim of monoculturalism. **(2)**

American history, as it was taught to us, began with Columbus's "discovery" of an apparently unnamed, unpeopled America, and moved on to the Pilgrims serving pumpkin pie to a handful of grateful red-skinned folks. College expanded our horizons with courses called Humanities or sometimes Civ, which introduced us to a line of thought that started with Homer, worked its way through Rabelais and reached a poignant climax in the pensées of Matthew Arnold. Graduate students wrote dissertations on what long-dead men had thought of Chaucer's verse or Shakespeare's dramas; foreign languages meant French or German. If there had been high technology in ancient China, kingdoms in black Africa or women anywhere, at any time, doing anything worth noticing, we did not know it, nor did anyone think to tell us. **(3)**

Our families and neighborhoods reinforced the dogma of monoculturalism. In our heads, most of us '50s teenagers carried around a social map that was about as useful as the chart that guided Columbus to the "Indies." There were "Negroes," "whites" and "Orientals," the latter meaning Chinese and "Japs." Of religions, only three were known—Protestant, Catholic and Jewish—and not much was known about the last two types. The only remaining human categories were husbands and wives, and that was all the diversity the monocultural world could handle. Gays, lesbians, Buddhists, Muslims, Malaysians, Mormons, etc. were simply off the map. **(4)**

So I applaud—with one hand, anyway—the multiculturalist goal of preparing us all for a wider world. The other hand is tapping its fingers impatiently, because the critics are right about one thing: when advocates of multiculturalism adopt the haughty stance of political correctness, they quickly descend to silliness or worse. It's obnoxious, for example, to rely on university administrations to enforce P.C. standards of verbal inoffensiveness. Racist, sexist and homophobic thoughts cannot, alas, be abolished by fiat but only by the time-honored methods of persuasion, education and exposure to the other guy's—or, excuse me, woman's—point of view. **(5)**

And it's silly to mistake verbal purification for genuine social reform. Even after all women are "Ms." and all people are "he or she," women will still earn only 65¢ for every dollar earned by men. Minorities by any other name, such as "people of color," will still bear a hugely disproportionate burden of poverty and discrimination. Disabilities are not just "different abilities" when there are not enough ramps for wheelchairs, signers for the deaf or special classes for the "specially" endowed. With all due respect for the new politesse, actions still speak louder than fashionable phrases. **(6)**

But the worst thing about the P.C. people is that they are such poor advocates for the multicultural cause. No one was ever won over to a broader, more inclusive view of life by being bullied or relentlessly "corrected." Tell a 19-year-old white male that he can't say "girl" when he means "teen-age woman," and he will most likely snicker. This may be the reason why, despite the conservative alarms, P.C.-ness remains a relatively tiny trend. Most campuses have more serious and ancient problems: faculties still top-heavy with white males of the monocultural persuasion; fraternities that harass minorities and women; date rape; alcohol abuse; and tuition that excludes all but the upper fringe of the middle class. **(7)**

So both sides would be well advised to lighten up. The conservatives ought to realize that criticisms of the great books approach to learning do not amount to totalitarianism. And the advocates of multiculturalism need to regain the sense of humor that enabled their predecessors in the struggle to coin the term P.C. years ago—not in arrogance but in self-mockery. **(8)**

Beyond that, both sides should realize that the beneficiaries of multiculturalism are not only the "oppressed peoples" on the standard P.C. list (minorities, gays, etc.). The "unenlightened"—the victims of monoculturalism—are oppressed too, or at least deprived. Our educations, whether at Yale or at State U, were narrow and parochial and left us ill-equipped to navigate a society that truly is multicultural and is becoming more so every day. The culture that we studied was, in fact, *one* culture and, from a world perspective, all too limited and ingrown. Diversity is challenging, but those of us who have seen the alternative know it is also richer, livelier and ultimately more fun. **(9)**

SUMMARIZING

The purpose of a summary is to give a reader a condensed and objective account of the main ideas and features of a text. Usually, a summary has between one and three paragraphs or one hundred to three hundred words, depending on the length and complexity of the original essay and the intended audience and purpose. Typically, a summary will do the following:

Inferences about the writer's intentions appear to be an essential building block—one that readers actively use to construct a meaningful text.

—LINDA FLOWER,

AUTHOR OF "THE CONSTRUCTION OF PURPOSE"

- **Cite the author and title of the text.** In some cases, the place of publication or the context for the essay may also be included.
- **Indicate the main ideas of the text.** Accurately representing the main ideas (while omitting the less important details) is the major goal of a summary.
- **Use direct quotation of key words, phrases, or sentences.** *Quote* the text directly for a few key ideas; *paraphrase* the other important ideas (that is, express the ideas in your own words).
- **Include author tags** ("according to Ehrenreich" or "as Ehrenreich explains") to remind the reader that you are summarizing the author and the text, not giving your own ideas. ***Note:*** Instead of repeating "Ehrenreich says," choose verbs that more accurately represent the purpose or tone of the original passage: "Ehrenreich argues," "Ehrenreich explains," "Ehrenreich warns," "Ehrenreich asks," "Ehrenreich advises."
- **Avoid summarizing specific examples or data** unless they help illustrate the thesis or main idea of the text.
- **Report the main ideas as objectively as possible.** Represent the author and text as accurately and faithfully as possible. Do not include your reactions; save them for your response.

SUMMARY OF "TEACH DIVERSITY—WITH A SMILE"

Following is a summary of Ehrenreich's essay. Do *not* read this summary, however, until you have tried to write your own. After you have made notes and written a draft for your own summary, you will more clearly understand the key features of a summary. Note: There are many ways to write a good summary. If your summary conveys the main ideas and has the features described previously, it may be just as good as the following example. (Key features of a summary are annotated in the margin.)

Title and author

In "Teach Diversity—with a Smile," journalist Barbara Ehrenreich explains the current conflict between people who would like to replace our Eurocentric bias in education with a multicultural approach and those critics and conservative scholars who are leading the backlash against multiculturalism and "political correctness." Writing for [readers of *Time* magazine,] Ehrenreich uses her own experience growing up in the 1950s to explain that her narrow education left her a "victim of monoculturalism," ill-equipped

Main idea
Paraphrase
Context for essay

to cope with America's growing cultural diversity. Ehrenreich applauds multiculturalism's goal of preparing people for a culturally diverse world, but she is impatient at the "haughty stance" of the P.C. people because they mistake "verbal purification for genuine social reform" and they arrogantly bully people and "correct" their language. Since actions speak louder than words, Ehrenreich argues, the multiculturalists should focus more on genuine social reform—paying equal salaries for men and women, creating access for people with disabilities, and reducing date rape and alcohol abuse. The solution to the problem, according to Ehrenreich, is for both sides to "lighten up." The conservatives should recognize that criticizing the great books of Western civilization is not totalitarian, and the multiculturalists should be less arrogant and regain their sense of humor.

Author tag

Direct quotations

Main idea

Paraphrase
Author tag

Main idea
Paraphrase

VIUTI
Buenos Aires
ARGENTINA

VIUTI

Cartoonists & Writers Syndicate

Courtesy of Cartoonists & Writers Syndicate.

Reading the world always precedes reading the word, and reading the word implies continually reading the world.

—PAULO FREIRE,

AUTHOR OF LITERACY: READING THE WORD AND THE WORLD

RESPONDING

A response requires your reaction and interpretation. Your own perspective—your experiences, beliefs, and attitudes—will guide your particular response. Your response, as the preceding Viuti cartoon illustrates, may be totally different from another reader's response, but that does not necessarily make yours better or worse. Good responses say what you think, but then they *show why* you think so. They show the relationships between your opinions and the text, between the text and your experience, and between this text and other texts.

Depending on its purpose and intended audience, a response to a text can take several directions. Responses may focus on one or more of the following strategies. Consider your purpose and audience or check your assignment to see which type(s) you should emphasize.

Types of Responses

- **Analyzing the effectiveness of the text.** In this case, the response analyzes key features such as the clarity of the main idea, the organization of the argument, the quality of the supporting evidence, and/or the effectiveness of the author's style, tone, and voice.
- **Agreeing and/or disagreeing with the ideas in the text.** Often, responders react to the ideas or the argument of the essay. In this case, the responders show why they agree and/or disagree with what the author/text says.
- **Interpreting and reflecting on the text.** The responder explains key passages or examines the underlying assumptions or the implications of the ideas. Often, the responder reflects on how his or her own experiences, attitudes, and observations relate to the text.

Analyzing, agreeing/disagreeing, and interpreting are all slightly different directions that a response may take. But regardless of the direction, responses must be supported by evidence, examples, facts, and details. A responder cannot simply offer an opinion or agree or disagree. Good responses draw on several kinds of supporting evidence.

Kinds of Evidence

- **Personal experience.** Responders may use *examples* from their personal experiences to show why they interpreted the text as they did, why they agreed or disagreed, or why they reacted to the ideas as they did.
- **Evidence from the text.** Responders should cite *specific phrases* or sentences from the text to support their explanation of a section, their analysis of the effectiveness of a passage, or their agreement or disagreement with a key point.

- **Evidence from other texts.** If appropriate, responders may bring in ideas and information from other relevant essays, articles, books, or graphic material.

Not all responses use all three kinds of supporting evidence, but all responses *must* have sufficient examples to support the responder's ideas, reactions, and opinions. Responders should not merely state their opinions. They must give evidence to *show* how and why they read the text as they did.

One final—and crucial—point about responses: A response should make a coherent, overall main point. It should not be just a laundry list of reactions, likes, and dislikes. Sometimes the main point is that the text is not convincing because it lacks evidence. Sometimes the overall point is that the text makes an original statement even though it is difficult to read. Perhaps the basic point is that the author/text stimulates the reader to reflect on his or her experience. Every response should focus on a coherent main idea.

RESPONSE TO "TEACH DIVERSITY—WITH A SMILE"

Following is one possible response to Ehrenreich's essay. Before you read this response, however, write out your own reactions. You need to decide what you think before other responses influence your reading. There are, of course, many different but legitimate responses to any given essay. As you read this response, note the marginal annotations indicating the different types of responses and the different kinds of evidence this writer uses.

What I like best about Barbara Ehrenreich's article is her effective use of personal experience to clarify the issues on both sides of the multiculturalism debate. However, her conclusion, that we should "lighten up" and accept diversity because it's "more fun," weakens her argument by ignoring the social inequalities at the heart of the debate. The issue in this debate, I believe, is not just enjoying diversity, which is easy to do, but changing cultural conditions, which is much more difficult.

Analyzing effectiveness of text

Responder's main point

Ehrenreich effectively uses her own experiences—and her common sense—to let us see both the virtues and the excesses of multiculturalism. When she explains that her monocultural education gave her a social map that was "about as useful as the chart that guided Columbus to the 'Indies,'" she helps us understand how vital multicultural studies are in a society that is more like a glass mosaic than a melting pot. Interestingly, even her vocabulary reveals—

Evidence from text

perhaps unconsciously—her Western bias: "Jacobins," "pensées," "fiat," and "politesse" are all words that reveal her Eurocentric education. When Ehrenreich shifts to discussing the P. C. movement, her common-sense approach to the silliness of excessive social correctness ("the other guy's—or, excuse me, woman's—point of view") makes us as readers more willing to accept her compromise position.

Evidence from text

Reflecting on the text

My own experience with multiculturalism certainly parallels Ehrenreich's impatience with the "haughty stance" of the P.C. people. Of course, we should avoid racist and sexist terms and use our increased sensitivity to language to reduce discrimination. But my own backlash began several years ago when a friend said I shouldn't use the word "girl." I said, "You mean, not ever? Not even for a ten-year-old female child?" She replied that the word had been so abused by people referring to a "woman" as a "girl" that the word "girl" now carried too many sexist connotations. Although I understood my friend's point, it seems that "girl" should still be a perfectly good word for a female child under the age of twelve. Which reminds me of a book I saw recently, *The Official Politically Correct Dictionary*. It is loaded with examples of political correctness out of control: Don't say "bald," say "hair disadvantaged." Don't use the word "pet," say "non-human companion." Don't call someone "old," say that they are "chronologically gifted." One humorous example even suggested that George Bush was "electorally slighted" when he was not re-elected.

Personal experience

Evidence from other texts

Analyzing effectiveness of text

Ehrenreich does recommend keeping a sense of humor about the P.C. movement, but the conclusion to her essay weakens her argument. Instead of focusing on her earlier point that "it's silly to mistake verbal purification for genuine social reform," she advises both sides to lighten up and have fun with the diversity around us. Instead, I wanted her to conclude by reinforcing her point that "actions still speak louder than fashionable phrases." Changing the realities of illiteracy, poverty, alcohol abuse, and sexual harassment should be the focus of the multiculturalists. Of course, changing language is crucial to changing the world, but the language revolution has already happened—or at least begun. Ehrenreich's article would be more effective, I believe, if she concluded her essay with a call for both sides to help change cultural conditions rather than with a reference to the silly debate about what to call a teenage woman.

Responder's main point

SUMMARIZING AND RESPONDING TO AN ADVERTISEMENT

Summarizing and responding to graphic material, such as advertisements, is an excellent way to practice responding to texts. In this case, a summary must observe and describe the key features of the advertisement (layout, color, proportion, images, and copy). The response then "reads" the advertisement for the message, selling tactics, cultural stereotypes, or other implications. The focus of the response may be to analyze and explain the persuasive tactics, to interpret cultural values or stereotypes, to judge the effectiveness of the ad, and/or to reflect on assumptions and implications.

The following summary/response is to an advertisement for Fila jeans. Notice how the student writer, Karyn Lewis, carefully describes key features of the advertisement so her readers can clearly visualize it.

SOME DON'T LIKE THEIR BLUES AT ALL

Karyn M. Lewis

He strides toward us in navy and white, his body muscled and heavy-set, one arm holding his casually flung jeans jacket over his shoulder. A man in his prime, with just the right combination of macho and sartorial flair.

He is also black.

She is curled and giggling upon a chair, her hair loose and flowing around her shoulders, leaning forward innocently—the very picture of a blossoming, navy flower.

She is white.

They are each pictured on a magazine page of their own, situated opposite each other in a complementary two-page spread. They are stationed in front of a muted photograph which serves as a background for each one. They both merit their own captions: bold indigo letters presiding over them in the outer corners of each page.

His says: SOME LIKE THEIR BLUES HARD.

Hers says: SOME LIKE THEIR BLUES SOFT.

His background depicts a thrusting struggle between a quarterback and a leaping defender, a scene of arrested violence and high tension.

Her background is a lounging, bikini-clad goddess, who looks at the camera with intriguing, calm passion. She raises her hand to rest behind her head in a languid gesture as she tries to incite passion within the viewer.

At the bottom of the page blazes the proud emblem of the company who came up with this ad: FILA JEANS.

This advertisement blatantly uses stereotypes of men and women to sell its product. It caters to our need to fit into the roles that society has deemed for the individual sexes ever since patriarchal rule rose up and replaced the primitive worship of a mother goddess and the reverence of women. These stereotypes handed down to us throughout the centuries spell out to us that men are violence and power incarnate, and that the manly attitude brooks no room for weakness or softness of nature. And we find our role model of women in the compliant and eager female who obeys her man in all things, who must not say no to a male, and is not very bright—someone who flutters her eyelashes, giggles a lot, and uses tears to get her way.

This ad tells us, by offering the image of a hard, masculine male, who is deified in violence, that he is the role model men should aspire to, and that for women, their ideal is weak but sexual, innocent and at the same time, old enough to have sex. In viewing this ad, we see our aspirations clothed in FILA JEANS, and to be like them, we must buy the clothes pictured here. This ad also suggests that a man can become hard and powerful (or at least look it) dressed in these jeans; a woman can become sexually intense and desirable dressed in FILA's clothing

The words of the captions tantalize with their sexual innuendo. The phrase, "SOME LIKE THEIR BLUES HARD," hints at male sexual prowess. Most men and women in this country are obsessed with the male need to prove their virility, and FILA plays on this obsession. Females too have their own stereotype of what constitutes their sexuality. "SOME LIKE THEIR BLUES SOFT" exemplifies this ideal: A woman should be soft and yielding. Her soft, sensuous body parts which so excite her partners have been transformed into her personal qualities. By using the term "soft," FILA immediately links the girl with her sexuality and sexual organs.

We are shown by the models' postures that men and women are (according to FILA) fundamentally different and total antonyms of one another. He is standing and walking with purpose; she sits, laughing trivially at the camera. Even the background hints at separation of the sexes.

The football players on the man's page are arranged in a diagonal line which starts at the upper left-hand corner and runs to the opposite corner, which is the center of the ad. On her page, the enchanting nymph in the bathing suit runs on a diagonal, beginning where his ends, and traveling up to the upper right-hand corner of her page. These two photos in effect create a "V" which both links the two models, and also suggests movement away from one another. Another good example of their autonomy from one another is their skin color. He is a black man, she's white. Black is the opposite color of white on an artist's color wheel and palette, and symbolizes dynamically opposed forces: good and evil, night and day, man and woman. This ad hits us with the idea that men and women are not parallel in nature to one another, but are fundamentally different in all things. It alienates the sexes from each other. Opposites may attract, but there is no room for understanding a nature completely alien to your own.

So in viewing this ad, and reading its captions, the consumer is left with the view that a woman must be "soft" and sensual, a male's sexual dream, and somehow still retain her innocence after having sex. She must be weak, the opposite of the violence which contrasts with her on the opposite page. The men looking at this ad read the message that they are supposed to be well-dressed, powerful, and possess a strength that borders on violent. As we are told by the caption, men should be "hard." Furthermore, men and women are opposite creatures, as different as two sides of a coin.

This ad is supposed to cause us to want to meet these requirements, but it fills me with a deep-rooted disgust that we still perpetrate the myth that men are unyielding creatures of iron and women are silly bits of fluff. The ad generates no good role models to aspire to where men and women are equal beings, and both can show compassion and still be strong. FILA may like their blues hard and soft, but I don't like their blues at all.

■ WARMING UP: JOURNAL EXERCISES The following topics will help you practice your reading and responding. Read all of the following exercises and then choose two or three for practice.

1. Find an advertisement in a magazine and do a summary/interpretation, following the model provided by Karyn Lewis. First, describe the advertisement carefully so your readers can visualize its graphic features. Quote directly any key parts of the ad copy or language. Then offer your response to this ad. You may wish to analyze the effectiveness of the ad and/or offer your interpretation of its cultural significance.

2. Locate the textbook and class notes from a liberal arts course that you are currently taking. First, examine your textbook. What reading/writing strategies do you use as you study the text? Highlighting key passages? Underlining sentences? Writing notes and questions in the margins? Rereading key sections? Answering study questions? Writing out questions to ask in class? Now look at your class notes. Do you write down key ideas? Do you ask questions? Do you reread or review your notes after class? Do you reread your notes in a study group? List and describe the reading/writing strategies that you use. Be prepared to share your strategies with other students in class.

3. Because previewing material is an important part of active reading, most recent psychology or social science textbooks use previewing or prereading strategies at the beginning of each new chapter. Find one chapter in a textbook that uses these previewing techniques. How does the author preview the material? Does it help you understand the material in the chapter?

4. Practice your summarizing skills on the following two paragraphs from Peter Singer's book, *Animal Liberation.* Begin by referring to the author and title. As you write your summary, remind your reader occasionally that these are the author's ideas by using "author tags," such as "according to Singer" or "as Singer explains."

If a being suffers there can be no moral justification for refusing to take that suffering into consideration. No matter what the nature of the being, the principle of equality requires that its suffering be counted equally with the like suffering—insofar as rough comparisons can be made—of any other being. If a being is not capable of suffering, or of experiencing enjoyment or happiness, there is nothing to be taken into account. . . . To mark this boundary by some other characteristic like intelligence or rationality would be to mark it in an arbitrary manner. Why not choose some other characteristic, like skin color?

Racists violate the principle of equality by giving greater weight to the interests of members of their own race when there is a clash between their interests and the interests of those of another race. Sexists violate the principle of equality by favoring the interests of their own sex. Similarly, speciesists allow the interests of their own species to override the greater interests of members of other species. The pattern is identical in each case.

5. Reading the following paragraph illustrates how our prior experience can combine with our predictions to make meaning. The following passage describes a common procedure in our lives. Read the passage. Can you identify the procedure?

The procedure is actually quite simple. First you arrange things into different groups. Of course, one pile may be sufficient depending on how much there is to do. If you have to go somewhere else due to lack of facilities, that is the next step; otherwise you are pretty well set. It is important not to overdo things. That is, it is better to do too few things at once than too many. In the short run this may not seem important but complications can easily arise. A mistake can be expensive as well. At first, the whole procedure will seem complicated. Soon, however, it will become just another facet of life. It is difficult to foresee any end to the necessity for this task in the immediate future, but then one can never tell. After the procedure is completed, one arranges the materials into different groups again. Then they can be put into their appropriate places. Eventually, they will be used once more and the whole cycle will then have to be repeated. However, that is part of life.

As you read, record your guesses. What words helped to orient you? Where did you make wrong guesses? Discuss your reactions in class.

6. Study the print by Maurits Escher reproduced below. How many different ways of perceiving this picture can you see? Describe each perspective. How is "reading" this picture similar to reading a printed text? How is it different?

7. Reading is a gradual process of making guesses and then confirming or rejecting those guesses. To dramatize how the process works, find an essay or a short story that you have not read before. (Either Edward Abbey's essay, "The Damnation of a Canyon," in Chapter 10 or Kate Chopin's short story, "The Story of an Hour," in Chapter 11 work well.) Read two paragraphs and then stop. Write down what has happened and what you predict will happen next. Then read one more page and stop. Summarize in a sentence what has happened and predict what is coming. A third time, read one more page. Now stop and write. Then read the essay or the story through to the end. How accurately were

Day and Night by M. C. Escher. © 1997 Cordon Art-Baarm-Holland. All rights reserved.

you able to make predictions? Where did your guesses turn out to be wrong? If you read both the essay and the story, which was more predictable? Why?

READING: PROFESSIONAL WRITING

ANIMAL RIGHTS AND BEYOND

David Quammen

An award-winning writer of essays and fiction, David Quammen is best known for his regular column on nature in Outside *magazine. Essays originally published in his column appear in* Natural Acts: A Sidelong View of Science and Nature *(1985),* The Flight of the Iguana *(1988), and* The Song of the Dodo *(1996). Although Quammen often writes on the weird or offbeat curiosities of biology, such as the mating habits of the aphid, he can tackle subjects requiring philosophical depth as well as biological learning. "Animal Rights and Beyond," which appears in* Natural Acts, *shows Quammen's talent for understanding the difficult moral problems behind the animal rights movement and responding in a sensible but humorous manner. Do animals have moral rights? Should we cease all scientific experiments with animals? Should we all become vegetarians? Here is Quammen's summary of two books by animal rights philosophers—Peter Singer and Tom Regan—and his own responses to the difficult questions they raise.*

Do non-human animals have rights? Should we humans feel morally bound to exercise consideration for the lives and well-being of individual members of other animal species? If so, how much consideration, and by what logic? Is it permissible to torture and kill? Is it permissible to kill cleanly, without prolonged pain? To abuse or exploit without killing? For a moment, don't think about whales or wolves or the California condor; don't think about the cat or the golden retriever with whom you share your house. Think about chickens. Think about laboratory monkeys and then think about lab rats and then also think about lab frogs. Think about scallops. Think about mosquitoes. **(1)**

It's a Gordian question, by my lights, but one not very well suited to Alexandrian answers. Some people would disagree, judging the matter simply enough settled, one way or the other. *Of course they have rights. Of course they don't.* I say beware any such snappy, steel-trap thinking. Some folk would even—this late in the evolution of human sensibility—call it a frivolous question, a time-filling diversion for emotional hemophiliacs and cranks. *Women's rights, gay rights, now for Christ sake they want ANIMAL rights.* Notwithstanding the ridicule, the strong biases toward each side, it is certainly a serious philosophical issue, important and tricky, with almost endless implications for the way we humans live and should live on this planet. **(2)**

Philosophers of earlier ages, if they touched the subject at all, were likely to be dismissive. Thomas Aquinas announced emphatically that animals "are intended for man's use in the natural order. Hence it is not wrong for man to make use of them, either by killing or in any other way whatever." Descartes held that animals are merely machines. As late as 1901, a moral logician named Joseph Rickaby (who happened to be a Jesuit, but don't necessarily hold that against him) declared: "Brute beasts, not having understanding and therefore not being persons, cannot have any rights. The conclusion is clear." Maybe not quite so clear. Recently, just during the past decade, professional academic philosophers have at last begun to address the matter more openmindedly. **(3)**

Two thinkers in particular have been influential: an Australian named Peter Singer, an American named Tom Regan. In 1975 Singer published a book titled *Animal Liberation*, which stirred up the debate among his colleagues and is still treated as a landmark. Eight years later Tom Regan published *The Case for Animal Rights*, a more thorough and ponderous opus that stands now as a sort of companion piece to the Singer book. In between there came a number of other discussions of animal rights—including a collection of essays edited jointly by Singer and Regan. Despite the one-time collaboration, Peter Singer and Tom Regan represent two distinct schools of thought: They reach similar conclusions about the obligations of humans to other animals, but the moral logic is very different, and possibly also the implications. Both men have produced some formidable work and both, to my simple mind, show some shocking limitations of vision. **(4)**

I've spent the past week amid these books, Singer's and Regan's and the rest. It has been an edifying experience, and now I'm more puzzled than ever. I keep thinking about monkeys and frogs and mosquitoes and—sorry, but I'm quite serious—carrots. **(5)**

. . .

Peter Singer's view is grounded upon the work of Jeremy Bentham, that eighteenth-century British philosopher generally known as the founder of utilitarianism. "The greatest good for the greatest number" is a familiar cartoon version of what, according to Bentham, should be achieved by the ethical ordering of society and behavior. A more precise summary is offered by Singer: "In other words, the interests of every being affected by an action are to be taken into account and given the same weight as the like interests of any other being." If this much is granted, the crucial next point is deciding what things constitute interests and who or what qualifies as a *being*. Evidently Bentham did not have just humans in mind. Back in 1789, optimistically and perhaps presciently, he wrote: "The day may come when the rest of the animal creation may acquire those rights which never could have been withholden from them but by the hand of tyranny." Most philosophers of his day were inclined (as most in our day are still inclined) to extend moral coverage only to humans, because only humans (supposedly) are rational and communicative. Jeremy Bentham took exception: "The question is not, 'Can they *reason?*' nor, 'Can they *talk?*' but, 'Can they *suffer?*'" On this crucial point, Peter Singer follows Bentham. **(6)**

The capacity to suffer, says Singer, is what separates a being with legitimate interests from an entity without interests. A stone has no interests that must be respected, because it cannot suffer. A mouse can suffer; therefore it has interests and those interests must be weighed in the moral balance. Fine, that much seems simple enough. Certain people of sophistic or Skinnerian bent would argue that there is no proof a mouse can in fact suffer, that it's merely an anthropomorphic assumption; but since each of us has no proof that *anyone* else actually suffers besides ourselves, we are willing, most of us, to grant the assumption. More problematic is that very large gray area between stones and mice. **(7)**

Peter Singer declares: "If a being suffers, there can be no moral justification for disregarding that suffering, or for refusing to count it equally with the like suffering of any other being. But the converse of this is also true. If a being is not capable of suffering, or of enjoyment, there is nothing to take into account." Where is the boundary? Where falls the line between creatures who suffer and those that are incapable? Singer's cold philosophic eye travels across the pageant of living species—chickens suffer, mice suffer, fish suffer, um, lobsters most likely suffer, *look alive, you other creatures!*—and his damning stare lands on the oyster. **(8)**

No, I'm not making this up. The oyster, by Singer's best guess, doesn't suffer. Its nervous system lacks the requisite complexity. Therefore, while lobsters and crawfish and shrimp possess inviolable moral status, the oyster has none. It is a difficult judgment, Singer admits, by no means an infallible one, but "somewhere between a shrimp and an oyster seems as good a place to draw the line as any, and better than most." **(9)**

Moral philosophy, no one denies, is an imperfect science. **(10)**

Tom Regan takes exception with Singer on two important points. First, he disavows the utilitarian framework, with its logic that abuse or killing of animals by humans is wrong because it yields a net *overall* decrease in welfare, among all beings who qualify for moral status. No, argues Regan, that logic is false and pernicious. The abuse or killing is wrong in its *essence*—however the balance comes out on overall welfare—because it violates the rights of those individual animals. Individual rights, in other words, take precedence over the maximizing of the common good. Second, in Regan's opinion the capacity to suffer is not what marks the elect. Mere suffering is not sufficient. Instead he posits the concept of *inherent value,* a complex and magical quality possessed by some living creatures but not others. **(11)**

A large portion of Regan's book is devoted to arguing toward this concept. He is more uncompromisingly protective of certain creatures—those with rights—than Singer, but he is also more selective; the hull of his ark is sturdier, but the gangplank is narrower. According to Regan, individual beings possess inherent value (and therefore inviolable rights) if they "are able to perceive and remember; if they have beliefs, desires, and preferences; if they are able to act intentionally in pursuit of their desires or goals; if they are sentient and have an emotional life; if they have a sense of the future, including a sense of their own future; if they have a psychophysical identity over time; and if they have an individual experiential welfare that is logically independent of their utility for, and the interests of, others." So Tom Regan is not handing rights around profligately, to every cute little beast that crawls over his foot. In fact we all probably know a few humans who, at least on a bad night, might have trouble meeting those standards. But how would Regan himself apply them? Where does he see the line falling? Who qualifies for inherent value, and what doesn't? **(12)**

Like Singer, Regan has thought this point through. Based on his grasp of biology and ethology, he is willing to grant rights to "mentally normal mammals of a year or more." **(13)**

Also like Singer, he admits that the judgment is not infallible: "Because we are uncertain where the boundaries of consciousness lie, it is not unreasonable to advocate a policy that bespeaks moral caution." So chickens and frogs should be given the benefit of the doubt, as should all other animals that bear a certain degree of anatomical and physiological resemblance to us mentally normal mammals. **(14)**

But Regan does not specify just what degree. **(15)**

The books by Singer and Regan leave me with two very separate reactions. The first combines admiration and gratitude. These men are applying the methods of systematic philosophy to an important and much-neglected question. Furthermore, they don't content themselves with just understanding and describing a pattern of gross injustice; they also emphatically say, *"Let's stop it!"* They are fighting a good fight. Peter Singer's book in particular has focused attention on the outrageous practices that are routine in American factory farms, in "psychological" experimentation, in research on the toxicity of cosmetics. Do you know how chickens are dealt with on the large poultry operations? How veal is produced? How the udders of dairy cows are kept flowing? Do you know the sorts of ingenious but pointless torment that thousands of monkeys and millions of rats endure, each year, to fill the time and the dissertations of uninspired graduate students? If you don't, by all means read Singer's *Animal Liberation.* **(16)**

The second reaction is negative. Peter Singer and Tom Regan, it seems to me, share a breathtaking smugness and myopia not too dissimilar to the brand they so forcefully condemn. Theirs is a righteous and vigorous smugness, not a passive and unreflective one. But still. **(17)**

Singer inveighs against a sin he labels *speciesism*—discrimination against certain creatures based solely upon the species to which they belong. Regan uses a slightly less confused and less clumsy phrase, *human chauvinism,* to indicate roughly the same thing. Both of them arrive (supposedly by sheer logic) at the position that vegetarianism is morally obligatory: To kill and eat a "higher" animal represents absolute violation of one being's rights; to kill and eat a plant evidently violates nothing at all. Both Singer and Regan claim to disparage the notion—pervasive in Western philosophy since Protagoras—that "Man is the measure of all things." Both argue elaborately against anthropocentrism, while creating new moral frameworks that are also decidedly anthropocentric. Make no mistake: Man is still the measure, for Singer and Regan. The test for inherent value has changed only slightly. Instead of asking, *"Is the creature a human?,"* they simply ask, *"How similar to human is similar enough?"* **(18)**

Peter Singer explains that shrimp deserve brotherly treatment but oysters, so different from us, are fair game for the gumbo. In Tom Regan's vocabulary, the redwood tree is an "inanimate natural object," sharing that category with clouds and rocks. But some simple minds would say: Life is life. **(19)**

VOCABULARY

In your journal, write the meaning of each of the following words:

- A *Gordian* question **(2)**
- *Alexandrian* answers **(2)**
- perhaps *presciently* **(6)**
- people of *sophistic* or *Skinnerian* bent **(7)**
- *anthropomorphic* assumption **(7)**
- *inviolable* moral status **(9)**
- biology and *ethology* **(13)**

QUESTIONS FOR WRITING AND DISCUSSION

1. Which of the following non-human species should or should not have rights protected by humans? Where would you draw the line, and on what basis? Use the following species—or make up your own list.

whales	snakes	fish	trees
wolves	scorpions	squid	orchids
cats and dogs	spiders	lobsters	cabbage
chickens	mosquitoes	clams	carrots
mice and rats	chiggers	oysters	lichen

2. A good summary should mention the author and title, use direct quotations for key ideas, include author tags, and describe the main ideas objectively and fairly. Examine Quammen's summary of either Singer's or Regan's texts. Is his summary effective?

READING: PROFESSIONAL WRITING

3. Responses can focus on analyzing the effectiveness of the text, agreeing or disagreeing with the ideas in the text, or reflecting on the meaning of the text. Does Quammen use all three of these kinds of responses? Which one does he emphasize?

4. Quammen focuses on a difficult philosophical problem, but he makes the organization of his essay easy to follow. Below is the basic outline.

   I. Introduction to the question of animal rights

   II. Review of early philosophers' views on animal rights

   III. Summary and review of the books and philosophies of Singer and Regan

      A. Singer's philosophy

      B. Regan's philosophy

   IV. Quammen's responses to Singer and Regan

      A. Positive reactions

      B. Negative reactions

   For the above outline, indicate by numbers which paragraphs belong with each section. Then underline or write down the transitions or key words or phrases near the beginning of each section that *signal* for the reader the focus for that section. Where are his signals clear? Where should he use a better transition or more clearly state the focus?

5. A writer's tone and sense of humor can make a passage appealing to readers. Find three sentences where Quammen's sense of humor is apparent. In each instance, did Quammen's humor make the passage more interesting for you? Explain.

6. Reread Quammen's essay and write out your own responses to his essay. Then read Paula Fisher's essay on Quammen later in this chapter. Discuss your responses to both articles with your classmates. Then write your own summary and response to the conversation created by your classmates about these authors.

MASTERS OF DESIRE: THE CULTURE OF AMERICAN ADVERTISING

Jack Solomon

In this selection from The Signs of Our Time, *Solomon does a semiotic reading of several advertisements for automobiles and whisky. The term "semiotics" comes from the Greek word for "sign," and was used by seventeenth-century philosopher John Locke to describe a science of signs. More recently, European linguists and philosophers have applied this science of signs to literature and popular culture objects in order to "read" messages of power and culture that are "hidden" in language, symbols, and ordinary objects. Solomon's "reading" of automobile advertisements goes beyond describing typical Madison Avenue strategies to showing how the character of America is revealed in pictures, paper, and body language.*

Amongst democratic nations, men easily attain a certain equality of condition; but they can never attain as much as they desire.

—Alexis de Tocqueville

On May 10, 1831, a young French aristocrat named Alexis de Tocqueville arrived in New York City at the start of what would become one of the most famous visits to America in our history. He had come to observe first-hand the institutions of the freest, most egalitarian society of the age, but what he found was a paradox. For behind America's mythic promise of equal opportunity, Tocqueville discovered a desire for *unequal* social rewards, a ferocious competition for privilege and distinction. . . . We Americans dream of rising above the crowd, of attaining a social summit beyond the reach of ordinary citizens. And therein lies the paradox. **(1)**

The American dream, in other words, has two faces: the one communally egalitarian and the other competitively elitist. This contradiction is no accident; it is fundamental to the structure of American society. Even as America's great myth of equality celebrates the virtues of mom, apple pie, and the girl or boy next door, it also lures us to achieve social distinction, to rise above the crowd and bask alone in the glory. This land is your land and this land is my land, Woody Guthrie's populist anthem tells us, but we keep trying to increase the "my" at the expense of the "your." Rather than fostering contentment, the American dream breeds desire, a longing for a greater share of the pie. It is as if our society were a vast high-school football game, with the bulk of the participants noisily rooting in the stands while, deep down, each of them is wishing he or she could be the star quarterback or head cheerleader. **(2)**

For the semiotician, the contradictory nature of the American myth of equality is nowhere written so clearly as in the signs that American advertisers use to manipulate us into buying their wares. "Manipulate" is the word here, not "persuade"; for advertising campaigns are not sources of product information, they are exercises in behavior modification. Appealing to our subconscious emotions rather than to our conscious intellects, advertisements are designed to exploit the discontentments fostered by the American dream, the constant desire for social success and the material rewards that accompany it. America's consumer economy runs on desire, and advertising stokes the engines by transforming common objects—from peanut butter to political candidates—into signs of all the things that Americans covet most. **(3)**

In this [essay], we'll look at a representative sample of ads and what they say about the emotional climate of the country and the fast-changing trends of American life. Because ours is a highly diverse, pluralistic society, various advertisements may say different things depending on their intended audiences, but in every case they say something about America, about the status of our hopes, fears, desires, and beliefs. **(4)**

Let's begin with two ad campaigns conducted by the same company that bear out Alexis de Tocqueville's observations about the contradictory nature of American society: General Motors' campaigns for its Cadillac and Chevrolet lines. First, consider an early magazine ad for the Cadillac Allanté. Appearing as a full-color, four-page insert in *Time,* the ad seems to say "I'm special—and so is this car" even before we've begun to read it. Rather than being printed on the ordinary, flimsy pages of the magazine, the Allanté spread appears on glossy coated stock. The unwritten message here is that an extraordinary car deserves an extraordinary advertisement, and that both car and ad are aimed at an extraordinary consumer, or at least one who wishes to appear extraordinary compared to his more ordinary fellow citizens. **(5)**

Ads of this kind work by creating symbolic associations between their product and what is most coveted by the consumers to whom they are addressed. It is significant, then, that this ad insists that the Allanté is virtually an Italian rather than an American car, an automobile, as its copy runs, "Conceived and Commissioned by America's Luxury Car Leader—Cadillac" but "Designed and Handcrafted by Europe's Renowned Design Leader—Pininfarina, SpA, of Turin, Italy." This is not simply a piece of product information, it's a sign of the prestige that European luxury cars enjoy in today's automotive marketplace. Once the luxury car of choice for America's status drivers, Cadillac has fallen far behind its European competitors in the race for the prestige market. So the Allanté essentially represents Cadillac's decision, after years of resisting the trend toward European cars, to introduce its own European import—whose high cost is clearly printed on the last page of the ad. Although $54,700 is a lot of money to pay for a Cadillac, it's about what you'd expect to pay for a top-of-the-line Mercedes-Benz. That's precisely the point the ad is trying to make: the Allanté is no mere car. It's a potent status symbol you can associate with the other major status symbols of the 1980s. **(6)**

Status symbols, then, are signs that identify their possessors' place in a social hierarchy, markers of rank and prestige. We can all think of any number of status symbols—Rolls-Royces, Beverly Hills mansions, even Shar Pei puppies (whose rareness and expense has rocketed them beyond Russian wolfhounds as status pets and has even inspired whole lines of wrinkle-faced stuffed toys)—but how do we know that something *is* a status symbol? The explanation is quite simple: when an object (or puppy!) either costs a lot of money or requires influential connections to possess, anyone who possesses it must also possess the necessary means and influence to acquire it. The object itself really doesn't matter, since it ultimately disappears behind the presumed social potency of its owner. Semiotically, what matters is the signal it sends, its value as a sign of power. One traditional sign of social distinction is owning a country estate and enjoying the peace and privacy that attend it. Advertisements for Mercedes-Benz, Jaguar, and Audi automobiles thus frequently feature drivers motoring quietly along a country road, presumably on their way to or from their country houses. **(7)**

Advertisers have been quick to exploit the status signals that belong to body language as well. As Hegel observed in the early nineteenth century, it is an ancient aristocratic prerogative to be seen by the lower orders without having to look at them in return. Tilting his chin high in the air and gazing down at the world under hooded eyelids, the aristocrat invites observation while refusing to look back. We can find such a pose exploited in an advertisement for Cadillac Seville in which we see an elegantly dressed woman out for a drive with her husband in their new Cadillac. If we look closely at the woman's body language, we can see her glance inwardly with a satisfied smile on her face but not outward toward the camera that represents our gaze. She is glad to be seen by us in her Seville, but she isn't interested in looking at *us!* **(8)**

Secondly, ads that are aimed at a broader market take the opposite approach. If the American dream encourages the desire to "arrive," to vault above the mass, it also fosters a desire to be popular, to "belong." Populist commercials accordingly transform products into signs of belonging, utilizing such common icons as country music, small-town life, family picnics, and farmyards. All of these icons are incorporated in GM's "Heartbeat of America" campaign for its Chevrolet line. Unlike the Seville commercial, the faces in the Chevy ads look straight at us and smile. Dress is casual; the mood upbeat. Quick camera cuts take us from rustic to suburban to urban scenes, creating an American montage filmed from sea to shining sea. We all "belong" in a Chevy. **(9)**

Where price alone doesn't determine the market for a product, advertisers can go either way. Both Johnnie Walker and Jack Daniel's are better-grade whiskies, but where a Johnnie Walker ad appeals to the buyer who wants a mark of aristocratic distinction in his liquor, a Jack Daniel's ad emphasizes the down-home, egalitarian folksiness of its product. Johnnie Walker associates itself with such conventional status symbols as sable coats, Rolls-Royces, and black gold; Jack Daniel's gives us a Good Ol' Boy in overalls. In fact, Jack Daniel's Good Ol'Boy is an icon of backwoods independence, recalling the days of the moonshiner and the Whisky Rebellion of 1794. Evoking emotions quite at odds with those stimulated in Johnnie Walker ads, the advertisers of Jack Daniel's have chosen to transform their product into a sign of America's populist tradition. The fact that both ads successfully sell whisky is itself a sign of the dual nature of the American dream. **(10)**

VOCABULARY

In your journal, write the meaning of the following words:

- most *egalitarian* society **(1)**
- competitively *elitist* **(2)**
- *populist* anthem **(2)**
- *pluralistic* society **(4)**
- social *hierarchy* **(7)**
- aristocratic *prerogative* **(8)**
- these *icons* **(9)**

QUESTIONS FOR WRITING AND DISCUSSION

1. Look at the objects around you. Focus on one item. Design a full-page advertisement for this object to appear in one of the following magazines: *Time, Vogue,* or *Sports Illustrated.* Use appeals to social status to sell the object.

2. Explain the "paradox" referred to in the first paragraph of the essay.

3. In your own words, explain what Solomon means when he says, "The object itself really doesn't matter, since it ultimately disappears behind the presumed social potency of its owner." In particular, why does Solomon say that the object "disappears"?

4. Reread Solomon's article. Where does he help the reader by repeating main ideas, defining terms, or citing examples that trigger the reader's own experiences? Where could his explanations be clearer?

5. Find a full-page advertisement from a recent magazine. Write your own essay analyzing the signs in this ad. What is the written message or caption? What unwritten messages are conveyed by color, design, images, or body language? What does this ad say about American consumers?

READING AND WRITING PROCESSES

■ ASSIGNMENT FOR READING/WRITING   Write an essay that summarizes and then responds to one or more essays, articles, or advertisements. As you review your particular assignment, make sure you understand what text or texts you should respond to, how long your summary and response should be, and what type(s) of responses you should focus on.

Your purpose for this assignment is to represent the text(s) accurately and faithfully in your summary and to explain and support your response. Taken together, your summary and response should be a coherent essay, with a main idea and connections between summary and response. Assume that your audience is other members of the class, including the instructor, with whom you are sharing your reading.

CHOOSING A SUBJECT

Suggested processes, activities, and strategies for reading and writing will be illustrated in response to the following essay by Dudley Erskine Devlin.

CHILDREN AND VIOLENCE IN AMERICA

Dudley Erskine Devlin

Dudley Erskine Devlin was born in Syracuse, New York, and attended the University of Kansas. Originally trained as a scientist, he currently teaches English at Colorado State University and writes columns and editorials on contemporary problems. The targets for his editorials are often the large and complicated issues of the day, such as education, violence, health care, and the media. "My first goal as a writer," Devlin said in a recent interview, "is to provoke response. If just one reader is angry enough to write me a letter of response, then my time is not wasted." As you read Devlin's essay, note places where you agree or disagree with his ideas. How would you reply to Devlin's argument?

Violence seems to be everywhere in America, but increasingly both the victims and the perpetrators are likely to be children and teenagers. According to a recent Department of Education study, 81 percent of the victims of violent crimes are now preteens and teenagers. Teenagers also lead adults in the number of serious crimes committed. As if to prove this point, recently a stray bullet from gang violence in Denver struck a 10-month-old child who was visiting the zoo. In another incident, a 13-year-old boy accidently shot his friend, and then in despair shot and killed himself. Even this morning's newspaper carries the story of a 15-year-old boy who accidently shot his 9-year-old sister while showing her how to load and unload his father's .22 semi-automatic handgun. The gun went off, and the bullet shattered her spine. The 9-year-old girl is now paralyzed. When people read these shocking and unbelievable stories, they begin to wonder about the causes of the problem. Why are children so frequently the victims or the perpetrators of violence? **(1)**

The debate in America today is about the causes of violence involving children. But what exactly is the basic, underlying cause? Conventional explanations take an either/or approach: Either the cause lies in TV programs which promote violence or the cause is a society riddled with family instability, drugs, and poverty. It's a classic chicken-or-the-egg question: Does TV and movie violence promote social violence, or is social violence merely reflected in violent movies and television programs? **(2)**

I believe that we should not be fooled by this either/or logic. There is, after all, a third possible answer. Instead of the primary cause being TV violence or the decline in family values, I believe that the news media themselves are the underlying cause of our crisis. The truth is that the liberal media—particularly newspapers and network TV news—have cleverly staged this crisis of violence by hyping a few statistics and isolated cases of violence. To prove this claim, I need to review the conventional arguments. **(3)**

First, let's analyze the belief that violence on TV and in the movies is causing increased violence among children and teenagers. The self-appointed liberal reformers usually trot out a bunch of statistics and examples like the following:

- By the age of 18, the average American child will have seen 200,000 violent acts on television, including 40,000 murders. By the time an American child has left elementary school, he or she has witnessed 8,000 murders on TV.
- Today, television programs and films strive for high body counts, not high morals. *Terminator 2* seems like one long machine-gunning. In *RoboCop*, 32 people are killed. *Die Hard 2* may have the unofficial record with 264 people killed.
- In 1950, approximately 15 percent of America's homes had television; by 1990, 93 percent of America's homes had television. In that 40-year period, the murder rate per 100,000 people jumped from 5.3 to 10.2. That's almost a 100 percent increase in murders.

Using examples like these, the TV and media critics like Tipper Gore argue that children confuse images on TV with the real world, that they become desensitized to repeated acts of violence, and that they say that "it's fun" to do violence to others. Researchers like University of Illinois psychologists Leonard Eron and Rowell Huesmann argue that violence on TV does cause violent behavior: "Television violence affects youngsters of all ages, of both genders, at all socioeconomic levels. It cannot be denied or explained away." **(4)**

On the other side of this either/or argument are those who believe that social violence causes violent behavior in children and teenagers. Those who make this argument point to drug use, poverty, and the decline in family values. Their best evidence is that violence already exists in our children's public schools. They like to cite figures released by the National Education Association (NEA) that show that violence is an everyday part of every child's education. Every school day, the NEA claims, at least 100,000 students bring guns to school; 40 are hurt or killed by firearms; 6,250 teachers are threatened with bodily injury; and 260 teachers are physically assaulted. Everywhere, schools are installing metal detectors and police are stationed in the hallways. **(5)**

Obviously, each of these arguments represents a half-truth. Possibly there is some TV and movie violence that adds to the culture of violence in America. And yes, we can believe that there are a few, isolated pockets of violence in society and schools. But the real truth is that the newspaper media and the network news have actually invented this epidemic of violence in order to promote their product and frighten the public. Every day, reporters search for a few examples of violence to teens and children, plaster them on the front page, and blow the whole thing out of proportion. **(6)**

To be sure, there are violent TV shows and movies that a few people watch, but there are also family shows like *Home Improvement* and *Home Alone* that don't get the publicity of *RoboCop* or *Terminator 2*. There are, of course, one or two cities in America, like Los Angeles and Washington, D.C., where there is occasional violence on the streets and in children's schools. But the liberal establishment press has done its thing again, trying to scare the daylights out of the public in order to sell newspapers and raise their Neilsen ratings. **(7)**

So when you pick up your paper in the morning or turn on the TV news and see another story about teenage violence, take it with a big lump of salt and don't believe everything you read. As they say, one swallow doesn't make a summer, and one infant shot in the Denver Zoo does not mean that we have this huge crisis of violence. In terms of "telling it like it is," you'll find more truth if you turn to the comics and check out "Peanuts." When Lucy hits Charlie Brown, at least you know it's make-believe. **(8)**

COLLECTING

Once a text or texts has been selected or assigned for your summary and response, try the following reading/writing/discussing activities.

■ **PREREADING JOURNAL ENTRY**   In your journal, write what you already know about the subject of the essay. For an essay about children and violence, for example, the following questions will help you to recall your prior experiences and think about your own opinions before you read the essay. The purpose of this entry is to think about your own experiences and opinions *before* you are influenced by the arguments of the essay.

What experiences have you had with guns and violence?

What acts of violence to or by children can you recall?

What seems to be the cause of these violent acts?

What would you do to solve the problem?

TEXT ANNOTATION   Most experts on reading and writing agree that you will learn more and remember more if you actually write out your comments, questions, and reactions in the margins of the text you are reading. Writing your responses helps you begin a conversation with the text. Reproduced below are one reader's marginal responses to paragraphs 6 and 7 of Devlin's essay.

I think that both areas contribute to violence

Obviously, each of these arguments represents a half-truth. Possibly there is some TV and movie violence that adds to the culture of violence in America. And yes, we can believe that there are a few, isolated pockets of violence in society and schools. But the real truth is that the newspaper media and the network news have actually *invented* this epidemic of violence in order to promote their product and frighten the public. Every day, reporters search for a few examples of violence to teens and children, plaster them on the front page, and blow the whole thing out of proportion.

There's a lot of violence on TV and in society

? Network news didn't invent it, but they do hype it.

TV news does this every night

Home Alone was filled with violence

To be sure, there are violent TV shows and movies that a few people watch, but there are also family shows like Home Improvement and *Home Alone* that don't get the publicity of RoboCop or Terminator 2.
There are, of course, *one or two cities in America*, like Los Angeles and Washington, D.C., where there is occasional violence on the streets and in children's schools. But the liberal establishment press has done its thing again, trying to scare the daylights out of the public in order to sell newspapers and raise their Neilsen ratings.

Huh?
Violence exists in every city in America

Showing violence on TV does raise ratings

READING LOG   A reading log, like text annotation, encourages you to interact with the author/text and write your comments and questions as you read. While text annotation helps you identify specific places in the text for commentary, a reading log encourages you to write out longer, more thoughtful responses. In a reading log, you can keep a record of your thoughts *while you read and reread* the text. Often, reading-log entries help you focus on a key idea to develop later in your response.

Below is one reader's response to Devlin's claim in paragraphs 6 and 7 that the violence is isolated in just a few cities.

> When Devlin says that violence happens in only a few cities like L.A. or D.C., I really disagree. One would never expect to hear of violence in a sparsely populated state like Montana, but it does happen there. Peers in my school bring weapons daily—guns, knives, and the like. So far, only threats have been made, but everyone lives in fear that one day someone will get hurt. Schools don't have to be in the slums to have violence. Three years ago, a boy walked into his classroom in Lewistown, Montana, and killed his teacher and wounded two others. This student went to a safe school, in a safe city, but somehow the violence found a way into this haven.

DOUBLE-ENTRY LOG   One of the most effective strategies to promote active reading is a double-entry log. Draw a line down the middle of a page in your notebook. On the left-hand side, keep a running summary of the main ideas and features that you notice in the text. On the right-hand side, write your questions and reactions. A double-entry log, especially if used with the *Rereading Guide* that follows, can help you quickly organize your ideas for a summary/response essay.

Author and Title:

SUMMARY COMMENTS: MAIN IDEAS AND KEY FEATURES	RESPONSE: COMMENTS, REACTIONS, AND QUESTIONS

REREADING GUIDE   After you've read an essay once, let the following set of questions guide your *rereadings* of the text. The questions on the left-hand side will help you summarize and analyze the text; the questions on the right-hand side will help focus your response.

DESCRIPTION	RESPONSE

I. Audience/Reader

- Who is the *intended audience?*
- What *assumptions* does the author make about the reader's knowledge or beliefs?
- From what *point of view* is the author writing?

- Are you part of the intended audience?
- Does the author misjudge the reader's knowledge or beliefs?
- Do you share the author's point of view on this subject?

II. Thesis and Main Ideas

- What *questions* or *problems* does the author/text address?
- What is the author's *thesis?*
- What *main ideas* are related to the thesis?
- What are the *key moments* or *key passages* in the text?

- What assumptions does the essay make?
- What are the implications or consequences of the essay's ideas?
- Does the essay have contradictions or errors in logic?
- What ideas or arguments does the essay omit or ignore?
- What experience or prior knowledge do you have about the topic?
- Where do you agree or disagree?

III. Organization and Evidence

- Where does the author *preview* the essay's organization?
- How does the author *signal* new sections of the essay?
- What *kinds of evidence* does the author use (personal experience, descriptions, statistics, interviews, other authorities, analytical reasoning, or other)?

- At what point could you accurately predict the organization of the essay?
- At what points were you confused about the organization?
- What evidence was most/least effective?
- Where did the author rely on assertions rather than on evidence?
- Which of your own personal experiences did you recall as you read the essay?

IV. Language and Style

- What is the author's *tone* (casual, humorous, ironic, angry, preachy, academic, or other)?
- Are *sentences* and *vocabulary* easy, average, or difficult?
- What key *words* or *images* recur throughout the text?

- Did the tone support or distract from the author's purpose or meaning?
- Did the sentences and vocabulary support or distract from the purpose or meaning?
- Did recurring words or images relate to or support the purpose or meaning?

V. Purpose

- Describe the author's overall *purpose* (to inform, explore, explain, evaluate, argue, entertain, or other purpose).
- How does the author/text want to to *affect* or *change* the reader?

- Is the overall purpose clear or muddled?
- Was the actual purpose different from the stated purpose?
- How did the text actually affect you?

Remember that not all these questions will be relevant to any given essay or text, but one or two of these questions may suggest a direction or give a *focus* to your overall response. When one of these questions suggests a focus for your response to the essay, *go back to the text, to other texts, and to your experience* to gather *evidence* and *examples* to support your response.

DISCUSSION AND REREADING   After you have recorded your initial reactions in your reading log or double-entry log, discuss your reactions in small groups. Do a collaborative annotation of the text by recording your group's best responses in the margins of a photocopy of the text. Or perhaps your class or small group may want to debate the strengths and weaknesses of the text. After your class or small-group discussion activity, however, take time to enter your responses to the following questions:

What do you need to change in your summary?

What new responses did you hear?

Which of your original responses have you revised?

What will be the new focus or main emphasis of your response?

GUIDELINES FOR CLASS DISCUSSION

Class discussions are an important part of the reading/writing/discussing process. Often, however, class discussions are not productive because not everyone knows the purpose of the discussion or how to discuss openly and fairly. Following is a suggested list of goals for class discussion. Read them carefully. *Make notes about any suggestions, revisions, or additions for your class.* Your class will then review these goals and agree to adopt, modify, or revise them for your own class discussions for the remainder of the semester.

Discussion Goals

1. To understand and *accurately represent* the views of the author(s) of the essays. The first discussion goal should be to summarize the author's views fairly.

2. To understand how the views and arguments of individual authors *relate* to each other. Comparing and contrasting different authors' views helps clarify each author's argument.

3. To encourage all members of the class to articulate their *understanding* of each essay and their *response* to the ideas in each essay. Class discussions should promote multiple responses rather than focus on a single "right" interpretation or response.

4. To hear class members' responses in an *open forum.* All points of view must be recognized. *Discussions in class should focus on ideas and arguments, not on individual class members.* Class members may attack ideas but not people.

5. To relate class discussions to the *assigned reading/writing task.* What effective writing strategies are illustrated in the essay the class is discussing? How can class members use any of these strategies in writing their own essays?

SHAPING

Summaries and responses have several possible shapes, depending on the writer's purpose and intended audience. Keep in mind, however, that in a summary/response essay or critique, *the summary and the response should be unified by the writer's overall response.* The summary and the response may be organized or drafted separately, but they are still parts of one essay, focused on the writer's most important or overall response.

SUMMARY SHAPING

Summaries should convey the main ideas, the essential argument, or the key features of a text. The purpose should be to represent the author's/text's ideas as accurately and as faithfully as possible. Summaries rely on description, paraphrase, and direct quotation. Below are definitions and examples for each of these terms.

DESCRIPTION   The summary should *describe* the main features of an essay, including the author and title, the context or place of publication for the essay (if appropriate), the essay's thesis or main argument, and any key text features, such as sections, chapters, or important graphic material.

In an editorial entitled "Children and Violence in America," Dudley Erskine Devlin documents the increasing violence in America done to children and by children. In addressing the question of why the violence has increased, he reports on the debate between those people who think that television violence is the main cause and those who think that the decline of social values is the cause. Devlin suggests that each of these arguments represents only a half-truth. In fact, Devlin argues, the news media have largely invented this crisis of violence.

PARAPHRASE A paraphrase restates a passage or text in different words. The purpose of a paraphrase is to recast the author's/text's words in your own language. A good paraphrase retains the original meaning without plagiarizing from the original text.

Original: But the real truth is that the newspaper media and the network news have actually invented this epidemic of violence in order to promote their product and frighten the public.

Paraphrase: Television and print media have created an illusion that violence is widespread simply to attract anxious viewers and readers to their programs and news stories.

As you can see, a paraphrase does not necessarily condense a passage. Actually, the paraphrase may be nearly as long as the original. A summary includes occasional paraphrasing of a few, selected, main ideas.

DIRECT QUOTATION Often, summaries directly quote a few key phrases or sentences from the source. *Remember: Any words or phrases within the quotation marks must be accurate, word-for-word transcriptions of the original.* Guidelines for direct quotation and examples are as follows. Use direct quotations sparingly to convey the key points in the essay:

> Devlin's essay addresses a simple but difficult question: "Why are children so frequently the victims or the perpetrators of violence?"

Use direct quotations when the author's phrasing is more memorable, more concise, or more accurate than your paraphrase might be:

> Devlin argues that media reporters are trying to "scare the daylights out of the public" in order to sell their stories.

Use direct quotations for key words or phrases that indicate the author's attitude, tone, or stance:

> Television and the news media, Devlin claims, have "invented" this crisis of violence.

Don't quote long sentences. Condense the original sentence to the most important phrases. Use just a short phrase from a sentence or use an ellipsis (three spaced periods . . .) to indicate words that you have left out.

Original:	But the real truth is that the newspaper media and the network news have actually invented this epidemic of violence in order to promote their product and frighten the public.
Condensed Quotation:	"The real truth," according to Devlin, is that the media "have actually invented this epidemic . . . to promote their product and frighten the public."

SAMPLE SUMMARIES   Following are summaries of Devlin's essay written by two different readers. Notice that while both convey the main ideas of the essay by using description, paraphrase, and direct quotation, they are not identical. Check each summary to see how well it meets these guidelines:

- Cite the author and title of the text.
- Indicate the main ideas of the text.
- Use direct quotation of key words, phrases, or sentences.
- Include author tags.
- Do not summarize most examples or data.
- Be as accurate, fair, and objective as possible.

SUMMARY NO. 1

In "Children and Violence in America," Dudley Erskine Devlin takes a different approach to explaining the apparent increase of violence involving children. Devlin begins by describing several cases of children and violence, and then he outlines the two major explanations for violence that most social analysts subscribe to. The first is that television promotes violence, and the second is that the decline in family values causes children to kill children. Devlin then offers his theory—that there is no real increase in child violence. The apparent increase is, in fact, caused by the liberal media "blowing the whole thing out of proportion." Devlin closes by urging the reader to think before jumping to conclusions about the causes of teenage violence.

SUMMARY NO. 2

Dudley Erskine Devlin's editorial, "Children and Violence in America," attempts to refute the claims of some people that violence on television and in movies leads to violence involving young people in real life. Devlin also argues against the idea that family instability, drugs, and poverty cause violence among young Americans. While Devlin agrees that "possibly there is some TV and movie violence that adds to the culture of violence in America," he argues that the media has "actually invented this epidemic of violence" to "frighten the public" and thus sell their stories. In actuality, Devlin claims, there is no problem with violence among young people in America. It is just something made up by the media to promote business.

RESPONSE SHAPING

Strategies for organizing a response depend on the purpose for the response. Typically, responses combine several of the following three purposes:

- Analyzing the effectiveness of the text.
- Agreeing and/or disagreeing with the ideas in the text.
- Interpreting and reflecting on the text.

As the following explanations illustrate, each of these types of responses requires supporting evidence from the text, from other texts, and/or from the writer's own experience.

ANALYZING   Analysis requires dividing a whole into its parts in order to better understand the whole. In order to analyze a text for its effectiveness, start by examining key parts or features of the text, such as the purpose, the intended audience, the thesis and main ideas, the organization and evidence, and the language and style. Notice how the following paragraph analyzes Devlin's illogical use of *evidence.*

> Devlin's essay has some clear problems with supporting evidence. In one case, his evidence does not support his argument, and in another the evidence he gives refutes his main point. In Devlin's opening paragraph, two of his examples involve shooting *accidents,* not violent crimes. The boy who accidently shot his friend and the boy who accidentally shot his sister did not commit "violent crimes." To support his point in the first paragraph, Devlin needs examples showing children as victims and perpetrators of violent crime. Another obvious problem with supporting evidence occurs later in the essay. Devlin argues in paragraph 4 that TV and movie violence is not a major cause of teenage violence, but then he goes on to cite several convincing examples and statistics linking TV shows and movies with violence. In

this case, Devlin gives plenty of evidence, but it supports the argument that he dismisses both in this paragraph and at the end of the essay.

AGREEING/DISAGREEING   Often, a response to a text focuses on agreeing and/or disagreeing with its major ideas. Responses may agree completely, disagree completely, or agree with some points but disagree with others. Responses that agree with some ideas but disagree with others are often more effective because they show that the responder sees both strengths and weaknesses in an argument. In the following paragraphs, notice how the responder agrees and disagrees and then supports each judgment with evidence.

> I agree with the author that the news media blow many stories out of proportion. It seems that every time I see a story about a child-related violent crime on the news, I am always told to stay tuned for more information. They keep going back to the same reporter, giving the same information. They usually have a special "follow-up report" on the next night. The more violent the crime, the more attention it gets. For example, if there is a high-speed chase involving a teenager, it will be mentioned on the news. If the chase ends in a crash, however, the story will be repeated in depth for several days. The media can stretch one incident into a crime story that lasts all week. The media always dwell on the bad. If news stories mention a teenager on a good note, it is shown just once, not shown or reprinted the rest of the week.

> I have to disagree with the author as well. Violent TV shows can lead to an increase in violent crimes. To see the effects of violent movies, you don't have to look any farther than the toy store or your local Wal-Mart. For every movie such as *RoboCop* or *Terminator 2,* there is a new line of violent toys. As children grow up playing with these toys, they begin associating violent objects with fun. As they grow older, they begin looking for more violent "toys." Pretty soon you have a 16-year-old kid holding a real 9-mm pistol to his best friend's head.

INTERPRETING AND REFLECTING   Many responses contain interpretations of passages that might be read from different points of view or reflections on the assumptions or implications of an idea. An interpretation says, "Here is what the text says, but let me explain what it means, what assumptions the argument carries, or what the implications might be." Here is a paragraph from an interpretive response to Devlin's essay on children and violence:

> Finally, Devlin's closing line about Lucy hitting Charlie Brown really made me stop and think. Statistics show that 90 percent of domestic violence is perpetrated by men, not women. This example helped me realize that the real problem of violence goes deeper than the media. TV and movies only reflect a deeper culture of sexism in America. Movies constantly depict knifings and rapes and murders, most of them against women. Men will accept violence in the media as long as it's played out against women and children, but never, never against themselves. The movie "Thelma and Louise" created a firestorm of controversy simply because it showed a woman shooting a rapist. Until the day comes when women and children are treated as equals to men, and not their property, there will be violence in this country.

OUTLINES FOR SUMMARY/RESPONSE ESSAYS

Three common outlines for summary/response essays are as follows. Select or modify one of these outlines to fit your audience, purpose, and kind of response. Typically, a summary/response will take the following form:

- **I.**   Introduction to text(s)
- **II.**   Summary of text(s)
- **III.**   Response(s)
  - **A.**   Point 1
  - **B.**   Point 2
  - **C.**   Point 3, etc.
- **IV.**   Conclusion

A second kind of outline, illustrated by Quammen's essay in the chapter, focuses initially on key ideas or issues and then examines the text or texts for their contribution to these key ideas. This outline begins with the issues, then summarizes the text(s), and then moves to the reader's responses:

- **I.**   Introduction to key issues
- **II.**   Summary of relevant text(s)

III. Response(s)
- **A.** Point 1
- **B.** Point 2
- **C.** Point 3, etc.

IV. Conclusion

A third outline integrates the summary and the response. It begins by introducing the issue and/or the text, gives a brief overall idea of the text, but then summarizes and responds point-by-point.

I. Introduction to issues and/or text(s)

II. Summary of text's point 1/response to point 1

III. Summary of text's point 2/response to point 2

IV. Summary of text's point 3/response to point 3, etc.

V. Conclusion

DRAFTING

If you have been reading actively, you have been writing throughout the reading/writing/discussing process. At some point, however, you will gather your best ideas, have a rough direction or outline in mind, and begin writing a draft. Some writers like to have their examples and evidence ready when they begin drafting. Many writers have outlines in their heads or on paper. Perhaps you like to put your rough outline on the computer and then just expand each section as you write. Finally, most writers like to skim the text and *reread their notes* immediately before they start their drafts, just to make sure everything is fresh in their minds.

Once you start drafting, keep interruptions to a minimum. Because focus and concentration are important to good writing, try to keep writing as long as possible. If you come to a spot where you need an example that you don't have at your fingertips, just put a parentheses—(put the example about cosmetics and animal abuse here)—and keep on writing. Concentrate on making all your separate responses add up to a focused, overall response.

REVISING

Revision means, literally, *reseeing*. Revising requires rereading the text and rewriting your summary and response. While revision begins as you read and reread the text, it continues until—and sometimes after—you turn in a paper or send it to its intended audience.

A major step in your revision is receiving responses from peer readers and deciding on a revision plan, based on the feedback. Use the following guidelines as you read your peer's papers and respond to their advice.

PEER RESPONSE

The instructions below will help you give and receive constructive advice about the rough draft of your investigating essay. You may use these guidelines for an in-class workshop, a take-home review, or a computer e-mail response.

Writer: Before you exchange drafts with another reader, write out the following information about your own rough draft:

1. On your draft, *label* the parts that are summary and the parts that are your own response.

2. *Underline* the sentence(s) that signal to the reader that you are shifting from objective summary to personal response.

3. Explain *one or two problems* that you are having with this draft that you want your reader to comment on.

Reader: Without making any comments, read the *entire* draft from start to finish. As you *reread* the draft, answer the following questions.

1. Review the guidelines for writing summaries. Has the writer remained *objective* in his or her summary? Does the summary *omit* any key ideas? Does the writer use *author tags* frequently and accurately? Can you clearly understand the main ideas of the article? Is the summary written in language appropriate for the intended audience?

2. Review the guidelines for writing responses. What type(s) of response is the writer using? In the margin, label the types. What kinds of evidence does the writer use in support of his or her response? In the margin, label the kinds of supporting evidence. Is this response addressed appropriately to the audience?

3. In your own words, state the main idea or the focus that organizes the writer's response.

4. Write out your own reactions to the writer's response. Where do you disagree with the writer's analysis or interpretation? Explain.

5. Answer the writer's questions in number 3, above.

Guidelines for Revision

- **Review the purpose and audience for your assignment.** Is your draft addressed to the appropriate audience? Does it fulfill its intended purpose?
- **Continue to use your active reading/writing/discussing activities as you revise your draft.** If you are uncertain about parts of your summary or response, reread the text, check your notes, or discuss your draft with a classmate.
- **Reread your summary for key features.** Make sure your summary indicates author and title, cites main ideas, uses an occasional direct quotation, and includes author tags. Check your summary for accuracy and objectivity.
- **Check paraphrases and direct quotations.** If you are paraphrasing (without quotation marks), you should put the author's ideas into your own language. If you are quoting directly, make sure the words within the quotation marks are accurate, word-for-word transcriptions.
- **Review the purpose of your response.** Are you analyzing, agreeing/disagreeing, interpreting, or some combination of all three? Do your types of responses fit the assignment or address your intended audience and satisfy your purpose?
- **Amplify your supporting evidence.** Summary/response drafts often need additional, relevant evidence. Be sure you use sufficient personal experience, evidence from the text, or examples from other texts to support your response.
- **Focus on a clear, overall response.** Your responses should all add up to a focused, overall reaction. Delete or revise any passages that do not maintain your focus.
- **Revise sentences to improve clarity, conciseness, emphasis, and variety.** (See Handbook.)
- **Edit your final version.** Use the spell check on your computer. Have a friend help proofread. Check your Handbook for suspected problems in usage, grammar, and punctuation.

■ POSTSCRIPT ON THE WRITING PROCESS

1. As you finish your essay, what questions do you still have about how to summarize? What questions do you have about writing a good response?

2. Which paragraphs in your response contain your most effective supporting evidence? What kinds of evidence (analysis of the text, evidence from other texts, or personal experience) did you use?

3. What sentences in your response contain your overall reaction to the text?

4. If you had one more day to work on your essay, what would you change? Why?

5. What did you learn about reading that you applied to the writing of this essay? Where in your essay did you help your reader to make accurate predictions? Where did you use supporting evidence that might trigger your reader's prior knowledge?

READING: STUDENT WRITING

DRAWING THE LINE

Paula Fisher

Paula Fisher, from Salt Lake City, Utah, wrote her essay while she was an occupational therapy major at Colorado State University. She chose to write a summary/response to David Quammen's essay, "Animal Rights and Beyond," because she could draw on her own personal experiences, both in an animal rights course and in cattle ranching. While reading the essay and making notes for her double-entry log, which follows, Fisher says that she "specifically noticed that Quammen failed to present the anti-animal rights issue, a perspective I am familiar with, since all of my mother's side of the family are involved with cattle farming." As you read her essay, see if she clearly summarizes Quammen's essay and then supports her response with examples from her experience.

Fisher's writing process was to read the essay carefully and make notes on her copy of the essay. Then, working on her computer, she used the Rereading Guide to make a double-entry log. Once she completed the double-entry log, she completely drafted her essay. Reprinted below are her double-entry log and her final version.

Double-Entry Log: Notes from Rereading Guide

DESCRIPTION	RESPONSES
I. Audience	
• Begins with questions for the reader. Audience is readers of *Outside* magazine, so they're probably pro-animal rights.	• Questions make beginning interesting.

II. Thesis and Main Ideas

- Thesis: Animal rights is a complex issue with no easy answers.
- Talks about history of animal rights. Talks about Singer's and Regan's views.
- Singer: Greatest good for greatest number.
- Can animals suffer? Where is the boundary?
- Regan—Abuse wrong in essence. Argues for "inherent value" "mentally normal animals of 1 year or more"
- Quammen's responses, positive and negative:
  Positive—they're fighting the good fight
  Negative—they're too smug.
- They think everyone should be vegetarians.
- They are still chauvanistic—"How similar to human is similar enough?" Where do we draw the line?
- Doesn't everything have value?
- Quammen says man should not be the measure, since "Life is life."

- Difficult to pick out thesis—for me.
- Where is the boundary between those who suffer and those who don't—oysters? Quammen's references to issues in animal rights are vague or missing.

- My own experience—LD 50, humane society, cosmetics, animal testing, grad students, medical testing, farming
- What about the mentally retarded?

- I had to read several times to grasp the references to "carrots," etc.

- I agree that issues are complex, but he ignores legitimate uses of farm animals and medical testing.
- No rebuttal at end?

III. Organization and Evidence

- No preview of ideas
- New sections signaled by extra space

- What about anti-animal rights—he has no fair mention.

IV. Language and Style

- Tone is humorous, casual.
- Tad sarcastic, but well explained.

- Gordian reference—didn't know Righteous gumbo—good metaphor

V. Purpose

- Purpose to explain Singer's and Regan's ideas and give his responses. He wants to make us see animal rights as a complex issue.

- Succeeded in purpose.

DRAWING THE LINE

In David Quammen's essay, "Animal Rights and Beyond," he discusses the issue of animal rights, taking the stance that it is a "serious philosophical issue" with no quick answers and serious implications for the way humans should live. Quammen, a nature column writer for *Outside,* briefly presents the historical anti-animal rights view, but quickly dismisses it. He goes on to discuss the writings of Peter Singer, an important animal rights advocate. Singer is willing to grant rights to animals that suffer, concluding that anything below an oyster doesn't. Quammen next discusses Tom Regan's philosophy. Regan asserts that animals have rights because they have inherent value, but is only willing to grant this value to mentally normal mammals. Quammen first commends these authors for their willingness to take a stance on this issue, but he also reprimands them for their lack of vision. According to Quammen, "man is still the measure" for these two authors. They simply changed the question from "Is the creature human?" to "How similar to human is enough?" **(1)**

I think that Quammen makes an excellent point in his essay: Animal rights is not an issue that has black or white answers. Gray areas exist everywhere. Quammen asserts that animal rights is an "important and tricky" issue that needs to be thought out carefully. His purpose seems to be to make his readers think. This particular essay was published in an environmental magazine that probably has many readers who advocate animal rights. Quammen seems to be challenging them to consider why they believe in animal rights. Is it because of complicated philosophical arguments or simply because "life is life"? Either way, he asserts, and I agree, that it is a difficult issue. **(2)**

When Quammen comments on Singer's and Regan's theories, he compliments them for "fighting a good fight." He asserts that they are focusing attention on "outrageous practices" that are commonplace throughout America. Not only are they writing about it, they are exclaiming, "Let's stop it!" I see this as an important distinction. Tests that blatantly mistreat animals, such as the LD-50 test, where a large number of animals are given a substance until 50 percent of them die, is cruel and wasteful. It often serves no other purpose than to be another figure in a scientist's logbook. Purposeless experiments by graduate students and brutal practices by some American farmers and cosmetic companies also need to be examined and controlled. **(3)**

On the other hand, issues from the anti-animal rights point of view also need to be carefully considered and weighed. This is an issue that Quammen fails to address fairly and realistically. One of the major issues involves the use of animals in medical research. Where does one draw the line between animal suffering and human suffering? The use of animals in medical research can and has helped scientists make breakthroughs that have saved human lives. I would have a hard time looking someone in the eye and saying, "You can't have a cure for cancer because some rats would have to die." It is not an issue that I can easily resolve for myself, and I contend it needs careful analysis and review. **(4)**

Another dilemma emerges when considering the rights of farmers versus the rights of farm animals. I come from a long line of cattle farmers, people whose livelihood revolves around raising animals. It's true, some practices are cruel and unnecessary and need to be regulated, but once again we need to consider where the farmers' rights end and the animals' rights begin. **(5)**

All things considered, I believe that Quammen makes a good claim. The issue of animal rights is truly a complex and complicated issue with no easy answers; if we carry animal rights too far, we won't be able to walk for fear of stepping on an ant, but if we don't consider animal rights we are blind and allowing cruel and inhumane practices to continue. **(6)**

QUESTIONS FOR WRITING AND DISCUSSION

1. Reread David Quammen's article and make your own double-entry log. On the left-hand side of a piece of paper, record Quammen's main points; on the right-hand side, write your own questions and reactions. Compare your notes to Fisher's summary/response. How would you advise Fisher to revise her summary to make it more complete and accurate? What suggestions would you make about revising her response?

2. Supporting evidence in a summary/response may take the form of analysis of passages from the text, references to ideas or facts from outside texts, or specific examples from personal experience. Find examples of all three kinds of evidence in Fisher's essay. Which did she use most effectively?

3. Compare Fisher's notes in her double-entry log with her final essay. Which of those notes appears in her final version? Which do not? What ideas from her double-entry log would you suggest including or omitting in her final version? Explain your choices.

4. Using Quammen's article, Fisher's response, your class discussion, and your own ideas and experiences, write your own essay on the uses of animals in medical research. Should animals be used to develop cosmetics? To study neurotic behavior? To find a cure for cancer? Where would you draw the line—and why?

Two Responses to Deborah Tannen

Jennifer Koester and Sonja H. Browe

The two essays reprinted here are written in response to an essay by Deborah Tannen, "How Male and Female Students Use Language Differently," which appears in Chapter 7. Jennifer Koester and Sonja Browe have opposite responses to Tannen's essay. Jennifer Koester, a political science major at Colorado State University, argues that Tannen's essay is effective because she uses sufficient evidence and organizes her essay clearly. On the other hand, Sonja Browe, an English education major at the University of Wyoming, writes an essay that is critical of Deborah Tannen's focus and supporting evidence. Be sure to read Tannen's essay and decide for yourself before you read the following essays.

A Response to Deborah Tannen's Essay

Jennifer Koester

Deborah Tannen's "How Male and Female Students Use Language Differently" addresses how male and female conversational styles influence classroom discussions. Tannen asserts that women speak less than men in class because often the structure of discussion is more "congenial" to men's style of conversing. **(1)**

Tannen looks at three differences between the sexes that shape classroom interaction: classroom setting, debate format, and contrasting attitudes toward classroom discussion. First, Tannen says that during childhood, men "are expected to seize center stage: by exhibiting their skill, displaying their knowledge, and challenging and resisting challenge." Thus, as adults, men are more comfortable than women when speaking in front of a large group of strangers. On the other hand, women are more comfortable in small groups. **(2)**

Second, men are more comfortable with the debate format. Tannen asserts that many classrooms use the format of putting forth ideas followed by "argument and challenge." This too coincides with men's conversational experiences. However, Tannen asserts that women tend to "resist discussion they perceive as hostile." **(3)**

Third, men feel it is their duty to think of things to say and to voice them. On the other hand, women often regulate their participation and hold back to avoid dominating discussion. **(4)**

Tannen concludes that educators can no longer use just one format to facilitate classroom discussion. Tannen sees small groups as necessary for any "non-seminar" class along with discussion of differing styles of participation as solutions to the participation gap between the sexes. **(5)**

Three things work together to make Deborah Tannen's essay "How Male and Female Students Use Language Differently" effective: qualifications of her argument, evidence used, and the parallel format of comparison/contrast. **(6)**

First, Tannen's efforts to qualify her argument prevents her from committing logical errors. In the first paragraphs of her essay, she states, "This is not to say that all men talk in class, nor that no women do. It is simply that a greater percentage of discussion time is taken by men's voices." By acknowledging exceptions to her claim, Tannen avoids the mistake of oversimplification. She also strengthens her argument because this qualification tells the reader that she is aware of the complexity of this issue. **(7)**

Later, Tannen uses another qualification. She says, "No one's conversational style is absolute; everyone's style changes in response to the context and others' styles." Not only does this qualification avoid a logical fallacy, but it also strengthens Tannen's argument that classroom discussion must have several formats. By acknowledging that patterns of participation can change with the setting, Tannen avoids oversimplifying the issue and adds to her argument for classroom variety. **(8)**

Second, Tannen's evidence places a convincing argument before her reader. In the beginning of her essay, Tannen states that a greater percentage of discussion time in class is taken by men and that those women who attend single-sex schools tend to do better later in life. These two pieces of evidence present the reader with Tannen's jumping off point. These statistics are what Tannen wants to change. **(9)**

In addition, Tannen effectively uses anecdotal evidence. She presents the reader with stories from her colleagues and her own research. These stories are taken from the classroom, a place which her audience, as educators, are familiar with. Her anecdotal evidence is persuasive because it appeals to the common sense and personal experiences of the audience. While some might question the lack of hard statistics throughout the entire essay, the anecdotal evidence serves Tannen best because it reminds her audience of educators of their own experiences. When she reminds the audience of their experiences, she is able to make them see her logic. **(10)**

Third, the parallel format of comparison/contrast between the genders highlights for the reader Tannen's main points. Each time Tannen mentions the reactions of one gender she follows with the reaction of the other gender. For example, Tannen states, "So one reason men speak in class more than women is that many of them find the "public" classroom setting more conducive to speaking, whereas most women are more comfortable speaking in private to a small group of people they know well." Here, Tannen places the tendencies of men and of women together, thus preventing the reader from having to constantly refer back to another section of the essay. **(11)**

In an earlier example, Tannen discusses men's comfort with the debate format in class discussion. The majority of that paragraph relates why men feel comfortable with that format. After explaining this idea, Tannen then tells the reader how women feel about the debate structure. By placing how men and women feel about the debate format within a paragraph, the readers easily see the difference between the genders. Tannen's use of the parallel format in the above examples and the rest of the essay provides a clear explanation of the differences in men's and women's interactions in the classroom. **(12)**

Tannen writes her essay effectively. She makes the essay convincing by qualifying her claims about gender participation. This strengthens her argument that just as the classroom is diverse, so should the format be diverse. Her supporting evidence is convincing because it comes from Tannen's own experience, reminds the audience of its own experiences, and appeals to the audience's common sense. Finally, her parallel format for discussing the differences between men and women enhances the reader's understanding. Overall, Tannen's essay is effective because she qualifies her argument, uses convincing evidence, and makes clear how men and women use language differently through a parallel comparison/contrast format. **(13)**

IS DEBORAH TANNEN CONVINCING?

Sonja H. Browe

In her article entitled "How Male and Female Students Use Language Differently," Deborah Tannen explores the issue of gender as it affects the way we use language to communicate. Specifically, she discusses how differences in the way males and females are socialized to use language affects their classroom interactions. She explains that as females are growing up, they learn to use language to talk to friends, and to tell secrets. She states that for females, it is the "telling of secrets, the fact and the way they talk to each other, that makes them best friends." Boys, on the other hand, are "expected to use language to seize center stage: by exhibiting their skill, displaying their knowledge, and challenging and resisting challenge." **(1)**

According to Tannen, these differences make classroom language use more conducive to the way males were taught to use language. Tannen suggests that speaking in front of groups and the debatelike formats used in many classrooms are more easily handled by male students. **(2)**

Finally, Tannen describes an experiment she conducted in her own classroom which allowed students to evaluate their own conversation transcripts. From this experience, she deduced that small-group interaction is essential in the classroom because it gives students who don't participate in whole class settings the opportunity for conversation and interaction. **(3)**

Though Tannen's research is a worthwhile consideration and provides information which could be of great interest to educators, this particular article lacks credibility and is unfocused. The points she is trying to make get lost in a world of unsupported assertions and she strays from her main focus, leaving the reader hanging and confused. **(4)**

Tannen does take some time at the beginning of her article to establish her authority on linguistic analysis, but we may still hold her accountable for supporting her assertions with evidence. However, Tannen makes sweeping declarations throughout the essay, expecting the reader to simply accept them as fact. For example, when discussing the practice of the teacher playing devil's advocate and debating with the students, she states that "many, if not most women would shrink from such a challenge, experiencing it as public humiliation." Following such an assertion, we expect to see some evidence. Who did Tannen talk to? What did they say? What percentage of women felt this way? This sort of evidence is completely lacking, making what Tannen states as fact to appear more like conjecture. **(5)**

Tannen makes another such unsupported pronouncement when she discusses the debatelike formats used in many classrooms. She explains that in contrast to males, this type of classroom interaction is in opposition to the way that females approach learning. She states that "it is not that females don't fight, but that they don't fight for fun. They don't ritualize opposition." Again, where is Tannen's evidence to support such a claim? **(6)**

When Tannen does bother to support her assertions, her evidence is trite and unconvincing. For example, she reviews Walter Ong's work on the pursuit of knowledge, in which he suggested that "ritual opposition . . . is fundamental to the way males approach almost any activity." Tannen supports this claim of Ong's in parentheses, saying, "Consider, for example, the little boy who shows he likes a little girl by pulling her braids and shoving her." This statement may serve as an example, but is not enough to convince the reader that ritual opposition is fundamental to the way males approach "almost any activity." **(7)**

Other evidence which Tannen uses to support her declarations comes in the form of conversations she has had with colleagues on these issues. Again, though these may provide examples, they do not represent a broad enough data base to support her claims. **(8)**

Finally, Tannen takes three pages of her article to describe in detail an experiment she conducted in her classroom. Though the information she collected from this experiment was interesting, it strayed from the main point of the essay. Originally, Tannen's article was directed specifically at gender differences in communication. In this classroom activity, she looks at language-use differences in general, including cultural differences. She states that some people may be more comfortable in classes where you are expected to raise your hand to speak, while others prefer to be able to talk freely. She makes no mention of gender in regard to this issue. **(9)**

Finally, at the close of her essay when we can expect to get the thrust of her argument or at least some sort of summary statement which ties into her main thesis, Tannen states that her experience in her classroom convinced her that "small-group interaction should be a part of any classroom" and that "having students become observers of their own interaction is a crucial part of their education." Again, these are interesting points, but they stray quite a bit from the original intention of the article. **(10)**

In this article, Tannen discusses important issues with which those of us who will be interacting with students in the classroom should be aware. However, her article loses a great deal of its impact because she does not stay focused on her original thesis and fails to support her ideas with convincing evidence. **(11)**

QUESTIONS FOR WRITING AND DISCUSSION

1. Do your own double-entry log for Tannen's essay (see Chapter 7). On the left-hand side of a piece of paper, record Tannen's main points. On the right-hand side, write your own questions and reactions. Compare your notes to Koester's and Browe's responses. Whose response most closely matches your own? Where or how does your response differ from each?

2. Koester and Browe use different strategies for writing their summaries of Tannen's essay. Describe how the two summaries are different. Which summary is more accurate? Why?

3. Responses to texts may analyze the effectiveness of the text, agree or disagree with the ideas in the text, and/or interpret or reflect on the text. What kinds of responses do Koester and Browe give? Would a different kind of response work better for either writer? Why or why not?

4. Koester focuses on three writing strategies that Tannen uses to make her essay more effective. What are they? What weaknesses of Tannen's essay does Koester ignore or downplay?

5. Browe's response focuses on two criticisms of Tannen's essay. What are they? In which paragraphs does Browe develop each criticism? What strengths of Tannen's essay does Browe ignore or downplay?

6. Neither Browe nor Koester uses personal experience as supporting evidence. Think of one experience that you have had in a specific class illustrating the conversational preferences of men and

women. Write out that specific example. Could either Browe or Koester use such a specific example? Where might each writer use it in her response?

7. Reread the essays by Tannen, Koester, and Browe. Review your reactions with your classmates. Then write your own summary and response. In your response, mention both the strengths and weaknesses of Tannen's article. Then indicate whether or not you found Tannen's essay, in general, thought-provoking or convincing.

6 INVESTIGATING

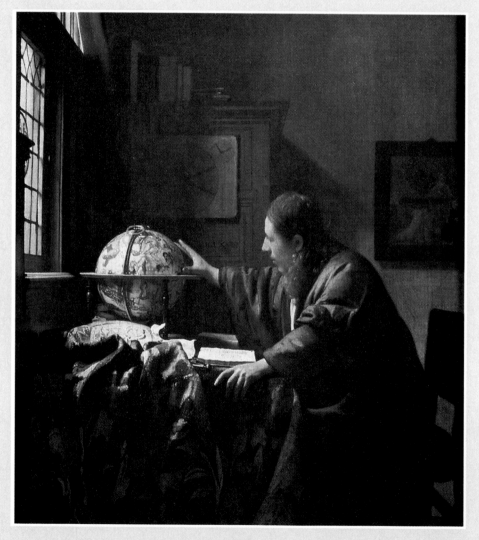

Vermeer van Delft, Jan (1632–1675) *The Astronomer.* Oil on canvas (1668)
31.5 x 45.5 cm. Louvre, Dep. de Peintures, Paris, France

YOUR BOSS AT THE LOCAL SELF-SERVICE GAS STATION WANTS TO EXPAND THE STATION'S RANGE OF CONVENIENCE ITEMS. CURRENTLY, YOU SELL ONLY SNACKS, such as soda pop, candy, and ice cream. Your boss asks you to find out what is sold at other gas-station convenience stores. Next, she wants you to design a survey for your customers, asking which items they would like to have the station carry. After tabulating questionnaires from thirty-five customers, you write a short report for the boss outlining what the competition stocks, how you designed your questionnaire, and what the responses from your customers indicate.

❧

WHILE WATCHING JOGGERS RUNNING IN THE PARK ONE DAY, YOU NOTICE THEIR STRAINING MUSCLES, THEIR LABORED BREATHING, AND THE GRIMACES ETCHED ON their faces. Why, you wonder, do people go through the pain of running? Does it have a physical or a psychological benefit? Or can it even become an addiction for those people who *have* to run every day? You decide to investigate this question in runners' magazines and professional journals and then interview a few serious runners to determine their motives and the effects that running has on them, both physically and psychologically. The results of your report, you hope, will prove interesting to those who run as well as to those who merely watch others run.

When you stop learning, stop listening, stop looking and asking questions, always new questions, then it is time to die.
—LILLIAN SMITH,
CIVIL RIGHTS ACTIVIST, JOURNALIST, AUTHOR OF <u>KILLERS OF THE DREAM</u>

❧

As the free press develops, the paramount point is whether the journalist, like the scientist or scholar, puts truth in the first place or in the second.
—WALTER LIPPMANN,
JOURNALIST AND AUTHOR

I NVESTIGATING BEGINS WITH QUESTIONS. WHAT CAUSES THE GREENHOUSE EFFECT? HOW DOES ILLITERACY AFFECT A PERSON'S LIFE? HOW WAS THE WORLD WIDE WEB CREATED? HOW DOES RAPE affect the lives of women in America? How do colleges recruit applicants? What can you find out about a famous person's personality, background, and achievements? At what age do children first acquire simple mathematical abilities? What kind of employee is most likely to be promoted? Why are sunsets yellow, then orange, red, and finally purple?

Investigating also carries an assumption that probing for answers to such questions—by observing and remembering, researching sources, interviewing key people, or conducting surveys—will uncover truths not generally known or accepted. As you dig for information, you learn *who, what, where,* and *when.* You may even learn *how* and *why.*

The purpose of investigating is to uncover or discover facts, opinions, and reactions for yourself and then to *report* that information to other people who want to know. A report strives to be as objective and informative as possible. It may summarize other people's judgments, but it does not editorialize. It may represent opposing viewpoints or arguments, but it does not argue for one side or the other. A report is a window on the world, allowing readers to see the information for themselves.

Curiosity is my natural state and has led me headlong into every worthwhile experience . . . I have ever had.

—ALICE
WALKER,
AUTHOR OF
THE COLOR PURPLE

TECHNIQUES FOR
INVESTIGATIVE WRITING

Investigative writing begins with asking questions and finding informed sources: published material, knowledgeable people, or both. In most cases, collecting information in an investigation requires the ability to use a library and then to summarize, paraphrase, and quote key ideas accurately from other people's writing. In addition, personal interviews are often helpful or necessary. For an investigation, you might talk to an expert or an authority, an eyewitness or participant in an event, or even the subject of a personality profile. Finally, you may wish to survey the general public to determine opinions, trends, or reactions. Once you have collected your information, you must then present your findings in a written form suitable for your audience, with clear references in the text to your sources of information.

Investigative writing uses the following techniques:

- **Beginning with an interesting title and a catchy lead sentence or paragraph.** The first few sentences arouse your readers' *interest* and focus their attention on the subject.

- **Giving background information by answering relevant who, what, when, where, and why questions.** Answering the *reporter's "Wh" questions* ensures that readers have sufficient information to understand your report.
- **Stating the main idea, question, or focus of the investigation.** The purpose of a report is to convey information as *clearly* as possible. Readers shouldn't have to guess the main idea.
- **Summarizing or quoting information from written or oral sources; citing sources in the text.** Quote *accurately* any statistics, data, or sentences from your sources. Cite authors and titles.
- **Writing in a readable and interesting style appropriate for the intended audience.** Clear, direct, and readable language is essential in a report. Use graphs and charts as appropriate.

The following reports illustrate three common types of investigative writing: the *summary* of a single book or article, the *investigation* of a controversial issue (using multiple sources), and the *profile* of a person. The three types may overlap (the investigation of a controversial issue may contain a personality profile, for instance), and all three types may use summaries of written material, questionnaires, and interviews. While some investigative reports are brief, intended to be only short news items, others are full-length features.

The intended audience for each report is often determined by the publication in which the report appears: *Psychology Today* assumes that its readers are interested in personality and behavior; *Discover* magazine is for readers interested in popular science; readers of *Ms.* magazine expect coverage of contemporary issues concerning women.

SUMMARY OF A BOOK OR ARTICLE

The following report from *Psychology Today,* by journalist Jeff Meer, summarizes information taken from an article by Charlene L. Muehlenhard and Melaney A. Linton that appeared in *Journal of Counseling Psychology.* Although the *Psychology Today* report summarizes only that one article, it demonstrates several key features of an investigative report.

Date Rape: Familiar Strangers

Attention-getting title

By now, everyone knows the scenario. Boy meets girl, they go to a party, get drunk, return to his apartment, and he forces her to have sex.

Lead-in paragraph

Most people assume that date rape occurs on a first or second date between relative strangers. But new research supports a different conclusion: The individuals involved generally know each other fairly well.

Focus of investigation or report

Who, what, where questions answered

Psychologist Charlene L. Muehlenhard and undergraduate Melaney A. Linton asked more than 600 college men and women about their most recent dates, as well as their worst experience with "sexual aggression"—any time a woman was forced to participate in acts, ranging from kissing to intercourse, against her will. More than three quarters of the women and more than half of the men admitted to having an experience with sexual aggression on a date, either

Summary of results

in high school or in college. And nearly 15 percent of the women and 7 percent of the men said they had intercourse against the woman's will.

The researchers found that when a man initiated the date, drove to and from and paid for the date, sexual aggression was more likely. They also found that if both people got drunk (at a party, for exam-

Summary of results

ple) and "parked," or found themselves in the man's dorm room or apartment, the date was more likely to end with the woman being forced to perform against her wishes. Men and women who thought of themselves as having traditional values and those who were more accepting of violence were also more likely to have been involved in date rape.

Summary of results

But contrary to what one might expect, date rape and sexual aggression were much more likely to happen between partners who knew each other. On average, students said they had known the partner almost a year before the incident. "If women were more aware of

Quotation

this, they might be less surprised and more prepared to deal with sexual aggression by someone they know well," Muehlenhard says.

Summary

She points out that communication is often a big problem on dates during which there is sexual aggression. Both men and women reported that the man had felt "led on" during such dates. Men said that women desired more sexual contact on these dates than had others on previous dates. Women said that they had desired less sexual contact than usual.

Quotation

Muehlenhard believes that a direct approach, such as a woman saying "I don't want to do anything more than kiss," might clear up confusion better than simply saying "No."

INVESTIGATION USING MULTIPLE SOURCES

Most investigative reports draw on multiple sources—books and articles, research studies, and interviews. The following article, which appeared in *Time* magazine has all the key features of an interesting investigative report.

The author, Anastasia Toufexis, focuses on the popular but controversial psychiatric drug Prozac. She catches our interest with personal case histories. She asks probing questions about the medical and psychological effects of the drug. She focuses her report on a best-selling book by Peter Kramer, but she also weaves in several interviews with other authorities on Prozac. Despite the controversial nature of her topic, however, Toufexis remains as neutral as possible. She presents the background information and lets the experts debate the issues so that her readers can judge for themselves.

THE PERSONALITY PILL

Susan Smith has everything going for her. A self-described workaholic, she runs a Cambridge, Massachusetts, real estate consulting company with her husband Charles and still finds time to cuddle and nurture their two young kids, David, 7, and Stacey, 6. What few people know is that Susan, 44, needs a little chemical help to be a supermom: she has been taking the antidepressant Prozac for five years.

Smith never had manic depression or any other severe form of mental illness. But before Prozac, she suffered from sharp mood swings, usually coinciding with her menstrual periods. "I would become highly emotional and sometimes very angry, and I really wasn't sure why I was angry," she recalls. Charles will never forget the time she threw her wedding band at him during a spat. Now, says Susan, "the lows aren't as low as they were. I'm more comfortable with myself." And she has no qualms about her long-term relationship with a psychoactive pill: "If there's a drug that makes you feel better, you use it."

Millions agree, making Prozac the hottest psychiatric drug in history. Since its introduction five years ago, 5 million Americans—and 10 million people worldwide—have used it. The drug is much more than a fad: it is a medical breakthrough that has brought unprecedented relief to many patients with severe depressions, phobias, obsessions and compulsions. But it is also increasingly used by people with milder problems, and its immense popularity is raising some unsettling questions. When should Prozac be prescribed? How does a doctor draw the line between illness and normal behavior? If you feel better after taking Prozac, were you ill before? When does drug therapy become drug abuse? Will Prozac become the medically approved feel-good drug, a cocaine substitute without the dangerous highs and lows?

At medical meetings or dinner parties, the talk turns more and more often to Prozac, and what frequently sets off the discussion is a provocative book about the drug—*Listening to Prozac: A Psychiatrist Explores Antidepressant Drugs and the Remaking of the Self* by Dr. Peter Kramer of Brown University. Having quickly become a must-read, the book has perched near the top of the best-seller lists for three months.

The author, who uses Prozac in his private practice, is both impressed by the drug and uneasy about what its widespread use may portend for human society. In case after case, he contends, Prozac does more than treat disease; it has the power to transform personality, instill self-confidence and enhance a person's performance at work and play. One of the patients profiled in the book, an architect named Sam, claims that the drug made him "better than well." His depression lifted, and he became more poised and thoughtful, with keener concentration and a more reliable memory than ever before. Prozac, writes Kramer, seems "to give social confidence to the habitually timid, to make the sensitive brash, to lend the introvert the social skills of a salesman."

The psychiatrist maintains that the power of Prozac challenges basic assumptions about the origins and uniqueness of individual personalities. They may be less the result of experiences and more a matter of brain chemistry. If temperament lies in a tablet, is there an essential, immutable Self? Ultimately, Kramer muses, society could enter a new era of "cosmetic psychopharmacology," in which changing personality traits may be as simple as shampooing in a new hair color. "Since you only live once, why not do it as a blond?" he asks, and "why not as a peppy blond?" Already, pharmaceutical houses are churning out a whole new class of similar drugs, including Paxil and Zoloft, that mimic the effects of Prozac.

So what makes Prozac any different from all the other popular mood-altering potions down through history, from alcohol, opium and marijuana to widely prescribed "mother's little helpers" such as Librium and Valium? Unlike the typical street drug, which sends people soaring and then crashing, Prozac has an effect that is even and sustained. And it seems safer and has fewer bothersome side effects than previous medicines prescribed to lift people out of depression. Prozac is what scientists call a "clean" drug. Instead of playing havoc with much of the brain's chemistry, the medication has a very specific effect: it regulates the level of serotonin, a crucial compound that carries messages between nerve cells. "Prozac makes people feel different without making them feel drugged," notes Kramer.

Patients don't all react the same way, of course; some don't feel a bit better. And many psychiatrists and patients don't agree with Kramer about the drug's transformative powers. "I have my ability to not snap at people back, my energy back," notes a rabbi who recently started taking Prozac for mild depression. But, he adds, "I don't feel like Superman, and I still can't stand parties."

"There's a lot less than meets the eye with Prozac," says Dr. Daniel Auerbach of the Veterans Health Administration in Sepulveda, California. "Nothing changes personality. What gets changed is symptoms of a disease." In other words, Prozac enables a person's true personality, often imprisoned by illness, to come out. Contends Dr. Hyla Cass, a psychiatrist in Santa Monica, California: "I don't think Prozac is manipulating people, turning them into feel-goods. It is correcting an imbalance, allowing people to be who they can be."

But, counters Kramer, doesn't that broaden the boundaries of mental illness to include any condition that responds to Prozac? If a person responds to an antidepressant, does that necessarily mean that he or she is suffering from depression? Kramer questions whether the "imbalances" cured by the drug are always bad; maybe they are just frowned upon by current society. Are the vivacity and blithe spirits often produced by Prozac superior to shyness and a touch of melancholy? Do decisiveness and vigor have more merit than reticence and calmness? Should a business executive who lacks aggressiveness feel compelled to take a pill?

Most psychiatrists argue that while Prozac may be abused, it is still a long way from being overused. A study by the National Institute of Mental Health shows that 40% to 50% of people with major depression are not receiving any kind of therapy.

With so many still going untreated, Kramer's book may do a service by alerting some of them to Prozac's potential benefits. But Kramer may also be raising expectations too high. Says Dr. Glen Gabbard, director of the Menninger Memorial Hospital in Topeka, Kansas: "We should not send patients rushing to their corner pharmacy in hopes of getting a magic chemical that will solve all their problems." For most people, happiness does not come packaged in a pill.

PROFILE OF A PERSON

The following passage is a *profile* of a person—a biographical sketch intended to give a sense of the person's appearance, behavior, character, and accomplishments. These paragraphs are part of a profile of Oprah Winfrey written by journalist Joan Barthel for *Ms.* magazine.

Here Comes Oprah!

A profile of Oprah Winfrey is not just the story of a survivor, though she obviously is one: besides that bottom-line day five years ago [when she wrote a suicide note], she's survived early adolescent years so troubled that she became a runaway and was nearly placed in a juvenile detention home.

Nor is it just a success story of a black woman who's made it in the white man's world of network television, though she's done that, too. At 19, she was anchoring the news in Nashville—the first woman, the first black. She worked for seven years in Baltimore, first paying her dues as a TV street reporter, "hating every minute of it," especially when she was required to ask a woman who'd just lost her children and her house in a fire how she felt. (When she didn't have the heart to do that piece, her boss told her to get it or lose her job. She came back to the studio with the story and, on the air live, apologized for it.) She did everything she was told, including trying to remake herself. "They told me my nose was too wide, my hair too thick and long, and they sent me to a place in New York to get my first perm. I felt the lotion burning my skull, and I kept saying, 'Excuse me, this is beginning to burn a little.' They kept saying, 'Oh, just a few more minutes.'" Within a week all her hair had fallen out. "You learn a lot about yourself when you're bald," she says now.

Nor is it even a rags-to-riches tale, though her dazzling condominium apartment (marble floors, four baths, including one with a gold swan as the tub faucet and another with adjoining sauna) is a glamorous world apart from the Milwaukee housing project where she spent part of her childhood. "I don't think of myself as a poor deprived ghetto girl who made good," she declares. "I think of myself as somebody who from an early age knew I was responsible for myself, and I *had* to make good."

Knowing did not always mean doing, though. Which is why a profile of Oprah Winfrey is, mostly, a look at a woman in process.

■ **WARMING UP: JOURNAL EXERCISES** The following exercises will help you practice investigative writing. Read all of the following exercises and then, in your journal, write on the three that interest you most. One of these exercises may suggest an idea for your investigating essay.

1. Write an "authority" list of topics about which you have some expertise or information. Consider your hobbies, academic interests, occupational skills, social problems, community concerns, art, sports, travel, animals, films, TV shows, and so forth. Jot down a few words or phrases indicating what you know about each item on your list. Emphasize what or who it is, how it happens or how to do it, and when or where it happens. Because one of these topics may develop into an essay for this course, spend at least fifteen minutes on this exercise.

2. Page through the notebooks and texts from another course you are currently taking. What subjects mentioned in class or referred to in the text might you investigate? Make a list of topics for investigation that would help you in that course. During that class, jot down any other suggestions that occur to you. While the topics

should not be topics for essays already assigned in that course, they could relate to relevant background reading.

3. Find a recent issue of a magazine you like to read—*Time, Science Digest, Ebony, Newsweek, Sports Illustrated, Ms., Rolling Stone, Playboy, Glamour, Jet, New Yorker,* and so forth. Your purpose is to determine current trends in magazine advertising. Using only the full-page ads as your subject, collect at least three ads and take notes on their important features: use of color, design, personalities, sex appeal, slogans, technology, or whatever else recurs frequently. What conclusions about advertising trends can you draw from your investigations?

4. Next semester, you will be taking a course in your major field, but you aren't sure which professor you should pick. To investigate the differences among the teachers, interview several students who have taken this course from different professors. Prepare questions that encourage factual responses: How many papers or tests does the teacher require? What is the grade distribution? What textbook was required? What was the reading or homework load? What were typical lecture topics? Was the teacher available outside of class?

5. As a member of the student governing board, your job is to solicit student opinions about some aspect of campus life that needs improving. Choose a subject such as dorms, classes, the library, parking, student clubs, the film or fine art series, or recreational opportunities. Then choose a question to focus your investigation and write a one-page questionnaire that you might distribute to students. (See the section on writing questionnaires in this chapter.)

6. Watch an investigative news show such as *60 Minutes* or *Nightline,* taking notes about the interviewer's techniques. Is there a sequence to the questions—say, from gentle and polite to critical or controversial? What information does the interviewer have *before* the interview? Can you tell which questions are planned or scripted and which are spontaneous? After taking notes on a show, explain what you think are the *three* most important tips for successful interviewing.

7. Interview a classmate for a 200- to 250-word "personality profile." Your object is to profile this person and one of his or her major interests. First, in your daybook, prepare questions you need to ask for biographical information. Then, in an eight- to ten-minute interview, ask questions about the person and about several topics

from that person's "authority" list. After the interview, take two or three minutes to review your notes. At home, write up the results of your interview, which will appear in your local or campus newspaper.

8. Start your own curiosity list by logging on the World Wide Web and using your browser to locate topics you might be interested in. Build your curiosity list by adding a **bookmark** at each place you want to remember to check out. Choose either topics from your authority list (above), or just use the search engines on your computer to explore interesting topics. The Web is a great starting place to investigate a possible new topic.

If you are still unfamiliar with how the Internet and the Web work, check out the following brief article, "How the Web Works," by Gene Cowan.

HOW THE WEB WORKS

Gene Cowan

1. When you enter a URL, or Universal Resource Locator, into your web browser, your computer sends that address to a computer called a name server which breaks it down into its parts, much like a mailing address. The Internet sees upper and lower case letters as being different, so it's important to enter a URL exactly as directed.

http://www.ncss.org/online/wwwhome.html

↑ ↑ ↑

The *protocol*, or method the computer will use for transferring the data. HTTP is Hypertext Transfer Protocol. Other protocols include FTP and *gopher*.

The name of the computer containing the file you want. The address is always decoded in reverse. *org* means a non-profit organization in the United States. *ncss* is the name of the organization. *www* directs you to a specific area on the computer set aside for World Wide Web users.

Everything after the computer name is a directory path on that computer to the document you want. In this case, *online* is a folder called "online" in the *ncss.org* computer. "wwwhome.html" is a file in that folder. *html* stands for HyperText Markup Language, the format that web pages are written in.

2. With the address decoded, the name server sends your request to the specific computer on the Internet you have asked for, using the best route possible. Because the Internet is actually over 7 million computers, all connected together, your request may be routed through a computer in China or Nigeria to make it to Washington, DC.

3. When the destination computer receives your request, it first checks to see if you are allowed to have the file you asked for. If you are, it sends the file back over the Internet—but with a twist. In order to use the network with maximum efficiency, the computer splits the file up into small pieces called *packets*. These packets of information are sent back, often by completely different routes. One bit may be sent via Australia, and one bit via North Carolina. Each packet has a destination address attached, so it won't get lost.

4. Finally, after an excruciating wait of seconds, the requested data begins to arrive back at your computer, and is re-assembled from the packets to create a full file. Your web browser decodes the file and displays the information according to the instructions contained within the file. It continues to repeat the process as often as necessary for each graphic referenced in the web page.

Glossary

- **browser** A program that accesses the World Wide Web. A browser decodes and displays HTML documents.
- **domain** The last part of an Internet address, such as *.org* or *.com*, it tells where to begin looking for a specific computer.
- **FTP** File Transfer Protocol. A method of copying files from one computer to another.
- **gopher** A method of retrieving files from another computer—as in "go fer."
- **http** HyperText Transfer Protocol. A method of retrieving files that will be decoded by a web browser.
- **HTML** HyperText Markup Language. A method of writing text files with special codes that direct a web browser to format documents on the screen and create links to other documents.
- **name server** A computer that decodes addresses and sends messages on to the destination.
- **URL** Universal Resource Locator. The address of the file you are searching for. A URL tells the Internet the location of one specific file out of the billions available on the Internet.

INVESTIGATING:

PROFESSIONAL WRITING

PLOTTING A NET GAIN

Connie Koenenn

In this profile of sociologist and computer guru, Sherry Turkle, Los Angeles Times *staff writer Connie Koenenn gives her readers information on
Turkle's new book,* Life on the Screen: Identity in the Age of the
Internet, *as well as a perspectives on Turkle's private life. In writing this
profile, notice how Koenenn interweaves material from interviews with
Turkle, quotations and information from Turkle's book, information from
a radio interview, and personal observations about Turkle's lifestyle.*

Microsoft Chairman Bill Gates looks at the Internet and sees a transformation in the way we get information. MIT sociologist Sherry Turkle looks
at the Internet and sees a transformation in the way we view ourselves. **(1)**

Despite all the hype and babble about the information superhighway,
Turkle says, most people actually have underestimated the coming knowledge revolution. When we log onto a bulletin board, chat room, forum or
other cyberspace sites, she says, we are entering a world of possibility. There,
we can change our name, our appearance, even our sex, and test ourselves in
that different persona. "We can easily move through multiple identities,"
Turkle says, "and we can embrace—or be trapped by—cyberspace as a way
of life." **(2)**

This is the theme of her new book, *Life on the Screen: Identity in the Age
of the Internet* (Simon & Schuster). It's based on her studies, which started 20
years ago when she noticed the way MIT students used computer language
("Let's debug this relationship") in everyday life. **(3)**

And although Turkle has been tracking the emerging computer culture
for two decades, the exploding popularity of the Internet world has turned a
new spotlight on her. *Newsweek* magazine listed her among "50 for the
Future" for 1995 and *Time* dubbed her the "Margaret Mead of Silicone." **(4)**

"Sherry Turkle is an important thinker and very perspicacious—she was
way ahead of the curve," says Constance Hale, associate managing editor of
Wired magazine, which is excerpting Turkle's book in its January issue. "Her
book is groundbreaking. Her theory—that the computer isn't a tool but that
it is giving you access to parts of yourself that you didn't have before—is revolutionary." **(5)**

Like Gates, Turkle says we are on the brink of a revolution, now that
computers inhabit life at every turn. But while Gates' new book, *The Road*

Ahead (Viking), focuses on the outward shapes of the computers and software (such as a wallet PC), Turkle is more concerned with the loosening of the boundaries between people and their computers. "If you want to call this an 'information revolution,' you can," she said on a recent visit to Los Angeles. "I think it is more than that." **(6)**

Turkle, 47, who was wearing a trim black pantsuit and carrying an immense leather handbag, had just been a guest on Michael Jackson's CABC-AM (790) talk show. The discussion had turned to such new phenomena as "cyber-infidelity." Turkle had mentioned a wife who decided her husband's online affair was better than his looking around for real-life women. **(7)**

That brought up the question of what constitutes infidelity in a world where nothing is physical. "I think when you can connect via the computer, you can adopt a persona somewhat different than the one you ordinarily have," she told the radio audience. "People feel that the anonymity and distance allow them to experience different aspects of themselves." **(8)**

Later, she elaborates. In person, Turkle is an engaging conversationalist, jumping from thought to thought with energy and humor. "People can experience other aspects of themselves online," she says. "I have seen it happen!" **(9)**

She has seen how people, talking online in a low-risk setting, have slowly developed social skills or been able to discuss physical problems, such as weight or disabilities, that they previously repressed. She has watched men and women gradually move from virtual online worlds into real relationships ("Rush Limbaugh met his wife on CompuServe," she says). **(10)**

Turkle put six years into writing *Life on the Screen*. Despite its catchy title and rich use of case studies, the heavily footnoted book, interweaving psychological and social analysis with an overview of intelligent machine development, is not light reading. "The meaning of the computer presence in people's lives is very different from what most expected in the late 1970s," Turkle writes. "One way to describe what has happened is to say we are moving from a modernist culture of calculation toward a postmodernist culture of simulation." In short, computers have moved from machines that do things for us (our tax returns or spreadsheets) to machines that do things to us, such as provide experiences that will affect our social and emotional life. **(11)**

Describing e-mail as a "return to conversation over the backyard fence," Turkle notes that in the Massachusetts Institute of Technology Media Lab, where she works, she can log on any morning and scroll through the staff messages. "Someone has died, someone has a baby, someone has won an award—it's like a small-town newspaper." **(12)**

Now, her interest is turning to families. She recently interviewed a woman whose son, just off to college, was studying for his first physics test. The woman had gotten America Online so they could keep in touch, and when she sent her first e-mail message, he replied, "Mom, you did it right!" She had insomnia and got up about 5 a.m. and, on an impulse, sent him another message. When he answered immediately, she realized he was very nervous about the test and had been studying all night. So she sent him a reassuring message that his parents will love him however he does on tests. "Here was a socially acceptable way to talk. She would never have called him at 5 in the morning, but this allows him to be in control, which is what kids that age need to be," Turkle says. **(13)**

Computers were not on the agenda when Turkle graduated in 1976 from Harvard with a double doctorate in sociology and personality psychology. She had spent a year in France analyzing how Freudian thought had been rejected and then accepted by the French; her first book, *Psychoanalytic Politics: Jacques Lacan & Freud's French Revolution,* has been reissued (Guilford Press, 1992). **(14)**

"I thought I would have a career studying how complicated ideas come into everyday life. I didn't anticipate the next set of ideas I would look at would be from computer science," Turkle says. **(15)**

She was hired because MIT wanted somebody who studied the cultural diffusion of scientific ideas. As technophobe Turkle began listening to the computer-savvy students, she realized they were using computer ideas (instead of "Freudian slip," they would say "information-processing error") to describe their lives. "It was like a 'Eureka!' experience to me," she says. **(16)**

Beginning in her own backyard, Turkle organized pizza parties for students playing MUDS (Multi-User Domains), the intricate online games in which participants can alter their real-life identities to improvise elaborate melodramas. She interviewed them at length about their experiences in the fantasies that grew out of the Dungeons and Dragons fantasy games of the early 1970s. She also studied children who were being introduced to computer toys. More recently, she began monitoring Internet chat and bulletin boards. **(17)**

"I just kept studying people and machines," says Turkle, who has steadily written articles for academic journals about the computer culture—about women and computers, physicists and computers, children and computers. Ten years ago she wrote *The Second Self: Computers and the Human Spirit* (Simon & Schuster). **(18)**

Turkle estimates that she has interviewed more than 1,000 people. Mitchel Resnick, a colleague at the MIT Media Lab, admires Turkle's ability to get people to open up in interviews. "She can make people feel comfortable sharing their deepest feelings," he says. "I think often they have been transformed by these [online] experiences and most people don't understand that world." **(19)**

Although Turkle may meet her subjects online, she insists on interviewing them in person, usually in her MIT office. She doesn't even have a computer there—it's reserved for seeing RL (real life) students and colleagues, she explains. **(20)**

She is, however, surrounded by computers at home. Turkle is married to consultant Ralph Willard, and they have a daughter, 4. Her routine in their Boston home is to wake up at 6 a.m. and devote two hours to e-mail, sitting at her Macintosh with a Powerbook nearby to receive faxes. "I have a little computer for my daughter and a palmtop I travel with. I don't watch TV and I write very few letters anymore—I spend a fair amount of time Internet-surfing." **(21)**

And although she signs on daily to a huge amount of e-mail, she says it is worth it. She recently heard from an old high school friend who had seen an article about her in a Boston paper. He had thought about contacting her previously, but with e-mail it was too easy to pass up, he said. She was delighted. "To me, making possible that kind of connection with your past, with people all over the world, is so precious. I am willing to bite the bullet and sort through all the e-mail." **(22)**

And although she acknowledges a darker side of cyberspace (people can get stuck in the selves they have created on the screen, or hurt by an online relationship that turns out to be fraudulent, she says), Turkle has great hopes for the emerging computer culture. **(23)**

"Here's the good news," she says briskly. "Being online can help you develop parts of yourself that have been underdeveloped and it can help your personal growth. Here's the bad news: Some people find themselves just acting out the same problems they have in real life in virtual life. If they've been hostile, they become the 'flamers' on the Internet, using the anonymity to act out their hangups." **(24)**

She doesn't like the question, "Is cyberspace good or bad?" The point is, it is, she says. "It's going to demand ongoing conversations about the new definition of work, of marriage, of sexuality, of child care, of every aspect of our lives." **(25)**

She thus welcomes the fuss over pornography on the Internet as a signal that we are living in a very different time. "It's setting the stage for that longer-term reflection. It's important to keep in mind that we are not going to sort this out in the next two months or two years." **(26)**

VOCABULARY

In your journal, write the meanings of the following words:

- *Margaret Mead* of Silicone **(4)**
- very *perspicacious* **(5)**
- *postmodernist* culture **(11)**
- cultural *diffusion* of scientific ideas **(16)**
- *technophobe* Turkle **(16)**
- *Freudian slip* **(16)**

QUESTIONS FOR WRITING AND DISCUSSION

1. Investigative essays focus on answering at least one key question. The question for Connie Koenenn's article might be, "Who is Sherry Turkle and what does she think about the Internet?" Reread the article, focusing on Koenenn's answer to the second part of that question. Find at least three specific passages that reveal what Turkle finds important about the Internet.

2. Without looking back at the article, list any key bits of information about Sherry Turkle and her books that you can remember. Then reread the article, jotting down any important facts or pieces of information that you forgot. What additional questions about Turkle or her ideas are not answered? Explain why you think Connie Koenenn does or does not effectively meet her purpose of reporting interesting information about Turkle and her ideas to her readers.

3. Reread Koenenn's article, looking for evidences of the sources she used in writing this essay. Next to major paragraphs, indicate the probable source of the quotations, facts, or information. Does Koenenn rely most on quotations and information from a personal interview, on information from Turkle's books, on outside biographical information, on additional third-party interviews, on transcripts of a radio interview, or on other sources? Write a list of the kinds of sources Koenenn probably used.

4. Write your own investigative profile about a person from your school, an employee at your place of work, or a member of your family. Schedule an interview to find out about this person. Use your own observations. Interview other people about their acquaintance with this person. Read anything this person may have written. Assume that your profile will appear in a local or campus newspaper.

THE TRIUMPH OF THE WHEEL

Lewis Grossberger

In this excerpt from an investigative piece that appeared in Rolling Stone *magazine, freelance writer Lewis Grossberger focuses on one question: Why has* Wheel of Fortune, *a television game show, become so popular that it has achieved virtual cult status? In seeking an answer to this question, he considers several possibilities: Is it just an entertaining family game? Is its popularity due to Vanna White's skill in turning letters? Is*

its popularity a reflection of American cultural values? In the process of his
investigation, Grossberger researches articles about the show's popularity,
observes how Wheel of Fortune *works, and interviews the show's key*
personalities.

The first time I saw *Wheel of Fortune,* I thought it was a vapid piece of fluff that could appeal only to brain-dead TV zombies. Five minutes of this tedious dreck was all it took to waft me sleepward. **(1)**

But the second time my reaction was different. The second time I realized—having been assigned meantime to write an article on the show that would bring a much-needed fee—that *Wheel of Fortune* was, in fact, a fascinating, deeply significant national phenomenon, the comprehension of which was essential to any proper understanding of our era. **(2)**

Thank God I'm open-minded. **(3)**

Soon I was wafting westward on an urgent sociophilosophical inquiry, clutching an envelope fat with press clippings that further impressed upon me the importance of my subject. The *Washington Post's* TV critic said *Wheel* is watched by 42 million people a day. *Time* said *Wheel* is the highest-rated syndicated series in television history. The *New York Times* said *Wheel* is so popular it has become a dominant factor in TV scheduling, sometimes wreaking havoc with local and network news. *People* said that Vanna White has blond hair, weighs 107, measures 36-23-33 and adores greasy hamburgers from White Castle. **(4)**

Vanna White is the hostess on *Wheel of Fortune,* which should not be confused with the master of ceremonies, who is Pat Sajak, although he is not called the MC but the host. Despite the fact that Vanna's function is mainly decorative and that she is rarely permitted to utter more than a parting "bye," she has become, *People* assured me, a bigger cult sensation than Paul Shaffer, Max Headroom or even Willard Scott. **(5)**

The only thing the press failed to tell me was why. **(6)**

Why a silly game show based on a simple children's spelling game and a cheezy carnival wheel so captivates the mightiest nation on earth. Now here was a journalistic challenge worthy of Murrow, of Woodward and Bernstein, perhaps even of the great Geraldo Rivera. Immune to the show's mysterious allure, I could operate with scientific detachment. By God, I would take up the gauntlet. I would find out why—or doze off trying. **(7)**

"I swear on the grave of every game-show host who ever lived that I have no idea," said Pat Sajak. **(8)**

Pat Sajak is overqualified for his job in that he is capable of wit. A former TV weatherman, he sounds a little like Bob Newhart and looks like . . . well, if Dick Clark went through that teleportation gizmo from *The Fly* and this time a chipmunk sneaked in, out would come Pat Sajak. **(9)**

I talked with Pat Sajak in his dressing room and found him a personable and modest man who readily admits that game-show hosting "is kind of a dopey way to make a living." I talked as rapidly as possible. When I arrived at the NBC studios in fabled Burbank, the publicity lady who collected me said that the staff would be taping five half-hour shows that night and that I could examine Pat and Vanna only during the fifteen-to-twenty minute breaks between shows. She was very apologetic, but, you know, everyone wants them, it's so exhausting, we have to protect them. I groused a bit—journalistic reflex—but, in truth, it didn't matter. Both host and hostess had been asked to explain the *why* before. They never could. **(10)**

"I mean, I know why it's successful," said Pat. "It's an easy game to play—you know, the people at home, unless you're a total moron, can generally solve the puzzles ahead of the people in the studio, so you feel kind of superior. It's a compelling game. You walk by the set and the puzzle's on and you tend to play along. But that just explains why it's a successful game show. Why it has gone beyond success to become—I don't know—part of the pop culture, I haven't the foggiest idea. I don't think anyone knows." **(11)**

I assured him that I would know. Soon. For that was my quest. My Grail. He responded politely enough, but I could see he was skeptical. It seemed like we'd been talking only a few minutes when a pounding on the door commenced, and a voice demanded Pat's presence, and he went forth to hostify. **(12)**

The *Wheel of Fortune* set looks like that of most Eighties game shows, decorated in feel-good Vegas Gaudy with bright splashes of color, flashing lights and revolving mounds of, as the announcer usually describes them, "fantastic prizes, fabulous and exciting merchandise." The studio audience of close to 200 well-behaved androids was stashed safely out of the way behind a sideline array of cameras, electronic gear, crew and staff. **(13)**

The actual gaming consists of a word puzzle and, naturally, a wheel. Large, multicolored, divided into slim wedges, each marked with a different dollar amount, the wheel is set horizontally in front of the three contestants, so they can lean forward and spin it. By doing so, they may accumulate a dollar account to be later spent on prizes. **(14)**

Between twirls, they take whacks at the word puzzle, which is basically that old childhood chestnut, hangman. The puzzle is mounted on a big vertical display board on a platform that's hauled on and off the set by crewmen at alarming speeds, usually with the courageous Vanna aboard. A display of blank tiles tells the contestants how many words and letters there are in a mystery phrase. As the contestants guess at the letters and Vanna rushes purposefully about, uncovering those correctly called out, the mystery phrase (usually something as banal as "walking on air" or "curiosity killed the cat") gradually emerges until someone identifies it. The winner then may go shopping among the pricetagged prizes until his or her account is exhausted. At the end of the proceedings, the champion tackles a bonus-round puzzle for a grand prize. **(15)**

During one break I was taken to meet the hostess. Vanna was in her dressing room, snacking from a take-out dish and wearing a snappy off-the-shoulder number. (She changes costume and hairdo for each show.) She was very energetic and cheerful and was able to maintain, under close interrogation, not only that Vanna White was her real name but also that she had known four other Vannas while growing up in South Carolina. **(16)**

A small-town girl, Vanna, who is not twenty-nine, drove to Hollywood in a U-Haul truck six years ago, because it was a childhood dream. Hollywood, not trucks. After landing some bit parts in movies, she heard that *Wheel of Fortune* needed a new hostess, and she beat out 200 other young women, even though in her final on-air audition she was so nervous her knees shook and she couldn't talk. Fortunately, speech was not a job qualification. **(17)**

Laboring under the cloud of bimbosity imposed by the alternately fawning and smirking media, Vanna told me what she always tells interviewers: "It's a lot harder than it looks. It really is." **(18)**

It seemed to me the wrong tactic. Were I her media adviser, I'd counsel this approach: "Hey, I look great, I walk sexy. For this they pay me a hundred big ones and put me on the cover of *People*. I should turn them down? Is it my fault I live in a society that accentuates superficial values?" **(19)**

Too soon came the inevitable pounding, and Vanna vanished, leaving me back on the set, watching a woman named Ruth win a Toyota by guessing "League of Women Voters." I talked to a contestant from Fresno named Bill. Bill told me that his family watches *Wheel of Fortune* all the time and that he was so good at it his wife got after him to become a contestant. He did. But he hadn't won a Toyota, and he seemed a little tense. **(20)**

I was not to meet *Wheel's* biggest winner. Who is that? Why, Merv Griffin. Yes, the same Merv Griffin who has spent the last twenty-three years demonstrating what Johnny Carson would be like without jokes. Merv always did seem a bit dazed, as though his mind were on something else. Now we know what. Puzzles. It was Merv who invented *Wheel of Fortune*, hired Pat Sajak and Vanna White and still approves every single puzzle. It was Merv who recently sold Merv Griffin Enterprises, which produces *Wheel* (not to mention *Jeopardy* and *Dance Fever*) to Coca-Cola for—my fingers go numb as I type this—a reported $250 million. According to Tom Shales, TV critic for *The Washington Post*, Merv was rumored to have run around his office waving his quarter-of-a-billion-dollar check in the air, joking that he couldn't find anyone to cash it. **(21)**

Puzzles. All this from puzzles. The man is a lifelong puzzle junkie. "You would think," said Sajak, "that a man who's worth $84 billion, or whatever he is, would have better things to do than make up puzzles—but he does. If you have lunch with Merv, the waiter comes over and says, 'May I take your order?' and Merv goes, 'Ooo! "May I take your order?" What a great puzzle!' and he writes it down." **(22)**

People, we underestimated Merv Griffin. We dismissed him as some kind of welfare agency for the Gabor sisters. But Merv figured out what America wanted, and he provided it. And became very, very rich. Much too rich to talk to the likes of me. But Nancy Jones, *Wheel's* producer, a woman who actually has puzzle meetings with Merv, did. Her take on *why* was family. "It's a show the whole family can enjoy. Anybody from six to a hundred can watch *Wheel of Fortune.* They're gonna understand what's going on. You know, there are kids in college now that learned their ABC's by watching *Wheel.*" Interesting, I thought, but not convincing. Not incisively all-encompassing. After all, there are plenty of family shows that don't have 42 million viewers. **(23)**

If stats like 42 million or quarter of a billion haven't sufficiently defined the scope of *Wheel's* triumph for you, surely Pat Sajak's parking spot will. It was one away from Johnny Carson's. Now *that's* success. I discovered this when Pat gave me a lift back to my hotel, a nice gesture. But he voiced a depressing vision. "This could literally be a show that is never canceled," he said. "You know, my grandkid will be up there, spinning the wheel, saying silly things and putting on hair spray." **(24)**

Considerably sobered, I retired and the next morning flew away. I'd already spent an evening on this investigation—in my view more than enough. Enroute to the airport, a chatty cabby pointed out an evocative sight: a new, exclusive real-estate development on a hill where, he said, the houses start at $1 million. The hill had previously served as a garbage dump, and the driver indicated a pumping station built to clear away the methane gas constantly seeping forth. So scarce is land in L.A. there had been no problem finding wealthy people to reside on top of Old Stinky. **(25)**

Soon afterward I was on the plane, thinking about *Wheel of Fortune,* which, as always, acted as a soporific. I dreamed of the lovely Vanna. She's in a terrific gold lamé jump suit, and she's starring in a big-budget disaster movie (a silent, oddly) about a gassy mountain threatening to explode and bury a nervous populace neck deep in putrid lava. Desperately trying to avert panic, Mayor Merv announces that the mountain, with its shining edifices concealing a rotten nether world, is merely a metaphor for an overly materialistic society, but then he whispers to me that only I can save the day—if I can complete this common, everyday phrase:

V _ _C_ _R_ _ _ _   _ _S THR_ _LLS

Then Pat Sajak's grandkid spins the wheel. The pointer falls on BANK-RUPT, and Swill Hill erupts, burying me neck deep in lethal sludge. I woke high over the Jersey swamps, and I had the answer. I knew *why.* **(26)**

Vicariousness. *Wheel of Fortune* creates the illusion for the hard-working, treadmill-trotting Middle American yearner that he or she is in the big game.

Viewers don't exactly identify with the contestants; they become the contestants. **(27)**

Look at the elements of the show. **(28)**

The Players: Wheel contestants are ordinary folk who serve as the viewers' surrogates. In the whoopee-cushion Seventies, game-show contestants screamed, bounced and wet themselves, but in the we-mean-business Eighties, Americans are cooler and less likely to appear in public dressed as yams. *Wheel* subtly de-emphasizes its contestants, who seem interchangeable. Pat introduces these undemonstrative, low-profile types with the briefest possible questioning, then the camera quickly moves off them and zooms in on the game. With the contestants relegated to the background, the viewer can put himself in their place and play. In your fantasy, you are the star. **(29)**

The Game: Both games promise easy success, one through luck, the other skill. The wheel—hypnotic, alluring, symbolic of nearly everything—is luckier than a roulette wheel, since it can yield only two bad outcomes: BANKRUPT or LOSE A TURN. Any other spin wins. Nice odds. The word puzzle is simple but compelling—it gets easier as you play, because more letters fill in. As Pat Sajak noted, viewers often solve the puzzle before contestants. With the whole family watching, someone at home is almost bound to. The result: You feel happy, excited, superior. You're chalking up wins. You're on a roll. **(30)**

The Payoff: During play, the wheel-whirling contestants (and, by extension, the viewers) are given credit. A nice touch. Who doesn't love credit? It's like betting on someone else's tab. And when you win, you don't win mere cash or some preordained prize. You go *shopping!* A brilliant touch. Shopping may be the ultimate thrill in this commodity-crazed era, an actual addiction for some. And it doesn't hurt *Wheel* in the yuppie department, either. Merv himself once said, "It's like being let loose on Rodeo Drive." As the winner shops, the camera lovingly roves around the prize showcase, as though the viewers' own eyeballs have been let loose amid the VCRs, Isuzu pickups, Tahitian vacations and ceramic Dalmations. *Wheel's* ambiance blends the organized excitement of the casino with the primal pull of the department store. **(31)**

The Cast: Game-show hosts are permitters and forgivers. Their benign presence signals that it's okay to indulge your greed, just in case some shred of conscience or old-fashioned values intrudes to make you feel guilty for craving wealth without work. Pat Sajak is today's kind of authority figure: casual, low-key, jocular, even a bit irreverent. Dignified and well dressed, he could be a yuppie cleric, lawyer or doctor. He could switch jobs with Ronald Reagan and little would change. **(32)**

And Vanna? Pat Sajak likes to say that Vanna's silence gives her a mysterious air. But there isn't any mystery. Her personality shines through without benefit of speech. She's a *cheerleader.* Your own personal cheerleader. Her most vital function is not really her letter turning (artistic though it is) but her clapping! She is forever clapping for the contestants (all of them—Vanna is impartial). When I asked if she'd been a cheerleader in high school, she said, "Of course. Who would have ever thought I'd still be a cheerleader?" **(33)**

And that's *why*. Now you know. Let me just add, before taking a well-deserved nap, that I doubt that Merv and his minions set out to design *Wheel of Fortune* around the Big V Principle or analyzed the economy. I think they just happened, by instinct, experience—and good luck—to hit on a formula that would make it the state-of-the-art Eighties game show. A formula that sucks the viewer through the screen and into that dazzling dreamscape—Vanna's Nirvana—where he is transformed from a nullity, a hapless anonymous bozo, a nobody from nowhere, to the only being now worth being: a Winner. Someone possessed of wealth, luck and, maybe more important, television exposure. Someone, in short, who finally exists. You know, a big wheel. **(34)**

VOCABULARY

In your journal, write the meanings of the following words:

- *vapid* piece of fluff **(1)**
- tedious *dreck* **(1)**
- take up the *gauntlet* **(7)**
- My *Grail* **(12)**
- well-behaved *androids* **(13)**
- acted as a *soporific* **(26)**
- *putrid* lava **(26)**
- rotten *nether* world **(26)**
- *vicariousness* **(27)**
- viewers' *surrogates* **(29)**
- Wheel's *ambiance* **(31)**
- *primal* pull **(31)**
- Merv and his *minions* **(34)**
- Vanna's *Nirvana* **(34)**

QUESTIONS FOR WRITING AND DISCUSSION

1. Grossberger has several *purposes* in this article: *entertaining* readers; *informing* readers about Pat Sajak, Vanna White, the game show, and its reception in the media; and *explaining* why the show is so popular. Based on your own reading, which of these purposes did he accomplish most effectively? Least effectively? Explain.

2. In collecting the information for this article, Grossberger used several kinds of sources: summaries or quotations from written

material, information and quotations from interviews, and observations of people, places, and events. Find one example of each kind of source.

3. Reread the article. Then give paragraph numbers identifying the following parts of the essay (each part may have several paragraph numbers):

Lead-in, catching the reader's interest	(_____)
Main idea, thesis, or focus of the investigation	(_____)
Narrative of writer's investigative steps	(_____)
Profile of key people	(_____)
Observation of the set and the game	(_____)
Analysis of the elements of the show	(_____)
Conclusion	(_____)

4. As a freelance journalist, Grossberger creates a role, or persona, as he writes. Which specific passages most clearly reveal his real or assumed personality? Explain.

5. As the editor of *TV Guide*, you want to use an excerpt from Grossberger's article. To do so, you will need to cut this piece by two-thirds and adapt it for the *TV Guide* audience. As you cut sections, consider your audience. How are readers of *TV Guide* likely to be different from the readers of *Rolling Stone*? (If you are not familiar with these magazines, look at current issues in your library.) What parts of this article will be most appealing to *TV Guide* readers?

THE HOMELESS
AND THEIR CHILDREN

Jonathan Kozol

In his most famous book, Illiterate America *(1985), Jonathan Kozol says that because more than one-third of America's adults are at least partially illiterate, we should organize a massive government and volunteer army to liberate people imprisoned by illiteracy. In "The Homeless and Their Children," taken from* Rachel and Her Children *(1988), Kozol investigates individual cases of poverty in a New York City welfare hotel. He uses his own observations and interview transcripts to demonstrate vividly the connection between illiteracy and poverty. However, instead of arguing indignantly for literacy programs to save the lives of the poor and illiterate, Kozol simply reports the case of a single illiterate woman trying to raise her four children. The woman he calls Laura cannot decipher labels on products at the grocery store, cannot read notices from the welfare office, and cannot understand letters from the hospital warning of her children's lead poisoning.*

The Martinique Hotel, at Sixth Avenue and Thirty-second Street, is one of the largest hotels for homeless people in New York City. When I visited it, in December of 1985, nearly four hundred homeless families, including some twelve hundred children, were lodged in the hotel, by arrangement with the city's Human Resources Administration. One of the residents I spoke to at some length was an energetic, intelligent woman I'll call Kim. During one of our conversations, she mentioned a woman on the seventh floor who had seemingly begun to find her situation intolerable. Kim described this woman as "a broken stick," and offered to arrange for us to meet. **(1)**

The woman—I will call her Laura, but her name, certain other names, and certain details have been changed—is so fragile that I find it hard to start a conversation when we are introduced, a few nights later. Before I begin, she asks if I will read her a letter from the hospital. The oldest of her four children, a seven-year-old boy named Matthew, has been sick for several weeks. He was tested for lead poisoning in November, and the letter she hands me, from Roosevelt Hospital, says that the child has a dangerous lead level. She is told to bring him back for treatment. She received the letter some weeks ago. It has been buried in a pile of other documents that she cannot read. **(2)**

Although Laura cannot read, she knows enough about the dangers of lead to grasp the darker implications of this information. The crumbling plaster in the Martinique Hotel is covered with sweet-tasting paint, and children eat or chew chips of the paint as it flakes off the walls. Some of the paint contains lead. Children with lead poisoning may suffer loss of coordination or undergo convulsions. The consequences of lead poisoning may be temporary or long-lasting. They may appear at once or not for several years. This final point is what instills so much uneasiness; even months of observation cannot calm a parent's fear. **(3)**

Lead poisoning, then, is Laura's first concern, but she has other problems. The bathroom plumbing has overflowed and left a pool of sewage on the floor. A radiator valve is broken, and every now and then releases a spray of scalding steam at the eye level of a child. A crib provided by the hotel appears to be unstable. A screw that holds two of its sides together is missing. When I test the crib with my hand, it starts to sway. There are four beds in the room, and they are dangerous, too. They have metal frames with unprotected corners, and the mattresses do not fit the frames; at one corner or another, metal is exposed.

If a child has the energy or the playfulness to jump or turn a somersault or wrestle with a friend, and if he falls and strikes his head against the metal corner, the consequences can be serious. The week before, a child on the fourteenth floor fell in just this way, cut his forehead, and required stitches. Most of these matters have been brought to the attention of the hotel management; in Laura's case, complaints have brought no visible results. **(4)**

All of this would be enough to make life difficult for an illiterate young woman in New York, but Laura has one other urgent matter on her hands. It appears that she has failed to answer a request for information from her welfare office, and, for reasons that she doesn't understand, she did not receive her benefits this week. The timing is bad; it's a weekend. The city operates a crisis center in the Martinique, where residents can go for food and other help, but today the crisis center is not open, so there's nobody around to tide her over with emergency supplies. Laura's children have been eating cheese and bread and peanut butter for two days. "Those on welfare," the Community Service Society of New York said in a report published in 1984, may be suddenly removed from welfare rolls "for reasons unrelated to their actual need," or even to eligibility standards. Welfare workers in New York City call this practice "churning." Laura and her children are being churned. **(5)**

The room is lighted by fluorescent tubes in a ceiling fixture. They cast a stark light on four walls of greenish paint smeared over with sludge draining from someone's plumbing on the floor above. In the room are two boys with dark and hollowed eyes and an infant girl. A third boy is outside and joins us later. The children have the washed-out look of the children Walker Evans photographed for "Let Us Now Praise Famous Men." Besides the four beds and the crib, the room contains two chairs, a refrigerator, and a television set, which doesn't work. A metal hanger serves as an antenna, but there is no picture on the screen. Instead, there is a storm of falling flakes and unclear lines. I wonder why Laura keeps it on. There are no table lamps to soften the fluorescent glare, no books, no decorations. Laura tells me that her father is of Panamanian birth but that she went to school in New York City. Spanish is her first language. I don't speak Spanish well. We talk in English. **(6)**

"I cannot read," Laura says. "I buy the New York *Post* to read the pictures. In the grocery, I know what to buy because I see the pictures." **(7)**

What of no-name products—generic brands, whose labels have no pictures but which could save her a great deal of money? **(8)**

"If there are no pictures, I don't buy it," she says. "I want to buy pancakes, I ask the lady, 'Where's the pancakes?' So they tell me." **(9)**

She points to the boys and says, "He's two. He's five. Matthew's seven. My daughter is four months. She has this rash." She shows me ugly skin eruptions on the baby's neck and jaw. "The carpets, they was filthy from the stuff, the leaks that come down on the wall. All my kids have rashes, but the worst she has it. There was pus all over. Somewhere here I have a letter from the nurse." She shuffles around but cannot find the letter. "She got something underneath the skin. Something that bites. The only way you can get rid of it is with a cream." **(10)**

She finds the letter. The little girl has scabies. **(11)**

Laura continues, "I have been living here two years. Before I came here, I was in a house we had to leave. There was rats. Big ones, they crawl on us. The rats, they come at night. They come into our house, run over my son's legs. The windows were broken. It was winter. Snow, it used to come inside. My mother lived with us before. Now she's staying at my grandma's house. My grandma's dying in the bed. She's sixty-five. My mother comes here once a week to do the groceries. Tomorrow she comes. Then she goes back to help my grandma. **(12)**

"I know my name, and I can write my name, my children's names. To read, I cannot do it. Medicines, I don't know the instructions. I was living here when I was pregnant with Corinne. No, I didn't see no doctor. I was hungry. What I ate was rice and beans, potato chips and soda. Up to now this week we don't have food. People ask me, 'Can you help? Do you got this? Do you got that?' I don't like to tell them no. If I have something, I give it. This week, I don't got. I can read baby books—like that, a little bit. If I could read, I would read newspapers. I would like to know what's going on. Matthew, he tells me I am stupid. 'You can't read.' You know, because he wants to read. He don't understand what something is. I tell him, 'I don't know it. I don't understand.' People laugh. You feel embarrassed. On the street. Or in the store." She weeps. "There's nothing here." **(13)**

Laura sweeps one hand in a wide arc, but I can't tell whether she means the gesture to take in the room or something more. Then she makes her meaning clear: "Everything I had, they put it on the sidewalk when I was evicted. I don't know if that's the law. Things like that—what is the law, what isn't? I can't read it, so I didn't understand. I lost everything I had. I sign papers. Somebody could come and take my children. They could come. 'Sign this. Sign that.' I don't know what it says. Adoption papers—I don't know. This here paper that I got I couldn't understand." **(14)**

She hands me another letter. This one is from the management of the hotel: "This notice is to inform you that your rent is due today. I would appreciate your cooperation in seeing to it that you go to your center today." Another form that she hands me asks her to fill out the names and the ages of her children. **(15)**

"Papers, documents—people give it to me. I don't know it: I don't understand." She pauses, and then says, "I'm a Catholic. Yes—I go two weeks ago to church. This lady say they have these little books that learn me how to spell. You see the letters. Put them together. I would like to read. I go to St. Francis' Church. Go inside and kneel—I pray. I don't talk to the priest. I done so many things—you know, bad things. I buy a bottle of wine. A bottle of beer. That costs a dollar. I don't want to say to God. I get a hundred and seventy-three dollars restaurant allowance. With that money I buy clothes. Food stamps, I get two hundred dollars. That's for groceries. Subway tokens I take out ten dollars. Washing machine, I do downstairs. Twenty-five dollars to dry and wash. Five dollars to buy soap. Thirty dollars twice a month." **(16)**

Another woman at the Martinique calculates her laundry costs at my request, and they come out to nearly the same figure. These may be the standard rates for a midtown site. The difficulty of getting out and traveling to find lower prices, whether for laundromats or for groceries, cannot be overstated. Families at the Martinique are trapped in a commercial district. **(17)**

I ask Laura who stays with the children when she does her chores. **(18)**

"My mother keeps the children when I do the wash," she replies. "If she can't, I ask somebody on the floor. 'Give me three dollars. I watch your kids.' For free? Nothing. Everything for money. Everybody's poor." **(19)**

Extending a hand, she says, "This is the radiator. Something's wrong." She shows me where the steam sprays out. I test it with my hand. "Sometimes it stops. The children get too close. Then it starts—like that! Leak is coming from upstairs down." I see the dark muck on the wall. "The window is broke. Lights broke." She points to the fluorescent tubes. They flicker on and off. "I ask them, 'Please, why don't you give me ordinary lights?' They don't do nothing. So it been two weeks. I go downstairs. They say they coming up. They never come. So I complain again. Mr. Tuccelli—Salvatore Tuccelli, the manager of the Martinique—said to come here to his office. Desks and decorations and a lot of pictures. It's above the lobby. So the manager was there. Mr. Tuccelli sat back in his chair. He had a gun. He had it here under his waist. You know, under his belt. I said, 'Don't show it to me if you isn't going to use it.' I can't tell what kind of gun it was. He had it in his waist. 'You are showing me the gun so I will be afraid.' If he was only going to show it, I would not be scared. If he's going to use it, I get scared. **(20)**

"So he says, 'You people bring us trouble.' I said, 'Why you give my son lead poison and you didn't care? My child is lead-poisoned.' He said, 'I don't want to hear of this again.' What I answer him is this: 'Listen. People like you live in nice apartments. You got a home. You got TV. You got a family. You got children in a school that learn them. They don't got lead poison.' **(21)**

"I don't know the reason for the guards. They let the junkies into the hotel. When my mother comes, I have to sign. If it's a family living good, they make it hard. If it's the drug dealers, they come in. Why they let the junkies in but keep away your mother? The guards, you see them taking women in the corner. You go down twelve-thirty in the night, they're in the corner with the girls. This is true. I seen it." **(22)**

She continues, "How I know about the lead is this: Matthew sits there and he reaches his fingers in the plaster and he put it in his mouth. So I ask him, 'Was you eating it?' He says, 'Don't hit me. Yes, I was.' So then I took him to the clinic and they took the blood. I don't know if something happen to him later on. I don't know if it affects him. When he's older . . ." **(23)**

I ask Laura why she goes to church. **(24)**

"I figure: Go to church. Pray God. Ask Him to help. I go on my knees. I ask Him from my heart. 'Jesus Christ, come help me, please. Why do you leave me here?' When I'm lying down at night, I ask, 'Why people got to live like this?' On the street, the people stare at you when you go out of the hotel. People look. They think, I wonder how they live in there. Sometimes I walk out this door. Garbage all over in the stairs. When it's hot, a lot of bugs around the trash. Sometimes there are fires in the trash. I got no fire escape. You have to get out through the hall. I got no sprinkler. Smoke detector doesn't work. When I cook and food is burning, it don't ring. If I smoke, it starts to ring. I look up. I say, 'Why you don't work? When I need you, you don't work. I'm gonna knock you down.' I did!" She laughs. **(25)**

There is a sprinkler system in the corridor. In 1987, the hotel management informed residents that the fire-alarm system was "inoperable." **(26)**

I ask Laura if the older children are enrolled in school. Nodding at Michael, her middle son, she says, "This one doesn't go to school. He's five. I need to call tomorrow. Get a quarter. Then you get some papers. Then you got to sign those papers. Then he can start school. **(27)**

"For this room I pay fifteen hundred dollars for two weeks. I don't pay. The welfare pays. I got to go and get it." The room, although it is undivided, was originally a two-room suite and is being rented at the two-room rate. "They send me this. I'm suppose to sign. I don't know what it is. Lots of things you suppose to sign. I sign it but I don't know what it is." **(28)**

While we are talking, Matthew comes in and sits beside his mother. He lowers his eyes when I shake his hand. **(29)**

Laura goes on, "Looking for a house, I got to do it." She explains that she's required to give evidence that she is searching for a place to live. "I can't read, so I can't use the paper. I get dressed. I put my makeup on. If I go like this, they look afraid. They say, 'They going to destroy the house!' You got to dress the children and look nice. Owners don't want homeless. Don't want welfare. Don't want kids. What I think? If they pay one thousand and five hundred dollars every two weeks, why not pay five hundred dollars for a good apartment?" **(30)**

She hands me another paper. "Can you tell me what is this?" **(31)**

It's a second letter from the hospital, telling her to bring her son for treatment. **(32)**

She says, "Every day, my son this week, last week was vomiting. Every time he eat his food, he throw it right back out. I got to take him to the clinic. **(33)**

"Christmas, they don't got. For my daughter I ask a Cabbage Patch. For my boys I ask for toys. I got them stockings." She shows me four cotton stockings tacked to the wall with nothing in them. "They say, 'Mommy, there's no toys.' I say not to worry. 'You are going to get something.' But they don't. They don't get nothing. I could not afford. No, this isn't my TV. Somebody lended it to me. Christmas tree I can't afford. Christmas I don't spend it happy. I am thinking of the kids. What we do on Christmas is we spend it laying on the bed. If I go outside, I feel a little better. When I'm here, I see those walls, the bed, and I feel sad. If I had my own apartment, maybe there would be another room. Somewhere to walk. Walk back and forth." **(34)**

I ask her, "How do you relax?" **(35)**

"If I want to rest, relax, I turn out the light and lie down on the bed," she says. "When I met his father, I was seventeen." She says she knew him before she was homeless, when she lived in Brooklyn with her mother. He was working at a pizza parlor near her mother's home. "One night, he bought me liquor. I had never tasted. So he took me to this hallway. Then my mother say that what I did is wrong. So I say that I already did it. So you have to live with what you did. I had the baby. No. I did not want to have abortion. The baby's father I still see. When he has a job, he brings me food. In the summer, he worked in a flower store. He would bring me flowers. Now he don't have any job. So he don't bring me flowers." **(36)**

She sweeps her hand in a broad arc and says again, "Nothing here. I feel embarrassed for the room. Flowers, things like that, you don't got. Pretty things you don't got. Nothing like that. No." **(37)**

In the window is a spindly geranium plant. It has no flowers, but some of the leaves are green. Before I go, we stand beside the window. Blowing snow hits the panes and blurs the dirt. **(38)**

"Some of the rooms high up, they got a view," Laura says. "You see the Empire State." **(39)**

I've noticed this—seen the building from a window. It towers high above the Martinique. **(40)**

"I talk to this plant. I tell him, 'Grow! Give me one flower!' He don't do it." Then, in an afterthought, "No pets. No. You don't got. Animals. They don't allow." **(41)**

It occurs to me that this is one of the few places I have been except a hospital or a reform school where there are hundreds of children and virtually no pets. A few people keep cats illegally. **(42)**

"I wish I had a dog," Laura says. "Brown dog. Something to hug." **(43)**

VOCABULARY

In your journal, write the meanings of the following words:

- the darker *implications* **(3)**
- call this practice *"churning"* **(5)**
- ugly skin *eruptions* **(10)**
- girl has *scabies* **(11)**

QUESTIONS FOR WRITING AND DISCUSSION

1. Describe your intellectual and emotional reaction to Kozol's article. What information about the lives of the poor and illiterate did you already know? What information surprised you? How did Kozol's essay make you feel about this problem?

2. The purpose of an investigative report is to give information without editorializing or arguing for or against a solution. In which paragraphs does Kozol remain most objective and unemotional? Which passages reveal Kozol's sympathy for Laura's situation? Does he avoid editorializing?

3. Reread the essay, marking those places where Laura's illiteracy causes her problems. Based on your notes, explain how her illiteracy (rather than her poverty) causes or magnifies her problems.

4. Describe the investigative techniques that Kozol probably used to write his essay. In addition to his interviews with Laura, what were his other probable sources of information?

5. According to the information provided by Kozol, what support does the welfare system provide Laura and her children? How does the welfare system encourage Laura to improve her life? List three changes that you believe the welfare system should make to solve Laura's problems and make her more self-sufficient.

6. On your next trip to the grocery store, see which products would appeal to an illiterate person. List the items (and their prices) that you might buy based on the pictures on the labels. Write a paragraph describing your findings. Is Kozol correct in assuming that Laura pays too much for her groceries?

INVESTIGATING:

THE WRITING PROCESS

■ ASSIGNMENT FOR INVESTIGATING   Choose a subject to investigate: one aspect of a current social or political policy, a scientific discovery or principle, a historical event, a profile of a controversial public figure, or perhaps just an ordinary event, person, process, or place that you find interesting. Your initial purpose should be to discover or learn about your subject. Then, with a specific audience in mind, report your findings. A report presents the information that you find; it should not argue for or against any idea or plan. With the final copy of your investigative report, you must turn in photocopies of any sources you have summarized or cited, notes from your interview(s), and/or copies of questionnaires that you used.

CHOOSING A SUBJECT

If one of your journal topics does not suggest a subject for your investigation, consider the following ideas. If you have a subject, go on to the collecting and shaping strategies.

- Choose some idea, principle, process, or theory discussed in a class that you are currently taking. Begin by interviewing classmates, graduate students, or a professor about how to investigate the history, development, or personalities behind this idea. With information from the interview, continue your investigation in the library, looking in appropriate magazines, books, or journals. As you read, focus your question on one narrow or specific area.

- Investigate and report on a campus or community service organization. Choose any academic, minority, cultural, or community organization. Visit the office. Interview an official. Read the organization's literature. Talk to students or community members who have used the service. Check the library for background information. Find people who are dissatisfied with or critical of the organization. Select an audience who might use this service or who might be interested in volunteering for the organization and report the relevant who, what, when, where, why and/or how information.

- At your workplace, investigate how something does or does not work, research how the business (or your part of the business) is organized, do a profile of a coworker, or survey your customers to find out what they like best or least about your store or company.

- Write an investigation of some aspect of your favorite hobby. No matter what the subject is, you will find several magazines in the library devoted to it: fashion, cars, rock climbing, music, cooking, fly fishing, photography, scuba diving, interior decorating, health foods, and so on. Find several magazines and browse through them. Based on what you find in the magazines, interview and/or survey other people interested in this subject. Focus your survey or interview on one specific aspect of this topic.

- Go back to your remembering essay. Do other people remember the person, place, or event? If so, interview one or more of them, either in person or on the phone. How do their recollections of the subject differ from yours? After investigating what happened from other points of view, rewrite your remembering essay to include the perspectives and memories of others.

*Had I known the
answer to any of these
questions, I would
never had needed
to write.*

—JOAN DIDION,

ESSAYIST AND NOVELIST

COLLECTING

The collecting strategies discussed in Chapters 3, 4, and 5 (brainstorming, clustering, looping, mapping, sketching, reading, summarizing, taking double-entry notes) may be useful as you collect ideas. Other strategies particularly useful for investigating are suggested here. Try each of the following collecting strategies for your subject.

ASKING QUESTIONS   Asking the *right questions* is crucial to investigative writing. Sets of questions (often called *heuristics*) will help you narrow and focus your subject and tailor your approach to the expectations or needs of your audience. You don't know what information you need to collect until you know what questions your investigation needs to answer.

1. The "reporter's" or the familiar "Wh" questions are one basic heuristic:

   Who? What? When? Where? Why?

   Asking these questions of a topic ensures that you're not leaving out any crucial information. If, for example, you are investigating recreational opportunities in your city or on campus, you might ask the following questions to focus your investigation (remember to ask the *negative* version of each question, too):

   - *Whom* is the recreation for?
   - *Who* runs the programs?
   - *Who* is excluded from the programs?
   - *Who* pays for the programs?
   - *What* is the program?
   - *What* sports are included in the program?
   - *What* sports are not included?
   - *What* is the budget for these programs?
   - *When* are these opportunities available or not available?
   - *Where* do the activities take place?
   - *Where* are they restricted?
   - *Why* are these programs offered?
   - *Why* are certain activities not offered?
   - *Why* have activities been changed?

   These questions might lead you to focus your investigation on the scheduling, on why soccer has been excluded, or on why participants are charged a fee for one class or program but not for another.

2. The classical "topics" provide a second set of questions for an investigation.

   Definition: What is it?
   Comparison: What is it like or unlike?

Relationship:	What caused it? What are its consequences?
Testimony:	What has been said or written about it?

These questions can be used in conjunction with the reporter's questions to focus an investigation. Applied to the topic on recreational opportunities, the questions might be as follows:

Definition:	What activities exist?
	How can the activities be described, classified, or analyzed?
Comparison:	What are similarities to or differences from other programs?
Relationship:	What caused these programs to be offered?
	What causes people to use or avoid these activities?
	What are the consequences of these programs?
Testimony:	What do students think about these activities?
	What do administrators think?
	What have other schools done?
	What does research show?
	What proverbs or common sayings apply here?

These two sets of questions will *expand* your information, helping you collect facts, data, examples, and ideas—probably more than you can use in a short essay. Once you have all of this information, you can then *narrow* your topic.

USING THE LIBRARY   Knowing how to use a library is crucial for most investigations. For this essay, you will not need to do exhaustive research on your topic, but you will need some background information, statistics, or information about current research, public opinion trends, or recent discoveries. Chapter 12, "Writing a Research Paper," will answer your research questions in more depth, but you can get information quickly in a library by using a few key sources.

- **Ask librarians for assistance.** Every library has librarians stationed at information desks, checkout counters, or reference desks whose job is to answer your questions. Be sure to ask for their advice when you need it. Because frustration is the number-one enemy of research projects, ask for assistance early in your investigation. The best procedure is simply to explain your project—what you intend to do and have done so far—and ask for advice or help. *There are no stupid questions in a library.*
- **Acquaint yourself with the basic sources of information in the library.** Most libraries offer group tours that familiarize their users with the location and use of the following:

  The online catalog

  CD-ROM access

  Internet and Web access

  Microfilm and microfiche room

  Current periodical room

  Basic references such as encyclopedias, almanacs, and dictionaries

USING THE INTERNET AND THE WEB   In the library, in a computer lab, or at home, you may be able to access the Internet to get information about your possible topic. Your browser—such as Netscape—will usually allow you quick access to a number of search engines, such as Alta Vista, Magellan, Lycos, Excite, Net Search, or Yahoo. Be sure to try a search on one of these, such as Alta Vista or Yahoo. There are some additional search tools that you may need a URL address to locate on your system. Below are some research sites you should definitely check out.

- *The Electric Library* at http://www.elibrary.com will give you access to articles on popular topics that you can usually *print out* right at your computer.
- *The Internet Public Library* at http://www.ipl.org will give you access to a library environment that looks like your public library at home.
- *The Internet Services List* at http://www.spectracom.com/islist is a Top 5% Point and Magellan 3 Star site that provides an excellent starting point for investigating a new topic.

- *The WWW Virtual Library* at http://www.w3.org/pub/DataSources/by
  Subject/Overview.html will get you to one of the best investigating
  sites on the Web.

For additional Web sites for investigating topics, see Chapter 12.

Using Written and Electronic Sources

- **When printed copies are not available directly from your computer
  access, make photocopies of relevant articles.** The small amount of
  money you spend on copies will enable you to reread articles if necessary, quote or paraphrase from them accurately, and cite them accurately as references. (The money you spend is also excellent anti-
  frustration insurance, in case you return to the library stacks and discover that someone else has checked out your magazine or book.) On
  your photocopies, be sure to write *source information:* magazine or
  book title, author, publisher, date and place of publication, volume,
  and page numbers. For this investigative report, remember that you
  must turn in photocopies of any pages of articles or books you use.
- **Make notes and summaries from your photocopied sources.** As you
  collect information from photocopied sources, jot down key facts,
  ideas, and direct quotations. For every note you take, record the
  author, title, publishing information, and page numbers. You may
  paraphrase another writer's ideas, examples, sentences, or short passages by writing them in your own words. Use *direct quotation* when
  words or phrases in a source are more striking than your paraphrase
  might be. You may edit a direct quotation by (1) deleting any irrelevant or unnecessary words or phrases by using ellipsis points (three
  spaced periods) to indicate the deleted words and by (2) inserting
  your own words in square brackets [ ] if you need to clarify a quoted
  passage. Otherwise, the words within the quotation marks must accurately reproduce the original: No altered spellings, changed words, or
  rephrasings are allowed.
- **Avoid plagiarism.** Use quotation marks whenever you quote more
  than a word or two from your source. Paraphrase in your own words
  rather than stringing together phrases and sentences written by someone else. Give credit for ideas, facts, and language by citing your
  sources. In informal investigative writing, you may simply mention
  the author and title of written sources, citing page numbers of direct
  quotations in parentheses. (All formal research papers and some
  investigative essays cite sources in full in a "Works Cited" section at
  the end. See Chapter 12, "Writing a Research Paper," for more
  details.)

SUMMARIZING   As explained in Chapter 5, a *summary* is a concise
explanation of the main and supporting ideas in a passage, report, essay, book,
or speech. It is usually written in the present tense. It identifies the author and

title of the source; it may refer to the context or the actual place where the study took place; it contains the passage's main ideas; and it may quote directly a few forceful or concise sentences or phrases. It will not usually cite the author's examples. A *paraphrase* usually expresses all the information in the passage—including examples—in your own words. Summary, paraphrase, and direct quotation often occur together as you use sources. (See Chapter 5 for more details.)

The following passage is a concise summary of Lewis Grossberger's article "The Triumph of the Wheel":

Source, author, title
Focus of article

In his *Rolling Stone* article, "The Triumph of the Wheel," Lewis Grossberger investigates why the television game show *Wheel of Fortune* has become so popular. Grossberger describes the workings of the game show, interviews the show's personalities (Pat Sajak and Vanna White) on location, describes Merv Griffin's role as producer and puzzle-maker for the show, and explains his own theory about why the show has reached the status of a "cult sensation."

Summary of article's
main ideas

Article's thesis

Wheel of Fortune is popular, Grossberger contends, because it gives its viewers a vicarious sense of participating in the excitement of solving a puzzle and winning thousands of dollars' worth of merchandise. The show's contestants are not stars, so the viewers at home can imagine that they are the contestants. The game itself involves a simple roulette wheel and the puzzles are easy to solve, giving home viewers a sense of accomplishment and superiority. The selection of prizes after the contestant has solved the puzzle similarly allows viewers to shop, vicariously, with the winner. Finally the show's personalities are familiar, people-next-door types: Pat Sajak is low-key and occasionally humorous; Vanna White is the show's bouncy cheerleader. *Wheel of Fortune,* Grossberger concludes, is a state-of-the-art show that "sucks the viewer . . . into that dazzling dreamscape—Vanna's Nirvana—where he [or she] is transformed from a nullity, a hapless anonymous bozo . . . [into] the only being now worth being: a Winner."

Summary of points that
support the article's thesis

Direct quotation from
article

CITING SOURCES IN YOUR TEXT   As you collect information, you should note authors, titles of books or magazines, dates of publication, publishers, and page numbers to give proper credit to your sources. For some journalistic writing, you may need to cite only the author, the title of your source, or both:

Time said that *Wheel* is the highest-rated syndicated series in television history. **(4)**

According to Tom Shales, TV critic for *The Washington Post*, Merv was rumored to have run around his office waving his quarter-of-a-billion-dollar check in the air, joking that he couldn't find anyone to cash it. **(21)**

According to the MLA (Modern Language Association) format, formal in-text citation requires that the author and page numbers be given, usually in parentheses, at the end of the sentence—for example, "(Grossberger 24–25)." If the author of the article you are citing is not known, use a shortened title—"(*Wheel* 27)."

If you refer to the author in the sentence introducing him or her, indicate just the page numbers in parentheses.

Grossberger implies that, by and large, viewers of *Wheel of Fortune* are a bunch of bozos. **(28)**

For additional information on formal, in-text citation, consult Chapter 12, "Writing a Research Paper."

INTERVIEWING   After you have done some initial research, interviews are a logical next step. Remember that the more you know about the subject (and the person you're interviewing), the more productive the interview will be. In planning an interview, keep the following steps in mind.

1. Make an *appointment* with the person you wish to interview. Although you may feel hesitant or shy about calling or e-mailing someone for an interview, remember that most people are flattered that someone else is interested in them and wants to hear their opinions or learn about their areas of expertise.

2. Make a *list of questions*, in an appropriate *sequence*, that you can ask during the interview. The interview itself will generate additional topics, but your list will jog your memory if the interview gets off the track. Begin with relatively objective or factual questions and work your way, gradually, to the more subjective questions or controversial issues. Try to phrase your questions so that they require more than a yes or no answer.

3. Begin the interview by introducing yourself and describing *your* investigation. Keep your biases or opinions out of the questions. Be sure to *listen* carefully and ask follow-up questions: "What information do you have on that? What do the statistical studies suggest? In your opinion, do these data show any trends? What memorable experiences have you had relating to this topic?" Like a dog with a good bone, a reporter doesn't drop a topic until the meat's all gone.

4. During the interview, *take notes*, and, if appropriate, use a tape recorder to ensure accuracy. Don't hesitate to ask your interviewee to repeat or

clarify a statement. Remember: People want you to get the facts right and quote them accurately. Especially if you're doing a personality profile, describe notable features of your interviewee: hair color, facial features, stature, dress, gestures, nervous habits, and details about the room or surroundings. Finally, don't forget to ask your interviewee for additional leads or sources. At the conclusion of the interview, express your thanks and ask if you can check with him or her later, perhaps by e-mail, for additional details or facts.

5. Immediately after the interview, go over your notes. If you recorded the interview, listen to the tape and transcribe important responses. List other questions you may still have.

WRITING QUESTIONNAIRES   Questionnaires are useful when you need to know the attitudes, preferences, or opinions of a large group of people. If you are surveying customers in your business, you may discover that 39 percent of those surveyed would prefer that your business stay open an additional hour, from 5 p.m. to 6 p.m. If you are surveying students to determine their knowledge of geography, you might discover that only 8 percent can correctly locate Beirut on a map of the Middle East. The accuracy and usefulness of a survey depend on the kinds of questions you ask, on the number of people you survey, and on the sample of people you select to respond to your questionnaire.

Open questions are easy to ask, but the answers can be difficult to interpret. For example, if you want to survey customers at a department store where you work, you might ask questions requiring a short written response:

- What is your opinion of the service provided by clerks at Macy's?
- What would make your shopping experience at Macy's more enjoyable?

While these questions may give you interesting—and often reliable—responses, the results may be difficult to tabulate. Open questions are often valuable in initial surveys because they can help you to determine specific areas or topics for further investigation.

Closed questions are more typical than open questions in surveys. They limit the responses so that you can focus on a particular topic and accurately tabulate the responses. Following are several types of closed questions:

- *Yes/No Questions:* Have you shopped at Macy's in the last three months?
  _____ Yes
  _____ No
- *Multiple Choice:* How far did you travel to come to Macy's?
  _____ 0–5 miles

_____ 5–10 miles

_____ 10–15 miles

_____ Over 15 miles

- How would you characterize the salespeople at Macy's?

  _____ Exceptionally helpful

  _____ Helpful

  _____ Indifferent

  _____ Occasionally rude

  _____ Usually rude

- *Checklists:* Which departments at Macy's do you usually visit?

  _____ Women's Wear

  _____ Sporting Goods

  _____ Children's Wear

  _____ Lingerie

  _____ Men's Wear

  _____ Household Goods

- *Ranking Lists:* Rank the *times* you prefer to shop (1 indicates most convenient time, 2 indicates slightly less convenient, and so on).

  _____ 9 a.m.–11 a.m.

  _____ 11 a.m.–1 p.m.

  _____ 1 p.m.–4 p.m.

  _____ 4 p.m.–8 p.m.

As you design, administer, and use your questionnaire, keep the following tips in mind:

- Limit and focus your questions so that respondents can fill out the questionnaire quickly.
- Avoid loaded or biased questions. For example, don't ask, "How do you like the high-quality merchandise in Macy's sports department?"
- At the top of your questionnaire, write one or two sentences describing your study and thanking participants.
- Pretest your questionnaire by giving it to a few people. Based on their oral and written responses, focus and clarify your questions.
- Use a large sample group. Thirty responses will give you more accurate information about consumer attitudes than will three responses.
- Make your sample as *random* or as evenly representative as possible. Don't survey customers on only one floor, in only one department, or at only one time of day.
- Be sure to include a copy of your questionnaire with your article or essay.

Note: If you intend to do a formal study using questionnaires, check your library for additional sources to help you design and administer statistically reliable surveys.

SHAPING

As you begin shaping your material, reconsider your purpose and audience. Limit your subject to create a *narrowed* and *focused* topic. Don't try to cover everything; focus on the *most interesting questions and information.* Take the time to write out a statement of your topic, key questions, purpose, and audience. Then try the following strategies.

But for whom have I tried so steadfastly to communicate? Who have I worried over in this writing? Who is my audience?

—CHERRIE MORAGA,

SOCIAL CRITIC AND POET

INVERTED PYRAMID   A common form for reports, especially in journalism, is the *inverted pyramid.* The writer begins with a succinct but arresting title, opens the story with a sentence or short paragraph that answers the reporter's "Wh" questions, and then fills in the background information and details in order of importance, from the *most important* to the *least important.*

Writers use the inverted pyramid when concrete information and the convenience of the reader are most important. The advantage of the inverted pyramid is that a hurried reader can quickly gather the most important information and determine whether the rest of the story is worth reading. The disadvantage is that some details or information may be scattered or presented out of clear sequence. In investigative writing, therefore, writers often supplement the inverted pyramid with other forms of development: chronological order, definition, classification, or comparison/contrast.

"Wh" question lead: Who, What, When, Where, Why
Most important information and details

Important information and details

Least important
information and
details

CHRONOLOGICAL ORDER   Often, writers present their information in the order in which they discovered it, enabling the reader to follow the research as though it were a "whodunit." In this format, you set forth the key questions for the investigation and then describe the *steps in your investigation,* from your earliest questions or clues to your final explanation or resolution.

Lewis Grossberger, for example, uses the chronology of his own investigation to shape his article about *Wheel of Fortune.* The following sentences—most of them appearing at the beginning of paragraphs—illustrate how he uses chronological order to shape his account:

> The first time I saw *Wheel of Fortune,* I thought it was a vapid piece of fluff . . .

> But the second time my reaction was different.

> Soon I was wafting westward on an urgent sociophilosophical inquiry . . .

> Now here was a journalistic challenge . . . By God, I would take up the gauntlet. I would find out why—or doze off trying.

> When I arrived at the NBC studios in fabled Burbank, the publicity lady who collected me said . . .

> During one break I was taken to meet the hostess. Vanna was in her dressing room . . .

> Too soon came the inevitable pounding, and Vanna vanished . . .

> Considerably sobered, I retired and the next morning flew away.

> Soon afterward I was on the plane, thinking about *Wheel of Fortune,* which, as always, acted as a soporific.

> I woke high over the Jersey swamps, and I had the answer. I knew *why.*

DEFINITION   Definitions are central to investigating and reporting, whether they shape only a sentence or two or several paragraphs. Grossberger uses informal definition to shape one paragraph in his article that explains the meaning of the word "vicariousness," the condition of imagined participation in another person's experience or emotions:

Vicariousness. *Wheel of Fortune* creates the illusion for the hard-working, treadmill-trotting Middle American yearner that he or she is in the game. Viewers don't exactly identify with the contestants; they *become* the contestants.

COMPARISON AND CONTRAST   Comparison and contrast are as essential to investigating and reporting as they are to observing and remembering. Consider how Lance Morrow uses comparison to shape the opening paragraphs of a *Time* magazine essay on AIDS. In this essay, entitled "The Start of a Plague Mentality," Morrow notes the similarities between attitudes created by a plague 200 years ago and contemporary attitudes toward AIDS.

> An epidemic of yellow fever struck Philadelphia in August 1793. Eyes glazed, flesh yellowed, minds went delirious. People died, not individually, here and there, but in clusters, in alarming patterns. A plague mentality set in. Friends recoiled from one another. If they met by chance, they did not shake hands but nodded distantly and hurried on. The very air felt diseased. People dodged to the windward of those they passed. They sealed themselves in their houses. The deaths went on, great ugly scythings. . . .

> In the past four years, some 6,000 people have died of AIDS in the U.S. From a statistical point of view, AIDS is not a major plague. Still, one begins to detect a plague mentality regarding the disease and those who carry it.

ANALYSIS   In the process of investigating any subject, writers frequently use analysis to organize or shape their writing. Analysis simply involves dividing a whole into its parts. In the process of analyzing *why Wheel of Fortune* is successful, for example, Grossberger devotes one paragraph to each of the four main elements of the show: the players, the game itself, the payoff, and the cast. Ask yourself, "What are the major components of my subject?" The answer may not only lead to some new ideas about your subject but may create a shape to help organize your material.

ADDITIONAL SHAPING STRATEGIES   Other shaping strategies, discussed in previous chapters, may be useful for your investigation, too. *Classifying people, places,* or *things* may help organize your investigation. *Simile, metaphor,* or *analogy* may develop and shape parts of your article. Even in investigative reporting, writers may create an identifiable *persona* or adopt a humorous tone. In the examples of reports given earlier in this chapter, Anastasia Toufexis, Jeff Meer, and Joan Barthel assume a reporter's objective persona and use a serious, straightforward tone. In contrast, Lewis Grossberger establishes a humorous persona and tone. He admits that *Wheel* is "tedious dreck" and is "soporific," he makes fun of Vanna when she says that turning the letters is a "lot harder than it looks," and he even recounts his own weird dream about Old Stinky.

TITLE, INTRODUCTION, AND CONCLUSION Especially in an investigative report, a catchy title is important to help get your readers' interest and attention. Jot down several ideas for titles now and add to that list *after* you've drafted your essay.

In your introductory paragraph(s), answering the "Wh" questions will help focus your investigation. Or you may wish to use a short *narrative.* Grossberger, for example, begins his article by describing how he became interested in his investigation: "The first time I saw *Wheel of Fortune*, I thought it was a vapid piece of fluff." Joan Barthel begins her article with stories from Oprah Winfrey's life, pointing out that her profile "is not just the story of a survivor, though she obviously is one." Other types of lead-ins, such as a short *description,* a *question,* a *statement of a problem,* a *startling fact* or *statistic,* or an arresting *quotation,* may get the reader's interest and focus on the main idea you wish to investigate. (See Chapter 7 for additional examples of lead-ins.)

The conclusion should resolve the question or questions posed in the investigation, summarize the most important information (useful primarily for long or complicated reports), and give the reader a sense of completion, often by picking up an idea, fact, quotation, narrative, or bit of description used in the introduction. Grossberger's conclusion, for example, mentions the formula used in *Wheel of Fortune,* reiterates the idea that viewers of *Wheel* want to be winners, and puns on the title of the show: "You know, a big wheel."

Some writers like to have a title and know how they're going to start a piece of writing before they begin drafting. However, if you can't think of the perfect title or introduction, begin drafting and continue working on the title, introduction, and the conclusion after the first draft.

All good writing is swimming under water and holding your breath.
—F. SCOTT FITZGERALD,
AUTHOR OF
THE GREAT GATSBY

DRAFTING

Before you begin a first draft, reconsider your purpose in writing and further focus your questions, sense of audience, and shaping strategies.

The actual drafting of an investigative essay requires that you have all your facts, statistics, quotations, summaries, notes from interviews, or results of surveys ready to use. Organize your notes, decide on an overall shaping strategy, or write a sketch outline. In investigative writing, a primary danger is postponing writing too long in the mistaken belief that if you read just one more article or interview just one more person, you'll get the information you need. At some point, usually *before* you feel ready, you must begin writing. (Professional writers rarely feel they know enough about their subject, but deadlines require them to begin.) Your main problem, you'll quickly discover, will be having too much to say rather than not enough. If you have too much, go back to your focusing questions and see whether you can narrow your topic further.

REVISING

After you have drafted your essay, you may wish to get some feedback from your peers about your work in progress. The peer response guidelines below will help you review your goals for this investigative assignment and construct a revision plan. When you read other students' drafts or ideas, be as constructively critical as possible. Think carefully about the assignment. Be honest about your own reactions as a reader. What would make the draft better?

PEER RESPONSE

The instructions that follow will help you give and receive constructive advice about the rough draft of your investigating essay. You may use these guidelines for an in-class workshop, a take-home review, or a computer e-mail response.

Writer:
Before you exchange drafts with another reader, write out the following on your essay draft or in an e-mail message:

1. *Purpose.* Briefly, describe your purpose and intended audience. For your audience, write out the title of a newspaper or magazine that might print your investigative report.

2. *Revision Plans.* Obviously, your draft is just a draft. What still needs work as you continue revising? Explain. (You don't want your reader to critique problems you are already intending to fix.)

3. *Questions.* Write out one or two questions that you still have about your draft. What questions would you like your reader to answer?

Reader:
First, read the entire draft from start to finish. As you reread the draft, answer the following questions:

1. *Purpose.* Remember that the purpose of this essay is to accurately and objectively report information, not argue or editorialize. Does this writer go beyond reporting to editorializing or arguing? If so, point out specific sentences that need revision.

2. *Evidence.* List the kinds of evidence the writer uses. What additional kinds of sources might the writer use: an additional interview? a source on the Web? personal observation? other print

---

continued

continued

> sources? a survey? Make a specific suggestion about additional, appropriate sources.
>
> 3. *Key Investigative Question.* When you read the essay, the key question should become apparent. Write it out. If there are places in the essay that don't relate to that key question, should they be omitted? Explain. Are there other aspects of the key question that the writer should address? Explain.
>
> 4. *Reader's Response.* An investigative essay should satisfy your curiosity about the topic. What did you want to learn about the topic that the essay did not answer? Write out any questions that you would like the writer to answer as he or she revises the essay.
>
> 5. *Answer the writer's questions in number 3.*

Guidelines for Revision

As you add, delete, substitute, or rearrange materials, keep the following tips in mind:

- **Reexamine your purpose and audience:** Are you doing what you intended? You should be *reporting* your findings; you should *not* be arguing for or against any idea.
- **Is the form of your essay or report responsive to audience needs and expectations?** Use samples of other writing for your audience (from newspapers, magazines, or journals) as models.
- **Can you add any of your own observations or experiences to the investigation?** Remember that your own perceptions and experiences as a reporter are also relevant data.
- **Review the reporter's "Wh" questions.** Are you providing your readers with relevant information *early* in the report and also catching their interest with a key statistic, fact, quotation, example, question, description, or short narrative?
- **Recheck your summaries, paraphrases, or direct quotations.** Are they accurate, and have you cited these sources in your text?
- **Use signals, cues, and transitions to indicate your shaping strategies:**

  Chronological Order: before, then, afterward, next, soon, later, finally, at last

  Comparison/Contrast: likewise, similarly, however, yet, even so, in contrast

  Analysis: first, next, third, fourth, finally

- **Revise sentences for directness, clarity, and conciseness.** Avoid unnecessary passive voice.
- **Edit your report for appropriate word choice, usage, and grammar.** Check your writing for problems in spelling and punctuation.

■ **POSTSCRIPT ON THE WRITING PROCESS**   While the process of writing an investigative essay is still fresh in your mind, answer the following questions in your journal.

1. What sources of information (articles, books, interviews, surveys) were most helpful in your investigation? Explain.

2. Most researchers discover that the more they learn, the more they still need to know about their subjects. If you had more time to work on this essay, which sources would you investigate further?

3. What was the most difficult problem you had to solve during your collecting, shaping, drafting, and revising? What helped you most as you tried to solve this problem (further reading, additional writing, advice from peers)? Explain.

4. What was the single most important thing you learned about investigating as you wrote this paper?

5. What do you like best about the final version of your investigative report?

INVESTIGATING:

STUDENT WRITING

SEE DICK RUN, RUN DICK RUN, WHY, WHY, WHY?

Jan Peterson

Jan Peterson, a jogger herself, decided to investigate why jogging is so popular. She read several articles from popular magazines, such as Runner's World, *and also found a relevant article in a technical journal,* Research Quarterly for Exercise and Sport. *Then she interviewed several joggers to profile their jogging behavior and attitudes. Shown below are notes from one of the articles she read, questions and notes from one interview, her first rough draft, and the revised version.*

NOTES FROM AN ARTICLE

Notes from a photocopy of Albert Mehrabian and Marijke Lynne Bekken, "Temperament Characteristics of Individuals Who Participate

in Strenuous Sports," Research Quarterly for
Exercise and Sport, 1986, Vol. 57, No.2, pp 160-166.

In their article, Mehrabian and Bekken found that
"those who participate in strenuous sports regularly and
intensively are healthier psychologically than the
general population" (160). Psychological health in this
case was composed of dominance, pleasantness and a
relaxed attitude. The authors also addressed the
question of whether certain personality types
gravitate towards certain types of sports, or whether
certain sports activities seem to create certain
temperament characteristics. They concluded that
certain people gravitate towards certain types of
sports (164). (Some of the language here was too
technical-PFQ scales and formulas.) Also important:
"Relaxed temperament is thus associated with low
fear and low anxiety levels and high tolerance for
discomfort and pain. Further, it is associated with
the ability to delay gratification; to endure discomfort, stress, and pain to achieve desired results;
and to cope with stressful situations or activities"
(164). The most important conclusion of the paper
appeared to be "that athletes are healthier
psychologically than the general population" (165).

QUESTIONS FOR AN INTERVIEW

1. How long have you been running?
2. Why did you start running?
3. Is running a personal thing – do you run
   alone or in a group?
4. Have your reasons for running changed
   over the years?
5. Do you experience a "runner's high"?
6. How do you feel after you run?
7. How do you feel when you don't run?
8. What do you think about when you run?
9. Do you compete at running?

NOTES FROM AN INTERVIEW

This runner started running in high school on cross country team – took up running again in 1979. Started running because he liked it and wanted to be on the track team – but wasn't fast enough to compete in shorter distances. He now runs to stay in shape, relax and relieve stress. However, he is unusual in that he enjoys several types of exercise – social forms – such as basketball where there is much more interaction between team members. Running relaxes him while he runs and those feelings of relaxation last long after the run ends. Not a "runner's high," as such. Things don't seem to bother him as much. He isn't extremely competitive – except with himself – he keeps track of his timed distances and tries to improve. He says he might have been an addicted runner had he started earlier.

FIRST DRAFT

Questions: Why do people run? **Audience:** General, readers of a local newspaper possibly **Purpose:** To report psychological effects of running

SEE JANE RUN—RUN, JANE, RUN— RUN, RUN, RUN

Why have so many thousands of people taken up a pastime lately which so closely resembles torture? You don't see runners or joggers smiling as they dash by you. What you see instead are painful grimaces etched into tight faces, and intense looks of concentration. What exactly is it that motivates these fanatics devoted to misery and self-abuse? **(1)**

According to Bruce Tuckman, author for *Runner's World* magazine, running can be "good medicine for bad moods." Tuckman says running has often been used as a treatment for clinical depression because "it incubates feelings of control, discipline, and self-worth in people who may have been feeling ineffectual." However, he also points out the possible dangers of developing a running addiction. This condition occurs in someone who depends too much on the good feelings provided by running, and is manifested in a person who can't and won't quit running. **(2)**

I interviewed one such person, who wishes to remain anonymous. Although he claims he is not addicted to running, I have suspicions to the contrary. Two days after a serious accident with a chainsaw in which he received 20 stitches in the middle of his shin, he attempted to hobble through his usual 6 mile course. The pain admittedly got to him, so he decided to wait 2 more days to try again. His repeated stressing of the injured leg resulted in a lump the size of a walnut on his shin bone. Perhaps he is not a total addict, as he did give up his passion for a few days, but I would surmise that addiction is just a matter of degree. Why is this person so dedicated to this form of self-abuse? **(3)**

It has been demonstrated that running causes biochemical as well as physiological changes in the body. In the past, endorphins, which are the body's naturally occurring opiates, were suspected to be at high levels in runners. But researchers were unable to detect a correlation between endorphins and runner's feelings of euphoria often known as a "runner's high." However, recently another drug has gained attention as a mood enhancer—the hormone noradrenaline. Tuckman claims that runners have higher levels of noradrenaline than do non-runners. **(4)**

However, the editors of *The Complete Runner* claim that the calming effect produced from running has its roots in our heredity. Our ancestors had only two options in how to react to threats: fight—that is stand their ground and club each other (or that growling saber-toothed tiger), or flight—that is, run away from the apparent danger. Options for dealing with stress today are no longer so clear-cut. If our boss threatens us, we can't very well punch him or her, or run away. Instead we are forced to stand there and just take the verbal abuse—somehow internalizing the stress. But, we still must deal with the stress. Some of us deal with stress by numbing the effects with drugs or alcohol. Others have come to depend upon strenuous exercise, such as running, for our tension releaser. This perhaps sounds strange—because when you run you tense your muscles and it would appear that the very act of tensing muscles would inhibit tension release. However, recent research reported by the editors of *The Complete Runner* has revealed that "relaxation is most pronounced after muscular work." **(5)**

REVISED VERSION

SEE DICK RUN. RUN, DICK, RUN. WHY, WHY, WHY?

Why have so many thousands of people taken up a pastime lately that so closely resembles self-abuse? You don't often see runners or joggers smiling as they trot past you—what you see instead are painful grimaces etched into tight faces and intense looks of concentration. What motivates these fanatics? What sort of satisfaction could they possibly be deriving from such agony? Or are they perhaps all just a bunch of masochists? **(1)**

People of all ages, shapes, and sizes have started running by the droves. You see them everywhere—at the park, downtown, on college campuses, at the beach, and in the mountains. Even more strange is the fact that once they start running, many of them won't, or can't quit. Now, I can understand the reasons why most people start a program of running—reasons such as wanting to lose weight or wanting to get into shape. What I fail to comprehend is why people continue to run after they find out what kind of pain is involved in the sport. **(2)**

Reasons for running are as varied and diverse as people are. One runner interviewed for this article claimed to have started running in high school. He said he joined the cross-country track team because he wanted to be a runner, but he was unable to compete effectively in shorter distance events. Now, however, he runs to stay in shape, relax, and relieve stress. A second interviewed runner began running in high school as well—also on the cross-country team. However, he ran only to be in better shape for his true love, wrestling. He says he runs now to stay in shape and keep his sanity. **(3)**

Runners may claim that running promotes sanity, but in fact there are both positive and negative psychological effects of running. In a recent *Runner's World* article entitled "Brighter Days," Bruce Tuckman explains that running can be "good medicine for bad moods." Tuckman says running has often been used as a treatment for clinical depression because "it incubates feelings of control, discipline, and self-worth in people who may have been feeling ineffectual." However, he also points out the possible dangers of developing a running addiction. This condition occurs in someone who depends too much on the good feelings provided by running and is manifested by a person who can't and won't quit running. **(4)**

One of the runners I interviewed provided a vivid example of the negative effects of running addiction. This person had an unfortunate encounter with a chain saw while cutting firewood. As a result of their rather abrupt meeting, he ended up with approximately twenty stitches in the middle of his shin. Two days after the accident occurred, he attempted to hobble through his usual six mile course. Crazy, you say? Not according to his philosophy—the more you use your body, the faster it heals! The result of this madness is a lump the size of a walnut in the middle of his shin, and a leg that still gives him problems. And he claims he runs just to stay in shape and keep his sanity—what sanity? **(5)**

Recent research has suggested that addiction to running may be caused, at least in part, by certain physiological or biochemical changes in the body. In the past, endorphins (the body's naturally occurring opiates) were suspected to be at high levels in runners. Researchers, however, were unable to detect a correlation between endorphins and runners' feelings of euphoria (often known as "runner's high"). Another mood-enhancing drug has gained attention more recently—the hormone noradrenaline. Tuckman claims runners have higher levels of noradrenaline than nonrunners. **(6)**

However, the editors of *The Complete Runner* argue that the calming effect produced by running has its roots in our heredity. Our ancestors had only two options for handling threats: fight (stand your ground and club each other) or flight (run away from that saber-toothed tiger that thinks you might make a scrumptious meal). Options for dealing with stress today are no longer so clear-cut. If your boss threatens you, you can't very well retaliate with a club. It probably wouldn't look too good if you ran away, either. So what are your choices? Stand there and internalize the stress, go home later and throw down a couple of martinis, yell at the wife and kids, and fall asleep watching television. This behavior, however, seems only to dull the tension rather than relieve it. The urges to fight or flee remain bottled up inside, and the stress is not alleviated. The only way we can release our stress and really relax is by voluntary muscular work. As the editors of *The Complete Runner* say, "Running offers one of the few chances left to get our feet on the ground—for the sake of our heads." **(7)**

Runners may be addicted psychologically or physiologically, but the result, some experts think, is positive. Albert Mehrabian and Marijke Bekken, writing in the *Research Quarterly for Exercise and Sport*, conclude that "those who participate in [running] regularly and intensively are healthier psychologically than the general population." These authors found that athletes in general have more dominant and pleasant temperaments than nonathletes. They also equated a relaxed temperament with those who run or exercise regularly. They defined "relaxed temperament" to be associated with "low fear and low anxiety levels and high tolerance for discomfort and pain. Further, it is associated with the ability to delay gratification; to endure discomfort, stress, and pain to achieve desired results; and to cope with stressful situations or activities." Do you suppose that the "chain-saw jogger" I interviewed may have a little more sanity than I previously gave him credit for? Maybe I'd better go put on my running shoes! **(8)**

QUESTIONS FOR WRITING AND DISCUSSION

1. One purpose of an investigative report is to give readers information. Without looking back at Peterson's revised article, recall the information you got from it. Were you confused at some points in the article? Explain.

2. What information, ideas, or quotations does Peterson pick up from her article notes and interview to use in her revised version? Was there anything else she should have used but didn't?

3. Which shaping strategies discussed in this chapter does Peterson use to organize the revised version of her article? Referring to paragraph numbers, identify two important shaping strategies.

4. Compare Peterson's first draft with her revised version. Find one change in content (added or deleted facts, examples, quotations). Is the change an improvement over the first draft? Find one change in shaping or organization (look particularly at transitions in the opening sentences of paragraphs). Is the revision an improvement? Finally, find one change in wording in a sentence. Does the rewording improve the clarity or appropriateness of the sentence? Explain.

MY FRIEND MICHELLE, AN ALCOHOLIC

Bridgid Stone

Bridgid Stone, a student at Southeast Missouri State University, decided to write her investigative essay on alcoholism. In the library, she was able to find quite a lot of information and statistics about alcohol. In her friend, Michelle, she had a living example of the consequences of alcohol abuse. The question, however, was how to combine the two. As you read her essay, notice how she interweaves description and dialogue with facts and statistics.

Five million teenagers are problem drinkers, according to *Group* magazine's article, "Sex, Drugs, and Alcohol." One of these five million teenagers is my friend, Michelle.

"I can't wait to go out tonight and get drunk," Michelle announces as she walks into my dorm room. I just sigh and shake my head. Michelle has been drunk every night since Wednesday. In the last three days, she has been to more fraternity parties than classes.

We leave a few hours later for a Sig Tau party. Even though I have been attending these parties for weeks now, the amount of alcohol present still amazes me. Almost everyone is walking around with a twelve-pack of beer. Others are carrying fifths of vodka or Jack Daniel's whiskey. As cited in *Fraternities and Sororities on the Contemporary College Campus,* seventy-three percent of fraternity advisors believe that alcohol is a problem in fraternities. I wish the other twenty-seven percent could be here now. Fraternities are synonymous with drinking.

Michelle and I both have innocent-looking squeeze bottles, but inside are very stiff screwdrivers. They probably have more vodka than orange juice. Michelle finishes her drink before I am halfway through with mine. So she finishes off mine too before disappearing into the throng of people at the party. The next time I see her, she is holding a beer in each hand. Her speech is slurred, and she can barely stand up on her own.

We head back to the dorm when Michelle starts vomiting. Once we are in her room, I help her undress and put her to bed.

"Bridgid, I am so sorry," Michelle cries, "I promise never to drink again."

"Okay, just get some sleep," I tell her as I leave.

It's Thursday night and Michelle is ready to party again.

"I haven't been to my Friday 8:00 class in a month. Do you think I should just stay up all night after the party and go to class drunk? Or should I just not go to class and sleep in?" Michelle asks.

"Don't go out and get drunk. Stay home tonight and get up and go to your classes tomorrow," I advise.

"I am just going to sleep in," Michelle informs me as she leaves for the party.

Like Michelle, an estimated 4.6 million adolescents experience negative consequences of alcohol abuse, such as poor school performance. This was reported in a survey conducted by NIAAA for a United States Congressional report.

Early Friday morning, I get a phone call from the on-duty resident advisor. Michelle has passed out in the lobby of the Towers Complex. She couldn't remember her phone number or even what floor she lived on, but I had written my phone number on Michelle's hand, so she could call me if she got into any trouble. The R. A. had seen my number and decided to call, since Michelle was too drunk to dial the four digits.

"Could you please escort your friend up to your room," the R. A. asks. She doesn't sound very happy.

"Sure, I will be down in a few minutes," I promise. It takes me and another girl from our floor to get Michelle onto the elevator. She keeps lying down or passing out. Thirty minutes later, we get Michelle into bed. She is mumbling incoherently, and she reeks of alcohol. Needless to say, Michelle doesn't make it to her 8:00 a.m. class, again.

Saturday afternoon, I confront Michelle about the Thursday night incident. This is rather hard to do, since she doesn't remember any of it.

"I just drink to loosen up. I'm much more fun if I've been drinking," Michelle tells me.

"You are not much fun when you are puking or passing out," I reply. A desire to loosen up is one of the main reasons that teenagers drink, reports *Group* magazine. Other reasons include a need to escape and to rebel.

"I have to release steam every once in awhile," she argues. "School is really stressing me out."

"Michelle, you don't even go to class," I tell her.

"Everyone else drinks!" she says. "Why are you picking on me?" She stomps out of my room.

Michelle was partially correct, though, when she stated, "Everybody else drinks." As reported in *Alcohol and Youth,* more than eighty percent of all college students surveyed had been drinking in the previous month. But this doesn't mean that what Michelle is doing is any less serious. In all probability, Michelle is an alcoholic.

A test that is often used to determine if someone has a drinking problem can be found in *Getting Them Sober,* by Toby Rice Andrews. There are twenty questions on the test. A "yes" answer to two of the questions indicates a possible drinking problem. Questions include: "Do you miss time from school or work due to drinking?" "Do you drink to escape from worries or troubles?" "Do you drink because you are shy?" "Have you ever had a memory loss due to drinking?" Michelle would probably have answered "yes" to all of the above questions.

I moved out of the dorm at the beginning of the second semester, so I haven't seen much of Michelle. The last time I saw her was about three weeks ago. She had gotten arrested while in New Orleans for spring break. Apparently, Michelle had been out drinking and eventually had been arrested for public drunkenness.

"It wasn't that bad," she told me. "I don't even remember being in the jail cell. I was pretty trashed."

Works Cited

Andrews, Toby Rice. *Getting Them Sober.* South Plainfield, New Jersey: Bridge Publishing, 1980

Barnes, Grace. *Alcohol and Youth.* Westport, Connecticut: Greenwood Press, 1982.

Pruett, Harold, and Vivian Brown. *Crisis Intervention and Prevention.* San Francisco: Jossey-Bass Inc., 1987.

"Sex, Drugs, and Alcohol." *Group,* February 1992: 17–20.

Van Pelt, Rich. *Intensive Care.* Grand Rapids, Michigan: Zondervan Publishing House, 1988.

Winston, Roger, William Nettles III, and John Opper, Jr. *Fraternities and Sororities on Contemporary College Campuses.* San Francisco: Jossey-Bass Inc., 1987.

QUESTIONS FOR WRITING AND DISCUSSION

1. Investigative reports should remain as objective as possible. Describe how Stone's essay affected you. Does Stone remain objective or does she become emotionally involved? Where is she most objective? Where does her point of view color her report? How successfully does Stone maintain her reportorial stance?

2. Who is Stone's audience for her essay? Where would you recommend that Stone send her essay for possible publication? List two possible publication sources (magazines or newspapers) and explain your choices.

3. If Stone were revising her essay, what advice would you give her about balancing statistics and personal experience? Should she have more statistics? Should she have more narrative? Refer to specific paragraphs and examples in your response.

4. Stone's use of present tense adds dramatic impact to her essay. Reread her essay, noticing where she uses present tense and where she shifts to past tense. Where was the use of present tense most effective? Did her tense shifting confuse you at any point? Where?

5. Compare Stone's essay with Kozol's essay earlier in this chapter. What reporting strategies does Stone adapt from Kozol? How are their reporting strategies different? Explain your response by referring to specific passages from each author.

7 EXPLAINING

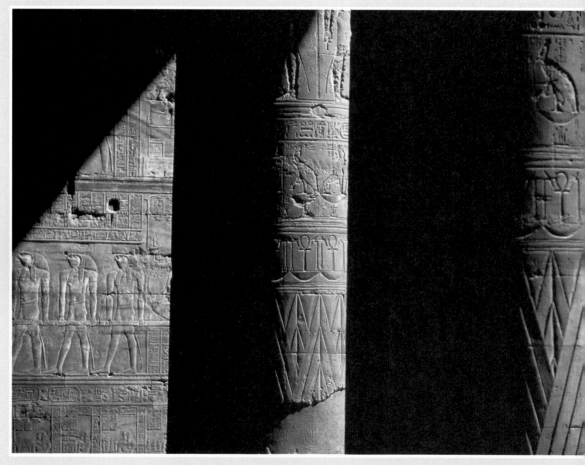

Ancient carvings, hieroglyphic columns.

YOU HAVE DECIDED TO QUIT YOUR PRESENT JOB, SO YOU WRITE A NOTE TO YOUR BOSS GIVING THIRTY DAYS' NOTICE. DURING YOUR LAST FEW WEEKS AT WORK, YOUR boss asks you to write a three-page job description to help orient the person who will replace you. The job description should include a list of your current duties as well as advice to your replacement on how to execute them most efficiently. To write the description, you record your daily activities, look back through your calendar, comb through your records, and brainstorm a list of everything you do. As you write up the description, you include specific examples and illustrations of your typical responsibilities.

AS A GYMNAST AND DANCER, YOU GRADUALLY BECOME OBSESSED WITH LOSING WEIGHT. YOU START SKIPPING MEALS, PURGING THE LITTLE FOOD YOU DO EAT, AND lying about your eating habits to your parents. Before too long, you weigh less than seventy pounds, and your physician diagnoses your condition: *anorexia nervosa*. With advice from your physician and counseling from a psychologist, you gradually begin to control your disorder. To explain to others what anorexia is, how it is caused, and what its effects are, you write an essay in which you explain your ordeal, alerting other readers to the potential dangers of uncontrolled dieting.

E XPLAINING AND DEMONSTRATING RELATIONSHIPS IS A FREQUENT PURPOSE FOR WRITING. EXPLAINING GOES BEYOND INVESTIGATING THE FACTS AND REPORTING INFORMATION; IT ANALYZES THE COMponent parts of a subject and then shows how the parts fit in relation to one another. Its goal is to clarify for a particular group of readers *what* something is, *how* it happened or should happen, and/or *why* it happens.

Explaining begins with *analysis:* You divide a thing or phenomenon (object, person, place, feeling, belief, event, process, or cause) into its various parts. Explaining how to learn to play the piano, for example, begins with an analysis of the parts of the learning process: playing scales, learning chords, getting instruction from a teacher, sight reading, and performing in recitals. Explaining why two automobiles collided at an intersection begins with an analysis of the contributing factors: the nature of the intersection, the number of cars involved, the condition of the drivers, and the condition of each vehicle. Then you bring the parts together and show their *relationships:* You show how practicing scales on the piano fits into the process of learning to play the piano; you demonstrate why one small factor—such as a faulty turn signal—combined with other factors to cause an automobile accident.

The emphasis you give to the *analysis* of the object or phenomenon and the time you spend explaining *relationships* of the parts depends on your purpose, subject, and audience. If you want to explain how a flower reproduces, for example, you may begin by identifying the important parts, such as the pistil and stamen, that most readers need to know about before they can understand the reproductive process. However, if you are explaining the process to a botany major who already knows the parts of a flower, you might spend more time discussing the key operations in pollination or the reasons why some flowers cross-pollinate and others do not. In any effective explanation, analyzing parts and showing relationships must work together for that particular group of readers.

Because its purpose is to teach the reader, *expository writing,* or writing to explain, should be as clear as possible. Explanations, however, are more than organized pieces of information. Expository writing contains information that is focused by your point of view, by your experience, and by your reasoning powers. Thus, your explanation of a thing or phenomenon makes a point or has a thesis: This is the *right* way to define "happiness." This is how one *should* bake lasagne or do a calculus problem. These are the *most important* reasons why the senator from New York was elected. To make your explanation clear, you show what you mean by using specific support—facts, data, examples, illustrations, statistics, comparisons, analogies, and images. Your thesis is a *general* assertion about the relationships of the *specific* parts. The support helps your reader identify the parts and see the relationships. Expository writing teaches the reader by alternating between generalizations and specific examples.

TECHNIQUES FOR EXPLAINING

Explaining requires first that you assess your subject and your audience. Although you will need to draw on your own observations and memories about this subject, you may also need to do some reading or perhaps interview an expert. As you consider your subject, keep in mind that while an explanation (involving both analysis and showing relationships) focuses on what, how, or why, it may involve all three. Following are five important techniques for writing clear explanations.

The main thing I try to do is write as clearly as I can.

—E. B. WHITE,
JOURNALIST AND
COAUTHOR OF
ELEMENTS OF STYLE

- **Getting the reader's attention and stating the thesis.** Devise an accurate but interesting *title*. Use an attention-getting *lead-in*. State the *thesis* clearly.
- **Defining key terms and describing *what* something is.** Analyze and *define* by describing, comparing, classifying, and giving examples.
- **Identifying the steps in a process and showing *how* each step relates to the overall process.** Describe how something should be done or how something typically happens.
- **Describing causes and effects and showing *why* certain causes lead to specific effects.** Analyze how several causes lead to a single effect or show how a single cause leads to multiple effects.
- **Supporting explanations with specific evidence.** Use descriptions, examples, comparisons, analogies, images, facts, data, or statistics to *show* what, how, or why.

In *Spirit of the Valley: Androgyny and Chinese Thought*, psychologist Sukie Colgrave illustrates many of these techniques as she explains an important concept from psychology: the phenomenon of "projection." Colgrave explains how we "project" attributes missing in our own personality onto another person—especially someone we love:

A one-sided development of either the masculine or feminine principles has [an] unfortunate consequence for our psychological and intellectual health: it encourages the phenomenon termed "projection." This is the process by which we project onto other people, things, or ideologies, those aspects of ourselves which we have not, for whatever reason, acknowledged or developed. The most familiar example of this is the obsession which usually accompanies being "in love." A person whose feminine side is unrealised will often "fall in love" with the feminine which she or he "sees" in another person, and similarly with the masculine. The experience of being "in love" is one of powerful dependency. As long as the projection appears to fit its object nothing awakens the person to the reality of the projection. But sooner or later the lover usually becomes aware of certain discrepancies between her or his

Explaining what: definition example

Explaining why: effects of projection

Explaining how: the process of freeing ourselves from dependency

desires and the person chosen to satisfy them. Resentment, disappointment, anger and rejection rapidly follow, and often the relationship disintegrates. . . . But if we can explore our own psyches we may discover what it is we were demanding from our lover and start to develop it in ourselves. The moment this happens we begin to see other people a little more clearly. We are freed from some of our needs to make others what we want them to be, and can begin to love them more for what they are.

EXPLAINING *WHAT*

Explaining *what* something is or means requires showing the relationship between it and the *class* of beings, objects, or concepts to which it belongs. *Formal definition*, which is often essential in explaining, has three parts: the thing or term to be defined, the class, and the distinguishing characteristics of the thing or term. The thing being defined can be concrete, such as a turkey, or abstract, such as democracy.

THING OR TERM	CLASS	DISTINGUISHING CHARACTERISTICS
A turkey is a	bird	that has brownish plumage and a bare, wattled head and neck; it is widely domesticated for food.
Democracy is	government	by the people, exercised directly or through elected representatives.

Frequently, writers use *extended definitions* when they need to give more than a mere formal definition. An extended definition may explain the word's etymology or historical roots, describe sensory characteristics of the term (how it looks, feels, sounds, tastes, smells), identify its parts, indicate how something is used, explain what it is not, provide an example of it, and/or note similarities or differences between this term and other words or things. The following extended definition of "democracy" begins with the etymology and then explains—using analysis, comparison, example, and description—what democracy is and what it is not:

Formal definition
Description: what democracy is
Etymology: analysis of the word's roots

Since democracy is government of the people, by the people, and for the people, a democratic form of government is not fixed or static. Democracy is dynamic; it adapts to the wishes and needs of the people. The term "democracy" derives from the Greek word *demos,* meaning "the common people," and *-kratia,* meaning "strength or power" used to govern or rule. Democracy is based on the notion that a majority of people creates laws and then everyone agrees to abide by those laws in the interest of the common good. In a democracy, people are not ruled by a king, a dictator, or a small group of powerful individuals. Instead, people elect officials who use the power temporarily granted to them to govern the society. For example, the people may agree that their government should raise money for defense, so the officials levy taxes to support an army. If enough people decide, however, that taxes for defense are too high, then they request that their elected officials change the laws or they elect new officials. The essence of democracy lies in its responsiveness: Democracy is a form of government in which laws and lawmakers change as the will of the majority changes.

Comparison: what democracy is not

Example

Formal definition

Figurative expressions—vivid word pictures using similes, metaphors, or analogies—can also explain what something is. During World War II, for example, the Writer's War Board asked E. B. White (author of *Charlotte's Web* and many *New Yorker* magazine essays) to provide an explanation of democracy. Instead of giving a formal definition or etymology, White responded with a series of imaginative comparisons showing the *relationship* between various parts of American culture and the concept of democracy:

Surely the Board knows what democracy is. It is the line that forms on the right. It is the don't in Don't Shove. It is the hole in the stuffed shirt through which the sawdust slowly trickles; it is the dent in the high hat. Democracy is the recurrent suspicion that more than half of the people are right more than half of the time. It is the feeling of privacy in the voting booths, the feeling of communion in the libraries, the feeling of vitality everywhere. Democracy is the score at the beginning of the ninth. It is an idea which hasn't been disproved yet, a song the words of which have not gone bad. It's the mustard on the hot dog and the cream in the rationed coffee. Democracy is a request from a War Board, in the middle of a morning in the middle of a war, wanting to know what democracy is.

Sometimes we think that technical subjects are by nature objective and denotative, but some of these subjects also use definitions that contain images and metaphors. Consider the following definition of Web robots—so-called "bots"—as defined by Andrew Leonard writing in *Wired* magazine:

Web robots—spiders, wanderers, and worms. Cancelbots, Lazarus, and Automoose. Chatterbots, soft bots, userbots, taskbots, knowbots, and mailbots. . . . In current online parlance, the word "bot" pops up everywhere, flung around carelessly to describe just about any kind of computer program—a logon script, a spellchecker—that performs a task on a network. Strictly speaking, all bots are "autonomous"—able to react to their environments and make decisions without prompting from their creators; while the master or mistress is brewing coffee, the bot is off retrieving Web documents, exploring a MUD, or combatting Usenet spam. . . . Even more important than function is behavior—bona fide bots are programs with personality. Real bots talk, make jokes, have feelings—even if those feelings are nothing more than cleverly conceived algorithms.

EXPLAINING *HOW*

Explaining *how* something should be done or how something happens is usually called *process analysis.* One kind of process analysis is the "how-to" explanation: how to cook a turkey, how to tune an engine, how to get a job. Such recipes or directions are *prescriptive:* You typically explain how something *should* be done. In a second kind of process analysis, you explain how something happens or is typically done—without being directive or prescriptive. In a *descriptive* process analysis, you explain how some natural or social process typically happens: how cells split during mitosis, how hailstones form in a cloud, how students react to the pressure of examinations, or how political candidates create their public images. In both prescriptive and descriptive explanations, however, you are analyzing a *process*—dividing the sequence into its parts or steps—and then showing how the parts contribute to the whole process.

Cookbooks, automobile-repair manuals, instructions for assembling toys or appliances, and self-improvement books are all examples of *prescriptive* process analysis. Writers of recipes, for example, begin with analyses of the ingredients and the steps in preparing the food. Then they carefully explain how the steps are related, how to avoid problems, and how to serve mouthwatering concoctions. Farley Mowat, naturalist and author of *Never Cry Wolf,* gives his readers the following detailed—and humorous—recipe for creamed mouse. Mowat became interested in this recipe when he decided to test the nutritional content of the wolf's diet. "In the event that any of my readers may be interested in personally exploiting this hitherto overlooked source of excellent animal protein," Mowat writes, "I give the recipe in full":

Souris à la Crème

Ingredients:

One dozen fat mice	Salt and pepper	One cup white flour
Cloves	One piece sowbelly	Ethyl alcohol

Skin and gut the mice, but do not remove the heads; wash, then place in a pot with enough alcohol to cover the carcasses. Allow to marinate for about two hours. Cut sowbelly into small cubes and fry slowly until most of the fat has been rendered. Now remove the carcasses from the alcohol and roll them in a mixture of salt, pepper and flour; then place in frying pan and sauté for about five minutes (being careful not to allow the pan to get too hot, or the delicate meat will dry out and become tough and stringy). Now add a cup of alcohol and six or eight cloves. Cover the pan and allow to simmer slowly for fifteen minutes. The cream sauce can be made according to any standard recipe. When the sauce is ready, drench the carcasses with it, cover and allow to rest in a warm place for ten minutes before serving.

Explaining *how* something happens or is typically done involves a *descriptive* process analysis. It requires showing the chronological relationship between one idea, event, or phenomenon and the next—and it depends on close observation. In *Lives of the Cell,* biologist and physician Lewis Thomas explains that ants are like humans: While they are individuals, they can also act together to create a social organism. Although exactly how ants communicate remains a mystery, Thomas explains how they combine to form a thinking, working organism:

[Ants] seem to live two kinds of lives: they are individuals, going about the day's business without much evidence of thought for tomorrow, and they are at the same time component parts, cellular elements, in the huge, writhing, ruminating organism of the Hill, the nest, the hive. . . .

A Solitary ant, afield, cannot be considered to have much of anything on his mind; indeed, with only a few neurons strung together by fibers, he can't be imagined to have a mind at all, much less a thought. He is more like a ganglion on legs. Four ants together, or ten, encircling a dead moth on a path, begin to look more like an idea. They fumble and shove, gradually moving the food toward the Hill, but as though by blind chance. It is only when you watch the dense mass of thousands of ants, crowded together around the Hill, blackening the ground, that you begin to see the whole beast, and now you observe it thinking, planning, calculating. It is an intelligence, a kind of live computer, with crawling bits for its wits.

At a stage in the construction, twigs of a certain size are needed, and all the members forage obsessively for twigs of just this size. Later, when outer walls are to be finished, thatched, the size must change, and as though given new orders by telephone, all the workers shift the search to the new twigs. If you disturb the arrangement of a part of the Hill, hundreds of ants will set it vibrating, shifting, until it is put right again. Distant sources of food are somehow sensed, and long lines, like tentacles, reach out over the ground, up over walls, behind boulders, to fetch it in.

EXPLAINING *WHY*

"Why?" may be the question most commonly asked by human beings. We are fascinated by the reasons for everything that we experience in life. We ask questions about natural phenomena: Why is the sky blue? Why does a teakettle whistle? Why do some materials act as superconductors? We also find human attitudes and behavior intriguing: Why is chocolate so popular? Why do some people hit small leather balls with big sticks and then run around a field stomping on little white pillows? Why are America's family farms economically depressed? Why did the United States go to war in Vietnam? Why is the Internet so popular?

Explaining *why* something occurs can be the most fascinating—and difficult—kind of expository writing. Answering the question "why" usually requires analyzing *cause-and-effect relationships*. The causes, however, may be too complex or intangible to identify precisely. We are on comparatively secure ground when we ask *why* about physical phenomena that can be weighed, measured, and replicated under laboratory conditions. Under those conditions, we can determine cause and effect with precision.

Fire, for example, has three *necessary* and *sufficient* causes: combustible material, oxygen, and ignition temperature. Without *each* of these causes, fire will not occur (each cause is "necessary"); taken together, these three causes are *enough* to cause fire (all three are "sufficient"). In this case, the cause-and-effect relationship can be illustrated by an equation:

CAUSE 1	+	CAUSE 2	+	CAUSE 3	=	EFFECT
(combustible material)		(oxygen)		(ignition temperature)		(fire)

Analyzing both necessary and sufficient causes is essential to explaining an effect. You may say, for example, that wind shear (an abrupt downdraft in a storm) "caused" an airplane crash. In fact, wind shear may have *contributed* to the crash (been necessary) but was not by itself the total (sufficient) cause of the crash: An airplane with enough power may be able to overcome wind-shear forces in certain circumstances. An explanation of the crash is not complete until you analyze the full range of necessary *and* sufficient causes, which may include wind shear, lack of power, mechanical failure, and even pilot error.

Sometimes, explanations for physical phenomena are beyond our analytical powers. Astrophysicists, for example, have good theoretical reasons for believing that black holes cause gigantic gravitational whirlpools in outer space, but they have difficulty explaining why black holes exist—or whether they exist at all.

In the realm of human cause and effect, determining causes and effects can be as tricky as explaining why black holes exist. Why, for example, do some children learn math easily while others fail? What effect does failing at math have on a child? What are necessary and sufficient causes for divorce? What are the effects of divorce on parents and children? Although you may not be able to explain all the causes or effects of something, you should not be satisfied until you have considered a wide range of possible causes and effects. Even then, you need to qualify or modify your statements, using such words as "might," "usually," "often," "seldom," "many," or "most," and then giving as much support and evidence as you can.

In the following paragraphs, Jonathan Kozol, a critic of America's educational system and author of *Illiterate America,* explains the multiple effects of a single cause: illiteracy. Kozol supports his explanation by citing specific ways that illiteracy affects the lives of people:

Illiterates cannot read the menu in a restaurant.

They cannot read the cost of items on the menu in the window of the restaurant before they enter.

Illiterates cannot read the letters that their children bring home from their teachers. They cannot study school department circulars that tell them of the courses that their children must be taking if they hope to pass the SAT exams. They cannot help with homework. They cannot write a letter to the teacher. They are afraid to visit in the classroom. They do not want to humiliate their child or themselves. . . .

Many illiterates cannot read the admonition on a pack of cigarettes. Neither the Surgeon General's warning nor its reproduction on the package can alert them to the risks. Although most people learn by word of mouth that smoking is related to a number of grave physical disorders, they do not get the chance to read the detailed stories which can document this danger with the vividness that turns concern into determination to resist. They can see the handsome cowboy or the slim Virginia lady lighting up a filter cigarette; they cannot heed the words that tell them that this product is (not "may be") dangerous to their health. Sixty million men and women are condemned to be the unalerted, high-risk candidates for cancer. . . .

Illiterates cannot travel freely. When they attempt to do so, they encounter risks that few of us can dream of. They cannot read traffic signs and, while they often learn to recognize and to decipher symbols, they cannot manage street names which they haven't seen before. The same is true for bus and subway stops. While ingenuity can sometimes help a man or woman to discern directions from familiar landmarks, buildings, cemeteries, churches, and the like, most illiterates are virtually immobilized. They seldom wander past the streets and neighborhoods they know. Geographical paralysis becomes a bitter metaphor for their entire existence. They are immobilized in almost every sense we can imagine. They can't move up. They can't move out. They cannot see beyond.

■ WARMING UP: JOURNAL EXERCISES The following exercises will help you practice writing explanations. Read all of the following exercises and then write on the three that interest you most. If another idea occurs to you, write about it.

1. Write a one-paragraph explanation of an idea, term, or concept that you have discussed in a class that you are currently taking. From biology, for example, you might define *photosynthesis* or *gene splicing*. From psychology, you might define *psychosis* or *projection*. From computer studies, you might define *cyberspace* or *morphing*. First identify someone who might need to know about this subject. Then give a definition and an illustration. Finally, describe how the term was discovered or invented, what its effects or applications are, and/or how it works.

2. Imitating E. B. White's short "definition" of democracy, use imaginative comparisons to write a short definition—serious or humorous—of one of the following words: *freedom, adolescence, mathematics, politicians, parents, misery, higher education, luck,* or a word of your own choice.

3. Novelist Ernest Hemingway once defined courage as "grace under pressure." Using this definition, explain how you or someone you know showed this kind of courage in a difficult situation.

4. When asked what jazz is, Louis Armstrong replied: "Man, if you gotta ask you'll never know." If you know quite a bit about jazz, explain what Armstrong meant. Or choose a familiar subject to

which the same remark might apply. What can be "explained" about that subject and what cannot?

5. Choose a skill that you've acquired (for example, playing a musical instrument, operating a machine, playing a sport, drawing, counseling others, driving in rush-hour traffic, dieting) and explain to a novice how he or she can acquire that skill. Reread what you've written. Then write another version addressed to an expert. What parts can you leave out? What must you add?

6. Three-year-old children are insatiably curious. They ask older people a never-ending series of "why" questions. Imagine you are going for a walk in a familiar place with a three-year-old. What questions might the child ask you about either strange or commonplace things or occurrences? Select one "why" question. First write out an explanation of that question for another adult. Then write your explanation for the three-year-old.

EXPLAINING: PROFESSIONAL WRITING

WELCOME TO CYBERSPACE

Philip Elmer-DeWitt

Philip Elmer-DeWitt was born in Boston and was educated at Oberlin College, Columbia University, and the University of California at Berkeley. Elmer-DeWitt currently writes for Time *magazine, where he has been since 1982. He has written several hundred articles, often on computer-related issues, including several* Time *cover stories, such as "Computer Viruses" (1988), "Supercomputers" (1988), "Cyberpunk" (1993), "Bards of the Internet" (1994), and "The Internet" (1994). "Welcome to Cyberspace" appeared as a* Time *magazine cover story in 1995. In this essay, Elmer-DeWitt explains what cyberspace is, how the Internet got started, and what questions we still have about future commercial and personal uses of the Net.*

It started, as the big ideas in technology often do, with a science-fiction writer. William Gibson, a young expatriate American living in Canada, was wandering past the video arcades on Vancouver's Granville Street in the early 1980s when something about the way the players were hunched over their glowing screens struck him as odd. "I could see in the physical intensity of their postures how *rapt* the kids were," he says. "It was like a feedback loop, with photons coming off the screens into the kids' eyes, neurons moving through their bodies and electrons moving through the video game. These kids clearly *believed* in the space the games projected." **(1)**

That image haunted Gibson. He didn't know much about video games or computers—he wrote his breakthrough novel *Neuromancer* (1984) on an ancient manual typewriter—but he knew people who did. And as near as he could tell, everybody who worked much with the machines eventually came to accept, almost as an article of faith, the reality of that imaginary realm. "They develop a belief that there's some kind of actual space behind the screen," he says. "Some place that you can't see but you know is there." **(2)**

Gibson called that place "cyberspace," and used it as the setting for his early novels and short stories. In his fiction, cyberspace is a computer-generated landscape that characters enter by "jacking in"—sometimes by plugging electrodes directly into sockets implanted in the brain. What they see when they get there is a three-dimensional representation of all the information stored in "every computer in the human system"—great warehouses and skyscrapers of data. He describes it in a key passage in *Neuromancer* as a place of "unthinkable complexity," with "lines of light ranged in the non-space of the mind, clusters and constellations of data. Like city light, receding. . . ." **(3)**

In the years since, there have been other names given to that shadowy space where our computer data reside: the Net, the Web, the Cloud, the Matrix, the Metaverse, the Datasphere, the Electronic Frontier, the information superhighway. But Gibson's coinage may prove the most enduring. By 1989 it had been borrowed by the online community to describe not some science-fiction fantasy but today's increasingly interconnected computer systems—especially the millions of computers jacked into the Internet. **(4)**

Now hardly a day goes by without some newspaper article, some political speech, some corporate press release invoking Gibson's imaginary world. Suddenly, it seems, everybody has an E-mail address, from Hollywood moguls to the Holy See. Billy Graham has preached on America Online; Vice President Al Gore has held forth on CompuServe; thousands chose to celebrate New Year's this year with an online get-together called First Night in Cyberspace. . . . **(5)**

One result of this drum roll is a growing public appetite for a place most people haven't been to and are often hard-pressed to define. In a *Time*/CNN poll of 800 Americans conducted in January by Yankelovich Partners, 57% didn't know what cyberspace meant, yet 85% were certain that information technology had made their life better. They may not know where it is, but they want desperately to get there. The rush to get online, to avoid being "left behind" in the information revolution, is intense. Those who find fulfillment in cyberspace often have the religious fervor of the recently converted. **(6)**

These sentiments have been captured brilliantly in an IBM ad on TV showing a phalanx of Czech nuns discussing—of all things—the latest operating system from Microsoft. As they walk briskly through a convent, a young novice mentions IBM's competing system, called Warp. "I just read about it in *Wired*," she gushes. "You get true multitasking . . . easy access to the Internet." An older sister glances up with obvious interest; the camera cuts to the mother superior, who wistfully confesses, "I'm dying to surf the Net." Fade as the pager tucked under her habit starts to beep. **(7)**

Cybernuns. **(8)**

What is cyberspace? According to John Perry Barlow, a rock-'n-roll lyricist turned computer activist, it can be defined most succinctly as "that place you are in when you are talking on the telephone." That's as good a place to start as any. The telephone system, after all, is really a vast, global computer network with a distinctive, audible presence (crackling static against an almost inaudible background hum). By Barlow's definition, just about everybody has already been to cyberspace. It's marked by the feeling that the person you're talking to is "in the same room." Most people take the spatial dimension of a phone conversation for granted—until they get a really bad connection or a glitchy overseas call. Then they start raising their voice, as if by sheer volume they could propel it to the outer reaches of cyberspace. **(9)**

Cyberspace, of course, is bigger than a telephone call. It encompasses the millions of personal computers connected by modems—via the telephone system—to commercial online services, as well as the millions more with high-speed links to local area networks, office E-mail systems and the Internet. It includes the rapidly expanding wireless services: microwave towers that carry great quantities of cellular phone and data traffic; communications satellites strung like beads in a geosynchronous orbit; low-flying satellites that will soon crisscross the globe like angry bees, connecting folks too far-flung or too much on the go to be tethered by wires. Someday even our television sets may be part of cyberspace, transformed into interactive "teleputers" by so-called full-service networks like the ones several cable-TV companies (including Time Warner) are building along the old cable lines, using fiber optics and high-speed switches. **(10)**

But these wires and cables and microwaves are not really cyberspace. They are the means of conveyance, not the destination: the information superhighway, not the bright city lights at the end of the road. Cyberspace, in the sense of being "in the same room," is an experience, not a wiring system. It is about people using the new technology to do what they are genetically programmed to do: communicate with one another. It can be found in electronic mail exchanged by lovers who have never met. It emerges from the endless debates on mailing lists and message boards. It's that bond that knits together regulars in electronic chat rooms and newsgroups. It is, like Plato's plane of ideal forms, a metaphorical space, a virtual reality. **(11)**

But it is no less real for being so. We live in the age of information, as Nicholas Negroponte, director of M.I.T.'s Media Lab, is fond of pointing out, in which the fundamental particle is not the atom but the bit—the binary digit, a unit of data usually represented as a 0 or a 1. Information may still be delivered in magazines and newspapers (atoms), but the real value is in the contents (bits). We pay for our goods and services with cash (atoms), but the ebb and flow of capital around the world is carried out—to the tune of several trillion dollars a day—in electronic funds transfers (bits). **(12)**

At this point, however, cyberspace is less about commerce than about community. The technology has unleashed a great rush of direct, person-to-person communications, organized not in the top-down, one-to-many structure of traditional media but in a many-to-many model that may—just may—be a vehicle for revolutionary change. In a world already too divided against itself—rich against poor, producer against consumer—cyberspace offers the nearest thing to a level playing field. **(13)**

Take for example, the Internet. Until something better comes along to replace it, the Internet *is* cyberspace. It may not reach every computer in the human system, as Gibson imagined, but it comes very close. And as anyone who has spent much time there can attest, it is in many ways even stranger than fiction. **(14)**

Begun more than 20 years ago as a Defense Department experiment, the Internet escaped from the Pentagon in 1984 and spread like Kudzu during the personal-computer boom, nearly doubling every year from the mid-1980s on. Today 30 million to 40 million people in more than 160 countries have at least E-mail access to the Internet; in Japan, New Zealand and parts of Europe the number of Net users has grown more than 1,000% during the past three years. **(15)**

One factor fueling the Internet's remarkable growth is its resolutely grass-roots structure. Most conventional computer systems are hierarchical and proprietary; they run on copyright software in a pyramid structure that gives dictatorial powers to the system operators who sit on top. The Internet, by contrast, is open (non-proprietary) and rabidly democratic. No one owns it. No single organization controls it. It is run like a commune with 4.8 million fiercely independent members (called hosts). It crosses national boundaries and answers to no sovereign. It is literally lawless. **(16)**

Although graphics, photos and even videos have started to show up, cyberspace, as it exists on the Internet, is still primarily a text medium. People communicate by and large through words, typed and displayed on a screen. Yet cyberspace assumes an astonishing array of forms, from the utilitarian mailing list (a sort of junk E-mail list to which anyone can contribute) to the rococo MUDS, or Multi-User Dungeons (elaborate fictional gathering places that users create one "room" at a time). All these "spaces" have one thing in common: they are egalitarian to a fault. Anybody can play (provided he or she has the requisite equipment and access), and everybody is afforded the same level of respect (which is to say, little or none). Stripped of the external trappings of wealth, power, beauty and social status, people tend to be judged in the cyberspace of the Internet only by their ideas and their ability to get them across in terse, vigorous prose. On the Internet, as the famous *New Yorker* cartoon put it, nobody knows you're a dog. . . . **(17)**

The Internet is far from perfect. Largely unedited, its content is often tasteless, foolish, uninteresting or just plain wrong. It can be dangerously habit-forming and, truth be told, an enormous waste of time. Even with the arrival of new point-and-click software such as Netscape and Mosaic, it is still too hard to navigate. And because it requires access to both a computer and a high-speed telecommunications link, it is out of reach for millions of people too poor or too far from a major communications hub to participate. **(18)**

But it is remarkable nonetheless, especially considering that it began as a cold war postapocalypse military command grid. "When I look at the Internet," says Bruce Sterling, another science-fiction writer and a great champion of cyberspace, "I see something astounding and delightful. It's as if some grim fallout shelter had burst open and a full-scale MardiGras parade had come out. I take such enormous pleasure in this that it's hard to remain properly skeptical." **(19)**

There is no guarantee, however, that cyberspace will always look like this. The Internet is changing rapidly. Lately a lot of the development efforts—and most of the press attention—have shifted from the rough-and-tumble Usenet newsgroups to the more passive and consumer-oriented "home pages" of the World Wide Web—a system of links that simplifies the task of navigating among the myriad offerings on the Internet. The Net, many oldtimers complain, is turning into a shopping mall. But unless it proves to be a total bust for business, that trend is likely to continue. **(20)**

The more fundamental changes are those taking place underneath our sidewalks and streets, where great wooden wheels of fiber-optic cable are being rolled out one block at a time. Over the next decade, the telecommunications systems of the world will be rebuilt from the ground up as copper wires are ripped up and replaced by hair-thin fiber-optic strands. **(21)**

The reason, in a word, is bandwidth, the information-carrying capacity of a medium (usually measured in bits per second). In terms of bandwidth, a copper telephone wire is like a thin straw, too narrow to carry the traffic it is being asked to bear. By contrast, fiber-optic strands, although hair-thin, are like great fat pipes, with an intrinsic capacity to carry tens of thousands of times as many bits as copper wire. **(22)**

It's not just the Internet surfers who are crying for more bandwidth. Hollywood needs it to deliver movies and television shows on demand. Video game makers want it to send kids the latest adventures of Donkey Kong and Sonic the Hedgehog. The phone companies have their eyes on what some believe will be the next must-have appliance: the videophone. **(23)**

There is a broad consensus in government and industry that the National Information Infrastructure, as the Clinton Administration prefers to call the info highway, will be a broadband, switched network that could, in theory, deliver all these things. But how it will be structured and how it will be deployed are not so clear. For example, if cable-TV and telephone companies are allowed to roll out the new services in only the richest neighborhoods—a practice known as "cream skimming"—that could exacerbate the already growing disparity between those who have access to the latest information and the best intelligence and those who must be content with what they see on TV. **(24)**

An even trickier question has to do with the so-called upstream capacity of the network. Everybody wants to build a fat pipeline going into the home; that's the conduit by which the new information goods and services will be delivered. But how much bandwidth needs to be set aside for the signal going from the home back into the network? In some designs that upstream pathway is quite narrow—allowing just enough bits to change the channel or order a zirconium ring. Some network activists argue that consumers will someday need as much bandwidth going out of the home as they have coming in. Only then can ordinary people become, if they choose, not just consumers of media but producers as well, free to plug their camcorders into the network and broadcast their creations to the world. **(25)**

How these design issues are decided in the months ahead could change the shape of cyberspace. Will it be bottom up, like the Internet, or top down, like broadcast television? In the best case, says Mitch Kapor, cofounder (with John Perry Barlow) of the Electronic Frontier Foundation, we could collectively invent a new entertainment medium, one that taps the creative energies of a nation of midnight scribblers and camcorder video artists. "In the worst case," he says, "we could wind up with networks that have the principal effect of fostering addiction to a new generation of electronic narcotics." **(26)**

If Kapor seems to be painting these scenarios in apocalyptic terms, he is not alone. There is something about cyberspace that sets people's imaginations blazing. Much of what has been written about it—in the press and on the networks—tends to swing from one extreme to the other, from hype and romanticism to fear and loathing. It may be that the near-term impact of cyberspace is being oversold. But that does not mean that real change isn't in the works. As a rule of thumb, historians say, the results of technological innovation always take longer to reach fruition than early champions of change predict. But when change finally comes, its effect is likely to be more profound and widespread and unanticipated than anyone imagined—even the guys who write science fiction. **(27)**

VOCABULARY

In your journal, write the meanings of the following words:

- *phalanx* of Czech nuns **(7)**
- a young *novice* **(7)**
- defined most *succinctly* **(9)**

- a *geosynchronous* orbit **(10)**
- *rococo* MUDS **(17)**
- *egalitarian* to a fault **(17)**
- *postapocalypse* military command grid **(19)**
- *exacerbate* the already growing *disparity* **(24)**
- longer to reach *fruition* **(27)**

QUESTIONS FOR WRITING AND DISCUSSION

1. Most readers of Elmer-DeWitt's article already know the basics about the Internet and the Web. In the form of a double-column log, write in the left-hand column what you already knew about the Internet. In the right-hand column, list the information that you learned from reading Elmer-DeWitt's article. Based on your list, do you think you are included in Elmer-DeWitt's target audience? Explain.

2. Explaining essays typically explain what something means (definition), how something works or was created (process analysis), and/or why something happens (cause-and-effect analysis). List the paragraph numbers of passages illustrating all three of these types of analysis (definition, process, cause/effect). Which of these types does Elmer-DeWitt rely on most frequently?

3. In his essay, Elmer-DeWitt defines key terms as he introduces them. The central word of the essay, "cyberspace," Elmer-DeWitt defines several times. Identify the different paragraphs in which he defines "cyberspace." Elmer-DeWitt also defines the following technical terms in the course of his essay: "feedback loop," "bit," "hierarchical and proprietary," "hosts," "MUDS," "bandwidth," and "upstream capacity." List the paragraph numbers in which each of these terms is defined. Overall, how effective is Elmer-DeWitt at defining key terms for his readers?

4. Elmer-DeWitt organizes his essay into clear sections. Referring to specific paragraph numbers, indicate where the following major divisions of the article begin and end.

    I. Introduction to cyberspace and William Gibson

    II. The growing popularity of cyberspace today

    III. Extended definition of cyberspace

    IV. The Internet and its history

    V. The future of cyberspace and the Internet

What clues did you use to discover Elmer-DeWitt's organization? Is his organization effective, or does it need clarification in places? Explain.

5. Explaining essays should use clear transitions between paragraphs to signal to the reader how the previous paragraph and the new paragraph topics are related. Choose any four consecutive paragraphs. Underline any transitional words or phrases (usually in the first sentence of each paragraph) that help the reader move from one paragraph to the next. Which transitions are effective? Which ones could be improved? Explain.

6. Write your own essay explaining some new technique for navigating the Web or some other aspect of the Internet or computer technology. Decide on your audience (novices, average computer users, or experts). Define key terms, explain processes, or analyze causes and effects.

7. In another *Time* magazine essay (July 4, 1994), "Bards of the Internet," Elmer-DeWitt argues that the kind of writing on the Internet is different—and inferior. Read this essay and investigate how electronic forms of writing have or have not created new rules or new forms for writing. Explain exactly how these new forms are or are not different or how they have or have not affected people.

To Dispel Fears of Live Burial

Jessica Mitford

In this selection from The American Way of Death, *Jessica Mitford illustrates the kind of investigative journalism (some call it "muckraking") that she has perfected. Other works by Mitford include* The Trial of Dr. Spock *(1969),* Kind and Unusual Punishment: The Prison Business *(1973), and* Poison Penmanship *(1979), a collection of articles. In "To Dispel Fears of Live Burial," Mitford explains what embalming is, shows how the process works, and suggests why funeral directors and the public agree to the whole affair. If writing exposition means the "act of exposing" as well as offering explanation, then Mitford is definitely writing "expository" prose. In fact, the exposure is so revealing that we are shocked by what we learn. As we read her essay, we begin to wonder about causes. Why doesn't the public know more about the funeral industry? Why are we so ignorant in these matters? Are we, as consumers, getting what we really want—and deserve?*

Embalming is indeed a most extraordinary procedure, and one must wonder at the docility of Americans who each year pay hundreds of millions of dollars for its perpetuation, blissfully ignorant of what it is all about, what is done, how it is done. Not one in ten thousand has any idea of what actually takes place. Books on the subject are extremely hard to come by. They are not to be found in most libraries or bookshops. **(1)**

In an era when huge television audiences watch surgical operations in the comfort of their living rooms, when, thanks to the animated cartoon, the geography of the digestive system has become familiar territory even to the nursery school set, in a land where the satisfaction of curiosity about almost all matters is a national pastime, the secrecy surrounding embalming can, surely, hardly be attributed to the inherent gruesomeness of the subject. Custom in this regard has within this century suffered a complete reversal. In the early days of American embalming, when it was performed in the home of the deceased, it was almost mandatory for some relative to stay by the embalmer's side and witness the procedure. Today, family members who might wish to be in attendance would certainly be dissuaded by the funeral director. All others, except apprentices, are excluded by law from the preparation room. **(2)**

A close look at what does actually take place may explain in large measure the undertaker's intractable reticence concerning a procedure that has become his major *raison d'être*. Is it possible he fears that public information about embalming might lead patrons to wonder if they really want this service? If the funeral men are loath to discuss the subject outside the trade, the reader may, understandably, be equally loath to go on reading at this point. For those who have the stomach for it, let us part the formaldehyde curtain. . . . **(3)**

The body is first laid out in the undertaker's morgue—or rather, Mr. Jones is reposing in the preparation room—to be readied to bid the world farewell. **(4)**

The preparation room in any of the better funeral establishments has the tiled and sterile look of a surgery, and indeed the embalmer-restorative artist who does his chores there is beginning to adopt the term "dermasurgeon" (appropriately corrupted by some mortician-writers as "demi-surgeon") to describe his calling. His equipment, consisting of scalpels, scissors, augers, forceps, clamps, needles, pumps, tubes, bowls and basins, is crudely imitative of the surgeon's, as is his technique, acquired in a nine- or twelve-month post-high-school course in an embalming school. He is supplied by an advanced chemical industry with a bewildering array of fluids, sprays, pastes, oils, powders, creams, to fix or soften tissue, shrink or distend it as needed, dry it here, restore the moisture there. There are cosmetics, waxes and paints to fill and cover features, even plaster of Paris to replace entire limbs. There are ingenious aids to prop and stabilize the cadaver: a Vari-Pose Head Rest, the Edwards Arm and Hand Positioner, the Repose Block (to support the shoulders during the embalming), and the Throop Foot Positioner, which resembles an old-fashioned stocks. **(5)**

Mr. John H. Eckels, president of the Eckels College of Mortuary Science, thus describes the first part of the embalming procedure. "In the hands of a skilled practitioner, this work may be done in a comparatively short time and without mutilating the body other than by slight incision—so slight that it scarcely would cause serious inconvenience if made upon a living person. It is necessary to remove the blood, and doing this not only helps in the disinfecting, but removes the principal cause of disfigurements due to discoloration." **(6)**

Another textbook discusses the all-important time element: "The earlier this is done, the better, for every hour that elapses between death and embalming will add to the problems and complications encountered. . . ." Just how soon should one get going on the embalming? The author tells us, "On the basis of such scanty information made available to this profession through its rudimentary and haphazard system of technical research, we must conclude that the best results are to be obtained if the subject is embalmed before life is completely extinct—that is, before cellular death has occurred. In the average case, this would mean within an hour after somatic death." For those who feel that there is something a little rudimentary, not to say haphazard, about this advice, a comforting thought is offered by another writer. Speaking of fears entertained in early days of premature burial, he points out, "One of the effects of embalming by chemical injection, however, has been to dispel fears of live burial." How true; once the blood is removed, chances of live burial are indeed remote. **(7)**

To return to Mr. Jones, the blood is drained out through the veins and replaced by embalming fluid pumped in through the arteries. As noted in *The Principles and Practices of Embalming,* "every operator has a favorite injection and drainage point—a fact which becomes a handicap only if he fails or refuses to forsake his favorites when conditions demand it." Typical favorites are the carotid artery, femoral artery, jugular vein, subclavian vein. There are various choices of embalming fluid. If Flextone is used, it will produce a "mild flexible rigidity. The skin retains a velvety softness, the tissues are rubbery and pliable. Ideal for women and children." It may be blended with B. and G. Products Company's Lyf-Lyk tint, which is guaranteed to reproduce "nature's own skin texture . . . the velvety appearance of living tissue." Suntone comes in three separate tints: Suntan; Special Cosmetic Tint, a pink shade "especially indicated for female subjects"; and Regular Cosmetic Tint, moderately pink. **(8)**

About three to six gallons of dyed and perfumed solution of formaldehyde, glycerin, borax, phenol, alcohol and water is soon circulating through Mr. Jones, whose mouth has been sewn together with a "needle directed upward between the upper lip and gum and brought out through the left nostril," with the corners raised slightly "for a more pleasant expression." If he should be bucktoothed, his teeth are cleaned with Bon Ami and coated with colorless nail polish. His eyes, meanwhile, are closed with flesh-tinted eye caps and eye cement. **(9)**

The next step is to have at Mr. Jones with a thing called a trocar. This is a long, hollow needle attached to a tube. It is jabbed into the abdomen, poked around the entrails and chest cavity, the contents of which are pumped out and replaced with "cavity fluid." This done, and the hole in the abdomen sewn up, Mr. Jones' face is heavily creamed (to protect the skin from burns which may be caused by leakage of the chemicals), and he is covered with a sheet and left unmolested for a while. But not for long—there is more, much more, in store for him. He has been embalmed, but not yet restored, and the best time to start the restorative work is eight to ten hours after embalming, when the tissues have become firm and dry. **(10)**

The object of all this attention to the corpse, it must be remembered, is to make it presentable for viewing in an attitude of healthy repose. "Our customs require the presentation of our dead in the semblance of normality . . . unmarred by the ravages of illness, disease or mutilation," says Mr. J. Sheridan Mayer in his *Restorative Art*. This is rather a large order since few people die in the full bloom of health, unravaged by illness and unmarked by some disfigurement. The funeral industry is equal to the challenge: "In some cases, the gruesome appearance of a mutilated or disease-ridden subject may be quite discouraging. The task of restoration may seem impossible and shake the confidence of the embalmer. This is the time for intestinal fortitude and determination. Once the formative work is begun and affected tissues are cleaned or removed, all doubts of success vanish. It is surprising and gratifying to discover the results which may be obtained." **(11)**

The embalmer, having allowed an appropriate interval to elapse, returns to the attack, but now he brings into play the skill and equipment of sculptor and cosmetician. Is a hand missing? Casting one in plaster of Paris is a simple matter. "For replacement purposes, only a cast of the back of the hand is necessary; this is within the ability of the average operator and is quite adequate." If a lip or two, a nose or an ear should be missing, the embalmer has at hand a variety of restorative waxes with which to model replacements. Pores and skin texture are simulated by stippling with a little brush, and over this cosmetics are laid on. Head off? Decapitation cases are rather routinely handled. Ragged edges are trimmed, and head joined to torso with a series of splints, wires and sutures. It is a good idea to have a little something at the neck—a scarf or a high collar—when time for viewing comes. Swollen mouth? Cut out tissue as needed from inside the lips. If too much is removed, the surface contour can easily be restored by padding with cotton. Swollen necks and cheeks are reduced by removing tissue through vertical incisions made down each side of the neck. "When the deceased is casketed, the pillow will hide the suture incisions . . . as an extra precaution against leakage, the suture may be painted with liquid sealer." **(12)**

The opposite condition is more likely to present itself—that of emaciation. His hypodermic syringe now loaded with massage cream, the embalmer seeks out and fills the hollowed and sunken areas by injection. In this procedure the backs of the hands and fingers and the under-chin area should not be neglected. **(13)**

Positioning the lips is a problem that recurrently challenges the ingenuity of the embalmer. Closed too tightly, they tend to give a stern, even disapproving expression. Ideally, embalmers feel, the lips should give the impression of being ever so slightly parted, the upper lip protruding slightly for a more youthful appearance. This takes some engineering, however, as the lips tend to drift apart. Lip drift can sometimes be remedied by pushing one or two straight pins through the inner margin of the lower lip and then inserting them between the two front upper teeth. If Mr. Jones happens to have no teeth, the pins can just as easily be anchored in his Armstrong Face Former and Denture Replacer. Another method to maintain lip closure is to dislocate the lower jaw, which is then held in its new position by a wire run through holes which have been drilled through the upper and lower jaws at the midline. As the French are fond of saying, *il faut souffrir pour être belle.* **(14)**

If Mr. Jones has died of jaundice, the embalming fluid will very likely turn him green. Does this deter the embalmer? Not if he has intestinal fortitude. Masking pastes and cosmetics are heavily laid on, burial garments and casket interiors are color-correlated with particular care, and Jones is displayed beneath rose-colored lights. Friends will say "How well he looks." Death by carbon monoxide, on the other hand, can be rather a good thing from the embalmer's viewpoint: "One advantage is the fact that this type of discoloration is an exaggerated form of a natural pink coloration." This is nice because the healthy glow is already present and needs but little attention. **(15)**

The patching and filling completed, Mr. Jones is now shaved, washed and dressed. Cream-based cosmetic, available in pink, flesh, suntan, brunette and blond, is applied to his hands and face, his hair is shampooed and combed (and, in the case of Mrs. Jones, set), his hands manicured. For the horny-handed son of toil special care must be taken; cream should be applied to remove ingrained grime, and the nails cleaned. "If he were not in the habit of having them manicured in life, trimming and shaping is advised for better appearance—never questioned by kin." **(16)**

Jones is now ready for casketing (this is the present participle of the verb "to casket"). In this operation his right shoulder should be depressed slightly "to turn the body a bit to the right and soften the appearance of lying flat on the back." Positioning the hands is a matter of importance, and special rubber positioning blocks may be used. The hands should be cupped slightly for a more lifelike, relaxed appearance. Proper placement of the body requires a delicate sense of balance. It should lie as high as possible in the casket, yet not so high that the lid, when lowered, will hit the nose. On the other hand, we are cautioned, placing the body too low "creates the impression that the body is in a box." **(17)**

Jones is next wheeled into the appointed slumber room where a few last touches may be added—his favorite pipe placed in his hand or, if he was a great reader, a book propped into position. (In the case of little Master Jones a Teddy bear may be clutched.) Here he will hold open house for a few days, visiting hours 10 a.m. to 9 p.m. **(18)**

Vocabulary

In your journal, write the meaning of the following words:

- *docility* of Americans **(1)**
- *intractable reticence* concerning a procedure **(3)**
- *raison d'être* [reason for being] **(3)**
- *loath* to discuss the subject **(3)**
- *rudimentary* and haphazard system **(7)**
- *somatic* death **(7)**
- splints, wires and *sutures* **(12)**
- that of *emaciation* **(13)**
- *il faut souffrir pour être belle* [one must suffer in order to be beautiful] **(14)**
- died of *jaundice* **(15)**

Questions for Writing and Discussion

1. What word best describes your initial reaction to this article: disgust, nausea, confusion, anger, surprise, amazement, disbelief, or some other word? Explain your reaction.

2. Funeral directors all over the country were outraged when *The American Way of Death* appeared. What passages from this selection would most likely anger them—and why?

3. Do you believe Mitford's *purpose* in this essay was just to *inform* us about the embalming procedure? To *explain* how and why it happens? To *persuade* us to adopt some belief or take action? What parts of the essay illustrate her purpose(s) most clearly? (Refer to paragraph numbers.)

4. The contrast between appearance and reality is a recurring theme in this essay—for instance, the lifelike appearance of the embalmed and prepared body versus the reality of death. Where in the essay is this contrast most obvious?

5. Mitford's essay illustrates organization by process analysis—her explanation of *how* the embalming process occurs. List the major steps in the embalming process. (Refer to paragraph numbers for each step.) What references to time or sequence does she use for transitions at the beginning of the paragraphs?

6. Without conducting a thorough investigation, Mitford could not have learned enough to write this explanation of embalming. What books, journals, or interviews does she refer to in her essay? What direct quotations does she use?

7. Describe the *persona* that Mitford projects in this essay. What is her *tone* or attitude toward her subject? Is she writing from the perspective of a sympathetic observer of the funeral industry or of one hostile to its pretensions? Where in the essay is her tone most obvious?

8. The funeral industry Mitford describes in 1963 has not changed much in the past four decades. For an update, read a recent article by Erik Larson (*Time,* December 9, 1996), which discusses current abuses. After reading about the current state of the funeral industry, write your own essay explaining how practices and attitudes have or have not changed in the past 35 years.

How Male and Female Students Use Language Differently

Deborah Tannen

Everyone knows that men and women communicate differently, but Deborah Tannen, a linguist at Georgetown University, has spent her career studying how and why their conversational styles are different. Tannen's books include Conversational Style: Analyzing Talk Among Friends *(1984) and her best-selling* You Just Don't Understand: Women and Men in Conversation *(1990). In the following article from* The Chronicle of Higher Education, *Tannen applies her knowledge of conversational styles to the classroom. How do men and women communicate differently in the classroom? What teaching styles best promote open communication and learning for both sexes? As you read her essay, think about your own classes. Do the men in your classes talk more than the women? Do men like to argue in large groups, while women prefer conversations in small groups? How clearly—and convincingly—does Tannen explain discussion preferences and their effects in the classroom?*

When I researched and wrote my latest book, *You Just Don't Understand: Women and Men in Conversation,* the furthest thing from my mind was reevaluating my teaching strategies. But that has been one of the direct benefits of having written the book. **(1)**

The primary focus of my linguistic research always has been the language of everyday conversation. One facet of this is conversational style: how different regional, ethnic, and class backgrounds, as well as age and gender, result in different ways of using language to communicate. *You Just Don't Understand* is about the conversational styles of women and men. As I gained more insight into typically male and female ways of using language, I began to suspect some of the causes of the troubling facts that women who go to single-sex schools do better in later life, and that when young women sit next to young men in classrooms, the males talk more. This is not to say that all men talk in class, nor that no women do. It is simply that a greater percentage of discussion time is taken by men's voices. **(2)**

The research of sociologists and anthropologists such as Janet Lever, Marjorie Harness Goodwin, and Donna Eder has shown that girls and boys learn to use language differently in their sex-separate peer groups. Typically, a girl has a best friend with whom she sits and talks, frequently telling secrets. It's the telling of secrets, the fact and the way that they talk to each other, that makes them best friends. For boys, activities are central: their best friends are the ones they do things with. Boys also tend to play in larger groups that are hierarchical. High-status boys give orders and push low-status boys around. So boys are expected to use language to seize center stage: by exhibiting their skill, displaying their knowledge, and challenging and resisting challenges. **(3)**

These patterns have stunning implications for classroom interaction. Most faculty members assume that participating in class discussion is a necessary part of successful performance. Yet speaking in a classroom is more congenial to boys' language experience than to girls', since it entails putting oneself forward in front of a large group of people, many of whom are strangers and at least one of whom is sure to judge speakers' knowledge and intelligence by their verbal display. **(4)**

Another aspect of many classrooms that makes them more hospitable to most men than to most women is the use of debate-like formats as a learning tool. Our educational system, as Walter Ong argues persuasively in his book *Fighting for Life* (Cornell University Press, 1981), is fundamentally male in that the pursuit of knowledge is believed to be achieved by ritual opposition: public display followed by argument and challenge. Father Ong demonstrates that ritual opposition—what he calls "adversativeness" or "agonism"—is fundamental to the way most males approach almost any activity. (Consider, for example, the little boy who shows he likes a little girl by pulling her braids and shoving her.) But ritual opposition is antithetical to the way most females learn and like to interact. It is not that females don't fight, but that they don't fight for fun. They don't *ritualize* opposition. **(5)**

Anthropologists working in widely disparate parts of the world have found contrasting verbal rituals for women and men. Women in completely unrelated cultures (for example, Greece and Bali) engage in ritual laments: spontaneously produced rhyming couplets that express their pain, for example, over the loss of loved ones. Men do not take part in laments. They have their own, very different verbal ritual: a contest, a war of words in which they vie with each other to devise clever insults. **(6)**

When discussing these phenomena with a colleague, I commented that I see these two styles in American conversation: many women bond by talking about troubles, and many men bond by exchanging playful insults and put-downs, and other sorts of verbal sparring. He exclaimed: "I never thought of this, but that's the way I teach: I have students read an article, and then I invite them to tear it apart. After we've torn it to shreds, we talk about how to build a better model." **(7)**

This contrasts sharply with the way I teach: I open the discussion of readings by asking, "What did you find useful in this? What can we use in our own theory building and our own methods?" I note what I see as weaknesses in the author's approach, but I also point out that the writer's discipline and purposes might be different from ours. Finally, I offer personal anecdotes illustrating the phenomena under discussion and praise students' anecdotes as well as their critical acumen. **(8)**

These different teaching styles must make our classrooms wildly different places and hospitable to different students. Male students are more likely to be comfortable attacking the readings and might find the inclusion of personal anecdotes irrelevant and "soft." Women are more likely to resist discussion they perceive as hostile, and, indeed, it is women in my classes who are most likely to offer personal anecdotes. **(9)**

A colleague who read my book commented that he had always taken for granted that the best way to deal with students' comments is to challenge them; this, he felt it was self-evident, sharpens their minds and helps them develop debating skills. But he had noticed that women were relatively silent in his classes, so he decided to try beginning discussion with relatively open-ended questions and letting comments go unchallenged. He found, to his amazement and satisfaction, that more women began to speak up. **(10)**

Though some of the women in his class clearly liked this better, perhaps some of the men liked it less. One young man in my class wrote in a questionnaire about a history professor who gave students questions to think about and called on people to answer them: "He would then play devil's advocate . . . *i.e.,* he debated us. . . . That class *really* sharpened me intellectually. . . . We as students do need to know how to defend ourselves." This young man valued the experience of being attacked and challenged publicly.

Many, if not most, women would shrink from such "challenge," experiencing it as public humiliation. **(11)**

A professor at Hamilton College told me of a young man who was upset because he felt his class presentation had been a failure. The professor was puzzled because he had observed that class members had listened attentively and agreed with the student's observations. It turned out that it was this very agreement that the student interpreted as failure: since no one had engaged his ideas by arguing with him, he felt they had found them unworthy of attention. **(12)**

So one reason men speak in class more than women is that many of them find the "public" classroom setting more conducive to speaking, whereas most women are more comfortable speaking in private to a small group of people they know well. A second reason is that men are more likely to be comfortable with the debate-like form that discussion may take. Yet another reason is the different attitudes toward speaking in class that typify women and men. **(13)**

Students who speak frequently in class, many of whom are men, assume that it is their job to think of contributions and try to get the floor to express them. But many women monitor their participation not only to get the floor but to avoid getting it. Women students in my class tell me that if they have spoken up once or twice, they hold back for the rest of the class because they don't want to dominate. If they have spoken a lot one week, they will remain silent the next. These different ethics of participation are, of course, unstated, so those who speak freely assume that those who remain silent have nothing to say, and those who are reining themselves in assume that the big talkers are selfish and hoggish. **(14)**

When I looked around my classes, I could see these differing ethics and habits at work. For example, my graduate class in analyzing conversation had twenty students, eleven women and nine men. Of the men, four were foreign students: two Japanese, one Chinese, and one Syrian. With the exception of the three Asian men, all the men spoke in class at least occasionally. The biggest talker in the class was a woman, but there were also five women who never spoke at all, only one of whom was Japanese. I decided to try something different. **(15)**

I broke the class into small groups to discuss the issues raised in the readings and to analyze their own conversational transcripts. I devised three ways of dividing the students into groups: one by the degree program they were in, one by gender, and one by conversational style, as closely as I could guess it. This meant that when the class was grouped according to conversational style, I put Asian students together, fast talkers together, and quiet students together. The class split into groups six times during the semester, so they met in each grouping twice. I told students to regard the groups as examples of interactional data and to note the different ways they participated in the different groups. Toward the end of the term, I gave them a questionnaire asking about their class and group participation. **(16)**

I could see plainly from my observation of the groups at work that women who never opened their mouths in class were talking away in the small groups. In fact, the Japanese woman commented that she found it particularly hard to contribute to the all-woman group she was in because "I was overwhelmed by how talkative the female students were in the female-only group." This is particularly revealing because it highlights that the same person who can be "oppressed" into silence in one context can become the talkative "oppressor" in another. No one's conversational style is absolute; everyone's style changes in response to the context and others' styles. **(17)**

Some of the students (seven) said they preferred the same-gender groups; others preferred the same-style groups. In answer to the question "Would you have liked to speak in class more than you did?" six of the seven who said yes were women; the one man was Japanese. Most startlingly, this response did not come only from quiet women; it came from women who had indicated they had spoken in class never, rarely, sometimes, and often. Of the eleven students who said the amount they had spoken was fine, seven were men. Of the four women who checked "fine," two added qualifications indicating it wasn't completely fine: One wrote in "maybe more," and one wrote, "I have an urge to participate but often feel I should have something more interesting/relevant/wonderful/intelligent to say!!" **(18)**

I counted my experiment a success. Everyone in the class found the small groups interesting, and no one indicated he or she would have preferred that the class not break into groups. Perhaps most instructive, however, was the fact that the experience of breaking into groups, and of talking about participation in class, raised everyone's awareness about classroom participation. After we had talked about it, some of the quietest women in the class made a few voluntary contributions, though sometimes I had to ensure their participation by interrupting the students who were exuberantly speaking out. **(19)**

Americans are often proud that they discount the significance of cultural differences: "We are all individuals," many people boast. Ignoring such issues as gender and ethnicity becomes a source of pride: "I treat everyone the same." But treating people the same is not equal treatment if they are not the same. **(20)**

The classroom is a different environment for those who feel comfortable putting themselves forward in a group than it is for those who find the prospect of doing so chastening, or even terrifying. When a professor asks, "Are there any questions?" students who can formulate statements the fastest have the greatest opportunity to respond. Those who need significant time to do so have not really been given a chance at all, since by the time they are ready to speak, someone else has the floor. **(21)**

In a class where some students speak out without raising hands, those who feel they must raise their hands and wait to be recognized do not have equal opportunity to speak. Telling them to feel free to jump in will not make them feel free; one's sense of timing, of one's rights and obligations in a classroom, are automatic, learned over years of interaction. They may be changed over time, with motivation and effort, but they cannot be changed on the spot. And everyone assumes his or her own way is best. When I asked my students how the class could be changed to make it easier for them to speak more, the most talkative woman said she would prefer it if no one had to raise hands, and a foreign student said he wished people would raise their hands and wait to be recognized. **(22)**

My experience in this class has convinced me that small-group interaction should be part of any class that is not a small seminar. I also am convinced that having the students become observers of their own interaction is a crucial part of their education. Talking about ways of talking in class makes students aware that their ways of talking affect other students, that the motivations they impute to others may not truly reflect others' motives, and that the behaviors they assume to be self-evidently right are not universal norms. **(23)**

The goal of complete equal opportunity in class may not be attainable, but realizing that one monolithic classroom-participation structure is not equal opportunity is itself a powerful motivation to find more-diverse methods to serve diverse students—and every classroom is diverse. **(24)**

VOCABULARY

In your journal, write the meanings of the following words:

- ritual opposition is *antithetical* **(5)**
- personal *anecdotes* **(8)**
- *conducive* to speaking **(13)**
- *ethics* of participation **(14)**
- *monolithic* classroom-participation structure **(24)**

QUESTIONS FOR WRITING AND DISCUSSION

1. Reread Tannen's essay, noting places where your experiences as a student match or do not match her observations. In what contexts were your experiences similar to or different from Tannen's? Explain what might account for the different observations.

2. In her essay, Tannen states and then continues to restate her thesis. Reread her essay, underlining all the sentences that seem to state or rephrase her main idea. Do her restatements of the main idea make her essay clearer? Explain.

3. Explaining essays may explain *what* (describe and define), explain *how* (process analysis), and/or explain *why* (causal analysis). Find one example of each of these strategies in Tannen's essay. Which of these three is the dominant shaping strategy? Support your answer with references to specific sentences or paragraphs.

4. Effective explaining essays must have supporting evidence—specific examples, facts, quotations, testimony from experts, statistics, and so on. Choose four consecutive paragraphs from Tannen's essay and list the kinds of supporting evidence she uses. Based on your inventory, rate her supporting evidence as weak, average, or strong. Explain your choice.

5. Does the style of Tannen's essay support her thesis that men and women have different ways of communicating? Does Tannen, in fact, use a "woman's style" of writing that is similar to women's conversational style? Examine Tannen's tone (her attitude toward her subject and audience), her voice (the projection of her personality in her language), and her supporting evidence (her use of facts and statistics or anecdotal, contextual evidence). Cite specific passages to support your analysis.

6. In another class where students discuss frequently, sit in the back row where you can observe the participation of men and women. First, record the number of men and the number of women in the class. Then, during one class period, record the following: (1) When the teacher calls on a student, record whether the student is male or female. (2) When students talk without raising their hands, record whether the student is male or female. (3) When students speak in class, record how long they talk and whether they are male or female. Once you have collected and analyzed your data, explain whether they seem to support or refute Tannen's claims.

EXPLAINING:

THE WRITING PROCESS

■ ASSIGNMENT FOR EXPLAINING   Explain *what* something means or is, *how* it should be done or how it occurs, and/or *why* something occurs. Choose from your personal experiences, talents, or interests or choose from ideas, concepts, theories, or strategies that you are learning in other courses. Your purpose is to explain something as clearly as possible for your audience by analyzing, showing relationships, and demonstrating with examples, facts, illustrations, data, or other information.

CHOOSING A SUBJECT

If one of your journal entries suggested a possible subject, go on to the collecting and shaping strategies. If you still need an interesting subject, consider the following suggestions:

- Reread your authority list or the most interesting journal entries from previous chapters. Do they contain ideas that you might define or explain, processes suitable for how-to explanations, or causes or effects that you could analyze and explain for a certain audience?
- Brainstorm a list of the five most important things that you've done in the last three years. Focus on one thing, event, or idea. Now imagine that your audience is someone like you, only three years younger. Explain this topic.
- Reread your notes from another class in which you have an upcoming examination. Select some topic, idea, principle, process, famous person, or event from the text or your notes. Investigate other texts, popular magazines, or journals for information on that topic. If appropriate, interview someone or conduct a survey. Explain this principle or process to a member of your writing class.

You can write about anything, and if you write well enough, even the reader with no intrinsic interest in the subject will become involved.

—TRACY KIDDER

NOVELIST

COLLECTING

QUESTIONS Once you have a tentative subject and audience in mind, consider which of the following will be your primary focus (all three may be relevant):

- *What* something means or is
- *How* something occurs or is done (or should be done)
- *Why* something occurs or what its effects are

To explain *what* something is, jot down answers to each of the following questions. The more you can write on each question, the more details you'll have for your topic.

- What are its class and distinguishing characteristics?
- What is its etymology?
- How can you describe it?
- What examples can you give?
- What are its parts or its functions?
- What is it similar to? What is it *not?*
- What figurative comparisons apply?
- How can it be classified?
- Which of the above is most useful to your audience?

To explain *how* something occurs or is done, answer the following questions:

- What are the component parts or steps in the whole process?
- What is the exact sequence of steps or events?
- Are several of the steps or events related?
- If steps or events were omitted, would the outcome change?
- Which steps or events are most crucial?
- Which steps or events does your audience most need to know?

To explain *why* something occurs or what its effects are, consider the following issues:

- Which are the necessary or sufficient causes?
- Which causes are remote in time and which are immediate?
- What is the order or sequence of the causes? Do the causes occur simultaneously?
- What are the effects? Do they occur in a sequence or simultaneously?
- Do the causes and effects occur in a "chain reaction"?
- Is there an action or situation that would have prevented the effect?
- Are there comparable things or events that have similar causes or effects?
- Which causes or effects need special clarification for your audience?

BRANCHING   Often, *branching* can help you visually analyze your subject. Start with your topic and then subdivide each idea into its component parts. The resulting analysis will not only help generate ideas but may also suggest ways to shape an essay:

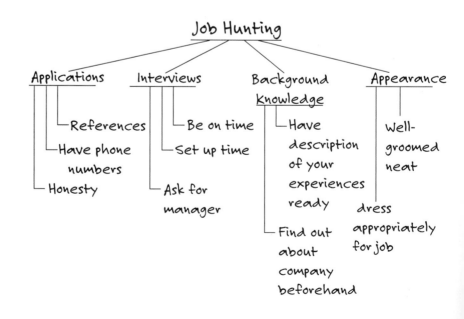

Branching can also take the form of a tree, with a main trunk for the subject and separate branches for each subtopic. For an essay on effective job hunting, information might be diagrammed like this:

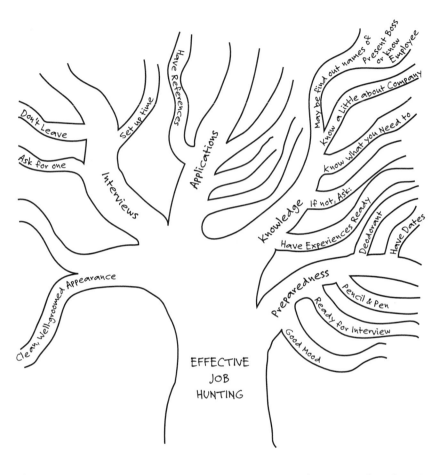

OBSERVING   If you can observe your subject, try drawing it, describing it, or taking careful notes. Which senses can you use to describe it—sight, sound, touch, smell, taste? If it is a scientific experiment that you can reproduce or a social situation you can reconstruct, go through it again and observe carefully. As you observe it, put yourself in your readers' shoes: What do you need to explain it to them?

REMEMBERING   Your own experience and memory are essential for explaining. *Freewriting, looping,* and *clustering* may all generate detailed information, good examples, and interesting perspectives that will make your explanation clearer and more vivid. (See Chapter 4 for an explanation of looping and clustering.)

READING   When you find written texts about your subject, be sure to use your active reading strategies. You may need only a few sources if you reread them carefully. Write out a short summary for each source. Respond to each source by analyzing its effectiveness, agreeing or disagreeing with its ideas, or interpreting the text. The quality of your understanding is more important than the sheer number of sources you cite.

INVESTIGATING   Use sources available in the library, textbooks containing relevant information, or interviews with teachers, participants, or experts. Interview your classmates about their own subjects for this assignment: Someone else's subject may trigger an idea that you can write about or suggest a fresh approach to the subject that you have already chosen.

RESEARCH TIPS

Review your topic for research possibilities. Four research strategies are direct *observation*, use of *memories* and personal experience, *field research* (including interviews and surveys), and *library research*. (See Chapter 6 for interview and survey techniques. See Chapter 12 on using and documenting sources.) Tips to remember: Make *photocopies* of all the sources that you plan to cite in your essay. When you make copies, be sure to *write all relevant information* on the photocopies, such as author, date, publisher, place of publication, journal title, and volume numbers. When you cite sources in the text, be sure to *introduce* your sources. Make sure your direct quotations are *accurate* word-for-word transcriptions.

SHAPING

As you collect information and generate ideas from your collecting activities, be sure to *narrow* and *focus* your subject into a topic suitable for a short essay. You will not be able to cover everything you've read, thought, or experienced about your subject. Choose the most interesting ideas—for you and for your audience—and shape, order, and clarify those ideas. In addition to *spatial order* and *comparison/contrast*, which are discussed in Chapters 3 and 4, one of the following shaping strategies may help you organize your essay.

DEFINITION AND CLASSIFICATION   An essay explaining *what* something means or is can be shaped by using a variety of definition strategies or by classifying the subject.

Definition itself is not a single organizing strategy; it supports a variety of strategies that may be useful in shaping your essay: description, analysis of parts or function, comparison/contrast, development by examples, or figures of speech such as simile, metaphor, and analogy.

Classification, on the other hand, is a single strategy that can organize a paragraph or even a whole essay quickly. Observers of human behavior, for example, love to use classification. Grocery shoppers might be classified by types: racers (the ones who seem to have just won forty-five seconds of free shopping and run down the aisles filling their carts as fast as possible), talkers (the ones whose phone must be out of order because they stand in the aisles gossiping forever), penny-pinchers (who always have their calculators out and read the unit-price labels for everything), party shoppers (who camp out in the junk-food aisles, filling their carts with potato chips, dip, candy, peanuts, and drink mixers), and dawdlers (who leave their carts crosswise in the aisles while they read twenty-nine different soup-can labels). You can write a sentence or two about each type or devote a whole paragraph to explaining a single type.

EXAMPLE   Development by example can effectively illustrate what something is or means, but it can also help explain how or why something happens. Usually, an example describes a specific incident, located at a certain place and occurring at a particular time, that *shows* or *demonstrates* the main idea. In the following paragraph from *Mediaspeak,* Donna Woolfolk Cross explains what effects soap operas can have on addicted viewers. This paragraph is developed by several examples—some described in detail, others referred to briefly:

> Dedicated watchers of soap operas often confuse fact with fiction. . . . Stars of soap operas tell hair-raising stories of their encounters with fans suffering from this affliction. Susan Lucci, who plays the promiscuous Erica Kane on "All My Children," tells of a time she was riding in a parade: "We were in a crowd of about 250,000 traveling in an antique open car moving ver-r-ry slowly. At that time in the series I was involved with a character named Nick. Some man broke through, came right up to the car and said to me, 'Why don't you give me a little bit of what you've been giving Nick?'" The man hung onto the car, menacingly, until she was rescued by the police. Another time, when she was in church, the reverent silence was broken by a woman's astonished remark, "Oh, my god, Erica prays!" Margaret Mason, who plays the villainous Lisa Anderson in "Days of Our Lives," was accosted by a

Readers may be strangers who have no immediate reason to care about your writing. They want order, clarity, and stimulation. . . .

—**ELIZABETH COWAN NEELD,**

TEACHER AND AUTHOR

woman who poured a carton of milk all over her in the supermarket. And once a woman actually tried to force her car off the Ventura Freeway.

VOICE AND TONE   Writers also use voice and tone to shape and control whole passages, often in combination with other shaping strategies. In the following paragraph, Toni Bambara, author of *The Salt Eaters* and numerous short stories, explains *what* being a writer is all about. This paragraph is shaped both by a single extended example and by Bambara's voice talking directly to the reader:

> When I replay the tapes on file in my head, tapes of speeches I've given at writing conferences over the years, I invariably hear myself saying—"A writer, like any other cultural worker, like any other member of the community, ought to try to put her/his skills in the service of the community." Some years ago when I returned south, my picture in the paper prompted several neighbors to come visit. "You a writer? What all you write?" Before I could begin the catalogue, one old gent interrupted with—"Ya know Miz Mary down the block? She need a writer to help her send off a letter to her grandson overseas." So I began a career as the neighborhood scribe—letters to relatives, snarling letters to the traffic chief about the promised stop sign, nasty letters to the utilities, angry letters to the principal about that confederate flag hanging in front of the school, contracts to transfer a truck from seller to buyer, etc. While my efforts have been graciously appreciated in the form of sweet potato dumplings, herb teas, hair braiding, and the like, there is still much room for improvement—"For a writer, honey, you've got a mighty bad hand. Didn't they teach penmanship at that college?" Another example, I guess, of words setting things in motion. What goes around, comes around, as the elders say.

CHRONOLOGICAL ORDER AND PROCESS ANALYSIS   Using chronological order for a *how* explanation creates a process analysis. For example, Jessica Mitford's explanation of embalming illustrates how chronological order or process analysis can shape a whole essay. Notice how the beginnings of several body paragraphs use transitions that *signal* to the reader the chronological order of the embalming process:

> The body is *first* laid out in the undertaker's morgue. . . . **(4)**

> Mr. John H. Eckels . . . describes the *first part* of the embalming procedure. . . . **(6)**

> *To return* to Mr. Jones, the blood is drained out through the veins. . . . **(8)**

The *next step* is to have at Mr. Jones with a thing called a trocar. **(10)**

The embalmer, *having allowed an appropriate interval to elapse, returns* to the attack. . . . **(12)**

The patching and filling *completed,* Mr. Jones is *now* shaved, washed and dressed. **(16)**

Jones is *now* ready for casketing. . . . **(17)**

Jones is *next* wheeled into the appointed slumber room. . . . **(18)**

CAUSAL ANALYSIS In order to explain *why* something happens or what the effects of something are, writers often use one of the following three patterns of cause and effect to shape their material:

Cause 1 + Cause 2 + Cause 3 . . . + Cause n → Effect

In the case of fire, for example, we know that three causes lead to a single effect. These causes do not occur in any special sequence; they must all be present at the same time. For historical events, however, we usually list causes in chronological order.

Sometimes one cause has several effects. In that case, we reverse the pattern:

Cause → Effect 1 + Effect 2 + Effect 3 . . . + Effect n

For example, an explanation of the collapse of the economy following the stock market crash of 1929 might follow this pattern. The crash (itself a symptom of other causes) led to a depreciated economy, widespread unemployment, bankruptcy for thousands of businesses, foreclosures on farms, and so forth. An essay on the effects of the crash might devote one or two paragraphs to each effect.

In the third pattern, causes and effects form a pattern of chain reactions. One cause leads to an effect that then becomes the cause of another effect, and so on:

Cause 1 → Effect 1 (Cause 2) → Effect 2 (Cause 3) → Effect 3

We could analyze events in the Middle East prior to the Persian Gulf War as a series of actions and reactions in which each effect becomes the cause of the next effect in the chain of skirmishes, car bombings, air raids, terrorist hijackings, and kidnappings. An essay on the chain reaction of events in the Middle East might have a paragraph or two on each of the links in this chain.

INTRODUCTIONS AND LEAD-INS   Often, the first sentences of the introductory paragraph of an essay are the hardest to write. You want to get your reader's attention and focus on the main idea of your essay, but you don't want to begin, boringly, with your thesis statement. Below are several kinds of opening sentences designed to grab your reader's interest. (All of these sample lead-ins are from essays reprinted in this text.) Consider your topic—see if one of these strategies will work for you.

A personal example

I knew my dieting had gotten out of hand, but when I could actually see the movement of my heart beating beneath my clothes, I knew I was in trouble.

—"Anorexia Nervosa," Nancie Brosseau

A description of a person or place

He strides toward us in navy and white, his body muscled and heavy-set, one arm holding his casually flung jeans jacket over his shoulder. A man in his prime, with just the right combination of macho and sartorial flair.

—"Some Don't Like Their Blues at All," Karyn M. Lewis

It's still there, the Chinese school on Yale Street where my brother and I used to go. Despite the new coat of paint and the high wire fence, the school I knew 10 years ago remains remarkably, stoically the same.

—"The Struggle to be an All-American Girl," Elizabeth Wong

An example from a case study

Susan Smith has everything going for her. A self-described workaholic, she runs a Cambridge, Massachusetts, real estate consulting company with her husband Charles and still finds time to cuddle and nurture their two young kids, David, 7, and Stacey, 6. What few people know is that Susan, 44, needs a little chemical help to be a supermom: she has been taking the antidepressant Prozac for five years.

—"The Personality Pill," Anastasia Toufexis

A startling statement, fact, or statistic

Embalming is indeed a most extraordinary procedure, and one must wonder at the docility of Americans who each year pay hundreds of millions of dollars for its perpetuation, blissfully ignorant of what it is all about, what is done, how it is done.

—"To Dispel Fears of Live Burial," Jessica Mitford

A statement from a book

The American novelist John Barth, in his early novel, *The Floating Opera*, remarks that ordinary, day-to-day life often presents us with embarrassingly obvious, totally unsubtle patterns of symbolism and meaning—life in the midst of death, innocence vindicated, youth versus age, etc.

> —"I'm O.K., But You're Not," Robert Zoellner

A literary allusion or quotation

"We began to sail up the narrow strait lamenting," narrates Odysseus. "For on the one hand lay Scylla, with twelve feet all dangling down; and six necks exceeding long, and on each a hideous head, and therein three rows of teeth set thick and close, full of black death. And on the other mighty Charybdis sucked down the salt sea water."

> —"Darwin's Middle Road," Stephen Jay Gould

A striking question or questions

Do non-human animals have rights? Should we humans feel morally bound to exercise consideration for the lives and well-being of individual members of other animal species? If so, how much consideration, and by what logic?

> —"Animal Rights and Beyond," David Quammen

A historical example

On May 10, 1831, a young French aristocrat named Alexis de Tocqueville arrived in New York City at the start of what would become one of the most famous visits to America in our history. He had come to observe firsthand the institutions of the freest, most egalitarian society of the age, but what he found was a paradox.

> —"Masters of Desire," Jack Solomon

A common error or mistaken judgment

There was a time when, in my search for essences, I concluded that the canyonland country has no heart. I was wrong. The canyonlands did have a heart, a living heart, and that heart was Glen Canyon and the golden, flowing Colorado River.

> —"The Damnation of a Canyon," Edward Abbey

Combined strategies

Last December a man named Robert Lee Willie, who had been convicted of raping and murdering an 18-year-old woman, was executed
in the Louisiana state prison. In a statement issued several minutes
before his death, Mr. Willie said: "Killing people is wrong. . . . It
makes no difference whether it's citizens, countries, or governments.
Killing is wrong."

—"Death and Justice," Edward Koch

LEAD-IN, THESIS, AND ESSAY MAP   The introduction to an
explaining essay—whether one paragraph or several—usually contains the
following features:

- *Lead-In:* Some example, description, startling statement, statistic,
  short narrative, allusion, or quotation to get the reader's interest *and*
  focus on the topic you will explain.
- *Thesis:* Statement of the main idea; a "promise" to the reader that the
  essay fulfills.
- *Essay Map:* A sentence, or part of a sentence, that *lists* (in the order
  in which the essay discusses them) the main subtopics for the essay.

In her essay on *anorexia nervosa* at the end of this chapter, Nancie Brosseau's
introductory paragraph has all three features:

Lead-in: startling state-ment

Description

Statistics
Thesis
Essay map

I knew my dieting had gotten out of hand, but when I could actually
see the movement of my heart beating beneath my clothes I knew I
was in trouble. At first, the family doctor reassured my parents that my
rapid weight loss was a "temporary phase among teenage girls." However, when I, at 14 years old and 5'0" tall, weighed in at 63 pounds, my
doctor changed his diagnosis from "temporary phase" to "anorexia
nervosa." Anorexia nervosa is the process of self-starvation that affects
over one hundred thousand young girls each year. Almost six thousand of these girls die every year. Anorexia nervosa is a self-mutilating
disease that affects its victim both physically and emotionally. **(1)**

The essay map is contained in the phrase "both physically and emotionally": The first half of the essay discusses the physical effects of anorexia nervosa; the second half explains the emotional effects. Like a road map, the
essay map helps the reader anticipate what topics the writer will explain.

PARAGRAPH TRANSITIONS & HOOKS   Transition words and paragraph hooks are audience cues that help the reader shift from one paragraph
to the next. These connections between paragraphs help the reader see the
relationships of the various parts. Transition words—"first," "second," "next,"
"another," "last," "finally," and so forth—signal your reader that a new idea or
a new part of the idea is coming up. In addition to transition words, writers

often tie paragraphs together by using a key word or idea from a previous paragraph in the opening sentence of the following paragraph to "hook" the paragraphs together. The following paragraphs from Mitford's essay on embalming illustrate how transition words and paragraph hooks work together to create smooth connections between paragraphs:

About three to six gallons of a dyed and perfumed solution of formaldehyde, glycerin, borax, phenol, alcohol and water is soon circulating through Mr. Jones. . . . If he should be bucktoothed, his teeth are cleaned with Bon Ami and coated with colorless nail polish. His eyes, meanwhile, are closed with flesh-tinted eye caps and eye cement. **(9)**

The *next step* is to have at Mr. Jones with a thing called a trocar. . . . This done, and the hole in the abdomen sewn up, Mr. Jones' face is heavily creamed . . . and he is covered with a sheet and left unmolested for a while. But not for long—there is more, much more, in store for him. He has been embalmed, but not yet restored, and the best time to start the restorative work is eight to ten hours after embalming, when the tissues have become firm and dry. **(10)**

Transition: "next step"

The object of all this attention to the corpse, it must be remembered, is to make it presentable for viewing in an attitude of healthy repose. . . . The funeral industry is equal to the challenge: "In some cases, the gruesome appearance of a mutilated or disease-ridden subject may be quite discouraging. The task of restoration may seem impossible and shake the confidence of the embalmer. . . . It is surprising and gratifying to discover the results which may be obtained." **(11)**

Hook: "Mr. Jones"
Hooks: "this attention,"
"corpse"

The embalmer, having allowed an appropriate interval to elapse, returns to the attack, *but now* he brings into play the skill and equipment of sculptor and cosmetician. Is a hand missing? Casting one in plaster of Paris is a simple matter. . . . **(12)**

Hooks: "embalmer,"
"attack"
Transition: "but now"

BODY PARAGRAPHS Body paragraphs in expository writing are the main paragraphs in an essay, excluding any introductory, concluding, or transition paragraphs. They often contain the following features:

- *Topic sentence:* To promote clarity and precision, writers often use topic sentences to announce the main ideas of paragraphs. The main idea should be clearly related to the writer's thesis. A topic sentence usually occurs early in the paragraph (first or second sentence) or at the end of the paragraph.

- *Unity:* To avoid confusing readers, writers focus on a single idea for each paragraph. Writing unified paragraphs helps writers—and their readers—concentrate on one point at a time.
- *Coherence:* To make their writing flow smoothly from one sentence to the next, writers supplement their shaping strategies with coherence devices: repeated key words, pronouns referring to key nouns, and transition words.

The following body paragraph from Mitford's essay illustrates these features. The paragraph begins with a topic sentence; it has unity because it focuses on a single idea (positioning the lips) and it uses transitions, pronouns, and repeated key words to promote coherence:

Topic sentence
Pronoun: "They"
Repeated key words:
"lips," "embalmer"

Transition: "however"

Repeated key word: "lip"

Transition: "Another"

Positioning the lips is a problem that recurrently challenges the ingenuity of the embalmer. Closed too tightly, they tend to give a stern, even disapproving expression. Ideally, embalmers feel, the lips should give the impression of being ever so slightly parted, the upper lip protruding slightly for a more youthful appearance. This takes some engineering, *however,* as the lips tend to drift apart. Lip drift can sometimes be remedied by pushing one or two straight pins through the inner margin of the lower lip and then inserting them between the two front upper teeth. If Mr. Jones happens to have no teeth, the pins can just as easily be anchored in his Armstrong Face Former and Denture Replacer. *Another* method to maintain lip closure is to dislocate the lower jaw, which is then held in its new position by a wire run through holes which have been drilled through the upper and lower jaws at the midline. As the French are fond of saying, *il faut souffrir pour être belle.* **(14)**

DRAFTING

Before you begin drafting, reconsider your purpose and audience. What you explain depends on what your audience needs to know or what would demonstrate or show your point most effectively.

As you work from an outline or from an organizing strategy, remember that all three questions—*what, how,* and *why*—are interrelated. If you are writing about causes, for example, an explanation of *what* the topic is and *how* the causes function may also be necessary to explain your subject clearly. As you write, balance your sense of plan and organization with a willingness to pursue ideas that you discover as you write. While you need to have a plan, you should be ready to change course if you discover a more interesting idea or angle.

REVISING

PEER RESPONSE

The instructions that follow will help you give and receive constructive advice about the rough draft of your explaining essay. You may use these guidelines for an in-class workshop, a take-home review, or a computer e-mail response.

Writer: Before you exchange drafts with another reader, write out the following on your essay draft:

1. **Purpose** Briefly, describe your purpose and intended audience.

2. **Revision Plans** What do you still intend to work on as you revise your draft?

3. **Questions** Write out one or two questions that you still have about your draft. What questions would you like your reader to answer?

Reader: First, read the entire draft from start to finish. As you reread the draft, answer the following questions:

1. **Clarity** What passages were clearest? Where were you most confused? Refer to specific sentences or passages to support your response. How and where could the writer make the draft clearer?

2. **Evidence** Where does the writer have good supporting evidence (specific examples, facts, analysis, statistics, interview results, or citations from sources)? Where does the writer need additional evidence? Refer to specific sentences or passages to support your response.

3. **Organization** Summarize or briefly outline the main ideas of the essay. Where was the organization most clear? Where were you confused? Refer to specific passages as you suggest ways to improve the draft.

4. **Purpose** Underline sentences that express the purpose or contain the thesis of the essay. Does your understanding of the essay's purpose match the writer's statement about purpose? Explain. How might the writer clarify the thesis?

5. **Reader's Response** Overall, describe what you liked best about the draft. Then identify one major area that the writer should focus on during the revision. Does your suggestion match the writer's revision plans? Explain. Answer the writer's own question or questions about the draft.

*I wish he would
explain his
explanation.*

—**LORD BYRON,**

POET

As you revise your explaining essay, concentrate on making yourself perfectly clear, on illustrating with examples where your reader might be confused, and on signaling the relationship of the parts of your essay to your reader.

Guidelines for Revision

- **Compare your thesis sentence with what you say in your conclusion.** You may have a clearer statement of your thesis near the end of your paper. Revise your original thesis sentence to make it clearer, more focused, or more in line with what your essay actually says.
- **Explaining means *showing* and *demonstrating* relationships.** Be sure to follow general statements with *specific examples, details, facts, statistics, memories, dialogues,* or other *illustrations.*
- **In a formal definition, be sure to include the class of objects or concepts to which the term belongs.** Avoid ungrammatical writing, such as "Photosynthesis is *when* plants absorb oxygen" or "The lymphatic system is *where* the body removes bacteria and transports fatty cells."
- **Avoid introducing definitions with "Webster says. . . ."** Instead, read definitions from several dictionaries and give the best or most appropriate definition.
- **Remember that you can modify the dictionary definition of a term or concept to fit your particular context.** For example, to you, "heroism" may mean having the courage to *say* what you believe, not just to endanger your life through selfless actions.
- **Don't mix categories when you are classifying objects or ideas.** If you are classifying houses *by floor design* (ranch, bilevel, split-level, two-story), don't bring in other categories, such as passive-solar, which could be incorporated into any of those designs.
- **In explaining *how* something occurs or should be done, be sure to indicate to your audience which steps are *most important.***
- **In cause-and-effect explanations, avoid *post hoc* fallacies.** This term comes from the Latin phrase *post hoc, ergo propter hoc:* "after this, therefore because of this." For example, just because Event B occurred after Event A, it does not follow, necessarily, that A caused B. If, for example, statistics show that traffic fatalities in your state actually declined after the speed limit on interstate highways was increased, you should not conclude that higher speeds actually caused the reduction in fatalities. Other causes—increased radar patrols, stiffer drunk-driving penalties, or more rigorous vehicle-maintenance laws—may have been responsible for the reduction.
- **As you revise to sharpen your meaning or make your organization clearer, use appropriate transitional words and phrases to signal the *relationships among the various parts of your subject.***

——*To signal relation in time:* before, meanwhile, later, soon, at last, earlier, thereafter, afterward, by that time, from then on, first, next, now, presently, shortly, immediately, finally

——*To signal similarity:* likewise, similarly, once again, once more

——*To signal difference:* but, yet, however, although, whereas, though, even so, nonetheless, still, on the other hand, on the contrary

——*To signal consequences:* as a result, consequently, therefore, hence, for this reason

■ POSTSCRIPT ON THE WRITING PROCESS Before you hand in your essay, reflect on your writing and learning process. In your journal, spend a few minutes answering each of the following questions:

1. Describe the purpose and intended audience for your essay.

2. What was the best workshop advice that you received? What did you revise in your draft because of that advice? What piece of advice did you ignore? Why?

3. What caused you the most difficulty with this essay? How did you solve the problem—or attempt to solve it? With what parts are you still least satisfied?

4. What are the best parts of your paper? Refer to specific paragraphs—what do you like most about them?

5. What was the most important thing you learned about writing or your writing process as you wrote this paper?

EXPLAINING: STUDENT WRITING

"THE POLICE WERE CALLING ME NAMES": AN EXPLANATION OF HARD-CORE PUNK ROCK

Dennis Alexander

Dennis Alexander's essay on hard-core punk rock explains what punk rock is, but he uses definition and analysis to make his own point: Punk rock, despite the charges of its detractors, is a legitimate form of music.

ALEXANDER'S POSTSCRIPT ON HIS WRITING PROCESS

When I was thinking about this paper, I wanted to write a cause-and-effect type of paper, but I couldn't seem to come up with any ideas I wanted to write on. Then one night I ordered a pizza and a really punked-out guy delivered it. I was playing some hard core and he said something about how few people understand it. This gave me my idea for the paper. I wanted to express the idea that punk was a real and legitimate form of music, so I spent some time looking up words in the dictionary, defining terms and finding the right words. I listened to a lot of music. This was harder than it sounds, going verse by verse to figure out the lyrics. I also listened to 180 minutes of interview tape from a radio interview with various hard-core artists. Then, after some brainstorming and outlining, I finally came up with a good thesis. When I had enough evidence to give good support to my thesis and also explain about punk, I wrote my essay and revised it.

NOTES FOR OUTLINE

Explaining Essay–
Support thesis and answer
                    questions: What is punk
                                 Why it is
Legit   or Viable   Who
Sanctioned
by law   workable and likely to
or custom   survive or to have real
                       meaning, pertinence, relevance
Comforming
to or abiding by
standards,
principles
Thesis: Hardcore Punk is a viable Musical
        Alternative

*It is alternative music
~~Just Beat~~
Revival of Old Rock
New Raw Rock & Roll
Not New Wave
Fast ~~Beat~~
(or satiric of other music

It is music
It is alternative
It is viable

Fits definition: Combination of vocal
and instrumental sounds or tones in
varying melody, harmony, rhythm, and
timbre so as to form structurally complete
and emotionally expressive compositions.

Fast Beat, Back Beat, 180 Beats/Min
Not as many chords, melody
* It is alternative

- Revival of Old Rock
- New Rock & Roll, Fun
- Satirical of other music/lifestyles
- Not New Wave

* It is viable
- it is workable
- provides for change
- doesn't cater to likes
- Likely to survive
- survived since origin in
early 70's in England
- Brought to USA

- Has meaning, pertinence, relevance
- commentary on war
- political statement
- social statement
- draws attention to community
problems (landlords/police or social
issues, war, politics, religion,
poverty, social welfare, police)

FIRST DRAFT

Purpose: To explain that hard-core is a viable musical alternative
Audience: General, but especially young people who like music but may not like hard-core—probably because they don't understand it.

Hard-Core

What you need boy is a holiday in Cambodia
Where you'll kiss ass or crack.
Sweat for the price of your life
With a bowl of rice as a snack.

—The Dead Kennedys
"Fresh Fruit for Rotting Vegetables"

Musical tastes vary as much as the people who like music. In any record store in America, it is not uncommon to find rock, country, and classical albums for sale. It is uncommon for a typical record store to have a variety of hard-core punk rock records for sale. This is unusual considering that hard core is a viable musical alternative. **(1)**

Some people think that punk is not music. Webster's dictionary defines music as combinations of vocal and instrumental sounds or tones in varying melody, harmony, rhythm and timbre so as to form structurally complete and emotionally expressive compositions. Hard-core punk fits this definition. Having developed from rock music in the early 70's punk inherited its rhythm and beat. The melody and harmony in rock and punk are also similar although punk has a much harsher, distorted sound. It is structurally complete and expresses a variety of emotions. Hard core may or may not sound as pleasant to the ear as other socially accepted forms of music. But this does not disqualify it as music. **(2)**

Most of all the other forms of music are accepted as legitimate. They conform and abide by socially accepted standards and customs. Because punk does not, it provides an alternative. It does not fit into other categories, it is non-conformist music. The names of common groups express this: The Germs, The Dead Kennedys, The Suicidal Tendencies, Two Sounds of Liberty (T.S.O.L.). In some ways, punk tries to revive old rock and roll into new raw rock. In other ways, punk music attempts to satirize other musical forms and the lifestyles they represent. Most importantly, punk is not new wave music. In the words of a singer from The Germs: "There was never any such thing as new wave. New wave was the polite thing to say when you were trying to explain you were not into the boring old rock but you didn't dare say punk because you were afraid to get kicked out of the f——— party." Because of the large difference between musical styles, punk is an excellent alternative. **(3)**

Despite its differences, hard-core is a viable form of music. It is workable. It can evolve and change. Because of its base on nonconformity, it easily provides for change and does not cater to sentiment. Punk is likely to survive. From its roots in the late 60's it has prospered, spread and is stronger than ever. Hard-core punk also has meaning, pertinence, and relevance. It often provides a satirical social comment. **(4)**

Punk highlights social problems by advocating crude solutions. Such satirically oriented songs are: "Kill the Poor," and "Lets Lynch a Landlord" by _____. Punk music is not afraid to hide opinion, in fact it is made blatantly clear. This opinion can be on such issues as war, religion and politics. Opinion is expressed in lyrics like "Army, Navy, Airforce, or jail" and "President Reagan can shove it" by T.S.O.L. In these ways, punk draws attention to community and social problems and reaffirms Americans' right to free speech. It is, therefore, viable. **(5)**

Because hard-core punk is a viable musical alternative there is no reason that it should be subject to undue discrimination or censorship. Just because it does not fit some people's idea of "good taste," it should not be cleared from the shelves. Hard-core punk is legitimate music that belongs on the shelves of music stores. **(6)**

REVISED VERSION

THE POLICE WERE CALLING ME NAMES: AN EXPLANATION OF HARD-CORE PUNK ROCK

I sat in my dorm room waiting for a pizza to be delivered. The Dead Kennedys blasted out through my stereo speakers. "What is that shit?" someone asked as he walked by with his fingers in his ears. The pizza guy finally arrived and walked into my room wearing combat boots, chains, spiked leather and a black and blonde mohawk. His foot tapped to the beat as I paid for the pie. He looked me over from my Levis jacket to my cowboy boots and said, "You listen to the D.K.? Way cool man!" Looking back on this incident, I think that the reaction of the pizza guy was normal while the attitudes of the dorm residents were narrow-minded. Hard-core punk rock is, in fact, a viable musical alternative. **(1)**

Is hard-core punk really music or is it just so much loud noise? Perhaps we need to define what music is. Music is a combination of vocal and instrumental sounds or tones that vary in melody, harmony, rhythm and timbre. The sounds should form a structurally complete and emotionally expressive composition. Hard-core punk fits this definition. Having developed from rock in the late 60s, punk inherited its rhythm and beat. The melody and harmony in rock and punk are also similar, although punk has a much harsher, distorted sound. It is also structurally complete and expresses a variety of emotions. Hard-core may or may not sound as pleasing to the ear as other socially accepted forms of music, but this does not disqualify it as music. **(2)**

Almost all of the other forms of music, such as country, rock, and classical, are accepted as legitimate. They conform to and abide by socially accepted standards and customs. Because punk does not, it provides an alternative. It does not fit into other categories; it is non-conformist music. The names of common groups express their nonconformity; "The Germs," "The Dead Kennedys," the "Suicidal Tendencies," "Religious Vomit," and "Two Sounds of Liberty." In some ways, punk tries to revive old music into new raw rock (Dead Kennedys, "Rawhide"). In other ways, punk attempts to satirize other musical forms and the lifestyles they represent. The Dead Milkmen do this in "Bitching Camaro" when they say, "Don't forget to buy your Motley Crue T-shirts, all proceeds go to get their lead singer out of jail." Most importantly punk is not new wave music. In the words of a singer for The Germs, "There was never any such thing as new wave. It was the polite thing to say when you were trying to explain that you were not into the boring old rock, but you did not dare say punk because you were afraid to get kicked out of the f———— party." Because of the noticeable difference in musical styles, punk is an excellent musical alternative. **(3)**

Despite its difference from rock, hard-core is a viable form of music. Let us consider some of the terms related to viability: ability to evolve, survivability, and relevance. Punk can evolve and change. Because of its basis in nonconformity, it easily provides for change and does not cater to fixed norms or sentiments. Punk is likely to survive. From its roots in the late 60s it has prospered and is stronger than ever. Hard-core punk also has meaning and relevance. It often provides a satirical social comment. Punk highlights social problems by advocating crude solutions. Such satirically oriented songs are "Kill the Poor" and "Let's Lynch a Landlord" by the Dead Kennedys. Punk music is not afraid to hide its opinion on relevant matters such as politics, war, religion, and human rights. Opinion is expressed in lyrics such as "Army, Navy, Air Force, or jail" and "President Reagan can shove it." In these ways punk draws attention to community and social problems and reaffirms the right to free speech. It is, therefore, viable. **(4)**

Whether people like hard-core rock or not, it is a viable musical alternative. It is a musical version of the freedom of speech guaranteed by our constitution. Punk music is an expression of feelings just like the pizza delivery man expresses his feelings through his mohawk and chains. So the next time you hear some punk music, don't plug your ears or slam the door. Listen to it as though it were real music: it is. **(5)**

QUESTIONS FOR WRITING AND DISCUSSION

1. Compare Alexander's first and revised drafts. Cite two specific changes that improved his revised version.

2. Alexander explains what punk music is, but he also takes a stand: He wants to convince his readers that it is a legitimate form of music. Where in his essay does he explain most clearly what punk music is? Where does he try to convince you that it is legitimate?

3. Assume that Alexander wants your advice before writing a third draft of this essay. What part of the writing process should he concentrate on: (1) collecting additional information and examples to clarify his explanation or make his thesis more convincing; (2) improving the organization, transitions, and coherence; or (3) editing sentences for grammar, punctuation, and clarity? Support your choice by citing a specific passage that needs improvement.

ANOREXIA NERVOSA

Nancie Brosseau

In her essay on anorexia nervosa, Nancie Brosseau writes from her own experience, explaining what anorexia nervosa is and what its effects are. Her essay succeeds not only because it is organized clearly, but also because it is so vivid and memorable. Relying on specific details, her explanation shows the effects of anorexia on her life.

I knew my dieting had gotten out of hand, but when I could actually see the movement of my heart beating beneath my clothes I knew I was in trouble. At first, the family doctor reassured my parents that my rapid weight loss was a "temporary phase among teenage girls." However, when I, at 14 years old and 5'0" tall, weighed in at 63 pounds, my doctor changed his diagnosis from "temporary phase" to "anorexia nervosa." Anorexia nervosa is the process of self-starvation that affects over one hundred thousand young girls each year. Almost six thousand of these girls die every year. Anorexia nervosa is a self-mutilating disease that affects its victim both physically and emotionally. **(1)**

As both a gymnast and a dancer, I was constantly surrounded by lithe, muscular people, all of them extremely conscious about their weight. Although I wasn't overweight to begin with, I thought that if I lost five to ten pounds I would look, feel, dance, and tumble better. I figured the quickest way to accomplish this was by drastically limiting my intake of food. By doing this, I lost ten pounds in one week and gained the approval of my peers. Soon, I could no longer control myself and ten pounds turned into twenty, twenty into forty, and so on, until I finally ended up weighing 58 pounds. **(2)**

Several serious health problems bombarded me, and it's a wonder I'm still alive. Because my body was receiving no nourishment at all, my muscles and essential organs, including my heart, liver, kidneys, and intestines, started to compensate by slowly disintegrating. My body was feeding on itself! As my weight plummeted, my circulation grew increasingly worse. My hands, feet, lips and ears took on a bluish-purple tint, and I was constantly freezing cold. My hair started to fall out and my whole body took on a very skeletal appearance. My eyes appeared to have sunken into my face, and my forehead, cheekbones, and chin protruded sharply. My wrists were the largest part of my entire arm, as were my knees the widest part of my legs. My pants rubbed my hips raw because I had to wear my belts at their tightest notch to keep them up. I would force myself to vomit as soon as possible if I was forced to eat. The enamel on my teeth started to be eaten away by the acid in the vomit, and my lips cracked and bled regularly. I stopped menstruating completely because I was not producing enough estrogen. Instead of improving my skills as a dancer and a gymnast, I drastically reduced them because I was so weak. One time, while executing a chain of back handsprings, I broke all five fingers on one hand and three on the other because my bones had become so brittle. My doctor realized the serious danger I was in and told me I either had to see a psychologist or be put in the hospital. I chose to see a psychologist, and she helped me sort out the emotional aspects of anorexia which in turn solved the physical problems. **(3)**

The emotional problems associated with anorexia nervosa are equally disastrous to the victim's health. Self-deception, lying, and depression are three examples of the emotions and actions an anorexic often experiences. During my entire bout with anorexia, I deceived myself into thinking I had complete control over my body. Hunger pains became a pleasant feeling, and sore muscles from over-exercising just proved to me that I still needed to lose more weight. When my psychologist showed me pictures of girls that were of normal weight for my age group, they honestly looked obese to me. I truly believed that even the smallest amount of food would make me extremely fat. **(4)**

Another problem, lying, occurred most often when my parents tried to force me to eat. Because I was at the gym until around eight o'clock every night, I told my mother not to save me dinner. I would come home and make a sandwich and feed it to my dog. I lied to my parents every day about eating lunch at school. For example, I would bring a sack lunch and sell it to someone and use the money to buy diet pills. I always told my parents that I ate my own lunch. I lied to my doctor when he asked if I was taking an appetite suppressant. I had to cover one lie with another to keep from being found out, although it was obvious that I was not eating by looking at me. **(5)**

Still another emotion I felt, as a result of my anorexia, was severe depression. It seemed that, no matter how hard I tried, I kept growing fatter. Of course, I was getting thinner all the time, but I couldn't see that. One time, I licked a postage stamp to put on a letter and immediately remembered that there was 1/4 of a calorie in the glue on the stamp. I punished myself by doing 100 extra situps every night for one week. I pinched my skin until it bruised as I lay awake at night because I was so ashamed of the way I thought I looked. I doomed myself to a life of obesity. I would often slip into a mood my psychologist described as a "blue funk." That is, I would become so depressed, I seriously considered committing suicide. The emotional instabilities associated with anorexia nervosa can be fatal. **(6)**

Through psychological and physical treatment, I was able to overcome anorexia nervosa. I still have a few complications today due to anorexia, such as dysmenorrhea (severe menstrual cramps), and the tendency to fast. However, these problems are minute compared to the problems I would have had if I hadn't received immediate help. Separately, the physical and emotional problems that anorexia nervosa create can greatly harm its victim. However, when the two are teamed together, the results are deadly. **(7)**

QUESTIONS FOR WRITING AND DISCUSSION

1. Without looking back at this essay, jot down the specific examples that you found most memorable. How would you describe these examples: tedious and commonplace, eye-opening, shocking, upsetting, persuasive? Explain.

2. Identify the thesis statement and essay map. Referring to paragraph numbers, show how the essay map sets up the organization of the essay.

3. Reread the opening sentences of each body paragraph. Identify one opening sentence that creates a smooth transition from the previous paragraph. Identify one opening sentence in which the transition could be smoother. Revise this sentence to improve the transition with a paragraph hook.

4. In this essay, Brosseau defines anorexia nervosa, explains its physical and emotional effects (and hints at its causes), and analyzes the process of the disorder, from its inception to its cure. Identify passages that illustrate each of these strategies: definition, cause-and-effect analysis, process analysis.

8 EVALUATING

Jacob Lawrence *The Curator*, 1937, Goauche on board 20 x 15.5"

I N A LETTER TO YOUR PARENTS, YOU EXPLAIN THAT YOU ARE CONSIDERING TRANSFERRING TO A DIFFERENT SCHOOL FOR THE FOLLOWING YEAR. YOU HAVE SOME MISGIVINGS about your decision to change, but after listing your criteria and ranking them in order from most to least important, you are convinced that you're making the right choice. In the letter, you explain your decision, based on your criteria, and ask that your parents continue to support your education.

❧

D URING YOUR FALL SEMESTER LIBRARY-ORIENTATION TOUR, YOU DISCOVER A SMALL OFFICE TUCKED AWAY IN THE CORNER OF THE LIBRARY BUILDING: THE INTERLIBRARY LOAN OFFICE. BECAUSE you occasionally need to see articles and books that your library does not have, you decide to investigate the interlibrary-loan service and evaluate the helpfulness of the staff as well as the convenience, speed, and cost of obtaining materials. As part of your evaluation, you interview the office coordinator as well as several teachers and students who have used the service. Their responses—combined with your own observations—indicate that although an interlibrary loan can sometimes take a couple of weeks, the loan office gets high marks for its service. The staff is always helpful and patient, the service is easily accessible through electronic mail, and the cost of books and articles is surprisingly low.

H ARDLY A DAY PASSES WHEN WE DO NOT EXPRESS OUR LIKES
OR DISLIKES. WE CONSTANTLY PASS JUDGMENT ON PEOPLE,
PLACES, OBJECTS, EVENTS, IDEAS, AND POLICIES IN THE
world around us. "Sue is a wonderful person." "The food in this cafeteria is
horrible." "That movie we saw Saturday night ought to get an Oscar nomi-
nation for best picture." "The Brady gun law is a good piece of legislation."
"The Vietnam War was a national tragedy." At the same time, we are constantly exposed to the opinions of our friends, family members, teachers, and
business associates. And, of course, the media barrages us with claims about
products, famous personalities, and candidates for public office.

A claim or opinion, however, is not an *evaluation*. Your reaction
to a person, a sports event, a meal, a movie, or a public policy
becomes an evaluation *only* when you support your value judgment with
clear standards and specific evidence. Your goal in evaluating something is not
only to express your viewpoint, but also to *persuade* others to accept your
judgment. You convince your readers by indicating the standards for your
judgment and then supporting it with evidence: "The food in this cafeteria is
horrible [your claim]. I know that not all cafeteria food tastes great, but it
should at least be sanitary [one standard of judgment]. Yesterday, I had to dig
a piece of green mold out of the meatloaf, and just as I stuck my fork into the
green salad, a large black roach ran out [evidence]."

Most people interested in a subject agree that certain standards are important—for example, that a cafeteria be clean and pest free. The standards that
you share with your audience are the *criteria* for your evaluation. You convince
your readers that something is good or bad, ugly or beautiful, tasty or nauseat-
ing by analyzing your subject in terms of your criteria. For each separate criterion, you support your judgment with specific *evidence:* descriptions, statistics,
testimony, or examples from your personal experience. If your readers agree
that your standards or criteria are appropriate, and if you supply detailed evidence, your readers should be convinced. They will take your evaluation seriously—and think twice about eating at that roach-infested cafeteria.

*It is as hard to find a
neutral critic as it is a
neutral country in a
time of war.*

**—KATHERINE
ANNE PORTER,**

NOVELIST AND SHORT
STORY WRITER

TECHNIQUES FOR WRITING

EVALUATIONS

Any writing that requires a *value judgment* uses the techniques of evaluating—whether you're writing about consumer products or services, works of

art, or performances by people. Effective evaluations use the following techniques:

- **Stating an *overall claim* about your subject.** This statement serves as the *thesis* for your evaluation.
- **Describing the person, place, object, text, event, service, or performance being evaluated.** Readers need basic information—*who, what, when,* and *where*—to form a clear judgment.
- **Clarifying the *criteria* for your evaluation.** A criterion is a standard of judgment that most people interested in your subject agree is important. A criterion serves as a yardstick against which you measure your subject.
- **Stating a *judgment* for each criterion.** The overall claim is based on your judgment of each separate criterion. Include both positive *and* negative judgments.
- **Supporting such judgment with *evidence*.** Support can include detailed description, facts, examples, testimony, or statistics.
- **Balancing your evaluation with both positive and negative judgments about your subject.** Evaluations that are all positive are merely advertisements; evaluations that are entirely negative may seem too harsh or mean spirited.

In the following evaluation of a Chinese restaurant in Washington, DC, journalist and critic Phyllis C. Richman illustrates the main features of an evaluation:

Hunan Dynasty

215 Pennsylvania Ave. SE. 546-6161   *Information &*
                                                                      description

Open daily 11 A.M. to 3 P.M. for lunch, 3 P.M. to 10 P.M. for dinner, until 11 P.M. on Friday and Saturday.

Reservations suggested for large parties.

Prices for lunch: appetizers $2 to $4.50, entrees $4.75 to $6.50. For dinner: appetizers $1 to $13.95 (combination platter), entrees $6.75 to $18.

Complete dinner with wine or beer, tax, and tip about $20 a person.

Chinese restaurants in America were once places one went just to   *Description*
eat. Now one goes to dine. There are now waiters in black tie, cloths
on the tables and space between those tables, art on the walls and
decoratively carved vegetables on the plate—elegance has become
routine in Chinese restaurants. What's more, in Chinese restaurants

the ingredients are fresh (have you ever found frozen broccoli in a Chinese kitchen?), and the cooking almost never sinks below decent. . . . And it is usually moderately priced. In other words, if you're among unfamiliar restaurants and looking for good value, Chinese restaurants now are routinely better than ever.

Overall claim

The Hunan Dynasty is an example of what makes Chinese restaurants such reliable choices. A great restaurant? It is not. A good value? Definitely. A restaurant to fit nearly any diner's need? Probably.

Criterion #1: nice setting
Judgment: attractive
Evidence

First, it is attractive. There are no silk tassels, blaring red lacquer or Formica tables; instead there are white tablecloths and subtle glass etchings. It is a dining room—or dining rooms, for the vastness has been carved into smaller spaces—of gracefulness and lavish space.

Criterion #2: good service

Judgment: often expert
Evidence

Second, service is a strong priority. The waiters look and act polished, and serve with flourishes from the carving of a Peking duck to the portioning of dishes among the diners. I have found some glitches—a forgotten appetizer, a recommendation of two dishes that turned out nearly identical—but most often the service has been expert. . . .

Criterion #3: good main dishes

Judgment: good but not memorable

As for the main dishes, don't take the "hot and spicy" asterisks too seriously, for this kitchen is not out to offer you a test of fire. The peppers are there, but not in great number. And, like the appetizers, the main dishes are generally good but not often memorable. Fried dishes—and an inordinate number of them seem to be fried—are crunchy and not greasy. Vegetables are bright and crisp. Eggplant with hot garlic sauce is properly unctuous; Peking duck is as fat-free and crackly-skinned as you could hope (though pancakes were rubbery). And seafoods—shrimp, scallops, lobster—are tenderly cooked, though they are not the most full-flavored examples of those ingredients.

Evidence

Criterion #3 cont.
Judgment: sometimes bad
Evidence

I have found only one dismal main dish in a fairly broad sampling: lemon chicken had no redeeming feature in its doughy, greasy, overcooked and underseasoned presentation. Otherwise, not much goes wrong. Crispy shrimp with walnuts might be preferable stir-fried rather than batter-fried, but the tomato-red sauce and crunchy walnuts made a good dish. Orange beef could use more seasoning but the coating was nicely crusty and the meat tender. . . .

Overall claim restated

So with the opening of the Hunan Dynasty, Washington did not add a stellar Chinese restaurant to its repertoire, but that is not necessarily what the city needed anyway. Hunan Dynasty is a top-flight neighbor-hood restaurant—with good food, caring service and very fair prices—that is attractive enough to set a mood for celebration and easygoing enough for an uncomplicated dinner with the family after work.

EVALUATING COMMERCIAL PRODUCTS OR SERVICES

Writers frequently evaluate commercial products or services. Consumer magazines test and rate every imaginable product or service—from cars and dishwashers to peanut butter and brokerage houses. Guidebooks evaluate tourist spots, restaurants, colleges, and hunting lodges. Specialty magazines, such as *Modern Photography, Road and Track, Skiing,* and *Wired,* often rate products and services of interest to their readers. To qualify as evaluation—and not just advertising—the authors and the publishers must maintain an independent status, uninfluenced by the manufacturers of the products or services they are judging.

Consider, first, the following "evaluation" of a wine, found on a bottle of Cabernet Sauvignon:

> "This Cabernet Sauvignon is a dry, robust, and complex wine whose hearty character is balanced by an unusual softness."

This "evaluative" language is so vague and esoteric that it may mean very little to the average consumer who just wants some wine with dinner. *Dry:* How can a liquid be dry? *Robust:* Does this refer to physique? *Soft:* Wine is not a pillow, though it might put you to sleep. *Complex:* Are they describing a wine or conducting a psychological analysis? While an independent evaluator may legitimately use these terms for knowledgeable wine drinkers, this particular description suggests that the wine is absolutely everything the buyer would like it to be—dry yet robust, hearty but at the same time soft. Apparently, the writer's purpose here is not to evaluate a product but to flatter readers who imagine themselves connoisseurs of wine.

Now consider the following report on the Yugo, in which *Consumer Reports* illustrates a more objective evaluation of a consumer product. In this brief excerpt, the editors present the criteria, the evidence, and their judgments. Clearly, this is not the language of advertising or uncritical promotion:

How Much Car for $3990?

An unusual new import, the *Yugo GV,* arrived in the U.S. last August. It's a tiny car—a couple of feet shorter than the *Chevrolet Chevette*—made in Yugoslavia by Zavodi Crvena Zastava (Red Flag Works).

But the most unusual thing about it is the advertised price—$3990. The price quickens the pulse at a time when the average car sells for nearly $12,000 and a similar-sized car, the Japanese-made *Chevrolet Sprint*, sells for about $5570.

Can you really buy a *Yugo* for $3990?

No. Dealer preparation, included in the base price of most other cars, is $90 extra, and the destination charge is $299. If you add the official *Yugo* stereo radio with two speakers and a cassette player for $265, you have a $4644 automobile.

Well, what's wrong with a *Yugo* for $4644? We'll let our test results speak for themselves.

Engine and Transmission

Acceleration. All-out acceleration from a standstill was adequate, but the *Yugo* struggled and strained to climb highway grades in high gear. Our 0–60 mph run took 18.5 seconds.

Transmission. Easily the worst we've encountered in years. The shifter was very imprecise and often balky. The sloppy shift linkage made it hard to tell which gear you were in.

Economy. Well below what you'd expect from a small car with such a small engine. Figure on averaging about 32 mpg. (The *Chevrolet Sprint*, a Japanese minicar, averages about 50 mpg). Cruising range is only about 250 miles.

Ride and Noise

Ride. Snappy and jerky on back roads, and harsh and busy even on expressways. But the *Yugo* took large bumps in stride. When the car carried its full recommended load—770 pounds—its ride softened just a bit.

Noise. Tiring. The small engine churned and buzzed on the highway. Coarse pavement increased the noise considerably. Wind noise, especially from the closed front vent windows, was also obtrusive.

Seating Accommodations

Driving position. Extremely awkward. The non-tilt steering wheel is too high, too far away, and too horizontal, and the steering column is angled toward the right. The pedals are too close to one another, and the intrusive wheel housing makes a very poor foot rest.

Rear seating. Unsuitable for adults. Six footers have to bow their head penitently and wrap their knees around the front seat back. The overly erect seatback forces passengers to slouch forward in a fetal tuck with all their weight on the base of their spine.

Our *Yugo* was a sorry sample indeed. We noted 21 defects attributable to sloppy assembly or incomplete dealer preparation. Oil dripped from the engine and coated the underbody as we drove. When it contacted the hot exhaust system, the car filled with acrid smoke. . . . The brakes squealed, and every so often they dragged so badly that we could barely coax the car to 45 mph on level pavement.

Recommendations

Is low price sufficient justification for buying the *Yugo?* We don't think so. Overall, the *Yugo* scored below every other small car we've tested in recent years. It's heavy for its size, and though its tiny engine revs willingly enough, it delivers weak performance and unimpressive fuel economy. Handling was competent and braking was very effective, but comfort, ride, shifting, heating, and the design of the controls were below par.

EVALUATING WORKS OF ART

Evaluations of commercial products and services tend to emphasize usefulness, practicality, convenience, and cost. Evaluations of works of art, on the other hand, focus on form, color, texture, design, balance, image, or theme. Even the phrase "appreciating a work of art" suggests that we are making a value judgment, though usually not one based on money. Through evaluation, writers teach us to appreciate all kinds of art: paintings, sculpture, photographs, buildings, antique cars or furniture, novels, short stories, essays, poems, and tapestries. A Dior fashion, a quilt, a silverware pattern, even an old pair of jeans might be evaluated primarily on aesthetic rather than practical grounds.

In the following selection, art critic Mark Stevens evaluates Francisco Goya's painting *Tre Maggio* [The Third of May], which is reprinted here. This painting depicts the execution of Spanish hostages by Napoleon's forces, in retaliation for an attack by a mob on the previous day. As Stevens explains, Goya does not portray the doomed hostages as heroic martyrs; instead, he tries to show the horrors of war and death. In doing that, Stevens believes, Goya "told the truth: what happened on the third of May was a butchering."

The iconography, the color and light, the composition—all contribute to the power of this picture. Its most impressive aspect, in my view, is that Goya . . . transformed the conventions of hope into those of despair. This makes the horror all the greater, for we can see what we have lost, in addition to what we have. In the background, for example, the spire of the church is a dark, dim reminder, certainly not a cause for hope. The cruelty of the execution, which takes place in a melodramatic light, reminds us of acts of martyrdom—but without the traditional promise of heavenly reward.

Of course, the outstretched arms of the central figure also recall the Crucifixion, and the man's hands bear stigmata. However, the traditional religious gesture of acceptance—the outstretched arms of Christ—has here been turned into an expression of outrage, terror and meaninglessness. What is the victim saying? There is nothing he can say, for his situation is one in which neither faith nor reason matter. His outflung arms are mirrored by those of the corpse in the foreground: such is the promise of resurrection. The corpse itself is perhaps the most truthful ever painted, for it exhibits the unbearable banality, the crumpled emptiness of death.

The men around the central victim display a variety of other reactions to their fate, none noble. One looks heavenward, but his expression is groveling. The praying man cannot raise his eyes. A third hides his face, as do the victims who await execution. Goya's use of light enhances their horror. The light contains no spiritual overtone, but rather emanates from a common lantern; an intense glow is cast on the small, grisly scene, but it cannot pierce the dark reaches. This light—glaring, without delicacy, lurid, almost artificial—seems peculiarly modern. . . .

In addition to his brilliant use of light and shade, which isolates the central figure, Goya used several other formal devices to make his point. He employed sweeping diagonal lines to scissor the picture into sharp, claustrophobic spaces. He foreshortened the corpse, so

Goya y Lucientes, Francisco de Goya (1746-1828). The Third of May, 1808. Scala. Museo del Prado, Madrid, Spain. Oil painting on canvas.

(detail) Goya y Lucientes, Francisco de Goya (1746-1828). The Third of May, 1808. Scala. Museo del Prado, Madrid, Spain. Oil painting on canvas.

that the body seems to draw toward the viewer. (It almost looks as though the dead man is bidding the viewer welcome.) Otherwise, Goya has positioned the figures so that the viewer, curiously, is placed on the side of the executioners. You and I, observing, are implicated in mankind's folly.

EVALUATING PERFORMANCES

Evaluating live, recorded, or filmed performances of people in sports, dance, drama, debate, public meetings or lectures, and music may involve practical criteria, such as the prices of tickets to sports events or rock concerts. However, there are also aesthetic criteria that apply to people and their performances. In film evaluations, for example, the usual criteria are good acting and directing, entertaining or believable story or plot, memorable characters, dramatic special effects, and so forth.

In the following review of *Malcolm X*, critic Peter Travers evaluates the film itself, the script and directing by Spike Lee, and the performances of the main actors and actresses. As you read this review, notice how Travers balances both positive and negative judgments as he evaluates the film.

THE YEAR OF MALCOLM X

IN SPIKE LEE'S STRIVING, UNEVEN but finally triumphant *Malcolm X*, Denzel Washington gives the performance of the year as the militant champion of black self-determination. Once a thief, an addict and a zoot-suited pimp, the Nebraska-born Malcolm Little experienced a spiritual enlightenment in prison during the fifties, joined the Nation of Islam (NOI) and preached the pursuit of black liberation "by any means necessary" until a 1964 pilgrimage to Mecca convinced him that racial harmony was possible, though never at the price of black subservience.

Gunned down in 1965 at thirty-nine, Malcolm X remains a focal point of the black struggle. And Washington brings it all home—the intelligence, the humor, the sexuality, the shame, the pride, the raised-fist indignation and, most of all, the stinging eloquence that continues to inspire and provoke any reader of the autobiography Malcolm wrote with Alex Haley, which Lee and co-writer Arnold Perl have adapted for the screen.

Though the sprawling, $35 million, three-and-a-half-hour film tries to touch all the bases, Lee's accommodations sometimes clash with his ambitions. He has toned down Malcolm's life to a PG-13 level to open the film to the widest possible audience. A compromise? You bet, but not a fatal one. Telling details emerge: Malcolm conks his hair with scalding lye to look more white; Malcolm learns the ropes from Harlem gangster West Indian Archie (a superb Delroy Lindo); Malcolm demands that his white mistress (Kate Vernon) kiss his feet and spoon-feed him in bed—an act of self-loathing masked as her subjugation.

Inexplicably, Lee squanders time on atmospherics like a jitterbug number; his own performance as Shorty, Malcolm's pimp pal, is vivid but extraneous. Flashbacks rush us through such vital events as the murder of Malcolm's father (Tommy Hollis) and the breakdown of his mother (Lonette McKee). Few links are made between his preacher father's activism and Malcolm's conversion. An exception is the KKK's torching of the Little home—camera wiz Ernest Dickerson realizes a *coup de cinéma* as white-sheeted horsemen ride off into a poisonously full moon.

Lee shows a surer hand when Malcolm emerges from prison in 1952 to begin his mission. Washington delivers Malcolm's words with a spellbinding urgency, revealing the brother-minister's growing confidence and ambition under the American leader of the NOI, Elijah Muhammad (a mesmerizing turn from Al Freeman Jr.).

In a searingly powerful reenactment, Malcolm leads a march on a Harlem police precinct, demanding that a Muslim victim of police brutality be given medical attention. Given the context of the fifties—exemplified by the insufferably banal sound of Perry Como's "Round and Round" on the radio—Malcolm is a storm unleashed. His victory in facing down the police builds Malcolm into an international figure that some saw as a protector and others as a threat.

Washington's fusion with the role is uncanny. He alone fills in some of the emotional and ideological transitions that the script misses as it moves in lock step through Malcolm's marriage to a nurse, Betty X (the very fine but underused Angela Bassett), the birth of their four daughters, the resentment his outspokenness engenders in his fellow ministers, his split from the NOI when Elijah Muhammad's sexual misconduct is revealed, his pilgrimage to Mecca, the firebombing of his house in Queens and the growing political fervor that made him a threat to the government as well as the NOI and led to his murder.

Lee's *Malcolm X* is far from the last word. It's more like a primer that illuminates its subject in brisk, broad strokes. But those who deride Lee as a self-promoter merely out to sell X hats and T-shirts and turn Malcolm into another manageable martyr for the white Hollywood Establishment just aren't paying attention. From the opening image of an American flag burning over the infamous video of the Rodney King beating in L.A. to Nelson Mandela's final eulogy, the film is a tribute to Malcolm's living, fighting spirit. Spike Lee has accomplished something historic in movies: a rousing, full-sized epic about a defiantly idealistic black hero whose humanism never extends to turning the other cheek.

■ WARMING UP: JOURNAL EXERCISES The following exercises will help you practice writing evaluations. Read all of the following exercises and then write on the three that interest you most. If another idea occurs to you, write about it:

1. Choose the best of the courses that you are currently taking. To persuade a friend to take it, evaluate the course, the teacher, or both. What criteria and evidence would you select to persuade your friend?

2. Evaluate an object related to one of your hobbies or special interests—stereo or video equipment, water or snow skis, a cooking appliance or utensil, diving or hiking equipment, photography or art equipment, ranching or farming apparatus, fishing rods or reels, some part of a car, or computers. Write an evaluation of that object following the format used by *Consumer Reports*.

3. Evaluate a TV show that you find particularly irritating, boring, or insipid, but which you find yourself watching occasionally anyway. Watch the show, taking notes about scenes, characters, dialogue, and plot. Write a critique of the show for other students in this class.

4. To gather some information for yourself about a possible job or career, interview a person in your prospective field about his or her job or profession. Focus your questions on the person's opinions and judgments about this career. What criteria does this person use to judge it? What other jobs serve as a good basis for comparison? What details from this person's daily routine support his or her judgments?

5. At your place of work, evaluate one of your products or services. Write down the criteria and evidence that your business might use to determine whether it is a "good" product or service. Then list the criteria and evidence that your customers or patrons probably use. Are these two sets of criteria and evidence identical? Explain.

6. Choose a piece of modern art (painting, drawing, poster, sculpture, ceramics, and so forth). Describe and evaluate it for an audience that is indifferent or possibly even hostile toward contemporary art. Explain why your readers should appreciate this particular art object.

7. Read James Gorman's essay "Man, Bytes, Dog." Imitating Gorman's essay, write a comparative evaluation of two dissimilar things.

MAN, BYTES, DOG

James Gorman

Many people have asked me about the Cairn Terrier. How about memory, they want to know. Is it I.B.M.-compatible? Why didn't I get the I.B.M. itself, or a Kaypro, Compaq, or Macintosh? I think the best way to answer these questions is to look at the Macintosh and the Cairn head on. I almost did buy the Macintosh. It has terrific graphics, good word-processing capabilities, and the mouse. But in the end I decided on the Cairn, and I think I made the right decision.

Let's start out with the basics:

MACINTOSH:

Weight (without printer): 20 lbs.

Memory (RAM): 128 K

Price (with printer): $3,090

CAIRN TERRIER:

Weight (without printer): 14 lbs.

Memory (RAM): Some

Price (without printer): $250

Just on the basis of price and weight, the choice is obvious. Another plus is that the Cairn Terrier comes in one unit. No printer is necessary, or useful. And—this was a big attraction to me—there is no user's manual.

Here are some of the other qualities I found put the Cairn out ahead of the Macintosh:

PORTABILITY: To give you a better idea of size, Toto in "The Wizard of Oz" was a Cairn Terrier. So you can see that if the young Judy Garland was able to carry Toto around in that little picnic basket, you will have no trouble at all moving your Cairn from place to place. For short trips it will move under its own power. The Macintosh will not.

RELIABILITY: In five to ten years, I am sure, the Macintosh will be superseded by a new model, like the Delicious or the Granny Smith. The Cairn Terrier, on the other hand, has held its share of the market with only minor modifications for hundreds of years. In the short term, Cairns seldom need servicing, apart from shots and the odd worming, and most function without interruption during electrical storms.

COMPATIBILITY: Cairn Terriers get along with everyone. And for communications with any other dog, of any breed, within a radius of three miles, no additional hardware is necessary. All dogs share a common operating system.

SOFTWARE: The Cairn will run three standard programs, SIT, COME, and NO, and whatever else you create. It is true that, being micro-canine, the Cairn is limited here, but it does load the programs instantaneously. No disk drives. No tapes.

Admittedly, these are peripheral advantages. The real comparison has to be on the basis of capabilities. What can the Macintosh and the Cairn do? Let's start on the Macintosh's turf—income-tax preparation, recipe storage, graphics, and astrophysics problems:

	TAXES	RECIPES	GRAPHICS	ASTROPHYSICS
Macintosh	yes	yes	yes	yes
Cairn	no	no	no	no

At first glance it looks bad for the Cairn. But it's important to look beneath the surface with this kind of chart. If you yourself are leaning toward the Macintosh, ask yourself these questions: Do you want to do your own income taxes? Do you want to type all your recipes into a computer? In your graph, what would you put on the *x* axis? The *y* axis? Do you have any astrophysics problems you want solved?

Then consider the Cairn's specialties: playing fetch and tug-of-war, licking your face, and chasing foxes out of rock cairns (eponymously). Note that no software is necessary. All these functions are part of the operating system:

	FETCH	TUG-OF-WAR	FACE	FOXES
Cairn	yes	yes	yes	yes
Macintosh	no	no	no	no

Another point to keep in mind is that computers, even the Macintosh, only do what you tell them to do. Cairns perform their functions all on their own. Here are some of the additional capabilities that I discovered once I got the Cairn home and housebroken:

WORD PROCESSING: Remarkably, the Cairn seems to understand every word I say. He has a nice way of pricking up his ears at words like "out" or "ball." He also has highly tuned voice-recognition.

EDUCATION: The Cairn provides children with hands-on experience at an early age, contributing to social interaction, crawling ability, and language skills. At age one, my daughter could say "Sit," "Come," and "No."

CLEANING: This function was a pleasant surprise. But of course cleaning up around the cave is one of the reasons dogs were developed in the first place. Users with young (below age two) children will still find this function useful. The Cairn Terrier cleans the floor, spoons, bib, and baby, and has an unerring ability to distinguish strained peas from ears, nose, and fingers.

PSYCHOTHERAPY: Here the Cairn really shines. And remember, therapy is something that computers have tried. There is a program that makes the computer ask you questions when you tell it your problems. You say, "I'm afraid of foxes." The computer says, "You're afraid of foxes?"

The Cairn won't give you that kind of echo. Like Freudian analysts, Cairns are mercifully silent; unlike Freudians, they are infinitely sympathetic. I've found that the Cairn will share, in a nonjudgmental fashion, disappointments, joys, and frustrations. And you don't have to know BASIC.

This last capability is related to the Cairn's strongest point, which was the final deciding factor in my decision against the Macintosh—user-friendliness. On this criterion, there is simply no comparison. The Cairn Terrier is the essence of user-friendliness. It has fur, it doesn't flicker when you look at it, and it wags its tail.

EVALUATING:

PROFESSIONAL WRITING

WATCHING THE EYEWITLESS NEWS

Elayne Rapping

Culture critic Elayne Rapping is a professor of communications at Adelphi University and is the author of several books, including The Looking Glass World of Nonfiction TV *(1987),* Mediations: Forays into the Culture and Gender Wars *(1994), and* The Culture of Recovery: Making Sense of the Self-Help Movement in Woman's Lives *(1996). She has also published dozens of articles about a variety of social, cultural and media-related issues. "Watching the Eyewitless News," which originally appeared as a column in* The Progressive, *evaluates the local "Eyewitness" news programs featured daily in regional television markets.*

Jimmy Cagney, the ultimate street-smart wise guy, used to snap, "Whadya hear? Whadya know?" in the days of black-and-white movies and READ ALL ABOUT IT! headlines. But that was then and this is now. Today, when gangsta rap has replaced gangster movies, and television has replaced newsprint as the primary source of information (for two-thirds of us, the *only* source), Cagney's famous question is not only antiquated, it is beside the point. What we hear when we consume "the news" has only the most marginal relationship to what we *know* about anything. **(1)**

I'm not referring here to CNN or the "evening news" on the national broadcast networks. I'm referring here to what passes for news in the homes and minds of the vast majority of Americans today: The Eyewitless, Happy

Talk local newscasts that run in many cities for as much as an hour and a half to two hours a day, on as many as seven or eight different channels. **(2)**

The rise of local news, the infotainment monster that ate the news industry, is a long and painful story about a key battle-front in the endless media war between capitalism and democracy, between the drive for profits and the constitutional responsibility of those licensed to use the airwaves to serve the public interest. We know who's winning, of course. The game was rigged from the start. . . . **(3)**

Local news as we know it was invented in 1970, the brainchild of a marketing research whiz hired by the industry to raise ratings by finding out what audiences "wanted to see." The Jeffersonian notion that public media should cover what citizens "need to know" was not a big consideration. Nor was it a concern to respect the audience's intelligence or diversity. **(4)**

The researchers offered a limited, embarrassingly vapid list of choices of formats and subjects, while ignoring the possibility that different groups might want different kinds of information and analysis. More annoying still, they ignored the possibility that individual viewers, of all kinds, might want and need different things at different times for different reasons. Nope, said the marketing whizzes, this master model of "The News" will buy us the most overall-ratings bang per buck. Wrap it up and send it out. **(5)**

And it worked. Their invention has conquered the TV world. The set, the news lineups, the anchors, the weather maps, the sports features—all developed for a New York City market—quickly became a universal formula, sent out to every network affiliate and independent station in America, complete with fill-in-the-blanks guidelines for adaptation to any community, no matter how large or small, urban or rural. Local news today is the single most profitable form of nonfiction television programming in the country and, for most stations, the only thing they actually produce. Everything else comes from the networks. As time went by, this tendency toward cookie-cutter formulas, exported far and wide from a central media source, reached ever more depressing depths. The trend has led to ever more nationally produced, generic features exported to local stations to be passed off as "local." **(6)**

So today we have a phenomenon euphemistically called "local news," although it is anything but, filled with images of a pseudo-community called "America," which is actually closer to Disney World in its representation of American life. But why should that surprise us, in a national landscape now filled, from coast to coast, with identical, mass-produced shopping malls that pass for town marketplaces, and hotels and airports that pass for village inns? In postmodern America, after all, this kind of brand-name synthetic familiarity appears to be the only thing that holds us—a nation of endlessly uprooted and mobile strangers—together. **(7)**

When you turn on the news, whether at home or in an airport of Holiday Inn in some totally strange locale, you see a predictable, comforting spectacle. The town or city in question, whether Manhattan or Moose Hill,

Montana, is presided over by a group of attractive, charming, well-dressed performers—whose agents, salaries, and movements up and down the ladder of media success, gauged by the size of the "market" they infiltrate, are chronicled each week in *Variety*. They seem to care endlessly for each other and us. "Tsk, tsk," they cluck at news of yet another gang rampage or Congressional scandal. "Ooh," they sigh, at news of earthquakes and plane crashes, far and near. **(8)**

If it bleeds, it leads is the motto of the commercial news industry and local news. Its endless series of fires, shootouts, collapsing buildings, and babies beaten or abandoned or bitten by wild dogs is the state-of-the-art showcase for the industry. As Don Henley once put it, in a scathing song about the local news phenomenon, "It's interesting when people die." And it's especially interesting when they die in bizarre or inhuman situations, when their loved ones are on camera to moan and wail, when a lot of them die at once. And since so much of our news is indeed personally terrifying and depressing, we need to have it delivered as cleverly and carefully as possible. And so we have the always smiling, always sympathetic, always confidently upbeat news teams to sugarcoat the bad news. **(9)**

Not that local news ignores the politically important stories. Well, not entirely anyway. When wars are declared or covered, when elections are won or lost, when federal budgets and plant closings do away with jobs and services or threaten to put more and more of us in jail, for less and less cause, the local news teams are there to calm our jagged nerves and reassure us that we needn't worry. **(10)**

This reassurance is sometimes subtle. National news items typically take up less than two minutes of a half-hour segment. And what's said and seen in that brief interlude is hardly enlightening. On the contrary, the hole for "hard news" is generally filled with sound bites and head shots, packaged and processed by the networks, from news conferences with the handful of movers and shakers considered "newsworthy"—the President and his key henchmen and adversaries, mostly. **(11)**

But even local issues of serious import are given short shrift on these newscasts. Hard news affecting local communities takes up only a minute or two more airtime than national events. And local teams are obsessed with "man-on-the-street" spot interviews. Neighbors on local TV are forever gasping and wailing the most clichéd of reflex responses to actual local horrors, whether personal or social. **(12)**

"It's so horrible," they say over and over again, like wind-up dolls with a limited repertoire of three-word phrases, when asked about a local disaster. And when the crisis affects them directly—a school budget cut or neighborhood hospital closing, for example—their on-air responses are equally vapid. "I don't know what we're going to do without any teachers or books," they say with puzzled, frenzied expressions as they try desperately to articulate some coherent reply to a complex issue they've just heard about. **(13)**

I am not suggesting that the news should not feature community residents' views and experiences. Of course it should. But the local news teams' way of presenting such community responses is deliberately demeaning and fatuous. No one could say much worth saying in such a format. And if someone managed to come up with something serious and intelligent, rest assured it would be cut in favor of a more sensational, emotional response. **(14)**

But real news, even about cats in trees or babies in wells, is hardly what takes up the most airtime. "Don't bother too much about that stuff," say the guys and gals in the anchor chairs. Here's Goofy Gil with the weather, or Snappy Sam with the sports—the two features which, on every local newscast, are given the longest time slots and the most elaborate and expensive props. The number and ornateness of the weather maps on local news, and the endlessly amazing developments in special-effects technology to observe climate changes and movements of impending "fronts" is truly mind-boggling. **(15)**

Who needs this stuff? But we're forgetting that this is not the question to ask. "Who wants it?" is the criterion for news producers, and it is, understandably, the weather and sports that most people, most of the time, are likely to sit still for. If local news is meant to be a facsimile of a sunny Disneyesque community of happy, cozy campers, in which the bothersome bad guys and events of the day are quickly dealt with so that community harmony may once more reign, at least for the moment—and that *is* the intended fantasy—then what better, safer, kind of information than weather reports. Historically, after all, the weather is the standard small-talk item for people wishing to be pleasant and make contact without getting into anything controversial or heavy. It is the only kind of news we can all share in—no matter what our race, class, gender, or political differences—as members of a common community. **(16)**

The researchers are not entirely wrong, after all, about what people in this kind of society want. They do want comfort, reassurance, and a community where they belong and feel safe. And why shouldn't they? They find precious little of those things in the streets and buildings they traverse and inhabit in their daily lives. In my urban neighborhood, parents warn children never to make eye contact with anyone on the street or subway; never to speak to anyone, even in case of tragedy or emergency; never to look at or listen to the pathetic souls who regularly beg for money or ramble incoherently in the hope that someone, anyone, will take pity and respond. **(17)**

Remember when California was God's country, the Promised Land of Milk and Honey, to which people migrated for clean air, good jobs, and single-dwelling homes? Try to find these things in overpopulated, polluted, socially vexed and violent LA today. . . . But if we can't all dream of moving to sunny California anymore, there's always TV, where something resembling that innocent dream still exists. Eyewitness News and its various clones allow us to believe, just for a moment, that there really is a Santa Claus, a Mary

Poppins, a Good Samaritan giving away fortunes to the needy, a spirit of Christmas Past to convert the most cold-hearted of corporate Scrooges. Indeed, this kind of "good news" is another staple of the genre. Charities, celebrations, instances of extraordinary good luck or good works by or for local residents are ever-present on local newscasts. Every day, in the midst of even the most dreadful and depressing news, there are legions of friends and neighbors to mourn and console each other, offering aid, bringing soup and casseroles to the victims of natural and man-made disasters, stringing lights and hanging balloons for festive neighborhood gatherings. **(18)**

The news teams themselves often play this role for us. They march at the head of holiday parades and shake hands and kiss babies at openings of malls and industrial parks. They are the neighbors—often thought of as friends by the loneliest among us—we wish we had in real life, there to do the right thing on every occasion. That is their primary function. They are not trained in journalism. They often cannot pronounce the local names and foreign words they read from teleprompters. But they sure can smile. . . . **(19)**

Sociologist Joshua Gamson has suggested, in an insightful essay, that there is a lesson to be learned from the enormous popularity of tabloid television—a category in which I would certainly include local news. The lesson is not that people are stupid, venal, "addicted," or otherwise blameworthy for their fascinated interest in junk TV. On the contrary, it is those responsible for the quality of our public life who are more deserving of such terms of contempt and opprobrium. For it is, says Gamson, "Only when people perceive public life as inconsequential, as not their own, [that] they readily accept the invitation to turn news into play." And people most certainly do perceive public life as inconsequential and worse these days, whether outside their doors or in Washington or on Wall Street. **(20)**

Only I don't think it is primarily the desire to "play" that drives people in droves to local newscasts, or even the trashier tabloid shows like *Hard Copy*. What people are getting from local newscasts—and here the researchers were right on the money, literally—is indeed what they want, in the most profound and sad sense of that phrase. They are getting what they always sought in fantasy and fiction, from *The Wizard of Oz* to *As the World Turns*. They are getting, for a brief moment, a utopian fantasy of a better, kinder, more decent and meaningful world than the one that entraps them. **(21)**

It is not only that public life is inconsequential, after all. It is, far more tragically, that public and private life today are increasingly unjust, inhumane, painful, even hopeless, materially and spiritually, for many of us. And there is no relief in sight except, ironically, on the local newscasts that are a respite from reality. Only, unlike the utopian villages of soap opera and fairy tale, these "imagined communities" are supposed to be, pretend to be, real and true. And for that reason they are more troubling than the trashiest or silliest of pop-culture fictions. **(22)**

VOCABULARY

In your journal, write down the meanings of the following words:

- is not only *antiquated* **(1)**
- *euphemistically* called "local news" **(7)**
- are given short *shrift* **(12)**
- a limited *repertoire* **(13)**
- equally *vapid* **(13)**
- demeaning and *fatuous* **(14)**
- be a *facsimile* **(16)**
- a *utopian* fantasy **(21)**

QUESTIONS FOR WRITING AND DISCUSSION

1. When you finish reading Elayne Rapping's essay, write out your personal responses. Did you agree or disagree with her analysis? Did you find her essay humorous or were you angry at her pronouncements? Were her judgments believable? Did her judgments fit with your own experiences watching your local news programs? Write out your reactions as fully as possible.

2. Reread Rapping's essay, identifying the criteria behind her judgments. In this case, criteria will be statements describing what an ideal news program should be—for example, "Good news programs should provide what the people need, not necessarily what they want." Find and list as many of these criteria as you can. Then make a three-column log for this essay, indicating the judgment that Rapping makes about each criterion and the supporting evidence that she provides.

3. Referring to the three-column log from Question 2, above, assess Rapping's use of supporting evidence—specific examples from local news shows illustrating her point. Which of Rapping's judgments have supporting evidence? Which are merely unsupported assertions? Based on your analysis, do you think Rapping has written an effective evaluative essay? Explain.

4. Observe a local news program. If possible, videotape the program. As you replay your videotape, list each segment of the news: local events, national news, weather, sports, business news, international news, medical and health issues, and so forth. Note any transitional sections (segues) that contain small talk among the anchors. Next to each segment, record the length of time. Next, indicate your opinion about quality or depth of coverage. Finally, record any evidence about the newscasters' personalities, on-camera style, or journalistic ability. Based on your observations and evidence, write an essay responding to Elayne Rapping. How accurately do

her observations apply to the case you have observed? What other general conclusions about Rapping's article or about local news programs might you make?

5. Using Rapping's method of cultural analysis, observe and then analyze/evaluate a particular social, cultural, or media-related event. You might choose hall or club meetings at your university, lecture or lab classes, sports events, class registration rituals, TV sitcoms, Internet home pages—the list is bounded only by your imagination. (Be sure to focus on only one particular kind of cultural event or media program.) Your purpose is both to evaluate these cultural "events" and to explain why the cultural event itself is or is not constructed to avoid limited, stereotypical visions of reality or of people.

FIRST BORN, LATER BORN

Geoffrey Cowley

As a medical and health writer for Newsweek *magazine, Geoffrey Cowley has published dozens of articles on issues such as the Persian Gulf War Syndrome, AIDS, abortion, gene tests, breast cancer, and Alzheimer's disease. His recent cover stories in* Newsweek *include "Herbal Warning," an article about dangerous herbal remedies; "Attention: Aging Men," an investigation of DHEA and hormonal treatments for men; and "Targeting a Deadly Scrap of Genetic Code," a report on current AIDS treatments. In "First Born, Later Born," Cowley turns to psychological issues to review Frank Sulloway's best-selling new book,* Born to Rebel *(Pantheon Books, 1996). Typically, book reviews have a dual purpose: to* inform *readers about the main ideas of the book and to* evaluate *the work's accuracy, interest level, and style. As you read Cowley's essay, think about your own relationship to your siblings. As a firstborn or later-born, do you—or your siblings—exhibit the personality traits Sulloway and Cowley describe?*

When 22-year-old Charles Darwin set out in 1831 to circle the globe on the HMS *Beagle,* his mind lay squarely in the mainstream. He assumed that life forms were fixed entities, each one hand-crafted by God for its special place in nature. But during his travels, Darwin started noticing things that didn't fit the paradigm. Why, he wondered, would finches and iguanas assume distinct but related forms on adjacent islands? And when Darwin proposed a revolutionary solution—that all nature's variety stems from a simple process that preserves useful variations and discards harmful ones—the authorities were appalled. "A scientific mistake," thundered Louis Agassiz, then the world's leading naturalist—"untrue in its facts . . . and mischievous in its tendency." **(1)**

What drives people like Darwin to stick pins in conventional wisdom? And why do radical innovations so enrage people like Agassiz? To Frank Sulloway, a science historian at MIT, it's no coincidence that Darwin was the fifth of six kids in his family, or that Agassiz was the firstborn in his. Sulloway has spent two decades gathering data on thousands of people involved in historic controversies—from the Copernican revolution to the Protestant Reformation—and running statistical tests to see what sets rebels apart from reactionaries. His findings, due out this month in a new book titled "Born to Rebel" (640 pages. *Pantheon Books*. $30), suggests that "the foremost engine of historical change" is not the church, state or economy but family structure. Sulloway makes a compelling case that firstborns, whatever their age, sex, class or nationality, specialize in defending the status quo while later-borns specialize in toppling it. Indeed, he says, people with the same birthranks have more in common with each other than they do with their own siblings. **(2)**

It's an audacious claim (Sulloway himself is a later-born), and not one that social scientists will flock to embrace. Birth-order research, for all its intuitive appeal, has a reputation for flakiness. "Both lay people and experts tend to overinterpret the importance of birth order," says Joseph Rodgers, a psychologist as the University of Oklahoma. "There are very few birth-order effects." In a 1983 review of 2,000 studies dating to the 1940s, the Swiss psychologists Cecile Ernst and Jules Angst declared that since most had failed to control for variables like social class and family size, none could be taken seriously. Sulloway agrees that much of the past research has been marred by weak hypotheses and poor methods. But his own study tackles many of the issues left unresolved by earlier ones, and some experts are raving about it. "It's a monumental work of scholarship," says Sarah Blaffer Hrdy, an anthropologist at the University of California, Davis. "I think it will change the way all of us think about ourselves and our families." **(3)**

Most of us already have a seat-of-the-pants sense of how birthrank affects personality. Firstborns are by reputation the list makers and control freaks. "Show me a librarian who's not a first born," says pop psychologist Kevin Leman, author of "The Birth Order Book" and "Growing Up First Born." "They live by the Dewey Decimal System." Firstborns are supposedly at home in trades like accounting and architecture—and maybe airline piloting. Walter Cronkite, Peter Jennings and Ted Koppel are all firstborns or only children. Chevy Chase, Danny DeVito and Jay Leno are last-borns. Psychologists have theorized about sibling differences since the 1920s, when Freud's estranged disciple Alfred Adler alleged that firstborns spend their lives getting over their displacement by younger brothers and sisters. But the models have been vague enough to accommodate almost any real-world observation—or its opposite. Adler, for example, argued that last-borns are often spoiled and lazy because they don't have younger siblings challenging them. He also characterized them as go-getters, hardened by incessant competition with their elders. Take your pick. **(4)**

Sulloway starts not by spinning random hypotheses but by thinking about the Darwinian pressures that foster sibling competition throughout the natural world. Parental support is often the key to a youngster's survival—and siblings are often the primary obstacle. When food is scarce, chicks in a nest may gang up to murder the youngest member of the brood, without a peep of parental protest. Humans harbor similar propensities. Many societies accord firstborns higher status than later-borns, and some still condone killing a newborn in times of scarcity, just to ensure an older child's survival. Sibling competition may take different forms in the New Jersey suburbs than it does among peasants facing starvation. But firstborns and later-borns still confront very different pressures and opportunities. And by Sulloway's reckoning, their experiences should foster very different qualities of character. **(5)**

How, exactly, should they differ? Firstborns, who grow up knowing they're "bigger, stronger and smarter than their younger siblings," should be more assertive and dominant. They should also be more jealous and status-conscious, having seen their untrammeled turf invaded by newcomers. Their early experience as parents' lieutenants should make them more conscientious than later-borns. And the favoritism they enjoy should leave them more closely wedded to their parents' values and standards. Later-borns, since they can't get their way by force or bluster, should be more sociable and agreeable. And their lesser state in the established family order should leave them more open to novelty and innovation. **(6)**

Sulloway has found ingenious ways of testing these hypotheses. By sifting through the 2,000 studies that Ernst and Angst discarded in 1983, he found 196 in which researchers had factored out differences in social class and family size before looking for birth-order effects. And those studies, which included nearly 121,000 participants, supported his predictions about each of the five personality dimensions that psychological tests look for. Birth order was a lousy predictor of extroversion, a category so broad that it could encompass both a firstborn's assertiveness and a later-born's backslapping sociability. But most studies found that firstborns were more neurotic than were later-borns, and more conscientious (as in responsible, organized and achievement-oriented). Later-borns were consistently deemed more agreeable, and they were overwhelmingly more open to experience. People without siblings fell somewhere between firstborns and later-borns on most personality measures, but they were no more open to experience than were firstborns. **(7)**

So far, so good. But did these psychological tests say anything about how people would behave out in the world? That's where Sulloway's historical surveys come into play. To get at the roots of real-life radicalism, he compiled biographical data on 6,566 people who have played public roles in scientific or political controversies over the past five centuries. By having panels of historians rate these payers on their resistance or receptivity to the innovations they confronted, he was able to plot their "openness to experience" in relation to everything from birth order to age, sex, race, temperament, social class, family size and even the tenor of their family relationships. **(8)**

In one case after another, the influence of birth order is remarkable. Later-borns were more likely than firstborns were to support each of the 61 liberal causes Sulloway surveyed, from the Protestant Reformation to the American civil-rights movement. Indeed birth order rivaled race as a predictor of who would support the abolition of slavery during the mid-1800s. Firstborns and later-borns differ more in their styles of thought than in their core beliefs—liberals can be rigidly doctrinaire and conservatives can be open to new ways of thinking. But the last-borns in Sulloway's survey were 18 times more likely to take up left-wing causes than to get involved in conservative ones, such as the temperance movement. Not surprisingly, Mahatma Gandhi and Martin Luther King Jr. were all later-borns, as were Leon Trotsky, Fidel Castro, Yasir Arafat and Ho Chi Minh. Rush Limbaugh, George Wallace and Newt Gingrich are all firstborns. **(9)**

The pattern was just as clear when Sulloway examined 28 scientific controversies. Later-borns were five times more likely than firstborns were to support the Copernican and Darwinian revolutions—and nine times more likely to embrace phrenology, a wacky 19th-century fad that involved divining character from the shape of a person's skull. By contrast, Sulloway found that "conservative innovations," such as the eugenics movement, have consistently been spearheaded by firstborns and opposed by later-borns. **(10)**

This isn't to say that birth order is all that counts in life, or even in the contentious worlds of science and politics. "These are statistical patterns, not physical laws," says Harvard evolutionist Ernst Mayr. "There are always exceptions." Isaac Newton was a firstborn, for example, and Adolf Hitler wasn't. Sulloway is the first to admit that the effects of birth order can be offset, exaggerated or even overridden by other factors. Indeed, he devotes much of the new book to plotting the ways in which different influences interact. Gender has a huge and obvious impact on personality. But studies have found that firstborn girls are typically more confident, assertive and verbally aggressive than their younger brothers or sisters are. By the same token, age makes most people less open-minded, regardless of their birthrank. Within Sulloway's sample, young later-borns were more than twice as likely as elderly ones were to embrace the idea of evolution during the 19th century. But 80-year-old later-borns were still more receptive than 30-year-old firstborns. **(11)**

Like age, certain features of a person's innate temperament can mask the effects of birth order. Congenital shyness, for example, tends to minimize birth-order differences. By placing a damper on other aspects of character, it makes firstborns less arch and later-borns less outwardly subversive. Likewise, extroversion tends to magnify the contrast. It might lead a firstborn to become a drill sergeant instead of a bank teller, and a last-born to do stand-up comedy instead of writing poems. Conflict with a parent can also offset a firstborn's conformist ways. Once estranged from the familial status quo and pushed into the underdog role, says Sulloway, anyone becomes more radical. **(12)**

Sulloway's findings are sure to strike a chord with lay readers, but social scientists may not appreciate his chutzpah. In the years since Ernst and Angst declared birth order meaningless, few researchers have bothered to look at it, and many of those who have tried have been disappointed. In a recent book titled "Birth Order and Political Behavior," Alfred University political scientist Steven Peterson and two colleagues describe how they analyzed a huge list of eminent figures to see if it was dominated by firstborns. When they came up dry, they assumed there was nothing left to study. "There are always some people who are going to say, 'Gee, you just didn't look at enough variables,'" says Peterson's collaborator Alan Arwine. "It's like trying to kill a vampire." But Arwine and Peterson's findings don't contradict Sulloway's. They merely answer a less interesting question. "The question isn't whether firstborns are more eminent than later-borns," Sulloway insists. "Eminence isn't even a personality trait. It's an outcome. What's interesting is that first-borns and later-borns become eminent in different ways." **(13)**

Other critics will dismiss Sulloway's whole approach. "From what I read, it's not scientific," says Toni Falbo, a professor of educational psychology at the University of Texas at Austin. "He looks at special cases. If you're looking at special cases, particularly in history, you can find a case that fits almost any hypothesis you want." By her logic, history is just an endless series of special cases, not a lawful process that can be illuminated through hypothesis testing. Sulloway's real accomplishment is to show that's not the case. His "special cases" span five centuries and many countries, yet they repeatedly confirm his predictions. "Frank attacks questions that could not be more contingent," says John Tooby, an anthropologist as the University of California, Santa Barbara—"why some countries ended up Protestant, why France resisted Darwinism, who ended up in which faction in the French National Assembly—and shows that they fit into larger patterns." **(14)**

Sulloway doesn't claim to have solved any ultimate questions. He plans to expand his database, test new predictions and publish a revised edition of the book every five years or so. "The publisher put that in my contract," he says. "It was the only way I could make myself stop and publish this." Anyone who can stomach a revolution should be glad that he did. **(15)**

VOCABULARY

In your journal, write the meanings of the following words:

- didn't fit the *paradigm* **(1)**
- defending the *status quo* **(2)**
- an *audacious* claim **(3)**
- spinning random *hypotheses* **(5)**

- humans harbor similar *propensities* **(5)**
- liberals can be rigidly *doctrinaire* **(9)**
- the *eugenics* movement **(10)**
- appreciate his *chutzpah* **(13)**
- firstborns are more *eminent* **(13)**
- could not be more *contingent* **(14)**

QUESTIONS FOR WRITING AND DISCUSSION

1. Reread Cowley's essay, underlining the major claim and the important ideas in Sulloway's book. Then write out Sulloway's major claim and the related key ideas (as summarized by Cowley). Which of those ideas do you personally agree or disagree with? Explain.

2. What does Cowley find to praise about Sulloway's book? What authorities does Cowley cite to support Sulloway's methods or claim? Where is Cowley skeptical about Sulloway's ideas or evidence? Why doesn't Cowley criticize Sulloway's lack of *female* firstborns or later-borns? What authorities does Cowley cite to question or refute Sulloway's ideas, evidence, or methods? Does Cowley offer an evaluation that sufficiently represents both the strengths and weaknesses of the book? Explain.

3. Do a sketch outline of Cowley's essay. Where is his introduction? Where are major divisions in the body of the essay? Where is his conclusion? Then, referring to the various types of lead-ins (see list in Chapter 7, pp. 292–294), identify the kind of lead-in Cowley uses. Did you find it effective? Choose three consecutive paragraphs in the body of Cowley's essay. What phrases or transitions does Cowley use to signal the connections between paragraphs? Are these transitions effective? Explain. Where is Cowley's conclusion? Explain why it is or is not effective.

4. Cowley's review article appeared in *Newsweek*. Find a recent copy of *Newsweek* and profile of the kind of reader it targets. Assume that you are assigned to adapt and revise Cowley's essay for your campus or local newspaper. How might you revise Cowley's essay? Consider length, depth of treatment, paragraphing, and style. Write out your revision plan for this adaptation. Include several specific examples (actual revisions of sample sentences or paragraphs) of how and where you might revise content, organization, or style.

5. Write your own essay in response to Cowley and Sulloway explaining how birth order has affected your personality and the personalities of your siblings. First, write out your thoughts about how birth order has or has not affected the personalities of yourself and your

siblings. Then call and interview your siblings about their opinions. (Be sure to ask them about their perceptions *before* you tell them about Sulloway's thesis or your own ideas.) Using your own perceptions (and supporting experiences), as well as the perceptions and experiences of your siblings, evaluate Sulloway's thesis. How well do Sulloway's ideas account for personality differences in your family?

I love criticism so long as it's unqualified praise.

—NOEL COWARD,

PLAYWRIGHT AND SONGWRITER

EVALUATING:

THE WRITING PROCESS

■ **ASSIGNMENT FOR EVALUATING** With a specific audience in mind, evaluate a product or service, a work of art, or a performance. Choose a subject that is *reobservable*—that you can revisit or review as you write your essay. Select criteria appropriate for your subject and audience. Collect evidence to support or determine a judgment for each criterion.

CHOOSING A SUBJECT

If you have already settled on a possible subject, try the following collecting and shaping strategies. If you have not found a subject, consider these ideas:

- Evaluating requires some expertise about a particular person, performance, place, object, or service. You generate expertise not only through experience but also through writing, reading, and rewriting. Review your authority list from Chapter 6. Which of those subjects could you evaluate? Reread your journal entries on observing and investigating. Did you observe or investigate some person, place, or thing that you could write about again, this time for the purpose of evaluating it?

- Comparing and contrasting leads naturally to evaluation. For example, compare two places you've lived, two friends, or two jobs. Compare two newspapers for their coverage of international news, local features, sports, or business. Compare two famous people from the same profession. Compare your expectations about a person, place, or event with the reality. The purpose of your comparison is to determine, for a specific audience, which is "better," based on the criteria you select and the evidence you find.

COLLECTING

Once you have a tentative subject and audience in mind, ask the following questions to focus your collecting activities:

- Can you narrow, restrict, or define your subject to focus your paper?
- What *criteria* will you use to evaluate your subject?
- What *evidence* might you gather? As you collect evidence, focus on three questions:
  What *comparisons* can you make between your subject and similar subjects?
  What are the *uses* or *consequences* of this subject?
  What *experiments* or *authorities* might you cite for support?
- What initial *judgments* are you going to make?

OBSERVING   Observation and description of your subject are crucial to a clear evaluation. In most cases, your audience will need to know *what* your subject is before they can understand your evaluation.

- Examine a place or object repeatedly, looking at it from different points of view. Take notes. Describe it. Draw it, if appropriate. Analyze its component parts. List its uses. To which senses does it appeal—sight, sound, touch, smell, taste? If you are comparing your subject to other similar subjects, observe them carefully. Remember: The second or third time you observe your subject, you will see even more key details.
- If you are evaluating a person, collect information about this person's life, interests, abilities, accomplishments, and plans for the future. If you are able to observe the person directly, describe his or her physical features, write down what he or she says, and describe the person's environment.
- If you are evaluating a performance or an event, a tape recording or videotape can be extremely useful. If possible, choose a concert, film, or play on tape so that you can stop and review it if and when necessary. If a tape recording or videotape is not available, attend the performance or event twice.

Making notes in a *three-column log* is an excellent collecting strategy for evaluations. Using the following example from Phyllis Richman's evaluation of the Hunan Dynasty restaurant, list the criteria, evidence, and judgments for your subject:

Subject: Hunan Dynasty Restaurant

CRITERIA	EVIDENCE	JUDGMENT
Attractive setting	No blaring red-lacquer tables	Graceful
	White tablecloths	
	Subtle glass etchings	
Good service	Waiters serve with flourishes	Often expert
	Some glitches, such as a forgotten appetizer	

REMEMBERING You are already an authority on many subjects, and your personal experiences may help you evaluate your subject. Try *freewriting, looping, branching,* or *clustering* your subject to help you remember relevant events, impressions, and information. In evaluating appliances for consumer magazines, for example, reporters often use products over a period of months, recording data, impressions, and experiences. Those experiences and memories are then used to support criteria and judgments. Evaluating a film often requires remembering similar films that you have liked or disliked. An evaluation of a great athlete may include your memories of previous performances. A vivid narrative of those memories can help convince an audience that a performance is good or bad.

READING Some of the ideas and evidence for your evaluation may come from reading descriptions of your subject, other evaluations of your subject, or the testimony of experts. Be sure you read these texts critically: Who is the intended audience for the text? What evidence does the text give? What is the author's bias? What are other points of view? Read your potential sources critically.

INVESTIGATING All evaluations involve some degree of formal or informal investigation as you probe the characteristics of your subject and seek evidence to support your judgments.

Using the Library or the Internet Check the library and Internet resources for information on your subject, for ideas about how to design and conduct an evaluation of that subject, for possible criteria, for data in evaluations already performed, and for a sense of different possible audiences. In its evaluation of chocolate-chip cookies, for example, *Consumer Reports* suggests criteria and outlines procedures. The magazine rated some two dozen popular store-bought brands, as well as four "boutique" or freshly baked varieties, on "strength of chocolate flavor and aroma, cookie and chip texture, and freedom from sensory defects." When the magazine's evaluators faced a problem sampling the fresh cookies in the lab, they decided to move the lab: "We ended up loading a station wagon with scoresheet, pencils, clipboards, water containers, cups, napkins . . . and setting off on a tasting safari to shopping malls."

Gathering Field Data You may want to supplement your personal evaluation with a sample of other people's opinions by using *questionnaires* or *interviews.* (See Chapter 6.) If you are rating a film, for example, you might give people leaving the theater a very brief *questionnaire,* asking for their responses on key criteria relating to the movie that they just saw. If you are rating a class, you might want to *interview* several students in the class to support your claim that the class was either effective or ineffective. The interviews might also give you some specific examples—descriptions of their experiences that you can then use as evidence to support your own judgments.

SHAPING

While the shaping strategies that you have used in previous essays may be helpful, the strategies that follow are particularly appropriate for shaping evaluations.

ANALYSIS BY CRITERIA   Often, evaluations are organized by criteria. You decide which criteria are appropriate for the subject and audience, and then you use those criteria to outline the essay. Your first few paragraphs of introduction establish your thesis or overall claim and then give background information: what the subject is, why you are evaluating it, what the competition is, and how you gathered your data. Then you order the criteria according to some plan: chronological order, spatial order, order of importance, or another logical sequence. Phyllis Richman's evaluation of the Hunan Dynasty restaurant follows the criteria pattern:

- Introductory paragraphs: *information* about the restaurant (location, hours, prices), general *description* of Chinese restaurants today, and *overall claim:* The Hunan Dynasty is reliable, a good value, and versatile.
- Criterion #1/Judgment: Good restaurants should have an attractive setting and atmosphere/Hunan Dynasty is attractive.
- Criterion #2/Judgment: Good restaurants should give strong priority to service/Hunan Dynasty has, despite an occasional glitch, expert service.
- Criterion #3/Judgment: Restaurants that serve moderately priced food should have quality main dishes/Main dishes at Hunan Dynasty are generally good but not often memorable. (Note: The most important criterion—the quality of the main dishes—is saved for last.)
- Concluding paragraphs: Hunan Dynasty is a top-flight neighborhood restaurant.

COMPARISON AND CONTRAST   Many evaluations compare two subjects in order to demonstrate why one is preferable to another. Books, films, restaurants, courses, music, writers, scientists, historical events, sports—all can be evaluated using comparison and contrast. In evaluating two Asian restaurants, for example, student writer Chris Cameron uses a comparison-and-contrast structure to shape her essay. In the following body paragraph from her essay, Cameron compares two restaurants, the Unicorn and the Yakitori, on the basis of her first criterion—an atmosphere that seemed authentically Asian:

> Of the two restaurants, we preferred the authentic atmosphere of the Unicorn to the cultural confusion at the Yakitori. At first impression, the Yakitori looked like a converted truck-stop, sparsely decorated with

a few bamboo slats and Japanese print fabric hanging in slices as Bruce Springsteen wailed loudly in the ears of the customers. The feeling at the Unicorn was quite the opposite as we entered a room that seemed transported from Chinatown. The whole room had a red tint from the light shining through the flowered curtains, and the place looked truly authentic from the Chinese patterned rug on the wall to the elaborate dragon on the ceiling. Soft oriental music played as the customers sipped tea from small porcelain cups and ate fortune cookies.

Cameron used the following *alternating* comparison-and-contrast shape for her whole essay:

- Introductory paragraph(s)
- *Thesis:* Although several friends recommended the Yakitori, we preferred the Unicorn for its more authentic atmosphere, courteous service, and well-prepared food.
- Authentic atmosphere: Yakitori vs. Unicorn
- Courteous service: Yakitori vs. Unicorn
- Well-prepared food: Yakitori vs. Unicorn
- Concluding paragraph(s)

On the other hand, Cameron might have used a *block* comparison-and-contrast structure. In this organizational pattern, the outline would be as follows:

- Introductory paragraph(s)
- Thesis: Although several friends recommended the Yakitori, we preferred the Unicorn for its more authentic atmosphere, courteous service, and well-prepared food.
- **The Yakitori:** atmosphere, service, and food
- **The Unicorn:** atmosphere, service, and food as compared to the Yakitori
- Concluding paragraph(s)

CHRONOLOGICAL ORDER   Writers often use chronological order, especially in reviewing a book or a film, to shape parts of their evaluations. Film reviewers rely on chronological order to sketch the main outlines of the plot as they comment on the quality of the acting, directing, or cinematography. At the end of this chapter, for example, Kent Y'Blood's review of the film *The Big Chill* uses chronological order to organize the middle paragraphs of his essay.

CAUSAL ANALYSIS   Analyzing the *causes* or *effects* of a place, object, event, or policy can shape an entire evaluation. Works of art or performances, for example, often measure the *effect* on the viewers or audience. Mark Stevens, for example, claims that Goya's painting has several definite effects on the viewer; those specific effects become the evidence that supports the claim:

- Criterion #1/Judgment: The iconography, or use of symbols, contributes to the powerful effect of this picture on the viewer.
  Evidence: The church as a symbol of hopefulness contrasts with the cruelty of the execution. The spire on the church emphasizes for the viewer how powerless the Church is to save the victims.
- Criterion #2/Judgment: The use of light contributes to the powerful effect of the picture on the viewer.
  Evidence: The light casts an intense glow on the scene, and its glaring, lurid, and artificial qualities create the same effect on the viewer that modern art sometimes does.
- Criterion #3/Judgment: The composition or use of formal devices contributes to the powerful effect of the picture on the viewer.
  Evidence: The diagonal lines scissor the picture into spaces that give the viewer a claustrophobic feeling. The corpse is foreshortened, so that it looks as though the dead man is bidding the viewer welcome.

RESEARCH TIP

Before you draft your evaluating essay, stop for a moment and *evaluate your sources* of information and opinion. If you are citing ideas or information from library articles—or especially from the Internet—be skeptical. How reliable is your source? What do you know about your source's reliability or editorial slant? Does the author have a particular bias? Be sure to *qualify* any biased or absolute statements you use from your sources. (See Chapter 12 for additional ideas on evaluating written sources.)

If you cite observations or field sources (interviews, surveys), evaluate the information you collected. Does it reflect only one point of view? How is it biased? Are your responses in surveys limited in number or point of view? Remember: You may use sources that reflect a limited perspective, but *be sure to alert your readers to those limitations.* For example, you might say, "Obviously, these reactions represent only four viewers who saw this film, but . . ." or "Of course, the administrator wanted to defend this student program when he said . . ."

I have to stop being afraid of being wrong; I can't wait until everything is perfect before the work comes out. I don't have that kind of time.

—SHERLEY ANNE WILLIAMS,

NOVELIST AND CRITIC

TITLE, INTRODUCTION, AND CONCLUSION Titles of evaluative writing tend to be short and succinct, stating what product, service, work of art, or performance you are evaluating ("The Big Chill" or "Watching the Eyewitless News") or suggesting a key question or conclusion in the evaluation ("How Much Car for $3990?").

Introductory paragraphs provide background information and description and usually give an overall claim or thesis. In some cases, however, the overall claim comes last, in a concluding "Recommendations" section or in a final summary paragraph. If the overall claim appears in the opening paragraphs, the concluding paragraph may simply review the strengths or weaknesses, or just advise the reader: This *is* or *is not* worth seeing, reading, watching, doing, or buying.

DRAFTING

With your criteria in front of you, your data or evidence at hand, and a general plan or sketch outline in mind, begin writing your draft. As you write, focus on your audience. If your evaluation needs to be short, you may have to use only those criteria that will appeal most effectively to your audience. As you write, check occasionally to be sure that you are including your key criteria. While some parts of the essay may seem forced or awkward as your write, other parts will grow and expand as you get your thoughts on paper. As in other papers, don't stop to check spelling or worry about an occasional awkward sentence. If you stop and can't get going, reread what you have written, look over your notes or sketch outline, and pick up the thread again.

REVISING

Remember that revision is not just changing a word here and there or correcting occasional spelling errors. Make your evaluation more effective for your reader by including more specific evidence, changing the order of your paragraphs to make them clearer, cutting out an unimportant point, or adding a point that one of your readers suggests.

I have rewritten— often several times— every word I have ever published. My pencils outlast their erasers.

—VLADIMIR NABOKOV,

NOVELIST

PEER RESPONSE

These guidelines will help you give and receive constructive advice about the rough draft of your evaluating essay.

Reader: Before you answer the following questions, read the entire draft from start to finish. As you *reread* the draft, do the following:

1. Underline the sentence(s) that state the writer's **overall claim** about the subject.
2. In the margin, put large brackets [ ] around paragraphs that *describe* what the writer is evaluating.

continued

3. On a separate piece of paper or at the end of the writer's essay, make a *three-column log* indicating the writer's criteria, evidence, and judgments. (Does the log include both positive and negative judgments?)

4. Identify with an asterisk (*) any passages in which the writer needs more *evidence* to support the judgments.

5. Write out one *criterion* that is missing or that is not appropriate for the given subject.

6. If possible, describe one of *your experiences* with this subject that the writer might find interesting or relevant.

Writer: As you read your peer reviewer's notes and comments, do the following:

1. Consider your peer reviewer's comments and notes. Has your reviewer correctly identified your overall claim? Do you need to add more description of your subject? Does the reviewer's three-column log look like yours? Do you need to revise your criteria or add additional evidence? Do you balance positive and negative judgments?

2. Based on your review, draw up a *revision plan.* Write out the three most important things you need to do as you revise your essay.

Guidelines for Revision

During your revision, keep the following tips in mind:

- **Criteria are *standards of value*.** They contain categories and judgments, as in "good fuel economy," "good reliability," or "powerful use of light and shade in a painting." Some categories, such as "price," have clearly implied judgments ("low price"), but make sure that your criteria refer implicitly or explicitly to a standard of value.

- **Examine your criteria from your audience's point of view.** Which criteria are most important in evaluating your subject? Will your readers agree that the criteria you select are indeed the most important ones? Will changing the order in which you present your criteria make your evaluation more convincing?

- **Include both positive and negative evaluations of your subject.** If all of your judgments are positive, your evaluation will sound like an advertisement. If all of your judgments are negative, your readers may think you are too critical.

- **Be sure to include supporting evidence for each criterion.** Without any data or support, your evaluation will be just an opinion that will not persuade your reader.
- **Avoid overgeneralizing in your claims.** If you are evaluating only three software programs, you cannot say that Lotus 1-2-3 is the best business program around. You can say only that it is the best among the group or the best in the particular class that you measured.
- **Unless your goal is humor or irony, compare subjects that belong in the same class.** Comparing a Yugo to a BMW is absurd because they are not similar cars in terms of cost, design, or purpose.
- **If you need additional evidence to persuade your readers, review the questions at the beginning of the "Collecting" section of this chapter.** Have you addressed all the key questions listed there?
- **If you are citing other people's data or quoting sources, check to make sure your summaries and data are accurate.**
- *Signal* **the major divisions in your evaluation to your reader using clear transitions, key words, and paragraph hooks.** At the beginning of new paragraphs or sections in your essay, let your reader know where you are going.
- **Revise sentences for directness and clairty.**
- **Edit your evaluation for correct spelling, appropriate word choice, punctuation, usage, and grammar.**

■ POSTSCRIPT ON THE WRITING PROCESS   When you finish writing your essay, answer the following questions:

1. Who is the intended audience for your evaluation? Write out one sentence from your essay in which you appeal to or address this audience.

2. Describe the main problem that you had writing this essay, such as finding a topic, collecting evidence, or writing or revising the draft.

3. What parts or paragraphs of your essay do you like best? Indicate the words, phrases, or sentences that make it effective. What do you like about them?

4. Explain what helped you most with your revision: advice from your peers, conference with the teacher, advice from a writing center tutor, rereading your draft several times, or some other source.

5. Write out one question that you still have about the assignment or about your writing and revising process.

EVALUATING:

STUDENT WRITING

BORROWERS CAN BE CHOOSY

Linda Meininger

Linda Meininger wrote her evaluation essay on the Interlibrary Loan Office at her campus library. Her purpose was to advise her readers— other students—about the usefulness of the interlibrary loan service. In order to gather information for her essay, she visited the office, learned how to access an interlibrary loan with her computer, interviewed the coordinator of the office, and surveyed nine people who had used the library service. Overall, she discovered that the interlibrary loan office provided a surprisingly convenient, helpful, and inexpensive service. Included on the next page are the following writing-process materials: a draft of her interview and survey questions, a three-column log, her first rough draft, questions for a conference with her instructor, and her final draft.

DRAFT OF INTERVIEW AND SURVEY QUESTIONS

Interview Questions for Interlibrary Loan Office (ILL) Coordinator

1. Have you surveyed your clients to get their impressions about the service? Results? Favorable—why? Unfavorable— why? Valid or not—why?

2. How do you and your employees rate your service?

3. Do you offer any special services for your clients?

4. Have you received any recognition for your work in The ILL?

5. What institutions lend documents to our library?

6. How convenient do you make it for clients to use your services?

Survey Questions

1. Were you satisfied with the interlibrary loan service you received? Why? Why not?

2. How often do you use the service?

3. How much lead time did you allow for your request?

4. What is your area of research?

5. What type of materials did you request? Periodicals? Books? Documents? Theses?

6. What was the cost of using the service?

DRAFT OF THREE-COLUMN LOG

Claim: The Interlibrary Loan Office runs a well organized and efficient operation.
Audience: Students
Purpose: To evaluate the service and encourage students to use it.

CRITERIA	EVIDENCE	JUDGMENT
1. Timely delivery of materials	Survey results	Mixed
2. Helpful service	Personal experience	Positive
3. Convenience for users	and survey	Positive
4. Scope of libraries available	Interview and brochure	Positive
5. Reasonable cost	Survey and interview	Positive

FIRST ROUGH DRAFT

Are you someone who has searched endlessly through the library's computer database or the card catalog only to have that elusive title never appear? Go directly to Room 210, Morgan Library and collect an Interlibrary Loan request card, or if that's too far to walk, place your order via e-mail from your PC. **(1)**

How useful can this service be to you? Stay tuned and I'll show you everything you need to know about Morgan Library Interlibrary Loan (ILL). In evaluating this service, available to all who are affiliated with CSU as a student or employee, I will be looking at the following criteria: convenience and ease of use; timely arrival of materials requested; cooperation and assistance from the ILL staff; and reasonable fees for use of loaned materials. **(2)**

Jane Smith of the ILL department informed me that request cards can be found in many locations in the library. These color-coded cards are used to request documents, periodicals, theses, or books. The color of the card corresponds to the type of material. Requests may be left at any of the reference desks or you may drop off your request in person in Room 210 of the library, Monday through Friday. **(3)**

Students and employees with a PC and a modem may request materials from their office or home. According to Jane Smith, electronic access was developed in-house by the ILL department. A new service has also been established, called the Library Retrieval and Delivery Service (LRDS). This is available to disabled students on campus. Requests may be made by the computer or manually. **(4)**

Jane Smith of the ILL office informed me that normal turnaround for requests is 24 hours. That translates to one day from the time the requests leave the ILL office for another lending institution. Unless . . . it's spring semester. Then, look out! Deadlines for theses and research are closing in and everyone is in need of the materials yesterday. Then the turnaround time is a week. Most likely materials will not arrive until the end of the school year. Requests at spring semester jump to 300–400 per day as compared to a normal of approximately 200 daily. **(5)**

I would say that being able to fill 300 requests for material is efficient by my standards. Jane was delighted to inform me that Morgan Library was chosen most efficient in the state by other ILL's in Colorado. I think that could be comparable to a Good Housekeeping Seal of Approval or a five-star rating by AAA. **(6)**

When I visited the ILL office I discovered a staff willing to answer my questions and with a sense of humor. They made me feel comfortable and at ease. One of the brochures I picked up was a pamphlet with their job descriptions: Queen of the World, Resident Geek, ILL's Mouthpiece, Double Agent, ILL's Movie Star and answer to Greta Garbo, and Leading (Lending) Lady. The pamphlet shows me that these people like what they do and can laugh at themselves and their idiosyncrasies. I believe this impression is relayed to their patrons. **(7)**

CONFERENCE QUESTIONS

1. Are the criteria I have sufficient? Should I have chosen more of the criteria from my log? Or other criteria from my list?

2. My development needs improvement. I need more evidence to substantiate my criteria. What If I didn't secure the surveys necessary (ten) to be fairly objective?

3. Should I introduce my criteria in a subtle manner, or just come right out and state them?

4. After class today, I felt that I needed to state judgments for each of my criteria, although they could change after the survey results.

5. Does it sound like I'm writing to a student audience?

REVISED VERSION

BORROWERS CAN BE CHOOSY

Are you someone who has searched endlessly through the library's computer listing, the card catalog, or even the stacks, only to have that elusive title never appear? Don't give up. Go directly to Room 210, Morgan Library, and collect an Interlibrary Loan request card. If that's too far to walk, just place your order via e-mail with your PC, a modem, and some communications software. **(1)**

This service can be useful to you during your four-year educational experience at Colorado State University. So stay tuned, and I'll review four characteristics of Morgan Library Interlibrary Loan (ILL). In evaluating this service, which is available to all CSU students, faculty, or staff, I will be looking at the following criteria: convenience and ease of use, timely arrival of materials requested, reasonable fees for materials, and cooperation and assistance from the ILL staff. To gain evidence about the performance of this department, I interviewed the staff, observed their operation, and conducted a survey of CSU students, faculty and employees (see Appendix for results of survey). Out of nine survey respondents, the level of usage varied from four one-time users to two weekly users. **(2)**

The convenience and ease of using the interlibrary loan service was definitely a high point. Jane Smith of the ILL department informed me that request cards have been placed in many locations in the library for convenient access. These color-coded cards are used to request documents, periodicals, theses, or books. The color of the card corresponds to the type of material requested. Cards may be left at any of the reference desks, or you may drop off your request in person in Room 210 of the library, just off to your left at the top of the stairs, Monday through Friday, 8:00 a.m.–5:00 p.m. **(3)**

The addition of computer access to interlibrary loan also adds to the ease of requesting materials. At the present time, students, faculty, and employees with a PC and a modem may request materials from their office or home. According to Ms. Smith, electronic access was developed in-house by the ILL department, making their service available 24 hours per day. Julie Wessling, coordinator of the Interlibrary Loan Department, said, "About one-third of our users request their specific information via our electronic service." **(4)**

The ILL has also established another convenient new service, called Library Retrieval and Delivery Service (LRDS). This is available to disabled students on campus and other off-campus users. Requests may be made by computer or by using the request cards. Delivery or notice of non-availability of materials will be made within 48 hours to three sites on campus: Braiden Hall, the RDS Office in 116 Student Services Building, and the ILL office. There is also dial-up access to the library's computer listings. This service is especially valuable to off-campus users or students with mobility problems. The ILL staff retrieves requests, most of which—according to Ms. Wessling—are in the CSU stacks, and then delivers them to one of the collection sites for pickup by the patron. **(5)**

Overall, I found the request forms and located the ILL office without any problem, and according to nine out of the nine people surveyed, the ILL service was "easy to use and locate." Judy Lira, a Rocky Mountain High School Media Specialist, faxes her requests and feels that the technology is a service to the staff and students at her school. Bonnie Mueller, a Morgan Library cataloguing employee, uses LAN to order materials, and she states, "It's wonderful!" While I was in the ILL office, a student was filling out request cards. I tried to enlist her aid for my survey, but she declined, saying that this was her first time using the interlibrary loan service. However, she did have one comment for me: "They [the ILL office] need to make us [students] more aware of this." It appears that the convenient access to the ILL system makes it an asset to CSU students and to the local schools. **(6)**

I wished to experiment personally with the ILL to evaluate the timely arrival of requests, but Ms. Smith explained to me that it would be impossible to receive anything within the time frame I was allotted to finish this essay. Therefore, I will be relying on the experiences and testimony of others. **(7)**

The normal processing turnaround time for requests, Ms. Smith informed me, is 24 hours. That means that it takes one day from the time the request is made by the borrower to the time it leaves the ILL office for another lending institution. Unless . . . it's spring semester. Then look out! Deadlines for theses and research papers are closing in, and students and faculty need their materials yesterday. Ms. Smith related the story of a student who recently came in on a Wednesday and wanted the item by Monday. She had to tell him, "Sorry, it's not possible, especially now." She said at this time of the year—spring semester—the processing time is approximately one week, and that's just until the request leaves the CSU ILL office. Most likely, materials will not arrive until April or the end of the school year. Normal arrival time seems to vary between ten days to two weeks, according to survey results. Requests at spring semester jump to 300–400 per day, and these requests include not only the CSU customers, but the borrowers from other institutions who are requesting materials from Morgan Library, reported Ms. Wessling. **(8)**

The normal processing time can be speeded up, however, in some cases. Ms. Wessling explained that "the use of e-mail allows us to locate and help process customers' requests faster. This allows the student or professor to receive the information more quickly. The only thing holding the process back is the time it takes to get the specific request in the mail." Also, articles from periodicals or a document can be sent electronically or by fax. When materials are needed in a hurry, a RUSH may be affixed to the card and a last usable date recorded. This will bring the request to the attention of the office, and they will give it priority to try to locate a copy at a nearby library for pickup by the client. Of the nine people I surveyed, six reported that their materials arrived within 24 hours to two weeks, but one person reported that it took eight weeks and didn't arrive in time to be of use. He allowed two weeks of lead time, but he ordered the material in April. Another person stated that she had to wait over six weeks for materials to arrive. Her materials were "very difficult to locate." My accounting professor, Dr. Middlemist, usually allows a two-week lead time when ordering and said that the "time taken to arrive depended on where the materials were coming from." Dr. Middlemist stated that she uses the service 10–12 times per year, maybe more, depending on what her needs are. **(9)**

By my standards, being able to fill 300 requests for materials is efficient. In addition, Ms. Smith was delighted to inform me that Morgan Library was chosen most efficient by other ILL's in Colorado and will be "looked over" by a team from the state so that their efficient and innovative ideas may be used in other libraries. I think that could be comparable to a Good Housekeeping Seal of Approval or a four-star rating by AAA. **(10)**

While the timely arrival of materials was a problem, especially in the spring semester, the cost of materials received was very reasonable. For most requests, there is no charge for the service. I found that only on the journal request card was there a line item for maximum cost. This is in the event that there could be photocopying charges. Eight of my nine respondents said they received their materials (books, theses, and journals) free of charge, and the other paid a reasonable fee for xeroxing one time. It is through the lending and borrowing reciprocal agreement between libraries that the ILL service can be offered at no cost or low cost to the user. **(11)**

Perhaps the strongest feature of the ILL service was the willingness of the staff to help patrons, answer questions, and keep their sense of humor. They made me feel comfortable and at ease. One of the brochures I picked up was a pamphlet with their job descriptions: Queen of the World, resident Geek, ILL's Mouthpiece, Double Agent, ILL's Movie Star and Answer to Greta Garbo, and Leading (Lending) Lady. This pamphlet shows that these people like what they do and can laugh at themselves and their idiosyncrasies. Something else Ms. Smith said really sticks in my mind. She said, "I think we're the only department in the whole library where everyone really likes what they do." I believe this impression is relayed to their patrons. My survey results concurred with this, as seven respondents felt that the staff was friendly and helpful. One dissenting student felt that the office could have presented the information she needed over the phone, saving her a trip to the library. The other person felt there wasn't any follow-up on a trace request to see if a book had been lost. Morgan Library has lost this patron to another library. Some of the positive comments received were as follows: "The ILL personnel went out of their way to help me." "What I needed was extremely obscure, and they got most of it." "They found a German book in Berlin, and they xeroxed it and sent the whole thing FREE!" **(12)**

As a result of my investigation and evaluation of the ILL office, I hope I have occasion to use their service in the future. I know from my conversations with the staff and other users of ILL that the service and staff are reliable and willing to assist at any time (during office hours, of course). The cost is well within the reach of all patrons, and we have two methods of booking our requests, manually on cards and electronically by computer. So the next time you need an item that the CSU library doesn't own, remember that you do have another resource available at your fingertips: Morgan Library's Interlibrary Loan. **(13)**

Works Cited

Interlibrary Loan. Fort Collins: Colorado State University, 1992.

It's Here! Fort Collins: Colorado State University, 1992.

Libraries Retrieval and Delivery Service. Fort Collins: Colorado State University, 1992.

Morgan Library Interlibrary Loan Survey. Personal Survey. 2 March 1992.

Self-Guided Tour of Morgan Library. Fort Collins: Colorado State University, 1992.

Smith, Jane. Personal Interview. 27 February and 2 March 1992.

Wessling, Julie. Personal Interview. 2 March 1992.

Appendix

Morgan Library Interlibrary Loan Survey

The following survey was completed by nine students and faculty members. Responses follow each question.

1. What was the subject area of the materials requested?

Accounting–1	Ben Jonson-17th C writer & critic–1
Agriculture–1	Cognitive Development–1
Ancient Roman Art–1	Popular Fiction–1
Anthropology–1	Travelogues-1800's–1
Archaeology–1	Various Subjects–1

2. What type of material did you request?

Book–7 Journal–6
Thesis–1 Documents–0

3. How much lead time did you allow the interlibrary loan office to secure your materials?

No deadline–5

24 hours–1

1 week–1

2 weeks–2

4. What time of the year did you request materials?

| Fall semester | Specify month | 3 in Oct, Nov and Dec |
| Spring semester | Specify month | 1-Jan, 4-Feb & Mar, 2-April, 1-May |

5. Did your materials arrive in a timely manner? How much time did it take?

24 hours–1	Very quickly–1
1 week–1	Not more than 1 1/2–2 months–1
8 weeks–1	Over 3 weeks–1
Typically timely–1	10 days–1

6. Were you satisfied with the service you received? Why? Why not?

No, not friendly, no follow-up if lost–1

Yes, friendly and helpful–1

Yes–2

Yes, very satisfied–1

Very, needed extremely obscure stuff-got most of it–1

Extremely satisfied, wonderful to have access to otherwise unreachable materials–1

No problem with service or individuals, satisfied–1

Friendly–1

7. How often do you use the service?

1 time–3	Weekly–1
2 times/year–1	One semester a lot of times–1
10–12 times/year–1	
Goes to Boulder-CU library–1	
2–3 times/week ave., usually turns in requests in batches–1	

8. Was there a charge for your requested materials? If so did you feel the charge was reasonable or not? How much was it?

No charge–8

Xeroxing charge, reasonable–1

9. Was the staff of the interlibrary loan office helpful? Friendly? Gave out of the ordinary service?

Not friendly, not helpful, no out of ordinary service–1

Could have presented info over phone, save trip to library–1

Staff went out of their way to help–1

Worked hard on obscure stuff–1

Always do their best–1

Very friendly–3	Friendly & helpful–3
Regular service–1	FAX requests–1

10. Did you feel that the service was convenient to use (i.e., easy to order materials and pick them up, forms to be filled out, the open hours of the office, etc.)?
Easy to use–2   Very–2   Yes–2
Used LAN–1

> Yes, feels guilty about amt. of paper involved in all of the requests–1

> Fax technology availability real service to students & staff–1

11. From which institution did you receive your materials?

> Northwestern–1

> Dartmouth–1

> Berlin–1

> Denver Public Library–1

> Oklahoma State University–1

> CU-Boulder–1

> Don't know–2

QUESTIONS FOR WRITING AND DISCUSSION

1. Evaluate Meininger's final draft, using the Peer Response guidelines in this chapter. What are the strengths and weaknesses of her essay? Now read Meininger's first rough draft. Which areas did she improve most in her revision?

2. Based on her final draft, make a revised version of Meininger's three-column log. Write out each criterion, the main supporting evidence for that criterion, and the judgment. Indicate the paragraphs (by number) that Meininger devotes to each of her criteria.

3. In her Postscript, Meininger wrote, "I revised my criteria and rearranged them in a different order after we talked in class. I didn't want to have my weakest criteria last." Compare her criteria (see her three-column log) with her revised draft. Explain how her additions, deletions, and reordering improved her criteria—and her essay.

4. Reread the questionnaire in Meininger's Appendix. How might she improve that questionnaire? What questions might she add or delete? How might she rephrase the questions?

5. Brainstorm a list of other campus services or organizations that you could evaluate. Choose one of those services or organizations and write a three-column log, indicating the subject, the audience, the criteria, and the possible kinds of evidence that you might collect for your essay.

"THE BIG CHILL"

Kent Y'Blood

In his review of The Big Chill, Kent Y'Blood writes a compact evalua-
tion of the film for a campus newspaper audience. Film-review writers
often need to walk a tightrope: They should give the basic information
about key characters and plot—without revealing too much about the
story; they should analyze and evaluate the film—without so much analy-
sis that the reader is bored. As you read the essay, decide how successful
Y'Blood is at both informing yet entertaining the reader.

"The Big Chill" is an actor's film in the very best sense. It's no easy task
to create eight major characters we can care about immediately without
resorting to some form of cinematic stereotyping, but director Lawrence Kasdan does it. We meet eight individuals whose stories of fading youthful opti-
mism are familiar in many ways. These characters are not mere representatives
of those stories but living, breathing people in a psychological comedy. **(1)**

And what a dark comedy it is. Death pervades every scene, and not just the
death of The Movement, or the death of Revolutionary Ideals, or the death of
The Spirit of a Generation. Those generalizations have little place here. "The
Big Chill" is about a real, particular death: that of Alex Marshall, permanent
dropout, college friend of Sam, Sarah, Michael, Nick, Harold, Meg and Karen.
He committed suicide in Harold's and Sarah's house where he was staying with
his young girlfriend Chloe. The old friends, who haven't seen much of each other
in years, regroup for his funeral and all decide to spend a weekend at Harold's and
Sarah's house in Georgia to try to sort out their confusion over Alex's act. **(2)**

At the beginning of the film, Kasdan packs plenty of character information into a relatively short space so that we get to know the people well. As
they make their various ways to the funeral, spread out across the country as
they are, we begin to learn about them. Sam (Tom Berenger) lines up four
miniature vodka bottles on his airplane tray and charms the stewardess out of
just one more. Nick (William Hurt) empties out a collection of pills on the
seat of his Porsche, downs a couple, and the car roars out ahead of the camera. We get glimpses of the other characters intercut with shots of a man
dressing in a pinstripe suit and white shirt, all to the tune of Marvin Gaye's
"I Heard It Through the Grapevine." Kasdan ends this scene with a shocker.
As a sewn-up wrist is slipped beneath a white cuff, we realize it was Alex's
corpse we saw being dressed. This combination of expository information
with emotionally powerful action is superb movie making, and Kasdan does
not let down after the promise of this opening sequence. **(3)**

At the funeral itself, we learn more about the principals. Michael (Jeff
Goldblum) obviously wants more than comfort from Chloe (Meg Tilly). Harold
(Kevin Kline) intones a eulogy and breaks down as he remembers "there was
something about Alex that was too good for this world." His wife Sarah (Glenn

Close) weeps but holds together admirably. Throughout the film, all the characters are true to our first impressions of them, but are not mechanically programmed to act predictably. They can still surprise us, and they all do. Later, when the characters get assigned their bedrooms, we get a glimpse of their luggage. Knowing who brings the economy-size bottle of Maalox, who the TV script and a volume of Kafka, and who has many pairs of designer men's underwear just adds that much more to our sense of who each of these people is. It is a weekend of talk, but the talk is supplemented by what we've observed about these people, so the dialogue doesn't have to carry all the weight in the film. **(4)**

When they do talk, the chat is brilliant. Their sentiment is constantly undercut by jokes that don't weaken their emotions, just complicate them. When Beth rises to play Alex's favorite song on the organ at the funeral (Rolling Stones' "You Can't Always Get What You Want"), it is simultaneously funny and heartbreaking. The friends collectively try to work out how they failed Alex, how they failed their younger selves by becoming successful and rich, and how the people they were became the people they are. **(5)**

"The Big Chill" is beautifully edited, masterfully acted, and has a script that has more depth than anything I've seen in a long time. The film directly confronts such tough themes as the endurance of friendship, the question of suicide, isolation, meaninglessness—and all to the '60s music of the Temptations, Smokey Robinson, and the Rascals. That's what I call a good movie. **(6)**

QUESTIONS FOR WRITING AND DISCUSSION

1. Profile yourself as a typical reader for this review: Give your age, note whether you frequently go to movies, describe the kinds of films you enjoy, describe your attitude toward music or events from the Sixties, and indicate whether or not you have seen *The Big Chill*. With these notes, come to class prepared to discuss whether or not Y'Blood's review succeeded. Did it make you want to see the movie? If you've seen the film already, was his evaluation convincing? Was it entertaining?

2. Y'Blood's writing-process materials are not reproduced here, but how do you suppose that he collected all the information and supporting evidence for his review? Describe a plausible sequence for his collecting activities.

3. In his review, Y'Blood emphasized Lawrence Kasdan's skills in directing this film. However, if he had chosen to focus on one particular actor's performance (for example, William Hurt's performance as Nick) or on the relationship of the songs to the story, how would that have changed the review? For practice, rewrite the opening paragraph of this review, focusing either on one principal actor or on the Sixties songs.

9 PROBLEM SOLVING

Miriam Schapiro, 1986, *Night Shade*, 1986. Acrylic and fabric collage on canvas 48'' x 96''. Private Collection, NY. Photo by Gamma One Conversions. Courtesy Steinbaum Krauss Gallery, NYC.

TRYING TO TAKE NOTES IN YOUR PSYCH I LECTURE CLASS— ALONG WITH 250 OTHER STUDENTS—YOU REALIZE THAT YOU ARE COMPLETELY LOST AND CONFUSED. SO YOU RAISE your hand to ask a question, but the professor keeps on talking, throwing out more new terms and examples. You look at your neighbor, who just shrugs and keeps on writing. After class, when you think about how hard you've worked to pay your tuition, you realize that you deserve better classes for your money. The problem, you decide, is in the large lecture format—there are just too many students for the teacher to answer questions and explain difficult concepts. So you decide to write a letter to the head of the psychology department (with a copy for the dean of Arts and Sciences) outlining the problems with this class and proposing that Psychology I be taught in classes no larger than fifty. Where the administrators get additional teachers, you decide, is their responsibility. You argue that, as administrators, it is their duty to give quality education the highest priority.

❧

IN YOUR WRITING CLASS, YOU READ A CONVERSATION BETWEEN TWO MINORITY WOMEN ABOUT RACIAL TEN- SIONS IN AFRICAN-AMERICAN AND ASIAN-AMERICAN COM- munities. The problems, you realize, are continuing and widespread. Publi- cized instances include a boycott by blacks on Korean shops in New York City and the looting of Korean stores during the Los Angeles riots. As a member of the American-Korean community, you decide to propose three solutions to promote education and understanding. First, encourage the American-Korean media to educate Koreans about cultural differences. Next, ask Korean-American churches to cooperate with churches in African- American communities. Finally, appeal to Korean businesspeople to invest in the black communities where they work. Communities, you argue, cannot wait for local or federal governments to solve these problems. They must take the initiative and work cooperatively to solve their problems.

This country has more problems than it should tolerate and more solutions than it uses.
—RALPH NADER, CONSUMER-RIGHTS ADVOCATE

❧

Whenever life doesn't seem to give an answer, we create one.
—LORRAINE HANSBERRY, AUTHOR OF A RAISIN IN THE SUN

357

W<small>E DON'T HAVE TO LOOK DILIGENTLY TO LOCATE PROB-</small>
<small>LEMS IN OUR LIVES. THEY HAVE A HABIT OF SEEKING US</small>
<small>OUT. IT SEEMS THAT IF SOMETHING CAN GO WRONG, IT</small>
will. Countries are fighting each other, the environment is polluted, unemployment is too high, prejudice is still rampant, television shows are too violent, sports are corrupted by drugs and money, education is too impersonal, and people drive so recklessly that you take your life in your hands every time you go across town. Everywhere we look, someone else creates problems for us—from minor bureaucratic hassles to serious or life-threatening situations. (On rare occasions, of course, we're part of the problem ourselves.)

If you write in order to *propose a solution* to some problem, you have no lack of subjects. First, however, you may well ask whether your problem is one that can be solved. As journalist Charles Dudley Warner once observed, "Everybody talks about the weather, but nobody does anything about it." For the short term, the weather is not a problem that has a solution. Although we can predict the weather (sometimes), experiment with cloud seeding, or prepare for the effects of hurricanes or blizzards, wisdom dictates that we accept the weather that comes. For the long term, however, we know that ozone depletion and global warming are serious weather-related problems that need worldwide planning and cooperation.

If the problem can be solved, the difficult part is to propose a solution and then persuade others that your solution will in fact solve the problem—without creating new problems and without costing too much. Because your proposal may ask readers to take some action, vote in a certain way, or actually work to implement your proposal, you must make sure that your readers vividly perceive the problem and agree that your plan outlines the most logical and feasible solution.

You see things; and you say, "Why?" But I dream things that never were; and I say, "Why not?"

—GEORGE
BERNARD
SHAW,

DRAMATIST

TECHNIQUES FOR PROBLEM SOLVING

Problem solving requires all your skills as a writer. You need to observe carefully to see if a problem exists. You may need to remember experiences that illustrate the seriousness of the problem. You need to read and investigate which solutions have worked or have not worked. You often have to explain what the problem is and why or how your proposal would remedy the situation. You may need to evaluate both the problem and alternative solutions. To help you identify the problem and convince your readers of the soundness of your proposal, keep the following techniques in mind:

- **Identifying and understanding your *audience*.** If you want something done, fixed, changed, improved, subsidized, banned, reorganized, or made legal or illegal, make sure that you are writing to the appropriate audience.
- **Demonstrating that a *problem exists*.** Some problems are so obvious that your readers will readily acknowledge them: high crime rates, conflicts in Africa and the Middle East, air pollution in industrialized nations, and drug and alcohol abuse. Often, however, you must first convince your audience that a problem exists: Are food preservatives really a serious problem, or would eliminating them cause even more problems?
- **Proposing a *solution* that will solve the problem.** After convincing your readers that a serious problem exists, you must then propose a remedy, plan, or course of action that will eliminate or reduce the problem.
- **Persuading your readers that your *proposal will work*,** that it is *feasible*, or that it is better than the *alternative solutions*. You convince your readers by supporting your proposal with *reasons* and *evidence*.

As you start your problem-solving paper, concentrate on ways to *narrow and focus* your topic. When you think about possible topics, follow the advice of environmentalists: "Think Globally, Act Locally." Rather than talk about education or drugs or crime or pollution on a national scale, find out how your community or campus is dealing with a problem. A local focus will help narrow your topic—and provide possibilities for using firsthand observations, personal experience, and interviews.

DEMONSTRATING THAT A PROBLEM EXISTS

A proposal begins with a description of a problem. Demonstrating that the problem exists (and is serious) will make your readers more receptive to your plan for a solution. The following selection from Frank Trippett's *Time* magazine essay, "A Red Light for Scofflaws," identifies a problem and provides sufficient examples to demonstrate that scofflawry is pervasive and serious enough to warrant attention. Even if we haven't been personally attacked while driving the Houston or Miami or Los Angeles freeways, Trippett convinces us that *scofflawry*—deliberately disobeying ("scoffing at") laws—is serious. His vivid description makes us aware of the problem:

> Law and order is the longest-running and probably the best-loved political issue in U.S. history. Yet it is painfully apparent that millions of Americans who would never think of themselves as lawbreakers, let alone criminals, are taking increasing liberties with the legal codes that are designed to protect and nourish their society.

Demonstrating that a problem exists

Evidence: authority

Indeed, there are moments today—amid outlaw litter, tax cheating, illicit noise, and motorized anarchy—when it seems as though the scofflaw represents the wave of the future. Harvard sociologist David Riesman suspects that a majority of Americans have blithely taken to committing supposedly minor derelictions as a matter of course. Already, Riesman says, the ethic of U.S. society is in danger of becoming this: "You're a fool if you obey the rules."

Evidence: examples

Evidence: statistics

The dangers of scofflawry vary wildly. The person who illegally spits on the sidewalk remains disgusting, but clearly poses less risk to others than the company that illegally buries hazardous chemical waste in an unauthorized location. The fare beater on the subway presents less threat to life than the landlord who ignores fire safety statutes. The most immediately and measurably dangerous scofflawry, however, also happens to be the most visible. The culprit is the American driver, whose lawless activities today add up to a colossal public nuisance. The hazards range from routine double parking that jams city streets to the drunk driving that kills some 25,000 people and injures at least 650,000 others yearly.

Evidence: authority

The most flagrant scofflaw of them all is the red-light runner. The flouting of stop signals has got so bad in Boston that residents tell an anecdote about a cabby who insists that red lights are "just for decoration." The power of the stoplight to control traffic seems to be waning everywhere. In Los Angeles, red-light running has become perhaps the city's most common traffic violation. In New York City, going through an intersection is like Russian roulette. Admits Police Commissioner Robert J. McGuire: "Today it's a 50–50 toss-up as to whether people will stop for a red light." Meanwhile, his own police largely ignore the lawbreaking.

Evidence: examples

The prospect of the collapse of public manners is not merely a matter of etiquette. Society's first concern will remain major crime, but a foretaste of the seriousness of incivility is suggested by what has been happening in Houston. Drivers on Houston freeways have been showing an increasing tendency to replace the rules of the road with violent outbreaks. Items from the Houston police department's new statistical category—freeway traffic violence: (1) Driver flashes high-beam lights at car that cut in front of him, whose occupants then hurl a beer can at his windshield, kick out his tail lights, slug him eight stitches worth. (2) Dump-truck driver annoyed by delay batters trunk of stalled car ahead and its driver with steel bolt. (3) Hurrying driver of 18-wheel truck deliberately rear-ends car whose driver was trying to stay within 55 m.p.h. limit.

PROPOSING A SOLUTION AND CONVINCING YOUR READERS

Once you have vividly described the problem, you are ready to propose a solution and persuade your readers. In the following selection from his book, *Fist Stick Knife Gun,* the essay "Peace in the Streets," as published in *The Utne Reader* magazine, Geoffrey Canada proposes ways to create a safer world for our children. Geoffrey Canada is president and CEO of Harlem's Rheedlen Center for Children and Families, an organization that serves at-risk inner-city children. For his work with Harlem's children, Canada received the Heinze Award celebrating the power of the individual in American society. As you read Canada's proposal, notice how he narrows the problem to saving the lives of inner-city children. When he makes a recommendation, he talks about the advantages of his solution, but he talks about *feasibility problems* and real drawbacks. At several points, he gives *reasons* why we must change and supports his reasons with *evidence* from statistics and from his own personal experience.

If I could get the mayors, the governors, and the president to look into the eyes of the 5-year-olds of this nation, dressed in old raggedy clothes, whose jacket zippers are broken but whose dreams are still alive, they would know what I know—that children need people to fight for them. To stand with them on the most dangerous streets, in the dirtiest hallways, in their darkest hours. We as a country have been too willing to take from our weakest when times get hard. People who allow this to happen must be educated, must be challenged, must be turned around.

Personal experience

If we are to save our children we must become people they will look up to. We must stand up and be visible heroes. I want people to understand the crisis and I want people to act: Either we address the murder and mayhem in our country or we simply won't be able to continue to have the kind of democratic society that we as Americans cherish. Violence is not just a problem of the inner cities or of the minorities in this country. This is a national crisis and the nation must mobilize differently if we are to solve it.

Proposal

Part of what we must do is change the way we think about violence. Trying to catch and punish people after they have committed a violent act won't deter violence in the least. In life on the street, it's better to go to jail than be killed, better to act quickly and decisively even if you risk being caught.

There are, however, things that governments could and should do right away to begin to end the violence on our streets. They include the following:

Specific recommendations

Specific details

Create a peace officer corps. Peace officers would not be police; they would not carry guns and would not be charged with making arrests. Instead they would be local men and women hired to work with children in their own neighborhoods. They would try to settle "beefs" and mediate disputes. They would not be the eyes and ears of the regular police force. Their job would be to try to get these young people jobs, to get them back into school, and, most importantly, to be at the emergency rooms and funerals where young people come together to grieve and plot revenge, in order to keep them from killing one another.

Recommendation

Reduce the demand for drugs. Any real effort at diverting the next generation of kids from selling drugs must include plans to find employment for these children when they become teenagers. While that will require a significant expenditure of public funds, the savings from reduced hospitalization and reduced incarceration will more than offset the costs of employment.

Reason + Evidence

Response to feasibility problems

And don't be fooled by those who say that these teenagers will never work for five dollars an hour when they can make thousands of dollars a week. I have found little evidence of this in my years of working with young people. Most of them, given the opportunity to make even the minimum wage, will do so gladly. The problem for many young people has been that they have looked for work year after year without ever finding a job. In some cities more than 40 percent of minority youth who want to work can't find employment.

Recommendation

Reduce the amount of violence on television and in the movies. Violence in the media is ever more graphic, and the justification for acting violently is deeply implanted in young people's minds. The movie industry promotes the message that power is determined not merely by carrying a gun, but by carrying a big gun that is an automatic and has a big clip containing many bullets.

Reason + Evidence

What about rap music, and especially "gangsta rap"? It is my opinion that people have concentrated too much attention on this one source of media violence. Many rap songs are positive, and some are neither positive nor negative—just kids telling their stories. But there are some rap singers who have decided that their niche in the music industry will be the most violent and vile. I would love to see the record industry show some restraint in limiting these rappers' access to fame and fortune.

Reduce and regulate the possession of handguns. I believe all hand-gun sales should be banned in this country. Recognizing, however, that other Americans may not be ready to accept a ban on handguns, I believe there are still some things we must do.

Recommendation

Licensing. Every person who wants to buy a handgun should have to pass both a written test and a field test. The cost for these new proce-dures should be paid by those who make, sell, and buy handguns. . . .

Evidence

Gun buy-backs. The federal government, which recently passed a $32 billion crime bill, needs to invest billions of dollars over the next ten years buying guns back from citizens. We now have more than 200 million guns in circulation in our country. A properly cared-for gun can last for decades. There is no way we can deal with handgun violence until we reduce the number of guns currently in circulation. We know that young people won't give up their guns readily, but we have to keep in mind that this is a long-term problem. We have to begin to plan now to get the guns currently in the hands of children out of circulation permanently.

Statistics

Response to feasibility problems

The truth of the matter is that reducing the escalating violence will be complicated and costly. If we were fighting an outside enemy that was killing our children at a rate of more than 5,000 a year, we would spare no expense. What happens when the enemy is us? What happens when those Americans' children are mostly black and brown? Do we still have the will to invest the time and resources in saving their lives? The answer must be yes, because the impact and fear of violence has overrun the boundaries of our ghettos and has both its hands firmly around the neck of our whole country. And while you may not yet have been visited by the spectre of death and fear of this new national cancer, just give it time. Sooner or later, unless we act, you will. We all will.

Evidence

Statistics

Call to action

■ **WARMING UP: JOURNAL EXERCISES** The following exercises will help you practice problem solving. Read all of the following exercises and then write on one or two that interest you most. If another idea occurs to you, write about it.

1. Wishful-Thinking Department: Assume that as a member of the stu-dent government, your organization has been given $10,000 to spend on a campus-improvement project. Think of some campus problem that needs solving. Describe why it is a problem. Then outline your plan for a solution, indicating how you would spend the money to help solve the problem.

A good solution solves more than one problem, and it does not make new problems. I am talking about health as opposed to almost any cure, coherence of pattern as opposed to almost any solution produced piecemeal or in isolation.

—WENDELL BERRY,

AUTHOR OF THE GIFT OF THE GOOD LAND

God, give us grace to accept with serenity the things that cannot be changed, courage to change the things which should be changed, and the wisdom to distinguish the one from the other.

—REINHOLD NIEBUHR,

AUTHOR AND THEOLOGIAN

2. Reread Frank Trippett's analysis of the scofflaw problem. Write a letter to the city council recommending a solution to one of the problems that Trippett identifies—a solution that the city council has the power to implement.

3. Eldridge Cleaver once said, "You're either part of the solution or part of the problem." Examine one of your activities or pastimes—sports, shopping, cruising, eating, drinking, or even studying. How does what you do possibly create a problem, from someone else's point of view? Explain.

4. "Let the buyer beware" is a time-honored maxim for all consumers. Unless you are vigilant, you can easily be ripped off. Write a letter to the Better Business Bureau explaining some consumer problem or rip-off that you've recently experienced and suggest a solution that will prevent others from being exploited.

5. Changing the rules of some sports might make them more enjoyable, less violent, or fairer: moving the three-point line further out, introducing the 30-second clock in NCAA basketball, using TV instant replays in professional and college football and basketball, imposing stiffer fines for brawls in hockey games, requiring boxers to wear padded helmets, giving equal pay and media coverage to women's sports. Choose a sport you enjoy as a participant or observer, identify and explain the problem you want to solve, and justify your solution in a letter to the editors of *Sports Illustrated*.

6. Sometimes problem solving requires great patience, compromise, and a lively sense of humor. We all invent rules for own lives—or, more likely, for lives of others—that will make life better or more tolerable. Read the following "Dog Rules Around Our House," and then write your own humorous rules for a problem you face in your everyday life.

Dog Rules Around Our House

1. The dog is not allowed in the house.
2. Okay, the dog is allowed in the house, but only in certain rooms.
3. The dog is allowed in all rooms, but has to stay off the furniture.
4. The dog can get on the old furniture only, but has to stay off the new couch.
5. Fine, the dog is allowed on all the furniture, but is not allowed to sleep with the humans on the bed.
6. Okay, the dog is allowed on the bed, but only by invitation.
7. The dog can sleep on the bed whenever he wants, but not under the covers.
8. The dog can sleep under the covers by invitation only.
9. The dog can sleep under the covers every night.
10. Humans must ask permission to sleep under the covers with the dog.

PROBLEM SOLVING:

PROFESSIONAL WRITING

SOLVING FOR PATTERN

Wendell Berry

A native of Kentucky and professor of English at the University of Kentucky, Wendell Berry is a prolific writer of poetry, fiction, and nonfiction. He is most noted for his essays and books on agricultural and ecological topics, including The Unforeseen Wilderness: An Essay on Kentucky's Red River Gorge *(1971),* The Unsettling of America: Culture and Agriculture *(1977),* The Gift of Good Land *(1981),* Home Economics *(1987), and* What Are People For? *(1990). In this selection from "Solving for Pattern," which appears in* The Gift of Good Land, *while Berry talks about solving specific problems in farming and agriculture, he focuses on the nature of problem solving itself. Although too many farm "solutions" (larger tractors, feed lots, overuse of fertilizers and pesticides) solve one problem, they create a host of destructive side effects. Good solutions, Berry argues, do not address problems in isolation. Good solutions must promote the harmony, health, and quality of the whole system.*

Our dilemma in agriculture now is that the industrial methods that have so spectacularly solved some of the problems of food production have been accompanied by "side effects" so damaging as to threaten the survival of farming. Perhaps the best clue to the nature and the gravity of this dilemma is that it is not limited to agriculture. My immediate concern here is with the irony of agricultural methods that destroy, first, the health of the soil and, finally, the health of human communities. But I could just as easily be talking about sanitation systems that pollute, school systems that graduate illiterate students, medical cures that cause disease, or nuclear armaments that explode in the midst of the people they are meant to protect. This is a kind of surprise that is characteristic of our time: The cure proves incurable; security results in the evacuation of a neighborhood or a town. It is only when it is understood that our agricultural dilemma is characteristic not of our agriculture but of our time that we can begin to understand why these surprises happen, and to work out standards of judgment that may prevent them. **(1)**

To the problems of farming, then, as to other problems of our time, there appear to be three kinds of solutions: **(2)**

There is, first, the solution that causes a ramifying series of new problems, the only limiting criterion being, apparently, that the new problems should arise beyond the purview of the expertise that produced the solution— as, in agriculture, industrial solutions to the problem of production have invariably caused problems of maintenance, conservation, economics, community health, etc., etc. **(3)**

If, for example, beef cattle are fed in large feed lots, within the boundaries of the feeding operation itself a certain factorylike order and efficiency can be achieved. But even within those boundaries that mechanical order immediately produces biological disorder, for we know that health problems and dependence on drugs will be greater among cattle so confined than among cattle on pasture. **(4)**

And beyond those boundaries, the problems multiply. Pen feeding of cattle in large numbers involves, first, a manure-removal problem, which becomes at some point a health problem for the animals themselves, for the local watershed, and for the adjoining ecosystems and human communities. If the manure is disposed of without returning it to the soil that produced the feed, a serious problem of soil fertility is involved. But we know too that large concentrations of animals in feed lots in one place tend to be associated with, and to promote, large cash-grain monocultures in other places. These monocultures tend to be accompanied by a whole set of specifically agricultural problems: soil erosion, soil compaction, epidemic infestations of pests, weeds, and disease. But they are also accompanied by a set of agricultural–economic problems (dependence on purchased technology; dependence on purchased fuels, fertilizers, and poisons; dependence on credit)—and by a set of community problems, beginning with depopulation and the removal of sources, services, and markets to more and more distant towns. And these are, so to speak, only the first circle of the bad effects of a bad solution. With a little care, their branchings can be traced on into nature, into the life of the cities, and into the cultural and economic life of the nation. **(5)**

The second kind of solution is that which immediately worsens the problem it is intended to solve, causing a hellish symbiosis in which problem and solution reciprocally enlarge one another in a sequence that, so far as its own logic is concerned, is limitless—as when the problem of soil compaction is "solved" by a bigger tractor, which further compacts the soil, which makes a need for a still bigger tractor, and so on and on. There is an identical symbiosis between coal-fired power plants and air conditioners. It is characteristic of such solutions that no one prospers by them but the suppliers of fuel and equipment. **(6)**

These two kinds of solutions are obviously bad. They always serve one good at the expense of another or of several others, and I believe that if all their effects were ever to be accounted for they would be seen to involve, too frequently if not invariably, a net loss to nature, agriculture, and the human commonwealth. **(7)**

Such solutions always involve a definition of the problem that is either false or so narrow as to be virtually false. To define an agricultural problem as if it were solely a problem of agriculture—or solely a problem of production or technology or economics—is simply to misunderstand the problem, either inadvertently or deliberately, either for profit or because of a prevalent fashion of thought. The whole problem must be solved, not just some handily identifiable and simplifiable aspect of it. **(8)**

Both kinds of bad solutions leave their problems unsolved. Bigger tractors do not solve the problem of soil compaction any more than air conditioners solve the problem of air pollution. Nor does the large confinement-feeding operation solve the problem of food production; it is, rather, a way calculated to allow large-scale ambition and greed to profit from food production. **(9)**

The real problem of food production occurs within a complex, mutually influential relationship of soil, plants, animals, and people. A real solution to that problem will therefore be ecologically, agriculturally, and culturally healthful. **(10)**

Perhaps it is not until health is set down as the aim that we come in sight of the third kind of solution: that which causes a ramifying series of solutions—as when meat animals are fed on the farm where the feed is raised, and where the feed is raised to be fed to the animals that are on the farm. Even so rudimentary a description implies a concern for pattern, for quality, which necessarily complicates the concern for production. The farmer has put plants and animals into a relationship of mutual dependence, and must perforce be concerned for balance or symmetry, a reciprocating connection in the pattern of the farm that is biological, not industrial, and that involves solutions to problems of fertility, soil husbandry, economics, sanitation—the whole complex of problems whose proper solutions add up to health: the health of the soil, of plants and animals, of farm and farmer, of farm family and farm community, all involved in the same internested, interlocking pattern—or pattern of patterns. **(11)**

A bad solution is bad, then, because it acts destructively upon the larger patterns in which it is contained. It acts destructively upon those patterns, most likely, because it is formed in ignorance or disregard of them. A bad solution solves for a single purpose or goal, such as increased production. And it is typical of such solutions that they achieve stupendous increases in production at exorbitant biological and social costs. **(12)**

A good solution is good because it is in harmony with those larger patterns—and this harmony will, I think, be found to have the nature of analogy. A bad solution acts within the larger pattern the way a disease or addiction acts within the body. A good solution acts within the larger pattern the way a healthy organ acts within the body. But it must at once be understood that a healthy organ does not—as the mechanistic or industrial mind would like to say—"give" health to the body, is not exploited for the body's health, but is a part of its health. The health of organ and organism is the same, just as the health of organism and ecosystem is the same. And these structures of organ, organism, and ecosystem belong to a series of analogical integrities that begins with the organelle and ends with the biosphere. **(13)**

VOCABULARY

In your journal, write the meanings of the following words:

- *ramifying* series of new problems **(3)**
- *purview* of the expertise **(3)**
- hellish *symbiosis* **(6)**
- soil *husbandry* **(11)**
- *analogical* integrities **(13)**
- begins with the *organelle* **(13)**

QUESTIONS FOR WRITING AND DISCUSSION

1. Reread your response to the freewriting exercise at the beginning of this chapter. What campus problem did you describe and what was your solution? Now, assume that you are Wendell Berry. Write one paragraph of Berry's response to your solution. Specifically, consider how well your solution meets Berry's goal of solving for the harmony, health, and quality of the whole college or university system.

2. Berry's essay explains three kinds of solutions. What are these three types of solutions and what makes the third kind the best?

3. In paragraph 1, Berry says that he "could just as easily be talking about sanitation systems that pollute, school systems that graduate illiterate students, [or] medical cures that cause disease." Choose one of these problems (or another common problem) and explain how Berry would analyze the problem.

4. Berry clarifies his explanation for his reader by using audience cues (transitions, paragraph hooks, and topic sentences) at the beginning of paragraphs. Choose any three successive paragraphs (for example, paragraphs 3, 4, and 5) and identify any words or phrases that (a) make a transition from the previous paragraph or idea and (b) announce or preview the subject of the new paragraph. Make a sketch outline of Berry's essay.

5. An analogy is a comparison between two things or processes in which a simple or familiar thing helps to explain a complex or unfamiliar thing. Thus, we can explain how the human heart works by drawing an analogy with a simple mechanical pump. In paragraph 13, Berry says that a "bad solution acts within the larger pattern the way a disease or addiction acts within the body."

Explain Berry's analogy. Then apply this analogy to one specific problem that you have discussed in class. Does Berry's organic analogy make sense in that particular case? Why or why not?

6. Apply Berry's ideas about "solving for pattern" to either the following essay by John Diebold or the subsequent essay by Neil Postman. How well do their arguments and solutions address the overall harmony, health, and quality of the system?

WHAT ARE WE WAITING FOR?

John Diebold

In a proposal written for Reader's Digest, *technology expert John Diebold examines the parallel problems of managing traffic in big cities and managing medical data in large hospitals. In both cases, Diebold argues, what we need is an "infostructure" that allows information to flow quickly to the people who need it most—the driver of the automobile and the doctor helping his patient. John Diebold, a Harvard MBA, has been a member of several technological organizations such as the International Cybernetic Association and has written many books on computers, business, and technology, including* Man and the Computer: Technology as an Agent of Social Change *(1969),* Making the Future Work *(1984),* Business in an Age of Information *(1985), and* The Innovators: The Discoveries, Inventions, and Breakthroughs of Our Time *(1990). As we face the next millennium, do Diebold's proposals present realistic solutions to our problems?*

Not long ago I hurt my back while sawing up a tree. Doctors ran a series of expensive tests and advised surgery. When I checked in for the operation two days later, they had to run the same tests all over again. The earlier results had been filed away, out of reach. **(1)**

Last summer, as I was driving to New York's Kennedy International Airport to catch a plane, hundreds of brake lights suddenly lit up ahead of me, and traffic slowed to a crawl. I finally realized that with the Mets playing at Shea Stadium, the toll booths ahead must be swamped. As precious minutes ticked by and tempers flared, I and hundreds of other travelers missed our flights. **(2)**

We've all had similar experiences—the frustration, expense, and sometimes harmful delays that occur when the information systems we rely on aren't up to the job. That traffic jam was really an information jam—too many drivers with too few facts about the traffic ahead and alternative routes. My hospital tests also reflected poor information: a filing system full of data, but none at hand. **(3)**

In the age of computers and instant communication, there's no excuse for such failures. We already have the technology to vastly speed the way we do things—from traffic and health care to shopping, education, emergencies, and public services. All we need is to put it to use. It's time to start building our "infostructure." **(4)**

The infostructure will underlie society in the same way as a traditional infrastructure of roads and rails. But the infostructure isn't made of steel or concrete. Instead, it uses revolutionary new technologies to make existing systems work better. Our highways and health system are good examples of where these technologies could make our lives easier. **(5)**

In the United States, 190 million vehicles jostle for room on 3.9 million miles of roads and streets. Traffic is growing almost twenty-five times faster than roads. The price tag on tie-ups is huge: The Federal Highway Administration calculates the cost of wasted time at over $100 billion a year. **(6)**

The solution? Intelligent Vehicle and Highway Systems (IVHS), which increase a road's carrying capacity by letting cars and traffic signals "talk" to each other. When a traffic jam threatens—cars streaming out of a stadium parking lot, for example—the system will automatically direct traffic to swifter routes. **(7)**

Simpler systems are already in use. Three years ago, street intersections in Detroit's suburban Oakland County were being paralyzed by mile-long backups. Expanding the infrastructure—the roads—would have cost $1 billion. Instead, the road commission has installed "smart signals" at one hundred intersections. Like old-time traffic cops, these signals "see" problems and respond—holding a green light longer for a bus about to cross, or keeping it green to clear out an unusual backup. You never have to wait at a red when nobody's coming; the light "reads" the empty road and turns green. **(8)**

Some trucks and buses are now being equipped with instruments once seen only in fighter jets. Trucker Jimmy Kennington, fifty-five, was gingerly guiding his eighteen-wheeler over a hill outside Bakersfield, California, when thick fog enveloped him. At that moment, a new collision-avoidance radar mounted on his front grille sounded a piercing alert. Kennington braked—safely escaping a smashup with a car stalled ahead. **(9)**

Radar and traffic networks are only part of IVHS. To see how a complete system could work, let's take a trip downtown. **(10)**

As you back your "smart" car out of the driveway after typing your destination on the keyboard on the dash, the vehicle's phone automatically calls ahead to reserve a parking space. It's a dark, wet morning, but a "slippery conditions" sign beside the road triggers an audible warning in your car. Infrared beams—probing five times farther than your eyes—alert you to a paper carrier up ahead, riding her bike without lights. **(11)**

Now your car projects an illuminated arrow, pointing right, that seems to float in the air ahead of the hood. A voice directs you to turn onto Columbus Avenue. Your "navigator," a dynamic route guidance system, is constantly analyzing traffic data picked up by sensors atop many of the town's signal lights. This morning, it calculates that Columbus offers you the clearest shot to the freeway. **(12)**

Once on the freeway, you click into "smart cruise." If the car in front slows down, so will yours. If it stops suddenly, your radar cuts your accelerator and hits the brakes. **(13)**

There's only a beep at the toll point as you zip past a scanner that subtracts the cost from a "smart card" on your windshield. Near the city, the voice and arrow alert you to a detour, and a map on your dashboard screen shows the new route. At the touch of a button you hear the reason: "Accident at Capitol Avenue blocking northbound traffic." **(14)**

You don't know this part of town, but the navigator safely directs you through it, back onto the freeway and eventually to your destination. At the parking-lot gate, a ticket pops out—stamped with the number of your reserved space. **(15)**

Painless, on-time drives like this are not a distant dream. Many of the technical elements exist and are already being put in place in Japan and Europe. Five automakers in Japan have fitted nearly half a million navigators as add-ons, and they are standard in Toyota's top model. (Later this year General Motors will offer computerized navigations systems in one of its Oldsmobile models.) In Germany, intersections in Berlin and Stuttgart are being wired for a new "Euro-Scout" in-car information system that will start up this spring. **(16)**

The benefits of building nationwide IVHS in the United States are potentially enormous. And the cost, estimated at $200 billion over twenty years, is roughly what highway inefficiency and accidents already cost the country *every year.* **(17)**

There is no reason for taxpayers to foot the entire bill, however. Good information about fast-changing conditions is a marketable commodity. Drivers would pay for useful services, such as dynamic route guidance, that save time and frustration—just as they today pay bridge tolls. **(18)**

State and local governments can now sell or lease property to private companies. Private firms are involved in a planned $300 million extension of the Dulles Toll Road in Virginia, for example. Besides Virginia, other states are organizing joint ventures between government and business. These changes will help make highway "infostructure" a mainstay of our lives. **(19)**

While easing traffic woes means gathering thousands of bits of ever-changing data, in health care the problem is the opposite: the system is drowning in data, but doctors can't use the information effectively. **(20)**

A patient's record is typically 1 1/2 pounds of barely legible notes, charts, and film stuffed into a folder, stored in the basement, and seldom transferred when the patient is moved. "Even in an advanced university hospital like this," says Dr. Otto Barnett of Massachusetts General in Boston, "there's about a one-in-ten chance your file simply can't be found when it's needed." **(21)**

Doctors spend a large portion of their time writing down or looking for patient histories. Paperwork consumes at least one-third of scarce nursing time too. My institute, undertaking a study funded by the Alfred P. Sloan

Foundation, estimated that, overall, wasteful effort in the health industry costs $90 billion a year—almost $1,000 per household. **(22)**

Computer technology could lift this costly burden—but, incredibly, fewer than 1 percent of the nation's hospitals keep patient records electronically. Sure, all hospitals have computers. But not enough are able to share information and put it to work for patient care. **(23)**

At the Regenstreif Institute of Indianapolis, a team led by Professor Clem McDonald devised an electronic system for thirty-five medical-care facilities. So far it has tracked more than a million patients, making their records instantly accessible from any computer workstation in the system. **(24)**

At Wishard Memorial Hospital in Indianapolis, connecting the ward and emergency-room computer workstations to each other and to the Regenstreif system cut patient charges an average of 13 percent and shortened the average hospital stay by twenty-one hours. In Boston, a computer system allowed Beth Israel Hospital to reduce its admitting staff even as patient admissions rose 67 percent. **(25)**

But what about patient privacy? Isn't it easier to snoop electronically? Not at all. Paper files can be open to anybody wearing a white coat and a serious expression. By contrast, Beth Israel's electronic system controls access with passwords—and keeps an automatic record of every inquiry so those who make one can be traced. **(26)**

Electronic information also saves lives. At the LDS Hospital in Salt Lake City, a computer system automatically checks drug prescriptions against patients' histories and symptoms. It alerted staff to adverse drug reactions in eighty-one times as many patients as traditional methods did. **(27)**

One of the biggest weaknesses in U.S. health care comes down to the startling fact that patients don't really know the relative merit of different treatments. The lack of comparative information suppresses competition and keeps people from making knowledgeable decisions about their care. **(28)**

Studies have revealed immense differences in methods of treatment. For instance, residents of New Haven, Connecticut, were found to undergo coronary-bypass operations at twice the rate of Boston patients. A hospital in Pennsylvania charged 90 percent more for cardiac surgery than one less than forty miles away, yet had a higher failure rate. **(29)**

But most of us are not aware of these differences, because the information is not readily accessible via computer. Doctors, too, are often in the dark about the statistics on treatments they advise. The brutal truth is, a child with a video game has more computing power in hand than the typical physician. **(30)**

Political debate rages about health care, while a solution—greater competition through easier comparison—lies under our noses. As with crowded roads, we can apply information technology to make much better use of the systems we already have. **(31)**

In the 1920s and '30s, American lives were transformed as households were connected by telephone and radio. In the 1950s and '60s, we were brought closer together by a network of interstate highways. Now an electronic infostructure can significantly improve our lives once more. Yet while Japan and Europe are moving ahead, U.S. progress has been disturbingly slow. **(32)**

The federal government urgently needs to:

- Promote a higher vision of what information technology can do for the nation. Right now, public officials seem focused only on the "information superhighway" that will deliver more TV channels to our homes. The potential is far greater than this.
- Challenge private industry to lead the way, by funding demonstration projects and awarding prizes for significant achievement.
- Bring its own systems up to date. Government generates and controls most of the data Americans rely on. Yet it's still buying typewriters and three-by-five cards.
- Press business and local governments to agree on compatible systems so networks can work with and "talk" to one another efficiently. **(33)**

Most of all, we need to recognize that information has a capital value, and encourage a free-market philosophy. The days of seemingly limitless public spending on services are gone; there simply is not enough money. But there is a huge market for smart, efficient uses of information technology. A new generation of private and public partnership can generate massive economic benefits—and help America make the leap to a new century. **(34)**

Ours is an exciting time—similar to the early days of the computer industry. We are now on the threshold of another technological adventure. Let us step boldly across. **(35)**

Vocabulary

In your journal, write the meanings of the following words:

- traditional *infrastructure* of roads and rails **(5)**
- *Infrared* beams **(11)**
- a marketable *commodity* **(18)**
- organizing joint *ventures* **(19)**
- *compatible* systems **(33)**
- a *capital* value **(34)**

Questions for Writing and Discussion

1. John Diebold's essay appeared in *Reader's Digest*. Profile the intended audience for Diebold's essay. To support your analysis, find at least three specific sentences or examples in the essay that seem to be directed toward that audience.

2. Effective problem-solving essays accomplish the following: 1) demonstrate to a particular audience that a serious problem exists, 2) propose a solution or plan of action that will solve the problem, and 3) persuade readers that the proposal will work—that it is feasible—by providing sufficient reasons and examples supporting the proposal. Analyze John Diebold's essay using these three criteria. Refer to specific paragraphs in the essay to support your judgments about each of the three criteria.

3. Based on your evaluation in question 2, what specific advice would you give to Diebold about revising his essay? What parts of his essay are strong and need little revision? What parts need more explanation, more examples, or more analysis of the problems or the solutions? Explain.

4. In addition to citing statistics and information from other studies, Diebold uses several kinds of *specific examples* to illustrate what the problem is and how the solution would work. From his essay, find at least one paragraph that illustrates each of the following kinds of specific examples: personal examples, specific examples from other people's experience, hypothetical examples, and historical precedents. (Which of these kinds of specific examples might work for your own essay?)

5. Later in this chapter, in the "Shaping" section of the writing process advice, there are four sample outlines for writing a problem-solving essay. Which of these outlines does Diebold follow? Would one of the other organizational patterns work better for his topic? Explain.

6. Do your own investigation of one of the two problems Diebold addresses. In your city or town, is the medical or traffic problem still a serious one? What special information problems exist? Which parts of Diebold's solutions are currently in place? What additional kinds of "infostructure" technology are in use that Diebold doesn't mention?

VIRTUAL STUDENTS, DIGITAL CLASSROOM

Neil Postman

No doubt the last two decades of the twentieth century in America will be remembered for the explosive increase in numbers of computers and numbers of computer-literate Americans. In America's schools, students now use computers and do Internet and Web research in virtually every field of study. As we face the twenty-first century, however, Neil Postman, professor of Communications at New York University, questions whether computers have, in fact, arrived on earth to save our students. Will computers enable all students—rich or poor, black, brown or white—to have equal access to the information so vital to their education? Will computers possibly make the school, as a place of learning, obsolete? In "Virtual Students, Digital Classrooms," Neil Postman critiques those computer-in-the-sky proposals and calls for a more conservative vision of the goals of education. Followers of Neil Postman's career as an educational reformist remind us that although Postman began his career with books such as Teaching as a Subversive Activity *(1969), which called for a radical reform of our nation's schools, his recent works advocate a more conservative vision of education. In the last two decades, Neil Postman's books include* Teaching as a Conserving Activity *(1979),* Amusing Ourselves to Death *(1985),* Technology: The Surrender of Culture to Technology *(1992), and* The End of Education: Redefining the Value of School *(1995). "Virtual Students, Digital Classroom," adapted from* The End of Education, *appeared in* The Nation.

If one has a trusting relationship with one's students, it is not altogether gauche to ask them if they believe in God (with a capital G). I have done this three or four times and most students say they do. Their answer is preliminary to the next question: If someone you love were desperately ill, and you had to choose between praying to God for his or her recovery or administering an antibiotic (as prescribed by a competent physician), which would you choose? **(1)**

Most say the question is silly since the alternatives are not mutually exclusive. Of course. But suppose they were—which would you choose? God helps those who help themselves, some say in choosing the antibiotic, therefore getting the best of two possible belief systems. But if pushed to the wall (e.g., God does not always help those who help themselves; God helps those who pray and who believe), most choose the antibiotic, after noting that the question is asinine and proves nothing. Of course, the question was not asked, in the first place, to prove anything but to begin a discussion of the nature of belief. And I do not fail to inform the students, by the way, that there has recently emerged evidence of a "scientific" nature that when sick people are prayed for they do better than those who aren't. **(2)**

As the discussion proceeds, important distinctions are made among the different meanings of "belief," but at some point it becomes far from asinine to speak of the god of Technology—in the sense that people believe technology works, that they rely on it, that it makes promises, that they are bereft when denied access to it, that they are delighted when they are in its presence, that for most people it works in mysterious ways, that they condemn people who speak against it, that they stand in awe of it, and that, in the "born again" mode, they will alter their life-styles, their schedules, their habits, and their relationships to accommodate it. If this be not a form of religious belief, what is? **(3)**

In all strands of American cultural life, you can find so many examples of technological adoration that it is possible to write a book about it. And I would if it had not already been done so well. But nowhere do you find more enthusiasm for the god of Technology than among educators. In fact, there are those, like Lewis Perelman, who argue (for example, in his book, *School's Out*) that modern information technologies have rendered schools entirely irrelevant since there is now much more information available outside the classroom than inside it. This is by no means considered an outlandish idea. Dr. Diane Ravitch, former Assistant Secretary of Education, envisions, with considerable relish, the challenge that technology presents to the tradition that "children (and adults) should be educated in a specific place, for a certain number of hours, and a certain number of days during the week and year." In other words, that children should be educated in school. Imagining the possibilities of an information superhighway offering perhaps a thousand channels, Dr. Ravitch assures us that:

> in this new world of pedagogical plenty, children and adults will be able to dial up a program on their home television to learn whatever they want to know, at their own convenience. If little Eva cannot sleep, she can learn algebra instead. At her home-learning station, she will tune in to a series of interesting problems that are presented in an interactive medium, much like video games. . . .
>
> Young John may decide that he wants to learn the history of modern Japan, which he can do by dialing up the greatest authorities and teachers on the subject, who will not only use dazzling graphs and illustrations, but will narrate a historical video that excites his curiosity and imagination. **(4)**

In this vision there is, it seems to me, a confident and typical sense of unreality. Little Eva can't sleep, so she decides to learn a little algebra? Where does Little Eva come from? Mars? If not, it is more likely she will tune in to a good movie. Young John decides that he wants to learn the history of modern Japan? How did young John come to this point? How is it that he never visited a library up to now? Or is it that he, too, couldn't sleep and decided that a little modern Japanese history was just what he needed? **(5)**

What Ravitch is talking about here is not a new technology but a new species of child, one who, in any case, no one has seen up to now. Of course, new technologies do make new kinds of people, which leads to a second objection to Ravitch's conception of the future. There is a kind of forthright determinism about the imagined world described in it. The technology is here or will be; we must use it because it is there; we will become the kind of people the technology requires us to be, and whether we like it or not, we will remake our institutions to accommodate technology. All of this must happen because it is good for us, but in any case, we have no choice. This point of view is present in very nearly every statement about the future relationship of learning to technology. And, as in Ravitch's scenario, there is always a cheery, gee-whiz tone to the prophecies. Here is one produced by the National Academy of Sciences, written by Hugh McIntosh.

> School for children of the Information Age will be vastly different than it was for Mom and Dad.

> Interested in biology? Design your own life forms with computer simulation.

> Having trouble with a science project? Teleconference about it with a research scientist.

> Bored with the real world? Go into a virtual physics lab and rewrite the laws of gravity.

> These are the kinds of hands-on learning experiences schools could be providing right now. The technologies that make them possible are already here, and today's youngsters, regardless of economic status, know how to use them. They spend hours with them every week—not in the classroom, but in their own homes and in video game centers at every shopping mall. **(6)**

The role that new technology should play in schools or anywhere else is something that needs to be discussed without the hyperactive fantasies of cheerleaders. In particular, the computer and its associated technologies are awesome additions to a culture, and are quite capable of altering the psychic, not to mention the sleeping, habits of our young. But like all important technologies of the past, they are Faustian bargains, giving and taking away, sometimes in equal measure, sometimes more in one way than the other. It is strange—indeed shocking—that with the twenty-first century so close, we can still talk of new technologies as if they were unmixed blessings—gifts, as it were, from the gods. Don't we all know what the combustion engine has done for us and against us? What television is doing for us and against us? At the very least, what we need to discuss about Little Eva, Young John, and McIntosh's trio is what they will lose, and what we will lose, if they enter a world in which computer technology is their chief source of motivation, authority, and, apparently, psychological sustenance. Will they become, as Joseph Weizenbaum warns, more impressed by calculation than human judgment? Will speed of response become, more than ever, a defining quality of intelligence? If, indeed, the idea of a school will be dramatically altered, what kinds of learning will be neglected, perhaps made impossible? Is virtual reality a new form of therapy? If it is, what are its dangers? **(7)**

These are serious matters, and they need to be discussed by those who know something about children from the planet Earth, and whose vision of children's needs, and the needs of society, go beyond thinking of school mainly as a place for the convenient distribution of information. Schools are not now and have never been largely about getting information to children. That has been on the schools' agenda, of course, but has always been way down on the list. For technological utopians, the computer vaults information access to the top. This reshuffling of priorities comes at a most inopportune time. The goal of giving people greater access to more information faster, more conveniently, and in more diverse forms was the main technological thrust of the nineteenth century. Some folks haven't noticed it, but that problem was largely solved, so that for almost a hundred years there has been more information available to the young outside the school than inside. That fact did not make the schools obsolete, nor does it now make them obsolete. **(8)**

Yes, it is true that Little Eva, the insomniac from Mars, could turn on an algebra lesson, thanks to the computer, in the wee hours of the morning. She could also, if she wished, read a book or magazine, watch television, turn on the radio or listen to music. All of this she could have done before the computer. The computer does not solve any problem she has but does exacerbate one. For Little Eva's problem is not how to get access to a well-structured algebra lesson but what to do with all the information available to her during the day, as well as during sleepless nights. Perhaps this is why she couldn't sleep in the first place. Little Eva, like the rest of us, is overwhelmed by information. She lives in a culture that has 260,000 billboards, 17,000 newspapers, 12,000 periodicals, 27,000 video outlets for renting tapes, 400 million television sets, and well over 500 million radios, not including those in automobiles. There are 40,000 new book titles published every year, and each day 41 million photographs are taken. And thanks to the computer, more than 60 billion pieces of advertising junk come into our mailboxes every year. Everything from telegraphy and photography in the nineteenth century to the silicon chip in the twentieth has amplified the din of information intruding on Little Eva's consciousness. . . . In the face of this we might ask, What can schools do for Little Eva besides making still more information available? If there is nothing, then new technologies will indeed make schools obsolete. But in fact, there is plenty. **(9)**

One thing that comes to mind is that schools can provide her with a serious form of technology education. Something quite different from instruction in using computers to process information, which, it strikes me, is a trivial thing to do, for two reasons. In the first place, approximately 35 million people have already learned how to use computers without the benefit of school instruction. In the second place, what we needed to know about cars—as we need to know about computers, television, and other important technologies—is not how to use them but how they use *us*. In the case of cars, what we needed to think about in the early twentieth century was not how to drive them but what they would do to our air, our landscape, our social relations, our family life, and our cities. Suppose in 1946 we had started to address similar questions about television: What will be its effects on our political institutions, our psychic habits, our children, our religious conceptions, our economy? Would we be better positioned today to control TV's massive assault on American culture? I am talking here about making technology itself an object of inquiry so that Little Eva and Young John are more interested in asking questions about the computer than getting answers from it. **(10)**

I am not arguing against using computers in school. I am arguing against our sleepwalking attitudes toward it, against allowing it to distract us from important things, against making a god of it. This is what Theodore Roszak warned against in *The Cult of Information:* "Like all cults," he wrote, "this one also has the intention of enlisting mindless allegiance and acquiescence. People who have no clear idea of what they mean by information or why they should want so much of it are nonetheless prepared to believe that we live in an Information Age, which makes every computer around us what the relics of the True Cross were in the Age of Faith: emblems of salvation." To this, I would add the sage observation of Alan Kay of Apple Computer. Kay is widely associated with the invention of the personal computer, and certainly has an interest in schools using them. Nonetheless, he has repeatedly said that any problems the schools cannot solve without computers, they cannot solve with them. What are some of those problems? There is, for example the traditional task of teaching children how to behave in groups. One might even say that schools have never been essentially about individualized learning. It is true, of course, that groups do not learn, individuals do. But the idea of a school is that individuals must learn in a setting in which individual needs are subordinated to group interests. Unlike other media of mass communication, which celebrate individual response and are experienced in private, the classroom is intended to tame the ego, to connect the individual with others, to demonstrate the value and necessity of group cohesion. At present, most scenarios describing the uses of computers have children solving problems alone; Little Eva, Young John, and the others are doing just that. The presence of other children may, indeed, be an annoyance. **(11)**

Like the printing press before it, the computer has a powerful bias toward amplifying personal autonomy and individual problem-solving. That is why educators must guard against computer technology's undermining some of the important reasons for having the young assemble (to quote Ravitch) "in a specific place, for a certain number of hours, and a certain number of days during the week and year." **(12)**

Although Ravitch is not exactly against what she calls "state schools," she imagines them as something of a relic of a pretechnological age. She believes that the new technologies will offer all children equal access to information. Conjuring up a hypothetical Little Mary who is presumably from a poorer home than Little Eva, Ravitch imagines that Mary will have the same opportunities as Eva "to learn any subject, and to learn it from the same master teachers as children in the richest neighborhood." For all of its liberalizing spirit, this scenario makes some important omissions. One is that though new technologies may be a solution to the learning of "subjects," they work against the learning of what are called "social values," including an understanding of democratic processes. If one reads the first chapter of Robert Fulghum's *All I Really Need to Know I Learned in Kindergarten,* one will find an elegant summary of a few things Ravitch's scenario has left out. They include learning the following lessons: Share everything, play fair, don't hit people, put things back where you found them, clean up your own mess, wash your hands before you eat, and, of course, flush. The only thing wrong with Fulghum's book is that no one has learned all these things at kindergarten's end. We have ample evidence that it takes many years of teaching these values in school before they have been accepted and internalized. That is why it won't do for children to learn in "settings of their own choosing." That is also why schools require children to be in a certain place at a certain time and to follow certain rules, like raising their hands when they wish to speak, not talking when others are talking, not chewing gum, not leaving until the bell rings, exhibiting patience toward slower learners, etc. This process is called making civilized people. The god of Technology does not appear interested in this function of schools. At least, it does not come up much when technology's virtues are enumerated. **(13)**

The god of Technology may also have a trick or two up its sleeve about something else. It is often asserted that new technologies will equalize learning opportunities for the rich and poor. It is devoutly to be wished for, but I doubt it will happen. In the first place, it is generally understood by those who have studied the history of technology that technological change always produces winners and losers. There are many reasons for this, among them economic differences. Even in the case of the automobile, which is a commodity most people can buy (although not all), there are wide differences between the rich and poor in the quality of what is available to them. It would be quite astonishing if computer technology equalized all learning opportunities, irrespective of economic differences. **(14)**

I do not say, of course, that schools can solve the problems of poverty, alienation, and family disintegration, but schools can *respond* to them. And they can do this because there are people in them, because these people are concerned with more than algebra lessons or modern Japanese history, and because these people can identify not only one's level of competence in math but one's level of rage and confusion and depression. I am talking here about children as they really come to us, not children who are invented to show us how computers may enrich their lives. **(15)**

I am a teacher myself and know how hard it is to contribute to the making of a civilized person. Can we blame those who want to find an easy way, through the agency of technology? Perhaps not. After all, it is an old quest. As early as 1918, H. L. Mencken (although completely devoid of empathy) wrote, "There is no sure-cure so idiotic that some superintendent of schools will not swallow it. The aim seems to be to reduce the whole teaching process to a sort of automatic reaction, to discover some master formula that will not only take the place of competence and resourcefulness in the teacher but that will also create an artificial receptivity in the child." **(16)**

Mencken was not necessarily speaking of technological panaceas but he may well have been. In the early 1920s a teacher wrote the following poem:

> *Mr. Edison says*
> *That the radio will supplant the teacher.*
> *Already one may learn languages by means of Victrola records.*
> *The moving picture will visualize*
> *What the radio fails to get across.*
> *Teachers will be relegated to the backwoods,*
> *With fire-horses,*
> *And long-haired women;*
> *Or, perhaps shown in museums.*
> *Education will become a matter*
> *Of pressing the button.*
> *Perhaps I can get a position at the switchboard.* **(17)**

I do not go as far back as the radio and Victrola, but I am old enough to remember when 16-millimeter film was to be the sure-cure. Then closed-circuit television. Then 8-millimeter film. Then teacher-proof textbooks. Now computers. **(18)**

I know a false god when I see one. **(19)**

VOCABULARY

In your journal, write the meanings of the following words:

- it is not altogether *gauche* **(1)**
- alternatives are not *mutually* exclusive **(2)**

- they are *bereft* **(3)**
- an *outlandish* idea **(4)**
- they are *Faustian* bargains **(7)**
- a most *inopportune* time **(8)**
- but does *exacerbate* one **(9)**
- mindless *allegiance* and *acquiescence* **(11)**
- technological *panaceas* **(17)**
- be *relegated* to the backwoods **(17)**

QUESTIONS FOR WRITING AND DISCUSSION

1. Reflect on your own use of computer technology in your education. Have computers had a positive effect on your schooling? Have they had a negative effect? Has computer technology been a mixed blessing for you? Describe one memorable incident in your education which illustrates the actual educational benefit (or harm) of computer technology.

2. What, exactly, is Postman's thesis in this essay? First, find three sentences in the essay that express the main idea of the essay. Of these, which sentence comes closest to explaining the main point of the essay? Explain your choice.

3. Postman gives several reasons why we should be skeptical of the ability of the computer to bring about an educational utopia. Find at least three passages where Postman critiques the technological optimists. Which of his reasons most effectively refutes their position? Explain your choice.

4. In this essay, Postman critiques the utopian point of view of critics such as Diane Ravitch, but he also offers his own proposal for improving education. Identify at least three of Postman's own recommendations. Did you find his recommendations persuasive? Explain.

5. A "motif" is a recurring thematic element or image used to develop a literary work. In his essay, Postman uses the images of the "god of Technology" and the little children (Eva and John) from Mars to help develop his main themes. Trace each of these images through the essay. Where does each motif reappear? Explain how each motif contributes to the overall thesis of the essay.

6. Reread Philip Elmer-DeWitt's essay, "Welcome to Cyberspace," and Connie Koenenn's essay, "Plotting a Net Gain." Then imagine that Elmer-DeWitt, Sherry Turkle, and Neil Postman are having

a round-table debate on the virtues of computers and their role in our lives in the twenty-first century. Write out the conversation they might have. Or, as an alternative, imagine how either Sherry Turkle or Elmer-DeWitt might respond to Neil Postman's argument.

7. Write your own investigative essay on the effects of computer technology on education. Interview several of your classmates in this class and/or in classes in your major field. Ask your interviewees a set of questions that will determine how much computer experience they have, how computers have or have not affected their fields of study, and whether they believe computers have or have not been helpful during their education. Explain how your results confirm or refute Postman's thesis.

PROBLEM SOLVING:
THE WRITING PROCESS

■ ASSIGNMENT FOR PROBLEM SOLVING   Select a problem that you believe needs a solution. Narrow and focus the problem and choose an appropriate audience. Describe the problem and, if necessary, demonstrate for your audience that it needs a solution. State your solution and justify it with reasons and evidence. Where appropriate, weigh alternative solutions, examine the feasibility of your own solution, and answer objections to your solution.

CHOOSING A SUBJECT

If one of your journal entries suggests a possible subject, try the collecting and shaping strategies below. If none of these leads to a workable subject, consider the following suggestions:

- Evaluating leads naturally into problem solving. Reread your journal entries and topic ideas for "evaluating." If your evaluation of your subject was negative, consider what would make your evaluation more positive. Based on your evaluation, write a proposal, addressed to the proper audience, explaining the problem and offering your solution.
- Organized groups are already trying to solve a number of national and international problems: homelessness, illegal aliens, the slaughter

of whales, acid rain, abuse of animals in scientific experiments, drug and alcohol abuse, toxic-waste disposal, and so forth. Read several current articles on one of these topics. Then narrow the problem to one aspect that students or residents of your town could help to resolve. Write an essay outlining the problem and proposing some *specific and limited* actions that citizens could take.

- Employers are always looking for workers with initiative and good ideas. At your place of work, take ten minutes during a break and observe what's going on around you. Take notes over a span of several days. Even though people may be getting the job done, would different procedures or policies improve efficiency, safety, quality, or personal relations? Write a letter to your boss identifying the problem that you've noticed and justifying your solution.

- Take an inventory of the personal problems that you regularly face, day to day. List the things that cost unnecessary amounts of time or money, that cause fear in your life, that increase your frustration level, or that simply make you less happy or productive than you could be. Then compare your inventory with a classmate's or friend's list. If there are common problems, discuss whether or how these problems might be solved.

"*I can't think of anything I have no problem with.*"

COLLECTING

With a possible subject and audience in mind, write out answers for each of the following topics. Remember that not all of these approaches will apply to your subject; some topics will suggest very little, while others may prompt you to generate ideas or specific examples appropriate for your problem and solution. A hypothetical problem—large classes that hinder learning—illustrates how these topics may help you focus on your subject and collect relevant ideas and information.

IDENTIFY AND FOCUS ON THE SPECIFIC PROBLEM. Answer the first four "Wh" questions:

Who: A Psychology I professor; the Psychology Department

What: Psychology I class

When: Spring semester (the structure of this class may be slightly different from previous semesters)

Where: University of Illinois (large lecture classes at one school may be different from those at another)

You may want to generalize about large lecture classes everywhere, but begin by identifying the specific problem at hand.

DEMONSTRATE THAT THE PROBLEM NEEDS A SOLUTION. Map out the *effects* of a problem. (See the diagram below.)

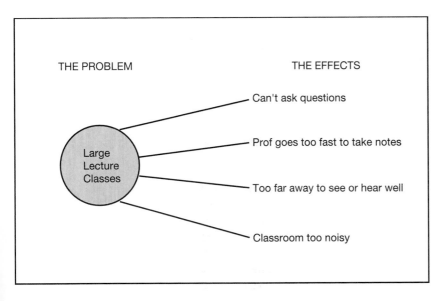

You may want to map out both *short-term effects* and *long-term effects.* Over the short term, large lecture classes prevent you from asking questions; over the long term, you may do poorly on examinations, get a lower grade in the class, lose interest in the subject, be unable to cope with your own and others' psychological problems, or end up in a different career or job.

DISCOVER POSSIBLE SOLUTIONS.   One strategy is to map out the history or the causes of the problem. If you can discover what caused the problem in the first place, you may have a possible solution. (See the diagram that follows.)

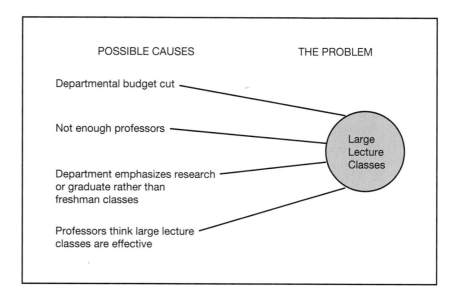

A second strategy takes the imaginative approach. Brainstorm hypothetical cases by asking, "What if . . ."

"What if students petitioned the president of the university to abolish all lecture classes with enrollments over 100 students?" Would that work?

"What if students invited the professor to answer questions at a weekly study session?" Would the professor attend? Would students attend?

"What if students taught each other in a psychology class?" How would that work?

EVALUATE POSSIBLE SOLUTIONS.   Apply the "If . . . then . . ." test on each possible solution: Consider whether each proposal would:

A.   actually solve the problem;

B.   meet certain criteria, such as cost-effectiveness, practicality, ethicality, legality;

C.   not create new problems.

"*If* classes were smaller, *then* students would learn more":

> If classes were smaller, students might learn more, but a small class size does not necessarily guarantee greater learning.
>
> Although students might learn more, do smaller classes meet other criteria? While they are legal and ethical, are they practical and cost-effective?
>
> Would smaller classes create new problems? Smaller classes might mean fewer upper-level course offerings. Is that a serious new problem?

CONVINCE YOUR READERS.   Support your proposed solutions by stating *reasons* and finding supporting *evidence:*

Reason: Smaller classes are worth the additional expense because students actually engage the material rather than just memorizing for exams.

Evidence: data from studies comparing large and small classes; personal testimony by students, interviews, or questionnaires; testimony or evidence from authorities on teaching.

ANSWER POSSIBLE OBJECTIONS TO YOUR PROPOSAL.
Every solution has a down side or possible drawbacks. You need to respond to the most important objections.

List Drawbacks

> Small classes cost more.
>
> Small classes might reduce course offerings.
>
> Small classes might mean less money for research.

List Your Responses

> Good education does cost more. The University of Illinois has a reputation as an excellent undergraduate institution, and small classes would help it maintain quality education.
>
> Perhaps some classes with low demand could be cut, but the necessary funds should not be taken out of upper-division classes for psychology majors or research projects.

LIST POSSIBLE STEPS FOR IMPLEMENTATION.   If appropriate, indicate the key steps or chronological sequence of your proposal:

> **1.** Poll students and teachers of large lecture classes to confirm that the problem warrants attention.

2. Gather evidence from other colleges or universities to show how they reduced class sizes.

3. Present results of polls and other evidence to the state legislature to request more funds.

RESEARCH TIP

As you begin researching your problem, *don't* rush off to the library and start collecting articles. *Do* start by interviewing people who may know about your problem. Use your investigating skills to locate authorities and interview them. (See Chapter 6.) Find out what other people have already done to solve the problem—or why current solutions are not working. Interview a teacher who knows about the problem, a student who has firsthand experience with the problem, an owner of a local business, or the coordinator of a community service. Save your library research until you know what the problem really is and what is currently being done to correct it.

OBSERVING   As you gather evidence and examples, use your observation skills. If the problem is large lecture classes, attend classes and *observe* the behavior of students and professors. Are students distracted by noise? Can they ask questions? Does the professor talk too softly to be heard in the back row? Remember that *repeated* observation is essential. If necessary, observe your subject over a period of several days or weeks.

The best time for planning . . . is when you're doing the dishes.

—AGATHA CHRISTIE,
MYSTERY WRITER

REMEMBERING   Use *freewriting, looping,* or *clustering* to help you remember examples from your experience of the problem or of possible solutions. Brainstorm or freewrite about previous class sessions in Psychology I. Do looping or mapping on other small-enrollment classes: What made these classes effective or ineffective? What teaching strategies, projects, or small-group activities were possible in these classes that would not be possible in a class of 250 students?

READING AND INVESTIGATING   *Use the library* to find books or articles about the particular problem. Other writers have no doubt offered solutions to your problem that you could consider. Articles may even suggest objections to your proposed solution that you need to answer.

Interview participants or authorities on the problem. The professor who is teaching your Psychology I class may have some ideas about a solution. Administrations—department chairs, deans, even the president—may agree to answer your questions and react to your possible solutions; schedule interviews.

Design a questionnaire that addresses aspects of your problem. Responses to questionnaires provide evidence that a problem is serious, immediate, and in need of a solution. If the results of a questionnaire show that 175 of the 200 people in Psychology I who returned it favor smaller sections, you can include that data in your letter to the head of the department and the dean of the college.

SHAPING

Writers of proposals often do the following:

- Identify and demonstrate problems
- Evaluate alternative solutions
- Make proposals
- Give reasons and evidence to support their proposals; answer objections, discuss feasibility and costs
- Indicate implementation or call for action

Of course not all problem-solving essays have all five elements. Some do not discuss feasibility or do not evaluate alternative solutions. Diebold's proposal, for example, suggests only four important ways to solve the problem—without considering alternative solutions.

OUTLINES FOR PROBLEM SOLVING   The following patterns indicate four possible ways to organize a problem-solving essay. One of these patterns may help you organize your proposal:

Problem-Solving Pattern

   I.   Introduction

  II.   The problem: identify and demonstrate

 III.   The solution(s)

 IV.   Answering possible objections, costs, drawbacks

  V.   Conclusion: implementation plan; call to action

Point-by-Point Pattern

   I.   Introduction

  II.   The overall problem: identify and demonstrate

 III.   One part of the problem, solution, evidence, answers to possible objections, feasibility

 IV.   Second part of the problem, solution, evidence, answers to possible objections, feasibility

V.   Third part of the problem, solution, evidence, and so on

VI.   Conclusion: implementation; call to action

Alternative Pattern

I.   Introduction

II.   The problem: identify and demonstrate

III.   Alternative solution 1; why it's not satisfactory

IV.   Alternative solution 2; why it's not satisfactory

V.   Alternative solution 3; why it works best: evidence, objections, feasibility

VI.   Conclusion: implementation; call to action

Step-by-Step Pattern

I.   Introduction

II.   The problem: identify and demonstrate

III.   Plan for implementing the solution or how solution has worked in the past:

    A.   Step one: reasons and evidence showing why this step is necessary and feasible

    B.   Step two: reasons and evidence showing why this step is necessary and feasible

    C.   Step three: reasons and evidence showing why this step is necessary and feasible

IV.   Conclusion

CAUSAL ANALYSIS   Causal analysis can be used to organize some paragraphs of a proposal. In arguing the benefits or advantages of a proposed solution, you are actually explaining the *effects* of your solution.

- The effects or advantages of smaller class sections in Psychology I would be greater student participation, fewer distractions, more discussion during lectures, and more individual or small-group learning.
- Shortening the work week to thirty-two hours would increase the number of jobs, reduce tensions for working parents, and give employees time to learn new skills.
- Eliminating steroid use among NFL athletes would reduce the impact of collisions and enable players to recover from injuries faster. Long-term effects of eliminating steroids would be to reduce incidence of cancers and urinary-tract problems.

In each of these cases, each effect or advantage can become a separate point and, sometimes, a separate body paragraph.

CRITERIA ANALYSIS   In some cases, the *criteria* for a good solution are quite clear. For example, cost effectiveness, feasibility, and worker morale might be important criteria for a business-related proposal. If you work in a fast-food restaurant and are concerned about the increasing number of crimes, for example, you might propose that your manager add a video surveillance system. In order to overcome the manager's resistance to spending the needed funds, you could defend your proposal (and answer possible objections) by discussing relevant criteria:

Proposal: To reduce theft and protect the employees of the restaurant by installing a video surveillance system.

- *Cost effectiveness.* Citing evidence from other stores that have video cameras, you could prove that the equipment would pay for itself in less than a year. In addition, you could argue that if the life of just one employee—or possibly one manager—were saved, the cost would be worth it.
- *Feasibility.* Installing a security system would not require any extensive remodeling or any significant training time for employees to learn how to operate the system.
- *Employee morale.* The benefits to employee morale would be significant: Workers would feel more secure, they would feel that the management cares about them, and they would work more productively.

CHRONOLOGICAL ORDER   If your proposal stresses the means of implementing your solution to a problem, you may organize several paragraphs or even an entire essay using a chronological order or step-by-step pattern.

A proposal to reduce boating accidents on a lake, for example, might involve a plan for educating boaters and enforcing regulations over a three-year period. During the first year, notices about dangers might be posted at key docks. During the second year, the county could pass a law requiring marinas to give a short instruction course for renters and set up voluntary classes on the lake for boat owners. Offenders might be given warnings and required to take classes. In the third year, offenders might face stiff fines.

A proposal to improve the reading skills of children might be justified by a series of coordinated steps, beginning by organizing seminars for teachers and PTA meetings to discuss possible solutions; establishing minimal reading requirements in grades K–6 that teachers and parents agree on; offering reading prizes; and organizing media coverage of students who participate in reading programs.

*Vigorous writing
is concise.*

**—WILLIAM
STRUNK, JR.,**

AUTHOR AND TEACHER

DRAFTING

Using your examples, recorded observations, reading, interviews, results from questionnaires, or your own experience, make a sketch outline and begin writing. As you write, let your own proposal and your intended audience guide you. In your first draft, get as much as possible on paper. Don't worry about spelling or awkward sentences. If you hit a snag, stop and read what you have written so far or reread your collecting-and-shaping notes.

REVISING

When you have a completed draft and are ready to start revising your essay, get another member of your class to read and respond to your essay. Use the Peer Response guidelines that follow to get—and give—constructive advice on your draft.

PEER RESPONSE

Writer: Provide the following information about your essay before you exchange drafts with a peer reader.

1. (a) audience
   (b) statement of problem
   (c) possible or alternative solutions
   (d) your recommended solution(s)
2. Write out one or two questions about your draft that you want your reader to answer.

Reader: Read the writer's entire draft. As you *reread* the draft, do the following:

1. Without looking at the writer's responses, describe (a) the essay's intended audience, (b) the main problem that the essay identifies, (c) the possible or alternative solutions, and (d) the writer's recommended solution. What feasibility problems or additional solutions should the writer consider? Why?
2. Indicate one paragraph in which the writer's evidence is strong. Then find one paragraph in which the writer needs more evidence. What additional *kinds* of evidence (personal experience, testimony from authorities, statistics, specific examples, etc.) might the writer use in this paragraph? Explain.

---

continued

3. Number the paragraphs in the writer's essay and then describe, briefly, the purpose or main idea of each paragraph. For example, paragraph 1 introduces the problem, paragraph 2 gives the writer's personal experience with the problem, etc. When you finish, explain how the writer might improve the organization of the essay.
4. List the three most important things that the writer should focus on during revision.
5. Respond to the writer's questions in number 2.

Writer: When your essay is returned, read the comments by your peer reader(s) and do the following:

1. Compare your description of the audience, the problem, and the solutions with your reader's description. Where there are differences, try to clarify your essay.
2. Reconsider and revise your recommended solution(s).
3. What additional kinds of evidence will make your recommendations stronger?
4. Make a revision plan. List, in order, the three most important things that you need to do as you revise your essay.

Use the following revising guidelines to identify areas for improving your draft. Even at this point, don't hesitate to collect additional information, if necessary, or reorganize your material. If a reader makes suggestions, reread your draft to see if those changes will improve your essay.

Guidelines for Revision

- **Have a classmate or someone who might understand your audience read your draft and play devil's advocate.** Have your reader pretend to be hostile to your solution and ask questions about alternative solutions or weaknesses in your own solution. Revise your proposal so that it answers any important objections.
- **Review your proposal for key elements.** If you are missing one of the following, would adding it make your proposal more effective for your audience? *Remember:* Proposals do not necessarily have to have all of these elements.

Develop the items that are most applicable to your proposal.

Show that a problem exists and needs attention

Evaluate alternative solutions

Propose your solution

Show that your solution meets certain criteria: feasibility, cost effectiveness, legality

Answer possible objections

Suggest implementation or call for action

- **Be sure that you *show* what you mean, using specific examples, facts, details, statistics, quotations from interviews or articles.** Don't rely on general assertions.
- **Signal the major parts of your proposal with key words and transitions.**
- **Avoid the following errors in logic and generalization.**

Don't commit an "either–or" fallacy. For example, don't say that "*either* we reduce class sizes *or* students will drop out of the university." There are more than two possible alternatives.

Don't commit an "ad hominem" fallacy by arguing "to the man" rather than to the issue. Don't say, for example, that John Diebold's proposal would never work because he's never been a city planner and therefore cannot understand traffic problems.

Test your proposal for "If . . . then . . ." statements. Does it really follow that "If we reduce class size, teaching will be more effective"?

Avoid overgeneralizing your solution. If all your research applies to solving problems in large lecture classes in psychology, don't assume that your solution will apply to, say, classes in physics or physical education.

- **If you are citing data or quoting sources, check to be sure that your material is accurately cited.**
- **Read your proposal aloud for flabby, wordy, or awkward sentences.** Revise your sentences for clarity, precision, and forcefulness.
- **Edit your proposal for spelling, appropriate word choice, punctuation, usage, mechanics, and grammar.** Remember that, in part, your form and audience help determine what is appropriate usage and mechanics.

■ POSTSCRIPT ON THE WRITING PROCESS   Before you turn in your essay, answer the following questions in your journal.

1. List the skills you used in writing this paper: observing people, places, or events; remembering personal experience; using questionnaires and interviews; reading written material; explaining ideas; evaluating solutions. Which of these skills was most useful to you in writing this essay?

2. What was your most difficult problem to solve while writing this paper? Were you able to solve it yourself, or did your readers suggest a solution?

3. In one sentence, describe the most important thing you learned about writing while working on this essay.

4. What were the most successful parts of your essay?

PROBLEM SOLVING:

STUDENT WRITING

NO PARKING

Kristy Busch, Steve Krause, and Keith Wright

Kristy Busch, Steve Krause, and Keith Wright worked together on a proposal to solve the parking problem at their university. They met several times to discuss the topic, select questions for the survey and interview, divide the research responsibilities, and determine who was going to draft each section. They agreed that Keith Wright would interview the director of parking management, and Kristy Busch and Steve Krause would survey students about the parking problem. After they collected their information, Wright drafted a first version of the section on the multilevel garage, Busch worked on the shuttle-bus proposal, and Krause wrote out the introduction and the rezoning proposal. Then they worked together to combine and revise their drafts, adding new information, reorganizing the paragraphs, and editing the final draft. Shown below are the questions for the interview, the results of the survey, the first draft of the introduction and rezoning proposal, and the revised draft of the entire proposal.

INTERVIEW

Interview Questions for Wes Westfall,
Director of Parking Management

1. Do you perceive a serious parking problem at CSU?

2. Do you think that students' arguments about lack of "X" parking spaces along the dorms on the north side of the campus are valid?

3. How many stickers for each zone are issued each year? Do these numbers fluctuate?

4. Are you in favor of building a multi-level parking facility?
   Where would you build such a structure?
   What would it cost? Is it feasible?
   How long would it take to build?

5. Have you considered a shuttle-bus system between Moby Gym and the central campus?
   What would it cost? Is it feasible?

6. Is rezoning possible? Is it currently under consideration? Would it solve the problem? Is it feasible? What would it cost?

PARKING SURVEY RESULTS

1. Do you drive to CSU?
   Yes: 36
   Occasionally: 53
   No: 11

2. Does CSU need more parking for students?
   Yes: 62
   No: 38

3. Would rezoning close-in lots to eliminate dorm parking help?
   Yes: 78
   No: 22

4. Class (Fr., Soph., Jr., Sr., Other)
   Fr: 33
   Soph: 20
   Jr: 22
   Sr: 13
   Other: 12

FIRST DRAFT

If you drive to CSU, you may already know how hard it can be to find a parking place. If not then now would be a good time to make the changes necessary to accommodate more cars (before you start driving). Not only is the parking inadequate for the number of cars, but it is also poorly organized and poorly distributed among the groups who use it. A very common occurrence is being forced to park very far from the building where you need to go. Not only students are affected; faculty, staff, and visitors also have problems finding somewhere to park. For a visitor this is very distressing and certainly doesn't present an attractive first impression of CSU. It is clear that something will have to be done; what is unclear is exactly what would be the most practical and cost effective solution. First, and probably the most effective for the immediate future would be to rezone the existing parking to better accommodate the users. A shuttle-bus system could also be used; however this could be costly and would have to be used a lot to make it a practical investment. The ominous "multilevel parking facility" is a drastic last measure that we would have a lot of trouble paying for. [add closing sentence]

The most cost-effective and probably the most immediately effective would be a partial rezoning of existing parking. This year, the office of parking management sold 7,641 parking stickers for an available 6,238 spaces, a difference of 1,703. This means that there are a lot more stickers than places to park. Granted, all these people do not drive at the same time, but enough do to cause a problem. In poll taken this March, 78 percent of the people said that they would like to see the parking rezoned. In rezoning we should first look at the parking areas which are not full and determine why and then shift the zones in a way in which they will help. For example, the western sections of the "Z" lot at Moby Gym could be changed to "X" for those dorm dwellers. Then the close-in lots could be changed to "Z" for the commuting students. Or we could eliminate the metered parking and put "Z" parking in its place. Rezoning the lots would seem to be the easiest solution to the problem, but it cannot be permanent, since if this school survives it will inevitably grow.

REVISED VERSION

NO PARKING

On Monday morning, Jennifer Martin left her apartment at 8:30 to drive to the Colorado State University campus, hoping to arrive on time for a test in her 9 a.m. sociology class. When she arrived at the student parking lot west of Aylesworth hall, there were no parking spots. So she began cruising up and down the lot, hoping that someone would soon pull out. As she drove slowly up and down the lanes, she muttered to herself and clenched her hands on the steering wheel. She did have a permit to park in the lot, but there were obviously more permits than spaces. About five minutes before class, a car pulled out of a place at the far end of the lot. She accelerated down the next lane, driving as fast as she could without running over other students, but just as she arrived, a green Ford Pinto cut in front of her and darted into the vacant space. She honked her horn and waved her fist, but the person got quickly out of the car and walked away. At this point, she realized that she had no choice. She wheeled into the area marked for motorcycles, parked her car, and raced for class. She was angry because she knew she was going to get a ticket even though she had a legal permit. **(1)**

If you drive to the CSU campus for classes, you have probably had a similar experience. But students are not the only ones who have parking problems on campus: faculty, staff, and visitors also have problems finding places to park. Especially for visitors, the overcrowded conditions don't present an attractive first impression of the campus. Clearly, something has to be done to improve parking facilities. After studying the problem, interviewing the director of parking management and polling one hundred students, we believe that there are three alternatives which the CSU administration should consider: building a multilevel parking facility, starting a shuttle-bus from remote lots, and rezoning the existing parking lots to better serve the users. **(2)**

A first possible solution to CSU's parking problem would be to build a multilevel parking facility. This sounds like a promising idea because it would allow more students, faculty, and staff to park over the same amount of ground space. CSU could build this facility at any of several locations. One place is on the west side of the Morgan Library, where the "A" parking zone—for faculty—is now. This location would provide parking convenient to classes, faculty offices, and the library. A second site would be the open parking lot west of Moby Gym. Although this location is further from classes, it would also be used during basketball games and concerts. A third location might be the large parking lot north of the Student Center. This too, like the library lot, would be close to classrooms and faculty offices. **(3)**

While these sites are all promising, we discovered that a multilevel parking facility has some serious drawbacks. Wes Westfall, manager of CSU parking, explained that there are several problems with these garages that most people don't consider. A first drawback to the parking garage is the expense. Westfall said that a multilevel garage would cost a minimum of $6,000 per parking space, raising the price of a parking permit from $30 to over $300. And that would be for a sticky piece of paper that still wouldn't guarantee a parking space for every car. Perhaps the president of the university could pay $300 a year, but most students can barely afford $30. **(4)**

A second drawback to a parking garage is that it doesn't last forever, and the maintenance costs can be considerable. Mr. Westfall has some frightening photographs of sections of strong, stable-looking concrete that has collapsed for no visible reason at all. One picture shows a whole garage leveled as though a good-sized bomb had hit it—nothing was left standing except for an occasional pillar here and there. Unless garages are carefully maintained, Westfall stated, they may not last over 20 years. The problem, he explained, lies in the rebarb (steel rods inside the concrete) that reinforces the concrete. Gas, oil, and anti-freeze from cars are gradually absorbed into the concrete, causing the rebarb to deteriorate and weaken the whole structure. The only way to check for this kind of damage, Westfall noted, is to use an expensive concrete X-ray machine. So even the maintenance for a garage can be an expensive proposition. **(5)**

The third and most serious problem, Westfall claims, is security. Parking garages can become just another place for sexual assault, drug trafficking, vandalism, and theft. Westfall commented that most garages have a monitor system and guards, but those precautions are not totally effective. By the time the guard detects a theft over the security system and arrives at the location, the thief has usually fled. In addition, any security system adds to the already high costs of a parking facility. Clearly, the problems connected with a multilevel garage make it a last resort for solving the parking problems on campus. **(6)**

A second alternative for solving the parking problems on the CSU campus is to use a bus shuttle service from the outlying "Z" lot at Moby Gym to the central campus. Students who responded to our survey frequently said that the lots on the perimeter of the campus were nearly empty, but they were too far away from the library and the classrooms. The shuttle would solve this problem by taking the following route: beginning at the Lory Student Center, the bus would head west down North Drive (along the residence halls) to the Moby Gym lot, and then stop and pick up drivers at both the north and south ends of the lot. It would then turn south onto Shields at the stoplight and turn east on South Drive, returning to central campus. This system would allow easier access to the core of the campus and, in return, put to full use the 539 parking spaces available in the Moby Gym parking lot. Of course, the shuttle, driver, and maintenance would cost money, so this solution would require a commitment from the university administration. **(7)**

The most cost-effective solution would be a partial rezoning of the parking lots. This past year, the office of parking management sold 7,461 parking stickers for an available 6,238 spaces, a difference of 1,403. This means that they sold 1,403 more stickers than there are places to park. Not all people need to park at the same time, but enough do to cause a problem. Of the 100 students that we polled, 78 percent said that they would like to see the central campus lots rezoned. In this scheme, students parking their cars for long periods of time would use the outlying lots and commuting students, faculty, and staff would use the closer lots. For example, if we changed the western section of the outlying "Z" lot to "X" for those students living in the dorms, the parking spaces near the dorms along South Drive could be made available to those who have to drive every day to campus to attend classes. Such rezoning seems to be the easiest and least expensive solution. **(8)**

One main problem to overcoming CSU's parking problem is money. A multilevel parking facility would accommodate more cars per acre of ground space, yet it is the most expensive solution. The shuttle-bus system—which could still be implemented—is more economical, but it would require raising additional revenue, most likely by raising the price of parking stickers. We certainly recommend that the university try a shuttle system on an experimental basis to determine the exact costs and see whether the number of riders justifies the expense. Rezoning the lots, however, is clearly the least complicated and most economical solution. Signs could be changed during the summer months, and new maps and brochures printed in time for the beginning of fall semester. Our group proposes that the university rezone the lots at the end of this academic year and start planning for a shuttle bus and a garage to meet the need in future years. With more careful management of the close-in lots, the new parking stickers might be more than just a hunting license. A person with a permit might actually be able to arrive at a lot at 8:45 and still make that nine o'clock class. **(9)**

Questions for Writing and Discussion

1. After reading the revised version, look again at the questions for the interview and the survey. How would you advise the authors to modify either set of questions? What questions would you add? What questions would you change or delete? Explain.

2. Compare the introduction in the first draft with the introduction in the revised version. Which is more effective? Jot down an idea for a third introduction that the authors might consider.

3. Reread the revised version and *outline* the major parts of the proposal. Then compare that outline with the authors' initial outline, given here:

    I.   Introduction

    II.   Rezoning proposal

    III. Shuttle-bus proposal

    IV.   Multilevel garage proposal

    V.   Conclusion

Do you think that their revised plan for organizing the paper was an improvement? Explain.

4. Who is the intended audience for this proposal? What revisions would make this proposal appeal even more strongly to that audience? (During the planning stages of this essay, the authors decided to send this proposal to Wes Westfall, director of parking management. How do you think Westfall would react to this proposal as it stands?)

WHO SHOULD TAKE CHARGE?

Eui Young Hwang

Eui Young Hwang, a student at the University of Illinois, wrote his problem-solving paper on the issue of black/Asian conflicts. After reading a conversation published in Ms. *magazine between Vicki Alexander, an African-American civil and medical rights activist, and Grace Lyu-Volckhausen, the Asian-American founder of the Korean YWCA, Hwang decided to enter their conversation by offering his own solutions to the racial tensions between the two communities. Hwang's solutions are to use the Korean-American media to help educate the community about cultural differences, to ask Korean-American churches to create religious and social opportunities for interaction, and to ask Korean-American businesses to return some profits to the African-American communities. Reprinted here is an excerpt from the* Ms. *conversation, followed by Hwang's own essay.*

BLACK/ASIAN CONFLICT: WHERE DO WE BEGIN?

Vicki Alexander and Grace Lyu-Volckhausen

Grace Lyu-Volckhausen: For me, being a feminist is in my genes. My grandmother was one of the earliest Korean feminists; my mom was one of the founders of the Korean Women's Association, and my father was one of the few Korean legislators who sponsored a women's rights bill. So when I came here in 1960 and women were fighting for their rights, I asked, "What is this? We have always been fighting."

I got involved with the women's movement here as a student in the 1960s. At that time, there were about 80 Koreans in New York, mostly students. Within five years, Koreans started to come in. I realized that Korean women were getting jobs in all kinds of labor markets and were getting taken advantage of. So we started the Korean YWCA; I worked with women's groups like Asian Women United. Now I spend most of my time and energy with immigrant women.

Vicki Alexander: I grew up in Los Angeles. My father was U.S. black, Blackfoot Indian, and Irish. Indians often allowed blacks or people escaping disasters like the Irish potato famine to stay on the reservation. We were welcomed there. My mother was a Polish-Russian Jew. My father was a union organizer, and from a very early age I was involved in progressive activities. In the early 1960s I married a college classmate—he was from Korea, a mathematician; he died in 1974 from a brain tumor.

I first was in the movement to free South Africa in the early 1960s, and then the movement for civil rights in this country. I had always wanted to be a doctor, but when I graduated from college I was not accepted by any medical school; after the civil rights movement, I reapplied and was accepted everywhere, with scholarships, and with no change in my record. So the civil rights movement was very important in my becoming a doctor. I decided to become an ob-gyn because the ones I saw didn't help women. . . .

Grace: The yearlong boycott of two Korean grocery stores by people in the African American community [on Church Avenue in the Flatbush section of Brooklyn] really soured a lot of things. I think it has soured New York as a whole. During the crisis I was behind the scenes trying to work things out. It was very frustrating.

Vicki: Well, everybody was talking about it. In the group I was in at the time, we were trying to analyze it and ask ourselves, "What's going on here? Should we take a side? Is there a side to take? Is there a middle road?" We tried to understand Korean immigration, because none of the people in the group were Korean.

Grace: So they just studied the situation.

Vicki: Right. We didn't engage in it. It was so nasty; it was terrible. All these guys, the black leaders, who have become discredited—the Sharptons and the Carsons—really discredited us.

Grace: I think Koreans wondered, why didn't David Dinkins [New York City's African American mayor] come down to the store? It took him eight months. When the crisis started, we asked him to come out right away—but he vacillated.

Our children remember these things. When they see their parents getting hurt, they remember it. And they have long memories.

Vicki: I think that among U.S. blacks there is a real hatred of people coming into our community and ripping us off. Once again getting ripped off by people who aren't us. Nationalism in the black community is very high, so blacks can come in and rip us off really badly, and they don't get chastised. The feeling gets fueled by racial incidents. And it's certainly been fueled on a national level by Reagan and Bush.

I feel that there is a long-standing kind of negativism that stems from nationalism; it says if it isn't black, it isn't good. No matter what. I think that's where a lot of the community is coming from. When you look historically at where black people have lived, we have not owned the stores. And on the whole, the money generated through the stores does not get reinvested in the community. So historically, you have a level of oppression not only based on class, but in the eyes of those blacks and in reality, based on race.

Then come Koreans. Koreans—and Arabs—own stores. But still, they are not black. There is that resentment, but what is clear about Arabs is that they are coming from a poor section of the world. So that's not as antagonistic as the white Jewish store owner. But then, in come Koreans, and nobody knows nothing about Koreans or the struggle in Korea—that's that world over there, Korea, China. The U.S. population is so ignorant, purposely so. But in the eyes of U.S. blacks, that is another body of folks coming over, taking over, and we don't know where they are from. So we must assume there is some money behind them. Maybe they don't have money, but we are assuming that they must have some money to come into our community and build whatever.

When it was just white–black, it wasn't as hard to understand. But when it is black–Asian–Arab, it starts to get very confusing, the class and race stuff starts to overlap. Because of the lack of education in the U.S., it's really a problem. What people need to start is a major education campaign.

Grace: From the Korean point of view, it doesn't matter what community we come into—black or white. The Koreans come in with a small amount of capital that they borrowed from their friends. They have trouble getting jobs because of discrimination, so they try to make a living by starting businesses that use the least amount of capital; they expend whatever amount of labor is necessary. Where do they go? The places with lowest rents, where there are not that many stores. So they end up going to black neighborhoods, where rent is cheap, where, if you work long hours, you can make profits—they all end up going there. But they don't know who these people are in the communities they go into.

Let me tell you an interesting story, an incredible misunderstanding between blacks and Koreans. Once a former black co-worker of mine was furious. He said, "You see that Korean woman there. I am so angry. She is insulting us." I asked, "What did she do?" He said, "Whenever I go there, the woman never puts the change in my hand, she always puts it on the counter." And I said, "Richard, this is because in Korea, a woman does not touch a man's hand. Except her own husband's—in private." He didn't know. It's just a little thing that becomes a big problem. I hear such comments all the time: "That Korean woman never smiles. They are so unfriendly." But in Korea, if you smile that much, they think you are stupid.

Vicki: Also, if you smile at men, it has a prostitution connotation.

Grace: Absolutely. This cultural gap is so great. Of course, Koreans will say, "These black people, they are always dancing, they are always loud."

Vicki: Or, "They're lazy. They don't work very hard."

Grace: My only regret in the Church Avenue crisis was that women were not able to get together. Korean women couldn't get together with African American women because we were just so engrossed in our own problems. We were all wringing our hands, "What do we do? What do we do?" And then all these politicians were running away from us. I felt like a pariah when I went to community meetings. People would see me and would not see me. They didn't want to deal with the Koreans because we were a time bomb.

I agonized that we could not pull our women together. Maybe next time there is a crisis we should bring our women together and tell these guys to shut up.

If I called you because of a black–Korean crisis, would you come out with your friends?

Vicki: Sure. You have to start building toward it now, at a time of no crisis. You have to establish a relationship with people. And one of the best places to do that is the Medgar Evers College women's center, a black women's center. I think it would be good if the overture came from Korean women, as people who come from an oppressed state. You were born in South Korea, an oppressed state, and I was born in the U.S., an oppressed state. We're both women oppressed within the oppressed state. There is a real commonality. We are struggling and fighting for our people, but to bridge some of those gaps, we have to start educating now.

WHO SHOULD TAKE CHARGE?

Eui Young Hwang

A boycott by blacks on a Korean grocery store in New York and lootings primarily on Korean-owned stores during the L.A. riots have focused Americans' attentions on racial conflicts between blacks and Koreans. Most Koreans are immigrants, not familiar to the American culture yet, and do business in poor black communities in the inner city. Vicki Alexander and Grace Lyu-Volckhausen, in "Black/Asian Conflict: Where Do We Begin?" assert that education on cultural differences and interactions is needed to reduce tension between blacks and Koreans. However, the authors fail to specify how to implement their solutions. Intervention by Korean American media, churches, and business organizations is needed in order to reduce racial conflict between blacks and Koreans caused by a lack of knowledge, few interactions, and Koreans' dominant business in black inner-city communities. **(1)**

Korean-American media can help to avoid misunderstandings between Koreans and blacks by educating Koreans about cultural differences. Korean merchants are often accused of insulting customers by not smiling and not putting change into a customer's hand. Lyu-Volckhausen explains that in Korean culture, a person smiling too often is considered stupid, and a woman does not touch a man's hand. Koreans, unaware of the cultural differences in America, often behave "rudely" to their black customers. Such little misunderstandings due to cultural differences often create an unfriendly relationship between blacks and Koreans. Korean-American media can readily educate Koreans about cultural differences. An organization might try to hold a program to educate Koreans on cultural sensitivities. Many Koreans are, however, too busy to attend any educational programs. The easiest way to get the attention of Koreans would be to use media in Korean communities. In big cities like New York, Los Angeles, and Chicago, where most Koreans live, there are a number of Korean-American television stations, radio channels, and newspapers. Korean-American media have large Korean audiences. With such big influences on Koreans, Korean-American media can easily get Koreans' attention in order to teach them about the cultural differences between Koreans and blacks. When compared to other organizations, Korean media provides the easiest method to reach and educate Koreans on cultural sensitivities. **(2)**

Korean-American churches can also increase cultural sensitivity and generate interactions between blacks and Koreans. Many Koreans think that blacks are lazy, untrustworthy, and violent. Blacks may perceive that Koreans have racism against blacks. On the other hand, Koreans may build bad images about blacks, since they often hear about blacks having no jobs, stealing, and murdering. To make matters worse, Koreans have too few contacts with blacks to overcome their stereotypical images about blacks. Therefore, frequent interactions between Koreans and blacks are necessary. Korean-American churches have the most potential in terms of promoting interactions between Koreans and blacks. One may argue that churches are too limited because they appeal to only Christians. On the contrary, churches include more Koreans than any other Korean-American organization, since many Koreans go to churches. Lyu-Volckhausen talks about blacks and Koreans singing together in church choirs and the opportunity it gives the two groups to get to know each other. Korean churches could cooperate with churches in black communities to hold religious activities and thus give both Koreans and blacks chances to establish friendly relationships. Korean-American churches can help Koreans to overcome stereotypical images of blacks by promoting interactions between blacks and Koreans and by holding religious activities with black churches. **(3)**

Finally, Korean-American business organizations need to reduce blacks' anger toward Korean businesses in black communities. They could begin by contributing some of their profits to black communities and helping blacks economically. Alexander points out that historically, blacks have not owned stores in their own communities, and the profit generated through stores does not get reinvested in black communities. Blacks often assume that Koreans take over black communities with money and that Koreans have an advantage over black businesses because they get money from secret financial sources, or were wealthy in Korea. Lyu-Volckhausen explains that Koreans with a small amount of capital often go to the poor black community because the rent is cheap and then make profits by working hard. There are several Korean-American business organizations which lead many Korean businesses. Those Korean-American business organizations can reduce hatred among blacks toward Koreans by contributing some of the profits of Korean businesses to black communities and helping blacks economically. In fact, some business organizations in Chicago have been trying to reduce tension between blacks and Koreans by donating scholarships to local black students, helping the homeless in black communities, encouraging Koreans to hire black employees, and helping local blacks' businesses by using their products. Some Koreans may say they should use their money however they want to. However, it may be more logical to contribute some of the profit to the community where they made the profit. By contributing a part of the profit to the black community, Korean business organizations can reduce not only the hatred among blacks toward Koreans but also the racial incidents like boycotts and lootings that have greatly hurt Koreans' businesses. **(4)**

Korean-American media, churches, and business organizations can greatly help to clear up misunderstandings and reduce tension between blacks and Koreans. Black organizations also need to cooperate with Korean-American organizations in order to establish friendly relationships between blacks and Koreans. Korean and black communities are too involved with each other to ignore the conflicts between them. That is, they need each other. First, Koreans and blacks need to show their willingness to listen to each other. Then, both Koreans and blacks should volunteer their efforts to reduce tension. Koreans and blacks cannot wait for the government to intervene to solve the conflicts between two communities. Conflicts between them hurt both Koreans and blacks too much to wait, and Koreans and blacks themselves are the only ones who can solve the problems. **(5)**

QUESTIONS FOR WRITING AND DISCUSSION

1. Before you read Hwang's essay, read the *Ms.* conversation and write your own response. Explain which of their ideas might work and which might not work. Then brainstorm a list of other actions that might reduce the racial tensions that Alexander and Lyu-Volckhausen describe.

2. Read Hwang's essay. In which paragraphs does he refer to ideas that Alexander and Lyu-Volckhausen discuss? Explain how his solutions further develop the ideas in their conversation.

3. Describe Hwang's three solutions. Which has the greatest promise for solving the problem? Which solution might not work or might cause other problems? What other solutions from your list might Hwang consider? Explain your responses.

4. In "Solving for Pattern," Wendell Berry argues that good solutions must consider the harmony, health, and quality of the overall system. How well does Hwang meet Berry's criterion for a good solution? Explain.

5. In which paragraphs does Hwang anticipate possible objections, analyze feasibility problems, or provide effective supporting evidence for his solutions? In which paragraphs should Hwang provide more analysis or more specific examples? Citing specific passages, point out strengths and suggest possible revisions for Hwang.

6. Use the excerpts from the *Ms.* conversation and Hwang's essay as starting points for your own essay on solving some aspect of interracial or intercultural tension. You may focus on conflicts between or among any racial or cultural groups. Draw on your own experience. Describe the problems and offer your solution(s).

10 ARGUING

Diana Ong, *Mingling*

AFTER BEING CITED FOR NOT WEARING A SEAT BELT WHILE OPERATING A MOTOR VEHICLE, YOU DECIDE THAT YOUR RIGHTS HAVE BEEN VIOLATED. IN ORDER TO WRITE A convincing argument to your representative that seat-belt laws are unfair, you research current articles about the law and interview a law professor on the issue. You decide to claim that the seat-belt laws should be repealed because they are a fundamental violation of individual liberty. You believe that the opposing argument—that seat belts save lives and reduce insurance rates for everyone—is not relevant to the issue of individual liberty. Because your representative has supported seat-belt laws, you present both sides of the issue but stress the arguments supporting your viewpoint.

❧

AFTER READING SEVERAL ACCOUNTS OF NEWS-MEDIA CENSORSHIP DURING THE PERSIAN GULF WAR, YOU DECIDE TO WRITE AN ESSAY ARGUING THAT CENSORSHIP IN THE NAME OF MILITARY security should not be tolerated. As you read about U.S. military censorship, you find other examples of censorship from World Wars I and II, from the Korean conflict and the Vietnam War, and from the operations in Grenada and Panama. Rather than putting soldiers' lives at risk, you believe, open coverage by the news media might actually reduce the death toll by shortening conflicts. Ultimately, you argue that a free society cannot tolerate any form of censorship that undermines its principles of freedom.

W HEN PEOPLE ARGUE WITH EACH OTHER, THEY OFTEN BECOME HIGHLY EMOTIONAL OR CONFRONTATIONAL. REMEMBER THE LAST HEATED ARGUMENT YOU HAD with a friend or family member—at the end of the argument, one person stomped out of the room, slammed the door, and didn't speak to the other for days. In the aftermath of such a scene, you felt angry with the other person and angry with yourself. Nothing was accomplished. Neither of you came close to achieving what you wanted when you began the argument. Rather than understanding each other's point of view and working out your differences, you effectively closed the lines of communication.

When writers construct arguments, however, they try, through reason and use of evidence, to avoid the emotional outbursts that often turn verbal arguments into displays of temper. Strong feelings may energize an argument—few of us make the effort to argue without emotional investment in the subject—but written argument stresses a fair weighing of pros and cons. While you advocate one position, you keep the lines of communication open by acknowledging and evaluating opposing arguments. Because written arguments are public, they take on a civilized manner. They implicitly say, "Let's be reasonable about this. Let's look at the evidence for *both* sides. Let's not shout or fight; let's be as objective as we can."

As writers construct written arguments, they carefully consider their audiences. Does the audience know about this controversy, or do they need background information? Do the readers hold an opposing viewpoint, or are they likely to listen to both sides and decide what to believe? What arguments will they find most persuasive? A written argument creates an atmosphere of reason, which encourages readers to examine their own views clearly and dispassionately. When successful, such argument convinces rather than alienates an audience. It changes people's minds or persuades them to adopt a recommended course of action.

All writing . . . is propaganda for something.

—ELIZABETH DREW,

WRITER AND CRITIC

TECHNIQUES FOR WRITING:

ARGUMENT

A written argument is similar to a public debate—between attorneys in a court of law or members of Congress who represent different political parties. It begins with a *debatable* issue: Is this a good bill? Should we vote for it? In such debates, one person argues for a position or proposal, while the other argues against it. The onlookers (the members of Congress, the jury, or the public) then decide what to believe or what to do. *Written argument imitates this situation by examining the opinions both for and against a position and then advocating one of the positions or proposing a solution.* Written argument evaluates the conflicting positions and then uses reasons and evidence to support the writer's claim. The writer represents the opposing arguments, responds to them, and advocates his or her own position. A sound written argument uses the following techniques:

- **Focusing on a *debatable* proposition or claim.** This claim becomes your thesis.
- *Analyzing the audience.* Knowing what your audience believes will help you convince them of your position or persuade them to act on your thesis.
- **Representing and evaluating the *opposing points of view* on the issue fairly and accurately.** The key to a successful arguing paper is anticipating and responding to the most important opposing positions.
- **Arguing reasonably *against the opposition* and *for your claim*.** State and refute opposing arguments. Present the best arguments supporting your claim. Argue reasonably and fairly.
- **Supporting your claims with *sufficient* evidence.** Use firsthand observations; examples from personal experience; statistics, facts, and quotations from your reading; and results from surveys and interviews.

In an article entitled "Active and Passive Euthanasia," James Rachels claims that active euthanasia may be defensible for patients with incurable and painful diseases. The following paragraphs from that article illustrate the key features of argument:

> The distinction between active and passive euthanasia is thought to be crucial for medical ethics. The idea is that it is permissible, at least in some cases, to withhold treatment and allow a patient to die, but it is never permissible to take any direct action designed to kill the patient. This doctrine seems to be accepted by most doctors. . . .

Opposing position

> However, a strong case can be made against this doctrine. In what follows I will set out some of the relevant arguments, and urge doctors to reconsider their views on this matter.

Claim
Audience

> To begin with a familiar type of situation, a patient who is dying of incurable cancer of the throat is in terrible pain, which can no longer be satisfactorily alleviated. He is certain to die within a few days, even if present treatment is continued, but he does not want to go on living for those days, since the pain is unbearable. So he asks the doctor for an end to it, and his family joins in the request.

Argument for claim
Example

Suppose the doctor agrees to withhold treatment, as the conventional doctrine says he may. The justification for his doing so is that the patient is in terrible agony, and since he is going to die anyway, it would be wrong to prolong his suffering needlessly. But now notice this. If one simply withholds treatment, it may take the patient longer to die, and so he may suffer more than he would if more direct action were taken and a lethal injection given. This fact provides strong reason for thinking that, once the initial decision not to prolong his agony has been made, active euthanasia is actually preferable to passive euthanasia, rather than the reverse. To say otherwise is to endorse the option that leads to more suffering rather than less, and is contrary to the humanitarian impulse that prompts the decision not to prolong his life in the first place.

CLAIMS FOR WRITTEN ARGUMENT

The thesis of your argument is a **debatable claim**. Opinions on both sides of the issue must have some merit. Claims for a written argument usually fall into one of four categories: claims of fact, claims about cause and effect, claims about value, and claims about solutions and policies. A claim may occasionally fall into several categories or even overlap categories.

Claims of Fact

- Grades do not measure intelligence or achievement.
- Polygraph tests do not accurately detect lies.
- Women face serious discrimination in the job market.

These claims are about matters of "fact" that are not easily measured or agreed upon. If I claimed that a Lhasa apso was an ancient Chinese ruler, you could check a dictionary and find out that I was wrong. A Lhasa apso is, in fact, a small Tibetan dog. There is no argument. But people do disagree about some *supposed* "facts": Do grades measure achievement? Are polygraph tests accurate? They also disagree about matters of "degree": Sexual discrimination exists in the marketplace, but is it "serious"? How prevalent and extreme are the economic inequities? What is "discrimination," anyway? *Definition* is a key to claims of fact: What do we mean by "detect lies"? Does "accurate" mean one hundred percent of the time? Ninety percent? Eighty percent? What does "serious discrimination" mean? Does the fact that female workers currently earn only sixty-seven cents for every dollar that male workers earn qualify as "serious discrimination"?

In an excerpt from a *Newsweek* column entitled "A Case of Severe Bias," Patricia Raybon makes a claim of fact when she argues that the news media's portrayal of black America is inaccurate, biased, and stereotyped:

This is who I am not. I am not a crack addict. I am not a welfare mother. I am not illiterate. I am not a prostitute. I have never been in jail. My children are not in gangs. My husband doesn't beat me. My home is not a tenement. None of these things defines who I am, nor do they describe the other black people I've known and worked with and loved and befriended over these 40 years of my life.

Nor does it describe most of black America, period.

Yet in the eyes of the American news media, this is what black America is: poor, criminal, addicted and dysfunctional. Indeed, media coverage of black America is so one-sided, so imbalanced that the most victimized and hurting segment of the black community— a small segment, at best—is presented not as the exception but as the norm. It is an insidious practice, all the uglier for its blatancy.

In recent months, oftentimes in this very magazine, I have observed a steady offering of media reports on crack babies, gang warfare, violent youth, poverty and homelessness—and in most cases, the people featured in the photos and stories were black. At the same time, articles that discuss other aspects of American life—from home buying to medicine to technology to nutrition—rarely, if ever, show blacks playing a positive role, or for that matter, any role at all.

Day after day, week after week, this message—that black America is dysfunctional and unwhole—gets transmitted across the American landscape. Sadly, as a result, America never learns the truth about what is actually a wonderful, vibrant, creative community of people.

Claims about Cause and Effect

- Cigarettes cause lung cancer.
- Capital punishment does not deter violent crime.
- Rock music weakens the moral fiber of America's youth.

Unlike the claim "Grades affect admission to college," these claims about cause and effect are debatable. The claim that cigarettes cause lung cancer is, of course, less debatable than it was twenty years ago, before the evidence demonstrating the link became overwhelming. The deterring effect of capital punishment is still an arguable proposition with reasonable arguments on both sides. The argument that rock music weakens the moral fiber of youth is certainly debatable; the writer would have to counter the argument that rock music sometimes raises social consciousness and fights world hunger.

In a selection from her book, *The Plug-In Drug: Television, Children, and the Family*, Marie Winn argues that television has a negative effect on family life. In her opening paragraphs, she sets forth both sides of the controversy and then argues that the overall effect is negative:

> Television's contribution to family life has been an equivocal one. For while it has, indeed, kept the members of the family from dispersing, it has not served to bring them *together*. By its domination of the time families spend together, it destroys the special quality that depends to a great extent on what a family does, what special rituals, games, recurrent jokes, familiar songs, and shared activities it accumulates.

> "Like the sorcerer of old," writes Urie Bronfenbrenner, "the television set casts its magic spell, freezing speech and action, turning the living into silent statues so long as the enchantment lasts. The primary danger of the television screen lies not so much in the behavior it produces—although there is danger there—as in the behavior it prevents: the talks, the games, the family festivities and arguments through which much of the child's learning takes place and through which his character is formed. Turning on the television set can turn off the process that transforms children into people."

> Yet parents have accepted a television-dominated family life so completely that they cannot see how the medium is involved in whatever problems they might be having. . . .

Claims about Value
- Boxing is a dehumanizing sport.
- The Ford Edsel is the ugliest automobile ever built in America.
- Toni Morrison is a great American novelist.

Claims about value lead to evaluative essays. All the strategies discussed in Chapter 8 apply here, with the additional requirement that you must anticipate and respond to alternate or opposing arguments. The argumentative essay that attempts to prove that boxing is dehumanizing must respond to the argument that boxing is merely another form of competition that promotes athletic excellence. Arguing that Morrison is a great American novelist requires setting criteria for great American novels and then responding to critics who argue that Morrison's talent does not reach those standards.

In "College Is a Waste of Time and Money," teacher and journalist Caroline Bird argues that many students go to college simply because it is the "thing to do." For those students, Bird claims, college is not a good idea:

> Nowadays, says one sociologist, you don't have to have a reason for going to college; it's an institution. His definition of an institution is an arrangement everyone accepts without question; the burden of proof is not on why you go, but why anyone thinks there might be a reason for not going. The implication is that an 18-year-old . . . should listen to those who know best and go to college.

> I don't agree. I believe that college has to be judged not on what other people think is good for students, but on how good it feels to the students themselves.

> I believe that people have an inside view of what's good for them. If a child doesn't want to go to school some morning, better let him stay at home, at least until you find out why. Maybe he knows something you don't. It's the same with college. If high-school graduates don't want to go, or if they don't want to go right away, they may perceive more clearly than their elders that college is not for them. It is no longer obvious that adolescents are best off studying a core curriculum that was constructed when all educated men could agree on what made them educated, or that professors, advisors, or parents can be of any particular help to young people in choosing a major or a career. High-school graduates see college graduates driving cabs and decide it's not worth going. College students find no intellectual stimulation in their studies and drop out.

Claims about Solutions or Policies

- Pornography on the Internet should be censored.
- The penalty for drunk driving should be a mandatory jail sentence and loss of driver's license.
- To reduce exploitation and sensationalism, the news media should not be allowed to interview victims of crime or disaster.

Claims about solutions or policies sometimes occur *along with* claims of fact, cause and effect, or value. Because grades do not measure achievement (argue that this is a fact), they should be abolished (argue for this policy). Boxing is a dehumanizing sport (argue this claim of value); therefore, boxing should be banned (argue for this solution). Claims about solutions or policies involve all the strategies used for problem solving (see Chapter 9), but with special emphasis on countering opposing arguments: "Although freedom of speech advocates suggest that we cannot suppress pornography on the Internet, in fact, we already have self-monitoring devices in other media that could help reduce pornography on the Internet."

In *When Society Becomes an Addict,* psychotherapist Anne Wilson Schaef argues that our society has become an "Addictive System" that has many characteristics in common with alcoholism and other addictions. Advertising becomes addictive, causing us to behave dishonestly; the social pressure to be "nice" can become addictive, causing us to lie to ourselves. Schaef argues that the solution for our social addictions begins when we face the reality of our dependency:

> We cannot recover from an addiction unless we first admit that we have it. Naming our reality is essential to recovery. Unless we admit that we are indeed functioning in an addictive process in an Addictive System, we shall never have the option of recovery. Once we name something, we own it. . . . Remember, to name the system as addict is not to condemn it: it is to offer it the possibility of recovery.

> Paradoxically, the only way to reclaim our personal power is by admitting our powerlessness. The first part of Step One of the AA [Alcoholics Anonymous] Twelve-Step Program reads, "We admitted we were powerless over alcohol." It is important to recognize that admitting to powerlessness over an addiction is not the same as admitting powerlessness as a person. In fact, it can be very powerfull to recognize the futility of the illusion of control.

Mere knowledge of the truth will not give you the art of persuasion.

—PLATO,

PHAEDRUS

APPEALS FOR WRITTEN ARGUMENT

To support claims and respond to opposing arguments, writers use *appeals* to the audience. Argument uses three important types of appeals: to *reason* (logic and evidence support the claim), to *character* (the writer's good character itself supports the claim), and to *emotion* (the writer's expression of feelings about the issue may support the claim). Effective arguments emphasize the appeal to reason but may also appeal to character or emotion.

APPEAL TO REASON An appeal to reason depends most frequently on *inductive logic,* which is sometimes called the "scientific method." Inductive logic draws a general conclusion from personal observation or experience, specific facts, reports, statistics, testimony of authorities, and other bits of data.

Experience is the best teacher, we always say, and experience teaches inductively. Suppose, using biologist Thomas Huxley's famous example, you pick a green apple from a tree and take a bite. Halfway through the bite you discover that the apple is sour and quickly spit it out. But, you think, perhaps the next green apple will be ripe and will taste better. You pick a second green apple, take a bite, and realize that it is just as sour as the first. However, you know that some apples—like the Granny Smith—look green even when they're ripe, so you take a bite out of a third apple. It is also sour. You're beginning to draw a conclusion. In fact, if you taste a fourth or fifth apple, other people may begin to question your intelligence. How many green apples from this tree must you taste before you get the idea that all of these green apples are sour?

Experience, however, may lead to wrong conclusions. You've tasted enough of these apples to convince *you* that all these apples are sour, but will others think that these apples are sour? Perhaps you have funny taste buds. You may need to ask several friends to taste the apples. Or perhaps you are dealing with a slightly weird tree—in fact, some apple trees are hybrids, with several different kinds of apples grafted onto one tree. Before you draw a conclusion, you may need to consult an expert in order to be certain that your tree is a standard, single-variety apple tree. If your friends and the expert also agree that all of these green apples are sour, you may use your experience *and* their testimony to reach a conclusion—and to provide evidence to make your argument more convincing to others.

In inductive logic, a reasonable conclusion is based on a *sufficient* quantity of accurate and reliable evidence that is selected in a *random* manner to reduce human bias or to take into account variation in the sample. The definition of "sufficient" varies, but generally the number must be large enough to convince your audience that your sample fairly represents the whole subject.

Let's take an example to illustrate inductive reasoning. Suppose you ask a student, one of fifty in a Psychology I class, a question of value: "Is Professor X a good teacher?" If this student says, "Professor X is the worst teacher I've ever had!" what conclusion can you draw? If you avoid taking the class based on a sample of one, you may miss an excellent class. So you decide to gather a *sufficient sample* by polling twenty of the fifty students in the class. But which twenty do you interview? If you ask the first student for a list of students, you may receive the names of twenty other students who also hate the professor. To reduce human or accidental bias, then, you choose a random method for collecting your evidence: As the students leave the class, you give a questionnaire to two out of every five students. If they all fill out the questionnaires, you probably have a *sufficient* and *random* sample.

Finally, if the responses to your questionnaire show that fifteen out of twenty students rate Professor X as an excellent teacher, what *valid conclusion* should you draw? You should not say, categorically, "X is an excellent teacher."

Your conclusion must be restricted by your evidence and the method of gathering it: "Seventy-five percent of the students polled in Psychology I believe that Professor X is an excellent teacher."

Most arguments use a shorthand version of the inductive method of reasoning. A writer makes a claim and then supports it with *reasons* and representative *examples* or *data:*

Claim: Professor X is an excellent psychology teacher.

Reason #1: Professor X is an excellent teacher because she gives stimulating lectures that students rarely miss.

Evidence: Sixty percent of the students polled said that they rarely missed a lecture. Three students cited Professor X's lecture on "assertiveness" as the best lecture they'd ever heard.

Reason #2: Professor X is an excellent teacher because she gives tests that encourage learning rather than sheer memorization.

Evidence: Seventy percent of the students polled said that Professor X's essay tests required thinking and learning rather than memorization. One student said that Professor X's tests always made her think about what she'd read. Another student said she always liked to discuss Professor X's test questions with her classmates and friends.

APPEAL TO CHARACTER   An appeal to your good character as a writer can also be important in argument. (The appeal to character is frequently called the "ethical" appeal because readers make a value judgment about the writer's character.) In a written argument, you show your audience—through your reasonable persona, voice, and tone—that you are a person who abides by moral standards that your audience shares: You have a good reputation, you are honest and trustworthy, and you argue "fairly."

A person's reputation often affects how we react to a claim, but also *the argument itself* should establish the writer's trustworthiness. You don't have to be a Mahatma Gandhi or a Mother Teresa to generate a strong ethical appeal for your claim. Even if your readers have never heard your name before, they will feel confident about your character if you are knowledgeable about your subject, present the pros and cons fairly, and support your own claim with sufficient, reliable evidence.

If your readers have reason to suspect your motives or think that you may have something personal to gain from your argument, you may need to bend over backward to be fair. If you do have something to gain, lay your cards on the table. Declare your vested interest but explain, for example, how your solution would benefit everyone equally. Similarly, don't try to cover up or distort the opponents' arguments; acknowledge the opposition's strong arguments and refute the weak ones.

APPEAL TO EMOTION Appeals to emotion can be tricky because, as we have seen, when emotions come in through the door, reasonableness may fly out the window. Argument emphasizes reason, not emotion. We know, for example, how advertising plays on emotions, by means of loaded or exaggerated language or through images of famous or sexy people. Emotional appeals designed to *deceive* or *frighten* people or to *misrepresent* the virtues of a person, place, or object have no place in rational argument. But emotional appeals that illustrate a truth or movingly depict a reality are legitimate and effective means of convincing readers.

COMBINED APPEALS Appeals may be used in combination. Writers may appeal to reason and, at the same time, establish trustworthy characters and use legitimate emotional appeals. The following excerpt from Martin Luther King's "Letter from Birmingham Jail" illustrates all three appeals. He appeals to reason, arguing that, historically, civil rights reforms are rarely made without political pressure. He establishes his integrity and good character by treating the opposition (in this case, the Birmingham clergy) with respect and by showing moderation and restraint. Finally, he uses emotional appeals, describing his six-year-old daughter in tears and recalling his own humiliation at being refused a place to sleep. King uses these emotional appeals legitimately; he is not misrepresenting reality or trying to deceive his readers.

One of the basic points in [the statement by the Birmingham clergy] is that the action that I and my associates have taken in Birmingham is untimely. Some have asked: "Why didn't you give the new city administration time to act?" The only answer that I can give to this query is that the new Birmingham administration must be prodded about as much as the outgoing one, before it will act. We are sadly mistaken if we feel that the election of Albert Boutwell as mayor will bring the millennium to Birmingham. While Mr. Boutwell is a much more gentle person than Mr. Connor, they are both segregationists, dedicated to the maintenance of the status quo. I have hoped that Mr. Boutwell will be reasonable enough to see the futility of massive resistance to desegregation. But he will not see this without pressure from devotees of civil rights. My friends, I must say to you that we have not made a single gain in civil rights without determined legal and nonviolent pressure. Lamentably, it is an historical fact that privileged groups seldom give up their privileges voluntarily. Individuals may see the moral light and voluntarily give up their unjust posture; but, as Reinhold Niebuhr has reminded us, groups tend to be more immoral than individuals.

Appeal to character and appeal to reason

Appeal to reason

Evidence

Appeal to character and reason

We know through painful experience that freedom is never voluntarily given by the oppressor; it must be demanded by the oppressed. Frankly, I have yet to engage in a direct-action campaign that was "well timed" in the view of those who have not suffered unduly from the disease of segregation. For years now I have heard the word "Wait!" It rings in the ear of every Negro with piercing familiarity. This "Wait" has almost always meant "Never." We must come to see, with one of our distinguished jurists, that "justice too long delayed is justice denied."

Appeal to emotion

Evidence

Appeal to emotion

Evidence

Appeal to emotion

Evidence

Appeal to character

We have waited for more than 340 years for our constitutional and God-given rights. . . . Perhaps it is easy for those who have never felt the stinging darts of segregation to say, "Wait." But when you have seen vicious mobs lynch your mothers and fathers at will and drown your sisters and brothers at whim; when you have seen hate-filled policemen curse, kick, and even kill your black brothers and sisters; when you see the vast majority of your twenty million Negro brothers smothering in an airtight cage of poverty in the midst of an affluent society; when you suddenly find your tongue twisted and your speech stammering as you seek to explain to your six-year-old daughter why she can't go to the public amusement park that has just been advertised on television, and see tears welling up in her eyes when she is told that Funtown is closed to colored children . . . when you take a cross-country drive and find it necessary to sleep night after night in the uncomfortable corners of your automobile because no motel will accept you; when you are humiliated day in and day out by nagging signs reading "white" and "colored"; when your first name becomes "nigger," your middle name becomes "boy" (however old you are) and your last name becomes "John" . . . —then you will understand why we find it difficult to wait. There comes a time when the cup of endurance runs over, and men are no longer willing to be plunged into the abyss of despair. I hope, sirs, you can understand our legitimate and unavoidable impatience.

ROGERIAN ARGUMENT

Traditional argument assumes that people are most readily convinced or persuaded by a confrontational "debate" on the issue. In a traditional argument, the writer argues reasonably and fairly, but the argument becomes a kind of struggle or "war" as the writer attempts to "defeat" the arguments of the opposition. The purpose of a traditional argument is thus to convince an undecided audience that the writer has "won a fight" and emerged "victorious" over the opposition.

In fact, however, there are many situations in which a less confrontational and less adversarial approach to argument is more effective. Particularly when the issues are highly charged or when the audience that we are trying to persuade is the opposition, writers may more effectively use negotiation rather than confrontation. *Rogerian argument*—named after psychologist Carl Rogers—is a kind of negotiated argument where understanding and compromise replace the traditional, adversarial approach. Rogerian, or *nonthreatening* argument, opens the lines of communication by reducing conflict. When people's beliefs are attacked, they instinctively become defensive and strike back. As a result, the argument becomes polarized: The writer argues for a claim, the reader digs in to defend his or her position, and no one budges.

Crucial to Rogerian argument is the fact that convictions and beliefs are not abstract but reside in people. If people are to agree, they must be sensitive to each other's beliefs. Rogerian argument, therefore, contains a clear appeal to character. While Rogerian argument uses reason and logic, its primary goal is not to "win" the argument but to open the lines of communication. To do that, the writer must be sympathetic to different points of view and willing to modify his or her claims in response to people who hold different viewpoints. Once the reader sees that the writer is open to change, the reader may become more flexible.

Once both sides are more flexible, a compromise position or solution becomes possible. As Rogers says, "This procedure gradually achieves a mutual communication. Mutual communication tends to be pointed toward solving a problem rather than toward attacking a person or group." Rogerian argument, then, imitates not a courtroom debate but the mutual communication that may take place between two people. Whereas traditional argument intends to change the actions or the beliefs of the opposition, Rogerian argument works toward changes *in both sides* as a means of establishing common ground and reaching a solution.

If you choose Rogerian argument, remember that you must actually be willing to change your beliefs. Often, in fact, when you need to use Rogerian argument most, you may be least inclined to use it—simply because you are inflexible on an issue. If you are unwilling to modify your own position, your reader will probably sense your basic insincerity and realize that you are just playing a trick of rhetoric.

Rogerian argument is appropriate in a variety of sensitive or highly controversial situations. You may want to choose Rogerian argument if you are an employer requesting union members to accept a pay cut in order to help the company avoid bankruptcy. Similarly, if you argue to husbands that they should assume responsibility for half of the housework, or if you argue to Anglo-Americans that Spanish language and culture should play a larger role in public education, you may want to use a Rogerian strategy. By showing that you empathize with the opposition's position and are willing to compromise, you create a climate for mutual communication.

Rogerian argument makes a claim, considers the opposition, and presents evidence to support your claim, but in addition it avoids threatening or adversarial language and promotes mutual communication and learning. A Rogerian argument uses the following strategies:

- **Avoiding** a *confrontational stance.* Confrontation threatens your audience and increases their defensiveness. Threat hinders communication.
- **Presenting** your *character* as someone who understands and can empathize with the opposition. Show that you understand by restating the opposing position accurately.
- **Establishing** *common ground* with the opposition. Indicate the beliefs and values that you share.
- **Being willing** *to change your views.* Show where your position is not reasonable and could be modified.
- **Directing your argument toward** *a compromise or workable solution.*

Note: An argument does not have to be either entirely adversarial or entirely Rogerian. You may use Rogerian techniques for the most sensitive points in an argument that is otherwise traditional or confrontational.

In his essay "Animal Rights versus Human Health," biology professor Albert Rosenfeld illustrates several features of Rogerian argument. Rosenfeld argues that animals should be used for medical experiments, but he is aware that the issues are emotional and that his audience is likely to be antagonistic. In these paragraphs, Rosenfeld avoids threatening language, represents the opposition fairly, grants that he is guilty of *speciesism,* and says that he sympathizes with the demand to look for alternatives. He indicates that his position is flexible: Most researchers, he says, are delighted when they can use alternatives. He grants that there is some room for compromise, but he is firm in his position that some animal experimentation is necessary for advancements in medicine.

States opposing position fairly and sympathetically

It is fair to say that millions of animals—probably more rats and mice than any other species—are subjected to experiments that cause them pain, discomfort, and distress, sometimes lots of it over long periods of time. . . . All new forms of medication or surgery are tried out on animals first. Every new substance that is released into the environment, or put on the market, is tested on animals. . . .

States opposing position fairly

In 1975, Australian philosopher Peter Singer wrote his influential book called *Animal Liberation,* in which he accuses us all of "speciesism"—as reprehensible, to him, as racism or sexism. He freely describes the "pain and suffering" inflicted in the "tyranny of human over nonhuman animals" and sharply challenges our biblical license to exercise "dominion over the fish of the sea, and over the fowl of the air, and over every living thing that moveth upon the Earth."

Well, certainly we are guilty of speciesism. We do act as if we had dominion over other living creatures. But domination also entails some custodial responsibility. And the questions continue to be raised: Do we have the right to abuse animals? To eat them? To hunt them for sport? To keep them imprisoned in zoos—or, for that matter, in our households? Especially to do experiments on these creatures who can't fight back?

Acknowledges common ground

Sympathetic to opposing position

Hardly any advance in either human or veterinary medicine—cure, vaccine, operation, drug, therapy—has come about without experiments on animals. . . . I certainly sympathize with the demand that we look for ways to get the information we want without using animals. Most investigators are delighted when they can get their data by means of tissue cultures or computer simulations. But as we look for alternative ways to get information, do we meanwhile just do without?

Suggests compromise position

■ WARMING UP: JOURNAL EXERCISES The following exercises will help you practice arguing. Read all of the following exercises and then write on the three that interest you most. If another idea occurs to you, write about it.

1. From the following list of "should" statements, choose one that relates to your experience and freewrite for ten minutes. When you finish your freewriting, state a claim and list arguments on both sides of the issue.

   • Tuition should be free at state universities.
   • Bicyclists should be subject to regular traffic laws, including DWI.
   • The sale of all handguns should be illegal.
   • Unions should be abolished.
   • NCAA football should have playoffs.
   • High-quality child care should be available to all working parents at public expense.
   • Computer literacy courses should be required at the college level.
   • Police should live in the neighborhoods they serve.
   • Fraternities and sororities should be forbidden to serve alcoholic beverages.

- Students should work for one year between high school and college.
- Businesses should be required to provide free health insurance for all employees.
- Rock music should be rated and labeled, from "PG" to "X," as films are.
- Unsportsmanlike behavior in tennis should result in a match forfeit.
- Drug tests should be required for your job or at your school.
- Nonmajor courses should be graded pass/fail.
- After committing three felonies, criminals should receive mandatory life sentences.

A society which is clamoring for choice. . . [is] filled with many articulate groups, each arguing its own brand of salvation. . . .

—MARGARET MEAD,

ANTHROPOLOGIST

2. Controversial subjects depend as much on the audience as they do on the issue itself. Make a quick list of things you do every day—the kind of clothes you wear, the food you eat, the books you read, the friends you have, the ideas you discuss. For one of these activities, imagine a person who might find what you do immoral, illogical, unjust, or unhealthy. What claim might they make about your activity? What reasons or evidence might they use to argue that your activity should be abolished, outlawed, or changed? Write for five minutes arguing *their* point of view.

3. Television and television advertising are often the subject of much criticism, such as in Marie Winn's excerpt from "The Effects of Television on Family Life." Write a letter to Marie Winn, to your local or college newspaper, or to members of the PTA in your city defending the *positive* effects or value of television. Cite one particular program or commercial as an example.

4. Grades are important, but in some courses they get in the way of learning. Choose an actual course that you have taken and write an open letter to the school administration, arguing for Credit/No Credit grading in that particular course. Assume that you intend to submit your letter to the campus newspaper.

5. News items often contain incidents that spark arguments about morality or justice. Choose a recent controversial news story and write out the arguments for or against the action taken in the case.

6. Does the cartoon on the opposite page from Gary Larson's "The Far Side" make a statement? Citing specific details from the cartoon, write a paragraph that explains the "point" of the cartoon. (If "The Far Side" is not one of your favorites, choose another cartoon that makes a controversial point and explain the "claim" it makes.)

7. The following essay by columnist Mike Royko appeared in the *Chicago Tribune*. Read Royko's essay. Next, write out your defini-

THE FAR SIDE By GARY LARSON

Copyright © 1984. Reprinted with the permission of Chronicle Features Syndicate.

tion for an effective written argument. Finally, write your own response to the essay, arguing that Royko's column does or does not meet your definition of an effective argumentative essay.

THE ETHICS OF ENDORSING A PRODUCT

Mike Royko

The man from an advertising agency had an unusual proposition. His agency does the TV commercials for a well-known chain of Mexican restaurants in Chicago.

"You may have seen our commercials," he said. "They include a cameo appearance by Lee Smith and Leon Durham of the Cubs. It shows them crunching into a tortilla."

No, I somehow missed seeing that.

"Well, anyway, we'd like to have you in a commercial."

Doing what?

"Crunching into a tortilla."

I thought tortillas were soft. I may be wrong, but I don't think you can crunch into a tortilla. Maybe you mean a taco.

"Well, you'd be biting into some kind of Mexican food."

What else would I have to do?

"That's it. It would be a cameo appearance. You'd be seen for about four seconds. You wouldn't have to say anything."

I'd just bite into a piece of Mexican food?

"Right. For a fee, of course."

How big a fee?

He named a figure. It was not a king's ransom, but it was more than walking-around money.

"It would take about 45 minutes to film," he said.

Amazing. In my first newspaper job almost 30 years ago, I had to work 12 weeks to earn the figure he had mentioned.

It was a small, twice-a-week paper, and I was the only police reporter, the only sports reporter, the only investigative reporter, the assistant political writer, and on Saturday I would edit the stories going into the entertainment page. The publisher believed in a day's work for an hour's pay.

Now I could make the same amount just for spending 45 minutes biting into a taco in front of a TV camera.

"Well, what do you think?" he asked.

I told him that I would think about it and get back to him.

So I asked Slats Grobnik, who has sound judgment, what he thought of the deal.

"That's a lot of money just to bite a taco on TV. For that kind of scratch, I'd bite a dog. Grab the deal."

But there is a question of ethics.

"Ethics? What's the ethics in biting a taco? Millions of people bite tacos every day. Mexicans have been biting them for hundreds of years. Are you saying that Mexicans are unethical? Careful, some of my best friends are Mexicans."

No, I'm not saying that at all. I like Mexicans, too, although I'm opposed to bullfighting."

"Then what's unethical?"

The truth is, I can't stand tacos.

"What has that got to do with it? I can't stand work, but I do it for the money."

It has everything to do with it. If I go on TV and bite into a taco, won't I be endorsing that taco?

"So what? You've endorsed politicians and I've never met a politician that I liked better than a taco."

But endorsing a taco I didn't like would be dishonest.

"Hey, that's the American way. Turn on your TV and look at all the people who endorse junk. Do you think they really believe what they're saying?"

Then it's wrong. Nobody should endorse a taco if they don't like a taco.

"Then tell them you'll bite something else. A tortilla or an enchilada."

But I don't like them, either. The truth is, I can't stand most Mexican food. The only thing I really like is the salt on the edge of a margarita glass.

"Can't you just bite the taco and spit it out when the camera is turned off?"

That would be a sham. Besides, even if I liked tacos or tortillas, what does it matter? Why should somebody eat in a restaurant because they see me biting into that restaurant's taco? Am I a taco expert? What are my credentials to tell millions of people what taco they should eat? I'm not even a Mexican.

"You're as Mexican as Jane Byrne, and she's doing it."

To get the Hispanic vote, she would go on TV and eat a cactus.

"Well, you're a sucker to turn it down. Why, it's almost un-American. Do you think that in Russia any newsman would ever have an opportunity to make that much money by biting into a pirogi?"

That may be so.

But maybe someday a food product will come along that I can lend my name to, something I can truly believe in.

"I doubt it. Not unless they start letting taverns advertise shots and beers on TV."

PROFESSIONAL WRITING

DEATH AND JUSTICE

Edward I. Koch

As a lifelong public servant and former mayor of New York City, Edward Koch has written several books on political issues, including Mayor *(1984),* Politics *(1985), and* Ed Koch on Everything *(1994). "Death and Justice," which appeared originally in* The New Republic, *is a classically organized essay arguing for the death penalty for convicted murderers. Koch represents opposing positions, uses appeals to reason, character, and emotion responsibly, and provides a variety of supporting evidence. This does not mean, of course, that you should necessarily be persuaded by his arguments or that his appeals, reasons, and evidence are flawless. Before you read Koch's essay, be sure to review the discussions of techniques, claims, and appeals for written argument in the opening sections of this chapter. Be prepared to evaluate Koch's argument. Where is his argument most or least persuasive?*

Last December a man named Robert Lee Willie, who had been convicted of raping and murdering an 18-year-old woman, was executed in the Louisiana state prison. In a statement issued several minutes before his death, Mr. Willie said: "Killing people is wrong. . . . It makes no difference whether it's citizens, countries, or governments. Killing is wrong." Two weeks later in South Carolina, an admitted killer named Joseph Carl Shaw was put to death for murdering two teenagers. In an appeal to the governor for clemency, Mr. Shaw wrote: "Killing is wrong when I did it. Killing is wrong when you do it. I hope you have the courage and moral strength to stop the killing." **(1)**

It is a curiosity of modern life that we find ourselves being lectured on morality by cold-blooded killers. Mr. Willie previously had been convicted of aggravated rape, aggravated kidnapping, and the murders of a Louisiana deputy and a man from Missouri. Mr. Shaw committed another murder a week before the two for which he was executed, and admitted mutilating the body of the 14-year-old girl he killed. I can't help wondering what prompted these murderers to speak out against killing as they entered the death-house door. Did their newfound reverence for life stem from the realization that they were about to lose their own? **(2)**

Life is indeed precious, and I believe the death penalty helps to affirm this fact. Had the death penalty been a real possibility in the minds of these murderers, they might well have stayed their hand. They might have shown moral awareness before their victims died, and not after. Consider the tragic death of Rosa Velez, who happened to be home when a man named Luis Vera burglarized her apartment in Brooklyn. "Yeah, I shot her," Vera admitted. "She knew me, and I knew I wouldn't go to the chair." **(3)**

During my 22 years in public service, I have heard the pros and cons of capital punishment expressed with special intensity. As a district leader, councilman, congressman, and mayor, I have represented constituencies generally thought of as liberal. Because I support the death penalty for heinous crimes of murder, I have sometimes been the subject of emotional and outraged attacks by voters who find my position reprehensible or worse. I have listened to their ideas. I have weighed their objections carefully. I still support the death penalty. The reasons I maintained my position can be best understood by examining the arguments most frequently heard in opposition. **(4)**

1. *The death penalty is "barbaric."* Sometimes opponents of capital punishment horrify with tales of lingering death on the gallows, of faulty electric chairs, or of agony in the gas chamber. Partly in response to such protests, several states such as North Carolina and Texas switched to execution by lethal injection. The condemned person is put to death painlessly, without ropes, voltage, bullets, or gas. Did this answer the objections of death penalty opponents? Of course not. On June 22, 1984, *The New York Times* published an editorial that sarcastically attacked the new "hygienic" method of death by injection, and stated that "execution can never be made humane through science." So it's not the method that really troubles opponents. It's the death itself they consider barbaric. **(5)**

Admittedly capital punishment is not a pleasant topic. However, one does not have to like the death penalty in order to support it any more than one must like radical surgery, radiation, or chemotherapy in order to find necessary these attempts at curing cancer. Ultimately we may learn how to cure cancer with a simple pill. Unfortunately, that day has not yet arrived. Today we are faced with the choice of letting the cancer spread or trying to cure it with the methods available, methods that one day will almost certainly be considered barbaric and would certainly delay the discovery of an eventual cure. The analogy between cancer and murder is imperfect, because murder is not the "disease" we are trying to cure. The disease is injustice. We may not like the death penalty, but it must be available to punish crimes of cold-blooded murder, cases in which any other form of punishment would be inadequate and, therefore, unjust. If we create a society in which injustice is not tolerated, incidents of murder—the most flagrant form of injustice—will diminish. **(6)**

2. *No other major democracy uses the death penalty.* No other major democracy—in fact, few other countries of any description—are plagued by a murder rate such as that in the United States. Fewer and fewer Americans can remember the days when unlocked doors were the norm and murder was a rare and terrible offense. In America the murder rate climbed 122 percent between 1963 and 1980. During that same period, the murder rate in New York City increased by almost 400 percent, and the statistics are even worse in many other cities. A study at M.I.T. showed that based on 1970 homicide rates a person who lived in a large American city ran a greater risk of being murdered than an American soldier in World War II ran of being killed in combat. It is not surprising that the laws of each country differ according to differing conditions and traditions. If other countries had our murder problem, the cry for capital punishment would be just as loud as it is here. And I daresay that any other major democracy where 75 percent of the people supported the death penalty would soon enact it into law. **(7)**

3. *An innocent person might be executed by mistake.* Consider the work of Adam Bedau, one of the most implacable foes of capital punishment in this country. According to Mr. Bedau, it is "false sentimentality to argue that the death penalty should be abolished because of the abstract possibility that an innocent person might be executed." He cites a study of the 7,000 executions in this country from 1893 to 1971, and concludes that the record fails to show that such cases occur. The main point, however, is this. If government functioned only when the possibility of error didn't exist, government wouldn't function at all. Human life deserves special protection, and one of the best ways to guarantee that protection is to assure that convicted murderers do not kill again. Only the death penalty can accomplish this end. In a recent case in

New Jersey, a man named Richard Biegenwald was freed from prison after serving 18 years for murder; since his release he has been convicted of committing four murders. A prisoner named Lemuel Smith, who, while serving four life sentences for murder (plus two life sentences for kidnapping and robbery) in New York's Green Haven Prison, lured a woman corrections officer into the chaplain's office and strangled her. He then mutilated and dismembered her body. An additional life sentence for Smith is meaningless. Because New York has no death penalty statute, Smith has effectively been given a license to kill. **(8)**

But the problem of multiple murder is not confined to the nation's penitentiaries. In 1981, 91 police officers were killed in the line of duty in this country. Seven percent of those arrested in the cases that have been solved had a previous arrest for murder. In New York City in 1976 and 1977, 85 persons arrested for homicide had a previous arrest for murder. Six of these individuals had two previous arrests for murder, and one had four previous murder arrests. During those two years the New York police were arresting for murder persons with a previous arrest for murder on the average of one every 8.5 days. This is not surprising when we learn that in 1975, for example, the median time served in Massachusetts for homicide was less than two-and-a-half years. In 1976 a study sponsored by the Twentieth Century Fund found that the average time served in the United States for first-degree murder is ten years. The median time served may be considerably lower. **(9)**

4. *Capital punishment cheapens the value of human life.* On the contrary, it can be easily demonstrated that the death penalty strengths the value of human life. If the penalty for rape were lowered, clearly it would signal a lessened regard for the victims' suffering, humiliation, and personal integrity. It would cheapen their horrible experience, and expose them to an increased danger of recurrence. When we lower the penalty for murder, it signals a lessened regard for the value of the victim's life. Some critics of capital punishment, such as columnist Jimmy Breslin, have suggested that a life sentence is actually a harsher penalty for murder than death. This is sophistic nonsense. A few killers may decide not to appeal a death sentence, but the overwhelming majority make every effort to stay alive. It is by exacting the highest penalty for the taking of human life that we affirm the highest value of human life. **(10)**

5. *The death penalty is applied in a discriminatory manner.* This factor no longer seems to be the problem it once was. The appeals process for a condemned prisoner is lengthy and painstaking. Every effort is made to see that the verdict and sentence were fairly arrived at. However, assertions of discrimination are not an argument for ending the death penalty but for extending it. It is not justice to exclude everyone from the penalty of the law if a few are found to be so favored. Justice requires that the law be applied equally to all. **(11)**

6. *Thou shalt not kill.* The Bible is our greatest source of moral inspiration. Opponents of the death penalty frequently cite the sixth of the Ten Commandments in an attempt to prove that capital punishment is divinely proscribed. In the original Hebrew, however, the Sixth Commandment reads, "Thou Shalt Not Commit Murder," and the Torah specifies capital punishment for a variety of offenses. The biblical viewpoint has been upheld by philosophers throughout history. The greatest thinkers of the 19th century— Kant, Locke, Hobbes, Rousseau, Montesquieu, and Mill—agreed that natural law properly authorizes the sovereign to take life in order to vindicate justice. Only Jeremy Bentham was ambivalent. Washington, Jefferson, and Franklin endorsed it. Abraham Lincoln authorized executions for deserters in wartime. Alexis de Tocqueville, who expressed profound respect for American institutions, believed that the death penalty was indispensable to the support of social order. The United States Constitution, widely admired as one of the seminal achievements in the history of humanity, condemns cruel and inhuman punishment, but does not condemn capital punishment. **(12)**

7. *The death penalty is state-sanctioned murder.* This is the defense with which Messrs. Willie and Shaw hoped to soften the resolve of those who sentenced them to death. By saying in effect, "You're no better than I am," the murderer seeks to bring his accusers down to his own level. It is also a popular argument among opponents of capital punishment, but a transparently false one. Simply put, the state has rights that the private individual does not. In a democracy, those rights are given to the state by the electorate. The execution of a lawfully condemned killer is no more an act of murder than is legal imprisonment an act of kidnapping. If an individual forces a neighbor to pay him money under threat of punishment, it's called extortion. If the state does it, it's called taxation. Rights and responsibilities surrendered by the individual are what give the state its power to govern. This contract is the foundation of civilization itself. **(13)**

Everyone wants his or her rights, and will defend them jealously. Not everyone, however, wants responsibilities, especially the painful responsibilities that come with law enforcement. Twenty-one years ago a woman named Kitty Genovese was assaulted and murdered on a street in New York. Dozens of neighbors heard her cries for help bud did nothing to assist her. They didn't even call the police. In such a climate the criminal understandably grows bolder. In the presence of moral cowardice, he lectures us on our supposed failings and tries to equate his crimes with our quest for justice. **(14)**

The death of anyone—even a convicted killer—diminishes us all. But we are diminished even more by a justice system that fails to function. It is an illusion to let ourselves believe that doing away with capital punishment removes the murderer's deed from our conscience. The rights of society are paramount. When we protect guilty lives, we give up innocent lives in exchange. When opponents of capital punishment say to the state: "I will not let you kill in my name," they are also saying to murderers: "You can kill in your *own* name as long as I have an excuse for not getting involved." **(15)**

It is hard to imagine anything worse than being murdered while neighbors do nothing. But something worse exists. When those same neighbors shrink back from justly punishing the murderer, the victim dies twice. **(16)**

VOCABULARY

In your journal, write the meanings of the following words:

- I have represented *constituencies* **(4)**
- find my position *reprehensible* **(4)**
- the most *flagrant* form of injustice **(6)**
- the most *implacable* foes **(8)**
- this is *sophistic* nonsense **(10)**
- capital punishment is divinely *proscribed* **(12)**
- one of the *seminal* achievements **(12)**

QUESTIONS FOR WRITING AND DISCUSSION

1. What exactly is Koch's thesis or overall claim? Find one or two sentences from Koch's essay that clearly express his thesis. In paragraph 13, Koch says "the state has rights that the private individual does not." Why is this statement important for Koch's thesis? Explain.

2. What are Koch's purposes in this essay? Is he making a claim of fact, value, cause-and-effect, or policy? Does he aim to convince us of a belief or persuade us to take some action? Cite specific passages from the essay to support your answer.

3. Koch's essay follows a classical argumentative organization. Review the six part classical structure in the "Shaping" section of this chapter. Does Koch's essay follow the sequence outlined there (Introduction, Narration, Partition, Argument, Refutation, and Conclusion)? How does he revise or adapt this structure?

4. For supporting evidence, Koch uses statistics, specific examples of criminals, and analogies. In the essay, find examples of each of these kinds of support. Evaluate his evidence. Are his specific examples appropriate and persuasive? Are his statistics timely and relevant? Are his comparisons or analogies effective? If you were giving Koch advice about revising and improving the evidence in his essay, what changes would you suggest?

5. In the past few years, films such as *Dead Man Walking* have focused on the issue of capital punishment. Check out *Dead Man Walking*—or another film focusing on capital punishment—from your local video store. Watch the film and take notes about the capital punishment issues that it raises. Is the film for or against capital punishment? Is it neutral? Write your own essay about the capital punishment issues raised in the film and in Koch's essay. How might Koch respond to this film?

6. Consider the arguing essay that you are currently writing. Keeping your own particular purpose and audience in mind, should you use Koch's classical organization? How do you intend to respond to opposing or alternative viewpoints? Should you use all three kinds of appeals (to reason, to character, and to emotion), as Koch does? What personal experiences, specific examples, statistics, quotations from authorities could you use? Which of Koch's strategies can you use and which do you need to revise?

DARWIN'S MIDDLE ROAD

Stephen Jay Gould

In his distinguished career as a spokesperson for the wonders of biology and the theory of evolution, Harvard professor Stephen Jay Gould has written dozens of scientific and popular articles and has published several collections of essays and award-winning books, including Ever Since Darwin *(1977),* The Panda's Thumb *(1980),* Hen's Teeth and Horse's Toes *(1983),* The Mismeasure of Man *(1981, 1996),* Bully for Brontosaurus *(1991),* Eight Little Piggies: Reflections in Natural History *(1993), and* Full House: The Spread of Excellence from Plato to Darwin *(1996). "Science is not a heartless pursuit of objective information," Gould has said. "It is a creative human activity." That idea is clearly illustrated in "Darwin's Middle Road." Gould opens the essay with an episode from Homer's epic poem* The Odyssey. *At one point during his adventures, Odysseus must sail between the horrible six-headed monster Scylla and the giant ocean whirlpool created by Charybdis. Odysseus's predicament dramatizes the focus of Gould's essay. Gould's subject is the nature of scientific creativity and his central question is whether great scientific theories are based on purely inductive, data-driven research or whether they arise primarily from intuition, hunches, and flashes of genius. Gould's claim is that the theory of natural selection sprang from Darwin's unique blending of careful, inductive observation with reflection, intuition, and synthesis.*

"We began to sail up the narrow strait lamenting," narrates Odysseus. "For on the one hand lay Scylla, with twelve feet all dangling down; and six necks exceeding long, and on each a hideous head, and therein three rows of teeth set thick and close, full of black death. And on the other mighty Charybdis sucked down the salt sea water. As often as she belched it forth, like a cauldron on a great fire she would seethe up through all her troubled deeps." Odysseus managed to swerve around Charybdis, but Scylla grabbed six of his finest men and devoured them in his sight—"the most pitiful thing mine eyes have seen of all my travail in searching out the paths of the sea." **(1)**

False lures and dangers often come in pairs in our legends and metaphors—consider the frying pan and the fire, or the devil and the deep blue sea. Prescriptions for avoidance either emphasize a dogged steadiness—the straight and narrow of Christian evangelists—or an averaging between unpleasant alternatives—the golden mean of Aristotle. The idea of steering a course between undesirable extremes emerges as a central prescription for a sensible life. **(2)**

The nature of scientific creativity is both a perennial topic of discussion and a prime candidate for seeking a golden mean. The two extreme positions have not been directly competing for allegiance of the unwary. They have, rather, replaced each other sequentially, with one now in the ascendency, the other eclipsed. **(3)**

The first—inductivism—held that great scientists are primarily great observers and patient accumulators of information. For new and significant theory, the inductivists claimed, can only arise from a firm foundation of facts. In this architectural view, each fact is a brick in a structure built without blueprints. Any talk or thought about theory (the completed building) is fatuous and premature before the bricks are set. Inductivism once commanded great prestige within science, and even represented an "official" position of sorts, for it touted, however falsely, the utter honesty, complete objectivity, and almost automatic nature of scientific progress towards final and incontrovertible truth. **(4)**

Yet, as its critics so rightly claimed, inductivism also depicted science as a heartless, almost inhuman discipline offering no legitimate place to quirkiness, intuition, and all the other subjective attributes adhering to our vernacular notion of genius. Great scientists, the critics claimed, are distinguished more by their powers of hunch and synthesis, than their skill in experiment or observation. The criticisms of inductivism are certainly valid and I welcome its dethroning during the past thirty years as a necessary prelude to better understanding. Yet, in attacking it so strongly, some critics have tried to substitute an alternative equally extreme and unproductive in its emphasis on the essential subjectivity of creative thought. In this, "eureka" view, creativity is an ineffable something, accessible only to persons of genius. It arises like a bolt of lightning, unanticipated, unpredictable and unanalyzable—but the bolts strike only a few special people. We ordinary mortals must stand in awe and thanks. (The name refers, of course, to the legendary story of Archimedes running naked through the streets of Syracuse shouting eureka [I have discovered it] when water displaced by his bathing body washed the scales abruptly from his eyes and suggested a method for measuring volumes.) **(5)**

I am equally disenchanted by both these opposing extremes. Inductivism reduces genius to dull, rote operations; eurekaism grants it an inaccessible status more in the domain of intrinsic mystery than in a realm where we might understand and learn from it. Might we not marry the good features of each view, and abandon both the elitism of eurekaism and the pedestrian qualities of inductivism. May we not acknowledge the personal and subjective character of creativity, but still comprehend it as a mode of thinking that emphasizes or exaggerates capacities sufficiently common to all of us that we may at least understand if not hope to imitate. **(6)**

In the hagiography of science, a few men hold such high positions that all arguments must apply to them if they are to have any validity. Charles Darwin, as the principal saint of evolutionary biology, has therefore been presented both as an inductivist and as a primary example of eurekaism. I will attempt to show that these interpretations are equally inadequate, and that recent scholarship on Darwin's own odyssey towards the theory of natural selection supports an intermediate position. **(7)**

So great was the prestige of inductivism in his own day, that Darwin himself fell under its sway and, as an old man, falsely depicted his youthful accomplishments in its light. In an autobiography, written as a lesson in morality for his children and not intended for publication, he penned some famous lines that misled historians for nearly a hundred years. Describing his path to the theory of natural selection, he claimed: "I worked on true Baconian principles, and without any theory collected facts on a wholesale scale." **(8)**

The inductivist interpretation focuses on Darwin's five years aboard the *Beagle* and explains his transition from a student for the ministry to the nemesis of preachers as the result of his keen powers of observation applied to the whole world. Thus, the traditional story goes, Darwin's eyes opened wider and wider as he saw, in sequence, the bones of giant South American fossil mammals, the turtles and finches of the Galapagos, and the marsupial fauna of Australia. The truth of evolution and its mechanism of natural selection crept up gradually upon him as he sifted facts in a sieve of utter objectivity. **(9)**

The inadequacies of this tale are best illustrated by the falsity of its conventional premier example—the so-called Darwin's finches of the Galapagos. We now know that although these birds share a recent and common ancestry on the South American mainland, they have radiated into an impressive array of species on the outlying Galapagos. Few terrestrial species manage to cross the wide oceanic barrier between South America and the Galapagos. But the fortunate migrants often find a sparsely inhabited world devoid of the competitors that limit their opportunities on the crowded mainland. Hence, the finches evolved into roles normally occupied by other birds and developed their famous set of adaptations for feeding—seed crushing, insect eating, even grasping and manipulating a cactus needle to dislodge insects from plants. Isolation—both of the islands from the mainland and among the islands themselves—provided an opportunity for separation, independent adaptation, and speciation. **(10)**

According to the traditional view, Darwin discovered these finches, correctly inferred their history, and wrote the famous lines in his notebook: "If there is the slightest foundation for these remarks the zoology of Archipelagoes will be worth examining; for such facts would undermine the stability of Species." But, as with so many heroic tales from Washington's cherry tree to the piety of Crusaders, hope rather than truth motivates the common reading. Darwin found the finches to be sure. But he didn't recognize them as variants of a common stock. In fact, he didn't even record the island of discovery for many of them—some of his labels just read "Galapagos Islands." So much for his immediate recognition of the role of isolation in the formation of new species. He reconstructed the evolutionary tale only after his return to London, when a British Museum ornithologist correctly identified all the birds as finches. **(11)**

The famous quotation from his notebook refers to Galapagos tortoises and to the claim of native inhabitants that they can "at once pronounce from which Island any Tortoise may have been brought" from subtle differences in size and shape of body and scales. This is a statement of different, and much reduced, order from the traditional tale of finches. For the finches are true and separate species—a living example of evolution. The subtle differences among tortoises represent minor geographic variation within a species. It is a jump in reasoning, albeit a valid one as we now know, to argue that such small differences can be amplified to produce a new species. All creationists, after all, acknowledged geographic variation (consider human races), but argued that it could not proceed beyond the rigid limits of a created archetype. **(12)**

I don't wish to downplay the pivotal influence of the *Beagle* voyage on Darwin's career. It gave him space, freedom and endless time to think in his favored mode of independent self-stimulation. (His ambivalence towards university life, and his middling performance there by conventional standards, reflected his unhappiness with a curriculum of received wisdom.) He writes from South America in 1834: "I have not one clear idea about cleavage, stratification, lines of upheaval. I have no books, which tell me much and what they do I cannot apply to what I see. In consequence I draw my own conclusions, and most gloriously ridiculous ones they are." The rocks and plants and animals that he saw did provoke him to the crucial attitude of doubt—midwife of all creativity. Sydney, Australia—1836. Darwin wonders why a rational God would create so many marsupials on Australia since nothing about its climate or geography suggests any superiority for pouches: "I had been lying on a sunny bank and was reflecting on the strange character of the animals of this country as compared to the rest of the World. An unbeliever in everything beyond his own reason might exclaim, 'Surely two distinct Creators must have been at work.'" **(13)**

Nonetheless, Darwin returned to London without an evolutionary theory. He suspected the truth of evolution, but had no mechanism to explain it. Natural selection did not arise from any direct reading of the *Beagle's* facts, but from two subsequent years of thought and struggle as reflected in a series of remarkable notebooks that have been unearthed and published during the past twenty years. In these notebooks, we see Darwin testing and abandoning a number of theories and pursuing a multitude of false leads—so much for his later claim about recording facts with an empty mind. He read philosophers, poets, and economists, always searching for meaning and insight—so much for the notion that natural selection arose inductively from the *Beagle's* facts. Later, he labelled one notebook as "full of metaphysics on morals." **(14)**

Yet if this tortuous path belies the Scylla of inductivism, it has engendered an equally simplistic myth—the Charybdis of eurekaism. In his maddeningly misleading autobiography, Darwin does record a eureka and suggests that natural selection struck him as a sudden, serendipitous flash after more than a year of groping frustration:

> In October 1838, that is, fifteen months after I had begun my systematic inquiry, I happened to read for amusement Malthus on Population, and being well prepared to appreciate the struggle for existence which everywhere goes on from long-continued observation of the habits of animals and plants, it at once struck me that under these circumstances favorable variations would tend to be preserved, and unfavorable ones to be destroyed. The result of this would be the formation of new species. Here, then, I had at last got a theory by which to work. **(15)**

Yet, again, the notebooks belie Darwin's later recollections—in this case by their utter failure to record, at the time it happened, any special exultation over his Malthusian insight. He inscribes it as a fairly short and sober entry without a single exclamation point, though he habitually used two or three in moments of excitement. He did not drop everything and reinterpret a confusing world in its light. On the very next day, he wrote an even longer passage on the sexual curiosity of primates. **(16)**

The theory of natural selection arose neither as a workmanlike induction from nature's facts, nor as a mysterious bolt from Darwin's subconscious, triggered by an accidental reading of Malthus. It emerged instead as the result of a conscious and productive search, proceeding in a ramifying but ordered manner, and utilizing both the facts of natural history and an astonishingly broad range of insights from disparate disciplines far from his own. Darwin trod the middle path between inductivism and eurekaism. His genius is neither pedestrian nor inaccessible. **(17)**

Darwinian scholarship has exploded since the centennial of the *Origin* in 1959. The publication of Darwin's notebooks and the attention devoted by several scholars to the two crucial years between the *Beagle's* docking and the demoted Malthusian insight has clinched the argument for a "middle path" theory of Darwin's creativity. Two particularly important works focus on the broadest and narrowest scales. Howard E. Gruber's masterful intellectual and psychological biography of this phase in Darwin's life, *Darwin on Man*, traces all the false leads and turning points in Darwin's search. Gruber shows that Darwin was continually proposing, testing, and abandoning hypotheses, and that he never simply collected facts in a blind way. He began with a fanciful theory involving the idea that new species arise with a prefixed life span, and worked his way gradually, if fitfully, towards an idea of extinction by competition in a world of struggle. He recorded no exultation upon reading Malthus, because the jigsaw puzzle was only missing a piece or two at the time. **(18)**

Silvan S. Schweber has reconstructed, in detail as minute as the record will allow, Darwin's activities during the few weeks before Malthus (The Origin of the *Origin* Revisited, *Journal of the History of Biology*, 1977). He argues that the final pieces arose not from new facts in natural history, but from Darwin's intellectual wanderings in distant fields. In particular, he read a long review of social scientist and philosopher Auguste Comte's most famous work, the *Cours de philosophie positive*. He was particularly struck by Comte's insistence that a proper theory be predictive and at least potentially quantitative. He then turned to Dugald Stewart's *On the Life and Writing of Adam Smith*, and imbibed the basic belief of the Scottish economists that theories of overall social structure must begin by analyzing the unconstrained actions of individuals. (Natural selection is, above all, a theory about the struggle of individual organisms for success in reproduction.) Then, searching for quantification, he read a lengthy analysis of work by the most famous statistician of his time—the Belgian Adolphe Quetelet. In the review of Quetelet, he found, among other things, a forceful statement of Malthus's quantitative claim—that population would grow geometrically and food supplies only arithmetically, thus guaranteeing an intense struggle for existence. In fact, Darwin had read the Malthusian statement several times before; but only now was he prepared to appreciate its significance. Thus, he did not turn to Malthus by accident, and he already knew what it contained. His "amusement," we must assume, consisted only in a desire to read in its original formulation the familiar statement that had so impressed him in Quetelet's secondary account. **(19)**

In reading Schweber's detailed account of the moments preceding Darwin's formulation of natural selection, I was particularly struck by the absence of deciding influence from his own field of biology. The immediate precipitators were a social scientist, an economist, and a statistician. If genius has any common denominator, I would propose breadth of interest and the ability to construct fruitful analogies between fields. **(20)**

In fact, I believe that the theory of natural selection should be viewed as an extended analogy—whether conscious or unconscious on Darwin's part I do not know—to the laissez faire economics of Adam Smith. The essence of Smith's argument is a paradox of sorts: if you want an ordered economy providing maximal benefits to all, then let individuals compete and struggle for their own advantages. The result, after appropriate sorting and elimination of the inefficient, will be a stable and harmonious polity. Apparent order arises naturally from the struggle among individuals, not from predestined principles or higher control. Dugald Stewart epitomized Smith's system in the book Darwin read:

> The most effective plan for advancing a people . . . is by allowing every man, as long as he observes the rules of justice, to pursue his own interest in his own way, and to bring both his industry and his capital into the freest competition with those of his fellow citizens. Every system of policy which endeavors . . . to draw towards a particular species of industry a greater share of the capital of the society than would naturally go to it . . . is, in reality, subversive of the great purpose which it means to promote.

As Schweber states: "The Scottish analysis of society contends that the combined effect of individual actions results in the institutions upon which society is based, and that such a society is a stable and evolving one and functions without a designing and directing mind." **(21)**

We know that Darwin's uniqueness does not reside in his support for the idea of evolution—scores of scientists had preceded him in this. His special contribution rests upon his documentation and upon the novel character of his theory about how evolution operates. Previous evolutionists had proposed unworkable schemes based on internal perfecting tendencies and inherent directions. Darwin advocated a natural and testable theory based on immediate interaction among individuals (his opponents considered it heartlessly mechanistic). The theory of natural selection is a creative transfer to biology of Adam Smith's basic argument for a rational economy: the balance and order of nature does not arise from a higher, external (divine) control, or from the existence of laws operating directly upon the whole, but from struggle among individuals for their own benefits (in modern terms, for the transmission of their genes to future generations through differential success in reproduction). **(22)**

Many people are distressed to hear such an argument. Does it not compromise the integrity of science if some of its primary conclusions originate by analogy from contemporary politics and culture rather than from data of the discipline itself? In a famous letter to Engels, Karl Marx identified the similarities between natural selection and the English social scene:

> It is remarkable how Darwin recognizes among beasts and plants his English society with its division of labor, competition, opening up of new markets, 'invention,' and the Malthusian 'struggle for existence.' It is Hobbes' *bellum omnium contra omnes* (the war of all against all).

Yet Marx was a great admirer of Darwin—and in this apparent paradox lies resolution. For reasons involving all the themes I have emphasized here—that inductivism is inadequate, that creativity demands breadth, and that analogy is a profound source of insight—great thinkers cannot be divorced from their social background. But the source of an idea is one thing; its truth or fruitfulness is another. The psychology and utility of discovery are very different subjects indeed. Darwin may have cribbed the idea of natural selection from economics, but it may still be right. As the German socialist Karl Kautsky wrote in 1902: "The fact that an idea emanates from a particular class, or accords with their interests, of course proves nothing as to its truth or falsity." In this case, it is ironic that Adam Smith's system of laissez faire does not work in his own domain of economics, for it leads to oligopoly and revolution, rather than to order and harmony. Struggle among individuals does, however, seem to be the law of nature. **(23)**

Many people use such arguments about social context to ascribe great insights primarily to the indefinable phenomenon of good luck. Thus, Darwin was lucky to be born rich, lucky to be on the *Beagle,* lucky to live amidst the ideas of his age, lucky to trip over Parson Malthus—essentially little more than a man in the right place at the right time. Yet, when we read of his personal struggle to understand, the breadth of his concerns and study, and the directedness of his search for a mechanism of evolution, we understand why Pasteur made his famous quip that fortune favors the prepared mind. **(24)**

VOCABULARY

In your journal, write the meanings of the following words:

- is *fatuous* **(4)**
- an *ineffable* something **(5)**
- the *hagiography* of science **(7)**
- the *nemesis* of preachers **(9)**
- the *marsupial fauna* of Australia **(9)**

- *speciation* **(10)**
- British Museum *ornithologist* **(11)**
- a created *archetype* **(12)**
- *metaphysics* on morals **(14)**
- *serendipitous* flash **(15)**
- the immediate *precipitators* **(20)**
- an extended *analogy* **(21)**
- *laissez faire* economics **(21)**
- harmonious *polity* **(21)**
- leads to *oligopoly* **(23)**

QUESTIONS FOR WRITING AND DISCUSSION

1. In your own words, explain the two "extremes" of inductivism and eurekaism. Describe Darwin's middle path through these extremes.

2. In the course of his essay, Gould defines both "genius" and "natural selection." Identify sentences from the essay that describe or define these terms.

3. Argument begins with a debatable proposition or question. In your own words, state the question that Gould addresses. Identify the "pro" side of this argument (Gould's position) and the "con" side (the position that Gould argues against).

4. In argument, refutations of opposing positions must be supported by evidence, testimony, facts, statistics, or other data. Find two paragraphs in which Gould refutes an opposing argument. List the evidence that Gould provides in that paragraph. Which evidence best supports Gould's argument?

5. Gould has written a monthly column, "This View of Life," for *Natural History* magazine. Review a copy of *Natural History* and then profile Gould's intended audience. Where in "Darwin's Middle Road" does Gould appeal to this audience?

6. Gould popularizes his subjects without trivializing them. Compare Gould's essay with Philip Elmer-DeWitt's essay in Chapter 7. Assuming that your class is the target audience, which essay does the best job of informing this audience about its subject? Cite examples from each essay of vocabulary, sentence length, tone, organization, and content to support your evaluation.

THE DAMNATION OF A CANYON

Edward Abbey

"In wildness is the preservation of the world." Henry David Thoreau's words serve to introduce Edward Abbey's own nature ethic. Beginning with the classic Desert Solitaire *(1968) and including* The Monkey Wrench Gang *(1975),* Abbey's Road *(1979), and* Down the River *(1982), Abbey's writings celebrate the American West, its deserts, canyons, mountains, and rivers. But always in full view are Abbey's villains in the black hats: Industrialists, Bureaucrats, and Developers. And Dammers. In this selection, taken from* Beyond the Wall *(1984), Abbey contrasts the Eden that was Glen Canyon with the stagnant, lifeless waters of Lake Powell. Abbey's argument is shaped by a clear outline—his claim, his refutation of the opposing view, his analysis of consequences, and his solution—but also by Abbey's insistent, cranky, and passionate voice that echoes throughout the essay.*

There was a time when, in my search for essences, I concluded that the canyonland country has no heart. I was wrong. The canyonlands did have a heart, a living heart, and that heart was Glen Canyon and the golden, flowing Colorado River. **(1)**

In the summer of 1959 a friend and I made a float trip in little rubber rafts down through the length of Glen Canyon, starting at Hite and getting off the river near Gunsight Butte—The Crossing of the Fathers. In this voyage of some 150 miles and ten days our only motive power, and all that we needed, was the current of the Colorado River. **(2)**

In the summer and fall of 1967 I worked as a seasonal park ranger at the new Glen Canyon National Recreation Area. During my five-month tour of duty I worked at the main marina and headquarters area called Wahweap, at Bullfrog Basin toward the upper end of the reservoir, and finally at Lee's Ferry downriver from Glen Canyon Dam. In a number of powerboat tours I was privileged to see almost all of our nation's newest, biggest and most impressive "recreational facility." **(3)**

Having thus seen Glen Canyon both before and after what we may fairly call its damnation, I feel that I am in a position to evaluate the transformation of the region caused by construction of the dam. I have had the unique opportunity to observe firsthand some of the differences between the environment of a free river and a powerplant reservoir. **(4)**

One should admit at the outset to a certain bias. Indeed I am a "butterfly chaser, googly eyed bleeding heart and wild conservative." I take a dim view of dams; I find it hard to learn to love cement; I am poorly impressed by concrete aggregates and statistics in the cubic tons. But in this weakness I am not alone, for I belong to that ever-growing number of Americans, probably a good majority now, who have become aware that a fully industrialized, thoroughly urbanized, elegantly computerized social system is not suitable for human habitation. Great for machines, yes: but unfit for people. **(5)**

Lake Powell, formed by Glen Canyon Dam, is not a lake. It is a reservoir, with a constantly fluctuating water level—more like a bathtub that is never drained than a true lake. As at Hoover (or Boulder) Dam, the sole practical function of this impounded water is to drive the turbines that generate electricity in the powerhouse at the base of the dam. Recreational benefits were of secondary importance in the minds of those who conceived and built this dam. As a result the volume of water in the reservoir is continually being increased or decreased according to the requirements of the Basin States Compact and the power-grid system of which Glen Canyon Dam is a component. **(6)**

The rising and falling water level entails various consequences. One of the most obvious, well known to all who have seen Lake Mead, is the "bathtub ring" left on the canyon walls after each drawdown of water, or what rangers at Glen Canyon call the Bathtub Foundation. This phenomenon is perhaps of no more than aesthetic importance; yet it is sufficient to dispel any illusion one might have, in contemplating the scene, that you are looking upon a natural lake. **(7)**

The utter barrenness of the reservoir shoreline recalls by contrast the aspect of things before the dam, when Glen Canyon formed the course of the untamed Colorado. Then we had a wild and flowing river lined by boulder-strewn shores, sandy beaches, thickets of tamarisk and willow, and glades of cottonwoods. **(8)**

The thickets teemed with songbirds: vireos, warblers, mockingbirds and thrushes. On the open beaches were killdeer, sandpipers, herons, ibises, egrets. Living in grottoes in the canyon walls were swallows, swifts, hawks, wrens and owls. Beaver were common if not abundant: not an evening would pass, in drifting down the river, that we did not see them or at least hear the whack of their flat tails on the water. Above the river shores were the great recessed alcoves where water seeped from the sandstone, nourishing the semitropical hanging gardens of orchid, ivy and columbine, with their associated swarms of insects and birdlife. **(9)**

Up most of the side canyon, before damnation, there were springs, sometimes flowing streams, waterfalls and plunge pools—the kind of marvels you can now find only in such small scale remnants of Glen Canyon as the Escalante area. In the rich flora of these laterals the larger mammals—mule deer, coyote, bobcat, ring-tailed cat, gray fox, kit fox, skunk, badger and others—found a home. When the river was dammed almost all of these things were lost. Crowded out—or drowned and buried under mud. **(10)**

The difference between the present reservoir, with its silent sterile shores and debris choked side canyons, and the original Glen Canyon, is the difference between death and life. Glen Canyon was alive. Lake Powell is a graveyard. **(11)**

For those who may think I exaggerate the contrast between the former river canyon and the present man-made impoundment, I suggest a trip on Lake Powell followed immediately by another boat trip on the river below the dam. Take a boat from Lee's Ferry up the river to within sight of the dam, then shut off the motor and allow yourself the rare delight of a quiet, effortless drifting down the stream. In that twelve-mile stretch of living green, singing birds, flowing water and untarnished canyon walls—sights and sounds a million years older and infinitely lovelier than the roar of motorboats—you will rediscover a small and imperfect sampling of the kind of experience that was taken away from everybody when the oligarchs and politicians condemned our river for purposes of their own. **(12)**

Lake Powell, though not a lake, may well be as its defenders assert the most beautiful reservoir in the world. Certainly it has a photogenic backdrop of buttes and mesas projecting above the expansive surface of stagnant waters where the speedboats, houseboats and cabin cruisers play. But it is no longer a wilderness. It is no longer a place of natural life. It is no longer Glen Canyon. **(13)**

The defenders of the dam argue that the recreational benefits available on the surface of the reservoir outweigh the loss of Indian ruins, historical sites, wildlife and wilderness adventure. Relying on the familiar quantitative logic of business and bureaucracy, they assert that whereas only a few thousand citizens even ventured down the river through Glen Canyon, now millions can—or will—enjoy the motorized boating and hatchery fishing available on the reservoir. They will also argue that the rising waters behind the dam have made such places as Rainbow Bridge accessible by powerboat. Formerly you could get there only by walking (six miles). **(14)**

This argument appeals to the wheelchair ethos of the wealthy, upper-middle-class American slob. If Rainbow Bridge is worth seeing at all, then by God it should be easily, readily, immediately available to everybody with the money to buy a big powerboat. Why should a trip to such a place be the privilege only of those who are willing to walk six miles? Or if Pikes Peak is worth getting to, then why not build a highway to the top of it so that anyone can get there? Anytime? Without effort? Or as my old man would say, "By Christ, one man's just as good as another—if not a damn sight better." **(15)**

It is quite true that the flooding of Glen Canyon has opened up to the motorboat explorer parts of side canyons that formerly could be reached only by people able to walk. But the sum total of terrain visible to the eye and touchable by hand and foot has been greatly diminished, not increased. Because of the dam the river is gone, the inner canyon is gone, the best parts of the numerous side canyons are gone—all hidden beneath hundreds of feet of polluted water, accumulating silt, and mounting tons of trash. This portion of Glen Canyon—and who can estimate how many cubic miles were lost?—*is no longer accessible to anybody.* (Except scuba divers.) And this, do not forget, was the most valuable part of Glen Canyon, richest in scenery, archaeology, history, flora and fauna. **(16)**

Not only has the heart of Glen Canyon been buried, but many of the side canyons above the fluctuating waterline are now rendered more difficult, not easier, to get into. This because the debris brought down into them by desert storms, no longer carried away by the river, must unavoidably build up in the area where flood meets reservoir. Narrow Canyon, for example, at the head of the impounded waters, is already beginning to silt up and to amass huge quantities of driftwood, some of it floating on the surface, some of it half afloat beneath the surface. Anyone who has tried to pilot a motorboat through a raft of half-sunken logs and bloated dead cows will have his own thoughts on the accessibility of these waters. **(17)**

Second, the question of costs. It is often stated that the dam and its reservoir have opened up to the many what was formerly restricted to the few, implying in this case that what was once expensive has now been made cheap. Exactly the opposite is true. **(18)**

Before the dam, a float trip down the river through Glen Canyon would cost you a minimum of seven days' time, well within anyone's vacation allotment, and a capital outlay of about forty dollars—the prevailing price of a two-man rubber boat with oars, available at any army-navy surplus store. A life jacket might be useful but not required, for there were no dangerous rapids in the 150 miles of Glen Canyon. As the name implies, this stretch of the river was in fact so easy and gentle that the trip could be and was made by all sorts of amateurs: by Boy Scouts, Camp Fire Girls, stenographers, schoolteachers, students, little old ladies in inner tubes. Guides, professional boatmen, giant pontoons, outboard motors, radios, rescue equipment were not needed. The Glen Canyon float trip was an adventure anyone could enjoy, on his own, for a cost less than that of spending two days and nights in a Page motel. Even food was there, in the water: the channel catfish were easier to catch and a lot better eating than the striped bass and rainbow trout dumped by the ton into the reservoir these days. And one other thing: at the end of the float trip you still owned your boat, usable for many more such casual and carefree expeditions. **(19)**

What is the situation now? Float trips are no longer possible. The only way left for the exploration of the reservoir and what remains of Glen Canyon demands the use of a powerboat. Here you have three options: (1) buy your own boat and engine, the necessary auxiliary equipment, the fuel to keep it moving, the parts and repairs to keep it running, the permits and licenses required for legal operation, the trailer to transport it; (2) rent a boat; or (3) go on a commercial excursion boat, packed in with other sightseers, following a preplanned itinerary. This kind of play is only for the affluent. **(20)**

The inescapable conclusion is that no matter how one attempts to calculate the cost in dollars and cents, a float trip down Glen Canyon was much cheaper than a powerboat tour of the reservoir. Being less expensive, as well as safer and easier, the float trip was an adventure open to far more people than will ever be able to afford motorboat excursions in the area now. **(21)**

All of the foregoing would be nothing but a futile exercise in nostalgia (so much water over the dam) if I had nothing constructive and concrete to offer. But I do. As alternate methods of power generation are developed, such as solar, and as the nation establishes a way of life adapted to actual resources and basic needs, so that the demand for electrical power begins to diminish, we can shut down the Glen Canyon power plant, open the diversion tunnels, and drain the reservoir. **(22)**

This will no doubt expose a drear and hideous scene: immense mud flats and whole plateaus of sodden garbage strewn with dead trees, sunken boats, the skeletons of long-forgotten, decomposing water-skiers. But to those who find the prospect too appalling, I say give nature a little time. In five years, at most in ten, the sun and wind and storms will cleanse and sterilize the repellent mess. The inevitable floods will soon remove all that does not belong within the canyons. Fresh green willow, box elder and redbud will reappear; and the ancient drowned cottonwoods (noble monuments to themselves) will be replaced by young of their own kind. With the renewal of plant life will come the insects, the birds, the lizards and snakes, the mammals. Within a generation—thirty years—I predict the river and canyons will bear a decent resemblance to their former selves. Within the lifetime of our children Glen Canyon and the living river, heart of the canyonlands, will be restored to us. The wilderness will again belong to God, the people and the wild things that call it home. **(23)**

Vocabulary

Look up the meanings of the following words:

- concrete *aggregates* **(5)**
- *aesthetic* importance **(7)**
- recessed *alcoves* **(9)**
- *oligarchs* and politicians **(12)**
- the wheelchair *ethos* **(15)**
- richest in . . . *archaeology* **(16)**
- preplanned *itinerary* **(20)**
- a *drear* and hideous scene **(23)**

Questions for Writing and Discussion

1. Do you consider yourself an "environmentalist"—someone who is in favor of preserving wild rivers, designating wilderness areas, and forbidding mining, grazing, or the use of motorized vehicles in national parks? Or do you believe that federal lands, parks, and

rivers should serve multiple uses? Explain, using a state or national park you have visited to give specific examples.

2. Which of Abbey's arguments did you find most persuasive? Which were least persuasive? Are there opposing arguments that Abbey does not answer? Explain, *referring to your own beliefs* outlined above.

3. An argument contains a *claim, reasons* that support the claim or refute the opposition, and *evidence.*

   - What sentence or sentences best illustrate Abbey's overall claim or thesis for this essay? Does he make a claim of fact, value, cause, or solution—or some combination of these? Explain.
   - List the *reasons* Abbey gives to support his claim and refute the opposing arguments.
   - For *one* of his reasons, list the evidence, facts, examples, or testimony that Abbey gives.

4. Note passages in which Abbey's *appeal to character* is evident. Where is he most reasonable? Where is he most cantankerous or even misanthropic? Are these facets of his character consistent with the persona portrayed in paragraph 5? In your judgment, does his appeal to character help or hurt his argument? Explain.

5. Cite one sentence in which Abbey uses an *emotional appeal.* Does this sentence make his argument more effective?

6. Assume you are the controller of the Glen Canyon dam. Write a short response to Abbey explaining why his solution—to "open the diversion tunnels, and drain the reservoir"—is absurd. Choose either an adversarial or a Rogerian strategy, whichever would work best for Abbey.

ARGUING:
THE WRITING PROCESS

■ ASSIGNMENT FOR ARGUING   For this assignment, choose a subject that interests you or relates to your own experience. You may even choose a subject that you have already written about for this class. Then examine the subject for a debatable claim of fact, value, cause and effect, or policy that you could make about it. If the claim is arguable, you have a focus for your arguing paper. Analyze your probable audience to guide your argumentative strategy. (Avoid ready-made pro/con subjects such as abortion, drinking age, drugs, and euthanasia *unless* you have clear beliefs based on your own experience.)

CHOOSING A SUBJECT

If a journal entry suggested a possible subject, do the collecting-and-shaping strategies. Otherwise, consider the following ideas:

You can write about anything, and if you write well enough, even the reader with no intrinsic interest in the subject will become involved.

—TRACY KIDDER,

NOVELIST

- Review your journal entries from previous chapters and the papers that you have already written for this class. Test these subjects for an arguable claim that you could make, opposing arguments you could consider, and an appropriate audience for an argumentative piece of writing.
- Brainstorm possible ideas for argumentative subjects from the other courses you are currently taking or have taken. What controversial issues in psychology, art, philosophy, journalism, biology, nutrition, engineering, physical education, or literature have you discussed in your classes? Ask current or past instructors for possible controversial topics relating to their courses.
- Newspapers and magazines are full of controversial subjects in sports, medicine, law, business, and family. Browse through current issues looking for possible subjects. Check news items, editorials, and cartoons. Look for subjects related to your own interests, your job, your leisure activities, or your experiences.
- Interview your friends, family, or classmates. What controversial issues are affecting their lives most directly? What would they most like to change about their lives? What has irritated or angered them most in the recent past?

COLLECTING

NARROWING AND FOCUSING YOUR CLAIM   Narrow your subject to a specific topic and sharpen your focus by applying the "Wh" questions. If your subject is "grades," your responses might be as follows:

Subject: Grades
- *Who:* College students
- *What:* Letter grades
- *When:* In freshman and sophomore years
- *Where:* Especially in nonmajor courses
- *Why:* What purpose do grades serve in nonmajor courses?

Determine what claim or claims you want to make. Make sure that your claim is *arguable*. (Remember that claims can overlap; an argument may combine several related claims.)

Claim of Fact:
- Letter grades exist. (not arguable)
- Employers consider grades when hiring. (slightly more arguable, but not very controversial)
- Grades do not measure learning. (very arguable)

Claim about Cause or Effect:
- Grades create anxiety for students. (not very arguable)
- Grades actually prevent discovery and learning. (arguable)

Claim about Value:
- Grades are not fair. (not very arguable: "fairness" can usually be determined)
- Grades are bad because they discourage individual initiative. (arguable)
- Grades are good because they give students an incentive to learn. (arguable)

Claim about a Solution or Policy:
- Grades should be eliminated altogether. (arguable—but difficult)
- Grades should be eliminated in humanities courses. (arguable)
- Grades should change to pass/fail in nonmajor courses. (arguable—and more practical)

Focusing and narrowing your *claim* helps determine what evidence you need to collect. Use your observing, remembering, reading, and investigative skills to gather the evidence. *Note:* An argumentative essay should not be a mathematical equation that uses only abstract and impersonal evidence. *Your experience* can be crucial to a successful argumentative essay. Start by doing the *remembering* exercises. Your audience wants to know not only why you are writing on this particular *topic*, but also why the subject is of interest to *you*.

REMEMBERING Use *freewriting, looping, branching,* or *clustering* to recall experiences, ideas, events, and people who are relevant to your claim. If you are writing about grades, brainstorm about how *your* teachers used grades, how you reacted to specific grades in one specific class, how your friends or parents reacted, and what you felt or thought. These prewriting exercises will help you understand your claim and give you specific examples that you can use for evidence.

OBSERVING If possible for your topic, collect data and evidence by observing, firsthand, the facts, values, effects, or possible solutions related to your claim. *Repeated* observation will give you good inductive evidence to support your argument.

INVESTIGATING For most argumentative essays, some research or investigation is essential. Because it is difficult to imagine all the valid counterarguments, interview friends, classmates, family, coworkers, and authorities on your topic. From the library, gather books and articles that contain arguments in support of your claim. *Note:* As you do research in the library, make photocopies of key passages from relevant sources to hand in with your essay. If you cite sources from your research, list them on a "Work Cited" page following your essay. (See Chapter 12 for the proper format.)

SHAPING

No one can write decently who is distrustful of the reader's intelligence, or whose attitude is patronizing.

—E.B. WHITE,
ESSAYIST

As you begin your shaping activities, reconsider your audience. Imagine one real person who might be among your readers. Is this person open minded and likely to be convinced by your evidence? Does this person represent the opposing position? Would a Rogerian strategy be effective in this case? Reread your collecting notes and *underline* the reasons and evidence that would be most effective for this reader. After reconsidering your audience and rereading your collecting notes, try the shaping strategies that follow.

LIST OF "PRO" AND "CON" ARGUMENTS Either on paper or in a computer file, write out your *claim* and then list the arguments for your position ("Pro") and the arguments for the opposing positions ("Con"). After you have made the list, match up arguments by drawing lines, as indicated. (On the computer file, move "Con" arguments so they appear directly opposite the corresponding "Pro" arguments.)

Claim: Grades should be changed to pass/fail in nonmajor courses.

PRO	CON
Grades inhibit learning by putting too much emphasis on competition.	Grades actually promote learning by getting students to study as hard as possible.
Pass/fail grading encourages students to explore nonmajor fields.	Students should be encouraged to compete with majors. They may want to change majors and need to know if they can compete.
Grade competition with majors in the field can be discouraging.	
Some students do better without the pressure of grades; they need	If students don't have traditional grading, they won't

PRO	CON
to find out if they can motivate themselves without grades, but they shouldn't have to risk grades in their major field to discover that.	take nonmajor courses seriously.

If some pro and con arguments "match," you will be able to argue against the con and for your claim at the same time. If some arguments do not "match," you will need to consider them separately. The outlines below suggest ways of organizing your pro and con arguments.

OUTLINES FOR ARGUMENTS   For more than two thousand years, writers and speakers have been trying to determine the most effective means to persuade audiences. One of the oldest outlines for a successful argument comes from classical rhetoric. The following six-part outline is intended as a guideline rather than a rigid list. Test this outline; see if it will work for *your* argument.

Introduction:	Announces subject; *gets audience's interest and attention;* establishes a trustworthy character for the writer
Narration:	Gives *background,* context, statement of problem, or definition
Partition:	States thesis or *claim,* outlines or *maps* arguments
Argument:	Makes *arguments* and gives *evidence* for the claim or thesis
Refutation:	Shows why *opposing arguments* are not true or valid
Conclusion:	Summarizes arguments, suggests solution, *ties into the introduction or background*

Most arguments have these features, but not necessarily in this order. Some writers prefer to respond to or refute opposing arguments before giving the arguments in support of their claims. When con and pro arguments match, refuting an argument followed by the argument for your claim may work best. As you organize your own arguments, put your strongest argument last and your weakest argument either first or in the middle.

Because most short argumentative essays contain the introduction, narration, and partition all in a few introductory paragraphs, you may use the following abbreviated outlines for argument:

Outline #1	Introduction (attention getter, background, claim or thesis, map)
	Your arguments
	Refutation of opposing arguments
	Conclusion
Outline #2	Introduction
	Refutation of opposing arguments
	Your arguments

Outline #3
Conclusion
Introduction
Refutation of first opposing argument that matches your first argument
Refutation of second opposing argument that matches your second argument, and so on
Additional arguments
Conclusion

For Rogerian arguments, you can follow one of the above outlines, but the emphasis, tone, and attitude are different:

Introduction:	Attention getter, background
	Claim (often downplayed to reduce threat)
	Map (often omitted)
	Appeal to character (crucial to Rogerian argument)
Opposing Arguments:	State opposing arguments fairly
	Show where, how, or when those arguments may be valid; establish common ground
Your Arguments:	State your position fairly
	Show where, how, or when your arguments are valid
Resolution:	Present compromise position
	State your solution to the problem and show its advantages to both sides

DEVELOPING ARGUMENTS   Think of your argument as a series of *because* statements, each supported by evidence, statistics, testimony, expert opinion, data, specific examples from your experience, or a combination of these.

Thesis or Claim: Grades should be abolished in nonmajor courses

Reason #1	Because they may keep a student from attempting a difficult nonmajor course
	Statistics, testimony, data, and examples
Reason #2	Because competition with majors in the field can be discouraging
	Statistics, testimony, data, and examples
Reason #3	Because grades inhibit students learning in nonmajor fields
	Statistics, testimony, data, and examples

You can develop each reason using a variety of strategies. The following strategies may help you generate additional reasons and examples.

Definition:	Define the crucial terms or ideas. (What do you mean by "learning"?)
Comparison:	Compare the background, situation, context with another similar context. (What other schools have tried pass/fail grading for nonmajor courses? How has it worked?)

Process: How does or should a change occur? (How do nonmajors become discouraged? How should a school implement pass/fail in grading?)

These strategies may help you develop an argument coherently and effectively. If several strategies are possible, consider which would be most effective for your *audience*.

RESEARCH TIP

When you draft your arguing essay, don't let your citations or direct quotations overpower your own argument. Two tactics will keep you in control of your argument:

First, "sandwich" your quotations. *Introduce* quotations by referring to the author, the source, and/or the author's study. *Follow* quotations with a sentence or two explaining how the author's evidence supports your argument. For examples, see paragraphs 8 and 9 in the essay by student writer Jim Haas.

Second, keep your direct quotations *short*. If possible, reduce a long passage to one sentence and incorporate the quoted material in the flow of your own language. For example, in his essay at the end of the chapter, Haas writes,

> In fact, twenty-nine other countries have mandatory seat belt laws. "Where statistics are available," Transportation Secretary Dole says, "they show that highway deaths have declined by an average of 25 percent." **(34)**

DRAFTING You will never really know "enough" about your subject or have "enough" evidence. At some point, however, you must stop collecting and start your draft. The most frequent problem with drafting an argumentative essay is delaying the actual writing too long, until the deadline is too close.

For argumentative essays, start with a working order or sequence and sketch an outline on paper or in your head. Additional examples and appeals to reason, character, or emotion may occur to you as you develop your argument or refute opposing arguments. In addition, if you have done some research, have your notes, photocopies of key data, statistics, quotations, and citations of authorities close at hand. As you write, you will discover that some information or arguments simply don't fit into the flow of your essay. Don't force arguments into your draft if they no longer seem to belong.

REVISING

Argumentation is the most public of the purposes for writing. It requires that you become aware of many different points of view. You must counter the arguments of others and recognize the flaws in your own logic. Test your argument by having friends or classmates read it. Explain your claim, your focus, and your intended audience. Ask your readers to look for possible opposing arguments that you need to counter or weaknesses in your own argument or evidence. Were your appeals effective? Ask them if your argument should be more adversarial or more Rogerian.

PEER RESPONSE

Writer: Before you exchange drafts with a peer reader, provide the following information about your essay:

1. (a) intended audience
   (b) primary claim or thesis
   (c) opposing arguments that you refute
   (d) arguments supporting your claim

2. Write out one or two questions about your draft that you want your reader to answer.

Reader: Read the writer's entire draft. As you reread, answer the following questions:

1. *Arguments.* Without looking at the writer's responses above, describe the essay's (a) target audience, (b) primary claim, (c) opposing arguments that are refuted, (d) arguments supporting the claim. Which of these did you have trouble identifying? What additional pro or con arguments should the writer consider?

2. *Organization.* Identify the following parts of the writer's draft: introduction, narration, partition, argument, refutation, and conclusion. Does the writer need all of these for his or her particular subject and audience? Why or why not? Where could the writer clarify transitions between sections? Explain.

3. *Appeals.* Identify places where the writer appeals to reason, to character, and to emotion. Where could these appeals be stronger? Identify sentences where the writer is overly emotional or illogical (see the section on "Revising Fallacies in Logic").

4. *Evidence.* Identify at least one paragraph in which the supporting evidence is strong. Then identify at least one paragraph in

continued

which the writer makes assertions without sufficient supporting evidence. What kind of evidence might the writer use—first-hand observation, personal examples, testimony from experts, interviews, statistics, or other? Explain.

5. *Revision Plan.* List three key changes that the writer should make during the revision.

6. Answer the writer's questions.

Writer: When your essay is returned, read the comments by your peer reader(s) and do the following:

1. Compare your descriptions of the audience, claim, and pro and con arguments with your reader's descriptions. Where there are differences, clarify your essay.

2. Read all of your peer reader's responses. List revisions that you intend to make in each of the following areas: *arguments, organization, appeals,* and *supporting evidence.*

Guidelines for Revision

- **When you finish your draft, reconsider your** *audience.* Persuading your audience requires that you tailor your reasons and evidence to your audience and situation. Do an audience analysis, and then reread your draft and make appropriate changes.
- **Ask a class member or friend to read your draft to determine the intended audience for your argument.** See which arguments your reader thinks would not be effective for your audience.
- **Ask your reader to tell you what kind of** *claim* **you are making, whether your arguments or counterarguments are logical, and whether your ethical or emotional appeals are effective for your audience.**
- **Which of your** *because* **arguments are most effective?** Least effective? Should you change the outline or structure that you initially chose?
- **Revise your draft to avoid fallacies or errors in reasoning.** Errors in logic create two problems: They can destroy your rational appeal and open your argument to a logical rebuttal, and they lessen your credibility—and thus reduce your appeal to your character. (Review the list below.)
- **Support your reasons with evidence:** *data, facts, statistics, quotations, observations, testimony, statistics,* **or** *specific examples from your experience.* Check your collecting notes once again for additional evidence to add to your weakest argument. Is there a weak or unsupported argument that you should simply omit?
- **Signal the major arguments and counterarguments in your partition or map.** Between paragraphs, use clear transitions and paragraph hooks.

- **If you cite sources in your essay, check the *accuracy* of statistics, quotations, and source references.** (See Chapter 12 for the proper format of in-text documentation and "Works Cited" page.)
- **Revise sentences to improve conciseness and clarity.**
- **Edit sentences for grammar, punctuation, and spelling.**

Revising Fallacies in Logic

Listed below are common fallacies in logic. Reread your draft or your peer's draft and revise as appropriate to avoid these logical errors.

- *Hasty Generalization:* Conclusion not logically justified by sufficient or unbiased evidence. If your friend Mary tells you that Professor Paramecium is a hard grader because he gave her a 36 percent on the first biology test, she is making a hasty generalization. It may be *true*—Prof P. may *be* a difficult grader—but Mary's logic is not valid. She cannot logically draw that conclusion from a sample of one; the rest of the class may have received grades of between 80 and 100.

- *Post Hoc Ergo Propter Hoc:* Literally, "after this, therefore because of this." Just because event B *occurred after* event A, it does not mean that A *necessarily caused* B. You washed your car in the morning, and it rained in the afternoon. Though we joke about how it always rains after we wash the car, there is, of course, no causal relationship between the two events. "I forgot to leave the porch light on when I went out last night, and someone robbed my house." Without further evidence, we cannot assume that the lack of light contributed to the robbery. A more obvious cause might be the back door you left unlocked.

- *Genetic Fallacy:* Arguing that the origins of a person, object, or institution determine its character, nature, or worth. Like the "post hoc" fallacy, the genetic fallacy is an error in causal relationships.

> This automobile was made in Detroit. It'll probably fall apart after 10,000 miles.
>
> He speaks with a funny German accent. He's really stupid, you know.
>
> He started Celestial Seasonings Herb Teas just to make a quick buck; it's just another phony yuppie product.

The second half of each statement *may* or *may not* be true; the logical error is in assuming that the origin of something will necessarily determine its worth or quality. Stereotyping is frequently caused by a genetic fallacy.

- *Begging the Question:* Loading the conclusion in the claim. Arguing that "pornography should be banned because it corrupts our youth" is a logical claim. However, saying that "filthy and corrupting pornography should be banned" is begging the question: the conclusion that the writer should *prove* (that pornography corrupts) is assumed in the claim. Other examples: "Those useless psychology classes should be dropped from the curriculum"; "Senator Swingle's sexist behavior should be censured by Congress"; "Everyone knows that our ineffective drug control program is a miserable failure." The writers must *prove* that the psychology classes are useless, that Senator Swingle is sexist, and that the drug program is a failure.

- *Circular Argument:* A sentence or argument that restates rather than proves. Thus, it goes in a circle: "President Reagan was a great communicator because he had that knack of talking effectively to the people." The terms in the beginning of the sentence ("great communicator") and the end of the sentence ("talking effectively") are interchangeable. The sentence ends where it started.

- *Either/Or:* An oversimplification that reduces alternatives to only two choices, thereby creating a false dilemma. Statements such as "love it or leave it" attempt to reduce the alternatives to two. If you don't love your school, your town, or your country, you don't have to leave: A third choice is to change it and make it better. Proposed solutions frequently have an "either/or" fallacy: "Either we ban boxing or hundreds of young men will be senselessly killed." A third alternative is to change boxing's rules or equipment. "If we don't provide farmers with low-interest loans, they will go bankrupt." Increasing prices for farm products might be a better alternative.

- *Faulty Comparison or Analogy:* Basing an argument on a comparison of two things, ideas, events, or situations that are similar but not identical. Although comparisons or analogies are often effective in argument, they can hide logical problems. "We can solve the cocaine problem the same way we reduced the DWI problem: Attack it with increased enforcement and mandatory jail sentences." Although the situations are similar, they are not identical. The DWI solution will not necessarily work on drugs. An analogy is an extended comparison that uses something simple or familiar to explain something complex or less familiar. "Solving a mathematics problem is like baking a cake: You have to take it one step at a time. First you assemble your ingredients or your known data. . . ." Like baking, solving a problem does involve a process; unlike baking, however, mathematics is more exact. Changing the amount of flour in a recipe by 1 percent will not make the cake fall; changing a numeric value by 1 percent, however, may ruin the whole problem. The point, however, is not to avoid comparisons or analogies. Simply make sure that your conclusions are qualified; acknowledge the *differences* between the two things compared as well as the similarities.

- *Ad Hominem (literally, "to the man"):* An attack on the character of the individual or the opponent rather than his or her actual opinions, arguments, or qualifications. "Susan Davidson, the prosecuting attorney, drinks heavily. There's no way she can present an effective case."

This is an attack on Ms. Davidson's character rather than an analysis of her legal talents. Her record in court may be excellent.

- *Ad Populum (literally, "to the people"):* An emotional appeal to positive concepts (God, mother, country, liberty, democracy, apple pie) or negative concepts (fascism, atheism) rather than a direct discussion of the real issue: "Those senators voting to increase the defense budget are really warmongers at heart." "If you are a true American, you should be for tariffs to protect the garment industry."

- *Red Herring and Straw Man:* Diversionary tactics designed to avoid confronting the key issue. *Red herring* refers to the practice of dragging a smelly fish across the trail to divert tracking dogs away from the real quarry. A "red herring" occurs when writers avoid countering an opposing argument directly: "Of course equal pay for women is an important issue, but I wonder whether women really want to take the responsibility that comes with higher-paying jobs? Do they really want the additional stress?" This writer diverts attention away from the argument about equal pay to another issue, stress—thus, a "red herring." In the *straw man* diversion, the writer sets up an artificially easy argument to refute in place of the real issue. Former President Richard Nixon's famous "Checkers" speech is a good example. Accused of spending $18,000 in campaign gifts for personal use, Nixon described how he received Checkers, a little black-and-white spotted cocker spaniel dog. Because his daughter Tricia loved this dog, Nixon decided to keep it. Surely, there's nothing wrong with that, is there? The "Checkers" argument is a "straw man" diversion: justifying his personal use of this gift is much easier than explaining how and why he spent the $18,000. Avoid "red herring" and "straw man" tactics by either refuting an argument directly or acknowledging that it has some merit. Don't just change the subject.

■ **POSTSCRIPT ON THE WRITING PROCESS** In your journal, answer the following questions.

1. Describe how your beliefs about your subject changed from the time you decided on your claim until you revised your essay. What caused the change in your views?

2. What opposing argument was most difficult to counter? Explain how you handled it.

3. Which was your strongest argument? Did you use logical appeals and evidence, or did you rely more on appeals to character or emotion? Explain.

4. How did your writing process for the argumentative essay change from previous essays? What steps or stages took longer? What stages did you have to go back and rework?

ARGUING:

STUDENT WRITING

PROTECT YOURSELF—
BUCKLE UP!

Jim Haas

Jim Haas decided to write his arguing paper about seat-belt laws, primarily because he had been in several accidents and had failed to fasten his own seat belt. He began collecting for this paper by writing a narrative of his own experience. Then, once he realized that he had a good subject, he read some articles in the library and clipped some stories from his hometown newspaper. Reproduced below are the narrative from his remembering exercise, a list of pro and con arguments, and the final draft.

REMEMBERING EXERCISE

Nick, Milo, D.J. and I were on our way back from a bar in Mondamin, Iowa, where we had spent the previous six hours drinking brandy and beer. We were all riding in the cab of Nick's pickup and we were almost to Nick's house where our girlfriends were making dinner. Nick turned off the road and drove down by the irrigation canal adjacent to his farm. He thought it would be fun to turn off his lights and drive around in the darkness. We were driving in the blackness when we told him to turn his lights back on and he did so just in time for us to see the ground go out from underneath us. We had just driven off a twenty-five foot cliff. We hit nose first, then flipped over the top. We all escaped serious injury. Milo and D.J. were not injured at all, Nick had to have his thumb sewn back on because the roof smashed down on the steering wheel where he was holding on, and I hit the dashboard and the roof with my face and forehead. I had two black eyes and had to eat soup for the next week because I ripped apart the inside of my mouth. I have been in two other automobile accidents and in all of them, the vehicle I was riding in was totalled, but I escaped serious injury. I consider myself lucky, because many people have died in lesser accidents. I was not wearing a seat belt when any of the accidents occurred. I think if I had been wearing a seat belt, I might have been saved the pain of injury and the bother of filling out insurance forms.

LIST OF PRO AND CON ARGUMENT

Claim: A mandatory seat belt law would save lives.

Pro	Con
Saves lives	Restricts freedom
Cut down on medical bills	Opens door for other laws which may restrict freedom
Will reduce insurance costs	
Saves money – will prevent manufacturers from using airbags, which will raise cost of automobiles	Cannot be fairly enforced
	Costs money for inspecting seat belts to make sure they are working
Reduce taxes spent on government subsidized medical care	Seat belts will trap people in burning vehicles
	People can avoid injury by bracing themselves before a crash

---

REVISED VERSION

PROTECT YOURSELF—BUCKLE UP!

Two men were killed early Sunday morning in separate car accidents in El Paso County. Steven D. Carmichael, 29, of Palmer Lake was pronounced dead at 12:45 a.m. Sunday after a pickup he was driving went off the road. Carmichael, who was alone in the truck, was not wearing a seat belt. In the second accident . . . Joseph David Vasquez, 21, of 22105 Farmer Road, died of massive head and chest injuries after he was thrown from a pickup truck just east of Enoch Road. . . . Vasquez wasn't wearing a seat belt. (Hill 3)

All too often, unfortunately, articles like this one appear in newspapers across the country. Even more unfortunate is the fact that many of these traffic-related deaths could be prevented if more people in the United States would use their seat belts. This has prompted fourteen states, so far, to pass mandatory seat belt laws, requiring all persons in automobiles to use safety belts, or risk paying fines if they're caught not using them (Sundstrom 16). Mandatory seat belt laws are opposed in some states, but the law is a good idea to immediately reduce deaths on our highways and cut the social costs that accompany them. **(1)**

U. S. Secretary of Transportation, Elizabeth Dole, states that "every year more than 40,000 persons are killed in auto accidents on our highways. . . . Car crashes are the leading cause of death of people up to [age] 34. For teenagers, car crash fatalities outnumber the next five causes of death combined" (33). These are sobering statistics, yet 85% of Americans still don't use the single most preventative measure to insure their survival in a car crash: seat belts (Horton 22). **(2)**

Seat belts save lives. The Highway Users Federation says that because 15% of Americans use seat belts, 1,800 lives are saved each year. They estimate that if 25% of all Americans used seat belts, 3,000 lives would be saved, and if 85% of Americans used seat belts, 9,600 human lives would be spared on our nation's highways each year (145). Philip Caldwell, Chairman of the Board at Ford Motor Company, explains: "Statistics show that in a typical auto accident, occupants restrained by standard safety belts have at least a 50% better chance of avoiding death or serious injury than those who are unrestrained" (38). **(3)**

Many opponents of seat belt usage believe it is safer to be thrown from a car than to be trapped in it, but according to Virginia Tech behavioral psychologist E. Scott Geller, who has been studying the use of seat belts for over six years, "being thrown from a car is twenty-five times more lethal than being 'trapped.' The exceptions are widely publicized, and that perpetuates the myth" (Horton 22). A friend of mine who works on an ambulance and who has helped many victims of automobile crashes reminded me of the value of seat belts when he said that he had never unbuckled a dead body from a seat belt. **(4)**

Other opponents are afraid that their car will end up underwater or on fire, and that they won't be able to escape. Actually the reverse is true. B. J. Campbell, director of Highway Safety Research Center at the University of North Carolina, tells us, "If you're wearing a [safety] belt, you've got a better chance of being conscious and not having your legs broken—distinct advantages in getting out of a dangerous situation" (Horton 22). **(5)**

Another myth about auto accidents is addressed by Roslyn Kaiser of the National Highway Traffic Safety Administration (NHTSA). She points out that most people don't understand the dynamics of crashes: "They think they can save themselves by bracing with their arms. But a ten-mile-an-hour collision is equivalent to catching a two-hundred-pound bag of cement dropped from a second-story window" (Horton 22). I can attest to that. I've been in three automobile accidents in my lifetime, and all three were potentially life-threatening, but two of them really proved Kaiser's point. The first accident happened when a pickup truck I was riding in went over a twenty-five foot cliff. I was not wearing a seat belt, but I had braced myself against the seat by placing my hands against the dashboard. The moment before we hit (we hit front-end first, then flipped over), I had my arms locked straight against the dashboard, but when we hit, I don't remember my arms giving way. I don't even remember hitting the dashboard because it happened so quickly, but I did hit it, receiving two black eyes and two gashes inside my mouth. **(6)**

My second accident also illustrated how helpless people are in an accident. I was a passenger in a 12-ton mobile drilling rig that rolled over while going about 50 miles per hour. I wasn't wearing a seat belt, and as the rig rolled over one and one-half times, I was thrown around like a rag doll. I received only minor injuries and was absent from work for only one week, but that accident impressed upon me how little control I had on the outcome of my life in such accidents. I definitely agree with Roger B. Smith, Chairman of General Motors, when he says, "The one sure way to achieve an immediate and dramatic reduction in accident injuries and fatalities is to get significantly more people to use the belt systems that are already in their cars" (35). **(7)**

If one proves that seat belt usage saves lives, the next step is to find out how to increase their use. I think the mandatory seat belt law is the answer. The United States is not the first country to implement such a law. In fact, twenty-nine other countries have mandatory seat belt laws. "Where statistics are available," Transportation Secretary Dole says, "they show that highway deaths have declined by an average of 25 percent" (34). Lee Iacocca of Chrysler agrees:

> In France, the automobile accident death rate has dropped 25 percent after their belt law was passed. In Australia, nearly 90 percent of the people are buckling up. Right across the river from Detroit, the Province of Ontario has enjoyed similar success. Not one nation, state or territory has repealed a belt use law once they've adopted it—because the laws work. (36)

Passing any kind of law is difficult, but the declining death rates indicate that the benefits from a mandatory seat belt law will be worth the effort. **(8)**

Some people are against mandatory seat belt laws because they believe passive restraints and automatic seat belts would be more effective. Those people need to realize that passive restraints, alone, are not as effective. Anyone who does not want seat belts would just disconnect the automatic seat belt, and they would be left with very little protection. In addition, air bags are effective only in front-end collisions. Writing in the National Safety News, Philip Caldwell says that "the air bag offers [only] supplemental protection. . . . The air bag offers added protection in frontal collisions at speeds greater than 12 to 15 miles per hour, but it does not provide protection, as safety belts do, in other kinds of accidents—like secondary collisions (after air bag deployment) and rollovers, or rear-end or side-impact collisions" (74). Dole, Iacocca, and Smith agree with Caldwell that safety belts are still the single most effective safety feature in the automotive industry, and they should not be substituted for, but supplemented with, air bags and other passive restraints. **(9)**

The most serious argument against the mandatory seat belt law is that it infringes on an individual's freedom to choose whether or not he or she wishes to use the safety belt. People who take this position believe seat belt use should be a private, personal choice, since it affects only the person who wears it. I once agreed with this view until I discovered that my choice affects all people in society. As Iacocca explains, "People who get injured because they don't use belts raise our taxes, increase our medical and hospitalization insurance, clog our courts, soak up social services for accident victims and survivors, and cause grief for friends and family. So the people who don't use belts because it hampers their freedom are already intruding on our freedom" (74). **(10)**

Of course wearing seat belts would not eliminate these effects, but it would reduce them. A Michigan state legislator notes, "It is estimated that each traffic fatality costs the state and family about $333,000. Injuries and lost wages, caused by the nonuse of belts, cost society $2,500 per accident" (Goodman 12). There is overwhelming evidence that the nonuse of safety belts has a significant effect on most people in society who have to give up part of their earned wage to pay for other people's failure to protect themselves. **(11)**

I think the heavy monetary cost that has to be absorbed by society as a result of death and injuries caused by the nonuse of seat belts, the loss of life itself, and the evidence that mandatory seat belt laws do reduce automobile fatalities are arguments that far outweigh any of the opposing arguments. Perhaps if our state had a seat belt law, I might have worn one and avoided the hospital costs and the days missed from work. More importantly, if Steven Carmichael and Joseph Vasquez had been required by law to wear seat belts, they might be alive today. Let's work together in an effort to reduce these tragic deaths on our nation's highways. Support the mandatory seat belt law, and in the meantime, protect your loved ones and protect yourself. Buckle up. **(12)**

Works Cited

Caldwell, Philip. "A Rational Approach to Car-Occupant Protection." *National Safety News* Feb. 1985: 38, 74–75.

Goodman, Walter. "Fair Game—Reflections on Forced Buckling." *New Leader* 26 Nov. 1985: 12.

Highway Users Federation. "Buckle Up." *Reader's Digest* Dec. 1985: 145.

Hill, David. "Two Men Killed in Separate Accidents." *Colorado Springs Sun* 9 Dec. 1985: 3.

Horton, Elizabeth. "Why Don't We Buckle Up?" *Science Digest* Feb. 1985: 22.

Iacocca, Lee A. "Grass-Roots Pressure Can Make Restraints Mandatory." *National Safety News* Feb. 1985: 36, 74.

Smith, Roger B. "Built-in Protection Complements Passenger Restraints." *National Safety News* Feb. 1985: 35, 74.

Sundstrom, Geoff. "40 Percent Now Covered by Belt Laws." *Automotive News* 5 Aug. 1985: 16.

Questions for Writing and Discussion

1. Does Haas make a claim of fact, value, cause and effect, policy, or some combination? Explain.

2. Were you convinced when you finished this essay? What evidence convinced you most? The personal experience? The statistics? The quotations from authorities? Explain.

3. Compare the version of Haas's personal experience in the remembering exercise with the account in the final version. What specific details were omitted in the final version? Would you recommend including them, leaving the final version the way it is, or condensing it even more? Explain.

4. Read the list of pro and con arguments. Which arguments were omitted from the essay? Were any added that were not on that original list? If you were writing the essay, which points would you include?

Games the Military Play

David Thomas

Should the U. S. military be permitted to control or censor news stories related to combat operations? David Thomas, a student majoring in business at Southeast Missouri State University, addresses a question with legitimate claims on both sides. The military believes that the security of war operations and the safety of individual soldiers requires some censorship of the news media. Private citizens, however, may argue that censorship violates their First Amendment rights and conceals vital information about the goals and conduct of a war. Citing examples from World War I to the Persian Gulf War, Thomas argues that censorship should not be tol-

erated—especially during times of war. As you read his essay, notice how Thomas counters opposing arguments. Are you persuaded by his reasons and examples?

The young lieutenant lay on a hospital bed, his face flushed with fever. Reporter Marguerite Higgens of the *New York Herald Tribune* leaned closer to hear, careful not to touch the bandages covering his shattered arm. The soldier looked up at her and asked, "Are you correspondents telling people back home the truth? Are you telling them that out of one platoon of twenty men we have three left? Are you telling them that we have nothing to fight with, and that this is an utterly useless war?" (Lubow 24). **(1)**

Yes, they did tell the people back home, at least until General Douglas MacArthur imposed formal censorship on all material concerning the Korean War. Do you remember reading or hearing a soldier making negative comments like that during the recent Persian Gulf War? In fact, can you remember hearing, reading, or seeing anything negative? Perhaps this is because the Pentagon imposed the strictest set of guidelines to control the media since the Revolutionary War. Citing "military security" or "compromising operations," the military infringed on our right to know during the Gulf War. In reality, protecting the image of the military and controlling public opinion are the real reasons our government tramples on our First Amendment rights. Censorship should not be tolerated in a democracy under any circumstances, least of all in times of war. **(2)**

Throughout our history, censorship in various forms has been used in times of war. In 1798, only seven years after passing the First Amendment guaranteeing our freedom of speech, Congress passed the Alien and Sedition Acts. These acts made it possible for people to be fined and jailed for speaking or writing against the government (Zinn 15). This was followed in 1917 with the passing of the Espionage Act. The government used this act to prosecute anyone who criticized the U.S. involvement in WW I (Zinn 17). Under the direction of the Office of Censorship and the Office of War Information, censorship was widely imposed during WW II (Lubow 24). During the Korean Conflict, censorship was imposed but not strictly enforced. In Vietnam, there was no formal declaration of war, therefore, censorship could not be enforced (Lubow 25). The startling footage of causalities, which contradicted the propaganda the government was feeding the public, finally began to erode public support for the Vietnam War. The myth that the press cost the United States victory in Vietnam is precisely why the military drafted a new set of rules concerning censorship, starting with Grenada in 1983. Very few members of the press were allowed on the island, and no reporters were allowed at the scene of battle. According to the belief that censorship worked so well, it was formally adopted in Panama, where the U.S. public has only a dim memory of what happened

(Galloway 49). In the Gulf War, censorship received an official name: Operation Annex Foxtrot. Its unstated purpose was to control the information and public opinion concerning the Gulf War. **(3)**

Officially, the reasons for censorship of news from the Gulf War were that operations, troop movements, and battle plans could be accidentally betrayed. While this is a valid concern, it is not justified. All members of the media are willing to hold back information that might jeopardize security. According to David Broder of the *The Washington Post,* members of the media found out about General Schwarzkopf's deceptive flanking maneuver in the Persian Gulf Sea and did not release the information until after the enemy had realized it (A2). As Henry Kissinger admitted after the Vietnam Conflict, the only stories released during Vietnam that had the potential to be security risks were leaked from the State Department in Washington D.C. In fact, out of hundreds of correspondents who wrote thousands of stories during Vietnam, only two reporters had their privileges revoked (Schanberg 23). **(4)**

Another reason frequently cited was that large numbers of reporters roaming around the desert would be dangerous because they could be captured and held as hostages. In fact, censorship was the reason many journalists ventured out on their own. Perhaps if they could have gotten all the information they needed, they would have stayed under the protection of the troops. One example of this is when Bob Simon, reporter for CBS News, frustrated by the censorship, struck out on his own and was captured by the Iraqis (Browne 45). **(5)**

A third reason the Pentagon decided to censor war news was the theory held by many people, including Saddam Hussein, that a prolonged war with heavy casualties would erode public support for the war (Schanberg 23). This may be true, but isn't that precisely why we need to know what is happening? Perhaps there is a good reason why a long war with heavy casualties would not be popular. Perhaps the people know how many soldiers are worth sacrificing to protect another country. How would we feel if the Gulf War were still going on today? And what if our death toll had reached two thousand? **(6)**

This is precisely why we should not have censorship. The public has a right to know. The Gulf War could easily have become another Vietnam, with a tremendous cost in human life. Fifty years ago there was another government that had complete censorship. The leader filled his people with propaganda and told them the war was a "just" war. After the war, many citizens of his country claimed they were kept in the dark and didn't know of the horrors he had committed. His name was Adolph Hitler. **(7)**

Keeping war news from the public will eventually raise suspicion from the public. At first, the public will accept token bits of information, but soon they will be asking, "What is the government hiding?" As Walter Cronkite said, "Hiding information will eventually lead to a breakdown in home-front confidence, just like Vietnam, which is precisely what the Pentagon fears the most" (43). The massive propaganda campaign the Johnson administration used during the Vietnam campaign conflicted with the truth. Eventually, the public realized this, and it wasn't long before public protests started. This loss of trust is what eventually undermined the war effort and ended the Johnson administration at the same time. **(8)**

The Gulf War has been over for several years now. According to our government it was an unequaled victory for the United States. Or was it? Thanks to military censorship we do not have enough information to give an intelligent answer. For example, we have no idea how many innocent Iraqi lives were lost. One hundred, a thousand, ten thousand? Censorship has not only denied us the right to decide if this was a "just" war, it also prevents us from using it as a guideline to decide whether or not to involve ourselves in the defense of another country. **(9)**

Our huge budget deficit is threatening the very economic security of our nation. One way to help the deficit is to cut unnecessary military spending. There is good reason to believe that the military consistently misleads us about the need of certain weapons systems. One specific example is the B-2 bomber. There has always been controversy about whether we actually need this plane. Of course, the military insists it is vital for our defense to maintain production, and they took measures in the Gulf War to protect its role as our primary bomber. One such measure is illustrated in a story by Malcolm W. Browne, a reporter for *The New York Times Magazine*. He filed a story about an air-raid attack on Baghdad, describing the F117-A as a fighter-bomber. Indeed, it had carried a heavy payload of bombs in the air attack. His story was censored, however, changing "fighter-bomber" to just "fighter." Apparently, the military is concerned that the public will wonder why we need the B-2 bomber if the F117-A can do the job (29). **(10)**

Military censorship has many forms. It could be outright censorship of a story, propaganda about our reasons for being in a war, misinformation about results of battles, or attempts to control public opinion by manipulating the media, which is illustrated in a story by Jason De Parle in the May 4 edition of *The New York Times*. During the buildup of troops in the Gulf War, correspondents from many large papers and magazines were denied access to the troops. However, reporters from small-town newspapers were not only allowed access, the military—in a program called Hometown News Program—provided free transportation and any equipment they might need to spend four days with troops from their hometowns. Why were those reporters allowed and not others? As the administrator of the program, Lieutenant Colonel Michael Cox of the Air Force admitted, "If they know they are getting a free ride, and they can't afford the $2,000 ticket, there is going to be a tendency to be sympathetic to our side" (A20). **(11)**

Whatever the disguise, censorship must not be allowed to interfere with our right to know. In the future, it is our duty to demand full disclosure about any military operations. After all, we are free people, governed by free people, and protected by an army of free people. And isn't that what the Gulf War was about, trying to keep the people of Kuwait free? **(12)**

Works Cited

Broder, David S. "The War Story," *The Washington Post* 11 Feb. 1991: A2.

Browne, Malcolm. "The Military vs. the Press." *The New York Times Magazine* 3 March 1991: 26–30, 44–45.

Cronkite, Walter. "What is There to Hide?" *Newsweek* 25 Feb. 1991: 43.

De Parle, Jason. "Long Series of Military Decisions Led to Gulf War News Censorship." *The New York Times* 4 May 1991: A1, A20.

Galloway, Joseph. "Who's Afraid of the Truth?" *U.S. News and World Report* 4 Feb. 1991: 49.

Lubow, Arthur. "Read Some About It: A Short History of Wartime Censorship." *New Republic* 18 March 1991: 23–25.

Schanberg, Sydney. "Censoring for Political Security." *Washington Journalism Review* March 1991: 23–25.

Zinn, Howard. "Second Thoughts on the First Amendment." *The Humanist* Nov.–Dec. 1991: 15–24, 42.

QUESTIONS FOR WRITING AND DISCUSSION

1. Assume that you were a soldier in the Persian Gulf War who believes that his or her safety would have been compromised by unlimited media coverage. Write a letter of response to Thomas. Explain when and how the military should restrict the media's access to news.

2. The "Shaping" section of this chapter identifies the six parts of a classical argument: introduction, narration, partition, argument, refutation, and conclusion. Identify by paragraph numbers the points at which Thomas uses each of these parts of a classical argument. Where does he alter the order? Should he reorganize his essay to follow the order indicated above? Explain why or why not.

3. Imitating the "pro" and "con" shaping strategy on page 450–451, make a list of the pro and con arguments that Thomas uses in his essay. (The pro arguments will be arguments in favor of eliminating military censorship; the con arguments are those supporting military censorship.) Which opposing arguments does he refute?

What additional arguments does he give in favor of complete freedom of the press?

4. List one piece of *evidence* that Thomas gives to support each of the following claims. (1) There was censorship during the Gulf War (claim of fact). (2) Censorship by the military is not good (claim of value). (3) Censorship may increase our budget deficit (claim of cause and effect). (4) Citizens should demand full disclosure about any military operations (claim of policy). Which claims and pieces of evidence were most persuasive? Where does Thomas need additional evidence?

5. One reader of this essay has charged that Thomas uses emotional appeals too strongly when he refers to the bandages covering the soldier's "shattered arm" in paragraph 1, when he uses loaded language in paragraph 3, and when he cites Adolph Hitler in paragraph 7. Assume that you are helping Thomas revise his essay. Should Thomas change these passages? Write a note explaining specifically how and why each passage should (or should not) be changed.

6. In a letter to Thomas Jefferson in 1798, James Madison wrote: "Perhaps it is a universal truth that the loss of liberty at home is to be charged to provisions against danger real or pretended from abroad." Explain what Madison meant and how this statement relates to Thomas's essay.

11 RESPONDING TO LITERATURE

Berthe Morisot, French 1841–1895, *La Lecture (Reading)*, 1888. Oil on canvas 29.25 x 36.5. Museum of Fine Arts, St. Petersburg, Florida. Given in memory of Margaret Acheson Stuart by family and friends.

I N A FILM CLASS, YOU WATCH ROMAN POLANSKI'S *TESS*, AN ADAPTATION OF THOMAS HARDY'S NOVEL *TESS OF THE D'URBERVILLES*. YOU DECIDE TO COMPARE THE FILM WITH the novel, focusing on four key episodes: the "strawberry scene," in which Tess meets Alec; the rape scene at night; the harvesting scene; and the final scene at Stonehenge. On the basis of your comparison, you argue that Polanski's interpretation (and the acting of Nastassia Kinski) retains Hardy's view of Tess as a victim of social and sexist repression.

❧

I N AN INTRODUCTION TO LITERATURE CLASS, YOU AND A FRIEND ARE ASSIGNED TO WORK COLLABORATIVELY ON AN ESSAY ABOUT EUDORA WELTY'S "A WORN PATH." YOU ARE both interested in how Phoenix Jackson's journey contains images of the phoenix: a mythological bird said to live for five hundred years, after which it burns itself to death and then rises from its ashes to become youthful and beautiful again. You draft your essays separately and then read each other's drafts. At that point, you collaborate on a single essay, combining the best ideas and evidence from your separate drafts. Your collaborative essay shows how Phoenix Jackson is characterized by birdlike images, how she calmly faces images of fire and death on her journey, and how her grandson represents her rebirth.

I hungered for new books, new ways of looking and seeing. It was not a matter of believing or disbelieving what I read, but of feeling something new, of being affected by something that made the look of the world different.
—RICHARD WRIGHT,
AUTHOR OF BLACK BOY

❧

No one else can read a literary work for us. The benefits of literature can emerge only from creative activity on the part of the reader.
—LOUISE ROSENBLATT,
AUTHOR OF LITERATURE AS EXPLORATION

RESPONDING TO LITERATURE REQUIRES THAT READERS PARTICIPATE IMAGINATIVELY WHILE THEY READ A LITERARY WORK, REREAD TO SEE HOW THE PARTS OF THE WORK relate to the whole, and share their interpretations of a piece of literature with other readers.

First, readers must *imagine* and recreate that special world described by the writer. The first sentences of a short story, for example, throw open a door to a world that—attractive or repulsive—tempts our curiosity and imagination. Like Alice in *Alice in Wonderland,* we cannot resist following a white rabbit with pink eyes who mutters to himself, checks his watch, and then zips down a rabbit hole and into an imaginary world.

Here are three opening sentences to three very different short stories:

> Young Goodman Brown came forth at sunset into the street at Salem village; but put his head back, after crossing the threshold, to exchange a parting kiss with his young wife.
>
> —Nathaniel Hawthorne, "Young Goodman Brown"

> As Gregor Samsa awoke one morning from uneasy dreams he found himself transformed in his bed into a gigantic insect.
>
> —Franz Kafka, "The Metamorphosis"

> The morning of June 27th was clear and sunny, with the fresh warmth of a full-summer day; the flowers were blossoming profusely and the grass was green.
>
> —Shirley Jackson, "The Lottery"

Whether our imaginations construct the disturbing image of a "gigantic insect" or the seemingly peaceful picture of a perfect summer day, we actively create each story. Responding to literature does not mean passively reacting to the writer's story. As readers, we should anticipate, imagine, feel, worry, and question. A story is like an empty balloon that we must inflate with the warm breath of our imagination and experience. Our participation makes us partners with the author in the artistic creation.

Responding to literature also requires that readers *reread*. If we read a story or a poem only once, we have misunderstood the whole point of literature. Great literature is worthy of study because the more we reread, the more we learn and discover. If we assume that the purpose of a story is merely to entertain us or to provide a moment's diversion, then we should stick to television sitcoms written for an audience of couch potatoes who want only predictable, unimaginative plots and canned studio laughter.

Rereading requires two distinct but related operations. First, you should *reread for yourself*—that is, reread to write down your ideas, questions, feelings, and reactions. To heighten your role in creating a story, you should note, in the margins, your questions and responses to important events, main characters, bits of description, and images that catch your attention: "What about the names Hawthorne uses? Is Young Goodman Brown really good? Is his wife, Faith, really faithful?" "I don't understand why Kafka's narrator thinks he is a gigantic insect. Is this happening, or is he dreaming?" "Why does Shirley Jackson's lottery happen on such a beautiful summer day?" Don't just underline or highlight passages. Actually *write* your responses in the margin.

Second, you should *reread with a writer's eye*. In fiction, identify the main and minor characters. Look for and note the conflicts between characters. Mark passages that contain *foreshadowing*—that urge you to think ahead imaginatively. Pinpoint sentences that reveal the narrative point of view. Use the appropriate critical terms (*character, plot, conflict, point of view, setting, style,* and *theme*) to help you reread with a writer's eye and to see how the parts of a story relate to the whole. Each critical term is a tool—a magnifying glass that helps you understand and interpret the story more clearly.

In addition to rereading, responding to literature requires that readers *share* ideas, reactions, and interpretations. Sharing usually begins in small-group or class discussions, but it continues as you explain your interpretation in writing. A work of literature is not a mathematical equation with a single answer. Great literature is worth interpreting precisely because each reader responds differently. The purpose of literature is to encourage you to reflect on your life and the lives of others—to look for new ways of seeing and understanding your world—and ultimately to expand your world. Sharing is crucial to appreciating literature.

> Hawthorne doesn't come right out and say that people become disillusioned by experiencing evil. He shows how it actually happens in the life of young Goodman Brown.

> Shirley Jackson's "The Lottery" helps me see that the notion of human sacrifice and the idea of the human scapegoat still exist in our culture today.

Writing about your responses and sharing them with other readers helps you "reread" your own ideas in order to explain them fully and clearly to other readers.

■ RESPONDING TO A SHORT STORY   Read and respond to Kate Chopin's "The Story of an Hour." Use your imagination to help create the story as you read. Then *reread* the story, noting in the margin your questions and responses. When you finish rereading and annotating your reactions, write your interpretation of the last line of the story.

THE STORY OF AN HOUR

Kate Chopin

Kate O'Flaherty Chopin (1851–1904) was an American writer whose mother was French and Creole and whose father was Irish. In 1870, she moved from St. Louis to New Orleans with her husband, Oscar Chopin, and over the next ten years she gave birth to five sons. After her husband died in 1882, Chopin returned to St. Louis to begin a new life as a writer. Many of her best stories are about Louisiana people and places, and her most famous novel, The Awakening, *tells the story of Edna, a woman who leaves her marriage and her children to fulfill herself through an artistic career.*

Knowing that Mrs. Mallard was afflicted with a heart trouble, great care was taken to break to her as gently as possible the news of her husband's death. **(1)**

It was her sister Josephine who told her, in broken sentences, veiled hints that revealed in half concealing. Her husband's friend Richards was there, too, near her. It was he who had been in the newspaper office when intelligence of the railroad disaster was received, with Brently Mallard's name leading the list of "killed." He had only taken the time to assure himself of its truth by a second telegram, and had hastened to forestall any less careful, less tender friend in bearing the sad message. **(2)**

She did not hear the story as many women have heard the same, with a paralyzed inability to accept its significance. She wept at once, with sudden, wild abandonment, in her sister's arms. When the storm of grief had spent itself she went away to her room alone. She would have no one follow her. **(3)**

There stood, facing the open window, a comfortable, roomy armchair. Into this she sank, pressed down by a physical exhaustion that haunted her body and seemed to reach into her soul. **(4)**

She could see in the open square before her house the tops of trees that were all aquiver with the new spring life. The delicious breath of rain was in the air. In the street below a peddler was crying his wares. The notes of a distant song which someone was singing reached her faintly, and countless sparrows were twittering in the eaves. **(5)**

There were patches of blue sky showing here and there through the clouds that had met and piled above the other in the west facing her window. **(6)**

She sat with her head thrown back upon the cushion of the chair quite motionless, except when a sob came up into her throat and shook her, as a child who has cried itself to sleep continues to sob in its dreams. **(7)**

She was young, with a fair, calm face, whose lines bespoke repression and even a certain strength. But now there was a dull stare in her eyes, whose gaze was fixed away off yonder on one of those patches of blue sky. It was not a glance of reflection, but rather indicated a suspension of intelligent thought. **(8)**

There was something coming to her and she was waiting for it, fearfully. What was it? She did not know; it was too subtle and elusive to name. But she felt it, creeping out of the sky, reaching toward her through the sounds, the scents, the color that filled the air. **(9)**

Now her bosom rose and fell tumultuously. She was beginning to recognize this thing that was approaching to possess her, and she was striving to beat it back with her will—as powerless as her two white slender hands would have been. **(10)**

When she abandoned herself a little whispered word escaped her slightly parted lips. She said it over and over under her breath: "Free, free, free!" The vacant stare and the look of terror that had followed it went from her eyes. They stayed keen and bright. Her pulses beat fast, and the coursing blood warmed and relaxed every inch of her body. **(11)**

She did not stop to ask if it were not a monstrous joy that held her. A clear and exalted perception enabled her to dismiss the suggestion as trivial. **(12)**

She knew that she would weep again when she saw the kind, tender hands folded in death; the face that had never looked save with love upon her, fixed and gray and dead. But she saw beyond that bitter moment a long procession of years to come that would belong to her absolutely. And she opened and spread her arms out to them in welcome. **(13)**

There would be no one to live for during those coming years; she would live for herself. There would be no powerful will bending her in that blind persistence with which men and women believe they have a right to impose a private will upon a fellow creature. A kind intention or a cruel intention made the act seem no less a crime as she looked upon it in that brief moment of illumination. **(14)**

And yet she had loved him—sometimes. Often she had not. What did it matter! What could love, the unsolved mystery, count for in face of this possession of self-assertion which she suddenly recognized as the strongest impulse of her being. **(15)**

"Free! Body and soul free!" she kept whispering. **(16)**

Josephine was kneeling before the closed door with her lips to the keyhole, imploring for admission. "Louise, open the door! I beg; open the door—you will make yourself ill. What are you doing, Louise? For heaven's sake open the door." **(17)**

"Go away. I am not making myself ill." No; she was drinking in a very elixir of life through that open window. **(18)**

Her fancy was running riot along those days ahead of her. Spring days, and summer days, and all sorts of days that would be her own. She breathed a quick prayer that life might be long. It was only yesterday she had thought with a shudder that life might be long. **(19)**

She arose at length and opened the door to her sister's importunities. There was a feverish triumph in her eyes, and she carried herself unwittingly like a goddess of Victory. She clasped her sister's waist, and together they descended the stairs. Richards stood waiting for them at the bottom. **(20)**

Someone was opening the front door with a latchkey. It was Brently Mallard who entered, a little travel-stained, composedly carrying his grip-sack and umbrella. He had been far from the scene of accident, and did not even know there had been one. He stood amazed at Josephine's piercing cry; at Richards's quick motion to screen him from the view of his wife. **(21)**

But Richards was too late. **(22)**

When the doctors came they said she had died of heart disease—of joy that kills. **(23)**

TECHNIQUES FOR RESPONDING

TO LITERATURE

As you read and respond to a work of literature, keep the following techniques in mind.

- **Understanding the assignment and selecting a possible purpose and audience.** Unless stated otherwise in your assignment, your purpose is to *interpret* a work of literature. Your audience will be other members of your class, including the teacher.
- **Actively reading, annotating, and discussing the literary work.** Remember that literature often contains *highly condensed experiences.* In order to give imaginative life to literature, you need to reread patiently both the major events and the seemingly insignificant passages. In discussions, look for the differences between your responses and other readers' ideas.
- **Focusing your essay on a single, clearly defined interpretation.** In your essay, clearly state your main idea or thesis, focusing on a single idea or aspect of the piece of literature. Your thesis should *not be a statement of fact.* Whether you are explaining, evaluating, or arguing, your interpretation must be clearly stated.
- **Supporting your interpretation with evidence.** Because your readers will probably have different interpretations, you must show which specific characters, events, conflicts, images, or themes prompted your response, and you must support your interpretation. *Do not merely retell the major events of the story—your readers have already read it.*

■ WARMING UP: JOURNAL EXERCISES   Read all of the following questions and then write for five minutes on two or three. These questions should clarify your perceptions about literature and develop your specific responses to "The Story of an Hour."

1. Describe a work of literature (a poem, short story, novel, or play) that you have read recently. Why did you read it? What did you like best about it? What did you not like about it?

2. On your bookshelves or in the library, find a short story or poem that you read at least six months ago. Before you reread it, write down the name of the author and the title of the work. Note when you read it last and describe what you remember about it. Then reread the story or poem. When you finish, write for five minutes, describing what you noticed that you did not notice the last time you read it.

3. Find a popular song whose lyrics describe a character and tell a story about that person. Listen to the recording and copy down the words. Compare it to Kate Chopin's "The Story of an Hour." Do the lyrics have the basic ingredients of short fiction (character, plot, point of view, setting, style, and theme)? Is it a miniature story? What elements does it lack?

4. Write out the *question* that "The Story of an Hour" seems to ask. What is your answer to this question? What might have been Kate Chopin's answer?

5. Read the Responding to Short Fiction section in this chapter. Review the descriptions of character, plot, point of view, setting, and style. Explain which of these terms and definitions best helps you find *evidence* in "The Story of an Hour" to answer the question that you identified in Question 4.

6. The words "heart," "joy," "free," "life," and "death" appear several times in "The Story of an Hour." Underline these words (or synonyms) each time they appear. Explain how the meaning of each of these words seems to *change* during the story. Is each word used ironically?

7. Write out a dictionary definition of the word "feminism." Then write out your own definition. Is Mrs. Mallard a feminist? Is Kate Chopin a feminist? What evidence in the story supports your answers?

8. Kate Chopin's biographer, Per Seyersted, says that Chopin saw that "truth is manifold" and thus preferred not to "take sides or point a moral." Explain how "The Story of an Hour" does or does not illustrate Seyersted's observations.

9. Literature often expresses common themes or tensions, such as the individual versus society, appearance versus reality, self-knowledge versus self-deception, or civilization versus nature. Which of these themes are most apparent in "The Story of an Hour"? Explain your choices.

PURPOSES FOR RESPONDING

TO LITERATURE

In responding to literature, you should be guided by the purposes that you have already practiced in previous chapters. As you read a piece of literature and respond in the margin, begin by writing *for yourself.* Your purposes are to observe, feel, remember, understand, and relate the work of literature to your own life: What is happening? What memories does it trigger? How does it make you feel? Why is this passage confusing? Why do you like or dislike this character? Literature has special, personal value. You should write about literature initially in order to discover and understand its importance in your life.

When you write an interpretative essay, however, you are writing *for* others. You are sharing your experience in working with the author as imaginative partners in recreating the work. Your purposes will often be mixed, but an interpretative essay often contains elements of *explaining, evaluating, problem solving,* and *arguing.*

- **Explaining.** Interpretative essays about literature explain the *what, why,* and *how* of a piece of literature. What is the key subject? What is the most important event or character? What are the major conflicts or the key images? What motivates a character? How does a character's world build or unravel? How does a story meet or fail to meet our expectations? How did our interpretations develop? Each of these questions might lead to an interpretative essay that explains the *what, why,* and *how* of your response.
- **Evaluating.** Readers and writers often talk about "appreciating" a work of literature. *Appreciating* means establishing its value or worth. It may mean praising the work's literary virtues; it may mean finding faults or weaknesses. Usually, evaluating essays measure *both strengths and weaknesses,* according to specific criteria. What important standards for literature do you wish to apply? How does the work in question measure up? What kinds of readers might find this story worth reading? An evaluative essay cites evidence to show why a story is exciting, boring, dramatic, puzzling, vivid, relevant, or memorable.

- **Problem Solving.** Writers of interpretative essays occasionally take a problem-solving approach, focusing on how the reader overcomes obstacles in understanding the story or how the author of a story solved problems in writing key scenes, creating characters, setting a plot in motion, and creating and resolving conflicts. Particularly if you like to write fiction yourself, you may wish to take the writer's point of view: How did the writer solve (or fail to solve) problems of setting, character, plot, or theme?

- **Arguing.** As readers share responses, they may discover that their interpretations diverge sharply from the ideas of other readers. Does "The Story of an Hour" have a "feminist" theme? Is it about women or about human nature in general? Is the main character admirable, or is she selfish? In interpretative essays, writers sometimes argue for their beliefs. They present evidence that refutes an opposing interpretation and supports their own reading.

Most interpretative essays about literature will be focused by these purposes, whether used singly or in combination. Writers should *select* the purpose(s) that are most appropriate for the work of literature and their own responses.

RESPONDING TO SHORT FICTION

RESPONDING AS A READER

Begin by noting in the margins your reactions at key points. *Summarize* in your own words what is happening in the story. Write down your *observations* or *reactions* to striking or surprising passages. Ask yourself *questions* about ambiguous or confusing passages. Following are examples written by students that illustrate all three kinds of responses.

Summary Comments

Mrs. Mallard is initially paralyzed by the news.

Mrs. Mallard feels her sister will protect her. She weeps in her sister's arms.

From the security of her chair, she stares at life outside her window.

Mrs. Mallard is young, but the lines on her face reveal repression.

Mrs. Mallard now feels "free, free, free" of the bonds of marriage.

News of her husband's death does not kill her, but news of his life does.

Observations and Reactions

Mrs. Mallard has "heart trouble"—possible double meaning.

Although Mrs. Mallard is experiencing shock and grief, outside her window the world is full of life.

The mistaken belief that men and women have a right to impose their will on others—this may be the point of the story.

Joy that kills = monstrous joy.

She does not die of the joy that kills—she dies of killed joy.

Questions

Why does the "storm" of grief come so quickly and then disappear?

She would live for herself: Is this selfishness or just a desire to be free?

Why does Chopin make Mrs. Mallard seem powerless, as though she was overcome by a fever?

Should we admire Mrs. Mallard for wanting her freedom?

Is this the story of an hour or the story of her life?

READING WITH A WRITER'S EYE

After you respond initially and make your marginal annotations, use the following basic elements of fiction to help you *analyze how the parts of a short story relate to the whole.* Pay attention to how setting or plot affects the character, or how style and setting affect the theme. Because analysis artificially separates plot, character, and theme, look for ways to *synthesize* the parts: Seeing how these parts relate to each other should suggest an idea, focus, or angle to use in your interpretation.

CHARACTER   A short story usually focuses on a *major character*—particularly on how that character faces conflicts, undergoes changes, or reveals himself or herself. *Minor characters* may be flat (one-dimensional), static (unchanging), or stereotyped. To get a start on analyzing character, diagram the *conflicts* between or among characters. Examine characters for motivation: What causes them to behave as they do? Is their behavior affected by *internal* or *external* forces? Do the major characters reveal themselves *directly* (through their thoughts, dialogue, and actions) or indirectly (through what other people say, think, or do)?

PLOT   *Plot* is the sequence of events in a story, but it is also the cause-and-effect relationship of one event to another. As you study a story's plot, pay attention to *exposition, foreshadowing, conflict, climax,* and *denouement.* To clarify elements of the plot, draw a time line for the story, listing in chronological order every event—including events that occur before the story opens. *Exposition* describes the initial circumstances and reveals what has happened before the story opens. *Foreshadowing* is an author's hint of what will occur before it happens. *Conflicts* within characters, between characters, and between characters and their environment may explain why one event leads to the next. The *climax* is the high point, the point of no return, or the most dramatic moment in a story. At the climax of a story, readers discover something important about the main character(s). *Denouement* literally means the "unraveling" of the complications and conflicts at the end of the story. In "The Story of an Hour," climax and denouement occur almost at the same time, in the last lines of the story.

NARRATIVE POINT OF VIEW   Fiction is usually narrated from either the first-person or the third-person point of view.

A *first-person narrator* is a character who tells the story from his or her point of view. A first-person narrator may be a minor or a major character. This character may be relatively *reliable* (trustworthy) or *unreliable* (naive or misleading). Although reliable first-person narrators may invite the reader to identify with their perspectives or predicaments, unreliable narrators may cause readers to be wary of their naive judgments or unbalanced states of mind.

A *third-person omniscient narrator* is not a character or participant in the story. Omniscient narrators are assumed to know everything about the characters and events. They move through space and time, giving readers necessary information at any point in the story. A *selective omniscient narrator* usually limits his or her focus to a single character's experiences and thoughts, as Kate Chopin focuses on Mrs. Mallard in "The Story of an Hour." One kind of selective omniscient point of view is *stream-of-consciousness narration,* in which the author presents the thoughts, memories, and associations of one character in the story. Omniscient narrators may be *intrusive,* jumping into the story to give their editorial judgments, or they may be *objective,* removing themselves from the action and the minds of the characters. Objective point of view creates the impression that events are being recorded by a camera or acted on a stage.

Reminder: As you reread a story, do not stop with analysis. Do not quit, for example, after you have identified and labeled the point of view. Determine how the point of view affects your reaction to the central character or to your understanding of the theme. How would a different narrative point of view change the story? If a different character told the story, how would that affect the theme?

SETTING   *Setting* is the physical place, scene, and time of the story. It also includes the social or historical context of the story. The setting in "The Story of an Hour" is the house and the room in which Mrs. Mallard waits, but it is also the social and historical time frame. *Setting is usually important for what it reveals about the characters, the plot, or the theme of the story.* Does the setting reflect a character's state of mind? Is the environment a source of tension or conflict in the story? Do changes in setting reflect changes in key characters? Do sensory details of sight, touch, smell, hearing, or taste affect or reflect the characters or events? Does the author's portrait of the setting contain images and symbols that help you interpret the story?

STYLE   *Style* is a general term that may refer to sentence structure, figurative language and symbols, as well as to the author's tone or use of irony. *Sentence structure* may be long and complicated or relatively short and simple. Authors may use *figurative language* (Mrs. Mallard is described in "The Story of an Hour" as sobbing, "as a child who has cried itself to sleep continues to sob in its dreams"). A *symbol* is a person, place, thing, or event that suggests or signifies something beyond itself. In "The Story of an Hour," the open window and the new spring life suggest or represent Mrs. Mallard's new freedom. *Tone* is the author's attitude toward the characters, setting, or plot. Tone may be sympathetic, humorous, serious, detached, or critical. *Irony* suggests a double meaning. It occurs when the author or a character says or does one thing but means the opposite or something altogether different. The ending of "A Story of an Hour" is ironic: The doctors say Mrs. Mallard dies "of joy that kills." In fact, she dies of killed joy.

THEME   The focus of an interpretative essay is often on the theme of a story. In arriving at a theme, ask how the characters, plot, point of view, setting, and style *contribute* to the main ideas or point of the story. The theme of a story depends, within limits, on your reactions as a reader. "The Story of an Hour" is *not* about relationships between sisters, nor is it about medical malpractice. It is an ironic story about love, personal freedom, and death, but what precisely is the *theme?* Does "The Story of an Hour" carry a feminist message, or is it more universally about the repressive power of love? Is Mrs. Mallard to be admired or criticized for her impulse to free herself? The theme of a story should not be trivialized by looking for some simple "moral." In describing the theme, you should deal with the complexity of life recreated in the story.

SHORT FICTION:

PROFESSIONAL WRITING

A WORN PATH

Eudora Welty

Eudora Welty was born in Jackson, Mississippi in 1909 and earned degrees from Mississippi State College, the University of Wisconsin, and Columbia University. While she was writing short stories during the early 1930s, Welty held jobs with the Works Progress Authority, a Jackson radio station, and local newspapers. Like Flannery O'Connor and William Faulkner, Eudora Welty wrote stories and novels set in the South. Her first major publication, A Curtain of Green, and Other Stories, *appeared in 1941 and was followed by three more collections of short stories. Her novels include* Delta Wedding *(1946) and* The Optimist's Daughter *(1972), which won a Pulitzer Prize. Welty's collection of reviews and essays,* The Eye of the Story *(1978), and her brief autobiography,* One Writer's Beginnings *(1984), provide insight into her fiction and her life.*

It was December—a bright frozen day in the early morning. Far out in the country there was an old Negro woman with her head tied in a red rag, coming along a path through the pinewoods. Her name was Phoenix Jackson. She was very old and small and she walked slowly in the dark pine shadows, moving a little from side to side in her steps, with the balanced heaviness and lightness of a pendulum in a grandfather clock. She carried a thin, small cane made from an umbrella, and with this she kept tapping the frozen earth in front of her. This made a grave and persistent noise in the still air, that seemed meditative like the chirping of a solitary little bird. **(1)**

She wore a dark striped dress reaching down to her shoe tops, and an equally long apron of bleached sugar sacks, with a full pocket: all neat and tidy, but every time she took a step she might have fallen over her shoe-laces, which dragged from her unlaced shoes. She looked straight ahead. Her eyes were blue with age. Her skin had a pattern all its own of numberless branching wrinkles and as though a whole little tree stood in the middle of her forehead, but a golden color ran underneath, and the two knobs of her cheeks were illuminated by a yellow burning under the dark. Under the red rag her hair came down on her neck in the frailest of ringlets, still black, and with an odor like copper. **(2)**

Now and then there was a quivering in the thicket. Old Phoenix said, "Out of my way, all you foxes, owls, beetles, jack rabbits, coons, and wild animals! . . . Keep out from under these feet, little bob-whites. . . . Keep the big wild hogs out of my path. Don't let none of those come running my direction. I got a long way." Under her small black-freckled hand her cane, limber as a buggy whip, would switch at the brush as if to rouse up any hiding things. **(3)**

On she went. The woods were deep and still. The sun made the pine needles almost too bright to look at, up where the wind rocked. The cones dropped as light as feathers. Down in the hollow was the mourning dove—it was not too late for him. **(4)**

The path ran up a hill. "Seem like there is chains about my feet, time I get this far," she said, in the voice of argument old people keep to use with themselves. "Something always take a hold of me on this hill—pleads I should stay." **(5)**

After she got to the top she turned and gave a full, severe look behind her where she had come. "Up through pines," she said at length. "Now down through oaks." **(6)**

Her eyes opened their widest, and she started down gently. But before she got to the bottom of the hill a bush caught her dress. **(7)**

Her fingers were busy and intent, but her skirts were full and long, so that before she could pull them free in one place they were caught in another. It was not possible to allow the dress to tear. "I in the thorny bush," she said. "Thorns, you doing your appointed work. Never want to let folks pass—no sir. Old eyes thought you was a pretty little green bush." **(8)**

Finally, trembling all over, she stood free, and after a moment dared to stoop for her cane. **(9)**

"Sun so high!" she cried, leaning back and looking, while the thick tears went over her eyes. "The time getting all gone here." **(10)**

At the foot of this hill was a place where a log was laid across the creek. **(11)**

"Now comes the trial," said Phoenix. **(12)**

Putting her right foot out, she mounted the log and shut her eyes. Lifting her skirt, leveling her cane fiercely before her, like a festival figure in some parade, she began to march across. Then she opened her eyes and she was safe on the other side. **(13)**

"I wasn't as old as I thought," she said. **(14)**

But she sat down to rest. She spread her skirts on the bank around her and folded her hands over her knees. Up above her was a tree in a pearly cloud of mistletoe. She did not dare to close her eyes, and when a little boy brought her a little plate with a slice of marble-cake on it she spoke to him. "That would be acceptable," she said. But when she went to take it there was just her own hand in the air. **(15)**

So she left that tree, and had to go through a barbed-wire fence. There she had to creep and crawl, spreading her knees and stretching her fingers like a baby trying to climb the steps. But she talked loudly to herself: she could not let her dress be torn now, so late in the day, and she could not pay for having her arm or her leg sawed off if she got caught fast where she was. **(16)**

At last she was safe through the fence and risen up out in the clearing. Big dead trees, like black men with one arm, were standing in the purple stalks of the withered cotton field. There sat a buzzard. **(17)**

"Who you watching?" **(18)**

In the furrow she made her way along. **(19)**

"Glad this not the season for bulls," she said, looking sideways, "and the good Lord made his snakes to curl up and sleep in the winter. A pleasure I don't see no two-headed snake coming around that tree, where it come once. It took a while to get by him, back in the summer." **(20)**

She passed through the old cotton and went into a field of dead corn. It whispered and shook and was taller than her head. "Through the maze now," she said, for there was no path. **(21)**

Then there was something tall, black, and skinny there, moving before her. **(22)**

At first she took it for a man. It could have been a man dancing in the field. But she stood still and listened, and it did not make a sound. It was as silent as a ghost. **(23)**

"Ghost," she said sharply, "who be you the ghost of? For I have heard of nary death close by." **(24)**

But there was no answer—only the ragged dancing in the wind. **(25)**

She shut her eyes, reached out her hand, and touched a sleeve. She found a coat and inside that an emptiness, cold as ice. **(26)**

"You scarecrow," she said. Her face lighted. "I ought to be shut up for good," she said with laughter. "My senses is gone, I too old. I the oldest people I ever know. Dance, old scarecrow," she said, "while I dancing with you." She kicked her foot over the furrow, and with mouth drawn down, shook her head once or twice in a little strutting way. Some husks blew down and whirled in streamers about her skirts. **(27)**

Then she went on, parting her way from side to side with the cane, through the whispering field. At last she came to the end, to a wagon track where the silver grass blew between the red ruts. The quail were walking around like pullets, seeming all dainty and unseen. **(28)**

"Walk pretty," she said. "This the easy place. This the easy going." **(29)**

She followed the track, swaying through the quiet bare fields, through the little strings of trees silver in their dead leaves, pass cabins silver from weather, with the doors and windows boarded shut, all like old women under a spell sitting there. "I walking in their sleep," she said, nodding her head vigorously. **(30)**

In a ravine she went where a spring was silently flowing through a hollow log. Old Phoenix bent and drank. "Sweet-gum makes the water sweet," she said, and drank more. "Nobody know who made this well, for it was here when I was born." **(31)**

The track crossed a swampy part where the moss hung as white as lace from every limb. "Sleep on, alligators, and blow your bubbles." Then the track went into the road. **(32)**

Deep, deep the road went down between the high green-colored banks. Overhead the live-oaks met, and it was as dark as a cave. **(33)**

A black dog with a lolling tongue came up out of the weeds by the ditch. She was meditating, and not ready, and when he came at her she only hit him a little with her cane. Over she went in the ditch, like a little puff of milk-weed. **(34)**

Down there, her senses drifted away. A dream visited her, and she reached her hand up, but nothing reached down and gave her a pull. So she lay there and presently went to talking. "Old woman," she said to herself, "that black dog come up out of the weeds to stall you off, and now there he sitting on his fine tail, smiling at you." **(35)**

A white man finally came along and found her—a hunter, a young man, with his dog on a chain. **(36)**

"Well, Granny!" he laughed, "what are you doing there?" **(37)**

"Lying on my back like a June-bug waiting to be turned over, mister," she said, reaching up her hand. **(38)**

He lifted her up, gave her a swing in the air, and set her down. "Anything broken, Granny?" **(39)**

"No sir, them old dead weeds is springy enough," said Phoenix, when she had got her breath. "I thank you for your trouble." **(40)**

"Where do you live, Granny?" he asked, while the two dogs were growling at each other. **(41)**

"Away back yonder, sir, behind the ridge. You can't even see it from here." **(42)**

"On your way home?" **(43)**

"No, sir, I going to town." **(44)**

"Why, that's too far! That's as far as I walk when I come out myself, and I get something for my trouble." He patted the stuffed bag he carried, and there hung down a little closed claw. It was one of the bob-whites, with its beak hooked bitterly to show it was dead. "Now you go on home, Granny!" **(45)**

"I bound to go to town, mister," said Phoenix. "The time come around." **(46)**

He gave another laugh, filling the whole landscape. "I know you old colored people! Wouldn't miss going to town to see Santa Claus!" **(47)**

But something held Old Phoenix very still. The deep lines in her face went into a fierce and different radiation. Without warning, she had seen with her own eyes a flashing nickel fall out of the man's pocket onto the ground. **(48)**

"How old are you, Granny?" he was saying. **(49)**

"There is no telling, mister," she said, "no telling." **(50)**

Then she gave a little cry and clapped her hands and said, "Git on away from here, dog! Look! Look at that dog!" She laughed as if in admiration. "He ain't scared of nobody. He a big black dog." She whispered, "Sic him!" **(51)**

"Watch me get rid of that cur," said the man. "Sic him, Pete! Sic him!" **(52)**

Phoenix heard the dogs fighting, and heard the man running and throwing sticks. She even heard a gunshot. But she was slowly bending forward by that time, further and further forward, the lids stretched down over her eyes, as if she were doing this in her sleep. Her chin was lowered almost to her knees. The yellow palm of her hand came out from the fold of her apron. Her fingers slid down and along the ground under the piece of money with the grace and care they would have in lifting an egg from under a sitting hen. Then she slowly straightened up, she stood erect, and the nickel was in her apron pocket. A bird flew by. Her lips moved. "God watching me the whole time, I come to stealing." **(53)**

The man came back, and his own dog panted about them. "Well, I scared him off that time," he said, and then he laughed and lifted his gun and pointed it at Phoenix. **(54)**

She stood straight and faced him. **(55)**

"Doesn't the gun scare you?" he said, still pointing it. **(56)**

"No, sir, I seen plenty go off closer by, in my day, and for less than what I done," she said, holding utterly still. **(57)**

He smiled, and shouldered the gun. "Well, Granny," he said, "You must be a hundred years old, and scared of nothing. I'd give you a dime if I had any money with me. But you take my advice and stay home, and nothing will happen to you." **(58)**

"I bound to go on my way, mister," said Phoenix. She inclined her head in the red rag. Then they went in different directions, but she could hear the gun shooting again and again over the hill. **(59)**

She walked on. The shadows hung from the oak trees to the road like curtains. Then she smelled wood-smoke, and smelled the river, and she saw a steeple and the cabins on their steep steps. Dozens of little black children whirled around her. There ahead was Natchez shining. Bells were ringing. She walked on. **(60)**

In the paved city it was Christmas time. There were red and green electric lights strung and crisscrossed everywhere, and all turned on in the daytime. Old Phoenix would have been lost if she had not distrusted her eyesight and depended on her feet to know where to take her. **(61)**

She paused quietly on the sidewalk where people were passing by. A lady came along in the crowd, carrying an armful of red-, green-, and silver-wrapped presents; she gave off perfume like the red roses in hot summer, and Phoenix stopped her. **(62)**

"Please, missy, will you lace up my shoe?" She held up her foot. **(63)**

"What do you want, Grandma?" **(64)**

"See my shoe," said Phoenix. "Do all right for out in the country, but wouldn't look right to go in a big building." **(65)**

"Stand still then, Grandma," said the lady. She put her packages down on the sidewalk beside her and laced and tied both shoes tightly. **(66)**

"Can't lace 'em with a cane," said Phoenix. "Thank you, missy. I doesn't mind asking a nice lady to tie up my shoe, when I gets out on the street." **(67)**

Moving slowly and from side to side, she went into the big building and into a tower of steps, where she walked up and around and around until her feet knew to stop. **(68)**

She entered a door, and there she saw nailed up on the wall the document that had been stamped with the gold seal and framed in the gold frame, which matched the dream that was hung up in her head. **(69)**

"Here I be," she said. There was a fixed and ceremonial stiffness over her body. **(70)**

"A charity case, I suppose," said an attendant who sat at the desk before her. **(71)**

But Phoenix only looked above her head. There was sweat on her face, the wrinkles in her skin shone like a bright net. **(72)**

"Speak up, Grandma," the woman said: "What's your name? We must have your history, you know. Have you been here before? What seems to be the trouble with you?" **(73)**

Old Phoenix only gave a twitch to her face as if a fly were bothering her. **(74)**

"Are you deaf?" cried the attendant. **(75)**

But then the nurse came in. **(76)**

"Oh, that's just old Aunt Phoenix," she said. "She doesn't come for herself—she has a little grandson. She makes these trips just as regular as clockwork. She lives away back off the old Natchez Trace." She bent down. "Well, Aunt Phoenix, why don't you just take a seat? We won't keep you standing after your long trip." She pointed. **(77)**

The old woman sat down, bolt upright in the chair. **(78)**

"Now, how is the boy?" asked the nurse. **(79)**

Old Phoenix did not speak. **(80)**

"I said, how is the boy?" **(81)**

But Phoenix only waited and stared straight ahead, her face very solemn and withdrawn into rigidity. **(82)**

"Is his throat any better?" asked the nurse. "Aunt Phoenix, don't you hear me? Is your grandson's throat any better since the last time you came for the medicine?" **(83)**

With her hands on her knees, the old woman waited, silent, erect and motionless, just as if she were in armor. **(84)**

"You mustn't take up our time this way, Aunt Phoenix," the nurse said. "Tell us quickly about your grandson, and get it over. He isn't dead, is he?" **(85)**

At last there came a flicker and then a flame of comprehension across her face, and she spoke. **(86)**

"My grandson. It was my memory had left me. There I sat and forgot why I made my long trip." **(87)**

"Forgot?" The nurse frowned. "After you came so far?" **(88)**

Then Phoenix was like an old woman begging a dignified forgiveness for waking up frightened in the night. "I never did go to school, I was too old at the Surrender," she said in a soft voice. "I'm an old woman without an education. It was my memory fail me. My little grandson, he is just the same, and I forgot it in the coming." **(89)**

"Throat never heals, does it?" said the nurse, speaking in a loud, sure voice to Old Phoenix. By now she had a card with something written on it, a little list. "Yes. Swallowed lye. When was it—January—two-three years ago—" **(90)**

Phoenix spoke unasked now. "No, missy, he not dead, he just the same. Every little while his throat begin to close up again, and he not able to swallow. He not get his breath. He not able to help himself. So the time come around, and I go on another trip for the soothing medicine." **(91)**

"All right. The doctor said as long as you came to get it, you could have it," said the nurse. "But it's an obstinate case." **(92)**

"My little grandson, he sit up there in the house all wrapped up, waiting by himself," Phoenix went on. "We is the only two left in the world. He suffer and it don't seem to put him back at all. He got a sweet look. He going to last. He wear a little patch quilt and peep out holding his mouth open like a little bird. I remembers so plain now. I not going to forget him again, no, the whole enduring time. I could tell him from all the others in creation." **(93)**

"All right." The nurse was trying to hush her now. She brought her a bottle of medicine. "Charity," she said, making a check mark in a book. **(94)**

Old Phoenix held the bottle close to her eyes and then carefully put it into her pocket. **(95)**

"I thank you," she said. **(96)**

"It's Christmas time, Grandma," said the attendant. "Could I give you a few pennies out of my purse?" **(97)**

"Five pennies is a nickel," said Phoenix stiffly. **(98)**

"Here's a nickel," said the attendant. **(99)**

Phoenix rose carefully and held out her hand. She received the nickel and then fished the other nickel out of her pocket and laid it beside the new one. She stared at her palm closely, with her head on one side. **(100)**

Then she gave a tap with her cane on the floor. **(101)**

"This is what come to me to do," she said. "I going to the store and buy my child a little windmill they sells, made out of paper. He going to find it hard to believe there such a thing in the world. I'll march myself back where he waiting, holding it straight up in this hand." **(102)**

She lifted her free hand, gave a little nod, turned round, and walked out of the doctor's office. Then her slow step began on the stairs, going down. **(103)**

QUESTIONS FOR WRITING AND DISCUSSION

1. Which of the following approximates your response(s) to the character of Phoenix Jackson: Surprise that she should be the subject of a story? Anger that no one helps her on her journey? Boredom that you just read a story in which nothing seems to happen? Puzzlement at her apparently senile behavior? Amazement at her determination and courage? Describe any other responses you may have.

2. According to legend, the Phoenix is a mythological bird that lives for five hundred years, burns itself to death, and then rises from its ashes in the freshness of youth to live through another life cycle. What *events, references,* and *images* in the story suggest that Welty's Phoenix Jackson is like the mythological bird?

3. One reader has suggested that during her journey, Phoenix encounters twelve obstacles (internal and external) that represent tests, or trials, of her faith and courage. How many of these tests can you find? Does she "pass" each test? What do these tests reveal about her character?

4. In an essay entitled "Is Phoenix Jackson's Grandson Really Dead?" Eudora Welty says, "The story is told through Phoenix's mind as she undertakes her errand. As the author at one with the character as I tell it, I must assume that the boy is alive. As the reader, you are free to think as you like, of course: the story invites you to believe that no matter what happens, Phoenix for as long as she is able to walk and can hold to her purpose will make her journey." Explain how the boy's actual condition might affect your interpretation of the story.

5. Kate Chopin's "The Story of an Hour" and Eudora Welty's "A Worn Path" are both stories about love. By way of contrast, what do the character and behavior of Mrs. Mallard tell you about Phoenix? What do the character and behavior of Phoenix reveal about Mrs. Mallard?

THE LESSON

Toni Cade Bambara

Toni Cade Bambara is an activist for the African-American community on many fronts—political, cultural, and literary. She has worked for political and social causes in urban communities, taught African-American Studies at half a dozen different colleges and universities, and is the author of several collections of short stories and novels, including Gorilla, My Love *(1972),* The Sea Birds Are Still Alive *(1977),* The Salt Eaters *(1980), and* If Blessing Comes *(1987). "The Lesson," which appears in* Gorilla, My Love, *dramatizes the gradual awakening of several children to the political and economic realities of contemporary urban life. As you read the story, pay attention to the narrator, Sylvia. What is the lesson and what does Sylvia learn?*

Back in the days when everyone was old and stupid or young and foolish and me and Sugar were the only ones just right, this lady moved on our block with nappy hair and proper speech and no makeup. And quite naturally we laughed at her, laughed the way we did at the junk man who went about his business like he was some big-time president and his sorry-ass horse his secretary. And we kinda hated her too, hated the way we did the winos who cluttered up our parks and pissed on our handball walls and stank up our hallways and stairs so you couldn't halfway play hide-and-seek without a goddamn gas mask. Miss Moore was her name. The only woman on the block with no first name. And she was black as hell, cept for her feet, which were fish-white and spooky. And she was always planning these boring-ass things for us to do, us being my cousins, mostly, who lived on the block cause we all moved North the same time and to the same apartment then spread out gradual to breathe. And our parents would yank our heads into some kinda shape and crisp up our clothes so we'd be presentable for travel with Miss Moore, who always looked like she was going to church, though she never did. Which is just one of the things the grownups talked about when they talked behind her back like a dog. But when she came calling with some sachet she'd sewed up or some gingerbread she'd made or some book, why then they'd all be too embarrassed to turn her down and we'd get handed over all spruced up. She'd been to college and said it was only right that she should take responsibility for the young ones' education, and she not even related by marriage or blood. So they'd go for it. Specially Aunt Gretchen. She was the main gofer in the family. You got some ole dumb shit foolishness you want somebody to go for, you send for Aunt Gretchen. She been screwed into the go-along for so long, it's a blood-deep natural thing with her. Which is how she got saddled with me and Sugar and Junior in the first place while our mothers were in a la-de-da apartment up the block having a good ole time. **(1)**

So this one day Miss Moore rounds us all up at the mailbox and it's puredee hot and she's knockin herself out about arithmetic. And school suppose to let up in summer I heard, but she don't never let up. And the starch in my pinafore scratching the shit outta me and I'm really hating this nappy-head bitch and her goddamn college degree. I'd much rather go to the pool or to the show where it's cool. So me and Sugar leaning on the mailbox being surly, which is a Miss Moore word. And Flyboy checking out what everybody brought for lunch. And Fat Butt already wasting his peanut-butter-and-jelly sandwich like the pig he is. And Junebug punchin on Q.T.'s arm for potato chips. And Rosie Giraffe shifting from one hip to the other waiting for somebody to step on her foot or ask her if she from Georgia so she can kick ass, preferably Mercedes's. And Miss Moore asking us do we know what money is, like we a bunch of retards. I mean real money, she say, like it's only poker chips or monopoly papers we lay on the grocer. So right away I'm tired of this and say so. And would much rather snatch Sugar and go to the Sunset and terrorize the West Indian kids and take their hair ribbons and their money too. And Miss Moore files that remark away for next week's lesson on brotherhood, I can tell. And finally I say we oughta get to the subway cause it's cooler and besides we might meet some cute boys. Sugar done swiped her mama's lipstick, so we ready. **(2)**

So we heading down the street and she's boring us silly about what things cost and what our parents make and how much goes for rent and how money ain't divided up right in this country. And then she gets to the part about we all poor and live in the slums, which I don't feature. And I'm ready to speak on that, but she steps out in the street and hails two cabs just like that. Then she hustles half the crew in with her and hands me a five-dollar bill and tells me to calculate 10 percent tip for the driver. And we're off. Me and Sugar and Junebug and Flyboy hangin out the window and hollering to everybody, putting lipstick on each other cause Flyboy a faggot anyway, and making farts with our sweaty armpits. But I'm mostly trying to figure how to spend this money. But they all fascinated with the meter ticking and Junebug starts laying bets as to how much it'll read when Flyboy can't hold his breath no more. Then Sugar lays bets as to how much it'll be when we get there. So I'm stuck. Don't nobody want to go for my plan, which is to jump out at the next light and run off to the first bar-b-que we can find. Then the driver tells us to get the hell out cause we there already. And the meter reads eighty-five cents. And I'm stalling to figure out the tip and Sugar say give him a dime. And I decide he don't need it bad as I do, so later for him. But then he tries to take off with Junebug foot still in the door so we talk about his mama something ferocious. Then we check out that we on Fifth Avenue and everybody dressed up in stockings. One lady in a fur coat, hot as it is. White folks crazy. **(3)**

"This is the place," Miss Moore say, presenting it to us in the voice she uses at the museum. "Let's look in the windows before we go in." **(4)**

"Can we steal?" Sugar asks very serious like she's getting the ground rules squared away before she plays. "I beg your pardon," say Miss Moore, and we fall out. So she leads us around the windows of the toy store and me and Sugar screamin, "This is mine, that's mine, I gotta have that, that was made for me, I was born for that," till Big Butt drowns us out. **(5)**

"Hey, I'm goin to buy that there." **(6)**

"That there? You don't even know what it is, stupid." **(7)**

"I do so," he say punchin on Rosie Giraffe. "It's a microscope." **(8)**

"Whatcha gonna do with a microscope, fool?" **(9)**

"Look at things." **(10)**

"Like what, Ronald?" ask Miss Moore. And Big Butt ain't got the first notion. So here go Miss Moore gabbing about the thousands of bacteria in a drop of water and the somethinorother in a speck of blood and the million and one living things in the air around us is invisible to the naked eye. And what she say that for? Junebug go to town on that "naked" and we rolling. Then Miss Moore ask what it cost. So we all jam into the window smudgin it up and the price tag say $300. So then she ask how long'd take for Big Butt and Junebug to save up their allowances. "Too long," I say. "Yeh," adds Sugar, "outgrown it by that time." And Miss Moore say no, you never outgrow learning instruments. "Why, even medical students and interns and," blah, blah, blah. And we ready to choke Big Butt for bringing it up in the first damn place. **(11)**

"This here costs four hundred eighty dollars," say Rosie Giraffe. So we pile up all over her to see what she pointin out. My eyes tell me it's a chunk of glass cracked with something heavy, and different-color inks dripped into the splits, then the whole thing put into a oven or something. But for $480 it don't make sense. **(12)**

"That's a paperweight made of semi-precious stones fused together under tremendous pressure," she explains slowly, with her hands doing the mining and all the factory work. **(13)**

"So what's a paperweight?" asks Rosie Giraffe. **(14)**

"To weigh paper with, dumbbell," say Flyboy, the wise man from the East. **(15)**

"Not exactly," say Miss Moore, which is what she say when you warm or way off too. "It's to weigh paper down so it won't scatter and make your desk untidy." So right away me and Sugar curtsy to each other and then to Mercedes who is more the tidy type. **(16)**

"We don't keep paper on top of the desk in my class," say Junebug, figuring Miss Moore crazy or lyin one. **(17)**

"At home, then," she say. "Don't you have a calendar and a pencil case and a blotter and a letter-opener on your desk at home where you do your homework?" And she know damn well what our homes look like cause she nosys around in them every chance she gets. **(18)**

"I don't even have a desk," say Junebug. "Do we?" **(19)**

"No. And I don't get no homework neither," says Big Butt. **(20)**

"And I don't even have a home," say Flyboy like he do at school to keep the white folks off his back and sorry for him. Send this poor kid to camp posters, is his specialty. **(21)**

"I do," says Mercedes. "I have a box of stationery on my desk and a picture of my cat. My godmother bought the stationery and the desk. There's a big rose on each sheet and the envelopes smell like roses." **(22)**

"Who wants to know about your smelly-ass stationery," say Rosie Giraffe fore I can get my two cents in. **(23)**

"It's important to have a work area all your own so that. . . ." **(24)**

"Will you look at this sailboat, please," say Flyboy, cuttin her off and pointin to the thing like it was his. So once again we tumble all over each other to gaze at this magnificent thing in the toy store which is just big enough to maybe sail two kittens across the pond if you strap them to the posts tight. We all start reciting the price tag like we in assembly. "Handcrafted sailboat of fiberglass at one thousand one hundred ninety-five dollars." **(25)**

"Unbelievable," I hear myself say and am really stunned. I read it again for myself just in case the group recitation put me in a trance. Same thing. For some reason this pisses me off. We look at Miss Moore and she lookin at us, waiting for I dunno what. **(26)**

"Who'd pay all that when you can buy a sailboat set for a quarter at Pop's, a tube of glue for a dime, and a ball of string for eight cents? It must have a motor and a whole lot else besides," I say. "My sailboat cost me about fifty cents." **(27)**

"But will it take water?" say Mercedes with her smart ass. **(28)**

"Took mine to Alley Pond Park once," say Flyboy. "String broke. Lost it. Pity." **(29)**

"Sailed mine in Central Park and it keeled over and sank. Had to ask my father for another dollar." **(30)**

"And you got the strap," laugh Big Butt. "The jerk didn't even have a string on it. My old man wailed on his behind." **(31)**

Little Q.T. was staring hard at the sailboat and you could see he wanted it bad. But he too little and somebody'd just take it from him. So what the hell. "This boat for kids, Miss Moore?" **(32)**

"Parents silly to buy something like that just to get all broke up," say Rosie Giraffe. **(33)**

"That much money it should last forever," I figure. **(34)**

"My father'd buy it for me if I wanted it." **(35)**

"Your father, my ass," say Rosie Giraffe getting a chance to finally push Mercedes. **(36)**

"Must be rich people shop here," say Q.T. **(37)**

"You are a very bright boy," say Flyboy. "What was your first clue?" And he rap him on the head with the back of his knuckles, since Q.T. the only one he could get away with. Though Q.T. liable to come up behind you years later and get his licks in when you half expect it. **(38)**

"What I want to know is," I says to Miss Moore though I never talk to her, I wouldn't give the bitch that satisfaction, "is how much a real boat costs? I figure a thousand'd get you a yacht any day." **(39)**

"Why don't you check that out," she says, "and report back to the group?" Which really pains my ass. If you gonna mess up a perfectly good swim day least you could do is have some answers. "Let's go in," she say like she got something up her sleeve. Only she don't lead the way. So me and Sugar turn the corner to where the entrance is, but when we get there I kinda hang back. Not that I'm scared, what's there to be afraid of, just a toy store. But I feel funny, shame. But what I got to be shamed about? Got as much right to go in as anybody. But somehow I can't seem to get hold of the door, so I step away for Sugar to lead. But she hangs back too. And I look at her and she looks at me and this is ridiculous. I mean, damn, I have never ever been shy about doing nothing or going nowhere. But then Mercedes steps up and then Rosie Giraffe and Big Butt crowd in behind and shove, and next thing we all stuffed into the doorway with only Mercedes squeezing past us, smoothing out her jumper and walking right down the aisle. Then the rest of us tumble in like a glued-together jigsaw done all wrong. And people lookin at us. And it's like the time me and Sugar crashed into the Catholic church on a dare. But once we got in there and everything so hushed and holy and the candles and the bowin and the handkerchiefs on all the drooping heads, I just couldn't go through with the plan. Which was for me to run up to the altar and do a tap dance while Sugar played the nose flute and messed around in the holy water. And Sugar kept givin me the elbow. Then later teased me so bad I tied her up in the shower and turned it on and locked her in. And she'd be there till this day if Aunt Gretchen hadn't finally figured I was lyin about the boarder takin a shower. **(40)**

Same thing in the store. We all walkin on tiptoe and hardly touchin the games and puzzles and things. And I watched Miss Moore who is steady watchin us like she waitin for a sign. Like Mama Drewery watches the sky and sniffs the air and takes note of just how much slant is in the bird formation. Then me and Sugar bump smack into each other, so busy gazing at the toys, 'specially the sailboat. But we don't laugh and go into our fat-lady bump-stomach routine. We just stare at that price tag. Then Sugar run a finger over the whole boat. And I'm jealous and want to hit her. Maybe not her, but I sure want to punch somebody in the mouth. **(41)**

"Watcha bring us here for, Miss Moore?" **(42)**

"You sound angry, Sylvia. Are you mad about something?" Givin me one of them grins like she tellin a grown-up joke that never turns out to be funny. And she's lookin very closely at me like maybe she plannin to do my portrait from memory. I'm mad, but I won't give her that satisfaction. So I slouch around the store bein very bored and say, "Let's go." **(43)**

Me and Sugar at the back of the train watchin the tracks whizzin by large then small then gettin gobbled up in the dark. I'm thinkin about this tricky toy I saw in the store. A clown that somersaults on a bar then does chin-ups just cause you yank lightly at his leg. Cost $35. I could see me askin my mother for a $35 birthday clown. "You wanna who that costs what?" she'd say, cocking her head to the side to get a better view of the hole in my head. Thirty-five dollars could buy new bunk beds for Junior and Gretchen's boy. Thirty-five dollars and the whole household could go visit Granddaddy Nelson in the country. Thirty-five dollars would pay for the rent and the piano bill too. Who are these people that spend that much for performing clowns and $1,000 for toy sailboats? What kinda work they do and how they live and how come we ain't in on it? Where we are is who we are, Miss Moore always pointin out. But it don't necessarily have to be that way, she always adds then waits for somebody to say that poor people have to wake up and demand their share of the pie and don't none of us know what kind of pie she talkin about in the first damn place. But she ain't so smart cause I still got her four dollars from the taxi and she sure ain't gettin it. Messin up my day with this shit. Sugar nudges me in my pocket and winks. **(44)**

Miss Moore lines us up in front of the mailbox where we started from, seem like years ago, and I got a headache for thinkin so hard. And we lean all over each other so we can hold up under the draggy-ass lecture she always finishes us off with at the end before we thank her for borin us to tears. But she just looks at us like she readin tea leaves. Finally she say, "Well, what did you think of F. A. O. Schwarz?" **(45)**

Rosie Giraffe mumbles, "White folks crazy." **(46)**

"I'd like to go there again when I get my birthday money," says Mercedes, and we shove her out the pack so she has to lean on the mailbox by herself. **(47)**

"I'd like a shower. Tiring day," say Flyboy. **(48)**

Then Sugar surprises me by sayin, "You know, Miss Moore, I don't think all of us here put together eat in a year what that sailboat costs." And Miss Moore lights up like somebody goosed her. "And?" she say, urging Sugar on. Only I'm standin on her foot so she don't continue. **(49)**

"Imagine for a minute what kind of society it is in which some people can spend on a toy what it would cost to feed a family of six or seven. What do you think?" **(50)**

"I think," say Sugar pushing me off her feet like she never done before, cause I whip her ass in a minute, "that this is not much of a democracy if you ask me. Equal chance to pursue happiness means an equal crack at the dough, don't it?" Miss Moore is besides herself and I am disgusted with Sugar's treachery. So I stand on her foot one more time to see if she'll shove me. She shuts up, and Miss Moore looks at me, sorrowfully I'm thinkin. And somethin weird is goin on, I can feel it in my chest. **(51)**

"Anybody else learn anything today?" lookin dead at me. I walk away and Sugar has to run to catch up and don't even seem to notice when I shrug her arm off my shoulder. **(52)**

"Well, we got four dollars anyway," she says. **(53)**

"Uh hunh." **(54)**

"We could go to Hascombs and get half a chocolate layer and then go to the Sunset and still have plenty money for potato chips and ice cream sodas." **(55)**

"Uh hunh." **(56)**

"Race you to Hascombs," she say. **(57)**

We start down the block and she gets ahead which is O.K. by me cause I'm going to the West End and then over to the Drive to think this day through. She can run if she want to and even run faster. But ain't nobody gonna beat me at nuthin. **(58)**

QUESTIONS FOR WRITING AND DISCUSSION

1. Describe one incident when a parent, friend, or family member tried to get you to do something that you didn't want to do. How did you react? How was your behavior similar to or different from the reaction of Sylvia, the narrator in "The Lesson"?

2. Reread the opening sentence of the story. What does the first half of that sentence reveal about the character of the narrator? Does the rest of the story confirm that initial impression? Explain.

3. Locate at least one sentence or passage describing the reactions of each of the following children to the merchandise at F.A.O. Schwarz: Sylvia (the narrator), Sugar, Flyboy, Mercedes, Big Butt, Junebug, Rosie Giraffe, and Q.T. How do their reactions to the toys and their prices affect the narrator? Why does Bambara include all of these children in the story rather than tell it using just Miss Moore, Sylvia, and Sugar?

4. Miss Moore is the "teacher" for this "lesson," but what kind of teacher is she and how do her students react to her? What strategies does she use to help the children learn? Are her methods effective? How do the children react to each other's learning? Does Miss Moore make some mistakes?

5. What evidence (cite specific sentences) suggests that Sylvia is learning more from this lesson than she wants to? What exactly is she learning? Describe what she might do in the future as a result of what she learns.

6. Explain how each of the following quotations from Sylvia's thoughts relates to the theme or main idea of "The Lesson":

   "White folks crazy."

   "I mean, damn, I have never ever been shy about doing nothing or going nowhere."

"If you gonna mess up a perfectly good swim day least you could do is have some answers."

"But ain't nobody gonna beat me at nuthin."

7. Write two paragraphs comparing and contrasting the "awakenings" of Mrs. Mallard in "The Story of an Hour" and Sylvia in "The Lesson." What—and how—does each character learn? How do they react to what they learn? What do we, as readers, learn?

RESPONDING TO LITERATURE:
THE WRITING PROCESS

■ ASSIGNMENT FOR RESPONDING TO LITERATURE
Choose one of the short stories from this chapter (or a work of literature assigned in your class) and read it actively, reread and annotate the work, and share your responses with others in the class. Then write an interpretative essay. Assume that you are writing for other members of your class (including your instructor) who have read the work but who may not understand or agree with your interpretation.

COLLECTING

In addition to reading, rereading, annotating, and sharing your responses, try the following collecting strategies:

- **Collaborative Annotation.** In small groups, choose a work of literature or select a passage that you have already annotated. In the group, read each other's annotations. Then discuss each annotation. Which annotations does your group agree are the best? Have a group recorder record the best annotations.
- **Elements of Fiction Analysis.** Reread the paragraphs defining character, plot, point of view, setting, and style. Choose three of these elements that seem most important in the story that you are reading. Reread the story, annotating for these three elements. Then freewrite a paragraph explaining *how these three elements are interrelated or how they explain the theme.*
- **Time Line.** In your journal, draw a time line for the story. List above the line everything that happens in the story. Below the line, indicate where the story opens, when the major conflicts occur, and where the climax and the denouement occur. For "The Story of an Hour," student writer Karen Ehrhardt drew the following time line:

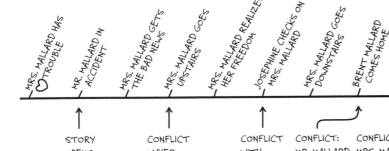

TIME LINE FOR "THE STORY OF AN HOUR"

MRS. MALLARD HAS TROUBLE — STORY OPENS: CONFLICT

MR. MALLARD IN ACCIDENT — CONFLICT W/HER FEELINGS

MRS. MALLARD GETS THE BAD NEWS

MRS. MALLARD GOES UPSTAIRS

MRS. MALLARD REALIZES HER FREEDOM — CONFLICT WITH JOSEPHINE

JOSEPHINE CHECKS ON MRS. MALLARD

MRS. MALLARD GOES DOWNSTAIRS — CONFLICT: MR. MALLARD ALIVE. CLIMAX

BRENT MALLARD COMES HOME — CONFLICT: MRS. MALLARD DIES. DENOUEMENT

MRS. MALLARD DIES OF THE JOY THAT KILLS

- **Feature List.** Choose a character trait, repeated image, or idea that you wish to investigate in the story. List, in order of appearance, every word, image, or reference that you find in the story.
- **Scene Vision or Revision.** Write a scene for this story in which you change some part of it. You may *add* a scene to the beginning, middle, or end of the story. You may *change* a scene in the story. You may write a scene in the story from a different character's point of view. You may change the style of the story for your scene. How, for example, might Eudora Welty have described the opening scene of "The Story of an Hour"?
- **Story Picture.** Draw a picture of the story, based on the time line and conflict mapping, that represents the entire story. Use the information from your character analysis, time line, and character conflicts to help you draw a single picture of the complete story. Student writer Lori Van Skike drew a picture for "The Story of an Hour" that shows how the rising and falling action of the plot parallels Mrs. Mallard's ascent and descent of the stairs:

The Story of an Hour

Story Picture: The Rising/Falling Action

(4b) landing: Louise's hopes are dashed

her death

(1) notice of death

(2) stairs: rising to knowledge of self-awareness

(3) upstairs room/windows: realization of her happiness

front door

(4a) death walks in

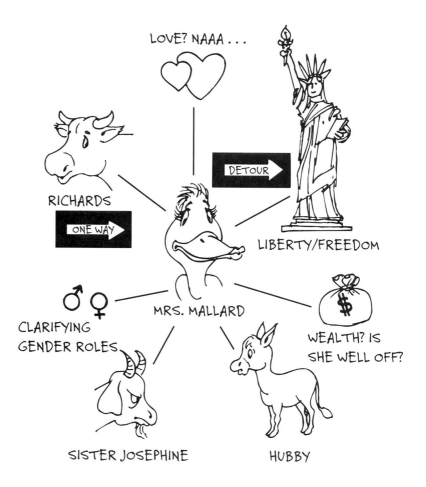

LOVE? NAAA...

RICHARDS

ONE WAY

DETOUR

LIBERTY/FREEDOM

♂ ♀
CLARIFYING
GENDER ROLES

MRS. MALLARD

WEALTH? IS
SHE WELL OFF?

SISTER JOSEPHINE

HUBBY

- **Character Conflict Map.** Start with a full page of paper. Draw a main character in the center of the page. Locate the other major characters, internal forces, and external forces (including social, economic, and environmental pressures) in a circle around the main character. Draw a line between each of these peripheral characters or forces and the main character. For his character conflict map for "The Story of an Hour," student writer Darren Marshall used images from his computer program to surround his picture of Mrs. Mallard.
- **Background Investigation.** Investigate the biographical, social, historical, or geographical context for the story. Locate a biography of the author. How are the major events of the author's life relevant to the story? Read about the historical or economic background of the story. Look at maps or descriptions of the setting for the story. How do these background sources increase your appreciation or widen your understanding of the story?

- **Reconsideration of Purposes.** What idea, theme, or approach most interests you? Will you be explaining, evaluating, problem solving, or arguing? Are you combining purposes? Do these purposes suggest what kinds of information you might collect?

SHAPING

Test each of the following possible shapes against your ideas for your essay. Use or adapt the shape or shapes that are most appropriate for your own interpretation.

EXPLAINING RELATIONSHIPS   Often interpretative essays analyze how the parts of a story relate to the whole. As you explain these relationships, you should show how key lines or scenes contribute to the portrait of the major character or to the overall theme of the story. Your focus might be on how *plot* or *character conflicts* affect your understanding of the major character, on how the *setting* reflects the theme, or on how *images* reveal character and/or contribute to the theme.

Introduction and thesis:	The images in story "X" reveal that the theme is "Y."
First scene or part:	How key images contribute to theme
Second scene or part:	How key images contribute to theme
Third scene or part:	How key images contribute to theme
Conclusion:	

EVALUATING   If your response suggests an evaluating purpose, you may wish to set up *criteria* for an effective short story and then provide evidence that shows how the particular story does or does not measure up to your standards. Your thesis might be "Story 'X' is highly dramatic because the main character undergoes emotional changes, the character conflicts heighten the tension, and the theme is controversial." A similar shaping strategy might be to set a *definition* of a "hero" or "heroine" and then analyze how the main character fits your definition.

Introduction and thesis:	Story "X" is highly dramatic.
Criteria #1:	A dramatic short story should focus on a character who changes his or her behavior or beliefs. Judgment and evidence for criteria #1:
Criteria #2:	A dramatic story must have striking conflicts that lead to a crisis or a predicament. Judgment and evidence for criteria #2:
Criteria #3:	A dramatic story should have a theme that makes a controversial point. Judgment and evidence for criteria #3:
Conclusion:	

ARGUING   During class discussion, you may disagree with another person's response. Your thesis may then take the form, "Although some readers believe this story is about 'X,' the story is really about 'Y.'" In an argumentative structure, you counter opposing interpretations by first pointing to evidence in the story and then supporting your interpretation with evidence.

Introduction and thesis:	Although some readers suggest that the story is about "X," it is really about "Y."
Body paragraphs:	State the opposing interpretation and give evidence that this interpretation cites: State your interpretation and give evidence (description, dialogue, images, points of conflict, incidents from the plot):
Conclusion:	

INVESTIGATING CHANGES IN INTERPRETATION   Often, readers *change* interpretations during the course of responding to a piece of literature. Thus, your main point might be, "Although I initially thought 'X' about the story, I gradually realized the theme of the story was 'Y.'" If that sentence expresses your main idea, you may wish to organize your essay following the *chronology* or the *steps* in the changes in your interpretation:

Introduction and thesis:	Although I initially thought "X," I now believe "Y."
Body paragraphs:	First step (your original interpretation of the story and supporting evidence): Second step (additional or contradictory ideas and evidence that forced you to reconsider your interpretation): Third step (your final interpretation and supporting evidence):
Conclusion:	

Note: One strategy you should *not* use is to simply retell the main events of the story. A review of the plot is not an acceptable interpretation. Your audience has already read the story. They want you to state your interpretation and then use details from the story to show how and why your interpretation is credible. *Although you will cite events from the plot, you must explain how or why these events support your interpretation.*

DRAFTING

To prepare to draft your essay, read through your annotations and gather your collecting and shaping notes. Some writers prefer to write one-sentence statements of their main ideas at the top of the page to keep them focused as they write. Other writers prefer to make rough outlines to follow, based on their adaptations of one of the preceding shaping strategies. When you begin drafting, you may wish to skip your introduction and start with the body of your essay. You can fill in the introduction after you have written a draft.

Once you start writing, keep your momentum going. If you draw a blank, reread what you have already written or look at your notes. If you cannot think of a particular word or are unsure about a spelling, draw a line _____ and keep on writing.

REVISING

Use the following guidelines as you read your classmates' drafts and revise your own essay. Be prepared to make changes in your ideas, organization, and evidence, as well as to fix problems in sentences and word choice.

Guidelines for Revisions

- **Clarify your main idea or interpretation.** Ask your readers to write, in one sentence, the main point of your interpretation. If their statements do not exactly match your main point, clarify your thesis. Your interpretation (not a statement of fact) should be clearly stated early in your essay.
- **Do not give a plot summary.** Your readers have read the story, so do not simply retell the plot. Do, however, give ample evidence. You must also explain how that evidence supports your main point.
- **Support each part of your interpretation with references to specific passages from the text.** Do not be satisfied with one piece of evidence. Find as many bits of evidence as possible. The case for your interpretation grows stronger with each additional piece of evidence.
- **Explain how each piece of evidence supports your interpretation.** Do not just cite several pieces of evidence and go on to your next point. Explain for your readers *how* the evidence supports your interpretation.
- **Define key terms in your essay.** If you are writing about the *hero* in a story, define what you mean by "hero" or "heroine." If you are arguing that "The Story of an Hour" has a *feminist* theme, define "feminism."
- **Signal the major parts of your interpretation.** Let your readers know when you shift to a new point. Use transitions and paragraph hooks at the beginning of body paragraphs.
- **Use the present tense as you describe the events in the story.** If you are describing the end of "The Story of an Hour," write "Mrs. Mallard descends the stairs and learns the 'good news' about her husband."

- **Quote accurately and cite page numbers for each reference.** Double-check your quotations to make sure they are accurate, word-for-word transcriptions. Following each direct quotation, cite page references as follows: In the first sentence, Kate Chopin says, "Mrs. Mallard was afflicted with a heart trouble" *(479). Note:* The period goes outside the parentheses. See Chapter 12 for correct documentation style.
- **Revise your essay for sentence clarity and conciseness.** Read your essay aloud or have a classmate read it. Reduce unnecessary repetition. Use active verbs. Rework awkward or confusing sentences.
- **Edit your essay.** Check your essay for correct spelling, word choice, punctuation, and grammar.

■ POSTSCRIPT ON THE WRITING PROCESS   Before you turn in your essay, answer the following questions in your journal.

1. Explain what part of this essay (collecting ideas and evidence, focusing on your interpretation, shaping your essay, drafting, or revising) was most difficult for you. How did you work around that problem?

2. What do you like best about your essay? Refer to specific places in the essay (lead-in, thesis, pieces of evidence, ideas, conclusion). Which specific paragraphs did you like best? Why?

3. What did you learn about the story by writing your interpretation? What do you realize now that you did not understand when you first read the story?

4. If you had two more hours to work on this essay, what would you change? Why?

RESPONDING TO LITERATURE:

STUDENT WRITING

A WORN PATH

Julia MacMillan and Brett MacFadden

Julia MacMillan and Brett MacFadden collaboratively wrote their essay on the Phoenix imagery in Eudora Welty's "A Worn Path." They drafted their own essays separately and then collaborated on a revision that shared their interpretations and their best textual evidence. The following are their original separate notes and drafts, their plans for their collaborative revision, and their final revised interpretation. Read their separate versions first, and then see how they collaborated to produce their revised essay.

ROUGH DRAFTS

JULIA MACMILLAN

The journey that Phoenix Jackson makes in Eudora Welty's "A Worn Path" is very similar to that made by the mythological phoenix on its way to rebirth. Much of the symbolism and figurative language throughout the story shows the succession of events that parallel a Phoenix-like ending to the old woman.

We can feel, almost from the beginning, that Phoenix's long life is coming to an end. She is described with "the two knots of her cheeks illuminated by a yellow burning under the dark" (289). In only a few more sentences, however, we hear the mourning dove, apparently mourning for Phoenix. The yellow burning under the dark is almost a desperate, final fiery burst in the face of oncoming death.

Her death is also foreshadowed in the mention of a buzzard, watching her from the tall, dead trees. She asks of him, "Who are you watching?" as if she knows it is herself. Further in her journey, upon meeting the white hunter, her impending death as well as her expectation of it are shown. The little bob-white, "its beak hooked bitterly to show it was dead" (262), that the hunter was carrying on his bag quite forcefully shows us her death. The fact that she does not fear, but expects this death is shown when the hunter points his gun at Phoenix, and she "stood straight and faced him" quite fearlessly (263). In not fearing this death and seeming to understand its nearness, Phoenix Jackson becomes more like the bird she is named for.

It is most clearly seen that the author intended her reader to see the Phoenix imagery when the grandson is introduced near the end of the story. On page 264, she "entered a door, and there she saw the document that had been stamped with the gold seal and framed in the gold frame, which matched the dream that was hung up in her head." The gold in this passage seems to represent flame—the flame of her funeral pyre and the dream in her head of perpetuation and reincarnation through her grandson's life. It is even more clearly stated when, once in the doctor's office, she goes into a strange trance, becoming unable to answer the agitated nurse's questions. When finally asked, "He isn't dead, is he?" a "flutter, then a flame of comprehension comes across her face" (265). These flames are symbolic of her death, yet they are caused by her remembering the importance of her grandson's life to her. This life is most precious to her, because it is through her grandson that Phoenix, like the mythological bird, will live again.

BRETT MACFADDEN

In many ways Phoenix Jackson is like the mythical bird she is named after; her physical characteristics, her purpose in life, and her extreme age and nearness to death all support her likeness to the mythological Phoenix.

The Phoenix is a bird of myth that lives for 500 years and then burns itself to death, rising from its ashes renewed and beautiful. Phoenix Jackson in the story "A Worn Path" by Eudora Welty is a very old black woman near the end of her life cycle who takes a long walk through the woods to town in order to get medicine for her ailing grandson. The core story is very simple, and it is because of this simplicity that the reader is forced to look beyond the core for a more complex tale. One of the first clues toward the inner story is the name of the main character, Phoenix. With the knowledge of what a Phoenix is, we can find many clues supporting the idea of the old woman living her life as a Phoenix.

Throughout the short story, words and phrases that describe the old woman might also describe the mythological bird. Her skin is black with a "golden color underneath" (259) and the "two knobs of her cheeks were illuminated by a yellow burning under the dark" (259). Both the golden color and especially the yellow burning are colors of fire, symbolizing the bird's fiery death. A red rag that she wears on top of her head is also another color of flame. Her black, wrinkled skin can be thought of as looking quite like ashes, and assuming that her grandson is a blood relative, his skin should also be the color of charred ash. She is like a fire that is almost out. It is mostly black, but there is the small flicker of flame to show you it is not yet extinguished.

Assuming the reader chooses to believe that Phoenix does in fact have a grandson and he is in fact sick, then the main purpose of her trip is to get the boy his medicine. This idea goes along nicely with the phoenix theme because she is giving everything she has left for the benefit of her grandson. She is essentially burning herself up so that the new person can exist. We can assume from the physical appearance and actions of Phoenix that she is pretty nearly burnt out. Phoenix knows her grandson is the one with the potential now, and so she gives all the effort she has to get him his medicine. Her only wish is to see him rise from his sick bed.

There are many hints to Phoenix's extreme age. At one time she tells herself, "I is the oldest person I ever know" (261), indicating that she has lived longer than most. Another time the hunter that she came across estimated that she was "a hundred years old" (263). Much of the imagery in the story symbolizes her oncoming death. The fact that it is winter can be seen as the winter of her life. Other death images include the big dead trees, the buzzard, the scarecrow she mistakes for a ghost, and the black dog that knocks her into the ditch.

A SINGULAR PERPETUATION

Brett MacFadden and Julia MacMillan

Phoenix Jackson, in the story "A Worn Path," by Eudora Welty, is in many ways like the mythological bird she is named after. Her purpose in life, birdlike characteristics, and nearness to death all support a clear parallel between the character and her namesake. The story is very simple, and because of this simplicity the reader is forced to search for a more meaningful tale. One of the first clues towards the inner story is the name of the main character, Phoenix. With the knowledge of what a Phoenix is, it is possible to find many clues supporting the idea of the old woman living her life as a Phoenix, burning herself out for the benefit of the new bird, her grandson. **(1)**

The Phoenix is a mythological bird who after living for 500 years, burns itself to ashes on a pyre, and rises renewed to live another cycle. Phoenix Jackson journeys through the woods to town to get medicine for her ailing grandson. This idea parallels the Phoenix theme, because she is making what appears to be her final journey, in order that her grandson may rise from his sickbed. The legend of the Phoenix is one of singular perpetuation; only one exists in the world. This is shown when she tells the nurses that "We is the only two left in the world" (255). Phoenix is concerned because if both of them were to die, then it would result in the extinction of the species. As much as she worries about him surviving, she is confident that he, like the immortal bird, will survive. Speaking to the nurses again, she says, "He suffer and it don't seem to put him back at all. . . . He going to last" (265–66). As well as his immortality, his birdlike characteristics and dependence on Phoenix for his perseverance are shown when he peeps out of his quilt "holding his mouth open like a little bird" (266). He is her reincarnation, and she is devoted to his successful ascension. **(2)**

Throughout the story many words and phrases that describe the old woman might also describe the mythological bird. Her skin is described as black with "a golden color underneath," and the "two knobs of her cheeks were illuminated by a yellow burning under the dark" (259). She wears on top of her head a red rag. Both the "golden color," and the "yellow burning," as well as the red of her rag are colors of fire, symbolizing her approaching death. As she walks, the tapping of her umbrella sounds like "the chirping of a solitary little bird" (259). Her likeness to a bird is evidenced when, in passing a scarecrow in a field, she is frightened, as a bird would be. When startled by a dog, she fell into a ditch "like a little puff of milk-weed" (262). This gives the appearance that she is a light creature, mostly flame and feather. These birdlike characteristics of Phoenix seem to imply that the author intended her to represent the mythical bird. **(3)**

The myth of the Phoenix holds that when ". . . its eyes begin to grow dim, it knows that the time of death has come" (Oswalt 239). When we are first introduced to the main character, as well as being old, she is described as having "eyes . . . blue with age" (259). Many images of death, some quite vivid, link Phoenix Jackson's impending death to that of the Phoenix of myth. At one point in her journey she stoops and looks upwards exclaiming, "Sun so high! Time getting all gone here" (260). This clearly indicates her knowledge of her approaching death. Her death is also foreshadowed by the mention of several images that bombard us from the dawn of the story. Early on she reflects on the call of a mourning dove—mourning being something done in the wake of death. Later she comes upon a buzzard sitting in a dead tree. She asks of him, "Who you watching?" (261), as if she knows it is herself. Her death is foreshadowed further when walking through a cornfield she happens upon what she perceives to be a ghost. Upon closer inspection, the ghost turned out to be a scarecrow. However, she shows no fear approaching what she thinks is a ghost, which demonstrates that she is comfortable with dying. The black dog that knocks her into a ditch is another vivid image of death. Further in her journey, upon meeting a white hunter, her impending death as well as her expectation of it are shown. The little bob-white, "its beak hooked bitterly to show that it was dead" (262) that the hunter was carrying on his bag quite forcefully shows us her anticipated death. The fact that she does not fear, but expects this death is shown when the hunter pointed his gun at Phoenix, and she "stood straight and faced him" quite fearlessly" (263). In not fearing this death and seeming to understand its nearness, Phoenix Jackson becomes more like the bird she is named for. **(4)**

A carefully wrought story, "A Worn Path" is more than a tale of an old woman's formidable journey. It is the rebirth of an age-old myth wrapped in the cloak of conventionality. In examining some of the symbols, allusions, and the underlying legend, we find a well hidden but evident parallel between the lives of the main character and her namesake, the Phoenix. **(5)**

Works Cited

Oswalt, Sabine G. *Concise Encyclopedia of Greek and Roman Mythology.* Chicago: Follett Publishing Co., 1969.

■ POSTSCRIPT ON THE COLLABORATIVE REVISION
We began this collaboration by reading each other's papers and rereading our own in order to find the strengths and weaknesses of each paper. Then together we combed through each paper, pulling out what we both agreed were our strongest points and compiled these into a thesis. For our thesis, we used the second sentence in the first paragraph: "Her [Phoenix's] purpose in life, her birdlike characteristics, and her nearness to death support a clear parallel between the character and her namesake."

Having decided on a thesis and a rough plan of action, we then went to the computer lab and began writing. At this point, the paper became more difficult because we had to narrow two papers into one and decide what we should omit. For example, Julia's paper discussed the emblem on the doctor's office wall as another symbol of Phoenix's fiery death. After discussing this scene, we decided that the symbolism was not strong enough and should be left out. We both knew each other before deciding to write the collaborative essay, so we were both comfortable around each other and were able to say what we really thought about each other's writing. We knew also that our basic writing styles were opposing. Brett's was concise, while Julia's was more flowing. Our different writing styles had to be combined into one smooth style. We did this by having one person dictate and the other type, which caused an intertwining of our styles by the time the words hit the screen. We had fun working on this paper and learned quite a bit about collaboration in the process. For example, we found it challenging because we had to work on one sentence at a time, making sure each sentence was right before we went on to the next one. This process made the revision take far longer to complete than if it had been done by one person.

QUESTIONS FOR WRITING AND DISCUSSION

1. What are the best ideas or evidence in this essay? Explain the points at which you might disagree with the writers' interpretation.

2. Compare MacMillan's and MacFadden's drafts with the final version of their essay. Explain how their interpretation changed as they worked collaboratively on the final version. What did they add to their final version? What did they omit from the earlier drafts?

3. In the final version, MacMillan and MacFadden do not cite evidence from the final part of the story. Explain why the events in town support or do not support the Phoenix parallels.

4. Review the Guidelines for Revision. In the authors' essay, underline sentences that contain the *main idea*, that *define key terms*, that contain *evidence* or support, that *explain* how the evidence supports the thesis, that *signal* major parts of the interpretation, and that contain *accurate quotations*. Based on your annotations, what suggestions for further revision do you have for the authors?

DEATH: THE FINAL FREEDOM

Pat Russell

Following a class discussion of the feminist theme in Kate Chopin's "The Story of an Hour," Pat Russell wrote in his journal, "Is the story a feminist one? No. It is not just about feminism but about how people stifle their own needs and desires to accommodate those of their mate." In his essay, Russell argues that the traditional feminist reading limits the universal theme of the story. As you read his essay, see if you are persuaded by his argument.

The poor treatment of women and their struggle for an individual identity is a major underlying theme of Kate Chopin's stories. Although many regard Chopin's "The Story of an Hour" as a feminist story, today a more universal interpretation is appropriate. This story is not about the oppression of a woman, but about how people strive to maintain the normalcy and security of their relationships by suppressing their own individual wants and needs. **(1)**

Evidence in favor of the feminist argument begins with the period the story was written in, sometime around the turn of the century. Society prevented women from coming out of the household. Most women weren't allowed to run a business, and for that matter, they couldn't even vote. Their most important jobs were wife and mother. This background sets the tone for the main character's life. In the beginning we are told Mrs. Mallard has a "fair, calm face whose lines bespoke repression" (414). There is also evidence that suggests her husband was ignorant of her ideas and forceful with his own. Chopin writes: "There would be no powerful will bending her in that blind persistence with which men and women believe they have a right to impose a private will upon a fellow creature" (415). In addition, Mrs. Mallard is described early on as fearful and powerless, and later as a triumphant "goddess of Victory," indicating her rebirth. These citations suggest that this is a feminist story, but this label limits the meaning behind the story. **(2)**

Many people who are unhappy with their marriages either fail to recognize their unhappiness or refuse to accept responsibility for it. I feel sorry for those who don't recognize their unhappiness. However, it is pathetic to see someone such as Mrs. Mallard hold onto a relationship simply because she doesn't know how to let go. "And yet she had loved him—sometimes. Often she had not" (415). She continuously fell in and out of love with her husband until he "died," at which point she told herself that love didn't matter compared to the self-assertion "which she suddenly recognized as the strongest impulse of her being" (415). It is as if she had waited for all of her life for this moment; she prayed for a long life, when only the day before she had dreaded it. She wept for him but at the same time compared her husband to a criminal, a man whom she had lived her life for, never once thinking of herself. But now "there would be no one to live for during those coming years; she would live for herself" (415). She was lucky in that she felt "free." Her emotional suppression was over, and she would no longer have anyone to blame for her unhappiness. **(3)**

It is important not only to try to interpret the author's intended meaning of the story, but also to think about what message "The Story of an Hour" has for us today. As a feminist story, the lesson "The Story of an Hour" teaches is one dimensional. Interpreting it as a story about the struggle of all people opens up the possibility of teaching others that selfishness and selflessness are both good, when used in moderation. In Mrs. Mallard's case, correcting this balance became a matter of life and death. In the face of her suppressor, her desperation for freedom forced her to choose death. **(4)**

QUESTIONS FOR WRITING AND DISCUSSION

1. With what parts of Russell's interpretation do you agree? What additional evidence from the story might Russell cite in support of his interpretation? What ideas or sentences might you challenge? What evidence from the story might refute those statements?

2. Write out your definition of *feminism*. Where does or should Russell explain his definition? How should Russell clarify his definition?

3. Write out Russell's main idea or thesis. Explain why his thesis is an interpretation and not just a statement of fact.

4. What shaping strategy does Russell use to organize his essay?

5. Write out two other possible titles for Russell's essay. Explain why your alternate titles are (or are not) better than Russell's title.

12

WRITING A RESEARCH PAPER

Raphael. *The School of Athens* 1508. Stanze di Raffaello, Vatican Palace, Vatican State

WHILE READING TONI MORRISON'S <u>SONG OF SOLOMON</u> AND TALKING WITH RELATIVES ABOUT YOUR OWN FAMILY TREE, YOU DECIDE TO LEARN MORE ABOUT YOUR ancestors—where they came from, what jobs they held, which ones were famous and which were not, and why these people lived the lives they did. In the process, you hope to learn more about yourself and your immediate family. During your research, you read family records and letters, interview your parents and grandparents, check county records, and research genealogies in the library. You intend to write an investigative paper documenting not only what you find but the process of your search and the discoveries that you make along the way.

❧

AFTER SPENDING TWO MONTHS IN FRANCE LIVING WITH A FAMILY AND TRYING TO UNDERSTAND THEIR DINNER CONVERSATION, YOU WONDER WHY YOU—AND OTHER Americans—know so little about foreign languages. After reflecting on your inadequate background in French language and culture, you decide to investigate the current state of foreign-language studies in the United States. During your research, you discover that Americans know very little about foreign languages and cultures simply because foreign languages are rarely required of students either in high school or in college. You decide to write a research paper that documents the current state of foreign-language studies and demonstrates a need for a mandatory foreign-language requirement for secondary schools. You hope that it will persuade more students to study foreign languages and encourage some schools to revise their requirements.

ALTHOUGH THE WORDS "RESEARCH PAPER" SOUND IMPOSING TO MOST PEOPLE, RESEARCH IS REALLY A NATURAL AND ENJOYABLE PART OF OUR EVERYDAY EXPERIENCE, BOTH OUT-side and inside college classrooms. We pride ourselves on being good detectives—whether it's window-shopping for a good bargain, finding the hottest used sports car, asking coworkers for tips on the best Mexican food in town, or just browsing in bookstores for something fun to read. Even in college classes, curiosity leads us to discover new ideas. Whenever we wonder about what causes ozone holes, why teenagers commit suicide, what makes the Internet work, how artists turn clay into beautiful pottery, or what the national debt means, the seed for a research idea drops into our minds. At some point, the idea becomes a question, takes root, and begins to grow. When that happens, we want to learn about something, to find out what others already know or don't know. Curiosity blooms into research when we'd rather discover the answers for ourselves instead of being handed an answer—an "answer" that may have the manufactured feel of a plastic flower.

Whether or not you called it by that name, the essays that you have already written in this course have involved research. The word *research* literally means "to seek out" or "to search again." All writing requires research. Your observing essay, for example, required you to "look again" at your subject in order to describe it well. For your remembering essay, you recalled special events from the past, researching your mind for memories. You have also investigated topics by searching in written documents and by doing surveys and interviews. You have explained, evaluated, argued, and even explored subjects using research. In short, you are already a researcher with considerable experience in presenting the results of your research to a chosen audience. A research paper—sometimes called a "term paper"—is simply a more thorough and systematic extension of skills that you have already practiced.

This chapter will show you how to write a research paper—preparing, locating sources, taking notes, collecting and shaping information, revising, and documenting your sources. As in other writing assignments, the process is recursive. Often, you will need to back up, collect new information, redraft parts of your paper, or refocus your subject during the writing process. At the end of this chapter, student writer Kate McNerny's paper, "Foreign Language Study: An American Necessity" illustrates the important features of a research paper. During the chapter, however, samples from her research log, bibliography, notes, drafts, and documentation illustrate various stages in one writer's process of writing a research paper.

TECHNIQUES FOR WRITING

A RESEARCH PAPER

Criticism [is] a disinterested endeavor to learn and propagate the best that is known and thought in the world.

—MATTHEW ARNOLD,

POET AND ESSAYIST

Like other kinds of writing, a research paper requires that you focus on a particular subject, develop a claim or thesis, and support your position with convincing evidence: background information, facts, statistics, descriptions, and other people's evaluations and judgments. The evidence that you present in a research paper, however, is more detailed than that in an essay, and the sources must be cited in the text and documented at the end of the paper.

In a sense, a research paper is like a scientific experiment. **Your readers should be able to trace your whole experiment—to see what ideas and evidence you worked with, where you found them, and how you used them in your paper.** If readers have any questions about the information you've presented or the conclusions you've reached, they can start with your sources and recreate or check the "experiment" for themselves. If they want to investigate your subject further, your sources will guide their reading. As you write your research paper, keep the following techniques in mind:

- Using *purpose, audience,* and *form* **as your guides for writing.** Research is just a method of collecting and documenting ideas and evidence. Purpose, audience, and form should still direct your writing.
- **Finding the** *best that has been written or said* **about your subject.** Instead of trying to reinvent the wheel, discover what other people or writers already know (or don't know) and then build on what they have learned. Learn to evaluate your sources—be especially critical of Internet or Web sources.
- **Using sources to make** *your* **point.** As you gather information, you may revise your thesis in light of what you learn, but don't let the tail wag the dog. Don't allow raw information to control you or your paper.
- *Documenting* **your sources, both in the text and at the end of the paper.** Using ideas, information, or actual language from your sources without proper documentation is *plagiarism.*

USING PURPOSE, AUDIENCE, AND FORM AS GUIDES

Like any other kind of writing, research papers have a *purpose.* Reporting, explaining, evaluating, problem solving, and arguing are all purposes for research papers. Purposes may appear in combinations, as in a paper that summarizes current research and then proposes a solution to a problem. Research papers, however, are not just reports of other people's ideas or evidence. What you, the researcher, observe and remember and learn is important, too. Most subjects are not interesting until writers make them so. Your curiosity, your interest in the subject, your reason and intuition establish why the subject is worth researching in the first place—and why a reader would want to read the paper once it is finished.

Research papers have a defined *audience,* too. The subject you choose, the kind of research you do, the documentation format, the vocabulary and style you use—all should be appropriate for your selected audience. If you write a senior research paper in your major, you will write for a professor and for a community of people knowledgeable about your field. If you are a legal assistant or a junior attorney in a law firm, a superior may ask you to research a specific legal precedent. If you work for a manufacturer, a manager may assign you a research report on the sales and strategies of a competitor. Although your classmates and teacher will probably read the research paper that you write for this class, you will ask them to role-play your audience. They will try to read your paper from the point of view of a defined audience—an employer, a politician, a nutritionist, an artist, an astronomer, or a senior law partner. In fact, your instructor may ask you to send your paper to some person or persons who actually are part of your audience.

Finally, your research paper will follow a *form* that fits your purpose and meets the expectations and needs of your audience. First, form is controlled by purpose. If you are writing a research paper evaluating some product or performance, it may look like an evaluating paper, organized around your claims, criteria, judgments, and evidence. If you are writing a problem-solving paper, you will demonstrate the problem, propose a solution, and convince your readers that your proposal is necessary or will work. If you are arguing for a position or claim, you will present research showing both sides of the controversy and then try to convince your reader to believe or act on your claim. In each case, however, you will cite your sources in the body or text of your paper and include a list of your sources (a *bibliography*) at the end.

The *form* for your research paper is also affected by your intended audience. If you are researching new advances in sports medicine for an audience of experts, you may choose an elaborate form, with an abstract or summary of your ideas at the beginning, a section reviewing and evaluating current research, subsections for each of your main points with diagrams and charts, and an appendix with supplementary materials. If, however, you are writing primarily for jogging enthusiasts, your research paper may look more like an informal essay. Magazines and journals in the field illustrate a variety of appropriate forms for research papers. The student essay by Kate McNerny at the end of this chapter illustrates one form.

FINDING THE BEST SOURCES

Accessing information from both published and unpublished sources is central to all research. To find good sources, you need to hone your detective skills. Unfortunately, Hollywood has promoted the myth that good detectives follow their suspects in high-speed car chases or through glamorous affairs. Of course, that's just fantasy. Detectives must do actual research—paperwork and legwork—to track down leads. Writers are, in a real sense, also detectives, constantly researching their own experiences and the experiences of others. Journalists, lawyers, psychologists, doctors, businesspeople, coaches, scientists, novelists—all sorts of people practice their skills in locating key bits of information and tracking down good leads.

Research combines careful planning with good luck, mindless drudgery and moments of inspiration, many dead ends and a few rare discoveries. As coaches sometimes say, those who prepare and work hard make their own luck. The following excerpt from the introduction to Pauli Murray's *Proud Shoes: The Story of an American Family* recounts her research into her family genealogy, which included slaves, free blacks, some racially mixed family members, and other relatives who were white and socially prominent. Although her detective work took several years and involved both library and field research, her account reflects the problems and successes that all researchers experience.

> My field research had the thrill of detection when the clues panned out. Rigorous discipline was needed for the drudgery of sifting through masses of documentary material in search of one relevant fact or one confirmation of a family legend. The trail of the Fitzgerald family led me into nearly a dozen localities in several states. It took me into musty basements of old courthouses to pore over dust-silted and sometimes indecipherable handwritten entries in old volumes. I found that each locality had its own captivating legends preserved in family papers; its traditions recorded in pamphlets and privately published little books; its stories printed in almanacs, newspapers, business directories. Almost every place had "the oldest living inhabitants" and their recollections. Most important, almost every locality had its own regional-history enthusiasts, who welcomed me into a fellowship of digging into the past. Some of them gave me expert guidance which improved the efficiency of my research and shortened my labors.

USING SOURCES TO MAKE YOUR POINT

When your hard work does yield a source that has good information and ideas on your exact subject, don't be tempted to let that source take over your paper. If you start stringing together passages from only one or two key sources, you'll be summarizing rather than doing research. You'll be letting the sources tell you what to think, what information is important, or what conclusions to reach. Use your sources, then, to support *your* point. Write your own paper; don't let your sources write it for you.

DOCUMENTING YOUR SOURCES

Documenting your sources is an important part of writing a research paper. Documentation takes place in two stages: first, in the body or text of your paper, you give credit to any material that you have taken from your sources. Then, at the end of the paper, you include a list of "Works Cited" or "Works Consulted" that gives fuller information about these sources for your readers. If your readers doubt a fact or statistic, they can check your sources for themselves. If your readers want more information, your documentation enables them to track down the sources. *Note:* Decide on the documentation format (usually MLA or APA styles) before you begin your research. You need to know what relevant bibliographical information you need to record in your notes.

PREPARING YOURSELF

FOR THE RESEARCH PROCESS

Writing a research paper involves the same process that you used in writing essays. The major difference is that each stage or dimension of the process takes longer. You may spend two weeks just collecting sources, reading articles and books, jotting down ideas, testing your ideas on classmates and friends, and narrowing and focusing your subject. And because you gather so much material, the shaping and organizing processes are also more demanding. Sometimes you may feel as if you're trying to put forty frogs in a dishpan: By the time you arrange ten, the first four have already jumped out. The revising also takes longer, partly because you have to include your documentation, but partly because the sections of the paper may not fit together as smoothly as you had hoped. There is really no way to rush research. If writing an ordinary paper is like fixing your lunch, then writing a research paper is like preparing

Thanksgiving dinner. You can't microwave a research paper. Good things take time.

The first step in writing a research paper is to *readjust your inner clock.* Initially, you'll think that you're not making much progress. You'll think that you're in a slow-motion movie or that you're trying to jog through butter. However, once you readjust your inner clock, set more modest goals, and content yourself with a slower but more persistent pace, you've won half the battle. By reducing the pressure on yourself, you'll feel less frustrated when you reach a dead end but also readier to appreciate valuable information when you discover it.

To help you adjust mentally and physically to a new pace and an extended writing process, begin your preparation by making a research notebook, outlining a realistic timetable for the paper, and selecting a documentation format.

■ WARMING UP: JOURNAL EXERCISES Do at least one of the following journal exercises to help get yourself into a research frame of mind or to discover a possible research subject.

1. In the library, find an issue of a magazine or newspaper published on or near the date and year of your birth. The issue may be on microfilm. Record the date and title of the newspaper or magazine. Browse through the issue, looking at headlines, articles, advertisements, editorials, comics, weather, sports, local news, and so forth. As you look through the issue, record any items, facts, or historical incidents that interest you. Photocopy one page that you find especially interesting. Explain why that page captured your attention.

2. Sit down with a family member, friend, or classmate. On a sheet of paper, write down the subject of the most interesting course that you are currently taking. Hand the sheet of paper to that person and ask him or her to write down questions for an interview designed to find out *why* you like this course and *what* you like best about it. Then have that person interview you and record your responses. At the end of the interview, discuss your responses. What ideas could you research in order to explain to your interviewer what is interesting about this subject?

3. If you are *not* in the library, try this exercise. Reread your authority list from the journal entries in Chapter 6, "Investigating." Choose one subject from that list. Assume that you are on a scavenger hunt, trying to track down bits of information about that subject without leaving the building that you are currently in. Anything is fair game:

a dictionary, a textbook, a telephone directory, a telephone, a computer terminal, a friend or roommate, this textbook, your journal, or anything you can observe or remember. You have twenty-five minutes to complete the hunt. Write down all the sources you use and the information you discover from each source.

4. In the library, wander down the stacks, looking at titles of books that might interest you. Choose one volume from the shelf. In your journal, record the basic information about that book: author, title, place of publication, publisher, date. In that book, find *three* specific sources that the author refers to or used to write the book. (If the book does not cite sources, choose another volume.) Does your library have these sources? If so, determine where these sources are located. Ask the reference librarian for help if you need it.

RESEARCH NOTEBOOK

Although some researchers still recommend using index cards for recording bibliographic entries and notes, for most shorter research projects (up to twenty pages), a notebook computer, a loose-leaf notebook, or a spiral notebook with pockets for additional papers and photocopies may be more functional. Divide your notebook into four sections: research log, bibliography, notes from sources (including photocopies), and drafts and ideas.

The *research log* section of your notebook serves as a scratch pad and log of your research progress. In it, you will record what you accomplish during each research session, potential references you need to check, reminders to yourself, questions to ask a librarian or your instructor, and notes about your problems, progress, and intended next steps. As you work, jot down what you did and what you still need to do. These notes about your problems, progress, questions, and next steps will help you maintain momentum on your research project. Each time you return to the library or to your research, you can check your notes to see what you need to do next.

Below is an excerpt from student writer Kate McNerny's research log:

4/26

4:30–6:00 p.m.

Still working on finding articles. Found the Delbert and Roberta Long article. It has some good stuff. Education is on microfilm, so I learned

how to photocopy from microfilm. Of course,
just when I had the machine turned to
exactly the right page, I discovered I didn't
have a dime for the copy machine, so I had
to leave the room (some guy waiting in line
looked irritated as I explained I'd be back in a
minute). I ran to the change machine, got
my nickels and copied the article!

April issue of <u>Parents</u> magazine missing
from the shelves. UGH – I hate that.

Question: Do I want to survey students to
find out about typical attitudes toward taking
foreign languages? What questions could I
ask?

Another question: Is this going to be an
arguing paper? Is there a controversy? Are
there two sides??

Try to find tomorrow: three <u>Education Digest</u>
articles on microfilm (L11/E3):   Oct. 94, p. 32
                                     Dec. 95, p. 89
                                     Mar. 96, p. 52

Check <u>Education Index</u>.

Remember that 5 – 6 p.m. is a good time
to work in the library. Everyone clears out,
so I don't have to fight over the Internet
computer, the photocopier, and the microfilm
machines.

In the *bibliography* section of your notebook, keep a list of every source
that you consult, with complete information about each source. If your
library's online catalog system shows the status of every source, be sure to
print out every source you want to check. If you cannot print the source, you'll
need to copy it in your notebook. Leave space between entries for additional
information, such as call numbers. This list becomes *your working bibliography.* McNerny's bibliography included the following entries:

Honan, William H. "Language Study Shifts Again: Chinese is up, Russian down." The New York Times 9 Oct. 1996: B9

AN 1. N4   Current issues in basement east wing; Older issues in microtext

Lambert, Richard D. "Some Issues in Language Policy for Higher Education" The Annals of the American Academy of Political and Social Science 532(1994): 123-37.

H 1 .A4   Current issues in current Periodicals Room; Older issues in Stacks

In the *source notes* section, leave plenty of pages to record direct quotations, paraphrases of key ideas, and facts from the sources in your bibliography list. Introduce each section with a reference to the author and a short version of the title. After each note, indicate the page number or numbers. One page of McNerny's notes contained the following entries:

Lambert, "Some Issues in Language Policy."

Lambert explains how the lack of coordination between secondary schools and higher education causes problems. As Lambert notes, "The result of this strong tradition of university autonomy is that in the United States, foreign language planning for higher education must take place one institution at a time and implementation of change must occur in house-to-house, hand-to-hand combat" (125).

Ranwez and Rogers, Status of Foreign Languages

91% of the 536 Colorado secondary schools responding to the questionnaire offered foreign languages, but 91% of schools responding didn't require any foreign language credits for graduation. pp. 99-100

For your source notes section, make *photocopies* of any valuable source materials. Write author, title, and page numbers on each photocopied source.

In the *drafts and ideas* section of the notebook, jot down brainstorms, looping or clustering exercises, sketch outlines, trial drafts, and examples from your own experience. During a research project, ideas can come to you at any time. When they do, take time to write them down. This section of your notebook serves as a journal devoted solely to your research paper. One example from McNerny's drafts and ideas section records her personal experience with foreign languages:

4/29

I can remember my mom always telling me, "Take French classes, learn how to speak French so that you can go visit your cousins in France some day." At the time (junior high school) though, learning a foreign language was low on my priority list. I did take French classes for two years – but dropped out after my sophomore year and immediately lost any basic competency I might have acquired.

In college, I'd like to take a language again, but it never seems to fit with my schedule. But last year, as my mom had promised, I got the opportunity to visit my cousins in France. For some reason, the fact that I couldn't speak French didn't seem to me like it would be a big problem. That was until I stepped off the train at Gare du Nord in Paris and couldn't find the relative who was supposed to meet me. After frantically searching the entire station several times, I had to break down and ask for help. At the information desk a few completely butchered French phrases escaped my lips – only to be received by an unimpressed, unresponsive station attendant. He muttered something about dumb Americans and then pointed me off

towards some unknown destination. Well I
survived that ordeal – but at the same time
swore to myself that I would never make
another trip to France until I could speak
the language.

RESEARCH TIME TABLE

Before you begin your research, write out a tentative schedule. Your instructor may assign due dates for specific parts of the paper (invention exercises, topic selection, working bibliography, rough draft), but you should make a schedule that fits your work habits and your weekly schedule.

The following schedule assumes that you have at least a month to work on your research paper. The amount of time required by each part depends on the amount of time you can work each day. On some days, you may have only thirty minutes. On other days, you may have several hours. The key is to do a little bit every day to keep your momentum going.

Prepare for research. Buy and organize a research notebook; set up a time table; select documentation format.   1–2 days

Choose a subject. Begin the narrowing and focusing process.   2–3 days

Collect sources. Find library sources; identify and find unpublished sources; do interviews or surveys; record personal experiences; browse sites on the Internet.

Evaluate source materials; take *notes* on selected sources; *photocopy* sources.   12–14 days

Shape and outline ideas; *reread* notes and photocopies; *draft* sections of essay. Continue to *focus* thesis while rereading, planning, and drafting.   6–10 days

Revise draft. Get peer response, collect additional information, sharpen thesis, reshape or revise outline, cite sources in the text and in the bibliographic list, and edit and proofread the paper.   6–8 days

Tailor your schedule to your own temperament and work habits. If you like to work exactly to a schedule or even finish early, design your schedule so you can finish a day or two before the due date. If you are like most writers—you love to procrastinate or you are often up all night just before an assignment is due—then use your schedule to set early target dates, to get your momentum going. When you finish drafting your schedule, put a copy in the *research log* section of your notebook, so that you can check your progress as you work.

DOCUMENTATION FORMAT: MLA AND APA STYLES

A final step in preparing for the research paper is to select a documentation style. This chapter illustrates both the MLA and APA styles. If you are writing a paper for the humanities, follow the Modern Language Association (MLA) style set forth in the *MLA Handbook for Writers of Research Papers*, 4th ed., (1995). If you are writing a paper in the behavioral sciences, use the American Psychological Association (APA) style as described in the *Publication Manual of the American Psychological Association*, 4th ed., (1994).

Leading academic and professional journals also illustrate the documentation styles customary in specialized fields. You may want to consult issues of those journals to determine the exact format for footnotes or in-text citation of sources. *Before you begin doing research, however, select a documentation style* that is appropriate for your subject, purpose, and audience. Then practice that style as you compile your working bibliography.

RESEARCH PAPER:

THE WRITING PROCESS

■ ASSIGNMENT FOR THE RESEARCH PAPER   Choose a subject that strongly interests you and about which you would like to learn more. It may be a subject that you have already written about in this course. Research this subject in a library and, as appropriate, supplement your library research with questionnaires, interviews, Internet research, or other unpublished sources of information. Check with your instructor for suggested length, appropriate number or kinds of sources, and additional format requirements. Use a documentation style appropriate for your subject, purpose, and audience.

CHOOSING A SUBJECT

For this research paper, choose a subject in which you already have personal interest or experience. Start by rereading your journal entries for possible research subjects. Even a personal entry may suggest an idea. If you wrote about how you fainted in the gym during aerobics or weight training, you might research the potential dangers of exercising in high heat and humidity or sitting in a sauna after hard exercise. If you wrote a journal entry about a friend's drinking problem, you might like to read more about the causes and treatments for alcoholism.

In addition, reread the essays that you have written to see whether one of them refers to a possible research subject. If your observing essay, for example, was about a tattoo parlor that you visited, use that essay as the starting point for further investigation and research. Who could you interview to find out more about tattooing? What is the history of tattooing? Is it becoming more popular? What controversies surround its use? What resources does your library have? What sites can you find on the Internet? You might also use a topic from your remembering, reading, or investigating essays as starting places for additional reading and research. *Build on what you already know and what already interests you rather than launch into an entirely unknown subject.*

NARROWING AND FOCUSING YOUR SUBJECT   Once you have a tentative idea, remember that you'll need to narrow it, focus it, or otherwise limit the subject. The topic of alcoholism is too general. Focus to a particular research question: "Do beer commercials on television contribute to alcoholism?" "Are there really positive effects to drinking moderate amounts of alcohol?" "What methods does Alcoholics Anonymous use to help people?" "Have DWI laws actually reduced the number of fatal automobile accidents?" Your research question may lead to a **thesis statement** that you will demonstrate in your research essay: "Although some studies show a definite link between consuming moderate amounts of white wine, the negative effects of alcohol consumption far outweigh the potential benefits."

Only after you've started your research, however, will you know whether your research question is still too broad (you can't begin to read everything about it in just two weeks) or too narrow (in two weeks, you can't find enough information about that question).

Two techniques may help narrow and focus your subject. You may wish to try these now, wait until you have done some initial reading, or do them several times during your collecting and shaping.

The first strategy is simply to think about your *purpose* and *audience.* The best way to focus your paper is to reflect on your purpose: What kinds of claims do you want to make about your topic? (If necessary, review the claims of fact, cause-and-effect, value, and policy outlined in Chapter 10, "Arguing.") As you collect articles, think about the kinds of claims you might want to make about your topic:

Claims of Fact: Are makers of hard liquor being discriminated against by not being allowed to advertise on TV? Is alcoholism a disease or just an addiction?

Claims of Cause-and-Effect: Does TV advertising increase alcohol consumption, or just affect the brands that are consumed? Can students who are "recreational" drinkers become alcoholics? Do recovery programs like Alcoholics Anonymous really work?

Claims of Value: Does beer have any nutritional value? Are micro-brews really made better or fresher than beers from larger breweries?

Claims of Policy: Do age-based drinking laws really work? Should liquor consumption be banned at campus sporting events? At dorms, fraternities, and sororities? At any campus function? Should makers of hard liquor be allowed to advertise on television?

Asking questions about your potential audience may also help you find a focus for your essay. If you are writing for a local audience, consider what they believe and what they might be interested in. Is the topic of alcohol regulation controversial? Who are your readers? What are they likely to believe on this issue? Profile your audience and brainstorm how you can connect your research question to those particular readers.

Question analysis is a second narrowing and focusing strategy. The who, what, when, where, and why questions that you use to focus your topic are the same questions that reference librarians use to help you focus your research in the library.

Who: What group of people are interested or affected?
What: How are key terms defined? What academic discipline is involved?
When: What is the period or time span?
Where: What continent, country, state, or town is involved?
Why: What are possible effects or implications?

Answering these questions—by yourself, in a group, or with a reference librarian—may suggest new angles, new avenues for research, or subtopics that could lead to a focus for your research paper. As you narrow your topic, you are narrowing and focusing the range of your research in the library. Student writer Kate McNerny, brainstorming with another class member, applied these questions to her subject about foreign-language study and came up with the following possibilities:

Foreign Language Study

Who?   Ans: I am interested in Americans. Specifically, I want to focus on why Americans should begin learning a foreign language early in school, in grade school, secondary school and college. Learning a foreign language would affect how foreigners see us.

What?   Ans: Key terms defined – perhaps what "learning" means. Does it mean just basic speaking competency? Probably. If I could have asked a few simple questions in the Gare du Nord, I wouldn't have felt so stupid. Academic discipline – learning the foreign language is important, but <u>culture</u> is part of it, too. History should teach us about foreign cultures. So should psychology – do the Japanese think differently from the Spanish? Why did the French seem rude and Italians friendly? Do I want to research the psychology of languages? I don't think so.

When?   Ans: I really want to know why foreign language studies are currently not emphasized. The 1990's. But what about trends – is it getting better or worse? Are more people learning foreign languages than a few years ago? I don't know.

Where? Ans: In the United States. In my home town. Why is it that in the French schools, children as a matter of course learn several languages while we aren't required to learn any? Supposedly, we are the "melting pot" for many different languages and cultures, but we don't know each other's languages.

Why?   Ans. I can make a long list of the effects
– We can't communicate when we're tourists
– We can't read anything printed in their language.
– We don't understand their culture.
– We don't even understand the cultures of the millions of Americans from other cultures.
– We isolate ourselves in business, too.

To avoid these effects, I want to argue for stronger foreign language requirements in secondary schools and colleges.

As a result of her question analysis, McNerny decided to discuss both language and culture, to focus on the current conditions, and to recommend that secondary schools require foreign languages. *In any research, however, what you look for and what you find are always different. You will need to modify your focus as you read and learn.*

COLLECTING

With ideas for a tentative subject, a possible purpose, and an audience, you can focus on collecting information. Collecting data for your research paper will require identifying and locating published and unpublished sources, evaluating your sources and choosing those that are the most appropriate for your needs, and then taking notes on your selected sources. *Remember, however, that finding sources—like writing itself—is an ongoing and recursive process.* You often identify new sources after you have taken notes on others. Although you may begin your search in the on-line catalog, in the reference section, or on the Internet, as you narrow and focus your topic or draft sections of your paper, you may come back and recheck the on-line catalog, basic references, periodical indexes, or bibliographies.

Use *informal contacts* with friends or acquaintances as an integral part of your collecting process. Friends, family members, business associates, or teachers may be able to suggest key questions or give you some sources: relevant books and magazine articles, television programs that are available in transcript, or local experts on your subject. One student, for example, was doing research on successful techniques for job interviews. She mentioned her project during a telephone conversation with her father. As it turned out, he regularly interviewed job applicants at his company. The student was able to interview him for specific recommendations. Another student was doing biographical research on television reporter Charles Kuralt. He mentioned his project to his journalism professor who, as it turned out, knew Kuralt personally and gave the student both some personal anecdotes and the titles of several recent articles. Most teachers, in fact, are happy to talk about their fields and recommend key sources of information.

UNPUBLISHED SOURCES Although the library may be your main source of information, other sources can be important, too. You may *interview* authorities on your subject or design a *questionnaire* to measure people's responses. (Interviews and questionnaires are discussed in Chapter 6.) *Phone calls* and *letters* to experts, government agencies, or businesses may yield background information, statistics, or quotations. *Notes from classes, public lectures, or television programs* are useful sources. Use a tape recorder to ensure that you transcribe your information accurately. A *scientific experiment* may even be appropriate. *Unpublished public documents,* such as deeds, wills, surveyors' maps, and environmental impact statements, may contain gold mines of information. Finally, don't ignore the most obvious sources: Your room, the attic in your home, or your relatives may have repositories of valuable unpublished data—private letters, diaries, old bills, or check stubs.

For her research paper, Kate McNerny decided to conduct an informal survey of attitudes toward foreign languages. She recorded the responses in the "Drafts and Ideas" section of her research notebook. When she drafted her paper, she used some of these responses in the introduction to her paper:

Q: Should foreign languages be required in Junior and Senior High?

A: (Mindy, 21, student) Yes, I think its a good idea – It would have been more valuable to me than some of the other required classes I took – like P.E.

A: (Jodi, 22, student) No, I had a hard enough time with English. Besides, I don't think I'd ever need to use it.

A: (Roger, 23, carpenter) Yes, I was in Europe last year and missed out on a lot because I couldn't speak any other language. Europeans don't speak English as much as we hear they do, but most of the people I Met there spoke at least two languages.

A: (Jim, 49, contractor) No, I've never gone to Europe and never needed to speak another language for any other reason. I had enough trouble getting through other classes.

A: (Carolyn, 59, teacher) Yes, when I was teaching there were few language classes available. But as a reading teacher I can see many ways in which language studies would have enhanced our program.

PRIMARY AND SECONDARY SOURCES   Some sources—accounts of scientific experiments, transcripts of speeches or lectures, questionnaires, interviews, private documents—are known as *primary sources.* They are original,
firsthand information, "straight from the horse's mouth." Secondhand reports,
analyses, and descriptions based on primary sources are known as secondary
sources. Secondary sources may contain the same information, but they are
once-removed. For example, a lecture or experiment by an expert in food irra-
diation is a primary source; the newspaper report of that lecture or experiment
is a secondary source.

The distinction between primary and secondary sources is important for
two related reasons. First, secondary sources may contain errors. The newspaper account, for example, may misquote the expert or misrepresent the experiment. If possible, therefore, find the primary source—a copy of the actual
lecture or a published article about the experiment. Second, finding the primary sources may make your research document more persuasive through an
appeal to character (see Chapter 10, "Arguing"). If you can cite the original
source—or even show how some secondary accounts distorted the original
experiment—you will gain your readers' trust and faith. Uncovering the primary data not only makes your research more accurate, but your additional
effort makes all your data and arguments appear more credible.

LIBRARY SOURCES   Before you begin collecting information, acquaint
yourself with the library itself. If you have not already done so, inquire at the
information desk about library tours or walk through the library with a friend
or classmate. Locate the *reference section;* the *on-line catalog* for books and articles; the *indexes* for newspapers, journals, and magazines; the *microfilm room;*
the *stacks;* and the *government documents* section. Don't assume that because
you've used one library, you can immediately start your research in a new
library. Remember: *Librarians* themselves are valuable sources of information.
Use their expertise early in your research.

BACKGROUND INFORMATION AND GENERAL REFERENCE   Before
you consult the on-line catalog, you may need a *general overview* of your subject. Start with an encyclopedia, dictionary, almanac, or biography for background information. Many people associate encyclopedias with their grade-
school "research"—when they copied passages out of *The World Book* or
Collier's Encyclopedia. But encyclopedias are an excellent source of basic information and terminology that may help you focus, narrow, and define your
subject. *Use them as background reading, however, not as major sources.*

In addition to the general encyclopedias, there are hundreds of references—one or two might just save you hours of research in the library and
lead you directly to key facts or important information on your topic. (You
may wish to begin your collecting in the reference room or check there only
after you have collected information from other books and articles. Often

these references are more valuable *after* you have done some reading on your subject.) Beyond the standard college dictionary or thesaurus, the *Oxford English Dictionary,* known as the *OED,* or *Webster's Third New International Dictionary of the English Language* may help you find key ideas or definitions.

There are also many specialized dictionaries for scientific terms, slang words, symbols, and a host of other specialized vocabularies. If you need facts, figures, or statistics, consult the *World Almanac,* the *Book of Facts,* or the *Statistical Abstract of the United States.* If your subject is a person, look at *Who's Who in America,* or check one of the references that indexes collections of biographies. *Biography and Genealogy Master Index* and *Biographical Dictionaries* reference more than three million biographical sketches.

The *librarian* is still the most valuable resource for your research. At some point during your research in the library, probably after you have a focused topic and have collected some sources, talk to a reference librarian. For many writers, asking for help can be really intimidating. To make the process of asking for help as painless—and productive—as possible, try saying something like the following: "Hi, I'm Kate McNerny. I'm doing a research project for my college writing course. My topic is foreign-language study in the United States. I'm trying to find information about the current state of foreign-language study in the United States and collect some arguments for increasing requirements in secondary schools and colleges. Here's what I've found so far [explain what you've done]. What additional reference books, indexes, dictionaries, or bibliographies might help me in my research?" The resulting conversation may be the most productive five minutes of your entire library research. After you've talked to the librarian once, it will be easier to return and ask a question when you hit a snag.

THE ON-LINE CATALOG   The good news for researchers as we face the twenty-first century is that computerized databases have revolutionized the whole process of library research. In most university libraries, a computer terminal can, in a few seconds, give you information that used to require hours of searching card catalogs or printed indexes. You can easily locate books, articles, and government documents relevant to your topic. You can find the library call numbers and locations of sources. You can determine if a source is available or checked out. Often, you can get an abstract or a short description of a source. For some systems, you can print out the bibliographic information so that you don't have to take notes. Occasionally, you can print out whole articles right there. Often you can access most of this information from a personal computer at home.

The only bad news is that nearly every on-line catalog system is different. Some colleges have OPAC's (On Line Public Access Catalogs) that allow you to access the library's holdings. Your college may use OCLC (On Line Computer Library System), which is the largest of the public-access catalogs,

Knowledge is of two kinds. We know a subject ourselves, or we know where we can find information upon it.

—SAMUEL
JOHNSON,

FROM BOSWELL'S LIFE OF
JOHNSON

or you may use systems such as NOTIS, RLIN, MELVYL, CARL, or SAGE. But whatever system your library uses, you need to spend time learning the tricks of that particular database. Don't try to learn the system by yourself. Take a library orientation tour. Collect the library's handouts about your computerized databases. Ask the librarians for help. And don't wait until your research paper is assigned to walk into the library. If you have to learn a new computer system *and* write your paper at the same time, you will be inviting massive frustration.

When McNerny started her search in her library's on-line database, she found the following sample entry on her topic. Notice that the information she received on her printout contained the following information: (1) the database she was searching; (2) the location of the periodical; (3) the author, title, and source; and (4) a short abstract. (For some of the references she found, she was able to print out the entire article.)

DATABASE:	Expanded Academic ASAP
KEY WORDS:	Language and languages study and teaching
LIBRARY:	Colorado State University
HOLDINGS:	Current issues in Current Periodicals Room. Older issues in Microtext, 1st floor, north wing. LB 2300 .C4
SOURCE:	*The Chronicle of Higher Education*, Nov 22, 1996 v43 n13 pA35(2).
TITLE:	A new program ends the stress of tackling a foreign language: NYU uses an informal approach to whet students' appetites for formal classes later. (New York University)
AUTHOR:	Amy Magaro Rubin
ABSTRACT:	New York University offers an experimental foreign language program called Speaking Freely, designed to encourage students to study foreign languages and travel abroad. The program incorporates music, food and other cultural aspects of the country and language being studied. Classes in French, Italian, Chinese, German, Japanese, Korean, Spanish, and Swahili have been well received by students and provides them a unique perspective on a culture as well as a refreshing approach to language study.

SEARCH STRATEGY   As you practice with your library's on-line or compact disk (CD-ROM) systems, you'll discover that the *search strategy* you use and the *key words* you enter become very critical. Should you use a *word* or a *subject* search? Should you use browse or express to search your database? You need to *practice with your library's system* to see *how it works*. Next, you need to pay careful attention to the key words you enter. If you are writing an essay about teenagers' psychological problems, entering the word "teen" may get you nowhere, while entering the word "adolescent" or even "teenage" may hit the jackpot. To help with your key-word search, try the following. First, make a list in your research notebook of all the possible terms that may relate to your subject. When you do an express search, note the other possible terms or headings given on the computer terminal. Second, stop and check a print source such as the *Library of Congress Subject Headings* (LCSH). Ask the reference librarian where the LCSH is located. Usually, it will be in the reference section or near the on-line terminals. Look up your topic in the LCSH and copy any headings or key words that are related to your subject. When McNerny looked in the LCSH under "Foreign Languages," she found "See Language and languages—Study and teaching" and "See Languages—Modern." So she checked under "Language and languages—Study and teaching" and found the following listings and cross references.

Language and languages
—Study and teaching
  Here are entered works which discuss the study and teaching of a second or foreign language. Works which discuss the social and psychological processes involved in learning a second language are entered under the heading Second language acquisition.
  UF   Foreign language study
  BT   Language and education
  RT   Language schools
  NT   Communication in foreign language education
       Immersion method (Language teaching)
       Inter language (Language teaching)
       Language transfer (Language learning)

From these entries, McNerny gathered several key-word entries, such as "foreign language study," "foreign language education," and "language and education." She was able to use these key words during her search on the library's on-line database, in subject indexes, and on the Internet. Then McNerny looked under "Languages, Modern" and found additional key words. As it turned out, finding the right key word or combination of key words was crucial to all her computer searches. If you are having trouble gathering information on your topic, be sure to consult a librarian and discuss your search strategy and the list of key words you are using for your search. *A brief discussion with a reference librarian will probably be the most productive ten minutes you will spend in the library!*

INTERNET SOURCES   Where should you start your search for relevant sources—in the library or on the Internet? The answer to that question depends on your topic, your purpose, and your audience. But the explosion of websites at the end of the 1990s indicates that, for many writers and topics, the Internet may well be the place to start. The immense variety of sources makes the Internet a great place to do your browsing—especially if you're not quite sure exactly what your topic will be or what angle you wish to investigate. Other writers—especially those who are already sure of their focus—may wish to begin with an on-line search in their library, and save their Internet research for later, when they want to find sources they cannot locate in the library. Whatever choice you make, you will probably want to browse the Internet at some point during your research.

Especially if you are not an expert at Internet research, you should think about the strengths and weaknesses of Internet research. The strengths of Internet research are many:

- The Internet has a mind-boggling number of sources, Usenet groups, and Web pages.
- The Internet can have an amazing retrieval speed for sources from around the world.
- The Internet gives you the ability to chat with other people who share similar interests.
- The Internet gives you personal access—from your library or your home—to key information from libraries, businesses, organizations, and governments.

Unfortunately, doing research on the Internet does have drawbacks that are often related to its strengths. Internet enthusiasts often praise the Web for creating a democratic space where every person and site is equal. On the downside, however, librarians often shudder at doing research on the Internet simply because everything is so decentralized and disorganized. And there are other problems as well:

- The sheer number of possible sources on the Internet may make finding the exact source you need very difficult.
- Gaining access to the Internet may be difficult, depending on how you are connected and what time of day you use the Internet.
- Browsing on the Web may be fun, but you may spend hours going from one site to the next without making any real progress.
- The increasing commercialization of websites may interfere with locating relevant information.
- Waiting for a source to download from a busy site can be tedious and frustrating.
- Sources on the Internet may not be accurate or reliable—and thus not appropriate for your paper.

With realistic estimations about the Internet's virtues and faults, however, you should be able to find relevant and even exciting sources that will help you learn about your topic and communicate your findings to your audience.

Note: As you continue to read in this section of the chapter, you may want to open a connection to the Internet so you can check out several of the sites. Also, remember to start making bookmarks for any sites you want to revisit later.

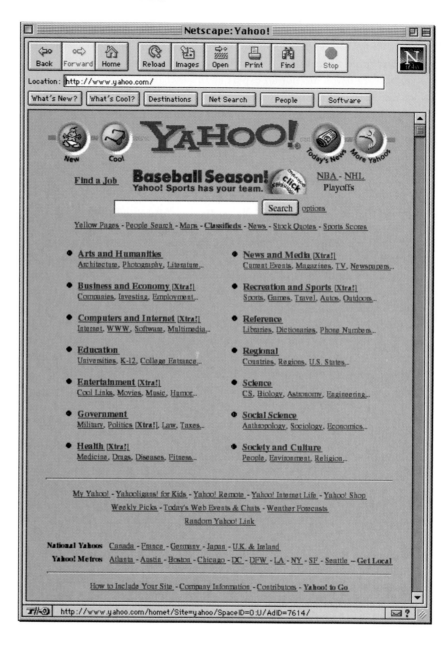

Internet Browsers and Search Engines

Once you have an idea for a possible topic, you can begin searching sites on the Internet for relevant information. If you need to review the basics of Internet research and terminology, refer to the Basic Internet Glossary on the next page. If you are sitting at a computer with a browser, such as Netscape or Internet Explorer, you can begin working on your topic right now by accessing one of the popular search engines described below. Of course, there are actually hundreds of such searching tools available on the Web, but the ones described here can get you started.

- **AltaVista http://altavista.digital.com** AltaVista is one of the most powerful search engines. It is especially effective if you are finished browsing through subject-directory searches such as Yahoo! and know your precise topic. You can then take advantage of the "Advanced" search screen.

- **Electric Library http://www.elibrary.com** Infonautics' Electric Library is not a search engine so much as it is an article retrieval service available on the Web. The Electric Library will search over 150 full-text newspapers, 800 magazines and journals, and 2,000 reference works, and actually print out an entire article on your computer's printer. The main drawback to Electric Library is that its sources are appropriate primarily for current, popular topics.

- **Excite http://www.excite.com** Excite is a competent search engine with Usenet connections as well as key-word text searching similar to but not as sophisticated as AltaVista. Excite gives its own reviews of websites.

- **InfoSeek http://www2.infoseek.com** InfoSeek provides a good search engine in both free and fee-based modes. The subscription fee allows access to several databases, including Usenet News and other areas in finance, business, health, and sports.

- **Internet Services List http://www.spectracom.com/islist** Internet Services provides a subject-based search like Yahoo! that also has FTP, GOPHER, and Telnet connections. Its general subjects tend to be more specialized that Yahoo!'s categories, with approximately a hundred topics, including subjects such as aviation, the Bible, disability, ham radio, java, kids, paranormal, parenting, recipes, shortwave, and women.

- **Lycos http://www.lycos.com** Lycos is similar to AltaVista in its ability to scan the text of each Web document with a text index in order to find hits or matches to the key words you enter. Try it once you have a fairly specific topic in mind.

- **Yahoo! http://www.yahoo.com** Yahoo! is an easily accessible search engine that provides a search of fourteen basic categories such as Arts, Business, Computers, Education, Health, Science, Sports, and Social Science. Yahoo! is like MetaCrawler in that it also searches Lycos, AltaVista, and WebCrawler.

- **MetaCrawler http://metacrawler.cs.washington.edu:8080/index. html** MetaCrawler is a powerful search site that can access multiple search engines *simultaneously*. When you type in your key words, MetaCrawler will search several sites, including Yahoo!, AltaVista, Excite, Lycos, Infoseek, and Inktomi.

Of course, websites and search engines are constantly changing. But the good news is that you can find comparative reviews of the various research tools and search engines right from your Internet access. For one review of search engines, try C/NET at <http://www.cnet.com/Content/Reviews>. For additional searching tips using these engines, see Peggy Zorn et al., "Advanced Searching: Tricks of the Trade," available at **<http://www.onlineinc.com/onlinemag/MayOL/zorn5>**.

BASIC INTERNET GLOSSARY

The URL (uniform resource locator) is the address that identifies each Internet site. In the address that follows, for example, **http** stands for "hypertext transfer protocol," **www** stands for World Wide Web, **Yahoo!** is the manager of the website, and **.com** indicates a commercial site.

URL: http://www.yahoo.com

In addition to commercial **(.com),** you can access a variety of locations, including educational **(.edu),** governmental **(.gov),** noncommercial **(.org),** military **(.mil),** and networking **(.net).** Other URLs can access GOPHER sites **(gopher://),** FTP **(ftp://),** newsgroups **(news://),** and so forth. For further explanation, see Gene Cowan's essay, "How the Web Works" in Chapter 6, "Investigating".

> *Note:* URLs have no spaces between any letters, periods, or slashes. URLs must be typed with complete accuracy—one missed slash or period or letter and your computer will not be able to find the correct address.

As you get started doing research on the Internet, acquaint yourself with the following key terms and definitions. If you know the basic language for navigating the Internet, you won't remain a newbie very long.

bookmark Your computer's browser (see below) will enable you to record each URL that you want to remember, so that the next time you want to visit that site, you merely have to click on the right line in your bookmark rather than type out a complete URL string. Remember to bookmark sites that look promising as you do your research!

browser Your computer needs a browser such as Netscape or Internet Explorer to help you access Telnet, GOPHER, or websites on the Internet. (A browser is not the same as a search engine such as Yahoo!, Excite, or Alta Vista—see listings that follow.)

cyberspace The on-line world created in electronic space or on the Internet. For a history of the Internet, read Philip Elmer-DeWitt's essay, "Welcome to Cyberspace" in Chapter 7, "Explaining".

FTP File Transfer Protocol is the set of commands that enables you to transfer files between two sites on the Internet.

gopher A program that "goes for" or finds items in a long list or menu is a gopher. Gopher addresses begin with "gopher://" rather than with "http://." Gopher was an early search program prior to the hypertext searches supported on the Web.

home page The home page is usually the first page of any website, and it identifies the author of the page, the location or sponsor of the site, and the basic information about the site.

hyperlink Often just called "links," these are highlighted words, icons, or bits of graphic that you can click on to move to a related site. A hypertext is simply a collection of documents or graphics connected by these links.

html Hypertext markup language is the computer code used to write pages on the Web.

listserv A listserv is a mail list that enables users to conduct an ongoing e-mail conversation about a particular topic.

MOO A multi-user domain, object oriented, provides a space in which people can meet, at a given time, to discuss a particular topic.

MUD A multi-user domain (or dungeon) enables simultaneous communication, often by role playing a certain character or persona.

newsgroup Any group of people who post messages on Usenet. Usenet is a network that gives access to an electronic discussion group.

search engine A program that enables Internet users to find relevant sites on the Internet. Popular search engines or search tools include Yahoo!, AltaVista, Excite, and Lycos.

Telnet An electronic program that enables you to communicate with another computer with a username and a password. If you access the Internet or the Web from your home, you probably need to "telnet" into America Online or an educational or commercial source in order to access the Internet.

This short list is just the tip of the iceberg of Internet terminology. If you want to know about **ASCII, baud rates, bytes, cookies, flame wars, MIMEs, POPs, spam, Veronica, WYSIWYG,** or literally hundreds of other terms, visit one of the dozens of Internet glossaries available on-line, such as the Internet Literacy Consultants' Glossary of Internet Terms at **http://www.matisse.net/files/glossary.html**. Check out this site and make a bookmark so you can return whenever you have a question.

Tips for Doing Research on the Internet

If you are still learning to use the Internet, here are some tips that may save you quite a bit of time during your research.

- The time of day you access the Internet may be crucial. Obviously, 3 A.M. is a good time for minimal Net traffic, but you do need your sleep. Log on at different times of the day to find out when is best for your location.
- Bring print sources to read while you wait for graphics or text to download to your computer. If you have the option on your browser or search engine, choose "text only" format for Web displays—downloading graphics adds significant time.
- If it takes more than a couple of minutes to get files from your site, click on the "Stop" button and try another source.
- Use the "bookmark" or "favorites list" to record your best sites. You may even want to organize your favorites or bookmarks into a folder designated specifically for the topic of this paper.
- Make sure your browser is set so that the location (URL), title, date, and page are recorded on the copies you print. If they do not appear, ask your laboratory monitor or teacher for assistance.
- Make sure you have enough information from your source (author, title, title of work, full URL address, and date of visit) so that you can write an in-text citation and a references citation in either MLA or APA format. (See the sections on MLA and APA citation of on-line sources later in this chapter.)

Useful Research Addresses

In some cases, instead of browsing through a search engine such as AltaVista or Yahoo!, you may wish to go directly to a reliable and relevant site. Here are a few you may wish to visit as you research your topic. Each of these sites offers links to other relevant sites.

- **ERIC http://www.cal.org/ericll** Your library will probably have an ERIC (Educational Resources Information Center) database on CD-ROM that you can conveniently search, but if you are not at a library, you can access the ERIC site at this URL. You may even order ready-made searches on popular topics such as "English Only/English Plus," "Teaching ESL Abroad," or "Peace Corps Language Teaching Materials."
- **Inter-Links Journals List http://www.nova.edu/Inter-Links/start.html** This service provides information about many electronic journals such as *The Chronicle of Higher Education* or *Journal of Political Ecology*. Also check out the Electronic Journal Collection from CICnet at <gopher://gopher.cic.net:2000/11/e-serials>. This site will give you access to electronic journals, e-zines (electronic magazines), and newspapers.
- **HyperNews http://union.ncsa.uiuc.edu** This website enables you to retrieve articles and contribute responses to new articles as they are posted on the site.

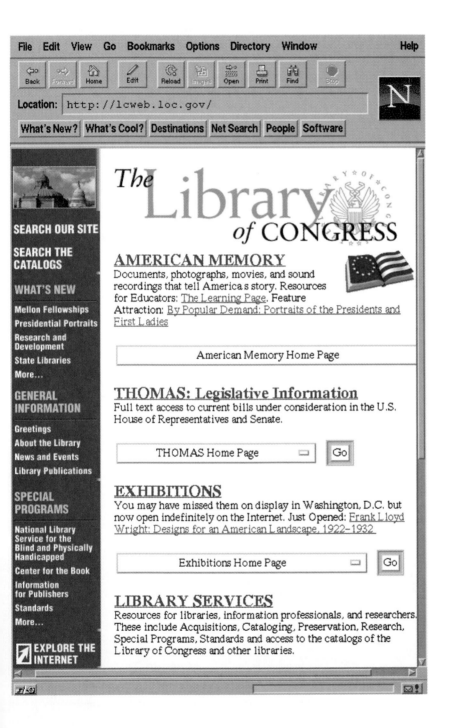

- **HYTELNET http://library.usask.ca/hytelnet** At this site, you can find Telnet addresses of library catalogs throughout the world. You can select from among research libraries, K–12 libraries, medical libraries, and public libraries.
- **The Library of Congress http://lcweb.loc.gov** The Library of Congress site can give you direct access to an immense range of government and library resources.
- *The New York Times* **http://www.nytimes.com** You will need to register with *The New York Times,* but then you can access the current paper or do a keyword search of relevant articles appearing in the *Times* by accessing <http://www.nytimes.com/search/daily>.
- **On-line Writing Centers** Check out the on-line writing centers at the following addresses for help with writing as well as with finding relevant research strategies and sites: Purdue University On-Line Writing Lab at <http://www.owl.trc.purdue.edu>; Colorado State University Online Writing Center at <http://www.ColoState.edu/Depts/WritingCenter>.

- **Popular Magazines** Many magazines, such as *Mother Jones* and *The Utne Reader* have home pages that allow you to access articles and participate in on-line "salon" conversations on current issues. Use your WWW search engine to find their URLs.
- **UnCover http://hplus.harvard.edu/alpha/CARL.html** If your library does not have direct access to UnCover, you may access it at this Harvard site. You can use this service to deliver indexed articles at around $9.00 per article.
- **U.S. Bureau of the Census http://www.census.gov** Want up-to-date information on demographic data from the Census Bureau? Access this site for news releases and statistics.

EVALUATING INTERNET SOURCES

Evaluating sources on the Internet requires much more care and attention than judging print sources. Printed sources in the library have often been screened and filtered for accuracy and reliability, whereas often Web sources may represent simply one person's opinion, reaction, or point of view. Even more problematic is our inability to judge the context of the information. When we read an article in *The New York Times,* for example, we can expect a certain level of accuracy and reliability; conversely, when we read an article in a supermarket tabloid, we know we should expect very little accuracy. We know not to quote a tabloid article about diet supplements when we are writing an academic paper about health and nutrition. Even in the television media, we know when we're watching *CNN News* and when we're seeing an infomercial. On the Internet, however, we may have very few context cues to help us judge what we're reading.

Internet sources must be evaluated with a critical eye. When we find a source, we need to ask some key questions: Who is the author? Is the author an expert, a salesperson, or a person with a reason to be biased? What organization is publishing this information? Where did the author find his or her sources? Can we verify the information in other reliable sources? How current is this information? As you read and download texts from the Internet, pay particular attention to five criteria below. (These criteria are adapted from guidelines designed by Elizabeth E. Kirk and are available on the Milton's Web Home Page at <http://milton.mse.jhu.edu:8001/research/education/net.html>. Ms. Kirk is the Library Instruction Coordinator for the Milton S. Eisenhower Library at The Johns Hopkins University. For additional checklists on evaluating websites, see the Widener University site at <http://www.science.widener.edu/withers/inform.htm>)

- **Authorship:** Who is the author? Is the author well known? Are the author's credentials or biographical information available on the

Internet or elsewhere? Does the author have a reason to be biased? Does the site give an e-mail address so you can request more information? The less you know about the author, the more cautious you need to be about using the source. *If you decide to use the source, indicate exactly what you know or don't know about the author's credentials.*

- **Publishing Organization:** Does the site indicate the organization responsible for the text? Is there information in the header or footer indicating the organization, webmaster, or designer of the home page? Is this organization recognized in its field? Is this organization's expertise relevant to your topic and your purpose? Is the organization selling something? Can you determine its bias? *If the organization or source has a clear bias, identify it if you quote from the source.*

- **Reference to Other Sources:** Does the author refer to other studies on your topic? Does the text contain references to other important studies? Does the text use citations or have a bibliography? Does the author acknowledge that his or her position is new or controversial? Does the author refer to alternate points of view? *Any source that has no references to other key works may simply be one writer's opinion and/or may contain erroneous information.*

- **Accuracy and Reliability:** Can the information in the text be verified for accuracy? Are the methods of gathering information indicated? Has this study been replicated elsewhere? If the accuracy or reliability are questionable or unknown, either do not use the text or else qualify your use of the source. *If you have reason to believe the source is not reliable or accurate, find other sources.*

- **Currency:** Depending on your purpose and audience, currency may or may not be important. If you are writing about the reception of Shakespeare's plays, information from texts written in the seventeenth century may be more relevant than current ones. If you are writing about censorship on the Internet, however, you need the most current available information. Can you determine the date the text was written? Can you find the date the information was posted to the site? Are cited statistics based on recent data?

As you gather sources from the Internet, be skeptical! Question the authority of the texts you find. If you think the source is not reliable, trust your judgment and don't use it. If the text seems accurate and reliable, but you cannot verify all of these criteria, indicate the problems in the source when you introduce your citation:

"Certainly Mind Extension University is in the business of selling on-line education, but they may be right when they claim that distance learning is the wave of the future."

"Karen Levine is a Spanish teacher at Thousand Oaks High School and has sponsored school to school exchange programs, but her testimonial for the International Education Forum's program—an exchange program for which she has worked—should be balanced against recommendations for other foreign language exchange programs."

If you have a question about the reliability, relevance, or accuracy of any source, check with your instructor or a librarian. *If you decide to use any questionable or biased sources, you need to qualify their findings and data when you introduce the source.* Otherwise, you reader may believe that your argument is based on biased, inaccurate, or unreliable data.

COMPUTERIZED DATABASES   In addition to the resources available on the Internet or in the library's on-line catalog, many libraries have other computerized databases to assist your research project. Some of these, such as ABI/INFORM (a general business database) or *InfoTrac* (database of general interest and current events), have no print equivalents. Your library may have one of the other popular computerized databases, such as the *Knowledge Index* or *DialogOnDisc. Ask your reference librarian to help you locate and use these databases.* Listed below are a few of the other commonly searched computerized databases:

- ERIC (Education Resources Information Center)
- NTIS (National Technical Information Service)
- SCI SEARCH (Science Citation Index)
- MLA (Modern Language Association International Bibliography)

PERIODICAL INDEXES   Magazines, journals, and newspapers are called "periodicals" because most are published on a daily, weekly, or monthly basis. An index is just a list of citations, organized for easy reference. Indexes may be in print or computerized form, such as CD-ROM. Just as the index of a textbook refers you to topics, ideas, or names in that book, a periodical index refers you to articles published in a certain group of magazines, journals, or newspapers. Periodical indexes, such as the *Readers' Guide to Periodical Literature,* are usually monthly, quarterly, or annual publications that refer to articles published in hundreds of different periodicals.

The library contains hundreds of periodical indexes, in print or computerized format, each referring to a slightly different subject or group of periodicals. A general index such as the *Readers' Guide* refers to approximately two hundred popular magazines. A general computerized database, such as *InfoTrac,* draws from more than one thousand current magazines, journals, and newspapers. A specialized index may focus on just one publication, such as *The New York Times Index,* or on just one subject, such as the *Art Index,* which indexes approximately three hundred periodicals in the arts.

Below is a list of frequently used indexes. When you discuss your research project with your instructor or with a reference librarian, ask which indexes will be most helpful for your topic and which are available in computerized format:

- *Applied Science & Technology Index*
- *Art Index*
- *Book Review Index*
- *Business Periodicals Index*
- *Consumers Index*
- *Education Index*
- *Humanities Index*
- *InfoTrac*
- *Psychological Abstracts*
- *Public Affairs Information Service Bulletin*
- *Readers' Guide to Periodical Literature*
- *Social Sciences Index*
- *The New York Times Index*

Since her subject was foreign language study, Kate McNerny decided to look through the *Education Index* under "Languages, Modern," for relevant articles. Below are some of the topics and entries she found:

Languages, Modern

Computer aids
E-mail: real-life classroom experiences with foreign languages.
  P.U. Silva and others. *Learn Lead Technol* v23 p10-12 F '96
Let your fingers do the talking [using computers in language
  teaching in Great Britain] E. Caldwell. il *Times Educ Suppl*
  no4160 p XI Mr 22 '96

Enrollment
Russian-language programs report sharp enrollment declines,
  M.C. Cage. *Chron Higher Educ* v42 p A19 O 20 '95

Motivation
Computer-assisted foreign language learning: effects of text,
  context, and gender on listening comprehension and motivation. S. Jakobsdottir and S. Hooper. bibl il *Educ Technol
  Res Dev* v43 no4 p43-59 '95

Standards
With nod to history, foreign-language standards unveiled.
  K. Diegmueller. *Educ Week* v15 p10 N 29 '95

The entries McNerny found in *Education Index* were not available on her other searches—on the Internet or on the library's *InfoTrac*—simply because those databases did not search the specialized journals in education, such as *The Chronicle of Higher Education* or the *Times Educational Supplement*. So remember: **Always check the specialized indexes relevant to your topic.** You may find just the sources you need.

GOVERNMENT DOCUMENTS   The largest publisher in the world is the United States Government Printing Office (G.P.O.). It publishes countless articles, pamphlets, and books on history, government, and law. Many of the publications cover an astonishing variety of everyday topics and are written in nontechnical language for the general public. Your library may have a separate government documents section, and the documents librarian can help you gain access to the collection.

EVALUATING LIBRARY SOURCES   Even with published library sources, you should appraise your sources with a critical eye, just as you do for Internet and Web sources. Just because something is published or printed does not mean that it is relevant, current, accurate, or reliable. Some will not relate specifically to your topic; others will be too superficial or too technical. Some will be out of date; others will be biased or simply inaccurate. Evaluate your printed sources based on the following criteria:

- **Sources should be relevant.** The sources you select should be relevant to your subject, your purpose, and your intended audience. If your narrowed topic is still too general, all your sources will look relevant. In that case, narrow your subject even more. Sources must also be relevant to your purpose. If you are writing an argumentative research paper, for example, you need sources representing both sides of the issue. If you are proposing a solution to a problem, look for sources describing the problem or the solution. Finally, sources should be appropriate for your intended audience. The articles that Kate McNerny found in *Foreign Language Annals* were more appropriate for her academic audience than was a brief and superficial article she found in *Parents* magazine.
- **Sources should be current.** As a rule of thumb, look for the most current sources—especially those on scientific or technical subjects. Research and data on AIDS is more accurate and complete now than it was in 1990. Sometimes, however, older books and articles are important. If you are doing historical research about the Great Depression in the United States, you may want to read key documents from the 1930s. In every academic discipline, some sources remain authoritative for decades. When you find that many writers refer to a single source, it may be valuable regardless of its date of publication.
- **Sources should be reliable.** Check for possible biases in articles and books. Don't expect the National Rifle Association to give an unbiased report on gun-control legislation. Don't assume that representatives of right-to-life or pro-choice groups will objectively represent the full range of facts about abortion. Because at least some bias is inevitable in any source, locate and use a variety of sources representing several points of view. If you are in doubt about an author's point of view or credibility, consult experts in the field or check book reviews. *Book Review Digest,* for example, contains references to reviews that may indicate the author's reputation or reliability.

TAKING NOTES   Taking careful notes from both published and unpublished sources is, of course, fundamental to accurate documentation. When a source appears relevant and useful, do the following:

1. *Record complete bibliographical information in the bibliography section of your research notebook (or in your computer notebook).* For many on-line library systems, you will be able to print out the bibliographical information you need right from your computer terminal. For *books,* you need authors, editors, titles, volumes, publishers, places of publication, and years of publication. For *articles,* you need authors, article titles, magazine or journal titles, volumes and numbers or dates, months, and years of publication, and beginning and ending page numbers. As Kate McNerny did in her log, leave a space between each entry to record call numbers or locations of documents:

(Book): Freed, Barbara F., ed. <u>Second Language Acquisition in a Study Abroad Context</u>. Philadelphia: John Benjamins, 1995.
    HF5549.A2P38   Current Periodical Room
(Article): Brady, Robert I. "English-only Rules Draw Controversy." <u>HR Focus</u> June 1996: 20.
    P118.2.S433   1995   First Floor East

If the source is unpublished—such as a telephone conversation, a letter, or a public document in the county courthouse—record all the information about it that your readers will need to identify and consult the source themselves. (See the Documenting Sources section in this chapter.) For printed sources, remember that the information you copy from a periodical index may be missing key information, such as the author's full name or page numbers for the article. *When you actually find each source, update your bibliographical information.*

2. *Record notes in the "Source Notes" section of your research notebook.* Identify each entry with the author's name and the title. If your notes fill two or more pages, put the author and title at the top of each page. Write on only one side of each page. Briefly *summarize* the main points made in the source, note specific information useful to you, paraphrase key ideas, transcribe interesting quotations, and jot down your own brief comments, questions, and memories. Place page numbers immediately following each paraphrase or quotation. Use direct quotation rather than paraphrase when the actual words in the source are more concise, authoritative, or persuasive than your paraphrase might be. *Be sure that direct quotations are accurate, word-for-word transcriptions from the original.*

3. *Photocopy important sources for later rereading and reference.* Make sure all photocopies clearly show authors, titles, and page numbers. (For some research projects, your instructor may request photocopies of every source you paraphrase or quote.) **Tip:** If you photocopy several pages, *copy title pages or the magazines' covers* and staple the copies together. Then, you will have all the necessary bibliographical information, and

you can underline key passages or make notes on the photocopies themselves.

Photocopying has distinct advantages. You can copy the relevant pages of a source so you don't have to lug thirty books home. (Leaving the sources in the library also helps other researchers.) Photocopies are good insurance against losing key information—in case the book or journal is checked out the next time you need it. Photocopies also allow you to reread sources *after* you have read other books or articles; often, on the first reading of a source, you're not certain what is important and what is not. Finally, photocopies allow you to recheck the final draft of your research paper against sources, to make sure that paraphrases, direct quotations, and page citations are accurate. You may save yourself an extra trip to the library to check a page number, a date, or a journal title. To avoid spending unnecessary amounts of money on photocopies, however, always read sources before making copies.

4. *As you read sources and take notes, record your own reactions and ideas in the "drafts and ideas" section of your research or computer notebook.* Be an active reader of your sources. When you agree or disagree with what you are reading, stop for a minute and jot down your ideas. When you think of a comparison, a process, a way to analyze or evaluate something, possible causes and effects, or examples from your own experience, *write out your ideas as completely as you can, right then, while they're fresh in your mind.* Don't get so absorbed in taking notes that you forget to record your own ideas. You don't have to collect twenty sources and *then* do a draft; instead, draft ideas *as* you collect information.

SHAPING

Once you've collected information for your research paper, you may feel overwhelmed by the task of shaping it into a coherent form. You can assert control over your data, however, and shape them into coherent form by reconsidering your purpose and thesis. *Reread your own notes and especially your draft sections from your research notebook.* Then, in the draft section of your notebook, answer the following questions:

Subject:	What is your general subject?
Narrowed topic or question:	What aspect of your subject is most interesting to you now? What question will you answer or explain?
Purpose:	Is your purpose primarily to inform, explain, evaluate, describe a problem and propose a solution, or argue a claim?
Working thesis:	What thesis, claim, or proposal do you want to impress upon your readers?

Writing is the hardest work in the world not involving heavy lifting.

—**PETER HAMILL,**

JOURNALIST

Writing a book is not as tough as it is to haul 35 people around the country and sweat like a horse five nights a week.

—BETTE MIDLER,

SINGER, ACTOR, AUTHOR

Audience: Analyze your audience. How can you interest them in your subject? What aspects of your collected data are most appropriate for your audience?

As you shape, draft, and revise your research paper, you may continue to refocus your topic and question, refine your thesis, or revise your sense of audience.

SHAPING STRATEGIES

Your goal now is to design some order, sequence, plan, or outline for your research paper. Forcing yourself to write an outline, however, simply may not work. You should have an idea from your previous papers about how your writing process works best, but if you're stuck, feeling frustrated, or overwhelmed, try several of the following strategies:

- *Review strategies for shaping* that are appropriate for your particular purpose. If you are arguing for a certain claim, reread shaping strategies in Chapter 10. If you are evaluating something or analyzing a problem and proposing a solution, review the strategies discussed in Chapter 8 or 9.
- *Explain to a friend or classmate your purpose, audience, and working thesis.* Then try to explain how you might proceed.
- *Try freewriting, looping, or clustering* to develop a plan.
- *Reread your notes and drafts* from your research notebook.
- *Take a break.* Let your ideas simmer for a while. Go for a walk. Work on assignments for another course. Go jogging or swimming. Let your mind run on automatic pilot for a while—the information and ideas in your mind may begin organizing themselves into an initial "sketch outline" without your conscious effort.
- *Try branching or treeing your main ideas.* On paper or at the chalkboard, begin with your topic and draw the trunk and main branches of your topics. Try to explain your sketch or chalkboard drawing to someone.

Think of these activities as a circle—begin at any point, work in either direction, repeat them as necessary. When something starts to work, stay with it for a while. If you start to block or become frustrated, go on to the next activity.

WORKING OUTLINE   If the shaping activities helped you discover a basic design or plan, translate it into a working outline. If not, you may need to begin drafting in order to discover an outline. Kate McNerny decided to follow a pattern for writing an argument. Although she modified it considerably to change her purpose to problem solving, the sketch outline helped her organize her ideas and source material so she could begin drafting.

Introduction:	Comments—quotations from informal survey—why people feel they don't need to know a foreign language. Mention study on misconceptions of school-aged children about Russian children.
I. Narration:	Foreign language studies position in other countries as opposed to U.S. Mention "Official English" here? Include example of European requirements? Statistics on how many Americans are actually competent in another language. Mention bills to require a state language? U.S. position in world as far as power-trade.
II. Partition:	American students should be required to study a foreign language throughout the 6 years of junior and senior high school. To increase number of students studying foreign language, we need changes in administrators and teachers, changes in students, and changes in state and national policies.
III. Arguments:	An increase in number of students studying foreign languages would: Help to improve diplomatic relations with other countries—peace cannot be achieved without this. Change American's attitudes toward foreigners and change foreigners' attitudes toward Americans. Facilitate international trade and other business. Increase jobs for students abroad and at home. Without requirement, no incentive for many students.
IV. Refutation:	Not necessary because other countries can speak English (This is more an argument against learning a language, not against a requirement.) Not essential for quality education. As requirement, would detract from other important subjects. Not enough federal, state or local money to change number of foreign language courses offered.
Conclusion:	Call for action on part of federal government. Contrary to popular belief, we are not an isolated country. A required study of languages will bring us one step closer to global understanding and peace.

ORGANIZING YOUR NOTES With a rough outline as a guide, reread your draft ideas, notes, and photocopies, and label them according to headings and subheadings in your working outline (for instance, I: Intro; II: Background and History; III: Required Changes; IV: Advantages of Changes; and V: Conclusion). Before you remove pages from the "source notes" section of your notebook or unstaple photocopied articles or sections of books, *make sure each entry or photocopy contains the author, title, and page numbers.* Now you are ready to arrange your notes and copies for use during drafting. Organize your notes into groups according to each section of your working outline. Reread each group, deciding which information should come first, in the middle, or last.

DRAFTING

At this point, some of the most difficult work is behind you. Congratulate yourself—there aren't many people who know as much as you do right now about your subject. You are an authority: You have information, statistics, statements, ideas from other writers and researchers, and your own experiences and observations at your fingertips. As you write, remember your purpose and audience. What is your purpose—to inform, explain, evaluate, offer a solution, or argue? Who exactly is your audience? What arguments and evidence will convince them? Your sources will become the evidence and support for *your ideas.* Remember that your voice and point of view should unify the information for your reader.

Many writers prefer to start a draft with the first main idea, leaving the introduction until later. As you write, you may discover a quotation, example, or narrative that doesn't fit anywhere else but that would be a perfect lead-in. Or you may already know how you want to start, using an idea that will help organize and direct your thoughts. As you draft, be guided by your working outline and your notes. Avoid copying passages verbatim from your own notebook ideas; instead, reread your notes and express those ideas in language that fits the idea you're working on.

If you get stuck, go back and reread what you have drafted so far or reread the source notes and ideas that you have assembled from your notebook and photocopies. Try to maintain your momentum by writing as quickly as possible. Don't be upset if the natural flow of your writing suggests a slightly different order or deviates from your working outline. Consider the new possibility. You may have discovered a better way to shape your material. If you are missing some fact or quotation, just leave a long line and keep writing. Later you can find the source and add the material you need.

USING SOURCES Proper use of sources requires both creativity and scrupulous honesty. On the one hand, you want to use other people's information and ideas when and where they serve *your* purpose and *your* ideas. A research paper is not simply a long string of quotations connected by a few transitions. On the other hand, the sources you cite or quote must be used *fairly* and *honestly*. You must give credit for other writers' ideas and information. You must quote accurately, cite your sources in your text, and document those sources accurately.

WHAT SOURCES TO CITE   You must cite a source for any fact or bit of information that is not *general knowledge*. Obviously, what is "general knowledge" varies from one writer and audience to another. **As a rule, however, document any information or fact that you did not know before you began your research.** You may know, for example, that America spends more money on defense than it does on education. However, if you state that the defense budget for the previous year is greater than the total amount spent on education for the past forty years, then cite the source for that fact.

Knowing when you must cite a source for an idea, however, can be tricky. You do not need to indicate a source for *your* ideas, of course. But if you find a source that agrees with your idea, or if you suspect that your idea may be related to ideas from a particular source, cite that source. A citation will give your idea additional credibility: You show your reader that another authority shares your perception.

HOW TO CITE SOURCES   In the text of your research paper, you will need to cite your sources according to either the Modern Language Association (MLA) style or the American Psychological Association (APA) style. Remember: Choose either the MLA style or the APA style and stick with it. Don't mix styles.

According to the MLA style, the in-text citation contains the author and page number of your source (Torres 50). No comma appears between author and page number. (If the author is unknown, identify the title and page number of your source. Underline book titles; place quotation marks around article titles.)

According to the APA style, the in-text citation contains author and date (Torres, 1996). Use a comma between author and date. If you refer to page number, it should appear after the author and date (Torres, 1996, p. 50). Use a "p." (or "pp." for more than one page) before the page number(s).

The in-text citation (either MLA or APA) refers readers to the end of your paper, where you give complete information about each source in a Works Cited (MLA) or References (APA) list. For illustration purposes, the following examples use MLA style. See Documenting Sources section (pp. 557–574) for examples of both APA and MLA styles.

IDENTIFY CITED REFERENCES   Once you have decided that a fact, a paraphrase, or a direct quotation contributes to your thesis and will make a strong impression on your reader, use the following guidelines for in-text citation.

- *Identify in the text the persons or source for the fact, paraphrased idea, or quotation:*

As two foreign language teachers noted: "Like it or not, we are members of a world community consisting of hundreds of nations, and our fates are closely intertwined" (Long and Long 366).

Note: The parentheses and the period *follow* the final quotation marks.

- *If you cite the author in your sentence, the parentheses will contain only the page reference:*

According to Paul Simon, former member of the President's Commission on Foreign Language, the United States should erect a sign at each port of entry that reads, "WELCOME TO THE UNITED STATES—WE CANNOT SPEAK YOUR LANGUAGE" (1).

- *Use block format (separated from the text by a blank line, indented ten spaces, and double-spaced) for quotations of five lines or more:*

Educator Gerald Unks points out two instances in which a lack of language proficiency caused companies to initiate fatal marketing programs.

> When Pepsi-Cola went after the Chinese market, "Come Alive with Pepsi" was translated into Chinese in Taiwan as "Pepsi Brings Your Ancestors Back from the Dead." No Sale! General Motors sought to sell its Nova in South America, oblivious to the fact that "No va" in Spanish means "It doesn't go." (24)

Note: In block quotations, the final period comes *before* the parentheses containing the citation of your source.

- *Vary your introductions to quotations:*

Educator Gerald Unks claims that "only 15 percent of American high school students study a foreign language. Only 8 percent of our colleges require credit in a foreign language for admission (down from 34 percent in 1966)" (24).

The problem is that high school students are not taking foreign languages, and most colleges no longer require a foreign language for admission: "Only 15 percent of American high school students study a foreign language. Only 8 percent of our colleges require credit in a foreign language for admission (down from 34 percent in 1966)" (Unks 24).

- *Edit quotations when necessary to condense or clarify.* Use three ellipsis points or spaced periods (. . .) if you omit words from the middle of a quoted sentence:

As two foreign language teachers noted, "We are members of a world community . . . and our fates are closely intertwined" (Long and Long 366).

If you omit words from the end of a quoted sentence or omit sentences from a long quoted passage, place a period after the last word quoted before the omission; follow it with three ellipsis points—for a total of four periods. (Be sure that you have a complete sentence both before and after the four periods.)

Paul Simon advises us that our nation's lack of language proficiency may have been a partial cause of our disastrous policies in Vietnam:

> Vietnam and the Middle East have taught us that our security position is not solely a matter of dealing with the Warsaw Pact countries or the giants among the nations. Before our heavy intervention in Vietnam, fewer than five American-born experts on Vietnam, Cambodia, or Laos . . . could speak with ease one of the languages of that area. . . . What if—a big if— we had had . . . a mere twenty Americans who spoke Vietnamese fluently, who understood their culture, aspirations, and political history? Maybe, just maybe, we would have avoided that conflict. (9)

Note: The first line is indented five spaces because in the source the quotation begins a new paragraph.

In some cases you may want to change the wording of a quotation or add explanatory words of your own to clarify your quotation. If you do so, clearly indicate your changes or additions by placing them within square brackets:

As Simon suggests, if only a few Americans knew Vietnamese then "maybe, just maybe, we would have avoided [the Vietnam War]" (9).

HOW TO AVOID PLAGIARISM Plagiarism is the act of passing off another researcher's or writer's *information, ideas, or language* as one's own. Whether intentional or not, plagiarism is a serious offense. In this class, the result may be a failing grade in both the research project and the course. In the working world, people have lost jobs and presidential candidates have been forced to end campaigns because they have been caught plagiarizing.

To avoid such consequences, be honest and give credit to the work of others by carefully documenting *all* facts, ideas, charts, diagrams, and actual phrases or sentences borrowed from your sources. Assume, for example, that an accurate quotation from your source would read as follows:

> "Most Americans take it for granted that English is the language of the United States and even imagine that every American speaks it fluently. According to the 1980 U.S. Census, however, 11 percent of Americans come from non-English-speaking homes, and over 1 percent of the U.S. population speaks English not well or not at all. No indicators suggest that these percentages will soon decrease" (Conklin and Lourie 3).

The most blatant form of plagiarism involves using *both* your source's information and your source's language (shown below in italics) without giving credit:

> It is ironic that *11 percent of Americans come from non-English-speaking homes,* and yet most Americans say they will never need to speak a foreign language.

A second form of plagiarism, equally serious, involves giving credit to a source for facts or ideas, but *failing to use quotation marks to indicate that you have borrowed the exact language from the source.* In essence, you are saying that these ideas and facts come from Conklin and Lourie, page 3, but that the language is your own. That, of course, is untrue:

> It is ironic that most Americans take it for granted that English is the language of the United States and even imagine that every American speaks it fluently (Conklin and Lourie 3).

Avoid plagiarism by documenting the passage as follows:

> It is ironic, as two researchers recently pointed out, that "most Americans take it for granted that English is the language of the United States and even imagine that every American speaks it fluently" (Conklin and Lourie 3).

What makes me happy is rewriting. . . . It's like cleaning house, getting rid of all the junk, getting things in the right order, tightening things up.

—ELLEN GOODMAN,

JOURNALIST

To avoid plagiarism, don't randomly copy out interesting passages. Take accurate notes and transcribe quotations *exactly* as they appear in sources. Either put quotation marks around the exact words of the source or paraphrase the main ideas in your own words.

REVISING

You have been revising your research essay since the first day of the project. You thought about several subjects, for example, but you chose only one. You started with a focus but revised it as you thought, read, and wrote more. You initially tested your ideas in the draft section of your research notebook, but you revised those ideas as you drafted. At this point, you are just continuing your revising; now, however, you have a complete draft to revise.

Start the revision of your complete draft by taking a break. Fix your schedule so that you can do something else for a couple of days. When you return and reread your draft, be prepared to be flexible. If there is something missing in your data, prepare yourself to track down the information. If a favorite source or quotation no longer seems relevant, have the courage to delete it. If an example on page 4 would work better as a lead-in for the whole paper, reorder your material accordingly. If the evidence for one side of an argument appears stronger than you initially thought, change your position and your thesis. *Being willing to make such changes is not a sign of poor research and writing. Often, in fact, it demonstrates that you have become more knowledgeable and sophisticated about your subject.*

After you have finished your rough draft, ask friends or classmates to give you their responses. Accept their criticism gracefully, but ask them to explain *why* they think certain changes would help. Would they help to make your purposes clearer? Would they be more appropriate for your audience? Don't be intimidated and feel that you must make every change that readers suggest. You must make the final decisions.

DOCUMENTING SOURCES

Both the MLA and APA documentation styles require citation of sources in the text of your paper, followed by a "Works Cited" (MLA style) or "References" list (APA style) at the end of your paper. Use footnotes only for content or supplementary notes that explain a point covered in the text or offer additional information. ***Note:*** MLA in-text documentation and "Works Cited" documentation are explained here. See pages 566–574 for APA in-text documentation and "References" format.)

IN-TEXT DOCUMENTATION: MLA STYLE In the MLA style, give the author's name and the page numbers in parentheses following your use of a fact, paraphrase, or direct quotation from a source. These in-text citations then refer your readers to the complete documentation of the source in a "Works Cited" or "Works Consulted" list at the end of the paper.

As you cite your sources in the text, use the following guidelines:

If you cite the author in the text, indicate only the page number in parentheses:

> According to Vicki Galloway, Project Director for the American Council on the Teaching of Foreign Languages, a student's horizons will not be broadened by "grammar lectures and manipulative classroom exercises" (33).

If the author is unknown, use a short version of the title in the parentheses:

> Most students in the United States would be surprised to learn that the
> Communist Party in Russia actually sponsors rock concerts (A Day in the
> Life 68).

If the source is unpublished, cite the name or title used in your bibliography:

> In an informal interview, one university administrator noted that funding
> foreign language study has steadily decreased over the past ten years
> (Meyers).

If the source is from the Internet or the Web, use the author, or if there is no author, use the title.

> Many Web sites now provide detailed information about how to plan a
> study abroad semester or year (Foreign Language).

If your bibliography contains more than one work by an author, cite the author, a short title, and page numbers. The following examples show various ways of citing a reference to Paul Simon, *The Tongue-Tied American:*

> In The Tongue-Tied American, Simon explains that students can earn a
> doctorate degree in the United States without ever studying a foreign
> language (2).

> As Simon notes, "it is even possible to earn a doctorate here without
> studying any foreign language" (Tongue-Tied 2).

> In the United States, one can earn a doctorate degree without studying
> a single foreign language (Simon, Tongue-Tied 2).

Note: Use a comma between author and title but not between title and page number.

If a source has two authors, cite both authors' names in the text or in the parentheses:

> A recent study sampling 536 secondary schools revealed that 91 percent
> did not require foreign language credits for graduation (Ranwez and
> Rodgers 98).

If a source has three or more authors, give the name of the author listed first in your bibliography followed by the abbreviation et al., meaning "and others":

> Teachers should integrate the study of history, culture, politics, litera-
> ture, and religion of a particular region with the study of language
> (Berryman et al. 96).

If a source has several volumes, precede the page number with the volume number and a colon, as indicated:

> Language and grammar can be taught with real-life contexts or scenarios (Valdman 3:82).

If you are citing a quotation or information from a source that itself cites another source, use the abbreviation "qtd. in" for "quoted in" to indicate that you have used an indirect source for your information or quotation. (If possible, however, check the original source.)

> As Sue Berryman et al. explain, "The course is developed as a world tour during which time the students take a vicarious trip . . . to become saturated in every aspect of a particular area of the globe" (qtd. in Simon 96).

If you cite two or more authors as sources for a fact, idea, or plan, separate the citations with a semicolon, as follows:

> Most recently, two prominent foreign language educators have published plans to coordinate foreign language studies (Lambert 9–19; Lange 70–96).

CONTENT OR SUPPLEMENTARY NOTES   You may use footnote numbers in the text of your paper to refer to a "Notes" section at the end of the paper. If you have an important idea, a comment on your text, or additional information or sources *that would interrupt the flow of your ideas in the text,* you may use that idea or comment in your supplementary Notes section. During her research, for example, McNerny read about the movement to make English the "official language" of the United States. She didn't want to digress in her paper, so she described the controversy in a supplementary note at the end of the paper. Here is a first draft of that note:

> [1]Several states currently have bills before their legislatures to make English the "official language." Proponents of these bills argue that immigrants need incentives to learn English. Many opponents from ethnic and civil-rights groups believe these bills are racist (McBee 64). If Americans were all educated in foreign languages, these bills would be unnecessary. Americans' ignorance and fear of foreign languages is probably a reason that these bills are so popular.

"WORKS CITED" LIST: MLA STYLE   After you have revised your essay and are certain that you will not change any in-text documentation, you are ready to write your list of sources. Depending on what you include, it will be one of the following:

- A "Works Cited" list (only those works actually cited in your essay)
- A "Works Consulted" list (works cited and works you read)

- A "Selected Bibliography" (works cited and the most important other works)
- An "Annotated List of Works Cited" (works cited followed by a short description and evaluation of each source)

A Works Cited list alphabetically orders, by author's last name, all published and unpublished sources cited in your research paper. If the author is unknown, alphabetize by the first word (excluding *A, An,* or *The*) of the title. As a general rule, underline or italicize titles of books, periodicals, and newspapers, but use quotation marks to enclose titles of newspaper and magazine articles. Use the following abbreviations for missing information (other than an unknown author): N.p. (no place of publication given), n.p. (no publisher given), n.d. (no date of publication given), or N. pag. (no pagination in source). The first line of each citation begins at the left margin, and succeeding lines are indented five spaces. Double-space the entire Works Cited list.

Following are examples of MLA style entries in a Works Cited list, organized by kind of source: books, articles, and unpublished sources. Use these as models for your own Works Cited list. For additional information and examples, see *MLA Handbook for Writers of Research Papers* (1995).

BOOKS: MLA STYLE

Order the information as follows, omitting information that does not apply:

Author's last name, first name. "Title of article or part of book." Title of
    Book. Ed. or Trans. Name. Edition. Number of volumes. Place of publi-
    cation: Name of publisher, Date of publication.

A Book by One Author

Gould, Stephen Jay. Bully for Brontosaurus: Reflections in Natural History.
    New York: Norton, 1991.

Additional Books by Same Author

Morrison, Toni. Song of Solomon. New York: Knopf, 1977.

    ---. Jazz. New York: Knopf, 1992.

A Book with Two or Three Authors

Conklin, Nancy F., and Margaret A. Lourie. A Host of Tongues: Language
    Communities in the United States. New York: Free Press, 1983.

Padilla, Amando M., Halford H. Fairchild, and Concepcion M. Valadez.
    Foreign Language Education. Newbury Park, CA: Sage, 1990.

A Book with More Than Three Authors

Comley, Nancy R., et al. Fields of Writing. New York: St. Martin's, 1997.

An Unknown or Anonymous Author

New York Public Library Student's Desk Reference. New York: Prentice, 1993.

A Book with an Author and an Editor

Austen, Jane. Pride and Prejudice. Ed. Mark Schorer. Boston: Houghton, 1956.

[The names of well-known publishers are often shortened to the first key word. Thus, "Houghton Mifflin Co." becomes "Houghton," and "Harcourt Brace Jovanovich, Inc." becomes simply "Harcourt."]

An Edited Book

Myers, Linda, ed. Approaches to Computer Writing Classrooms. Albany:
State University of New York Press, 1993.

A Translation

Allende, Isabel. Paula. Trans. Margaret Sayers Peden. New York:
HarperCollins, 1996.

An Article or Chapter in an Edited Book

Sophocles. Electra. Trans. David Grene. Greek Tragedies. Ed. David Grene
and Richmond Lattimore. Vol 2. Chicago: U of Chicago P, 1960. 2 vols.
45–109.

A Work in More Than One Volume

Morrison, Samuel Eliot, and Henry Steele Commager. The Growth of the
American Republic. 2 vols. New York: Oxford UP, 1941.

A Work in an Anthology

Blake, William. "The Tyger." The Norton Anthology of English Literature.
Ed. M. H. Abrams et al. 6th ed. Vol. 2. New York: Norton, 1993. 2 vols.
37–38.

An Encyclopedia or Dictionary Entry

"Don Giovanni." The Encyclopedia Americana. 1994 ed.

A Government Document—Known Author

Machenthun, Kenneth M. Toward a Cleaner Aquatic Environment.
Environmental Protection Agency. Office of Air and Water Programs.
Washington: GPO, 1973.
["GPO" stands for "Government Printing Office."]

A Government Document—Unknown Author

United States. Department of Health, Education, and Welfare. Infant Care.
Washington: GPO, 1972.

An Unpublished Dissertation

Burnham, William A. "Peregrine Falcon Egg Variation, Incubation, and
Population Recovery Strategy." Diss. Colorado State U, 1984.

A Pamphlet

Guide to Raptors. Denver: Center for Raptor Research, 1990.

PERIODICALS: MLA STYLE

For all articles published in periodicals, give the author's name, the title of the article, and the name of the publication. For newspapers and magazines, add complete dates and inclusive page numbers. Use the first page number and a plus sign if an article is not printed on consecutive pages. For most professional journals, add volume numbers, issue numbers if appropriate, years of publication, and inclusive page numbers.

An Article in a Weekly or Biweekly Magazine

Hull, Jon D. "A Boy and His Gun." Time 2 Aug. 1993: 22–27.

An Article in a Monthly or Bimonthly Magazine

Edwards, Mike. "Sons of Genghis Khan." National Geographic Feb. 1997: 2–35.

Morrison, Ann M., Randall P. White, and Ellen Van Velsor. "Executive Women:
Substance Plus Style." Psychology Today Aug. 1987: 18+.

An Unsigned Article in a Magazine

"Catching a Cold: It's Up in the Air." Science 86 July–Aug. 1986: 8.

An Article in a Professional Journal

Many professional journals have continuous page numbers throughout the year. The first issue of the year begins with page 1, but every issue after that begins with the number following the last page number of the previous issue. For such journals, give volume followed by the year.

Swope, Christopher. "Panel OKs Bill to Make English Official Government
Language." Congressional Quarterly Weekly Report 54 (1996): 2128–29.

[For page numbers over 100, use only two digits for final page citation: 2128–29.] If each issue of a professional journal begins with page 1, cite the volume number followed by a period, then the issue number, and year. In the following example, the article is in volume 9, issue 1, published in January 1987.

Brodkey, Linda. "Writing Ethnographic Narratives." Written Communication
9.1 (1987): 25–50.

An Article in a Newspaper

Omit the introductory article (*Wall Street Journal* instead of *The Wall Street Journal*). If the masthead includes an edition, include it in your entry.

Mundy, Alicia. "Attorney General of Social Work." Wall Street Journal 5 Jan.
1994: A14.

An Unsigned Article in a Newspaper

"Plastic Surgeon is Convicted of Disguising Wanted Man". New York Times
28 Feb. 1997, late ed.: A22.

An Editorial

Fish, Stanley. "When Principles Get in the Way." Editorial. New York Times
26 Dec. 1996, late ed.: A27.

An Unsigned Editorial

"European Summit of Uncertainty." Editorial. Los Angeles Times 7 Jan.
1994: B6.

A Review

Molotch, Harvey. Rev. of A Cycle of Outrage, by James Gilbert. Science 15
Aug. 1996: 794–95.

A Published Interview

Lamm, Richard D. "Governments Face Tough Times." With Robert Baun.
Coloradoan [Ft. Collins, CO] 30 Nov. 1995: B9.

ELECTRONIC AND INTERNET SOURCES: MLA STYLE

CD-ROMS and Other Portable Databases

Portable databases include CD-ROMS, diskettes, videodiscs, videotapes, and
magnetic tapes. Your citation should include the publication's medium, the
vendor name, and the date of electronic publication.

A Publication on CD-ROM

Godwin, M. E. "An Obituary to Affirmative Action and a Call for Self-
Reliance." ERIC. CD-ROM. SilverPlatter. Oct. 1992.

A Publication on Diskette

Lanham, Richard D. The Electronic Word: Democracy, Technology, and the
Arts. Diskette. Chicago: U of Chicago P, 1993.

The World Wide Web and the Internet itself are still under constant construction and revision. A standard format for citing electronic sources had not
yet evolved by the publication of the most recent MLA Handbook. For the
short term at least, formats for documenting electronic sources from the
Internet will be subject to revision. There are two widely consulted documents
for MLA style citation of Internet sources. The first, Janice R. Walker's
"MLA-Style Citations of Electronic Sources" (endorsed by the Alliance for
Computers and Writing), is available at **http://www.cas.usf.edu/english/
walker/mla.html.** The examples here follow Andrew Harnack and Gene

Kleppinger's "Beyond the MLA Handbook: Documenting Electronic Sources on the Internet," which is available at **<http://falcon.eku.edu/honors/beyond-mla/#ftp>**. Ask your instructor which format you should follow.

The basic features of an Internet or electronic citation are as follows:

- Name of author (if known)
- Title of document
- Date of publication or revision (if known)
- URL (in angle brackets) or message path
- Date of access, in parenthesis

A World Wide Web Site

For a WWW source, give the following information: **author's name; title of document,** in quotation marks; **title of complete work,** underlined or in italics; **date of publication or revision,** if known; **URL in angle brackets; date of access,** in parentheses.

> Tyler, Patrick E. "U.S. And Chinese Seen Near a Deal on Human Rights."
>
> The New York Times. <http://www.nytimes.com/yr/mo/day/news/
>
> world/exclusive-china-us-rights.html> (24 Feb. 1997).

If the author is not known, begin with title of document or title of work:

> "Foreign Language Study Abroad Service." <http://www.netpoint.net/flsas>
>
> (21 Jan. 1997).

Linkage Data: If you wish to show the hypertext context for a World Wide Web source, use the abbreviation Lkd. ("linked from") to indicate the access path and "at" to indicate additional linkage information:

> Fielder, John. "Photographing Colorado" Lkd. Local Photographers, at "All
>
> About Colorado." 10 Jan. 1997. <http:denverpost.com> (13 Jan. 1997).

An E-mail Message

For an e-mail message, give the following information: **author's name; author's e-mail address,** in angle brackets; **subject or title of posting** in quotation marks; **date of publication,** if known; **type** of communication (personal e-mail, distribution list, office communication); and **date of access,** in parentheses.

> Palmquist, Mike. <mpalmquist@vines.colostate.edu> "A Paradigm for Dis-
>
> tance Learning Courses." 20 Feb. 1997. Personal e-mail. (25 Feb. 1997).

FTP Site

To document a file available for downloading via FTP (File Transfer Protocol), give the following information: **author's name,** if known; **title of document,** in quotation marks; **date of publication,** if known; **abbreviation** "ftp"; **address of FTP site,** with no closing punctuation; **path** to locate document, with no closing punctuation; **date of access,** in parentheses:

Markham, Dave. "Using the World Wide Web." Oct. 1995. <bftp://ftp.

colostate.edu/bulletins/networks/NTO4%/3Awww> (3 Mar. 1997).

Burns, Pat and David C. M. Wood. "Westnet." Apr. 1988. <ftp://ftp.

colostate.edu/general.info/westnet.overview> (10 May 1997).

GOPHER Site

To document information available through a gopher search, give the following information: **Author's name,** if known; **title of document,** in quotation marks; **date of publication,** if known; **print publication information,** italicized or underlined; **URL,** in angle brackets; **date of access,** in parentheses.

Yates, Albert C. "A Community That Works: Colorado State and the Chal-

lenges Ahead." 16 Aug. 1995. <gopher://yuma.ACNS.ColoState.EDU:

70/00/ON/CAMP.SRV/ln37pubrel/speeches/fall-add.txt> (13 Mar. 1997).

Telnet Site

To document information available via Telnet, give the following information: **author's name,** if known; **title of document,** in quotation marks; **title of full work,** if applicable; **date of publication,** if known; the word **"telnet"; address of Telnet site,** with no closing punctuation; **date of access,** in parentheses.

Gomes, Lee. "Xerox's On-Line Neighborhood: A Great Place to Visit."

Mercury News. 3 May 1992. telnet lambda.parc.xerox.com 8888, @go

#50827, press 13 (5 Dec. 1994).

Synchronous Communication (MOOs, MUDs, IRCs)

To document a syncronous communication, give the following information: **author's name,** if known; **title of event,** in quotation marks; **date of event; type of communication** (group discussion, personal interview); **URL,** in angle brackets; **date of access.**

Harnack, Andrew. "Words." 4 Apr. 1996. Group discussion. <telnet moo.du.

org/port=8888> (5 Apr. 1996).

Newsgroup Message

To document newsgroup information, give the following information: **author's name,** if known; **author's e-mail address,** in angle brackets; **subject line from posting,** in quotation marks; **date of publication; name of newsgroup,** in angle brackets; and **date of access,** in parentheses.

Slade, Robert. <res@maths.bath.ac.uk> "UNIX Made Easy." 26 Mar. 1996.

<alt.books.reviews> (31 Mar. 1996).

Listserv Message

To document a listserv message, give the following information: **author's name,** if known; **author's e-mail address,** in angle brackets; **subject line from**

posting, in quotation marks; **date of publication; address of listserv,** in angle brackets; and **date of access,** in parentheses.

> Parente, Victor. <vrparent@mailbox.syr.edu> "On Expectations of Class
>   Participation." 27 May 1996. <philosed@sued.syr.edu> (29 May 1996).

OTHER SOURCES: MLA STYLE

For unpublished sources, give relevant information that may help your reader identify or locate the source.

Computer Software

Microsoft Word. Computer Software. Microsoft, 1992.

A Film

Star Trek IV: The Voyage Home. Dir. Leonard Nimoy. Perf. William Shatner
    and Leonard Nimoy. Paramount, 1986.

A Recording

Carey, Mariah. "Hero." Music Box. Sony Songs, Inc, Columbia Records, 1993.

A Television or Radio Program

"Not Quite Dead." Narr. Mike Wallace. Sixty Minutes. CBS. WCBS, New
    York. 13 Apr. 1997.

A Letter

Ehrlich, Gretel. Letter to the author. 15 Mar. 1997.

A Lecture or Speech

Gridley, Rita. Lecture on Texas Folklore. U of Kansas. Lawrence, 8 Mar. 1996.

If title is unknown, list type of oral presentation such as *Reading, Speech,* or *Lecture.*

A Personal Interview

Miller, J. Philip. Personal interview. 12 Mar. 1997.

A Personal Survey

Morgan Library Interlibrary Loan Questionnaire. Personal survey. 15 March
    1994.

A Cartoon

Roberts, Victoria. Cartoon. New Yorker 13 Jan. 1997: 47.

An Advertisement

Toshiba. Advertisement. Time 20 Jan. 1997: 35.

IN-TEXT DOCUMENTATION: APA STYLE   In the APA style, give the author's name and date in parentheses following your use of a summary or paraphrase. If you quote material directly, give author's name, date, and page number. (Use "p." for one page and "pp." for more than one page.) These citations will direct your reader to your References list, where you give complete bibliographical information. As you cite your sources, use the following guidelines:

If you do not cite the author in the text, give author, date, and page in parentheses at the end of the citation. If you are specifically citing a quotation or a part of a source, indicate the page with *p.* or the chapter with *chap.*

> In a recent survey, New Jersey secondary school administrators "rated social studies objectives as contributing most to the attainment of high priority goals, and foreign language as contributing least" (Koppel, 1982, p. 437).

If you cite the author in the text, indicate the date in parentheses immediately following the author's name, and cite the page number in parentheses following the quotation:

> According to Vicki Galloway (1984), a student's horizons will not be broadened by "grammar lectures and manipulative classroom exercises" (p. 33).

If you cite a long direct quotation (more than forty words), indent the passage five spaces from the left margin. Omit the enclosing direct quotation marks. Place the period at the end of the passage, not after the parentheses that include the page reference.

> Educator Gerald Unks (1985) points out two instances in which a lack of language proficiency caused companies to initiate fatal marketing programs:
>
> > When Pepsi-Cola went after the Chinese market, "Come Alive with Pepsi" was translated into Chinese in Taiwan as "Pepsi Brings Your Ancestors Back from the Dead." No Sale! General Motors sought to sell its Nova in South America oblivious to the fact that "no va" in Spanish means "It doesn't go." (p. 24)

If you are paraphrasing or summarizing material (no direct quotations), you may omit the page number.

> According to Coxe (1984), many top American businesspeople agree that students who combine some business or economics training with fluency in Japanese have unlimited job possibilities.

Note: Although the APA style manual says that writers may omit page citation for summaries and paraphrases, check with your instructor before you omit page references. If you have previously cited the author and date of a study, you may omit the date:

In addition, Coxe points out that many top American businesspeople agree that students who combine some business or economics training with fluency in Japanese have unlimited job possibilities.

If the work has between two and five authors, cite all authors in your text or in parentheses in the first reference. *Note:* In your text, write "Long and Long"; in parenthetical citation, use an ampersand: "(Long & Long)."

Long and Long (1985) refer to two foreign language teachers who noted, "We are members of a world community . . . and our fates are closely intertwined" (p. 366).

As two foreign language teachers noted, "We are members of a world community . . . and our fates are closely intertwinted" (Long & Long, 1985, p. 366).

For subsequent citations, cite both names each time if a work has two authors. If a work has three to five authors, give the last name of the first author followed by "et al." Include the year for the first citation within a paragraph.

Taylor et al. (1997) found . . .

If a work has six or more authors, use only the last name of the first author and the abbreviation et al. followed by the date for the first and subsequent in-text and parenthetical citations.

Teachers should integrate the study of history, culture, politics, literature, and religion of a particular region with the study of language (Berryman et al., 1988).

If a work has no author, give the first few words of the title and the year:

Most students in the United States would be surprised to learn that the Russian government has sponsored rock concerts (A Day in the Life 1988).

If the source is from the Internet or the Web, use the author, or if there is no author, use the title.

Many Web sites now provide detailed information about how to plan a study abroad semester or year (Foreign Language, 1997).

If the author is a corporation, cite the full name of the company in the first reference:

Foreign language study must be accompanied by in-depth understanding and experience of culture (University of Maryland, 1990).

If the source is a personal communication (letter, memo, interview, phone conversation), cite in text but do not include in your References list (personal communications are not recoverable data):

> As Professor Devlin (personal interview, September 21, 1996) explained, "Foreign language study encourages students to see their own language and culture in a fresh perspective."

If you are citing a government document, give the originating agency, its abbreviation (if any), the year of publication, and (if you include a direct quotation) the page number:

> Newcomers to a foreign culture should "pay attention to their health as well as their grammar. What the natives regularly eat may be dangerous to a foreigner's constitution" (Department of Health and Human Services [DHHS] , 1989, p. 64).

If your citation refers to several sources, list the authors and dates in alphabetical order:

> Several studies (Lambert, 1996; Lange, 1987; Long & Long, 1985) have documented severe deficiencies in America's foreign language preparation.

"REFERENCES" LIST: APA STYLE   If you are using the APA style, you should make a separate list, titled "References" (no underlining or quotation marks), that appears after your text but before any appendixes. Include only sources actually used in preparing your essay. List the sources cited in your text *alphabetically*, by author's last name. Use only *initials* for author's first and middle names. If the author is unknown, alphabetize by the first word in the title (not *A, An,* or *The*). In titles, capitalize only the first word, proper names, and the first word following a colon. Ask your instructor which of APA's two recommended formats you should use for Reference list entries: first line indented five spaces, subsequent lines full measure (as shown here), or first line full measure, subsequent lines indented five spaces. Double space the entire References list.

Following are samples of APA-style References list entries. For additional information and examples, consult the *Publication Manual of the American Psychological Association* (1994).

BOOKS: APA STYLE

A Book by One Author

Gould, S. J. (1991). Bully for brontosaurus: Reflections in natural history. New York: Norton.

Additional Books by Same Author

Morrison, T. (1977). <u>Song of Solomon</u>. New York: Knopf.

Morrison, T. (1992). <u>Jazz</u>. New York: Knopf.

A Book with Two or More Authors

Conklin, N. F., & Lourie, M. A. (1983). <u>A host of tongues: Language communities in the United States</u>. New York: Free Press.

An Unknown or Anonymous Author

<u>New York Public Library student's desk reference</u> (1993). New York: Prentice Hall.

Note: In titles of books and journals, capitalize the first word, the first word after a colon, and any proper names. (New York Public Library is a proper name.)

A Book with an Author and an Editor

Austen, J. (1956). <u>Pride and prejudice</u> (M. Schorer, Ed.). Boston: Houghton Mifflin.

Note: The APA style usually uses the full name of publishing companies.

A Work in an Anthology

Chopin, K. (1989). The story of an hour. In E. V. Roberts & H. E. Jacobs (Eds.), <u>Literature: An introduction to reading and writing</u> (pp. 304–306). Englewood Cliffs, NJ: Prentice Hall.

A Translation

Lefranc, J. R. (1976). <u>A treatise on probability</u> (R. W. Mateau & D. Trilling, Trans.). New York: Macmillan. (Original work published 1952).

Note: Titles of poems, short stories, essays, or articles in a book are not underlined or italicized or put in quotation marks. Only the title of the anthology is underlined.

An Article or Chapter in an Edited Book

Sophocles. (1960). <u>Electra</u> (D. Grene, Trans.). In D. Grene & R. Lattimore (Eds.), <u>Greek tragedies</u> (Vol. 2, pp. 45–109). Chicago: University of Chicago Press.

A Government Document

Machenthun, K. M. (1973). <u>Toward a cleaner aquatic environment.</u> Environmental Protection Agency. Office of Air and Water Programs. Washington, D.C.: U.S. Government Printing Office.

A Government Document—Unknown Author

United States Department of Health, Education, and Welfare. (1972). <u>Infant Care.</u> Washington, D.C.: U.S. Government Printing Office.

PERIODICALS: APA STYLE

The following examples illustrate how to list articles in magazines and periodicals according to APA style. *Note:* Do *not* underline or italicize or put quotation marks around titles of articles. Do underline (or italicize) titles of magazines or periodicals. Cite the volume number for magazines and omit the "p." or "pp." before any page numbers. If an article is not printed on continuous pages, give all page numbers, separated by commas.

An Article in a Weekly or Biweekly Magazine

Goodgame, D. (1997, January 20). Social security: Many happy returns. Time, 149, 28–29.

An Article in a Monthly or Bimonthly Magazine

Dunbar, D. (1997, February). White noise. Travel and Leisure, 27, 106–110, 150–158.

An Unsigned Article in a Magazine

Catching a cold: It's up in the air. (1986, July–August). Science 86, 8.

An Article in a Journal with Continuous Pagination

Underline the volume number and do not include "pp." Also, APA style requires repeating all number digits: Write 2552–2555.

Sady, S.P. (1986). Prolonged exercise augments plasma triglyceride clearance. Journal of the American Medical Association, 256, 2552–2555.

An Article in a Journal That Paginates Each Issue Separately

Underline the volume number followed by the issue number in parentheses.

Brodkey, L. (1987). Writing ethnographic narratives. Written Communication, 9 (1), 25–50.

An Article in a Newspaper

Use *p.* or *pp.* before newspaper section and page numbers.

Mundy, A. (1994, January 5). Attorney general of social work. The Wall Street Journal, p. A14.

An Unsigned Article in a Newspaper

Plastic surgeon is convicted of disguising wanted man. (1997, February 28). The New York Times, p. A22.

An Editorial

Fish, S. (1996, December 26). When principles get in the way. [Editorial.] The New York Times, p. A27.

An Unsigned Editorial

European summit of uncertainty. (1994, January 7). [Editorial.] Los Angeles Times, p. B6.

ELECTRONIC AND INTERNET SOURCES: APA STYLE

CD-ROM

An Abstract on CD-ROM

Roberts, J. T. (1995). An anatomy of home-study foreign language courses

[CD-ROM].System, 23, 513–530. Abstract from: SilverPlatter 3.11: ERIC

Item: EJ 521 628.

The World Wide Web and the Internet itself are still under constant construction and revision. A standard format for citing electronic sources had not yet evolved by the publication of the most recent APA Handbook. For the short term at least, formats for documenting electronic sources from the Internet will be subject to revision. The examples here follow Xia Li and Nancy B. Crane's "Bibliographic Formats for Citing Electronic Information," which is available at <**http://www.uvm.edu/~ncrane/estyles**>. Ask your instructor what format you should follow. The basic features of an Internet or electronic citation are as follows:

- Name of author (last name, first initial and any middle initials)
- Date of Internet publication, if known, in parentheses (year, month date)
- Document title (no quotation marks, no capital letters after first word)
- If appropriate, volume, followed by issue number in parentheses plus paging or indicator of length (number of paragraphs)
- "Available:" followed by URL or database identifier (Omit the unnecessary [online] designation.)
- Date of access, in square brackets

A World Wide Web Site

For a WWW source, give the following information: **author's name,** if known; **date of publication,** if known; **title of document; title of complete work,** underlined; page numbers and or length indicator; Available: followed by **URL; date of access (yr, mo day),** in square brackets.

Tyler, P. E. (1997, February 24). U.S. and chinese seen near a deal on human

rights. The New York Times 3-4 (9 paragraphs). Available: http://www.

nytimes.com/yr/mo/day/news/world/exclusive-china-us-rights.html

[1997, February 25].

If the author is not known, begin with title of document or title of work.

Foreign Language Study Abroad Service, 1. Available: http://www.netpoint.

net/~flsas [1997, April 4].

Linkage Data: If you wish to show the hypertext context for a World Wide Web source, use the abbreviation Lkd. ("linked from") to indicate the access path and "at" to indicate additional linkage information:

Fielder, J. (1997, January 10). Photographing Colorado, 1. Lkd. Local Photographers, at All About Colorado. Available: http:denverpost.com [1997, 13 January].

FTP Site

To document a file available for downloading via FTP (File Transfer Protocol), indicate the FTP site following "Available."

Markham, D. (1995, October). Using the world wide web (13 paragraphs). Available: ftp://ftp.colostate.edu/bulletins/networks/NTO4%3Awww [1997, 3 March].

GOPHER Site

To document information available through a gopher search, indicate GOPHER site following "Available."

Yates, A. C. (1995, August 16). A community that works: Colorado state and the challenges ahead (18 paragraphs). Available: gopher://yuma.ACNS. ColoState.EDU:70/00/ON/CAMP.SRV/ln37pubrel/speeches/fall-add.txt [1997, March 13].

Synchronous Communication (MOOs, MUDs, IRCs)

Following "Available," indicate address or directions for retrieving the information.

Harnack, A. (1996, April 4). Group Discussion. Available: telnet://moo.du. org/port=8888 [1996, April 4].

Mailing List or Newsgroup Message

Following "Available," indicate address or directions for retrieving the information.

Slade, R. (1996, March 26). UNIX made easy. Available: news://alt.books. reviews [1996, March 31].

Telnet Sites

To document information available via Telnet, indicate Telnet site following "Available."

Gomes, L. (1992, May 3). Xerox's on-line neighborhood: A great place to visit. Mercury News, 7-10. Available: telnet lambda.parc.xerox.com 8888, @go #50827, press 13 [1994, December 5].

An E-mail Message

The APA Publications Manual does not recommend including personal communications in the References section. However, since many writers wish to include and reference e-mail correspondence, use the following guidelines. For an e-mail message, give the following information: **sender's name,** if known; **sender's e-mail address,** in parentheses; **date of correspondence,** in parentheses; **subject of message; type of communication** (E-mail to recipient); **recipient's e-mail address,** in parentheses.

Palmquist, M. (mpalmquist@vines.colostate.edu). (1997, April 4). Pending ACL surgery. E-mail to Stephen Reid (sreid@vines.colostate.edu).

OTHER SOURCES: APA STYLE

In the APA system, unpublished letters and interviews are personal communications and do not represent recoverable data. Therefore, they should not appear in a References list. Do, however, cite personal letters or interviews in your text. (See In-text Documentation: APA Style.)

A Review

Molotch, H. (1986, August 15). A cycle of outrage. [Review of the book A cycle of outrage]. Science, 794–795.

Published Interview

Lamm, R. (1995, November 30). Governments face tough times. [Interview with Baun, R.] Coloradoan, p. B9.

Computer Software

Microsoft word. Vers. 5.0[Computer software]. (1992). Microsoft.

A Film

Nimoy, L. (Director). (1986). Star trek IV: The voyage home [Film]. Paramount.

A Recording

Carey, M. (1993). Hero. On Music box [CD]. New York: Columbia Records.

A Television or Radio Program

Bogdonich, R. (Producer). (1997, April 13). Sixty Minutes. New York: WCBS.

EDITING AND PROOFREADING   Edit your paper for conciseness, clarity, and accuracy of grammar, spelling, and punctuation. See your handbook for assistance in revising errors and improving usage. Check your direct quotations to make sure they are *accurate, word-for-word transcriptions* of the originals. Make sure that your in-text citation of sources is accurate. Proofread both the text *and* the Works Cited or References section. Finally, have someone else proofread your research paper for typos, spelling errors, missing words, or confusing sentences.

■ POSTSCRIPT ON THE WRITING PROCESS   As your final entry in your research notebook, answer the following questions:

1. Reread your "research log" section. Compare your initial schedule with your actual progress. What parts of the research paper took longer than you anticipated? What took less time?

2. What was the most difficult problem you encountered while writing the research paper? How did you try to solve that problem?

3. What do you like best about the final version of your research paper? Why? What do you like least? Why?

RESEARCH PAPER:

STUDENT WRITING

FOREIGN LANGUAGE STUDY: AN AMERICAN NECESSITY

Kate McNerny

Kate McNerny's final version of her research paper appears on page 576. Her purpose is to persuade students, administrators, and ordinary citizens that learning the language and culture of a foreign country is important, both to people as individuals and to America as a nation. In this paper, she uses interviews, library research, research on the Internet, and her own experience to alert her readers to the seriousness of the problem and to recommend a solution. She argues that American schools should require students to study at least one foreign language during junior and senior high school. McNerny follows the MLA style for in-text documentation, supplementary notes, and Works Cited list. The marginal annotations highlight key features of her research paper.

↑ 1"
↓ ½"
McNerny 1

Kate McNerny

Professor Thomas

English 101

18 November 1997

/double space

/double space

Foreign Language Study:

An American Necessity

/double space

For her lead-in, McNerny uses quotations she collected in her informal survey.

"Why should I learn a foreign language—everyone speaks English!" "I would never use another language—I never plan to leave the United States." "I had a hard enough time learning English!" These are only a few of the excuses people have given for opposing foreign language studies, and unfortunately they represent the ideas of more than a few American citizens. In possibly the most multicultural nation in the world, it is ironic that so many people—who themselves have come from foreign cultures and foreign languages—should want to remain isolated from international languages and cultures. A recent indication of the backlash against foreign languages came when the House of Representatives passed legislation recommending that English should be the official language of the U.S. Government.[1] In addition, 23 states already have Official English laws on the books (Swope 2128 and Torres 51). Because these attitudes are so widespread, we need a national policy supporting foreign language study in elementary and secondary schools. If we are to continue to develop as a people and a nation, we must be able to communicate with and understand the cultures of people from countries around the globe.

*McNerny gives first version of her **thesis** for her problem-solving essay: "We need a national policy supporting foreign language study."*

Historically, Americans' attitudes toward foreign languages have swayed from positive to negative, depending on current

McNerny presents historical background on the problem.

1"

1"

↕ 1"

McNerny 2

events around the world. Theodore Huebener's study, Why Johnny Should Learn Foreign Languages, shows how attitudes reflect the times. In 1940, in an isolationist period before World War II, a committee of the American Youth Commission issued a report labeling foreign language studies as "useless and time-consuming" (Huebener 13). An even more appalling statement came from a group of Harvard scholars. They suggested that "foreign language study is useful primarily in strengthening the student's English. . . . For the average student, there is no real need at all to learn a foreign language" (Huebener 14). With such attitudes, it is no wonder that students and administrators ignored foreign language programs during the 1940s and 1950s.[2] With the advent of Sputnik, however, interest in Russian increased, and with the growing trade with Pacific Rim countries in recent years, the United States has experienced short bursts of interest in Japanese and Chinese foreign language study.

Despite some occasional surges of interest, however, foreign language study still holds the weakest position of any other major subject in American secondary schools. A recent study of foreign language programs reports that "only 15 percent of American high school students study a foreign language. Only 8 percent of [American] colleges require credit in a foreign language for admission (down from 34 percent in 1966)" (Unks 24). Because available programs at the junior and senior high school level are generally limited in variety and scope, only a small percentage of those students who take a foreign language ever become fluent in it. A 1984

Ellipses points indicate material omitted from the source.

The footnote refers the reader to the "Notes" page for McNerny's comment on the history of the problem.

Square brackets in quoted material indicate a word added by McNerny to clarify the sentence.

In-text citation for a source with two authors.

study that sampled 536 secondary schools revealed that most offered a foreign language, but 91 percent did not require foreign language credits for graduation (Ranwez and Rodgers 98). In contrast, most European countries require all students to learn at east one, and often two, foreign languages. Norway, Spain, France, Sweden, Italy, England, Germany, and Finland all require at least one foreign language. According to Rune Bergentoft, currently a Mellon Fellow at the National Foreign Language Center, "Several [European] countries require knowledge of two foreign languages for entry to the upper secondary school; in the Netherlands, the requirement is three foreign languages" (18).

McNerny restates her thesis, using more specific language: "American students . . . should be required to study at least one foreign language during . . . junior and senior high school."

The United States cannot continue to lag behind other countries in language capability. As two foreign language researchers noted, "We are members of a world community consisting of hundreds of nations, and our fates are closely intertwined" (Long and Long 366). It is time to change attitudes and to recognize that in order to successfully interact with its "world community," the United States must drastically change its foreign language practices and policies. American students should be encouraged to start their language studies in elementary school and required to study at least one foreign language during their six years of junior and senior high school.

*McNerny's **essay map:** The solution requires changes by administrators, by students, and by national policy makers.*

How do we encourage more students to study a foreign language in our elementary and secondary schools? The solution requires changes on the part of administrators and teachers, changes in the attitudes and experiences of students

McNerny 4

themselves, and changes in our state and national foreign language policies.

School administrators across the country often oppose the idea of requiring foreign languages because they cannot see the contribution these studies make to the overall goals of the schools' curriculum. In a recent survey, New Jersey secondary school administrators "rated social studies objectives as contributing most to the attainment of high priority goals, and foreign language as contributing least" (Koppel 437). These administrators fail to realize that language studies can add a valuable dimension to a social studies program. Educators can use a combined program to emphasize a global perspective in language and cultural studies. "The world looks and sounds different when one is 'standing in the shoes' of another, speaking another language, or recognizing another's point of view based on an alternative set of values" (Bragaw 37). This global-awareness is crucial in our increasingly interdependent world.

Likewise, teachers need to continue to make changes in their foreign language courses to attract more students. More and more primary and secondary language courses already focus on cultural issues more than grammar, but now they need to use all the computer, online, and Internet resources currently available to attract and motivate their students. Linguist Mark Warschauer, in a preface to papers collected at a conference on Global Networking in Foreign Language Learning, asserts that "foreign language learners can communicate rapidly and inexpensively with other learners or speakers of the target language around the world. With the World Wide Web, learners can access a broad array of authentic foreign

*Notice **punctuation** for in-text citation: Source appears in parentheses after the quotation marks but **before** the period.*

*McNerny uses **personal experience** in her research paper. Her experience provides a great example to show why students can benefit from studying a foreign language.*

McNerny 5

language materials . . . or they can develop and publish their own materials to share with others across the classroom or across the globe" (Warschauer ix). Teachers need to make use of the Internet communication possibilities to help motivate and interest their students.

Of course, students themselves need motivation in order to enroll in foreign language classes. Many students simply fail to see why they will ever need to use a foreign language. I used to belong to that group. I remember my mom always telling me, "Take French classes. Learn how to speak French so you can visit your cousins in France someday." At the time, during junior high, I did take French classes for a while, but then dropped them when my schedule became "too busy." Then, as my mom had promised, I got the opportunity to visit my cousins in France. For some reason, the fact that I couldn't speak French didn't really hit me—until I stepped off the train at Gare du Nord in Paris and couldn't find the relative who was supposed to meet me. After frantically searching the entire station several times, I had to break down and ask for help. At the information desk, a few completely butchered French phrases escaped my lips—only to be received by an unimpressed, unresponsive station attendant. He muttered something about dumb Americans. Then, with a wave of his hand, he gestured toward some unknown destination. I did survive that painful ordeal, but I vowed I wouldn't embarrass myself—and other Americans—again.

Another way to change students' attitudes is to encourage them to participate in exchange programs or study abroad

McNerny 6

programs.[3] Again, the Internet and the World Wide Web offer students and their teachers immediate access to a variety of exchange and study abroad programs. The World Wide Web has hundreds of sites related to foreign language study that can help both teachers and students. The International House World Organization, at **http://www. international-house.org**, is "a worldwide network of language schools sharing a common commitment to the highest standards of teaching and training" (International). Students wishing to find out about exchange and study abroad programs should browse the web, perhaps beginning at a site such as Foreign Language Study Abroad Service at **http://www.netpoint.net/~flsas**. The Foreign Language Study Abroad Service was started in 1971 and is, according to their home page, "the oldest study abroad service in the U.S." (Foreign).

Study abroad programs and exchange programs help students learn the language, but just as important, they enable students to learn about different cultures. In his resource book, Teaching Culture, H. Ned Seelye, Director of Bilingual-Bicultural Education for the State of Illinois, cites just one of many cultural lessons that American students—and tourists—need to learn:

> At a New Year's Eve celebration in an exclusive Guatemalan hotel, one American was overheard telling another. "You see all these people? They're all my wife's relatives. And every damn one of them has kissed me tonight. If another Guatemalan man hugs and kisses me I'll punch him right in the face!" The

McNerny introduces the author, the title of the book, and the author's credentials to lend authority to the quoted passage.

At the end of the quotation, McNerny cites only the page number, since she has already introduced the author. Page number follows the period in indented block quotation.

Mc Nerny does not end her paragraph with a quotation; instead, she shows how this evidence supports her point.

irritated American was disturbed by two things: the extended kinship patterns of the group and the *abrazo de ano neuvo* as executed by the men (he did not complain of the female *abrazos*). Both customs—close family ties that extend to distant relatives and the *abrazo* given as a greeting or sign of affection devoid of sexual overtures—elicited hostility in the American who was bored by unintelligible language and depressed by nostalgia and alcohol. (85)

In order to prevent such linguistic and cultural misunderstandings, more and more Americans should take advantage of study abroad and exchange programs that will acquaint them with a variety of cultures and languages.

Finally, in order to coordinate our schools' foreign language studies, America needs changes in our state and national foreign language policies to ensure that every child receives some basic instruction in foreign languages and culture. Changes in our foreign language requirements would not only promote cultural understanding but also would strengthen the United States' international relations in business and diplomacy. International trade is continually increasing in the United States and has created a demand for business people competent in foreign languages. Many top American business people agree that students who combine some business or economics training with fluency in Japanese have unlimited job possibilities (Coxe 194). Company executives simply cannot expect to make efficient, sound decisions in their international markets without understanding and speaking

McNerny 8

the language of the country they are dealing with (Huebener 45). Educator Gerald Unks points out two instances in which a lack of language proficiency caused companies to initiate fatal marketing programs.

> When Pepsi-Cola went after the Chinese market, "Come
> Alive With Pepsi" was translated into Chinese in Taiwan as
> "Pepsi Brings Your Ancestors Back from the Dead." No
> Sale! General Motors sought to sell its Nova in South
> America oblivious to the fact that "No va" in Spanish
> means "It doesn't go." (24)

These examples illustrate that business people need thorough competence in, not just rudimentary knowledge of, foreign languages.

Finally, proficiency in foreign languages and culture is important not only for business and trade overseas, but also for jobs in America. Required foreign language study would help our future citizens understand and appreciate our multicultural heritage—and help them become employable. Verada Bluford, writing in Occupational Outlook Quarterly, argues that as our country "becomes more involved in foreign trade, tourism, and international cooperative ventures, the number of jobs open to fluent speakers of a foreign language increases" (25). Bluford explains that there are "language-centered jobs" such as teaching, translating, and interpreting, but there are also "language-related jobs," such as jobs in marketing and finance, engineering, airlines, banking, and government, where language skills are necessary. These "language-related jobs" will go to students who have language skills *in addition*

Before quoting from Bluford, McNerny introduces the author and the journal from which the article is taken.

to some other skill (Bluford 26). A foreign language requirement, whether mandated by each state or by Congress, would make all Americans better citizens of the world and their own country.

The need for required language study in the United States is urgent. Some states already require schools to introduce children to some foreign language during their grade school years (Kuo 2). For example, North Carolina, Arkansas, Louisiana, Arizona, and Oklahoma already have existing laws, while Oregon has a proposed new law that will require all tenth graders to know a language other than English (Kuo 2). Since some individual schools and states realize the benefits of foreign language requirements, Congress should guide all the states and formulate a national foreign language policy that would make all our schools more like the European model.

Although the ideas and the plans for a national policy exist, often the funds do not. Some funds can be diverted from within school districts, but the federal government must take some initiative. The current administration spends endless time and money subsidizing business interests and propping up weak foreign economies. Since foreign language knowledge contributes strongly to success in both these areas, however, it would be practical for the administration also to support expansion of language studies. Instead, it continues to reduce funding for special programs including language studies centers and international teaching facilities (Unks 25). Realistically, a foreign language requirement in junior and senior high school cannot be initiated without the support of both local school districts as well as the federal government. Americans must acknowledge the fact

McNerny begins her conclusion, citing precedents and calling for state and federal administrators to support a foreign language requirement.

that they are not isolated from the rest of the world. Successful interaction in the "world community" relies on our ability, as a nation, to effectively communicate with and understand people from other countries. Understanding, communication, and world peace cannot be achieved without cultural awareness and foreign language proficiency.

Notes

Content notes are placed on a separate page and double-spaced. Use raised footnote number and indent first line five spaces.

¹Americans not only hesitate to take a foreign language, but they also seem bent on keeping foreign languages officially "out of sight." The debate over "official English" has spilled over into the workplace, in the form of "English-only" rules in business. Robert Brady, writing in HR Focus, reviews the two sides of the English-only debate: "Advocates of English-only rules argue that a single language promotes good organizational communications, ensures workplace safety, improves service to the English-speaking customer base, and avoids discrimination" (20). On the other side, Brady says, opponents believe that requiring employees to speak English goes against the melting pot heritage of our country—and may violate Title VII of the Civil Rights Act (20). Many opponents from ethnic and civil-rights groups believe these bills and rules are racist (McBee 64). Americans' ignorance of foreign languages (and the fear that ignorance breeds) is an important cause for the popularity of both the "official English" laws and the "English-only" rules.

In her notes, McNerny includes her ideas about "English-only" and "official English" that would have been digressive in the text of her paper.

²One of the most disturbing facts is that although Huebener's study was done in 1961, very little has changed in almost forty years. Except for slight changes in statistics, dates, and names of wars, Americans have remained strikingly insular in their attitudes toward foreign languages and foreigners.

In this footnote, McNerny puts statistics that didn't seem to fit in the flow of her paragraph but are relevant to study abroad programs.

³Recent figures on study abroad programs illustrate the huge gap between the number of foreign students who study in the U.S. versus U.S. students who study abroad. In an article on language learning and study abroad, Barbara Freed gives the following figures: "Close to half a million international students came to the

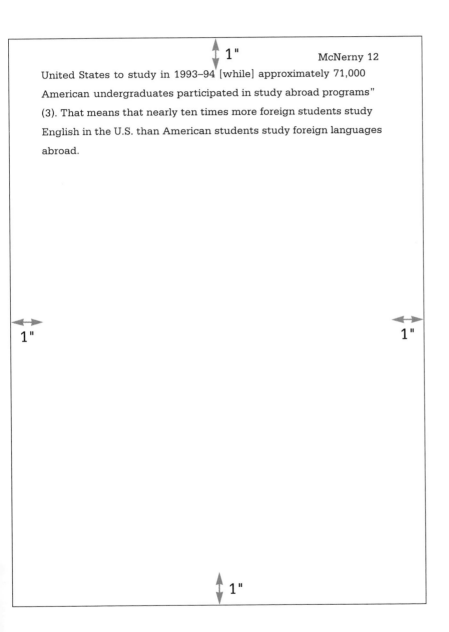

McNerny 12

United States to study in 1993–94 [while] approximately 71,000 American undergraduates participated in study abroad programs" (3). That means that nearly ten times more foreign students study English in the U.S. than American students study foreign languages abroad.

1"

½"

Works Cited

The Works Cited list begins a new page. List entries alphabetically by author's last name. If no author is given, list by first work in the title. Double-space all lines.

Bergentoft, Rune. "Foreign Language Instruction: A Comparative Perspective." The Annals of the American Academy of Political and Social Science 532 (1994): 8–34.

Bluford, Verada. "Working with Foreign Languages." Occupational Outlook Quarterly 38.4 (1994): 25–28.

Brady, Robert I. "English-Only Rules Draw Controversy." HR Focus June 1996: 20.

Bragaw, Donald H., and Helene Zimmer-Loew. "Social Studies and Foreign Language: A Partnership." Education Digest Dec. 1985: 36–39.

Coxe, Donald. "The Back Page." Canadian Business Feb. 1984: 194.

Foreign Language Study Abroad Service. http://www.netpoint.net/~flsas (21 Feb. 1997).

Indent five spaces after first line of each entry.

1"

1"

Freed, Barbara F. "Language Learning and Study Abroad." Second Language Acquisition in a Study Abroad Context. Ed. Barbara F. Freed. Philadelphia: John Benjamins, 1995. 3–33.

Book

Huebener, Theodore. Why Johnny Should Learn Foreign Languages. New York: Chilton, 1961.

Internet Web page

International House: The Worldwide Language Teaching Organization. http://www. international-house.org (2 Mar 1997).

Article from a journal with contiguous pagination

Koppel, Irene E. "The Perceived Contribution of Foreign Language to High Priority Education Goals." Foreign Language Annals 15 (1982): 435–37.

Kuo, Fidelius. "Foreign Language Proposal in Washington State Worthy." Northwest Asain Weekly 9 Dec. 1994: 4.

1"

McNerny 14

Long, Delbert H., and Roberta A. Long. "Toward the Promotion of Foreign Language Study and Global Understanding." Education 105 (1985): 366–68.

McBee Susanna. "A War Over Words." U.S. News and World Report 6 Oct. 1986: 64.

Ranwez, Alain D., and Judy Rodgers. "The Status of Foreign Languages and International Studies: An Assessment in Colorado." Foreign Language Annals 17 (1984): 97–102.

Seelye, H. Ned. Teaching Culture: Strategies for Foreign Language Educators. Skokie, IL: National Textbook, 1974.

Swope, Christopher. "Panel OKs Bill to Make English Official Government Language." Congressional Quarterly Weekly Report 54 (1996): 2128–29.

Torres, Joseph. "The Language Crusade." Hispanic 9.6 (1996): 50–54.

Unks, Gerald. "The Perils of Our Single-Language Policy." Education Digest Mar. 1985: 24–27.

Warschauer, Mark. Preface. Telecollaboration in Foreign Language Learning. By Warschauer. Ed. Mark Warschauer. Honolulu: Second Language Teaching & Curriculum Center, 1996.

1"

1"   1"

1"

For inclusive page numbers over 100, use only the last two digits in the second number (366–68).

Article from a monthly magazine

APPENDIX:

WRITING UNDER PRESSURE

The main chapters of this text describe purposes for writing and strategies for collecting, shaping, drafting, and revising an essay. These chapters assume that you have several days or even weeks to write your paper. They work on the premise that you have time to read model essays, time to think about ideas for your topic, and time to prewrite, write several drafts, and receive feedback from other members of your class. Much college writing, however, occurs on midterm or final examinations, when you may have only fifteen to twenty minutes to complete the whole process of writing. When you must produce a "final" draft in a few short minutes, your writing process may need drastic modification.

A typical examination has some objective questions (true/false, multiple choice, definitions, short answer) followed by an essay question or two. For example, with just twenty-five minutes left in your Western Civilization midterm, you might finish the last multiple-choice question, turn the page, and read the following essay question:

> Erich Maria Remarque's *All Quiet on the Western Front* has been hailed by critics the world over as the "twentieth century's definitive novel on war." What does Remarque's novel tell us about the historical, ideological, national, social, and human significance of twentieth-century warfare? Draw on specific illustrations from the novel, but base your observations on your wider perspective of Western Civilization. Good luck!

Overwhelmed by panic, the blood drains from your face and your fingers feel icy. You now have twenty-two minutes to write on the "historical, ideological, national, social, and human significance of twentieth-century warfare." Do you have to explain everything about modern warfare? Must you use specific examples from the novel? Good luck, indeed! Everything you remembered about the novel has now vanished. Bravely, you pick up your pen and start recounting the main events of the novel, hoping to show the instructor that you at least read it.

You can survive such an essay examination, but you need to prepare yourself emotionally and intellectually. Following is some advice from senior English majors who have taken dozens of essay examinations in their four years of college. These seniors answer the question, "What advice would you give to students who are preparing to take an essay examination?"

> Even though I'm an English major, I'm perfectly petrified of writing impromptu essays. My advice is to calm yourself. Read the question.

Study key words and concepts. Before beginning an essay question, write a brief, informal outline. This will organize your ideas and help you remember them as well. Take a deep breath and write. I would also recommend *rereading* the question while you are writing, to keep you on track.

The first step is to know the material. Then, before you begin, read the instructions. Know what the teacher expects. Then try to organize your thoughts into a small list—preferably a list that will become your main paragraphs. Don't babble to fill space. Teachers hate reading nonsense. Reread what you've written often. This will ensure that you won't repeat yourself. Proofread at the end.

Organization is important but difficult in a pressure situation. Well-organized essays do have a tendency to impress the professor, sometimes more than information-packed essays. Organize your notes and thoughts about those notes as you study (not necessarily in a chronological order, but rather in a comprehensible order). Good luck.

Read the question carefully.

Get your thoughts in order.

Write what the question asks, not what you hope it says.

Don't ramble.

Give textual facts or specific examples.

Summarize with a clear, understandable closure.

Proofread.

Keep calm. Your life doesn't depend on one test.

My advice would be first to learn how to consciously relax and practice writing frequently. *Practice!!!* It's important to practice writing as much as possible in any place possible, because the more writing you do, the better and easier it becomes. Also, your belief that it *can* be done is critical!

Know the information that you will be tested over well enough that you can ask yourself tough and well-formed questions in preparation. You should be able to predict what essay questions your professor will ask, at least generally. I always go to the test file or ask friends for sample essay questions that I can practice on. Then I practice writing on different areas of the material.

The common threads in these excerpts of advice are to know your audience, analyze key terms in the question, make a sketch outline, know the material, practice writing before the test, and proofread when you finish writing. Knowing how to read the question and practicing your writing before the test will help you relax and do your best.

KNOW YOUR AUDIENCE

Teachers expect you to answer a question exactly as it is asked, not just to give the information that you know. Because teachers must read dozens of essays, they are impressed by clear organization and specific detail. As one senior says, teachers hate babble because they cannot follow the thread of your argument. Although they demand specific examples and facts from the text, they want you to explain how these examples *relate* to the overall question. In a pile of two hundred history exams graded by one professor, margins featured comments like "Reread the question. This doesn't answer the question." "What is your main point? State your main point clearly." "Give more specific illustrations and examples." Keep this teacher in mind as you write your essay response.

ANALYZE KEY TERMS

Understanding the key terms in the question is crucial to writing an essay under pressure. Teachers expect you to respond to *their* specific question, not just to write down information. They want you to use your writing to *think* about the topic—to analyze and synthesize the information. In short, they want you to make sense of the information. Following are key terms that indicate teachers' expectations and suggest how to organize your answer.

DISCUSS: A general instruction that means "write about." If the question says "discuss," look for other key words to focus your response.

DESCRIBE: Give sensory details or particulars about a topic. Often, however, this general instruction simply means "discuss."

ANALYZE: Divide a topic into its parts and show how the parts are related to each other and to the topic as a whole.

SYNTHESIZE: Show how the parts relate to the whole or how the parts make sense together.

EXPLAIN: Show relationships between specific examples and general principles. Explain what (define), explain why (causes/effects), and/or explain how (analyze process).

DEFINE: Explain what something is. As appropriate, give a formal definition, describe it, analyze its parts or function, describe what it is not, and/or compare and contrast it with similar events or ideas.

COMPARE: Explain similarities and (often) differences. Draw conclusions from the observed similarities and differences.

CONTRAST: Explain key differences. Draw conclusions from the observed differences.

ILLUSTRATE: Provide specific examples of an idea or process.

TRACE: Give the sequence or chronological order of key events or ideas.

EVALUATE: Determine the value or worth of an idea, thing, process, person, or event. Set up criteria and provide evidence to support your judgments.

SOLVE: Explain your solution; show how it fixes the problem, why it is better than other alternatives, and why it is feasible.

ARUGE: Present both sides of a controversial issue, showing why the opposing position should not be believed or accepted and why your position should be accepted. Give evidence to support your position.

INTERPRET: Offer your understanding of the meaning and significance of an idea, event, person, process, or work of art. Support your understanding with specific examples or details.

MAKE A SKETCH OUTLINE

The key terms in a question should not only focus your thinking but also suggest how to organize your response. Use the key terms to make a sketch outline of your response. You may not regularly use an outline when you have more time to write an essay, but the time pressure requires that you revise your normal writing process.

Assume that you have twenty-five minutes to read and respond to the following question from a history examination. Read the instructions carefully, not the key terms, and make a brief outline to guide your writing.

- Answer *one* of the following. Draw on the reading for your answer. (25 pts)

1. Explain the arguments that the balance of power does and does not work in the nuclear age (discuss and illustrate both sides of the argument). Then take a stand—citing the evidence for your position.

2. Explain the arguments that the United Nations does and does not play a positive role in international relations (discuss and illustrate

both sides of the argument). Then take a stand—citing the evidence for your position.

Let's assume that because you know more about the United Nations, you choose the second question. First, you should identify and underline key words in the question. The subject for your essay is the *United Nations* and its role in *international relations*. You need to *explain* the reasons why the UN does or does not have a positive effect on international relations. You will need to *discuss* and *illustrate* (give specific examples of) both sides of the controversy. Finally, you need to *take a stand* (argue) for your belief, citing *evidence* (specific examples from recent history) of how the UN has or has not helped to resolve international tensions.

Based on your rereading and annotation of the key words of the question, make a quick outline or list, perhaps as follows:

I.   Reasons (with examples) why some believe the UN is effective

    A. Reason #1 + example

    B. Reason #2 + example

II.   Reasons (with examples) why some believe the UN is not effective

    A. Reason #1 + example

    B. Reason #2 + example

III.   Reasons why you believe the UN is effective

    Refer to reasons and examples cited in I, above, but explain why these reasons and examples outweigh the reasons cited in II, above.

With this sketch outline as your guide, jot down reasons and examples that you intend to use and then start writing. Your outline will make sure that you cover all the main points of the question, and it will keep your essay organized as you concentrate on remembering specific reasons and examples.

■   **JOURNAL EXERCISE**   For practice, analyze at least one question from two of the following subject areas. First, underline key terms. Then, in your journal explain what these terms ask you to do. Finally, sketch an outline to help organize your response. If you are not familiar with the topics, check a dictionary or encyclopedia. (Do not write the essay.)

Biology

- Describe the process by which artificial insulin was first produced.
- What is reverse transcriptase and how was it used in genetic engineering?
- Humans—at least most of us—walk on two legs as opposed to four. How might you account for this using a Darwinian, Lamarckian, and Theistic model?

History

- Discuss the significant political developments in the English colonies in the first half of the eighteenth century.
- Account for the end of the Salem witchcraft delusion and discuss the consequences of the outbreak for Salem Village.

Human Development

- Discuss evidence for nature versus nurture effects in human development.
- Contrast Piaget's, Vygotsky's, and Whorf's ideas on connections between language and thought.

Humanities

- How and why did early Christian culture dominate the Roman Empire? In terms of art and architecture, discuss specific ways in which the early Christians transformed or abolished the Greco-Roman legacy.

Literature

- Aristotle wrote that a tragedy must contain certain elements, such as a protagonist of high estate, recognition, and reversal, and should also evoke pity and fear in the audience. Which of the following best fits Aristotle's definition: *Hamlet, Death of a Salesman,* or *The Old Man and the Sea?* Explain your choice.

Philosophy

- On the basis of what we have studied in this class, define "philosophy." Taking your major subject of study (for example, biology, history, literature), discuss three philosophical problems that arise in this field.
- Write an essay explaining the following statement. Be clear in your explanation and use specific examples. "Egoism allows for prudent altruism."

Political Science

- Evaluate the achievements of the current administration's policy in Africa in recent years.
- Analyze the role of force in the contemporary international system.

Psychology

- Contrast Freud's and Erikson's stage theories of personality.

- What is meant by triangulation of measurement (multiple method-ology)?

KNOW THE MATERIAL

It goes without saying that you must know the material in order to explain the concepts and give specific examples or facts from the text. But what is the best way to review the material so that you can recall examples under pressure? The following three study tactics will improve your recall.

First, read your text actively. Do not just mark key passages in yellow highlighter. Write marginal notes to yourself. Write key concepts in the margin. Ask questions. Make connections between an idea in one paragraph and something you read earlier. Make connections between what you read in the text and what you heard in class.

Second, do not depend only on your reading and class discussion. Join or form a study group that meets regularly to review course material. Each person in the group should prepare some question for review. Explaining key ideas to a friend is an excellent way to learn the material yourself.

Finally, use your writing to help you remember. Do not just read the book and your notes and head off for the test. Instead, review your notes, *close* your notebook, and write down as much as you can remember. Review the assigned chapters in the text, close the book, and write out what you remember. If you can write answers to questions with the book closed, you know you're ready for an essay examination.

■   JOURNAL EXERCISE   Get out the class notes and textbook for a course that you are currently taking. Annotate your notes with summary comments and questions. In the margins, write out the key ideas that the lecture covered. Then write out questions that you still have about the material. Open your textbook for that class. Annotate the margins of the chapter that you are currently reading. Write summary comments about important material. Write questions in the margins about material that you do not understand. Note places in the text that the instructor also covered in class.

PRACTICE WRITING

As several of the senior English majors suggested, practicing short essays *before* an examination will make you feel comfortable with the material and reduce your panic. A coach once noted that while every athlete wants to win, only the true winners are willing to *prepare* to win. The same is true of writing an examination. Successful writers have already completed 80 percent of the writing process *before* they walk into an examination. They have written notes in the margins of their notebooks and textbooks. They have discussed the subject with other students. They have closed the book and written out key definitions. They have prepared questions and practiced answering them. Once they read a question, they are prepared to write out their "final" drafts.

■ JOURNAL EXERCISE   For an upcoming examination in one of your other courses, write out three possible essay questions that your instructor might ask. For each question, underline the key words and make a sketch outline of your response. Set your watch or timer for fifteen minutes and actually write out your response to *one* of your questions.

PROOFREAD AND EDIT

In your normal writing process, you can put aside your draft for several days and proofread and edit it later. When you are writing under pressure, however, you need to save three or four minutes at the end to review what you have written. Often, you may be out of time before you have finished writing what you wanted to say about the question. At this point, one effective strategy is to draw a line _____ at the end of what you have written, write "Out of Time," and then write one or two quick sentences explaining what you planned to say: "If I had more time, I would explain how the UN's image has become more positive following the crises in Israel and Iraq." Then use your remaining two or three minutes to reread what you have written, making sure that your ideas are clear, that you have written in complete sentences and used correct spelling and punctuation. If you don't know how to spell a word, at least write "sp?" next to a word to show that you think it is spelled incorrectly.

SAMPLE ESSAY QUESTIONS AND RESPONSES

The following are sample essay questions, student's responses, and instructors' comments and grades.

HISTORY 100: WESTERN CIVILIZATION   Examination II over Chapter 12, class lectures, and Victor Hugo's *The Hunchback of Notre Dame*

Essay I (25 Points)

What was the fifteenth-century view of "science" as described in *The Hunchback?* How did this view tend to inhibit Claud Frollo in his experiments in his closet in the cathedral?

An excellent response. Your focus on superstition and heresay along with the specific examples of the roasted mouse, the "Philosopher's Stone," and La Esmeralda's goat illustrate the fifteenth-century view of science and its inhibiting effect.
Grade: A

Give more examples from the novel and show how the fifteenth-century view actually <u>inhibited</u> Frollo. Otherwise, generally good response. (Why was creating the Earth such a religious "ordeal"?)
Grade: B

Needs more specific illustrations from the novel. Frollo was inhibited by his lack of

ANSWER 1

The fifteenth-century view of "science" was characterized by superstition and heresy. In the *Hunchback of Notre Dame,* for example, we see superstition operating when the king's physician stated that a gunshot wound could be cured by the application of a roasted mouse. Claud Frollo, a high-ranking church official, had a thirst for knowledge, but unfortunately it pushed beyond the limits of knowledge permitted by the church. When he worked in his closet on the art of alchemy and searched for the "Philosopher's Stone" (gold), he was guilty of heresy. Frollo read and mastered the arts and sciences of the university and of the church, and he wanted to know more. He knew that if he pressed into the "Black Arts," the Devil would take his soul. And indeed, the "Devil" of passion did. Frollo felt inhibited because many of the experiments he performed would have made him guilty of heresy and witchcraft in the eyes of the church. And this seemed to be the case in almost anything "new" or out of the ordinary. La Esmeralda, for instance, was declared "guilty" of witchcraft for the training of her goat. Her goat appeared to have been possessed by the Devil himself. When in fact, all the girl was guilty of was training the goat to do a few simple tricks. All in all, the fifteenth-century view of "science" was not one of favor, but of oppression and fear. Thankfully, the Renaissance came along!

ANSWER 2

The fifteenth-century view of science was that according to the Bible. God was the creator of all and as to scientific theory, the subject was moot. No one was a believer in the scientific method—however we do find some science going on in Claud Frollo's closet, alchemy. At that time he was trying to create gold by mixing different elements together. Though alchemy seems to be the only science of that time period, people who practiced it kept it to themselves. We even find King Louis IX coming to Frollo, disguised, to dabble in a little of the science himself. At this time people were rejecting the theory of the Earth revolving around the sun because, as a religious ordeal, God created the Earth and man and they are the center of all things so there were no questions to be answered by science, because the answer was God.

ANSWER 3

According to The Hunchback of Notre Dame, the view of "science" in the fifteenth century was basically alchemy, that is being able to turn back metals into gold. Everything else that we would regard as scientific today was regarded as sorcery or magic in the fifteenth century. What inhibited Claud Frollo in his experiments of turning bare metals into gold was that, according to the laws of alchemy, one needed "The Philosopher's Stone" to complete the experiment and Claud Frollo was unable to find this particular stone.

ANSWER 4

During the period that the *Hunchback* took place, the attitude toward science was one of fear. Because the setting was in the medieval world, the people were afraid to admit to doing some things that were not being done by a majority of people. The overall views during that period was to keep one's own self out of trouble. The fright may be the result of the public executions which was perhaps Claud Frollo's deterrent in admitting to performing acts of science which others are uneducated in. Claud Frollo was outnumbered in the area of wanting to be "educated" and he kept to himself because he feared the people. He was in a position that didn't give him the power to try and overcome people's attitude of fear toward science. If he tried, he risked his life.

scientific method and the censure of the church. Underline title of novels: The Hunchback Of Notre Dame. *Grade: C*

State your ideas more clearly. Your response doesn't answer the question. Very limited in your examples of science. Grade: D

BIOLOGY 220: ECOLOGY
FINAL EXAMINATION

ESSAY II (20 POINTS)

Water running down a mountainside erodes its channel and carries with it considerable material. What is the basic source of the energy used by the water to do this work? How is the energy used by water to do this work related to the energy used by life in the stream ecosystem?

ANSWER 1

The process begins with the hydrologic cycle. The sun radiates down and forces evaporation. This H2O gas condenses and forms rain or snow which precipitates back to earth. If the precipitation falls on a mountain, it will eventually run down the hillside and erode its channel. (Some water will evaporate without running down the hill.) The energy used by water to do its work relates directly to the energy used by life in the stream system. The sun is an energy input. It is the source of energy for stream life just as it is the source of energy for the water. Through photosynthesis, the energy absorbed by the stream is used by higher and higher trophic levels. So the sun is the

Good response. Clear focus on the hydrologic cycle, photosynthesis, and solar energy and the source of energy for both the stream and its ecosystems. Grade: A

energy source for both running water and the life in the stream. It all starts with solar energy.

Very clear explanation of the hydrologic cycle, but response doesn't explain how source of energy for the streams ecosystems is related, through photosynthesis, to solar energy. Grade: B

___

ANSWER 2

Ultimately, the sun is the basic source of energy which allows water to do the work it does. Solar power runs the hydrologic cycle, which is where water gets its energy. Heat evaporates water and allows molecules to rise in the atmosphere where it condenses in clouds. Above the ground, but still under the effects of gravity, water has potential energy at this point. When enough condensation occurs, water drops back to the ground, changing potential energy to kinetic energy, which is how water works on mountainsides to move materials. As water moves materials, it brings into streams a great deal of organic matter which is utilized by a number of heterotrophic organisms. That is the original source of energy for the ecosystems, and also how energy used by water is related to the energy that is used by life in streams.

Reread the question. The basic source of energy is solar power, You almost discover the answer when you discuss photosynthesis, but after that, you get off track again. Grade: C−

___

ANSWER 3

The actual energy to move the water down the mountains is gravitation pull from the center of the earth. The stream's "growth" from the beginning of the mountain top to the base starts out with being a heterotrophic system. This is because usually there is not enough light to bring about photosynthesis for the plants and in turn help other organism's survival so the streams use outside resources for energy. Once the stream is bigger (by meeting up with another stream), it is autotrophic. It can produce its own energy sources. When the water reaches the base and becomes very large, it falls back to heterotrophic system because the water has become too deep for light to penetrate and help with photosynthesis.

Handbook

A piece of writing is never finished. It is delivered to a deadline, torn out of a typewriter on demand, and sent off with a sense of accomplishment and shame and pride and frustration. If only there were a couple more days, time for just another run at it, perhaps then . . . .

—DONALD MURRAY,

TEACHER AND WRITER

SECTION 4

PUNCTUATION AND MECHANICS

If you have problems using commas, semicolons, colons, or dashes, this section will help you pinpoint errors and fix them. The examples show you how to revise comma splices and fused sentences, how to punctuate dialogue, and how to use numbers, apostrophes, italics, and capitals.

The information in this Handbook will help you with the final stages of the revising process: editing and proofreading. Most writers and researchers agree that editing and proofreading should wait until the end of the writing process, when you are least likely to interrupt the flow of your ideas. During this final stage, you should clarify your sentences and correct any errors in grammar, usage, diction, spelling, and mechanics. As you edit, concentrate on polishing the surface blemishes in your writing, but don't get so locked in on punctuation or grammar that you ignore the meaning, organization, or development of your essay. Even when you are proofreading, you may find an occasional spot to add another bit of detail, take out a repetitious phrase, or sharpen a transition.

To be a good editor, you need to understand the *conventions* of language and *expectations* of the reader instead of memorizing rules. In fact, the "rules" of grammar, punctuation, and usage may vary from one occasion to the next. A sentence fragment or a substandard usage such as "ain't" may be appropriate for one situation but not for another. Moreover, the notion of "rules" tends to suggest that language is static or unchanging. In fact, the opposite is true: Vocabulary, acceptable usage, even grammatical choices depend on current conventions and expectations. What is acceptable for one occasion or audience may be totally inappropriate for another. If you are not aware of these conventions, all your hard work in collecting, shaping, drafting, and revising may be wasted. A sloppy job of editing can ruin the best of essays.

This chapter describes standard conventions of editing for formal American English usage. As you edit your writing, however, remember that your purpose and audience should be your final guide.

WHY EDIT AND PROOFREAD?

Most writers and readers agree that grammar, usage, spelling, and mechanics are less important than content and ideas. But writers should realize that readers react not only to the ideas in an essay but also to the clarity, accuracy, and even the surface appearance of the writing. Often, writers will say, rather defensively, "Of course there are a few typos and grammar problems in my essay, but readers can still get the message. After all, it's my *ideas* that count." Unfortunately, ideas count only if the reader *gets* them. If the reader becomes irritated by unclear sentences and errors in spelling or usage, your good ideas may never reach their destination.

Writers who say that surface errors are unimportant are either rationalizing or living in a fantasy world. In the real world, most readers react negatively if writing is not neat, accurate, and readable. If your friend or roommate leaves a scrawled note that says, "I borried your shert for too day—hope you do'nt mind!" you may worry about the "shert"—and look for a new roommate. If your bank statement has misspellings, crossed-out numbers, or penciled-in debits, you may change banks in a hurry. If your doctor writes a note saying, "In my opinnion you should have bone serjury immediately!" you may rush to get another "opinnion" before agreeing to "serjury." The medium may communicate the real message: If the medium—your language—is flawed by surface errors, readers often suspect that the message is flawed, too.

Some readers believe that writers who do not edit or proofread are just lazy. Although you need time to polish your writing, effective editing and proofreading are not just matters of effort or willpower. Rereading your essay ten times will not necessarily resolve all the problems. Editing is often difficult because many of your errors really don't look like mistakes—primarily because *you already know what you are trying to say*. When you reread what you have written, you tend to recall the idea already in your mind instead of reading the words exactly as they are written on the page.

Easy writing's curst hard reading.
—**RICHARD BRINSLEY SHERIDAN,**
DRAMATIST

The man snoozing in his chair with an unfinished magazine open on his lap is a man who was being given too much unnecessary trouble by the writer.
—**WILLIAM ZINSSER,**
WRITER AND TEACHER

If you live with a friend or roommate, try this experiment. Sit in a neutral corner of the room and look at your desk. It looks relatively clean, right? A few books, papers, and pencils are scattered here and there, but you know where everything is. It has an order. It makes sense. The math book is on the corner of the desk—under the notebook, the sock, and the coffee—just where you left it last night. The psychology book is open to Chapter 4, right underneath the sweatshirt and the lecture notes that you're going to study after dinner. Stuff is kind of stacked up, but not really messy. Now look at your friend's desk. Everything looks disorganized, as if it were dumped upside down from a backpack. You count four books, two spiral notebooks, four dog-eared sheets of paper, one cup of stale coffee, a broken ballpoint pen, and a T-shirt. It's a mess, right? And sometimes it really irritates you. *How can your roommate stand to live in such chaos?* But wait. Your roommate's desk has some order to it, too, just as yours does. You just can't see the order for the mess.

Unfortunately, the same is true for writing: In your *own* writing, all you see is the meaning—the order that is in your mind. In other people's writing, you see the errors first and then, only after careful reading, the meaning. The bedrock truth is that readers will more easily see your mess than your meaning. Your writing will be more effective if your readers aren't irritated about the mess that they have had to read through. Errors or surface distractions may even undermine your credibility as a writer. For some kinds of writing—letters of application or essays for classes—the result of a few errors may be more than irritation; you simply may not be admitted, get the job, or get a passing grade.

How to Edit and Proofread

The purpose of editing is, of course, to keep language problems from interfering with the ideas or message—to make language work for your purpose rather than against it. Editing usually requires that you read over your work several times, checking for errors and anticipating problems that your readers might have. However, because you literally may not see many "obvious" errors, have friends or classmates look over your draft for problems or mistakes. When you use other readers, however, explain your purpose and audience. Then ask them to use conventional proofreading and editing marks to indicate their suggestions. *Remember: Your editors' marks are suggestions.* If they mark errors you've simply overlooked, make the correction. But if they mark something that you don't understand, check the appropriate section in this Handbook. If you disagree with their marks or suggestions, ask them to explain why they are suggesting the change. *You are responsible for deciding whether and how to make the change.*

Begin your editing and proofreading process for each essay by *reviewing your previous essays.* What problems and errors did your peer readers notice or your teacher mark? If you are keeping a log in your journal of your problems in grammar, usage, punctuation, or mechanics, review your entries. If you typically have punctuation problems and wordy sentences, reread those sections in this Handbook and focus on those specific items as you edit.

To improve your editing and proofreading skills, learn the following proofreading marks and correction symbols.

PROOFREADING MARKS

∧	Insert comma
embařassing	Insert letter or word
hot tub.ᵛᵛ	Insert quotation marks
south‿bound	Close up
¶	Begin a new paragraph
NO ¶	Do not begin a new paragraph
down his face ⊙	Add period
hop#back	Add space
peice of pie	Transpose letters
left/will\that/	Transpose words
in a ~~large~~ sweat	Delete words
encounter, is	Delete punctuation
Los Angel∅s ᵉ	Replace a letter
deep ~~inhilations~~ **breaths**	Replace a word
Ḿanure	Use lowercase
friday	Capitalize

The following paragraph by student writer Kenneth Clause illustrates how to use these proofreading marks.

My Home Town, LA Style

It is 11:00 p.m. on a chilly friday night. We are travelling South on the 405 freeway and have just entered Los Angeles city limits. A thick, damp fog rolls in from the ocean to blanket the city. Visibility is low. The vehicle discends through a sharp, banked turn and the headlights reveal the first glimpse of "it" looming in the distance. What my weary travelling companion from New York is about to encounter, is the most embarrassing and horrifying beast known to residents of Los Angeles. I break out in a ~~large~~ sweat, realizing there are no exits left will that detour this formation. In a moment of desperation, I step on the accelerator. Perhaps I can speed by this ~~depraved~~ ugly monument so my friend will not notice. Unfortunately, I'm too late. In that instant, he begins howling with laughter. We are suddenly upon it. The head-lights reveal a heaping pile of Manure ~~appears~~ with a sign posted on the pinnacle that says, "Welcome to Los Angeles! A town where the grass is greener . . . on the other side of the hot tub." Well, no use in trying to hide any longer. I hit the brakes and pull the car over to the side of the road. Immediately, my jovial friend from New York opens the door and falls to the pavement with tears of laughter streaming down his face. The last thing he expected to see among the palm trees of California was a huge dungheap. The laughter of my merry schoolmate quickly ceases after a few deep ~~inhilations.~~ breaths The foul stench of this revolting glob of dung is enough to make even his pollution-hardened lungs feel weak. Upon my request, we hop back in the car and head for home. After recieving such a shock to his senses, his only hope for revival is a long shower and a peice of my dad's hot apple pie.

EDITING SYMBOLS

As you edit someone else's draft, use the following symbols to refer the writer to problems discussed in this Handbook. Your instructor may also use these correction marks to guide your own editing. Listed here are some of the most common symbols, with an explanation and reference to the section number in this Handbook.

adj	use adjective, 1C
adv	use adverb, 1C
cs	comma splice, 4B
d	revise diction (word choice)
dm	dangling modifier, 2C
frag	sentence fragment, 2A
fs	fused sentence, 4B
mm	misplaced modifier, 2C
//	revise faulty parallelism, 2D
p	punctuation needed, 4A–J
pn agr	make pronoun agree with antecedent, 2I
ref	pronoun referent problem, 2I
sp	spelling error

sxt	sexist language, 3E
sv agr	subject–verb agreement error, 2G
t	verb tense error, 1D, 2H
trans	needs transition
v	verb form problem, 1D
wdy	wordy—omit needless words, 2F, 3A, 3B
wc	revise word choice

TIPS FOR EDITING AND PROOFREADING

1. Review sections of this chapter just before you begin editing. If you need to review basic grammatical terms, begin with Section 1. Otherwise, review appropriate parts of Sections 2, 3, or 4.

2. Practice your editing and proofreading skills first on others' essays. You will see others' problems much more readily than you will see your own. Becoming a good editor of their writing will, in turn, help you recognize your own problems more easily.

3. As you edit, look for one problem at a time. Concentrate, for example, just on punctuation, or just on subject–verb agreement, or just on diction or word choice.

4. Have a friend or classmate read your essay aloud. Listen as the person reads. If you notice something that is not clear, stop and revise the sentence. If the reader does not understand what he or she is reading, stop and revise.

5. If you are writing on a computer, reformat and print out your essay, double-spaced, in narrow columns, forty to forty-five spaces wide. Many obvious errors will jump out at you as you reread your writing in a new format.

6. For proofreading, place a ruler or a blank piece of paper underneath the line you are checking. If you are proofreading for typos, try reading backward, one word at a time, from the bottom of the page to the top.

SECTION 1

....

REVIEW OF BASIC SENTENCE ELEMENTS

This section reviews the names and definitions of basic sentence elements. Other sections in this Handbook use the terms defined and illustrated in this section.

1A SENTENCE STRUCTURE

A sentence is a group of words beginning with a capital letter and ending with a period or other end mark; it has a subject and a predicate and expresses a complete thought. The *subject* is the word or group of words that is the topic

1A struc

or focus of the sentence. It acts, is acted upon, or is described. The *predicate* gives information about the subject: what the subject is, what it is doing, or what is done to it.

SUBJECT	PREDICATE
Piranhas	bite!
The McNeils	dig clams at the seashore.
Bubble gum	can cause cancer in rats.

Sentences may contain the following elements: subject (S), verb (V), direct object (DO), indirect object (IO), subject complement (SC), object complement (OC), modifier (M), and conjunction (+).

S   V
Piranhas bite.

S   V   DO +   DO   M
Piranhas attack fish or animals in their waters.

S   V   IO   M   DO
Andrea gave Carlos two piranhas.

S   V   DO   OC
Carlos considers Andrea a prankster.

S   V   SC
Andrea is a prankster.

Subjects may be nouns, pronouns, noun phrases, or noun clauses.

Verbs may be single words *(bite)* or verb phrases *(will have bitten)*. Verbs may be transitive or intransitive; verbs have tense, voice, and mood.

Direct objects can be nouns, pronouns, noun phrases, or noun clauses. A direct object receives the action of a transitive verb. Direct objects usually answer the question "What?" or "Whom?" about the subject and verb:

Piranhas bit [whom?] *people.*

Indirect objects can be nouns, pronouns, noun phrases, or noun clauses. The indirect object answers the question "To whom?" or "For whom?" about the subject and verb:

Andrea gave [to whom?] *Carlos* two piranhas.

Complements occur in the predicate of the sentence following a "to be" or linking verb. Subject complements rename or describe the subject. Object complements rename or describe the object:

1A
struc

SC

Carlos is *upset*.

OC

Carlos named one piranha *Bucktooth*.

Modifiers describe or limit a subject, verb, object, or complement. They may be single words, groups of words, or entire clauses:

M

Piranhas have a *nasty* disposition.

Conjunctions are words that link words, phrases, clauses, or sentences. The word *conjunction* means "join together." (See Section 4a for additional examples of conjunctions.)

- *Coordinating conjunctions (and, but, or, yet, for, nor, so)* join equal sentence elements:

  Carlos is angry, *but* Andrea is laughing.

- *Correlative conjunctions (both . . . and, either . . . or)* also join equal sentence elements:

  Neither Carlos *nor* his aquarium fish are particularly happy about the piranhas.

- *Subordinating conjunctions (because, since, although, if, until, while,* and others) begin many dependent clauses:

  If Andrea plays another joke on Carlos, she may lose a good friend.

1B NOUNS AND PRONOUNS

A *noun* names a person, place, object, or idea. Nouns may be grouped in several classes:

- *Proper nouns* name specific people, places, or things

  Abraham Lincoln, Cape Hattaras, Buick

- *Common nouns* name all nouns that are not proper nouns

  cat, ocean, helicopter

- *Concrete nouns* name things that can be sensed

  table, waves, coat

- *Abstract nouns* name things not knowable by the senses

  justice, pity, freedom

1B
n/pr

- *Collective nouns* name groups

  family, committee, team

- *Compound nouns* are several words joined by hyphens to form a noun

  brother-in-law, commander-in-chief

A *pronoun* takes the place of a noun. Pronouns must meet three requirements:

- *Reference:* A pronoun must refer to a specific, identifiable word, phrase, or clause. This referent or antecedent occurs within the sentence or in a preceding sentence. (See Section 2j for examples of how to solve problems in pronoun reference.)

  Evelyn has the flu. *She* has missed two classes. [*Evelyn* is the referent for *she.*]

- *Agreement:* A pronoun must agree with or correspond to the noun that it replaces. A pronoun must agree in *person* (first, second, or third person), *number* (singular or plural), and *gender* (he, she, it). (See Section 2i for examples of how to solve problems in pronoun agreement.)

  Each girl should check on *her* friend. [*Her* agrees in person (third person), in number (singular), and gender (feminine) with the referent, *girl.*]

- *Case:* Pronouns must take the appropriate case (subjective, objective, possessive):

  Subjective pronouns (*I, you, he, she, it, we, they, who*) should be the subject or the complement in a sentence.

  They have the flu. [Subject]

  Who is sleeping there? It is she. [Complement]

  Objective pronouns *(me, you, her, him, whom, us, you, them)* should act as objects in a sentence:

  Evelyn gave *me* the flu. [Indirect object]

  Possessive pronouns (*my, mine, your, yours, his, her, hers, its, our, ours, their, theirs, whose*) show possession:

  I am sick as a dog with *her* flu virus.

Pronouns may be grouped in several classes:

- *Personal pronouns (I, me, mine, we, us, our, ours, you, yours, she, her, hers, he, him, his, it, its, they, them, theirs)* refer to people or things:

  She bought a cat for *him.*

- *Relative pronouns (that, who, whom, which, what, whose, whoever)* introduce clauses:

  Whoever fed the cat made a mistake.

- *Interrogative pronouns (who, whose, what, which, whom)* introduce a question:

  Which cat is the mother?

- *Reflexive* and *intensive pronouns (myself, yourself, herself, ourselves,* and so on) refer back to a pronoun or antecedent or intensify the antecedent:

  She says she paid for the cat *herself.* I *myself* suspect she just found it.

- *Indefinite pronouns (all, anyone, another, anybody, both, each, few, most, some, several, none, someone, something, such,* and so on) refer to nonspecific persons or things:

  Someone will turn up and claim the cat.

- *Demonstrative pronouns (this, that, these, those)* refer to an antecedent:

  On Tuesday morning, I must pay my bill. *That* will be a painful moment.

1C ADJECTIVES AND ADVERBS

Adjectives are modifiers that limit, describe, or add information about nouns and pronouns:

> Secretariat was my *favorite* horse. [modifies noun, *horse*]
> Even standing still, he looked *dynamic.* [modifies pronoun, *he*]

Adverbs limit, describe, or add information about verbs, adjectives, or other adverbs, and they complete sentences:

> He won *overwhelmingly.* [modifies verb, *won*]
> The Kentucky Derby was a *very* important victory. [modifies adjective, *important*]
> On that day, he ran *extremely* fast. [modifies adverb, *fast*]
> *Fortunately,* he won the Triple Crown. [modifies whole sentence]

1D VERBS

The *verb* is the heart of most sentences. Verbs can set up equations or definitions ("A flotilla *is* a small fleet of ships"). They can describe states of being ("Fear and confusion *exist* in Lebanon"). They can explain occurrences ("The players *became* angry at the referee's call") or describe actions ("The candidate

1D
verbs

defeated her opponent"). When sentences communicate clearly, verbs often deserve the credit.

The great variety of verb forms creates a richness in the language. This richness, however, can create confusion. Some verbs are regular; others, irregular. In some cases, combinations of verb tense, voice, and mood may entangle sentences. The following explanations and examples will help you resolve problems in verb forms so that you can communicate precisely and vividly.

PRINCIPAL PARTS OF VERBS

Verbs have three principal parts: simple form, past tense, and past participle:

SIMPLE FORM (INFINITIVE)	PAST TENSE	PAST PARTICIPLE
live (to live)	lived	lived
go (to go)	went	gone

REGULAR AND IRREGULAR VERBS *Regular verbs* form the past tense and past participle by adding *-ed* or *-d* to the simple form:

SIMPLE FORM	PAST TENSE	PAST PARTICIPLE
count	counted	counted
dance	danced	danced
create	created	created

Irregular verbs can cause problems because they form the past tense and past participle by changing letters, sounds, or entire words. Check your dictionary to determine if a verb is irregular. If the dictionary gives only two forms *(catch, caught)*, the past participle is the same as the past tense *(caught)*. Following are some examples of the nearly two hundred irregular English verbs:

SIMPLE FORM	PAST TENSE	PART PARTICIPLE
sing	sang	sung
begin	began	begun
break	broke	broken
drive	drove	driven
sink	sank, sunk	sunk
sleep	slept	slept
read	read	read
eat	ate	eaten
see	saw	seen
slide	slid	slid

LINKING VERBS *Linking verbs (is, becomes, seems, looks, and so on)* equate subjects with predicates, so that the word or words in the predicate rename or describe the subject. A linking verb creates a subject complement (SC)—a word or words that complete the equation:

```
  S    V    SC          M
```
Lillian was president of the company. [Lillian = president]

```
  S    V    SC
```
The storm seemed threatening. [Storm = threatening]

AUXILIARY VERBS *Auxiliary verbs,* also called "helping verbs," combine with main verbs to show tense, voice, or mood. The verbs *be, do,* and *have* are common auxiliary verbs:

She is running a marathon. [auxiliary verb = is]
They did enjoy the dinner. [auxiliary verb = did]
He had left before she arrived. [auxiliary verb = had]

TENSE *Tense* tells *when* a verb's action, occurrence, or state of being takes place. The six verb tenses in English are illustrated here with the regular verb *create.* The parentheses contain the *progressive* form (*-ing*) to show continual or ongoing action, occurrence, or state of being:

Present   I create (I am creating)
Past   I created (I was creating)
Future   I will create (I will be creating)
Present Perfect   I have created (I have been creating)

The present perfect tense describes actions occurring or conditions existing at an unspecified time in the past and continuing into the present: *I have created several award-winning recipes for chili.*

Past Perfect   I had created (I had been creating)

The past perfect tense describes actions occurring or conditions existing before a specific time in the past: *I had created three different recipes for extra-hot chili before I won my first award.*

Future Perfect   I will have created (I will have been creating)

The future perfect tense describes actions that have already occurred or conditions that will exist by a specific future time: *I will have created a new salsa recipe before the county fair begins.*

TRANSITIVE AND INTRANSITIVE Many verbs in English can be either transitive or intransitive, depending on the sentence. *Transitive* verbs take objects. As the prefix *trans-* suggests, they carry the action across to the object:

**1D
verbs**

<pre>
     S   V   DO
</pre>
Myrna developed the film.

<pre>
     S   V   DO
</pre>
Michael sees the oncoming car.

Intransitive verbs do not take objects:

<pre>
     S   V   M
</pre>
Myrna developed early. [*Early* is not a direct object; it describes when Myrna developed]

<pre>
     S   V   M
</pre>
Michael sees in the dark. [*In the dark* is not a direct object]

VOICE   Verbs have *active* and *passive* voice. *Active voice* means that the subject of the sentence performs the action. *Passive voice* means that the subject is acted upon. A passive-voice sentence uses a form of "be" plus a past participle. (For additional discussion of active and passive voice, see Section 2e.)

Active Voice	Inuits *build* stone and peat houses.
Passive Voice	Stone and peat houses *are built* by Inuits. [Contains a form of "be" + past participle: are + built]

MOOD   Verbs have three moods that indicate a writer's attitude toward a statement. *Indicative mood* expresses a statement of fact or asks a question. *Imperative mood* expresses commands or directives. *Subjunctive mood* expresses a wish or condition contrary to fact:

Indicative	She has perfect pitch. [fact]
	Why does she sing opera? [question]
Imperative	Pay attention to the music. [command]
	Turn and face the spotlight. [directive]
Subjunctive	I wish that I were more talented. [wish]
	If she were to catch a cold, she would not sing on opening night. [condition contrary to fact]

1E PHRASES AND CLAUSES

PHRASES

A *phrase* is a group of related words that does not contain a subject or a predicate:

Prepositional Phrase	He wrote *on the computer.*
Noun Phrase	A *notebook computer* is handy.
Appositive Phrase	The Apple II, *the first popular school computer,* is the Model T of home computers. [An appositive phrase identifies or provides more information about the preceding noun or pronoun.]

A *verbal phrase* is a group of related words that contains a verbal: an infinitive (to talk), a present participle (talking), or a past participle (talked). There are three kinds of verbals:

- *Infinitives* usually use *to + simple verb;* they function as nouns, adjectives, or adverbs:

Infinitive	*To talk*
Infinitive Phrase	He planned *to talk for three minutes.* [infinitive phrase = direct object] *To listen carefully* was his first objective. [infinitive phrase = subject]

- *Gerunds* are nouns made from the *"-ing"* or present participle form of the verb:

Gerund	*Talking* got her into trouble. [*Talking* is a gerund; gerund = subject]
Gerund Phrase	*Talking during the lecture* got her into trouble. [gerund phrase = subject]

- *Participles* are adjectives made from verb forms. As adjectives, they modify nouns or pronouns. They can use either the *"-ing"* (present participle) or the *"-ed"* (past participle) verb form:

Participle	*Coughing* students may bother the teacher. [Participle modifies *students.*] *Whispered* conversations may distract students. [Participle modifies *conversations.*]
Participial Phrases	*Rustling their papers and snapping their notebooks closed,* they prepare to leave the lecture hall. [Participial phrase modifies *they.*] Several students, *entranced by the final scene in the film,* write quietly for a few moments. [Participial phrase modifies *students.*]

**1E
ph/cl**

CLAUSES

A *clause* is a group of words containing a subject and a verb. It need not be an entire sentence or a complete thought. Clauses can be independent (main) or dependent (subordinate):

- *Independent or main clause:* A group of words containing a subject and a verb that can stand by itself as a complete thought:

  We drank decaffeinated coffee.

- *Dependent clause:* A group of words that contains a subject and verb but cannot stand by itself as a complete thought:

  Because we drank decaffeinated coffee

- *Subordinate clauses* (sometimes called *adverb clauses*) are dependent clauses that begin with a subordinating conjunction, such as *because, if, although, unless, when, while, since, as, until, before,* and *after:*

  Although I drank coffee, everyone else drank tea.

- *Relative clauses* (also called *adjective clauses*) are dependent clauses that begin with *when, where, why,* or with relative pronouns *(who, that, which, whom, whoever, whomever, whatever)*:

  Driving *when you are under the influence of alcohol* may result in a mandatory jail sentence. [Adjective clause modifies *driving.*]
  Free coffee, *which the bar serves after midnight,* is part of a campaign for responsible drinking. [Adjective clause modifies *coffee.*]
  The policeman gave a ticket to the woman *who was driving the red pickup truck.* [Adjective clause modifies *woman.*]

1F ARTICLES, PREPOSITIONS, INTERJECTIONS

ARTICLES

Articles (a, an, the) often appear before nouns. They are modifiers that limit a noun. *A* and *an* are less limiting than *the:*

  I have *a* plan to solve our problems.
  I have *the* plan to solve our problems. [*The* suggests that the plan is more definitive.]

The article *a* appears before words that begin with a *consonant sound* (not necessarily a consonant): *a* kite, *a* hammer, *a* university, *a* one-sided victory.

The article *an* appears before words that begin with a *vowel sound* (not necessarily a vowel): *an* opening, *an* egg, *an* old shirt, *an* honor, *an* E.

PREPOSITIONS

Prepositions (*in, on, up, to, after, by, for, across, within,* and others) usually occur in prepositional phrases with a noun or pronoun that is the object of the preposition:

In the hot sun *by* the edge *of* the water, a small turtle lay perfectly still.

Note that some words can function as either prepositions or conjunctions:

We will row home *after* lunch. [preposition]
After you finish your sandwich, we will row home. [conjunction]

INTERJECTIONS

Interjections (*oh, alas, yea, damn, hooray, ouch,* and others) are words conveying strong feeling or surprise. Interjections occasionally appear in informal writing or in a dialogue:

The Cardinals won the pennant *(yea!)* but lost the World Series *(boo, hiss).*
Alas, their hitting was anemic.
"*Oh,* she moped about it for days."

SECTION 2
....
SENTENCE STRUCTURE AND GRAMMAR

When sentences don't follow standard American English conventions, readers may become aggravated, confused, or simply lost. While some deviations from established conventions barely distract the reader, others totally scramble meaning. If "sickening grammar" detracts from your meaning, your readers may react uncharitably. If you write a confusing sentence fragment, some readers will think, "This writer doesn't know what a sentence is." If you have a problem in subject–verb agreement, readers may think, "This writer didn't reread the sentence or doesn't know what the subject of the sentence is." If you write a sentence with a dangling modifier, the reader may think, "The writer doesn't know how comical this sounds." This section will help you avoid those embarrassing problems that confuse readers or invite them to think about your grammar rather than your meaning.

I've noticed a good deal, and there's no bird, or cow, or anything that uses as good grammar as a bluejay. You may say a cat uses good grammar. Well, a cat does— but you let a cat get excited once; you let a cat get to pulling fur with another cat on a shed, nights, and you'll hear grammar that will give you the lockjaw. Ignorant people think it's the noise which fighting cats make that is so aggravating, but it ain't so; it's the sickening grammar they use.

—MARK TWAIN,
BAKER'S BLUEJAY YARN

1F
art

2A FRAGMENTS

Use sentence fragments only for special emphasis. A *fragment* is an incomplete sentence. A fragment may lack a subject or verb, or it may be only a dependent clause. *Test* for sentence fragments by taking the group of words out of context. If the group of words cannot stand by itself as a complete thought, it is a fragment.

Revise sentence fragments by adding a subject or verb or by combining the fragment with the preceding sentence:

Fragment:	I still remember the championship basketball game when I scored forty points. *Breaking the existing conference record.* ["Breaking the existing conference record" is not a complete sentence. It cannot stand by itself as a complete thought. Combine with previous sentence.]
Revision:	I still remember the championship basketball game when I broke the existing conference record by scoring forty points.
Fragment:	At home I enjoy many water sports. *Waterskiing and sailing, which are my two favorites.* ["Waterskiing and sailing, which are my two favorites" cannot stand by itself as a complete thought. Revise to make one complete sentence.]
Revision:	At home, I enjoy my two favorite water sports: waterskiing and sailing.
Fragment:	She stood in line for four hours in the freezing rain. *To get tickets for the rock concert.* ["To get tickets for the rock concert" cannot stand by itself as a complete thought. Combine with previous sentence.]
Revision:	To get tickets for the rock concert, she stood in line for four hours in the freezing rain.
Fragment:	After a tough class, I took a long shower, dried my hair, and put on my underwear. Then I walked into the living room. *Because I thought no one was home.* Was I surprised to discover my mother talking to Reverend Jones! ["Because I thought no one was home" cannot stand by itself as a complete thought. It is a dependent clause or fragment.]
Revision:	After a tough class, I took a long shower, dried my hair, and put on my underwear. Because I thought no one was home,

I walked into the living room. Was I surprised to discover my mother talking to Reverend Jones!

Fragment: At the end of the game, the frustrated fans began to throw snowballs on the field. *The score being 42–0.*
["The score being 42–0" is not a complete sentence. Change *being* to *is* or *was.*]

Revision: At the end of the game, the frustrated fans began to throw snowballs on the field because the score was 42–0.

For special emphasis, however, sparingly used sentence fragments can be effective. In context, the following are examples of effective sentence fragments:

When the river was dammed almost all of these things were lost. Crowded out—or drowned and buried under mud.

—Edward Abbey

Head off? Decapitation cases are rather routinely handled.

—Jessica Mitford

When I finally did fall asleep, I had that same hideous nightmare in which a woodchuck is trying to claim my prize at a raffle. Despair.

—Woody Allen

EXERCISE
In the following passage, identify all sentence fragments. Then revise the passage to eliminate inappropriate fragments.

(1) Most people think that a library is as quiet as growing grass, but often it is the noisiest place on campus to study. (2) The worst time being finals week. (3) Some of the chatter is from people who come to the library just to visit: "How did you like the party Saturday night?" (4) "Did you get the notes from chemistry?" (5) The chatter goes on continually, punctuated by coughs, gasps, and giggles. (6) Just when I start to panic about my calculus examination. (7) Someone across the table tells a joke, and they all start laughing. (8) They try to cover their laughter with their hands, but the sound explodes out anyway. (9) Irritating ten other students who are trying to study. (10) Sometimes I wish the library had its own police force. (11) To arrest those gabby, discourteous "party people." (12) I would sit there smiling as they handcuffed these party people and dragged them out of the library. (13) Ah, the sweet revenge of daydreams.

2B Mixed Constructions and Faulty Predication

Mixed Constructions

Occasionally, writers begin sentences with one structure and then switch, right in the middle, to another. Revise sentences with mixed constructions by choosing one structure and sticking to it:

Mixed: Because the repairs were so expensive is why I ended up selling the car.

Revised: Because the repairs were so expensive, I sold the car.

Mixed: By getting behind in math classes is a quick way to flunk out.

Revised: Getting behind in math classes is a quick way to flunk out.

Faulty Predication

Sometimes the predicate does not *logically* fit with the subject. Remember that the verb *"to be"* is an *equals* sign. Revise faulty predication by changing either the subject or the predicate:

2B
mx con

Faulty: Freestyle ski jumping is where skiers take crazy chances in midair.
Note: "Ski jumping" is an activity, not a place. It is illogical to say "ski jumping is where . . ."

Revised: Freestyle ski jumping is a sport that encourages skiers to take crazy chances in midair.

Faulty: My dog Noodles is the reason I'm feeling depressed.
Note: "My dog Noodles" is a specific animal, not a "reason." Missing Noodles, however, could be a cause for depression.

Revised: I'm feeling depressed because I miss my dog Noodles.

Faulty: Real intelligence is when you can say no to that third piece of chocolate cream pie.
Note: Intelligence is or equals a mental condition, not a *when.*

Revised: Saying no to that third piece of chocolate cream pie requires real intelligence.

Exercise

In the following passage, identify sentences with mixed constructions, faulty predication, or both, and then revise them.

(1) After my sophomore year, I intend to transfer to Boston College. (2) Basically, I want to attend a school that has a city environment and a diverse population of students. (3) I suppose my sister Nadine is a big reason I want to transfer. (4) She wants me to move closer to home. (5) Also, by attending a city school will enable me to see plays, to visit museums occasionally, and to eat out at good restaurants. (6) Finally, I'd like to meet all sorts of students. (7) A good university is when a student can meet people from all walks of life. (8) Because Boston College has diversity is really why I intend to transfer.

2C DANGLING MODIFIERS AND MISPLACED MODIFIERS

DANGLING MODIFIERS

Modifying phrases must clearly describe, qualify, or limit some word in the sentence. When the modifying phrase occurs at the beginning of a sentence, the word that is modified must appear *immediately* following the phrase. Otherwise, the modifying phrase "dangles" or is logically "unattached" to the sentence. Such sentences are confusing and often comical:

2C dm/mm

Faulty: Rushing to get to class on time, my shoelace broke.
            [*Who* was rushing to get to class? The shoelace? Revise by indicating the person immediately after the comma.]
Revised: Rushing to get to class, I broke a shoelace.

Faulty: Flying at 5,000 feet, the cars looked like tiny toys.
            [*Who* is flying at 5,000 feet? The cars? Revise by indicating that person immediately after the comma.]
Revised: Flying at 5,000 feet, I saw cars that looked like tiny toys.

Faulty: From birth until the first grade, one parent should be home with the children.
            [Does the opening phrase, "From birth until the first grade," modify *parent* or *children?* Revise by placing the appropriate word immediately following the introductory phrase.]
Revised: From birth until the first grade, children should have one parent at home.

Faulty: Sue practiced her freestyle stroke until she knew she could swim faster than Flipper, being a fanatical swimmer.
            [Who is the fanatical swimmer—*Sue* or *Flipper?* When modifying phrases "dangle" from the *end* of a sentence, revise by placing the phrase next to the word it modifies.]

Revised: Being a fanatical swimmer, Sue practiced her freestyle stroke until she knew she could swim faster than Flipper.

MISPLACED MODIFIERS

Place a modifying word, phrase, or clause immediately before or after the word it modifies. In the following sentences, notice how changing the placement of the word "only" changes the meaning of the sentence:

Only I tasted grandfather's pumpkin pie. [I was the only one who tasted it.]

I only tasted grandfather's pumpkin pie. [I only tasted it; Pete actually ate it.]

I tasted only grandfather's pumpkin pie. [I didn't taste anything else; I didn't even taste Aunt Margaret's pecan pie.]

I tasted grandfather's only pumpkin pie. [Grandfather made only one pumpkin pie, and I tasted it.]

Confusing: He borrowed a computer from his professor with a faulty memory.
                     [*Who* or *what* has the faulty memory? Place the phrase "with a faulty memory" next to the word it modifies ("computer").]

Revised: He borrowed a computer with a faulty memory from his professor.

Confusing: The hamburgers have been horrible in the fast-food restaurants that I've eaten.
                     [Did the writer eat restaurants or hamburgers? Revise by placing the clause "that I've eaten" next to the word it should modify ("hamburgers").]

Revised: The hamburgers that I've eaten in fast-food restaurants have been horrible.

EXERCISE

In the following passage, identify sentences with dangling modifiers and misplaced modifiers, and then revise each faulty sentence.

(1) SP302, History of Film, is a worthwhile class to take. (2) Occurring on Tuesday night from 7:00 P.M. to 9:45 P.M., Professor Hancock teaches the class so that it coincides with dollar movie night at the campus theater. (3) Normally, a long class would be boring because of the Nod Factor. (4) However, Professor Hancock keeps everyone awake and entertains the students, being very energetic. (5) Her lecture on *Citizen Kane* was a particularly good example. (6) Unfortunately, the film began before she finished her lecture. (7) Rushing across the stage just as the film was beginning, an elec-

trical cord tripped her up, causing her to lose her balance and fall. (8) She regained her composure in time to remind us that Orson Welles also wrote and performed the famous broadcast about the invasion of the Martians on the radio. (9) We certainly were relieved to get that important information!

2D FAULTY PARALLELISM

Repeated elements in a sentence that are similar in meaning or function should be *parallel* in grammatical form. The parallel form should, in turn, help to emphasize the meaning. Any repeated sentence elements, from subjects and verbs to prepositional phrases, may occur in parallel form:

Parallel Clauses	*I came, I saw, I conquered.*
Parallel Adverbs	He read *slowly* and *thoroughly.*
Parallel Prepositional Phrases	She walked *through the archway, across the quadrangle,* and *into the library.*

Identifying and numbering the repeated elements may help you see the parallel elements in a sentence:

2D //

She walked	(1) through the archway,
	(2) across the quadrangle
	and
	(3) into the library.

Faulty: Walking, biking, and automobiles are the three most popular modes of transportation.
[Identify and number elements that should be parallel. "(1) *Walking,* (2) *biking,* and (3) *automobiles* are the three most popular modes of transportation." Revise, choosing one pattern for all three elements.]

Revised: Walking, biking, and driving are the three most popular modes of transportation.

Faulty: Traveling abroad last summer, John increased his social awareness, his cultural knowledge, and overall sophistication.
[Identify and number elements that should be parallel. "Traveling abroad last summer, John increased (1) *his social awareness,* (2) *his cultural knowledge,* and (3) _____ *overall sophistication.*" Then revise, choosing one grammatical pattern for all three elements.]

Revised: Traveling abroad last summer, John increased his social awareness, his cultural knowledge, and his overall sophistication.
[or]

Revised: Traveling abroad last summer, John increased his social awareness, cultural knowledge, and overall sophistication.

Faulty: There are three commandments for college students: Thou shalt go to class; thou shalt read the text; and be sure to borrow your neighbor's notes.
[Identify and number elements that should be parallel. Since the first and second "commandments" set the grammatical pattern, the reader expects the third commandment to take the same "thou shalt" form.]

Revised: There are three commandments for college students: Thou shalt go to class; thou shalt read the text; and thou shalt borrow thy neighbor's notes.

Faulty: She was angry not only because he was late but also he forgot the tickets.
Note: Compared or contrasted sentence elements introduced by "either . . . or," "both . . . and," or "not only . . . but also" must be parallel.
[Identify and number elements that should be parallel. "She was angry not only (1) because he was late but also (2) _____ he forgot the tickets." Revise to make (1) and (2) parallel.]

Revised: She was angry not only because he was late but also because he forgot the tickets.

EXERCISE

In the following passage, identify and revise any sentences with faulty parallelism.

(1) Alcohol abuse is a primary cause of spectator violence at college football games. (2) On average, the police department makes between five and ten arrests at each home football game. (3) These arrests are for property destruction, public intoxication, and occasionally when students conduct themselves in a disorderly manner. (4) When spectators consume too much alcohol not only do they hurt themselves but also act obnoxiously toward others. (5) Following a recent fight, ambulance attendants said that some drunken spectators or "animals" actually pelted them with sod while they tried to assist an injured man. (6) The attendants tried pleading, reason, and shouting, but to no avail. (7) To reduce these ugly incidents and

2D
//

restoring the enjoyment of the game, alcohol should not be sold at football games after the beginning of the second half.

2E ACTIVE AND PASSIVE VOICE

Verbs that can have direct objects (transitive verbs) are in the *active voice* when the subject of the sentence *acts upon the object:*

The wolfhound bit Perry.

Wolfhound, the subject of the sentence, *acts upon the object, Perry.* The arrow shows that in the active voice, the action of the verb *bit* goes forward, toward the object, *Perry.*

Verbs that can have objects (transitive verbs) are in the *passive voice* when the *subject is acted upon.* The passive voice uses a form of *be (is, am, are, was, were, been, being)* followed by the past participle of the main verb (in this case, *bitten*):

Perry was bitten by the wolfhound.

The verb *was bitten* is transitive, but *Perry,* now the subject of the sentence, is acted upon. The arrow shows that the action of the verb goes backward, so that *Perry* receives the action.

Notice the following *differences* between active and passive voice:

The active-voice sentence, "The wolfhound bit Perry," uses two fewer words than the passive version, its action moves in a normal forward direction, and it clearly identifies the actor.

The passive-voice sentence, "Perry was bitten by the wolfhound," uses two more words, and it inverts the direction of the action in the sentence. In some cases, the passive voice may omit the actor altogether: "Perry was bitten on Friday." In that case, the reader does not know who or what bit Perry.

ACTIVE VOICE

Usually, *active voice* is preferable because it is more direct, vivid, and concise than passive voice. Remember, however, that sentences must be judged *in the context* of the writer's purpose, audience, and focus.

Following are examples of passive-voice constructions that, in context, may be more effective in the active voice. To change from passive to active, move the actor (often identified in the "by" phrase) to the subject of the sentence:

Passive: Children's unruly behavior cannot be accepted by their parents.

Note: The actor in the "by" phrase is *parents*. Change to active voice by making *parents* the subject of the sentence.

Active: Parents cannot accept their children's unruly behavior. [The active-voice version places the actor in the subject of the sentence and has two fewer words.]

Passive: It is argued by the members of our class that the teacher grades too hard.

Note: The *actor* in the "by" phrase is *members*. Change to active voice by making *members* the subject of the sentence.

Active: Members of our class argue that the teacher grades too hard. [This active-voice version is more direct and has four fewer words.]

Passive: Under the current proposal, property taxes will be raised $1,000 dollars over the next two years.

Note: The *actor* is not identified in a "by" phrase; however, the *governor* actually proposed the tax increase. Change to active–voice by making *governor* the subject of the sentence.

Active: The governor currently proposes to raise property taxes by $1,000 over the next two years. [The active-voice version reveals who, in fact, is responsible. It adds information without increasing the length of the sentence.]

PASSIVE VOICE

The *passive voice* is appropriate when the actor is unknown or is less important than the action or the receiver of the action. Use the passive voice in the following situations:

When the actor is unknown:

When her sports car swerved off the road and into the river, Carolyn was killed. [We don't know who or what actually killed her.]

When you want to emphasize that some person or thing is helpless or is a victim:

The small Kansas town was leveled by the tornado.
Our football team was mauled by the Bears, 42–0.
The bag lady was mugged in broad daylight.

When the scientific experiment and the results should be the focus of the sentence or the passage (scientific writing typically uses the passive voice to lend objectivity to the findings):

The first recordings of humpback whales were obtained in 1952 from a U.S. Navy hydrophone installation.
The titration experiment was performed under careful laboratory conditions.

2E
act

One typical *abuse of passive voice* occurs when writers omit the actor in order to conceal responsibility:

> The tuition for nonresident students was increased by $500 for the upcoming academic year.

This sentence, which was written by university officials, omits the actor or the agency responsible for the change. Because tuition increases are unpopular with students, university officials may have deliberately omitted the responsible actor or agency to avoid confrontation or blame. Careful readers should recognize such deceptive uses of passive voice.

Caution: Don't assume that all verbs that follow the pattern, "be" verb form + past participle ["was _____ed"], are necessarily passive voice. In the sentence "I was scared," for example, the verb "scared" can be either transitive or intransitive, depending on the context. Only *transitive verbs* can be either active or passive voice:

Transitive Active	A horrible Halloween mask scared me.
Transitive Passive	I was scared by a horrible Halloween mask.
Intransitive	At the Cave of Horrors, I was upset and scared.
Transitive Active	The boss fired me.
Transitive Passive	I was fired.
Intransitive	I was tired.

Test: To distinguish between intransitive and transitive passive, try adding the word *very*. If *very* cannot logically be used, the construction is passive voice:

> I was [very] tired. [*Very* works; *tired* is intransitive.]
> I was [very] fired. [*Very* doesn't work; *fired* is transitive passive.]

In addition, a good dictionary will indicate whether a verb is transitive, intransitive, or both.

EXERCISES

Identify sentences containing passive voice. Change passive-voice sentences into active voice:

1. People communicate using body movements.
2. A nod, gesture, or a glance can be interpreted by people in several ways.
3. A wave and a smile mean one thing, but a wave and a tear can be interpreted to mean something else.
4. In addition, some people may be irritated by a continual or intense stare.

2E
act

5. We may also be intimidated by a person who talks to us at very close range.

Read the following passage and identify sentences that are in the active or passive voice. Then determine which sentences should be active voice and which should be passive voice. Revise the passage, leaving sentences as they are, changing active-voice sentences to passive, or changing passive-voice sentences to active—as appropriate for the context.

(1) Writing on a word processor can transform the act of writing, but only if the writer has some rudimentary typing skills. (2) Unfortunately, many men have a sexist hang-up about typing so that their writing on a computer is inhibited. (3) Traditionally, it has been felt by most men that only females—i.e., secretaries—should type. (4) Only the macho Hemingways and Mailers of the world actually type their own novels and stories. (5) Now, however, many male business executives are caught by conflicting role-images. (6) It is socially acceptable for them to be computer literate, but it is still somehow demeaning to sit at a keyboard and practice the "female" skill of typing. (7) One more example of how notions about sexist roles can hurt men as well as women is thus provided by word-processing.

2F NOMINALS AND "BE" VERBS

NOMINALS

Nominals (also called nominalizations) are *nouns* created from verbs. Nominals often make sentences less dynamic because they disguise or eliminate the action in a sentence. Frequently, nominals are nouns ending in *-ment, -ance, -ence, -ion,* and *-ing.* Each of the following nominals "contains" a verb: expectation (expect), description (describe), solution (solve), resistance (resist), government (govern), preference (prefer), meeting (meet). For many purposes and audiences, you can make your writing more vigorous, dynamic, and readable by changing nominals into verbs:

Nominal: Bill's *expectation* was to win the marathon.

Revised: Bill *expected* to win the marathon.

Nominal: The owner's manual contains a *description* of how to adjust the timing.

Revised: The owner's manual *describes* how to adjust the timing.

Nominal: On this campus, there exists some *resistance* among students to the tuition increases.

Revised: On this campus, students *resist* tuition increases.

Nominal:	*Dissatisfaction* with drinking-policy *decisions* is likely to be a major *contribution* to student *objections*.
	Note: When repeated nominals obscure the meaning, rewrite the whole sentence, making the primary *actor* the subject of the sentence.
Revised:	Students object to the drinking policy.

"BE" VERBS

"Be" verbs *(is, am, are, was, were, been, being)* are effective for stating conditions, definitions, or concepts:

> Edgar Allan Poe's "The Raven" *is* a literary classic.
> An "iconoclast" *is* one who destroys sacred images or seeks to overthrow popular ideas or institutions.

Often, however, "be" verbs create static, flat, or lifeless sentences. Where appropriate, make your writing more dynamic by replacing "be" verbs with action verbs.

Eliminate "be" verbs by changing passive voice to active voice, by changing nominals or adjectives into verbs, by selecting a more vigorous verb, or by combining sentences:

"Be" Verb:	The classical mythology course that *is* offered by the English department is fascinating.
Revised:	The English department *offers* a fascinating course in classical mythology.
"Be" Verb:	The driving force for many workaholics *is* their fear of failure.
Revised:	Fear of failure *drives* many workaholics.
"Be" Verb:	AIDS *is* a simple but sometimes lethal malfunction of the immune system. AIDS *is* a disease that can lead to the physical and mental destruction of its victim.
Revised:	AIDS, a simple but sometimes lethal malfunction of the immune system, can *destroy* its victim physically and mentally.

EXERCISE

In the following passage, identify *nominals* and *"be"* verbs. Then revise the passage to make it more vivid, energetic, and concise by eliminating inappropriate nominals and "be" verbs.

(1) As parents, we know that many young people love to ride motorcycles, motorbikes, and motorscooters. (2) Today, however, our ten-year-old kids have some attraction to those off-road three-wheelers.

(3) Although kids get enjoyment from riding three-wheelers in the hills, these vehicles can be the cause of serious injury. (4) Unfortunately, these young drivers—and their parents—do not receive sufficient education from salespeople about the potential dangers. (5) As a result, some activist groups are in opposition to the sales of all three-wheelers. (6) These groups want regulations for the industry in order to make riding safer for children and adults. (7) The efforts of these groups to reform the industry are commendable to every responsible parent.

2G SUBJECT–VERB AGREEMENT

A verb must agree *in number* with its subject. Remember: *-s* or *-es* added to a noun makes it plural: *whale, whales.* Adding *-s* to a present-tense verb makes it singular: *whales sing; whale sings.*

2G
sv agr

1. Many agreement problems occur when plural words come between a singular subject and its verb. To correct a subject–verb error, first identify the actual subject and then use the correct verb ending for that subject:

    Faulty: A list of campaign promises often hurt the candidate.

    [Put brackets around any prepositional phrases. The subject of the sentence is never in a prepositional phrase. "A list [of campaign promises] often hurt the candidate." *List* is the subject and *hurt* is the verb. Read without the words inside the brackets and revise the verb.]

    Revised: A *list* of campaign promises often *hurts* the candidate.

    Faulty: This company, with few skilled mechanics and electricians, do not guarantee any repairs.

    [Put brackets around the prepositional phrase. "This company [with few skilled mechanics and electricians], do not guarantee any repairs." Read the sentence without the words in brackets and revise the verb.]

    Revised: This company, with few skilled mechanics and electricians, *does* not guarantee any repairs.

2. Two subjects connected by *and* take a plural verb. "The sergeant and his recruits march double-time across the grounds." When two subjects are connected by *or* or *nor*, however, the verb agrees with the closer subject:

    Faulty: Neither the recruits nor the sergeant know how to march.

Revised: Neither the recruits nor the sergeant *knows* how to march.
[or]

Revised: Neither the sergeant nor the recruits *know* how to march.

3. Indefinite pronouns *(each, one, either, everyone, neither, everybody, nobody, no one, none, somebody, someone)* usually take a singular verb:

Faulty: Each of the books cost twenty dollars.
[Remove the prepositional phrase: "Each [of the books] cost twenty dollars." *Each* is singular, so the verb should be *costs.*]

Revised: Each of the books *costs* twenty dollars.

Faulty: Everybody in all three classes are going to see the film.
[Remove the prepositional phrase: "Everybody [in all three classes] are going to see the film." *Everybody* is singular, so the verb should be *is.*]

Revised: Everybody in all three classes *is* going to see the film.

4. A collective noun as a subject takes a singular verb. Collective nouns *(family, committee, audience, class, crowd,* and *army)* usually refer to a single *unit* or *group* of several individuals or elements, and thus they take a singular verb:

Faulty: The audience at the concert whistle its approval.

Revised: The audience at the concert *whistles* its approval.
Note: When referring to the action or condition of *several individuals* within a group, use the phrase *the members of* or the phrase *a number of* followed by the plural verb. The members of the committee argue about the policy.

5. Even when the normal subject–verb order is reversed, the verb should agree in number with the subject:

Faulty: For such a small dormitory, there is far too many students.
[Put the subject and verb in their normal order: Too many students are in the small dormitory. (Students is the subject, so the verb is plural: *are.*)]

Revised: For such a small dormitory, there *are* far too many students.

EXERCISE

In the following passage, revise all errors in subject–verb agreement.

2G
sv agr

(1) If you have friends or a family member who smoke, I have some suggestions to help this person quit. (2) First, if the family are supportive, try talking openly about the facts. (3) There is a few public service agencies that will provide evidence demonstrating the link between smoking and cancer. (4) Next, investigate this person's behavior: What does this person do just before he or she smokes? (5) To quit smoking, the smoker must disrupt the patterns of behavior that leads to smoking. (6) An inventory of the activities and places that cause a person to smoke provide key information. (7) For example, if the person always smokes after dinner, suggest eating snacks over a two-hour period instead of having a sit-down meal. (8) If he or she always smoke in a certain chair in the living room, change the furniture. (9) Breaking any habit is always easier if you break the entire behavior pattern. (10) Of course, each of these smokers need to want to stop smoking.

2H VERB TENSE

Avoid unnecessary shifts in verb tense:

Shift: After they *ate* ice cream and cake for dessert, they *are* ready to relax.

Revised: After they *ate* ice cream and cake for dessert, they *were* ready to relax.

Shift: Peter *ate* dinner before you *had offered* to cook tacos.

Revised: Peter *ate* dinner before you *offered* to cook tacos.

Shift: At one point in the film, Gandhi *gathered* his followers together to discuss strategy. Suddenly, a British general *gave* an order to fire upon them. People then *scurry* around and *try* to protect themselves and their children from the hail of bullets.

Note: For summaries or accounts of artistic works, films, literary works, or historical documents, use the present tense.

Revised: At one point in this film, Gandhi *gathers* his followers together to discuss strategy. Suddenly, a British general *gives* an order to fire upon them. People then *scurry* around and *try* to protect themselves and their children from the hail of bullets.

EXERCISE

In the following passage, revise any unnecessary shifts in tense.

(1) In Sophocles' play, *Antigone,* two characters are tragic figures: Antigone and Creon. (2) In the play, Antigone faced a choice of conscience. (3) Should she be loyal to her family and bury her brother, or should she have been loyal to the state and obeyed the edict of Creon,

the King of Thebes? (4) She assumes that she knew the best way to handle the situation and willfully chooses her own death. (5) Creon also faced a choice of conscience. (6) Should he punish someone who has betrayed the state, even if that person is a member of his family? (7) Like Napoleon and General Custer, Creon thought primarily about himself and his public image. (8) In Creon's case, ego or "hubris" leads to tragic results for the people around him.

21 PRONOUN AGREEMENT

A pronoun must agree in number and person with the noun to which it refers:

Faulty:	One of the scientists signed their name to the report. [Because the subject is never in the prepositional phrase, put parentheses around the prepositional phrase ("of the scientists"). Now look for another noun that could be the subject of the sentence. "One" is the subject of the sentence, and it is a singular noun. Change "their" to the singular form, "his" or "her."]
Revised:	One of the scientists signed her name to the report.
Faulty:	Each of the students felt cheated on their test. *Note: Each* is singular: *their* is plural.
Revised:	The *students* felt cheated on *their* tests.
Faulty:	Everyone brought their gift to the party.
Revised:	Everyone brought *his* or *her* gift to the party. *Note:* Avoiding sexist language by using "his or her" can be wordy or awkward in some contexts. Rewrite the sentence with a plural subject and plural pronoun.
Revised:	The *guests* brought *their* gifts to the party.

Avoid shifts in person. Avoid shifting between third person *(people, one, they, he, she)* and second person *(you):*

Faulty:	When *you* come to the party, *everyone* should bring a friend. *Note: You* is second person; *everyone* is third person. Revise the sentence, using either second or third person throughout.
Revised:	When *you* come to the party, bring a friend.
Faulty:	A good party should make *people* feel at ease, so *you* can make new friends.
Revised:	A good party should make *people* feel at ease, so *they* can make new friends.
Revised:	A good party should make *you* feel at ease, so *you* can make new friends.

2J PRONOUN REFERENCE

A pronoun should refer clearly and unambiguously to its antecedent:

Unclear: Joan told Bev that her bank account was overdrawn. [Whose bank account is overdrawn?]

Revised: When Joan discovered that her bank account was overdrawn, she told Bev.

Unclear: If people do not take care of their cats, we should turn them into the humane society. [Who should be turned in—the cats or their owners?]

Revised: If people do not take care of their cats, we should report the owners to the humane society.

EXERCISE

In the following passage, correct problems in pronoun agreement and reference.

(1) People use the term *best friend* to describe a person who has a special warmth and friendliness. (2) I still remember when Michelle Martin, one of my best friends, said that they really like me, too. (3) I called her my best friend; we stood by each other. (4) One time at a party, I saw her talking angrily to another woman. (5) It turned out that she had dated Tom, the guy she was going with at the time. (6) Each of them felt cheated by their boyfriend. (7) Before I knew what was happening, they were screaming at each other. (8) When I tried to stick up for her, she took a swing at me, and so I swung back with my best left hook, popping her in the right eye. (9) As a result, I was suspended from school for a week. (10) It just goes to show that when you have a best friend, everyone expects that you'll help them if you can.

SECTION 3
....
DICTION AND STYLE

Effective writing hides a curious paradox. On the one hand, good writing contains vivid detail. Good writing does not merely assert that thus-and-so is true; it supports a claim or assertion with evidence. It recreates an experience, shows exactly how the writer feels, or communicates precisely what the writer thinks. To accomplish this, writers *add* specific details, examples, facts, or other data. On the other hand, good writing is also concise. Good writers *take out* vague words, weak verbs, and empty language. Their writing is as lean and sinewy as a long-distance runner. As you edit your writing for diction (choice of words) and clarity of style, you should *add* specific examples but *remove* vague, imprecise language. Your details should be ample; your diction and style spare.

3A VAGUE WORDS

Replace vague words with more specific or concrete language.

1. The following *nouns* are vague or unspecific. Vague nouns encourage writers to *tell* rather than to *show* with specific details or examples. Vague nouns may also lead to wordy and imprecise sentences. In most cases, *replace* the following nouns with more specific words, details, or examples:

thing	situation	difficulty
something	type	feeling
anything	way	beauty
someone	fun	people
some	trouble	deal
area	problem	place
case	field	character
manner	nature	appearance
factor	aspect	

Vague: During their freshman year, students worry about all sorts of *things*. [Be specific: What things?]

Revised: During their freshman year, students worry about leaving their families, making new friends, and passing their courses.

Vague: I have taken courses in the *field* of statistics for two years, and it has changed my *feeling* toward studying in the *area* of mathematics.

Revised: After taking statistics courses for two years, I no longer hate studying mathematics.

Vague: Meteorologists occasionally have a great *deal of trouble* in forecasting a *situation* where an upper-level disturbance becomes a *factor* in local weather. [Be specific: What kind of trouble? Be concise: Omit unnecessary, vague words.]

Revised: When an upper-level disturbance affects local weather, meteorologists occasionally miss a forecast.

2. The following *modifiers* are weak, vague, or unspecific. Replace them with stronger modifiers or add specific details:

very	a lot	pretty
really	good	bad
a few	certain	happy
many	nice	much
regular	similar	soon

3A
wdy

Vague:	I *really* liked *certain* classes in high school *very much,* but I just couldn't stand *a lot* of the *really boring* courses. [Be specific: What *certain classes?* Be specific: How or why were they *really boring?*]
Revised:	I really looked forward to learning about the turtles, snakes, and birds in the biology lab, but I couldn't stand just sitting still and practicing grammar hour after hour in French class.
Vague:	Overall, *The Cosby Show* is pretty good, but sometimes it gets somewhat unreal. [Be specific: What makes it pretty good? What makes it unreal?]
Revised:	*The Cosby Show* has entertaining stories about family problems—I still remember the episode when Theo decides he just has to join the Blue Angels—but in many episodes, the family seems to resolve the conflict too easily and simply.

3. The following *verbs* are weak, vague, or unspecific. Where appropriate, replace them with more active, energetic, or vivid verbs. When these verbs occur with nominals or passive voice, change to active verbs or active voice. Always test your revision: In your context, is the change more effective, concise, or vivid?

deals with	take	get
involved with	relate to	go
has to do with	make	give

Vague:	He gets some enjoyment from sky diving.
Revised:	He enjoys sky diving.

Vague:	Her job deals with collecting rare species of lizards.
Revised:	She collects rare species of lizards.

Vague:	Jogging along the path, she got involved with a rattlesnake in a serious way. [How exactly was she "involved" with this rattlesnake?]
Revised:	Jogging along the path, she was seriously bitten by a rattlesnake.

EXERCISE

In the following passage, substitute specific and vivid words or phrases for all vague nouns, verbs, and modifiers.

(1) When I was separated from my girlfriend, I missed her a lot.
(2) Being alone sometimes gave me a pretty empty type feeling.
(3) When I called her on the phone, we talked about all the nice times we spent together, not about all the very big fights we used to

have. (4) Since there was no stress to deal with, we had a fun-filled, long-distance relationship. (5) I know that one aspect of this relationship will improve the way we get along, now that we're back together. (6) We always had difficulty talking in a serious manner about our future. (7) Now we are more involved with each other and can really talk about all sorts of things. (8) For anyone who is having troubles, I recommend this kind of separate situation because, in the long run, the relationship will be much happier.

3B WORDINESS

1. The following wordy phrases can be stated more concisely:

WORDY	CONCISE
due to the fact that	because
despite the fact that	though
regardless of the fact that	although
at this point in time	now
at the present time	now
until such time as	until
in the event that	if, when
at all times	always
there is no doubt that	doubtless
in a deliberate manner	deliberately
by means of	by
the reason is that	[omit]

2. The following phrases are redundant—they say the same thing twice or repeat unnecessarily:

REDUNDANT	CONCISE
new innovation	innovation
disappear from view	disappear
repeat again	repeat
reflected back	reflected
circle around	circle
few in number	few
cheaper in cost	cheaper
oblong in shape	oblong
blue in color	blue
consensus of opinion	consensus
important essentials	essentials
resulting effect	effect
cooperate together	cooperate

3B
wdy

3. Where appropriate, be more concise by omitting *there is, there are, it is,* and *this is* constructions:

Wordy:	There are seven people living in that apartment.
Revised:	Seven people live in that apartment.
Wordy:	This is the step that is crucial for getting a job.
Revised:	This step is crucial for getting a job.

4. Some *who, which,* and *that* clauses can be changed into modifying words or phrases:

Wordy:	Cheryl Stickfinger, who is the mayor, is accused of embezzling city funds.
Revised:	Mayor Cheryl Stickfinger is accused of embezzling city funds.
Wordy:	Then they each wolfed down a banana split that contained 500 calories.
Revised:	Then they each wolfed down a 500-calorie banana split.
Wordy:	The police officer, who was frustrated about missing his promotion, started taking kickbacks.
Revised:	The police officer, frustrated about missing his promotion, started taking kickbacks.

3C
wdy

EXERCISE

Revise the following passage to reduce wordiness.

(1) One of the most recent new discoveries in medicine is the so-called diving reflex. (2) When people fall into water that is icy, their circulation slows down due to the fact that the water is so cold. (3) In addition, the metabolism of every cell that is in the body slows down, conserving oxygen. (4) In a recent case, Alvaro Garza, who is eleven years old, disappeared from view underneath the ice for 45 minutes. (5) When rescuers finally pulled him at long last from beneath the ice, he was unconscious, his body temperature was cold and below normal, and his skin was grayish-blue in color. (6) Regardless of the fact that rescuers could find no pulse or heartbeat, they began CPR (cardiopulmonary resuscitation) immediately. (7) Within a few days, Alvaro began to recover in a steady manner, and soon he was asking for a hamburger and French fries. (8) Although he may have some lingering effects from his ordeal that do not go away in a short period of time, the unexplainable miracle is that he survived.

3C COLLOQUIAL LANGUAGE AND SLANG

Your audience and purpose should determine whether conversational language is appropriate. In informal or expressive writing, colloquial language (spoken language), slang, or trendy expressions may be vivid and effective. In conversation or informal writing, we may say that something is *cool, hip, gross, weak, sweet,* or *too much.* We may call a friend *dude,* a skateboarder a *thrasher,* or someone we don't like a *wimp* or *geek.*

In formal writing, however, you should avoid colloquial expressions and slang. Your readers may not know the expressions, they may find some slang offensive, or they may think "gross" is simply too vague to describe what really happened. Slang, in fact, tends to become a shorthand for a whole experience and thus invites *telling* ("This guy was a real geek") rather than *showing* ("Rudolph had messy hair, wore adhesive tape on his glasses, and always had one green and one orange sock sticking out of his polyester pants. He lived out of a forty-pound bookpack, watched *Dr. Who* on TV every day, and spoke like William F. Buckley").

3D CLICHÉS AND JARGON

CLICHÉS

Some expressions are so commonly used that they have become automatic, predictable, trite, or hackneyed. The phrases in the left-hand column, for example, may have been fresh and original once, but now they are as stale as dirty dishwater and about as exciting as a secondhand sock. The expressions in the right-hand column, for example, are so predictable that we can easily guess the missing word:

tried and true	strong as an _____
needle in a haystack	dark as _____
easier said than done	heavy as _____
burning the midnight oil	cold as _____
didn't sleep a wink	busy as a _____
crack of dawn	happy as a _____
dead of night	white as _____
last but not least	quick as a _____
birds of a feather	blind as a _____
hit the nail on the head	sober as a _____
face the music	tough as _____
straw that broke the camel's back	gentle as a _____

JARGON

Jargon is the technical vocabulary of any specialized occupation, field, or profession. In technical or specialized writing, writers should use the vocabulary of their fields. In the following passage, the specialized vocabulary *(homeotic, mutant, rudimentary,* and *thoracic)* is entirely appropriate:

> In the cockroach *Bletella germanica,* a homeotic mutant produces rudimentary wings on the first thoracic segment. No modern insect

normally bears wings on its first thoracic segment, but the earliest winged fossil insects did!

—Stephen J. Gould, *Hen's Teeth and Horse's Toes*

Jargon, however, is also a generic label for impressive words used for their own sake. Any specialized vocabulary is inappropriate when used not to *inform* but to *impress* an audience with the writer's intelligence. When writers use jargon inappropriately, they are not communicating—they're showing off.

Below is a jargon-filled parody, in legalese, of the simple, clear sentence, "Have an orange." This passage, by the editors of *Labor Magazine,* appears in Stuart Chase's essay, "Gobbledygook":

> I hereby give and convey to you, all singular, my estate and right, title, claim and advantages of and in said orange, together with all rind, juice, pulp and pits, and all rights and advantages therein . . . anything hereinbefore or herinafter or in any other deed or deeds, instrument or instruments of whatever nature or kind whatsoever, to the contrary, in any wise, notwithstanding.

Sometimes writers use jargon not to make themselves sound impressive but to promote the *subject* they're writing about. We commonly call the result "advertising." Here is a sample of a Nike advertisement for a walking shoe:

> Walking. To you, it's a simple matter of putting one foot in front of another. To Nike, it's an entire science.

> In fact, we have studied walking in one of the world's leading biome-chanical labs. Our own. And as a result, we've designed a technically advanced shoe specifically for the walking motion. The EXW. We built it close to the ground for stability. With a tri-density midsole that supports and centers your foot. A vented toe area for cool com-fort. Flex grooves that bend with your foot. And a Nike-Air cushion-ing system that makes you feel, literally, like you're walking on air.

> Now, all this technology may seem a bit much. But try on a pair. You'll see that the EXW doesn't make walking more complicated. It just takes it one step further.

Nike hopes the inflated language and technical jargon in this passage will make you feel better about spending eighty dollars for a walking shoe. "World's leading biomechanical labs," "advanced shoe specifically for the walking motion," "tri-density midsole," "vented toe area," and "flex grooves"— all this jargon does seem a bit much. We may ridicule such language, but remember that if the advertisement causes us to buy the shoe, the language is appropriate for the audience.

3D wdy

EXERCISE

In the following passage, replace clichés with fresh, figurative language and eliminate or replace inappropriate jargon.

(1) The television news media in America needs to be reformed. (2) The bottom line is that serious news has been lost as stations rush to entertain the viewer. (3) Trying to find an informative story on the evening news is like looking for a needle in a haystack. (4) The station executives who finalize the programmatic output for the evening news believe that the average American is dumber than an ox. (5) As a result, viewers see in-depth stories about a sex scandal involving a local politician, but only a few seconds explaining why the stock market is scraping the bottom of the barrel. (6) Newscasters attempt to maximize their humor by telling jokes that go over like a lead balloon rather than informing the viewer about the latest decision-making process on armament restrictions. (7) If station programmers actually interfaced with the public occasionally, they would recognize the error of their ways.

3E SEXIST LANGUAGE

Do not use language that unfairly stereotypes people or discriminates against either women or men. Just as you would avoid racist terms, you should avoid language that stereotypes people's roles, occupations, or behavior by gender. Sentences such as "A doctor always cares for his patient" or "A secretary should always help her boss" imply that all doctors are men and all secretaries are women. Phrases such as *female logic, male ego, emotional woman,* or *typical male brutality* imply that all women are excessively emotional and all men are egotistical brutes. In fact, those stereotypes are not true. If you use sexist language, you will offend your readers. Even more important, your language should not encourage you or your reader to see the world in sexist stereotypes.

1. Avoid words that suggest sexist roles:

SEXIST	REVISED
man	people, person
chairman	chair, head
businessman	businessperson
policeman	police officer
mankind	humanity
congressman	representative
statesman	politician, diplomat
lady lawyer	lawyer
career girl	professional woman

SEXIST	REVISED
coed	student
mailman	letter carrier
old wives' tale	superstition

Note, however, that some words that link occupation with gender are still appropriate. Most writers still use *actor* and *waiter* for men and *actress* and *waitress* for women. Other words, however, such as *stewardess* or *seamstress,* are often replaced with *flight attendant* or *garment worker.*

2. Be consistent in your use of people's names. If you write *Ernest Hemingway,* then write *Emily Dickinson,* not *Miss Dickinson.* If you write *Lennon* instead of *John Lennon,* then write *Parton,* not *Dolly Parton* or *Dolly.*

3. Avoid using the pronouns *he, his,* or *him* when you are referring to activities, roles, or behavior that could describe either sex:

Sexist:	A doctor should listen carefully to his patient.
	Note: Use plural if it does not alter your meaning.
Revised:	Doctors should listen carefully to their patients.
Sexist:	An effective teacher knows each of her students.
	Note: You may use *his or her* sparingly, but avoid using the construction *s/he.*
Revised:	An effective teacher knows each of his or her students.
Sexist:	Everyone hopes that he will survive the first year of college.
	Note: Often, you can revise the sentence by using first or second person or by omitting the pronoun.
Revised:	I hope to survive the first year of college.
Revised:	All of us hope to survive the first year of college.
Revised:	You hope to survive the first year of college.
Revised:	Everyone hopes to survive the first year of college.
	Note: Do *not* mix singular and plural by saying, "Everyone hopes *they* will survive the first year of college."

EXERCISE

Revise the following passage to eliminate sexist language.

(1) Everyone in college now is looking for that special job that will match his talents and yet bring him sufficient income. (2) Teaching is a low-paying but good career if you don't mind being a professor who spends his life reading papers, getting grants, and serving on committees. (3) A secretary or stewardess can begin her career with

minimal training, but a nurse must dedicate herself to rigorous medical schooling. (4) In business and entertainment, girls can work right alongside the men. (5) In the entertainment field, many people dream of being a Bruce Springsteen or a Tina Turner, although most singers don't have Springsteen's talent or Tina's perseverance. (6) A businessman often works his way up the ladder and becomes chairman of the company. (7) Even staying at home and raising a family is a respectable career for either a man or his wife, though most men simply don't have the temperament to raise children. (8) Whatever your chosen career, from mailman to congressman, hard work and dedication are the keys to landing and keeping that important job.

3F DENOTATION AND CONNOTATION

The *denotation* of a word is its literal or dictionary definition. Both *house* and *home* refer, denotatively, to a structure in which people live. Many words have, in addition, a *connotation* or emotional association that can be negative, neutral, or positive. *House* has, for most people, a *neutral* or sterile connotation, whereas *home*, for most people, has a *positive* connotation, suggesting warmth, comfort, security, and family.

Choose words appropriately for their connotative value:

Inappropriate:	Dr. Aileen Brown, a *notorious* scientist, just received the Nobel prize for her work with superconductors. [*Notorious* people are usually famous for their *misconduct.*]
Revised:	Dr. Aileen Brown, a *famous* scientist, just received the Nobel prize for her work with superconductors.
Inappropriate:	Beverly looked at her friend Steve and said, "Why don't you finish your dinner? You need the food—you're already a bit *scrawny* looking." [Steve prefers to think of himself as *thin* or *slim* rather than scrawny.]
Revised:	Beverly looked at her friend Steve and said, "Why don't you finish your dinner? You need the food—you're already a bit *thin.*"
Inappropriate:	Lynn's father told Paul that the apartment was decorated *cheaply* but tastefully. [Paul's feelings may be hurt. He does have good taste in furnishings, and he did the best he could on his tight budget.]
Revised:	Lynn's father told Paul that the apartment was decorated tastefully but *inexpensively.*

3F
dn/cn

EXERCISE

The following groups of words have similar denotative meanings but vary widely in their emotional associations or connotative meanings. Rank the words in each group from most negative, to neutral, to most positive.

- social drinker, wino, lush, reveler, alcoholic, sot, party animal, elbow bender, inebriate, problem drinker, booze hound, bar hopper
- scholar, intellectual, four-eyes, walking encyclopedia, geek, savant, bookworm, genius, pedant, bibliophile
- thrifty, penny-pinching, frugal, miserly, tight-fisted, cheap, economical, prudent, stingy
- steady, loyal, stubborn, firm, unyielding, dedicated, obstinate, devoted

3G USAGE GLOSSARY

This glossary alphabetically lists words and phrases that frequently cause problems for writers. In many cases, writers disagree about the preferred usage in formal writing. If you are in doubt, check a dictionary, such as *The American Heritage Dictionary, The Random House Dictionary,* or a guide, such as Margaret Bryant's *Current American Usage.*

Because this glossary references only the most obvious usage errors, refer to a standard or unabridged dictionary for items not included.

a, an: Use *a* when the following word begins with a *consonant sound:* a book, a clever saying, a hat. Use *an* when the following word begins with a *vowel sound:* an apple, an old building, an honor.

accept, except: *Accept* is a verb meaning "to receive": "I accept the gift." *Except* is a preposition meaning "other than" or "excluding": "Everyone received a gift except John." Rarely, *except* is a verb meaning "to exclude": "The editor excepted the footnote from the article."

advise, advice: *Advise* is a verb: "I advise you to exercise regularly." *Advice* is a noun: "Please take this advice."

affect, effect: *Affect* is a verb: "The flying beer cups did not affect the outfielder's concentration." *Effect* is a noun: "His obvious poise had a calming effect on the crowd." *Remember:* If you can say, "The effect," then you are correctly using the noun form. Less often, *effect* is also a verb: "His behavior effected a change in the crowd's attitude."

all right, alright: *All right,* two words, is the accepted spelling. *Alright* is nonstandard, in the opinion of most experts.

already, all ready: *Already* means "by now" or "previously": "The essay was already completed." *All ready* means "completely prepared": "The paragraphs were all ready to be printed."

a lot: *A lot* is always two words that mean "many." Wherever possible, however, *avoid* using *a lot*. Replace with more specific description. See Section 3a.

among, between: Use *among* for *three or more* people or things: "We should distribute the winnings among all the players." *Note: Between* is used for three or more items when location or a reciprocal relationship is indicated: "They found the treasure at a point equidistant between the three trees." "Through careful negotiations, a nonaggression treaty was reached between the four nations."

amount, number: *Amount* refers to quantity: "He saved a large amount of food for the winter months." *Number* refers to countable items: "She owned a large number of expensive sports cars."

anyone, any one: *Anyone* is a pronoun: "Anyone who likes Mayan art should hear the lecture." *Any one* is an adjective phrase modifying a noun: "He owns more Mayan art than any one person could possibly appreciate."

bad, badly: *Bad* is an adjective used in the predicate ("After a week of the flu, she looked bad") or before a noun ("She caught my cold at a bad time"). "She felt bad because she had a bad cold." *Badly* is an adverb: "He wrote badly because he had a high fever."

being, being that: *Being* cannot be used as a complete verb. "The seat being taken" is not a complete sentence. *Being that* is nonstandard: "Being that the bus was late, we missed the show." Use *because* or *since:* "Because the bus was late, we missed the show."

beside, besides: *Beside* is a preposition meaning *next to* or *by the side of:* "Peggi sat beside the senator." *Besides* is a preposition meaning *moreover* or *in addition to:* "Besides, the senator likes several people besides George."

can, may: In formal writing, use *can* for ability: "I can take out the garbage." Use *may* for permission: "May I have the honor of taking out the garbage?" Also use *may* for possibility: "If I have time, I *may* take out the garbage."

center around: Illogical: One can "circle around" but not "center around." Replace with "center on" or "focus on": "The controversy focused on the right of the worker to a safe, smoke-free environment."

cite, site: *Cite* is a verb meaning "to quote as an authority or to mention": "She cited Newcastle's blue law, which forbade card playing on Sunday." *Site* is a noun meaning "a place or location": "The church basement was, in fact, the site of Newcastle's first bingo game."

continual, continuous: *Continual* means "frequently repeated": "Most soap operas have continual interruptions for commercials." *Continuous* means "unceasing": "Throughout the broadcast, we heard a continuous buzzing sound."

could of, should of: Nonstandard. Use *could have* or *should have*.

data, media, criteria: The singular forms are *datum, medium,* and *criterion*. In formal writing, use plural verbs and pronouns with the plural noun. "Our data reveal a sharp increase in rapes and assaults since last year." "The media use their own criteria for sex and violence."

different from, different than: For prepositional phrases, use *different from:* "His chili recipe is different from yours." Although "different from" is preferred, sometimes "different than" results in a more concise sentence. "She is a different player than she used to be" is less wordy than "She is a different player from the player she used to be."

disinterested, uninterested: *Disinterested* means "objective or impartial": "As a disinterested third party, Marji resolved our dispute." *Uninterested* means "lack of interest": "We were uninterested in the outcome of the hall elections."

farther, further: *Farther* usually refers to distance: "How much farther are we going to jog?" *Further* refers to additional time, amount, or degree: "Furthermore, if you cannot hire me, I will go further into debt."

fewer, less: *Fewer* refers to numbers or countable items: "Fewer teenagers smoke than a decade ago." *Less* refers to amount ("less sugar") or degree ("less important"): "Teenagers spend less money on cigarettes than they did a decade ago."

hopefully: *Hopefully* means "with hope," or "in a hopeful manner": "Charlene waited hopefully for a letter from home." Most good writers still object to the colloquial usage of *hopefully* (meaning, "I hope," or "it is to be hoped"): "Hopefully, Charlene will get her letter from home." Change to: "I hope Charlene gets her letter from home."

imply, infer: *Imply* means to suggest without directly stating: "The news report implied that the president was seriously ill." *Infer* means to draw a conclusion: "I inferred from the news report that the president was seriously ill." Writers and speakers *imply;* readers and listeners *infer*.

its, it's: *Its,* like *his* or *her,* is a possessive pronoun: "The tree is losing its leaves." *It's* is a contraction of *it is:* "It's your turn to rake the leaves."

lay, lie: *Lay* is the transitive verb (lay, laid, laid) meaning "put" or "place." "Please lay the book on the table." *Lie* is an intransitive verb (lie, lay, lain) meaning "recline" or "occupy a place": "The books lie on the table."

like, as, as if: *Like* is a preposition: "A great race driver is like an opera singer—vain and arrogant." *As* can be a preposition ("His mission as a driver was to demonstrate his grace and courage"), but it can also introduce a clause: "Even at the end of the race, he looked as if he had just stepped off the cover of a magazine."

lose, loose: *Lose* is a verb meaning "misplace" or "be deprived of": "Good detectives never lose their nerve." *Loose* is an adjective meaning "free" or "not tight": "The psychopath got loose by climbing through the ventilating system."

principal, principle: *Principal* as an adjective means "major" or "main"; as a noun, *principal* refers either to a "chief official" or to a "capital sum of money": "The principal of the high school listed as his principal debt the $50,000 he owed on the principal of his house mortgage." *Principle* is a noun meaning "basic truth," "rule," or "moral standard": "He learned the principles of accounting and finance."

quote, quotation: *Quote* is a verb: "I quoted the passage from Thoreau's *Walden*." Do not use *quote* as a noun ("The following quote from *Walden*"); instead, use "quotation," "remark," or "passage": "The following passage from *Walden* illustrates Thoreau's politics."

that, which: *That* always introduces restrictive clauses: *which* introduces either restrictive or nonrestrictive clauses. Some writers prefer, however, to use *that* only for restrictive clauses and *which* only for nonrestrictive. "The hat that has the pheasant feather was a birthday present." The clause, "that has the pheasant feather" restricts, limits, and identifies which hat was the present. "The hat, which is nearly ten years old, was a birthday present." The clause, "which is nearly ten years old," is only incidental information; it does not specify which hat was the present.

their, they're, there: *Their* is a pronoun: "She is playing with their tennis balls." *They're* is a contraction: "They're really upset that she didn't even ask." *There* is an adverb or an expletive: "She's practicing over there. There are the tennis balls."

to, too, two: *To* is a preposition: "I am writing to Bev." *Too* is an adverb meaning "in addition" or "also": "You too can write her a letter." *Too* also is an intensifier meaning "very": "Dad expects me to write too often." *Two* is a number: "I have written two times this month."

used to, supposed to: Use the past tense ("used to") not ("use to"): "I used to go there every weekend." "I was supposed to be swimming practice at 3:30 P.M. this afternoon."

SECTION 4
. . . .
PUNCTUATION AND MECHANICS

The purpose of punctuation is to clarify meaning and promote communication. Commas, periods, semicolons, dashes, and other punctuation marks guide readers to meanings, just as traffic signals, double yellow lines, turning lanes, and one-way signs guide motorists to destinations. The conventions of punctuation create *expectations* in the reader. Just as you are surprised when a car runs a red light and nearly hits you, readers are surprised when writers fail to follow the conventions of punctuation.

Punctuation—or the lack of it—can change the entire meaning of a sentence. In actual conversation, pauses, inflections, intonation, gestures, and facial expressions do the work of punctuation. In writing, however, punctuation must provide these clues.

Read the following sentences. How many different ways can you find to punctuate each sentence? How does each version alter the meaning?

> Give the peanuts to my daughter Ella
> She said walk quietly
> Let's go see the lions eat Marcia.

Sometimes writers unintentionally create confusion by omitting important punctuation. Notice how the appropriate use of commas in the following sentences prevents a possible surprise and clarifies the meaning:

Confusing: To keep the pipes from freezing the plumber advised us to run the water all night. [How exactly did the pipes freeze the plumber?]

Revised: To keep the pipes from freezing, the plumber advised us to run the water all night.

Confusing: On the menu for lunch was ham and Sam was doing the cooking. [Is Sam on the menu?]

Revised: On the menu for lunch was ham, and Sam was doing the cooking.

The guidelines for punctuation and mechanics in this section will help you avoid unintentional problems and clarify your writing. Review these guidelines as you edit your own and other people's writing.

4A SENTENCE PUNCTUATION

Much of the confusion about punctuation occurs because connecting words often have similar meanings but signal different punctuation conventions. A stop sign, a red light, and a blinking red light, for example, all mean that motorists must stop, but each signals a slightly different procedure. In English, *but, although,* and *however* mean that a contrast is coming, but each requires different punctuation:

> We won the volleyball game, *but* our best hitter broke her wrist.
> *Although* we won the game, our best hitter broke her wrist.
> We won the game; *however,* our best hitter broke her wrist.

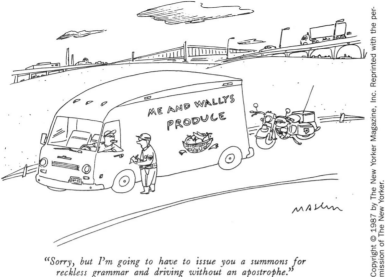

"Sorry, but I'm going to have to issue you a summons for reckless grammar and driving without an apostrophe."

Using commas and semicolons to punctuate sentences and clauses requires knowing the three basic types of connecting or *conjunctive* words.

Coordinate conjunctions: "Conjunction" means "join together"; "coordinates" are "equals." A coordinate conjunction (coord. conj.) joins equals together. The acronym BOYFANS will help you remember the coordinate conjunctions:

B	O	Y	F	A	N	S
but	or	yet	for	and	nor	so

Subordinating conjunctions: A subordinate conjunction (sub. conj.) joins a dependent or subordinate clause to an independent or main clause. The following are the most common subordinating conjunctions:

after	before	since	until
although	even if	so that	when
as	even though	than	whenever
as if	if	that	where
as though	in order that	though	wherever
because	rather than	unless	while

Adding a subordinating conjunction changes an independent clause (IC) to a dependent clause (DC):

	IC
Independent clause	He buys a newspaper.

	SUB	
	CONJ	DC
Dependent clause	*If* he buys a newspaper	

	DC	IC
Complete sentence	If he buys a newspaper, he will see the story.	

Conjunctive adverbs: A conjunctive adverb (conj. adv.) acts as a transitional phrase. Following are the most common conjunctive adverbs:

accordingly	however	meanwhile	still
also	incidentally	moreover	thereafter
consequently	indeed	nevertheless	therefore
furthermore	instead	otherwise	thus
hence	likewise	similarly	

If you are uncertain whether a connecting word is a conjunctive adverb, *test* by moving the connecting word to another place in the clause. Conjunctive adverbs can be moved; subordinating conjunctions (such as *if* or *because*) and coordinating conjunctions *(but, or, yet, for, and, nor, so)* cannot.

Conjunctive adverbs can be moved:

We won the game; *however,* our best hitter broke her wrist.
We won the game; our best hitter, *however,* broke her wrist.
We won the game; our best hitter broke her wrist, *however.*

Subordinating conjunctions cannot be moved:

Although our best hitter broke her wrist, we won the game.
Our best hitter, *although,* broke her wrist, we won the game.
[Obviously, *although* cannot be moved to another position in the clause.]

Coordinating conjunctions cannot be moved:

We won the game, *but* our best hitter broke her wrist.
We won the game, our best hitter, *but,* broke her wrist.
[Moving a coordinating conjunction scrambles the sentence.]

Follow these rules for joining independent clauses (IC) and dependent clauses (DC):

1. Join two independent clauses with a *comma* and a *coordinating conjunction:*

	COORD	
IC,	CONJ	IC
The pizza is good,	*but* the mystery meat is disgusting.	

2. Join two independent clauses with a *semicolon* and a *conjunctive adverb:*

> CONJ
>
> IC;   ADV   IC.
>
> The pizza is good; however, the mystery meat is disgusting.

3. Join two independent clauses with a *semicolon:*

> IC;   IC.
>
> The pizza is good; the mystery meat is disgusting.

4. Join a dependent clause to an independent clause with a *comma:*

> DC,   IC.
>
> Although mystery meat tastes all right, it looks disgusting.

4B COMMA SPLICES AND FUSED SENTENCES

Two common errors in joining independent clauses are the *comma splice* and the *fused sentence* (also called a *run-on sentence*). Revise by following one of the patterns in 1–3 in the rules just cited:

4B
cs/fs

Comma Splice:	[IC, IC.] I know that airplanes are safer than cars, I still have a fear of flying.
Revised:	I know that airplanes are safer than cars, *but* I still have a fear of flying.
Comma Splice:	[IC, Conj. Adv., IC.] I know that airplanes are safer than cars, however I still have a fear of flying.
Revised:	I know that airplanes are safer than cars; *however,* I still have a fear of flying.
Fused Sentence:	[IC IC.] I know that airplanes are safer than cars I still have a fear of flying.
Revised:	*Although* I know that airplanes are safer than cars, I still have a fear of flying.

EXERCISE

In the following passage, correct all comma splices and fused sentences.

(1) For years, scientists have attempted to teach animals to communicate for the most part, their efforts have failed. (2) In the 1950s, psychologists failed to teach a chimpanzee to speak, the ape was able to grunt only a few words. (3) In the 1960s, however, a chimp named Washoe learned the sign language of the deaf. (4) Washoe came to understand hundreds of words, he used them to communicate and express original ideas. (5) As it turns out, the great apes have the capacity to learn language, but they cannot speak. (6) This research

proved that humans are not the only animal capable of using language they are, however, the most sophisticated users of language.

4C COMMAS

COMMAS FOR INTRODUCTORY ELEMENTS

Use commas to set off most introductory elements:

> Because I broke three flasks, I'm going to have a large bill for chemistry lab. [introductory dependent clause]
> In the middle of finals week last semester, I became seriously depressed. [long introductory prepositional phrase]
> Jogging home after classes, I see children playing in the schoolyard. [introductory participial phrase]
> To save money, I often take the bus. [introductory infinitive phrase]
> Incidentally, I hope my roommate will be here this weekend. [introductory adverb]

ITEMS IN A SERIES

Use commas to separate items in a series (a, b, and c). Generally, use a comma before the *"and."* In some cases, omitting the comma before the final item in the series may cause confusion:

Confusing: She rented an apartment with a convection oven, a microwave, a refrigerator with an icemaker and a garbage disposal. [Does the refrigerator have a built-in icemaker and garbage disposal?]

Revised: She rented an apartment with a convection oven, a microwave, a refrigerator with an icemaker, and a garbage disposal.

EXERCISE

Revise the punctuation in the following passage.

(1) Everyone can have fun outside in the wintertime by following some common-sense rules. (2) If you are going to be outside for several hours be sure to eat a nutritious meal before leaving. (3) On cold damp or windy days wear clothes that are warm and dry. (4) To stay warm protect yourself against moisture that builds up from the inside. (5) Most experts recommend dressing in layers. (6) The inner layer wicks moisture away from your body the middle layer provides thermal protection and the outer layer protects against rain or wind. (7) Curiously enough most people tend to put on too many clothes,

underestimating their body's ability to exercise comfortably naturally and safely in cold weather.

NONRESTRICTIVE ELEMENTS

Nonrestrictive modifiers should be separated from the sentence by commas. Always *test* the phrase or clause. If it can be removed from the sentence without changing the meaning, use commas:

Nonrestrictive: Coach Hall, who was invited to the party, celebrated the victory.
[The clause, "who was invited to the party," is incidental information. It does not restrict or specify which coach was celebrating. The two commas indicate that removing the clause from the sentence will not change the meaning: "Coach Hall celebrated the victory."]

Nonrestrictive: Seattle, which has a reputation as a rainy city, is actually drier than New Orleans.
[Remove the clause, and the meaning of the sentence is not altered. "Seattle is actually drier than New Orleans."]

Nonrestrictive: Charles, the man in the gray suit, eats fried grasshoppers when no one is looking.
[The appositive, "the man in the gray suit," can be removed from the sentence without altering the meaning.]

Restrictive: Demonstrators who hurled bricks were arrested by the police.
[The meaning is that *only those* demonstrators *who hurled bricks* were arrested by the police. The phrase *who hurled bricks* cannot be removed from the sentence without changing this meaning. Do *not* use commas to separate restrictive elements.]

Nonrestrictive: The class, which was taught by Anne Perkins, met at eight o'clock in the morning.
Note: This sentence says that the class met at eight o'clock, and Anne Perkins was, incidentally, the teacher. (Usually use *which* for nonrestrictive clauses.)

Restrictive: The class that was taught by Anne Perkins met at eight o'clock in the morning.
Note: This sentence says that the particular class taught by Professor Perkins met at eight o'clock. Other classes met at some other time. (Use *that* for restrictive clauses. Do not use commas.)

4C
,

UNNECESSARY COMMAS

Do not use a comma to separate a subject and a verb:

Faulty: My toughest class of the day, met at eight o'clock.

Revised: My toughest class of the day met at eight o'clock.

Do not use a comma to separate compound subjects or predicates:

Faulty: The Dean of Students, and the Chancellor decided to cancel classes. [compound subject]

Revised: The Dean of Students and the Chancellor decided to cancel classes.

Faulty: Because of the heavy snowfall, I stayed inside all afternoon, and popped popcorn. [compound predicate]

Note: When coordinate conjunctions do not join independent clauses or items in a series, a comma is usually not necessary (see Section 4A for appropriate use of commas with coordinate conjunctions).

Revised: Because of the heavy snowfall, I stayed inside all afternoon and popped popcorn.

COORDINATE ADJECTIVES

Use a comma to separate coordinate (equal) adjectives. Test for coordinate adjectives: (1) insert an "and" between the adjectives and (2) reverse the order of the adjectives. If the meaning of the sentence remains unchanged, the adjectives are equal or coordinate:

Example: It was a dull dark day.

[Insert "and"; reverse adjectives. *It was a dull and dark day. It was a dark and dull day.* Since the meaning of the sentence has not changed, these are coordinate or equal adjectives. Remove the *and* and add a comma.]

Revised: It was a dull, dark day.

Example: The car had studded snow tires.

[Insert "and"; reverse adjectives. *The car had studded and snow tires. The car had snow and studded tires.* The meaning of the original sentence is changed; therefore, the adjectives are not coordinate. Do *not* separate with comma.]

Revised: The car had studded snow tires.

DIALOGUE

Use commas to set off a direct quotation or dialogue.

Direct quotation:

> The author points out, "One of the effects of embalming by chemical injection, however, has been to dispel fears of live burial."
>
> —Jessica Mitford

Dialogue:

> "We'll try it," the professor said to me, grimly, "with every adjustment of the microscope known to man."
>
> —James Thurber

In fiction or nonfiction, indent (begin a new paragraph) when the dialogue shifts from one person to the next:

> A white man finally came along and found her—a hunter, a young man, with his dog on a chain.
>
> "Well, Granny!" he laughed, "what are you doing there?"
>
> "Lying on my back like a June-bug waiting to be turned over, mister," she said, reaching up her hand.
>
> He lifted her up, gave her a swing in the air, and set her down. "Anything broken, Granny?"
>
> "No sir, them old dead weeds is springy enough," said Phoenix, when she had got her breath. "I thank you for your trouble."
>
> —Eudora Welty, "A Worn Path"

ADDRESSES, DATES, DEGREES

Use commas to set off addresses, dates, degrees/titles:

Addresses:	What Cheer, Iowa, is his home town.
Dates:	On December 7, 1941, the Japanese bombed Pearl Harbor.
Degrees:	Randall Beaver, D.D.S., is my orthodontist.

EXERCISE

Revise the punctuation in the following passage.

(1) Dinosaurs which have been extinct for millions of years are making news again. (2) At a meeting of the Geological Society of America in November 1987 scientists announced a startling discovery. (3) Dinosaurs, that lived 80 million years ago, benefited from an atmosphere that contained nearly 50 percent more oxygen than it does now. (4) Gary Landis geochemist for the U.S. Geological Ser-

vice and Robert Berner professor at Yale University reached that conclusion after analyzing, air bubbles trapped in bits of amber. (5) They found that the tiny, air bubbles contained 32 percent oxygen, compared with 21 percent in the modern atmosphere. (6) When asked whether a decreasing oxygen supply, could have caused the extinction of the dinosaurs, Berner explained "It was a very gradual change, and most organisms easily adapt." (7) "The large slow-moving dinosaurs probably became extinct" he said "following some cataclysmic, geological, event."

4D PERIODS AND SEMICOLONS

PERIODS

Use periods at the end of sentences, indirect questions, and commands:

Sentence:	The Statue of Liberty was officially rededicated.
Indirect Question:	I asked my friend when he was going to stop taking pictures.
Command:	Wait until the ship moves into the picture.

SEMICOLONS

Use a semicolon to join related independent clauses. Remember to test for independent clauses by using a period. If you can use a period at the end of each independent clause, and if the sentences are related, you may wish to use a semicolon. Remember, however, that semicolons are usually more appropriate in formal writing:

> Nowadays, says one sociologist, you don't have to have a reason for going to college; it's an institution. His definition of an institution is an arrangement everyone accepts without question; the burden of proof is not on why you go, but why anyone thinks there might be a reason for not going.
>
> —Caroline Bird

> I take a dim view of dams; I find it hard to learn to love cement.
>
> —Edward Abbey

Use a semicolon to separate items in a series that already have internal punctuation:

> We quickly meet the "good guys" of *Star Wars:* Luke Skywalker, played by Mark Hamill; Ben "Obi-Wan" Kenobi, played by Alec Guinness; and Han Solo, played by Harrison Ford.
>
> —Judith Crist

Do *not* use a semicolon to join dependent with independent clauses:

> Harrison Ford played the leading role in *Raiders of the Lost Ark;* which made him an instant star.

4E COLONS AND DASHES

COLONS

Use a colon to introduce a list or an explanation. Colons often create formal, structured sentences:

> When you go to the grocery store, please get the following items: two boxes of frozen peas, five pounds of baking potatoes, and a package of stuffing for the turkey.

> There is only one guaranteed method to lose weight: eat less and exercise more.

Usually, a colon following a verb is unnecessary:

Unnecessary: The best way to lose weight is: eat less and exercise more.

Revised: The best way to lose weight is to eat less and exercise more.

Unnecessary: I need: peas, baking potatoes, and stuffing.

Revised: I need peas, baking potatoes, and stuffing.

DASHES

Use a single dash for an abrupt shift. Use a pair of dashes for an interrupting or parenthetical comment. Use a dash instead of a comma, colon, or parentheses when you want a sentence to have a more informal, colloquial flavor:

> At last a happy thought struck me—I would draw the fish.
>
> —Samuel Scudder

> Indeed, there are moments today—amid outlaw litter, tax cheating, illicit noise, and motorized anarchy—when it seems as though the scofflaw represents the wave of the future.
>
> —Frank Trippett

EXERCISE

In the following passage, insert semicolons, colons, or dashes at the appropriate places. In some cases, there are several ways to punctuate the sentence correctly, so be prepared to explain your choice.

4E
: / —

(1) Yo-yo dieting the process of repeatedly losing and gaining weight is common today. (2) Instead of changing eating habits and exercise patterns, the yo-yo dieter uses three common strategies to lose weight taking diet pills, drinking diet liquids, and fasting outright. (3) The yo-yo dieter, however, needs to know the truth about dieting diet cycles decrease the muscle-to-fat ratio in the body and decrease the body's ability to lose weight during the next dieting cycle. (4) Quick-fix diets, in other words, will lead to rapid weight losses however, they will be followed by an even faster weight gain. (5) Ultimately, crash diets do more harm than good the body just wasn't designed to be a yo-yo.

4F EXCLAMATION POINTS AND QUESTION MARKS

EXCLAMATION POINTS

Use exclamation points sparingly, for stylistic emphasis:

> I saw the sleek gray-haired manager standing near the dance floor, snapping his fingers and smiling. . . . I bet myself that he owned one of the few blow-dryers in Moscow. . . . He was watching the growing success of the only Western-style club in town and thinking: These kids! Right on! Crazy, but I love 'em!
>
> —Andrea Lee

> Bicyclists often ride as though two-wheeled vehicles are exempt from all traffic laws. Litterbugs convert their communities into trash dumps. . . . And then there are (hello, Everybody!) the jaywalkers.
>
> —Frank Trippett

QUESTION MARKS

Use a question mark after a direct question:

> What is your first childhood memory?

Do not combine question marks with commas or periods.

> "What is your earliest memory?" she asked me. [Do *not* use a comma and a question mark: "What is your earliest memory?," she asked me.]

4G QUOTATION AND ELLIPSIS MARKS

QUOTATION MARKS

Use quotation marks to indicate a writer's or speaker's exact words:

4G
" " / . . .

> Marya Mannes says, "Woman, in short, is consumer first and human being fourth."

Use quotation marks for titles of *essays, articles, short stories, poems, chapters,* and *songs*—any title that is part of a larger collection:

> "Television: The Splitting Image" is the title of an essay by Marya Mannes.

Use single quotation marks for quotations within a quotation:

> James said, "I know I heard her say, 'Meet me outside the east door.'"

ELLIPSIS MARKS

Use ellipsis marks (three *spaced* periods) to indicate material omitted from a direct quotation:

> Marya Mannes said, "Woman . . . is consumer first and human being fourth." [The ellipsis indicates that words are omitted from the middle of the sentence.]

Use a period *plus* three spaced periods to signal either omitted words at the end of a sentence or omitted intervening sentence(s):

> Marya Mannes said, "Woman, in short, is consumer first and human being fourth. . . . The conditioning starts very early. . . ."

PUNCTUATION WITH QUOTATION MARKS

The following guidelines will help you to punctuate sentences with quotation marks. Periods and commas go *inside* quotation marks:

> According to biologist Julie Earwig, "Penguins are more densely covered with feathers than any other bird—nearly 180 feathers per square inch."

Colons and semicolons go *outside* quotation marks:

> Recent data about the eagle's feathers may revise the old saying "light as a feather": the vaned feathers on a bald eagle weigh more than its entire skeleton.

Exclamation points and question marks go *inside or outside* quotation marks. They go *inside* if they are a part of the quoted material:

> The award for the highest number of feathers, according to Earwig, "goes to the whistling swan with a staggering 25,000 feathers!" [The original sentence ends with an exclamation point.]

They go *outside* if they are not a part of the quoted material:

> Is it true that, as Earwig claims, "the tiny ruby-throated hummingbird has 940 feathers"? [The original sentence ends with a period.]

4G
" " / . . .

4H ITALICS

Most word-processing programs allow you to *italicize* certain words for emphasis. When using a typewriter or writing by hand, use underlining to indicate words that should be set in italics.

Titles:
"Down the River" is the most interesting chapter in Edward Abbey's *Desert Solitaire.*
[Underline (or italicize) titles of books, magazines, films, paintings, newspapers—any work published separately. Use quotation marks for titles of chapters, articles, or poems—any title that is part of some collection in a book or magazine.]
Exceptions: Do not underline the Bible or titles of legal documents, such as the Deed of Trust or the United States Constitution.

Names:
The most famous travel ships used to be the *Santa Maria,* the *Titanic,* and the *Queen Mary.* Now the great ones are the *Apollo* and the *Challenger.*
[Underline (or italicize) names of ships, trains, aircraft, or spacecraft.]

Foreign Words:
He graduated *cum laude,* while his friend, who barely passed freshman mathematics, graduated *magna cum laude. "C'est la vie,"* he thought.
[Note, however, that some foreign words (burrito, bourgeois, genre, cliché, junta, and many others) have been incorporated into the language and do not need italics. Consult your dictionary if you are in doubt.]

Words or Letters:
Suppose to should have a *d:* supposed to.
[Quotation marks are also used to indicate italics in handwritten or typed manuscripts.]
Note: Do not underline or put quotation marks around the title of your essay when it appears on a title page or the first page of your manuscript.

EXERCISE

Revise the following passage, underlining appropriate words and titles.

(1) Tom Wolfe, author of The Right Stuff, has written a novel about a Wall Street broker in his newest work, The Bonfire of the Vanities. (2) This novel first appeared in twenty-seven installments in Rolling Stone magazine. (3) Wolfe's style has always been au courant, and Bonfire is no exception. (4) This novel features New York characters who

run the gamut from drug pushers to the cunning and ambitious young lions of the investment world. (5) It is not a cliché to say that this book is difficult to put down.

4I PARENTHESES AND BRACKETS

PARENTHESES

Use parentheses ( ) to set off additional information, examples, or comments:

> Writing a film review requires that you carefully examine the criteria for your judgment (see Chapter 7).

> Outside our lifeboat, let us imagine another 210 million people (say the combined populations of Colombia, Ecuador, Venezuela, Morocco, Pakistan, Thailand, and the Philippines), increasing at a rate of 3.3 percent per year.
>
> —Garrett Hardin

BRACKETS

Use brackets [ ] to set off editorial remarks in quoted material. Brackets indicate that you, as an editor, are adding comments to the original material:

Original: After you hear my arguement, you will reelect Eastwood.

Edited: After you hear my arguement [sic], you will reelect [Mayor Clint] Eastwood. [As editor, you add information about Clint Eastwood and indicate by using "sic" ("thus it is") that the misspelling, grammatical mistake, or inappropriate usage occurs in the original source and is not your error.]

4J APOSTROPHES AND HYPHENS

APOSTROPHES

Use apostrophes for contractions, possession, and some plurals:

Contractions: It's too bad you don't agree.

Possession: The wind blew the student's notes across the front lawn. [The notes belonging to one student blew across the lawn.]
The wind blew the students' notes across the front lawn. [The notes belonging to several students blew across the lawn.]
Your sister-in-law's accident was someone else's fault. [For compounds, make the last word possessive.]

4J
'/ -

Plurals	The 1980's [or 1980s] were the Yuppie years. Eliminate unnecessary *which's* in your sentences.

HYPHENS

Use hyphens for compound words, compound adjectives before nouns, some prefixes, and some numbers. When in doubt, always check a good dictionary.

Compounds:	cross-reference; president-elect
Adjectives:	a twentieth-century writer; the slate-blue sea; the three-year-old child *Note:* When the compound adjectives follow a noun, omit the hyphen: He is a writer well known only in Vermont.
Prefixes:	ex-President Reagan; self-motivation
Numbers:	twenty-six; one hundred sixty-five; one-fifth

4K CAPITALS AND NUMBERS

CAPITALS

4K cap

Capitalize proper nouns and adjectives, professional titles, principal words in titles of books or articles, and regional locations:

Proper Names:	Judson Smith, Atlanta, Los Angeles, Missouri River, English, Swahili, American, Labor Day, Christmas, Hanukah, Wednesday, October [Do not capitalize seasons or terms: autumn, spring, summer, fall semester, freshman year.]
Titles:	Senator Kennedy, President Lincoln, Professor Findlay, Associate Dean Natalie Renner, Uncle Don, Father [Do not capitalize family titles preceded by a pronoun: my mother, my uncle, our grandfather.]
Titles:	*Gone with the Wind,* "The Short Happy Life of Francis Macomber," "The Triumph of the Wheel," *Star Wars* [Some style manuals suggest capitalizing only the first word in a title. If you are citing titles in a bibliography or list of works cited, check your style manual.]
Regions:	the South, the Northwest, the Middle East [Do *not* capitalize directions: traveling east, walking due north.]

NUMBERS

Conventions regarding numbers vary. Generally, except in scientific or technical writing, spell out numbers of one hundred or less or numbers that require two words or less. If a passage requires many numbers, be consistent in your usage:

> This stadium seats fifty thousand people, but adding the end-zone bleachers increases the seating to fifty-seven thousand. [Hyphenated words count as one word.]
>
> Our chemistry lecture hall seats 425 students, but only 310 are enrolled this semester in Chemistry 201. [However, at the beginning of sentences, spell out numbers (Three hundred and ten students are enrolled this semester) or rewrite the sentence (In Chemistry 201, 310 students are enrolled).]

EXERCISE

Revise the following passage for proper use of apostrophes, hyphens, capitals, italics, and numbers. Use your dictionary to help you edit this passage.

(1) The advertisement shows a sky-diver floating down to earth, and the pictures caption says, "I take vitamin supplements every day, just to be on the safe side." (2) Self styled experts, from your local pharmacist to physicians from the mount Sinai school of Medicine in New York city, encourage the public to believe that vitamins are a cure all. (3) There are only thirteen known vitamin deficiencies (such as scurvy, which is a Vitamin C deficiency), but nearly sixty percent of the two hundred fifty two american's responding to our questionnaire believed in taking vitamin supplements. (4) These days, its almost patriotic to take vitamins—even your Mother says, "Don't forget to take your vitamins!" (5) During the 1980's, vitamins popularity rose an astonishing twenty nine percent, and revenue from vitamin sale's jumped to nearly three billion. (6) Although sales are generally higher in the west, some Eastern cities such as boston and Philadelphia have also shown dramatic increase's in sales. (7) If you want to learn more about vitamins, read The Vitamin-Pushers in a recent issue of Consumer Reports.

4K
cap

INDEX

ALPHABETICAL REFERENCE TO THE HANDBOOK